GERMAN LAW ACCESSIBLE

Marius Mann

Commercial Contracts in Germany

# Commercial Contracts in Germany

by

Marius Mann

2024

C.H.BECK

**beck.de**

ISBN Print: 978 3 406 80991 0


Wilhelmstraße 9, 80801 München
Druck und Bindung: Beltz Grafische Betriebe GmbH
Am Fliegerhorst 8, 99947 Bad Langensalza

Satz: Fotosatz Buck
Zweikirchener Straße 7, 84036 Kumhausen
Umschlag: Druckerei C.H.Beck Nördlingen

myclimate
shape our future

chbeck.de/nachhaltig

Gedruckt auf säurefreiem, alterungsbeständigem Papier
(hergestellt aus chlorfrei gebleichtem Zellstoff)

# Preface

Despite the internationalisation and harmonisation of law, national laws still play a significant role in international trade and commerce. This is particularly true for German commercial and contract law, as German manufacturers and intermediaries continuously enter into contracts with customers and suppliers from all over the world thereby choosing German law to govern their contractual relationships.

My aim with this second edition is to offer a practice-oriented summary of important aspects of German commercial and contract law and to provide both non-German and German businesspersons and lawyers with a quick and practical overview. At the same time, this book serves as a reference work for specific issues that often arise in business relations, in particular in the field of commercial and distribution law.

This book also contains relevant statutory materials such as important provisions of the German Commercial Code, the German Product Liability Act and the Supply Chains Due Diligence Act. Whereas translations of the German Civil Code are publicly available, this is not the case for the German Commercial Code or the Supply Chains Due Diligence Act. For the user's convenience, a German-English glossary with definitions and corresponding translations of some of the most important legal terms is attached at the end of the book.

Stuttgart, December 2023 *Dr. Marius Mann*

# Author

Rechtsanwalt **Dr. Marius Mann**, born 1979, studied law at the Universities of Constance, Heidelberg and Oxford (M. Jur. 2008). He holds an MBA from the Swiss EGSM. Dr. Mann practises as a lawyer in Stuttgart and advises clients – from the automotive, machine building, service and wholesale industry in particular – on commercial and contract law matters. He has considerable experience in related commercial litigation and arbitration, including the settlement of cross-border disputes, and disputes in the field of distribution, product liability, logistics, and plant construction.

# Summary table of contents

## PART II
## RELEVANT STATUTORY MATERIALS



## PART III
## GERMAN-ENGLISH GLOSSARY

# Table of contents



## PART I
## COMMERCIAL CONTRACTS IN GERMANY

## PART II
## RELEVANT STATUTORY MATERIALS



## PART III
## GERMAN-ENGLISH GLOSSARY

# List of abbreviations

| | |
|---|---|
| AcP | Archiv für zivilistische Praxis |
| ADSp | German forwarding agents standard terms and conditions (*Allgemeine Deutsche Spediteurbedingungen*) |
| AG | Die Aktiengesellschaft |
| AG | District Court (*Amtsgericht*) |
| AktG | Stock Corporation Act (*Aktiengesetz*) |
| b2b | business to business |
| b2c | business to consumer |
| BAG | Federal Labour Court (*Bundesarbeitsgericht*) |
| BauR | Zeitschrift für das gesamte öffentliche und zivile Baurecht |
| BB | Betriebs-Berater |
| BeckOGK | beck.online.Grosskommentar |
| BeckOK | Beck'scher Online-Kommentar |
| BeurkG | Authentication Act (*Beurkundungsgesetz*) |
| BGB | Civil Code (*Bürgerliches Gesetzbuch*) |
| BGH | Federal Court of Justice (*Bundesgerichtshof*) |
| BT-Drs. | Bundestag-Drucksache |
| BVerfG | Federal Constitutional Court (*Bundesverfassungsgericht*) |
| BvR | Aktenzeichen des Bundesverfassungsgerichts |
| Ch. | Chapter |
| CISG | United Nations Convention on Contracts for the International Sale of Goods of 11 April 1980 |
| DB | Der Betrieb |
| DIHK | Association of German Chambers of Commerce and Industry (*Deutsche Industrie- und Handelskammer*) |
| DIS | German Institution of Arbitration (*Deutsche Institution für Schiedsgerichtsbarkeit e.V.*) |
| DNotZ | Deutsche Notar-Zeitschrift |
| DStR | Deutsches Steuerrecht |
| DZWIR | Deutsche Zeitschrift für Wirtschafts- und Insolvenzrecht |
| ECJ | European Court of Justice |
| ed. | editor (plural: eds) |
| edn | edition |
| e.g. | exempli gratia/for example |
| EEA | European Economic Area |
| et seqq. | et sequentes/and the following |
| etc. | etcetera/and so forth |
| EU | European Union |
| GG | Basic Law/German Constitution (*Grundgesetz*) |
| GmbH | Limited Liability Company (*Gesellschaft mit beschränkter Haftung*) |

| | |
|---|---|
| GmbHG | Law on Limited Liability Companies (*Gesetz betreffend die Gesellschaften mit beschränkter Haftung*) |
| GRUR | Gewerblicher Rechtsschutz und Urheberrecht |
| GRURInt | Gewerblicher Rechtsschutz und Urheberrecht Internationaler Teil |
| GWB | Act against Restraints of Competition (*Gesetz gegen Wettbewerbsbeschränkungen*) |
| HGB | Commercial Code (*Handelsgesetzbuch*) |
| i.e. | id est/that is |
| IP | Intellectual Property (*Geistiges Eigentum*) |
| JuS | Juristische Schulung |
| JZ | Juristen-Zeitung |
| LG | Regional Court (*Landgericht*) |
| LkSG | Supply Chains Due Diligence Act (*Lieferkettensorgfaltspflichtengesetz*) |
| LMuR | Lebensmittel & Recht |
| LSG | Higher Social Court (*Landessozialgericht*) |
| M&A | mergers and acquisitions |
| MDR | Monatsschrift für Deutsches Recht |
| MMR | MultiMedia und Recht |
| mn. | margin number |
| MPR | Medizin Produkte Recht, Zeitschrift für das gesamte Medizinproduktrecht |
| MüKo | Münchener Kommentar |
| NJOZ | Neue Juristische Online-Zeitschrift |
| NJW | Neue Juristische Wochenschrift |
| NJW-RR | NJW-Rechtsprechungs-Report Zivilrecht |
| no. | number/pl. nos. |
| NZA | Neue Zeitschrift für Arbeitsrecht |
| NZG | Neue Zeitschrift für Gesellschaftsrecht |
| OEM | Original Equipment Manufacturer |
| OLG | Higher Regional Court (*Oberlandesgericht*) |
| p. | page (plural: pp.) |
| ProdHaftG | Product Liability Act (*Produkthaftungsgesestz*) |
| ProdSG | Product Safety Act (*Produktsicherheitsgesetz*) |
| RdA | Recht der Arbeit |
| RG | Supreme Court of the German Reich (*Reichsgericht*) |
| RGZ | Entscheidungen des Reichsgerichts in Zivilsachen |
| SPA | Share Purchase Agreement |
| StGB | Criminal Code (*Strafgesetzbuch*) |
| suppl. | supplement |
| SZR | special drawing right (*Sonderziehungsrecht*) |
| TranspR | Zeitschrift für Transportrecht |
| VIZ | Zeitschrift für Vermögens- und Immobilienrecht |
| VVG | Insurance Contracts Act (*Versicherungsvertragsgesetz*) |
| WM | Zeitschrift für Wirtschafts- und Bankrecht |
| WRP | Wettbewerb in Recht und Praxis |
| ZErb | Zeitschrift für die Steuer- und Erbrechtspraxis |

| | |
|---|---|
| ZGR | Zeitschrift für Unternehmens- und Gesellschaftsrecht |
| ZIP | Zeitschrift für Wirtschaftsrecht |
| ZPO | Code of Civil Procedure (*Zivilprozessordnung*) |
| ZR | Aktenzeichen des Bundesgerichtshofs in Zivilsachen |
| ZRP | Zeitschrift für Rechtspolitik |
| ZVertriebsR | Zeitschrift für Vertriebsrecht |

# Introductory remarks

Commercial contracts play a significant and substantial role in the regulation of trade and mercantile relations. The number of commercial contracts concluded in national and international trade exceeds most other contract forms. Commercial contracts such as purchase agreements, framework and supply agreements, commercial agency agreements, distribution and authorised dealer agreements, commission agency agreements, franchise agreements, transport agreements, and warehousing agreements are discussed in this manual. These types of contracts all regulate – directly or indirectly – the distribution of goods (and in some cases, services as well). Supplemental agreements such as pre-contracts, option contracts, quality assurance agreements, confidentiality agreements or standard terms and conditions are not commercial contracts in the narrow sense as they do not govern the procurement, exchange or supply of goods. They are, however, often concluded together with commercial contracts and are therefore also discussed in this manual.

The law of commercial contracts consists of general contract law, including the law of standard terms and conditions, which is regulated in the Civil Code (*Bürgerliches Gesetzbuch* – BGB). Yet, German law also provides specific sets of rules for specific contract types which are either regulated in the BGB and the Commercial Code (*Handelsgesetzbuch* – HGB) or are developed by court practices.

This manual first discusses how commercial contracts may be concluded validly, then elaborates on specific contracts on the supply and procurement of goods, and finally discusses contracts governing logistics. In addition to typical issues that may arise when negotiating and concluding commercial contracts, this manual also goes beyond mere contract law into areas important to many commercial players such as insolvency or competition law.

# PART I
# COMMERCIAL CONTRACTS IN GERMANY

## Chapter 1
## Fundamentals of the law of contracts

**Bibliography:** Bälz, 'Der Ausschluss des Ausgleichsanspruchs in internationalen Handelsvertreterverträgen', NJW 2003, 1559; Graf v. Westphalen/Thüsing (eds), Vertragsrecht und AGB-Klauselwerke, 49th edn, Munich 2023; Grüneberg (ed.), Bürgerliches Gesetzbuch: BGB, 82nd edn, Munich 2023; Heidel et al. (eds), Bürgerliches Gesetzbuch (BGB), Band 1: Allgemeiner Teil – EGBGB (NK-BGB), 4th edn, Baden-Baden 2021; Heussen/Pischel (eds), Handbuch Vertragsverhandlung und Vertragsmanagement, 4th edn, Cologne 2014; Hopt (ed.), Handelsgesetzbuch: HGB, 42nd edn, Munich 2023; Jauernig, BGB, 18th edn, Munich 2021; Kolbe, 'Schweigen auf einseitige Preiserhöhungen' BB 2010, 2322; Lorenz, 'Im BGB viel Neues: Die Umsetzung der Fernabsatzrichtlinie' JuS 2000, 833; Mann, 'Vertragsgestaltung beim IT-Outsourcing: Besonderheiten und Fallstricke', MMR 2012, 499; Mann/Waschkowski, 'Vertragsstörungen in Krisenzeiten', BB 2022, 1285; Markesinis/Unberath/Johnston, The German Law of Contract, 2nd edn, Oxford 2006; Oetker (ed.), Handelsgesetzbuch: HGB, 7th edn, Munich 2021; Scholz, 'Strafbarkeit juristischer Personen?', ZRP 2000, 435; Schöner/Stöber, Grundbuchrecht, 16th edn, Munich 2020; Schulze/Dörner/Ebert et al, Bürgerliches Gesetzbuch: BGB (HK-BGB), 11th edn, Baden-Baden 2022; Strick, 'Die Anfechtung von Arbeitsverträgen durch den Arbeitgeber', NZA 2000, 695; Wagner/Mann, 'Tips und Tricks zur Kündigung von Verträgen', BB 2012, 2842.

## A. Introduction

The law of contracts governs the formation, effect and performance of contracts and is regulated in the Civil Code (*Bürgerliches Gesetzbuch* – BGB), which consists of five books.[1] Although contract law is by far the most significant topic regulated in the BGB, it does not contain a chapter that deals exclusively with the law of contracts. The design of the BGB is somewhat abstract and not very 'user friendly'. The important rules when it comes to the law of contracts can generally be found in the first and second books of the BGB (general part and law of obligations). 1

Lawyers from other jurisdictions may consider the high degree of abstraction, especially in the first book of the BGB, ambiguous. The general rules of the first book are to be applied throughout the entire civil law, e.g. in all books of the BGB, unless a special provision establishes a departure from the rule. For example, the first book of the BGB provides rules for the interpretation of declarations of intent and the interpretation of contracts (§§ 133, 157 BGB) that also govern the interpretation of contracts of work, rent, services, commercial agency, transport and freight, warehousing and many others. As an exception, the legislator considered it necessary to provide special rules for the interpre- 2

[1] General Part (Book 1), Law of Obligations (Book 2), Property Law (Book 3), Family Law (Book 4) and Law of Succession (Book 5).

tation of testaments (§ 2084 BGB) which prevail over §§ 133, 157 BGB when it comes to the interpretation of the last will of the bequeather.

3 The BGB, which came into force on 1 January 1900, is based on the overriding principle of the freedom of contract. It is possible for two parties to agree on any content of a contract if the content (i) does not violate a statutory prohibition (§ 134 BGB), (ii) does not violate public policy (§ 138(1) BGB) and (iii) does not give rise to a grossly disproportionate and unduly obtained bargain (§ 138(2) BGB). In recent years, the law of terms and conditions and other consumer protection rules (primarily promulgated by regulations and directives of the European Union) have had a further restrictive effect on the general principle of freedom of contract which also applies in business relations aiming to protect the weaker party to the contract.[2]

4 In addition to the freedom of contract the BGB is shaped by further principles. Numerous sections of the BGB may be better understood when taking into account the impact of social balancing of the BGB or parts thereof. This applies, in particular, to labour law and residential tenancy law.[3] However, the legislator also saw a need to protect the typically weaker party in business relationships and therefore provided, at least in part, binding sections in the HGB to secure protection for the agent[4] or the carrier[5]. In these fields of law, mandatory provisions (*zwingende Regelungen*) aim to ensure that the parties do not agree on rules that discriminate against the typically weaker party. Unfortunately, these provisions are only binding in very few cases, which makes legal counsel essential, especially when negotiating contracts in the fields of product supply, agency, distribution, transport or labour law.

# B. Formation of contracts

5 A contract essentially requires two corresponding declarations of intent (*Willenserklärungen*). If more than two parties are involved – which may be the case when corporate groups enter into contracts with suppliers – each party that wishes to become a party to the contract must issue a corresponding declaration of intent. In these cases, multiple declarations of intent are required of the parties that are obliged under the contract.

## I. Offer and acceptance

### 1. Definition

6 Declarations of intent can be categorised into offer and acceptance. In commercial relations it is not always entirely clear which party made the offer and which party accepted it. However, if there are corresponding declarations of intent, this does not cause major problems. The actual designation of a declaration of intent as an offer, order, acceptance

---

[2] See e.g. Council Directive 93/13/EEC of 5th April 1993 on unfair terms in consumer contracts, which also heavily influences business relationships due to restrictive case law. The German legislator implemented this Directive in §§ 305–310 BGB, → Ch. 2 mn. 3 et seqq.

[3] See e.g. § 577a BGB.

[4] See e.g. § 89b HGB, which obliges the entrepreneur to pay termination compensation to the agent once the commercial agency agreement is terminated.

[5] See e.g. §§ 449, 466 HGB, which provide constraints for the parties to agree on limitations of liability.

or the like does not have any legal effect. Offer and acceptance are regulated in §§ 145 to 157 BGB comprehensively.

## 2. Offer

An offer is binding for the declaring party unless it has excluded the binding character of the offer (§ 145 BGB). This does not lead to a disproportionate burden for the offering party, as offers may only be accepted immediately (when making the offer to a person who is present or by telephone or chat, § 147(1) BGB) or until the time when the offeror can expect to receive an answer under ordinary circumstances (when the other person is absent, § 147(2) BGB). The interpretation of 'ordinary circumstances' depends on the specific features of the case, in particular the content, complexity, and the commercial consequences of the possible contract. Whereas in an ongoing commercial distribution relationship the periods tend to be very short (a few days), this might be different in cases where (large) entities or (local) authorities are involved which have to follow internal approval procedures involving panels and committees.[6] Courts have developed customs and practices that may help identify certain periods for certain categories of cases: when accepting an offer to buy real estate, a period of four weeks is commonly expected.[7] When concluding a tenancy agreement, a period of two to three weeks is to be considered acceptable.[8] 7

## 3. *Essentialia negotii*

The essential content of an offer is called *essentialia negotii*. When concluding a contract concerning the sale of goods, the *essentialia negotii* are (i) the sold goods, (ii) the purchase price, and (iii) the parties to the contract, which need to be identifiable. It is sufficient if the *essentialia negotii* are identifiable based on the circumstances of the case. There is no rule under German law that requires the contract to be concluded in a certain form or by expressly referring to the *essentialia negotii*. The *essentialia negotii* may differ depending on the type of contract. In practice, it is important to identify and define the parties' main obligations in full. The parties' rights and duties are usually defined in the very first paragraphs of the contract. As a general rule: when problems or lack of clarity arise in this context, the contract is not void as long as the will of the parties can be determined by interpretation. 8

## 4. Acceptance

The acceptance must be unreserved and not contain any new elements. An acceptance containing expansions, restrictions, or other alterations, even if it is designated as an 'order confirmation', is considered a new offer and therefore does not result in a contract unless it is – without limitation – accepted by the addressee in turn (§ 150(2) BGB). A late acceptance is likewise treated as a new offer. Due to the freedom of contract, the addressee of an offer is in general free to accept or reject it. There are only a few cases in which, under very narrow circumstances, the addressee is obliged to enter into a contract with the party making the offer. Two exceptions should be mentioned here: (i) services for the public (gas, electricity, water, public transport) and (ii) enterprises that hold a highly 9

---

[6] MüKoBGB/Busche BGB § 147 mn. 38.
[7] Cf. BGH V ZR 85/09, NJW 2010, 2873 (2874).
[8] Cf. OLG Naumburg 9 U 3/04, NZG 2005, 75 (76).

dominant market position may, pursuant to §§ 19 et seqq. GWB (*Gesetz gegen Wettbewerbsbeschränkungen* – Act against Restraints of Competition), be obliged to enter into contracts in order to avoid discriminatory practices.[9]

## II. Intent of legal responsibility

10 A declaration of intent must be precise, complete, and identifiable. A prudential receiver (often defined as an impartial third party) must also be able to understand and identify the intent to assume legal responsibility of the declaring party. In other words, it is necessary that the offer and acceptance contain evidence of seriousness. It is essential to distinguish the declarer's intent to assume legal responsibility from a non-binding willingness to conclude a contract.[10] However, a declaration of intent does not have to be given expressly or in written form. In fact, a binding declaration of intent is often given through implied behaviour, especially when it comes to common everyday shopping situations in which a legal transaction is carried out without a single word being exchanged. The same can be found in (ongoing) commercial supply relationships in which goods are exchanged and money is transferred without express oral or written declarations.

11 A declaration of intent is binding unless the declaring party clearly indicates that the declaration of intent shall not be binding or shall be binding only under certain circumstances or for a specific period. In practice, such cases are frequently seen in trade practices. Terms like 'subject to change' (*freibleibend*), 'without obligation' (*ohne obligo*) or 'non-binding' (*unverbindlich*) are common when one of the parties submits an offer. Whether such a declaration is seen as an offer that may be revoked until the other party accepts it, or if it is only an invitation to the other party to make a binding offer (*invitatio ad offerendum*) is subject to interpretation. In the latter case, the declaration is not a binding offer.[11] It is undisputed that declarations in catalogues, on internet sites, price lists or the like are generally not to be regarded as binding offers.[12]

## III. Silence as a declaration of intent

### 1. General principle

12 Silence in response to a declaration of intent does not generally constitute a declaration of intent and therefore does not result in a contract. This is not true when the parties have agreed upon the fact that, in a specific case, silence shall have a particular meaning (e.g. negotiated silence: *beredtes Schweigen*).[13] In this context it is necessary to distinguish between silence and implied behaviour. Silence is a non-reaction, whereas implied behaviour (e.g. nodding, reception of goods) makes clear that the declaring party wishes to express a declaration of intent.

---

[9] See Markesinis/Unberath/Johnston, p. 71; MüKoBGB/Busche BGB vor § 145 mn. 16.
[10] See RG VII 2/32, RGZ 136, 132, 135.
[11] See BGH VII ZR 177/82, NJW 1984, 1885; BGH X ZR 135/93, NJW 1996, 919.
[12] BGH VIII ZR 32/08, NJW 2009, 1337 (1338); HK-BGB/Heinrich Dörner BGB § 145 mn. 5.
[13] See BGH X ZR 135/93, NJW 1996, 919.

### 2. Silence in commercial relations

An important exception to the rule that silence does not constitute a declaration of intent can be found in commercial relations. When an offer is made to a merchant whose business includes solicitation or conclusion of business transactions for others, and such an offer originates from someone with whom the merchant has a previous business relationship and concerns such transactions on behalf of the offeror, the merchant is obliged to reply immediately. Otherwise, silence will be deemed an acceptance of the offer (§ 362(1) sentence 1 HGB). Pursuant to § 362(1) sentence 2 HGB, the same applies if the merchant receives an offer to conclude transactions from someone to whom he has offered his services in concluding such transactions. **13**

### 3. Commercial letter of confirmation

The commercial letter of confirmation (*kaufmännisches Bestätigungsschreiben*) applies to commercial interactions and is aimed at accelerating trade. Although there is no written rule expressly governing the commercial letter of confirmation, it is acknowledged as a commercial custom (§ 346 HGB) developed and applied by German courts. The commercial letter of confirmation results in a legal presumption that a contract with the content of the confirmation letter has been concluded between the sender and addressee, irrespective of whether the parties have actually concluded such a contract.[14] A commercial letter of confirmation that merely reflects what the parties have agreed on in their oral negotiations is not an order confirmation but rather a certificate of proof (*deklaratorisches Bestätigungsschreiben*). However, if the parties believe that they have reached an agreement even though their respective declarations do not correspond, the commercial letter of confirmation (*konstitutives Bestätigungsschreiben*) results in a contract. The doctrine of the commercial letter of confirmation is subject to certain requirements: **14**

- it only applies to commercial interactions between two merchants or between persons who take part in commerce;
- the confirmation letter (which may also be sent, for example by email or text message) must refer to recent oral negotiations between the parties;
- the sender must, in good faith, believe that a valid contract has already been concluded even though the recent negotiations resulted in two declarations of intent with (slightly) different content;[15]
- lastly, the confirmation letter must contain an acceptable content for the receiving party, which is not the case if the confirmation letter includes extreme and extraordinary additional contract conditions.[16]

In practice, the commercial letter of confirmation has two remarkable effects: first, a contract may be concluded through silence on the part of the addressee. Second, a confirmation letter with content that slightly deviates from what the parties originally negotiated may still be acceptable and therefore lead to a (slight) contract change. **15**

## IV. Agency

A declaration of intent may not always be given by the person for whom the contract will be concluded. Agency (also proxy) establishes the opportunity for a party (the prin- **16**

---

[14] BGH II ZR 305/51, NJW 1952, 1369.
[15] See Hopt/Leyens HGB § 346 mn. 20–27.
[16] BGH VIII ZR 44/64, NJW 1966, 1070 (1071); Hopt/Leyens HGB § 346 mn. 27.

cipal) to grant power of representation to another person (the agent), who then acts on behalf of the principal when dealing with a third person (the contract partner). Agency is an essential instrument for organisations and corporate bodies (*juristische Personen*), since it enables these artificial persons to be able to act. The fundamentals of agency are regulated in §§ 164 to 181 BGB.

17 Agency is typically conferred on the agent by means of a unilateral declaration of intent of the principal to the agent. However, the law also allows for the principal to confer power of representation on the agent by making such declarations not to the agent, but to the third party (§ 167(1) BGB). It is important to note that the underlying contract between the principal and agent (commonly a service contract) is separate from the power of representation given to the agent. Consequently, the power of representation remains unaffected in cases where the underlying contract between the principal and agent is void for any reason.

### 1. Elements of agency

18 To make a valid declaration of intent on behalf of the principal, four criteria need to be met by the agent: (i) Agency must be **permissible**, which is not the case only in very limited circumstances, such as when drafting a testament or in case of marriage. (ii) The agent has to issue his own, **separate declaration of intent**, meaning that the principal must have granted the agent discretion to make his own decision and to not only forward a declaration of intent of the principal (in the latter case, the person working for the principal is a mere messenger). (iii) It must be apparent for the third party that the **agent is acting** not for himself but **on behalf of the principal** (*Offenkundigkeitsprinzip*). This requirement aims to protect the contract partner, as the party with whom it is concluding the contract, especially when it comes to solvency and performance, might be relevant for the contract partner. There are, however, cases in which it is either not of relevance to the third party or is typically apparent from the circumstances of the case who is to become party to the contract. In common everyday shopping situations, a supermarket owner is not concerned with the identity of his contractual partner (business for whom it may concern: *Geschäft für den, den es angeht*). Of greater relevance in commercial relations is the company-related transaction (*unternehmensbezogenes Geschäft*),[17] whereby the contract is concluded between the principal and the third party (contract partner) although the agent has not disclosed his agency. In this scenario, it must be evident from the circumstances of the transaction that the owner of the enterprise – not the person acting (agent) – shall become party to the contract. This may be the case, for instance, in commercial relations in which an employee from the purchasing department of a company negotiates and concludes supply agreements with one of the company's suppliers.

19 Finally, it is essential that (iv) the agent has been granted actual **power of representation** (authority) by law or by legal act of the principal. Cases in which authority is given to the agent by law can be found in company law where directors have the duty and power to represent their company.[18] The names of the directors are entered into the commercial register. In addition, sub-authority given to employees of the company by its officers or directors is considered authority given by means of a legal act of the principal. In practice, employees are often granted agency for certain types of transactions or defined business areas (§ 54(1) HGB).

---

[17] BGH II ZR 311/88, NJW 1990, 2678.

[18] See § 78(1) AktG (*Aktiengesetz* – Stock Corporation Act) and § 35(1) GmbHG (*Gesetz betreffend die Gesellschaften mit beschränkter Haftung* – Limited Liability Companies Act).

## 2. General commercial authority

A special and unique type of agency is the general commercial authority (*Prokura*). 20
It is an authority of unlimited scope granted by the company to a registered manager (*Prokurist*) (§§ 48 to 53 HGB). There are generally no form requirements for granting agency. However, the unlimited scope of the general commercial authority makes this form of agency especially risky for all parties involved. As a result, it must be entered into the commercial register when granted and revoked, and is therefore publicly verifiable.[19] Whereas commercial power of attorney according to § 54(1) HGB grants authority to the agent only for certain types of transactions or defined business areas, general commercial authority also gives the registered manager the right to carry out intersectoral transactions. It is an unlimited power of representation. Only fundamental transactions (*Grundlagengeschäfte*) and contracts for the transfer of real estate property are not within the scope of general commercial authority, meaning that the registered manager is not allowed to discontinue the business, sell the company or change the name of the company.[20]

## 3. Apparent and tolerated authority

Under narrow circumstances the agent can legally bind the principal without actually 21
having power of representation. The rationale behind this rule is the need to protect third party interests in situations where the principal deserves less protection than the third party. Two cases of apparent authority are well-acknowledged in judicial practice: apparent authority (*Anscheinsvollmacht*) and tolerated authority (*Duldungsvollmacht*).

### a) Apparent authority

A person may bind the principal by way of apparent authority when (i) a person re- 22
peatedly acts on behalf of the principal, (ii) the principal actually *does not have knowledge* of but is negligently unaware of the person acting on behalf of him and (iii) the third party supposes, in good faith, that the acting party has power of representation.[21] As an example, apparent authority can result from the repeated use of the company's stamp by an employee that has not actually been granted power of representation.

### b) Tolerated authority

A person may bind the principal by way of tolerated authority when (i) a person acts 23
on behalf of the principal, (ii) the principal does not intervene although he *has knowledge* of this and (iii) the third party supposes, in good faith, that the acting party has power of representation.[22] Unlike in the case of apparent authority, repeated action is not necessary to establish tolerated authority. The doctrine of tolerated authority may, for instance, apply in a case in which an employee, in the presence of his manager, signs a contract that he (the employee) has essentially negotiated although he does not actually have power of representation, which the third party is not aware of.

---

19 A missing registration, however, does not make the general commercial authority void. The registration merely protects good faith, cf. RG II B 30/31, RGZ 134, 303, 307. A third party dealing with the registered manager in good faith after the revocation of his authority – but prior to the publication of the revocation – will be protected, see § 15(1) HGB.

20 See Hopt/Hopt HGB § 49 mn. 2.

21 BGH I ZR 96/51, NJW 1952, 657 (658).

22 BGH I ZR 96/51, NJW 1952, 657 (658).

### 4. Agency and certain types of distribution

24 Commercial agents, commission agents and brokers entail certain elements of agency. These types of agents, however, which are often found in a distribution context, are not agents within the meaning of the BGB. They will be discussed separately in depth later (→ Ch. 11 mn. 1 et seqq.; → Ch. 13 mn. 1 et seqq.).

### 5. Unauthorised agency

25 §§ 177 to 179 BGB regulate unauthorised agency. As a rule, when an agent exceeds the authority granted to him, the principal can either approve the unauthorised transaction or reject it (§ 177(1) BGB). The other party (contract partner) may withdraw from the unauthorised transaction prior to approval (§ 178 BGB). If the principal does not approve the transaction, the other party may, at its free discretion, either demand performance of the contract or payment of damages from the unauthorised agent (*Vertreter ohne Vertretungsmacht*) (§ 179(1) BGB). However, the agent is not liable if the other party knew or ought to have known about the lack of authority.

## V. Legal capacity; capacity to contract

### 1. Beginning and end

26 Legal capacity, capacity to contract (business capacity) and tort capacity (which will not be discussed as it has no practical relevance in a business context) are explicitly regulated in the BGB. Legal capacity starts with the completion of birth (§ 1 BGB) and ends when the brain ceases to function, whereas the unlimited capacity to contract occurs when a person reaches the age of 18 (§§ 2, 106 BGB) and ceases if he is in a state of pathological mental disturbance (§ 104 sentence 2 BGB), which prevents the free exercise of will. A declaration of intent made by a person without capacity to contract is void (§ 105 BGB).

### 2. Definition

27 Legal capacity determines when a person can be a subject of rights and obligations, whereas capacity to contract determines when a natural person may conclude a contract involving rights and duties. A natural person acting in commercial transaction must be 18. Yet, there are several exceptions in which persons aged between 7 and 18 years, who have limited capacity to contract, may conclude transactions. This may be the case where (i) a particular transaction is solely legally advantageous for the minor (not from an economic but legal perspective), (ii) the legal representative authorises or approves a particular transaction (§§ 107, 108, 112, 113 BGB) or (iii) the legal representative, with the approval of the family court, gives authorisation to operate a trade or business independently (§ 113 BGB).

28 **Corporate bodies** have legal capacity, which means they can become subject to rights and duties. Corporate bodies can sue and be sued; however, they cannot be subject to criminal penalties and criminal sanctions.[23]

---

[23] Unlike in other jurisdictions, only natural persons may be subject to criminal sanctions, Scholz, ZRP 2000, 435. However, according to § 30 OWiG (*Ordnungswidrigkeitengesetz* – Administrative Offences Act), administrative penalties may be imposed upon corporate bodies (which are often given in competition law).

## VI. Multilateral agreements

The principle of freedom of contract includes the opportunity to conclude not only bilateral contracts but also contracts between multiple parties. In practice, multilateral agreements are often concluded between suppliers and companies in corporate groups where not only one division but multiple divisions need to be supplied with certain goods. In these cases, it is essential to secure correct and therefore valid power of representation of the companies that become parties to the contract. The commercial register helps to identify who has power of representation and how a company is represented. This is also crucial when terminating an agreement. A declaration of termination made without proper power of representation may be challenged without having to state a reason and is therefore void according to § 174 BGB. This of course does not keep the person terminating the contract from expressing the declaration of termination (*Kündigungserklärung*). However, a second declaration of termination does not have a retroactive effect on the first (and void) declaration. Consequently, a specific notice period for termination might be missed if the first termination was made without proper power of representation and was successfully challenged. 29

# C. Paving the way for a contract

## I. Contract design

The design of a contract may differ in each individual case depending on the needs and expectations of the parties. External lawyers or in-house counsels usually have access to many drafts or model contracts. In practice, the use of model documents is inevitable. However, recourse to pre-formulated drafts or model contracts may have significant legal consequences, as this increases the risk of being subjected to the test of reasonableness (*Inhaltskontrolle*) according to §§ 305 et seqq. BGB (→ Ch. 2 mn. 3 et seqq.). 30

In every jurisdiction, contracts commonly begin with a preamble, which opens the contract, and a severability clause, which concludes the document. Some authors recommend a basic structure of six blocks containing the necessary content of a contract.[24] Although the need for a different structure may exist in individual cases, this basic structure is advisable and may help non-lawyers build a set of rules covering the necessary scope of regulation. The six blocks are: 31

**Part 1 – Contractual basis.** This part contains all information that will – in case of a gap in the provisions and dispute – help interpret the true intentions of the parties. In addition to the purposes and propositions of the parties, part 1 commonly also contains definitions. 32

**Part 2 – Contractual content**. The second part includes the rules necessary to describe the parties' performance obligations. This is a description of the main obligations (in complex contracts, annexes may be used) as well as the payment obligations. In sales agreements, part 2 contains the purchased goods (and other performances the parties may agree on, such as maintenance & service) and the purchase price. In commercial agency agreements, part 2 specifies, among other things, (i) the contractual territory, (ii) 33

[24] Heussen/Pischel, p. 138.

the products to be procured by the agent, (iii) the commission to be paid, and (iv) the payment date.

34 **Part 3 – Security of performance.** This complex contains representation and warranties, warranty of merchantability and guarantees. In supply agreements, the supplier (seller) should insist on a retention-of-title clause (*Eigentumsvorbehalt*) to protect his payment claim between delivery of the purchased item and actual payment. Furthermore, non-compete clauses, rules on confidentiality and limitation of liability are commonly specified in this part.

35 **Part 4 – Contract management.** This section illustrates how performance will be provided. It differs from part 2 in that it describes the steps that have already been taken in the past and the ones that need to be taken in the future. Whereas in sales contracts part 4 might be negligible, in complex ongoing continuing obligations such as transportation contracts or IT-outsourcing agreements, part 4 may constitute the contract's core. For example, a transportation contract must describe where the freight is picked up, how it is loaded, what safety regulations need to be adhered to, where and how embarkation needs to be carried out, what means of transportation shall be used, etc. As a rule, one must ensure that an issue is never regulated twice in a contract. Otherwise, inconsistent or slightly deviating provisions may result in conflicting contract clauses and can therefore give rise to gaps and/or disputes.

36 **Part 5 – General provisions.** This part normally governs miscellaneous provisions that are usually not – or only rarely – disputed between the parties. This is comprised of, among other things, a written form clause, a severability clause, an interpretation clause, a choice of law clause and a jurisdiction or arbitration clause.

37 **Part 6 – Annexes.** Annexes usually contain business details regarding performance, payment or delivery. However, annexes are equally relevant to provisions regulated in the text of the contract itself. It is a mistake to believe that a change to an annex will not constitute a change of the contract itself, even though a change to an annex is usually easier for editorial and practical reasons. As a rule, the draft and negotiation of annexes require the same degree of diligence as the provisions of the contract itself.

## II. Contract negotiation

38 The freedom of contract involves the right of the parties to determine whether and with what content the parties wish to contract. It also includes the right of the parties to determine if, how, and to what extent they want to negotiate a contract. There are no rules obliging the parties to adhere to a certain negotiation procedure. At the beginning of contract negotiations, the parties may draft a schedule that sets forth not only the timeframe for negotiations but also the order (exchange of drafts) and possible fixed dates. When preparing for face-to-face negotiations, the parties usually agree on one party providing the draft. In M&A transactions this is often the seller – although this may also differ depending on the economic strength of the parties. The draft is then forwarded to the other party, providing it with the opportunity to comment on, amend or supplement the draft. In practice, this is done by compiling a 'mark-up' or 'redline' version of the first draft. When exchanging the revised drafts (as the case may be, in several rounds of negotiations) the parties are given the opportunity to identify the big issues, which are later discussed in face-to-face negotiations. Emotions, social background, customs, motives (whether known or unknown), respect, psychological power games, trust, or suspicion may greatly influence the success of negotiations and should therefore not be underestimated, especially when it comes to final face-to-face negotiations. Where intercultural

contract negotiations are taking place, it is advisable to learn about the 'dos and don'ts' prior to the start of negotiations.[25]

## III. Letter of intent

Before entering into negotiations or while negotiating a contract, one of the parties may feel the need to enter into a letter of intent (*Absichtserklärung*). In such a declaration signed by both parties, the parties typically declare that they will (i) faithfully negotiate with the other party, (ii) not negotiate with competitors, (iii) not disclose confidential information of the other party, and/or (iv) bear the negotiation expenses separately. Moreover, a letter of intent may also regulate the conditions under which a due diligence is to be conducted (costs, access to information, duration, consequences of failure, etc.). Depending on the particular matter, it may also be essential for one party to have certain expenditures remunerated even before the actual contract is signed. However, the purpose of a letter of intent is mainly to give one or both parties certainty with regard to upcoming or ongoing negotiations. Therefore, in practice, most letters of intent contain only a few binding provisions. **39**

## IV. Pre-contract

Unlike a letter of intent, a pre-contract (*Vorvertrag*) is generally binding. A pre-contract gives the parties the opportunity to make a legally binding agreement consisting of the obligation to enter into the actual contract at a later stage. The need for a pre-contract may arise in practice if, for instance, the parties need more time to discuss the details of the main contract (delivery conditions, details of the order system, minimum purchase requirement) or are waiting for administrative approval (commission's decision, trademark admissions, registration) or other conditions have not yet been fulfilled (due diligence report). However, to be valid, a pre-contract must contain all terms necessary for an actual contract. This requires that the party's main duties be sufficiently certain or at least ascertainable under the pre-contract.[26] Whether the parties actually want to be legally bound when making a declaration or whether the declaration is merely a non-binding letter of intent is subject to interpretation. Decisive for interpreting the will of the parties is, for instance, the point in time of the declaration, the value and the consequences of the transaction, and the economic importance of the transaction for the parties. If the primary contract requires a certain form, the pre-contract must meet this form requirement too. This applies, for example, when a pre-contract is concluded to oblige the parties enter into termination agreement. In labour law, a pre-contract in which the parties to the employment contract agree to conclude a termination agreement has to be concluded in writing like the termination agreement to be effective.[27] **40**

[25] For further reference regarding contract negotiation in the USA, Russia, China, Japan, and Brazil, see Heussen/Pischel, p. 969 et seqq.
[26] RG VI 701/28, RGZ 124, 81.
[27] BAG 6 AZR 242/09, NZA 2010, 273.

## V. Option contract

41 Unlike a pre-contract, an option contract (*Optionsvertrag*) gives one party the unilateral legal option to force a contractual relationship on the other party. With respect to formalities, a pre-contract and an option contract are identical. If the primary contract requires a certain form, this form must be met by the option contract as well to be valid. The party in possession of the option is – in the absence of a divergent agreement – free to decide whether and at what time it wants to exercise the option. Legal options are common in stock and financial trade but can hardly be found in commercial distribution.

## VI. *Culpa in contrahendo* and abandonment of negotiations

42 As a general principle, no duties for either party arise from the contract negotiations. However, a pre-contractual liability may arise for the parties under narrow circumstances in accordance with the principle of *culpa in contrahendo.* Before being implemented in § 311(2) and (3) BGB, this legal doctrine was developed by case law and numerous legal publications. The doctrine has a wide scope of application and was first applied in cases in which a party seriously intending to conclude a contract with another party was injured by the other party. This category also includes cases of culpable abandonment of contractual negotiations, which are of considerable significance in practice.

43 Yet the conditions under which a party may require compensation for culpable abandonment of contractual negotiations are restrictive. It is not sufficient that the parties have negotiated in a significantly serious manner or that one of the parties has forgone other business opportunities or has incurred expenses in expectation of the contract being concluded.[28] A party may demand compensation for the culpable estoppel (abandonment) of contractual negotiations only if the following requirements are met: (i) The other party has cause to have particular confidence that the future contract will be concluded, (ii) the party claiming compensation has incurred expenses or damages in expectation of the contract, and (iii) the other party has stopped the negotiations without a material reason for doing so.[29]

# D. Ineffectiveness

44 As described below (→ Ch. 2 mn. 16), contract terms or even entire contracts are ineffective if they unreasonably disadvantage the other party to the contract (§§ 307 et seqq. BGB). Contracts that pass the test of reasonableness may still violate other provisions of German law and therefore be ineffective. A contract is ineffective if it violates a form requirement (§ 125 BGB), a statutory prohibition (unless the statute leads to a different conclusion) (§ 134 BGB), or if it is contrary to public policy (§ 138 BGB).

---

[28] BGH V ZR 17/73, NJW 1975, 43 (44); BGH VII ZR 360/98, NJW-RR 2001, 381 (382).
[29] BGH III ZR 48/76, NJW 1978, 1802 (1803).

## I. Form requirements

### 1. General

The freedom of contract which dominates German civil law ensures that contracts may generally be concluded without adhering to any form requirement. Only in limited cases does the law require that the parties use a specific form. This applies, in particular, when real estate is sold (contracts on plots of land, § 311b(1) sentence 1 BGB), company shares are transferred (§ 15(3) GmbHG), a suretyship is granted (§ 766 sentence 1 BGB), or a gift is promised (§ 518(1) BGB). 45

### 2. Types

§ 126 to § 129 BGB describe the specific types of form requirements that are found in German civil law and their respective content. These are: (i) the written form according to § 126 BGB (document signed by the issuer), (ii) the electronic form according to § 126a BGB (the issuer must add his name to the declaration and furnish the electronic document with a qualified electronic signature in accordance with the Electronic Signature Act: *Signaturgesetz* – SigG), (iii) the text form according to § 126b BGB (declaration in a manner suitable for permanent reproduction such as a letter, email, USB-drive, and the like),[30] (iv) an agreed form between the parties, according to § 127 BGB, (v) the notarial recording according to § 128 BGB (the notary has an obligation to read, explain, and instruct according to the Authentication Act: *Beurkundungsgesetz* – BeurkG), and (vi) the official certification according to § 129 BGB (a signature certified by a notary without examination of content). Despite the introduction of § 126a BGB and with it, the possibility to replace the written form with the electronic form, the latter's use in Germany remains insignificant.[31] The requirement of a qualified electronic signature is accompanied with high costs and technical expenses that prevent companies from widespread adoption of this possibility. 46

### 3. Functions

The respective form requirements fulfil different functions, namely (i) warning, (ii) counselling, and (iii) proof. Depending on the consequences that specific categories of transactions usually trigger, the German legislator has established form requirements intended to prevent parties (or one of the parties) from entering into contracts while overlooking the potential consequences. Therefore, when parties enter into a contract for real estate, the contract must be recorded by a notary (§§ 128, 311b(1) sentence 1 BGB). The same applies when shares of a limited liability company (not a stock corporation) are transferred from one shareholder to another (§ 128 BGB, § 15(3) GmbHG). The rationale is that the parties are protected from over-hasty decisions if the notary explains the legal consequences of a land transaction or the transfer of shares. 47

### 4. Extent

The notarial record is necessary for any sort of contract that directly or indirectly obliges a party to transfer or acquire real estate, irrespective of whether this is a pre-con- 48

---

[30] See Grüneberg/Ellenberger BGB § 126b mn. 3.
[31] BeckOK BGB/Wendtland BGB § 126a mn. 1.

tract, a cancellation agreement or a subcontract.[32] In the case of composed contracts which, in addition to the obligation to sell or buy a plot of land, contain further obligations such as the obligation to transfer rights of exploitation, IP rights, or a client base, the entire contract has to be recorded by a notary. This is always the case where an internal connection may exist between the transfer of property and other contractual obligations.[33]

### 5. Legal consequences

49 If a form requirement exists but is not met, this constitutes a breach of form. In certain cases, the law provides the opportunity to cure such a breach, for instance if the promise of a gift was not recorded by a notary but the gift was actually rendered to the receiver (§ 518(2) BGB), or if the transfer or acquisition of ownership of a plot of land was not recorded by a notary but the declaration of conveyance and registration in the land register has been effected (§ 311b(1) sentence 2 BGB). If a legal transaction does not adhere to the form prescribed by statute, and the conditions for a cure of such a breach are not fulfilled, the contract is void according to § 125 sentence 1 BGB.

## II. Statutory prohibitions

50 Legal transactions that violate a statutory prohibition are void unless the statute leads to a different conclusion (§ 134 BGB). § 134 BGB limits the freedom of contract, as statutory prohibitions are not at the disposal of the parties.[34] The general rule is that a violation of a statutory prohibition results in the invalidity of the legal transaction. Therefore, a contract in which the parties agree on insurance fraud pursuant to § 265(1) StGB (*Strafgesetzbuch* – Criminal Code) or one that obliges the selling of alcohol to persons under 16 (§ 9(1) no. 2 JuSchuG: *Jugendschutzgesetz* – Law for the Protection of the Youth) is void. Although statutory prohibitions can be found in all areas of law, important ones are contained in the StGB. The main difficulty in interpreting this statute is determining the legal consequence of a violation. § 134 BGB stipulates the invalidity of a legal transaction only if the statute does not lead to a different conclusion. A different legal consequence exists, if the respective prohibition of a rule is directed only against the **formality** of a contract (no invalidity) and not its content (invalidity). For example, a contract concluded in breach of the Shops Closing Act (*Ladenschlussgesetz* – LadSchlG) is not void, as the content of the contract is not objectionable but only the time at which it was concluded.

## III. Legal transaction contrary to public policy

51 According to § 138(1) BGB, a legal transaction that violates *bonos mores* (public policy) is void. § 138 BGB restrains the freedom of contract in so far as the legal system does not accept contracts which content is contrary to public policy. The definition of 'public policy' or '*bonos mores*' is, in a fast-paced modern society, in urgent and constant need of interpretation and clarification. The courts have developed a set phrase to give shape to this amorphous definition: a violation exists, in so far as the contract breaches the sense

---

[32] Cf. Schöner/Stöber GrundbuchR mn. 3112 et seqq.
[33] BGH V ZR 111/72, DNotZ 1975, 87.
[34] BGH VII ZR 42/07, ZIP 2008, 1636 (mn. 13).

of decency of all right and proper-thinking persons.[35] Although this generic set phrase contributes little to a specification of the term, it enables changing social values to be considered. Behaviour and agreements that were considered outrageous 50 years ago may be socially acceptable today. In practice, case groups have formed which are comprised of, among others, (i) usury (§ 138(2) BGB – as a special case of violation of *bonos mores*), (ii) excessive demands of a structurally weaker party, (iii) economically oppressive contracts, or (iv) excessive security. The application of § 138 BGB serves as a last resort and will lead to the invalidity of a contract in extreme cases only.

## IV. Lack of seriousness and sham transaction

A declaration of intent made to another person is void according to § 117 (1) BGB if it is – with the consent of the other person – only made for the sake of appearance. In these cases, there is a lack of real intent to transact. A declaration of intent made in the expectation that its lack of serious intention will be recognised is also void pursuant to § 118 BGB (e.g. a joke declaration). However, if contrary to the expectation of the declaring party, the other party takes the declaration seriously, the declaring party is liable for damages according to § 122 BGB. **52**

## V. Avoidance

In cases where actual intent and declaration diverge without the awareness of the declaring party (unconscious divergence) or where a party is induced to make a declaration of intent by deceit or unlawfully by duress, the BGB provides the opportunity for the party making the declaration of intent to contest/avoid such declaration. The different reasons that give the declaring party the right to contest his/her declaration of intent are listed in §§ 119(1) and (2), 120 and 123 BGB. The results of avoidance are twofold: first, the initial declaration of intent is void from the outset (§ 142(1) BGB).[36] Consequently only one declaration of intent remains and the entire contract is ineffective. Second, if a declaration of intent is void, the person avoiding the declaration is liable to compensate the other party for damage that the other party suffers as a result of relying on the validity of the declaration of intent (*Vertrauensschaden*). However, the compensation payment cannot exceed the total amount of the interest the other or third party has regarding the validity of the declaration (*Erfüllungsinteresse*). **53**

A successful avoidance requires the fulfilment of the following conditions: **54**

1. a reason for avoidance,
2. causation between the reason for avoidance and the conclusion of the contract,
3. a declaration of avoidance according to § 143 BGB, and
4. observance of the avoidance period (§§ 121, 124 BGB).

The types of reasons for avoidance established by German law are examined below. As a rule, before assessing whether a party has the right of avoidance, one must clarify whether the true meaning of the declaration can be determined using the rules of interpretation, pursuant to §§ 133, 157 BGB. Only in cases where interpretation does not help **55**

---

[35] RG VI 443/1900, RGZ 48, 114, 124; BGH II ZR 217/03, NJW 2004, 2668 (2670).

[36] Exceptions are acknowledged for ongoing obligations, e.g. employment contracts, commercial agency agreements or authorised dealer agreements. In such cases, avoidance results in the invalidity of the transaction from the time of the declaration of avoidance (*ex nunc*), see Strick, NZA 2000, 695.

identify the true meaning of the declaration do the following reasons for avoidance give the declaring party the right to contest his/her declaration of intent.

## 1. Mistake

### a) Content and meaning

56 The mistake of content or meaning (*Inhaltsirrtum*) is regulated in the first alternative of § 119(1) sentence 1 BGB. Mistake of content or meaning occurs when the person making a declaration of intent is mistaken about the actual (legal) content of the declaration made. This applies in cases where the parties have used technical terms, and one of the parties has a wrong understanding of such terms (unconscious ignorance of the real facts). This also happens in situations in which, for instance, scale units,[37] the identity of the contract partner, or the scope of supply and service[38] were assessed erroneously. For example, if a person, who is not able to speak German, signs a contract of guarantee in German, and it later turns out that the signed document deviated considerably from what the signing guarantor thought it would mean, the guarantor can avoid his declaration of intent pursuant to the first alternative under § 119(1) sentence 1 BGB if he can prove that he would not have signed the document had he known the actual meaning.[39]

57 Yet, this type of mistake does not cover situations in which both parties to the contract use the same wrong term to mean the same thing (mutual mistake, e.g. if both parties consider the term 'ctb.' as an abbreviation for 'metric ton' instead of a 'container batch'). In this case, the actual meaning understood by both the parties becomes the subject matter of the contract.

### b) Expression

58 The mistake of expression (*Erklärungsirrtum*) is regulated in the second alternative of § 119(1) sentence 1 BGB. Mistake of expression typically involves mistyping, misprinting or misspelling words.

### c) Characteristics

59 As a general principle, mistakes about the motive of a party or a third person do not fall under § 119 BGB. Therefore, a person buying a diamond ring in the belief that his spouse will like it does not have a right to avoid his declaration of intent if it later turns out that his spouse does not like it. However, as an exception, § 119(2) BGB contains an established case of an error in motive: the mistake about the characteristics (*Eigenschaftsirrtum*). Pursuant to § 119(2) BGB, a mistake about the characteristics occurs where a person is mistaken about such characteristics of a person or a thing that are customarily regarded as essential. This includes all permanent characteristics influencing the value of the object. A characteristic is essential when it has an objective importance for the contract and therefore was made the basis of the contract. Essential characteristics, depending on the particular case, can include: origin and genuineness of artwork, position or development-potential of a plot of land, age or year of manufacture, usability of a machine for a certain application, the existence of a licence agreement with regard to a patent, or the age, knowledge, qualities, trustworthiness and credibility of a person. The mere value or price, however, is never an essential characteristic.

---

[37] LG Hanau 1 O 175/78, NJW 1979, 721.
[38] MüKoBGB/Armbrüster BGB § 119 mn. 80.
[39] Cf. BGH IX ZR 168/93, NJW 1995, 190.

#### d) Transmission

The mistake of transmission (*Übermittlungsirrtum*) is regulated in § 120 BGB. A declaration of intent that has been mistakenly transmitted by the person or facilities used for its transmission may be avoided. This is the case, for instance, where an assistant or other third party (the transmitter), by mistake, hears or writes something incorrectly and this is conveyed to the other party. § 120 BGB only covers unintentional mistakes of transmission.[40] **60**

### 2. Deceit or duress

The principle of freedom of contract requires that the will of a party to enter into a contract is protected. Therefore, a person giving a declaration under deceit or duress can avoid such declaration according to the criteria stipulated in § 123(1) BGB. The law provides that the deceived or coerced party be given free choice as to whether it wants to avoid the declaration, thereby annulling the contract, or adhere to the contract (for the unlikely case that the contract is beneficial). §§ 134 and 138 BGB prevail over § 123 BGB as they provide that the contract shall be void. Moreover, §§ 134 and 138 BGB are intended to regulate the content of a contract rather than its formation.[41] **61**

#### a) Deceit

Deceit (*arglistige Täuschung*) exists when a party creates a false impression or mistake in the mind of the other party, thereby causing the other party to make a declaration of intent. Deceit can either occur through active behaviour (e.g. lying, manipulating the speedometer when selling a car, making a misrepresentation to the buyer about the earning potential when selling a corporation) or by omission (concealment). However, concealment and suppression of the truth only constitute deceit if there is a duty to inform. Courts have established case groups according to which a duty to inform exists when (i) the other party expressly asks, (ii) certain circumstances are obviously of particular importance for the other party (e.g. severe defects of the object of purchase[42]), or (iii) mutual trust between the parties exists (e.g. in longstanding contractual relationships, in ongoing obligations where the parties are in close personal contact, or due to a certain professional position, such as bankers). One must keep in mind that with regard to employment relationships, the courts have developed the 'right to lie' in exceptional circumstances, in particular, if the (potential) employer asks prohibited questions (e.g. about pregnancy, certain infections or diseases of the potential employee, trade union membership, etc.).[43] In such cases, the employer has no right to avoid the employment contract if it turns out that the (potential) employee has answered these questions incorrectly. **62**

#### b) Duress

Duress (*Drohung*) is defined as the threat of a future evil that the person making the threat has or pretends to have control over. The threat must be unlawful and causal for the declaration of intent made by the addressee. In such a case, the threatened party may avoid its declaration of intent. **63**

---

[40] A person intentionally transmitting a declaration of intent in a false manner is to be treated as an unauthorised agent, OLG Oldenburg 1 U 88/77, NJW 1978, 951 (952).
[41] See BGH ZR 245/86, NJW 1988, 2599 (2601).
[42] BGH V ZR 246/87, NJW 1990, 975.
[43] For further reference see HK-BGB/Heinrich Dörner BGB § 123 mn. 4.

### 3. Period for declaration of avoidance

64 Pursuant to § 143(1) BGB, the declaration of avoidance must be made to the contract partner. In the cases established under §§ 119 and 120 BGB, avoidance must be declared by the mistaken party without culpable (undue) delay (§ 121(1) BGB). This period begins after the party entitled to avoid its declaration of intent obtains knowledge of the grounds for avoidance. The absolute preclusion period amounts to ten years from the time the declaration of intent was made (§ 121(2) BGB). Avoidance due to duress or deceit may, however, be declared within one year. In the case of deceit, the period commences when the deceived person discovers the deceit. In the case of duress, the period commences when the duress stops (§ 124(1) and (2) BGB).

## VI. Invalidity and partial invalidity

65 If a part of a legal transaction is void, then the entire legal transaction is generally also void (§ 139 BGB). The freedom of contract ensures that the parties are prevented from entering into a contract which they did not actually want to conclude. This general rule, however, is modified in cases in which the parties to the contract would have undertaken the transaction even without the void part (§ 139 BGB). Whether the parties would have entered into the contract without the void part is subject to interpretation (§§ 133, 157 BGB). For example, an invalid framework agreement typically does not affect the validity of the single purchase orders concluded under it. An arbitration or jurisdiction clause remains generally valid even though the contract is otherwise entirely invalid. On the flip side, an invalid arbitration clause of a contract generally does not lead to the invalidity of the contract itself.[44]

# E. Execution

## I. Performance of obligations

### 1. Types of obligations

66 A validly concluded contract gives either party the right to demand performance of the other party's obligations (§ 241(1) sentence 1 BGB). Depending on the contract, such performance can be either a one-time obligation of the obligor (*Schuldner*) or an ongoing obligation. As an example, the seller is obliged to hand over the object of purchase under a purchase agreement, whereas in a tenancy agreement the landlord shall provide the property to the tenant on a continuous basis. In the same vein, a commercial agent or distributor must provide his services to the entrepreneur continuously for the duration of the agreement and not only once. This type of contract is called an ongoing continuing obligation (*Dauerschuldverhältnis*).

[44] BGH III ZR 18/77, NJW 1979, 2567 (2568).

### 2. Claim for performance

If a party does not perform as contractually promised and thus breaches the contract, such a breach gives the other party the right to claim performance pursuant to § 241(1) BGB or – in cases of causative damage – to claim compensation for the damage incurred (§§ 280 et seqq. BGB).[45] In contrast to many common law jurisdictions, where a party can claim specific performance in court only under narrow circumstances, German law allows for this as long as the specific performance is not impossible. For example, if a party does not deliver the desired goods, the other party can only claim monetary damages in an English court. In contrast, a German court could order the other party to deliver the goods and fulfil the contract. 67

#### a) Sub-contracting

Basically, a party is not obliged to perform personally and may engage a third party to render performance (§ 267(1) BGB). Whether the obligor has to perform in person depends on the nature of his obligation as well as on the intention of the parties. German law stipulates that the performance of some contract types must be rendered in person, such as employment and service contracts (§§ 611, 613 BGB) or the contract of mandate (§§ 662, 664 BGB). In these cases, sub-contracting is generally not permitted, unless the contract specifically allows for this. In contrast, sub-contracting is generally permissible in contracts to produce a work (*Werkvertrag*). For example, sub-contracting plays an important role in the construction industry. 68

#### b) Main contractor

In construction law it is common that a main or general contractor organises and coordinates the construction of a work and must hand over the work ready-to-use. This is advantageous for the buyer since there is only one obligor that owes the entire construction. In the event of the illiquidity of a sub-contractor or defects, the general contractor is liable towards the buyer. The main contractor carries the entrepreneurial risk to subrogate against his sub-contractors. Of course, the buyer must pay the main contractor, who usually demands as fair remuneration a price above the mere sum of what all sub-contractors would cost him. 69

## II. Written and unwritten contractual obligations

### 1. Mandatory law

The content of a contract largely establishes the rights and duties of the parties. In general, statutory law provides default rules for the parties only in cases where they have merely agreed on the contract's basic content (*essentialia negotii*). For a purchase contract: price, product, and the parties constitute the *essentialia negotii*. If, for instance, the parties of a purchase agreement did not come to an agreement on warranty, guarantee, or liability, statutory law helps fill the gap. This is not the case if it becomes apparent from the circumstances that the parties had deviating intentions (e.g. they implicitly excluded an independent guarantee but did not do so in all previous purchase contracts). In such cases, interpretation helps fill the gap. 70

[45] With detailed and further illustration, Markesinis/Unberath/Johnston, pp. 444–474.

71 However, deviating intentions of the parties (implied or explicit) are irrelevant when the law provides mandatory rules that may not be disposed of by the parties. This is the case, for instance, largely in the commercial law of agency (§§ 84 et seqq. HGB), in labour law, and in consumer protection law. In these fields of law, the legislator intended to protect the structurally weaker party (commercial agent, employee, and consumer). This goal could be undermined if the parties are able to simply opt out of the protective statutory provisions. For example, it is not possible for the parties to a commercial agency agreement to exclude compensation if they terminate their contract (§§ 89b HGB).[46]

### 2. Subsidiary and protective obligations

72 In addition to the contractual main and subsidiary obligations, both parties have the duty to respect and to consider the other party's rights, legal interests, and other interests (§ 241(2) BGB). This obligation applies irrespective of whether the parties have agreed on these subsidiary and protective obligations (*Neben- und Schutzpflichten*). Subsidiary and protective obligations include the duty to inform the other party about important facts or developments and the duty to protect the physical integrity and property of the other party. Under certain circumstances (e.g. when starting serious negotiations), such subsidiary obligations may even arise prior to the conclusion or after termination of the contract (§ 311(2) BGB). Subsidiary and protective obligations may be waived only to the extent that their core protective effect is left in place.

## III. Gaps and interpretation

### 1. Interpretation

73 If the content of a contract or a single contractual provision remains unclear, German law provides for the instrument of interpretation. §§ 133, 157 BGB govern interpretation of the declaration of intent and therefore also of the resulting contract. Interpretation is also necessary where gaps in a contract arise due to the parties not considering specific situations when entering into the contract. Interpretation is of tremendous practical importance in all areas of civil law and helps clarify unclear contractual clauses, which is crucial for keeping the economic system running. Interpretation is aimed at identifying the true intention of the parties.

### 2. Standard of interpretation

74 Depending on the particular type of declaration, the standard of interpretation may be either (i) the subjective true intention of the declaring party (e.g. in unilateral legal transactions like the declaration of termination of a contract or the creation of a will) or (ii) the understanding of an objective reasonable addressee.[47] The latter standard of interpretation is applied in most cases, as it governs the interpretation of bilateral legal transactions such as most types of contracts (e.g. purchase contracts, agency or distribution contracts, supply agreements, etc.).

[46] Cf. BVerfG 1 BvR 1624/92, NJW 1996, 381; for further reference see Bälz, NJW 2003, 1559.
[47] See Grüneberg/Ellenberger BGB § 133 mn. 9.

### 3. Four-step test

The interpretation of a contract or a declaration of intent is governed by the following process. First, the judge (or, if the dispute is not yet pending, a party) interpreting the respective clause must look at the wording, spirit, and purpose of the contract. Second, the circumstances surrounding a contract may help (specific circumstances, formation of the contract, expressions of a party before or even after[48] the contract was concluded) identify the parties' actual intention. Third, the interests of the parties when entering into the contract need to be taken into account. Fourth, good faith and common practices are considered. 75

### 4. Legal assumptions

If these steps do not result in an unambiguous interpretation, German law provides for legal assumptions (*Auslegungsregeln*) for special types of situations (e.g. §§ 364(2), 2097, 2304 BGB). Moreover, the law also sets forth rules for clarifying specific types of cases. If a standard term is unclear, doubts are resolved to the detriment of the standard term's user (§ 305c(2) BGB). This also applies in insurance law when the insurance provider uses unclear contract clauses or certificates. 76

## IV. Contract types

### 1. Contract types provided by law

German law expressly regulates a number of contracts in the second book of the BGB, such as purchase contracts (§§ 433 et seqq. BGB), tenancy contracts (§§ 535 et seqq. BGB), service contracts (§§ 611 et seqq. BGB), construction contracts (§§ 650a et seqq. BGB), package travel contracts (§§ 651a et seqq.), brokerage contracts (§§ 652 et seqq. BGB), and many more. However, numerous types of contracts have been established in German civil law that are not regulated in the BGB, the HGB, or any other code. Contracts that are not regulated in a code – but whose existence is undisputed – are regularly subsumed under § 311(1) and (2) BGB (e.g. cancellation agreement) if they cannot be allocated to any other type of expressly regulated contract. An example is leasing contracts in the b2b context, which were not yet invented when the BGB came into force in 1900. Leasing agreements are to a large extent subsumed under the law of tenancy. 77

### 2. Developed contract types

The rights and duties of combined or composed contracts are defined according to case law as well as acknowledged customs and practices. Maintenance contracts, hospitality contracts, or retirement home contracts are, for example, mixed contracts (*typengemischter Vertrag*) or combined contracts (*zusammengesetzter Vertrag*). If a contract type is not expressly regulated but there is a close similarity to a specific and regulated contract type, such regulated contract type may be applied analogously (if certain conditions are fulfilled). This is true, for instance, in the case of distributorship agreements (application of the law of agency to a large extent (§§ 84 et seqq. HGB), → Ch. 12 mn. 5). 78

---

[48] BGH VIII ZR 136/04, NJW 2005, 3205 (3207).

## V. Modification and change

79 The principle *pacta sunt servanda* requires that the contract parties fulfil their contractual obligations under the contract. Non-fulfilment of respective obligations constitutes a breach of the contract (*pact*). The principle *pacta sunt servanda* binds the parties to the contract by what they have agreed on when concluding it. Therefore, contract changes or any other modification of the contract requires consent of the parties.

### 1. Contract modifications

80 Generally, there is no obligation on the part of either party to agree to any proposed change or modification by the other party. However, in practice, contract changes are often simply conducted by one party (the stronger one) and tolerated by the other (weaker) party. Depending on the individual case, this implied behaviour might constitute a contract change. Whether the conditions for such a change by implied behaviour are fulfilled is subject to interpretation.

81 For example, if the purchaser of services or goods continuously pays invoices of his supplier that feature increased prices, he generally consents to the price increase.[49] The continued performance of the job by the employee without objection may constitute the employee's acceptance of an offered contract change by the employer.[50] However, the unilateral cut by the entrepreneur to the commission payments of the commercial agent does not generally constitute a valid contract change (commission reduction) by implied agreement, even if the agent did not object to such a reduction.[51] This may not be the case if the behaviour of the commercial agent can be interpreted as consent (e.g. discussions about reduction without objection to the reduction, unchallenged confirmation letter about receipt of payment).

### 2. Contract change clauses

82 To keep contracts in fast-moving business environments (e.g. IT outsourcing agreements[52] or ongoing continuing obligations with an extensive time period) from losing their economic balance, parties may agree on specific contract change procedures (e.g. for prices). Such contract change procedures regularly only establish an obligation on the parties to negotiate in good faith on a price adjustment. These contract change clauses provide no obligation on the part of either party to consent to a change request made by the other party; such an obligation to consent would give the requesting party the right to modify the content of the contract unilaterally and is not recognised in German law.

### 3. Price index clauses

83 The freedom of contracts allows the parties to agree on price index clauses, which adjusts the price to be paid if certain conditions are satisfied. When drafting these clauses, one should pay special attention to the specific conditions that must be met and their consequences. Depending on the circumstances, the parties may agree on an increase in manufacturing costs, in the costs of living, or on other factors to be the trigger. If these

[49] BGH VIII ZR 36/06, NJW 2007, 2540 (gas price adjustment); for further reading, see Kolbe, BB 2010, 2322.
[50] BAG 4 AZR 129/00, MDR 2002, 37.
[51] BGH VIII ZR 293/94, NJW 1996, 588.
[52] See Mann, MMR 2012, 499.

conditions are met, the contract may allow for a contracting or a third party to determine a fair price, for the price of the goods to be pegged to manufacturing costs, or obligate the parties to negotiate a fair price.[53] If these clauses are imposed on a party in standard terms, the user must ensure that they do not unfairly disadvantage the other party. Otherwise, they will be invalid according to § 307 BGB.

## 4. Doctrine of interference with the basis of transaction

Under very narrow circumstances the BGB provides an opportunity to adapt contractual obligations pursuant to § 313 BGB including an adjustment of prices. This doctrine is called interference with the basis of transaction *(Störung der Geschäftsgrundlage).* It applies when (i) circumstances that became the **basis of a contract** have (ii) **significantly changed** since the contract was entered into, (iii) the parties would **not have entered** into the **contract** or would have entered into it **with different content** if they had foreseen this change, and (iv) one of the parties **cannot** reasonably **be expected** to **uphold** the contract without alteration. Under these conditions, adaptation of the contract may be demanded. § 313 BGB does not give the parties a right to unilaterally alter the contract. It only establishes a claim for alteration, which, in case of dispute, has to be executed and enforced by courts. However, the party seeking adaption under § 313 BGB initially has the duty to ask the other party for an adaption of the respective contractual obligation. If adaption is not possible or reasonable, § 313(3) BGB provides the disadvantaged party with a right to revoke the contract. **84**

The standard for applying § 313 BGB is high, as it falls within the responsibility of both parties to receive adequate performance and to negotiate the contract accordingly. However, the application of § 313 BGB is acknowledged, e.g. in the case of severe inflation, massive devaluation or massive increase of the value of performance due to legislative amendments, unforeseeable governmental intervention in economic policies impacting the contractual obligations. **85**

## 5. Price adaption in times of Covid-19, armed conflict, and inflation

We live in times of crisis. The Covid-19 pandemic, the raw material and semiconductor shortages, and also the war in Ukraine have introduced massive problems to trade. In particular, they have created structural imbalances between contracting parties. While one party may insist on the fulfilment of the contract in the agreed upon terms, the provider of these goods or services may not be able to do so without substantial losses and even jeopardy to its entire business. There are contractual and legal instruments that can correct these imbalances. Contractually, the parties can agree on the aforementioned price index clause or a *force majeure* clause.[54] Even if the contract does not contain such clauses, the disadvantaged party may be able to request adaption under § 313 BGB[55] or, in the case of an ongoing continuing obligation, be able to terminate the contract pursuant to § 314 BGB. Businesses are well-advised to regulate price adaption contractually to hedge their liabilities since the legal remedies often prove to be inadequate. **86**

---

[53] For a detailed discussion on the different types of price index clauses, see Mann/Waschkowski, BB 2022, 1283–1285.

[54] Mann/Waschkowski, BB 2022, 1285.

[55] For the extent in which § 313 BGB can be applied to crises, see: Mann/Waschkowski, BB 2022, 1286–1288.

# F. Extinction and termination

## I. Extinction by performance, impossibility, and set-off

87 A contract is extinguished according to § 362(1) BGB if the performance owed is rendered to the obligee (*Gläubiger*). This is the case if the performance owed is provided to the right obligee at the right place and the right time. Ongoing continuing obligations are not extinguished through performance of the obligor but rather when terminated by a lapse of time period or declaration of either party. § 275(1) BGB stipulates another scenario that may lead to the extinction of a contract. This is the case when the performance is impossible for the obligor (e.g. if the sold but not yet transferred factory burns down). In such a case the consideration is dispensed with (§ 326(1) BGB). A single claim may also be extinguished by setting it off against a claim of the other party (§§ 387 et seqq. BGB). The BGB permits a party that has an enforceable claim against another person to set off (*aufrechnen*) its claim against the enforceable claim of the other person. Furthermore, a contract may be extinguished by lapse of time or if the parties conclude a cancellation agreement, which frequently happens in practice.

## II. Revocation, rescission, and cancellation

### 1. Revocation

88 Revocation (*Widerruf*) provides the opportunity for consumers (§ 13 BGB) to revoke certain types of contracts within a period of 14 days after their conclusion and a corresponding instruction referring to the right to revoke the contract was made to the consumer in text form (§ 355 BGB). The types of transactions conferring a right of revocation are, for example, off-premises contracts (§ 312b BGB), distance selling contracts (§ 312c BGB), and consumer loan contracts (§ 491 BGB).[56] The right of revocation is intended to protect consumers in situations in which a threat or effect of surprise pressures him into concluding a contract that he may regret after consideration, or in situations in which the consumer does not have the opportunity to examine the goods in person until after the contract has been concluded. Enterprises specialising in these types of businesses (e.g. distance or online selling) need to ensure that the mandatory instruction of their right to revocation is properly issued to the consumers. Otherwise, the consumer may still have a right of revocation a year and 14 days after entering into the contract with the entrepreneur (§§ 356(3) BGB). However, it is important to note that in b2b contracts the right of revocation pursuant to § 355 BGB does not exist, unless that parties explicitly agree on a right of revocation of the contract.

### 2. Rescission

89 Recission (*Rücktritt*) must be distinguished from revocation. Revocation does not require good cause or any other reason to be triggered, whereas a reason is necessary in the case of rescission. §§ 323 and 324 BGB specify the potential statutory reasons that may give the parties a right to rescind the contract. This is the case, in particular, if a party is in breach of contractual duties after a new time limit for performance set by the

[56] For a brief overview, see Lorenz, JuS 2000, 833.

obligee has expired. After the declaration of rescission, the contract is transformed into an obligation of restitution (*Rückgewährschuldverhältnis*), meaning performances received and payments taken must be returned. In so doing, the parties return all performances they have received from one another, including any profit obtained in accordance with its intended use. If the contract for the sale of an industrial machine is rescinded, the seller has to return the purchase price whereas the purchaser has to give back the machine plus any emoluments taken (such as the benefits from the usage of the machine). If the sold good (e.g. the machine) has been used up, resold, processed, or redesigned, the sold good has deteriorated or been destroyed, or if emoluments may not be returned, the obligor must provide compensation to the obligee. In the case at hand, the purchaser would have to compensate the loss in value due to the usage of the machine plus expenses saved from not having to rent an alternative machine. Compensation is usually made by means of a monetary payment. If the parties do not agree on the compensation, the judge has discretion to estimate its value (§ 287 ZPO).[57]

### 3. Cancellation

Cancellation (*Vertragsaufhebung*) is not regulated in German law. A party therefore **90** does not have a right to unilaterally cancel a contract that has been concluded, but is bound according to the principle *pacta sunt servanda*. However, the parties may by mutual agreement cancel a contract (→ Ch. 11 mn. 60 et seqq.).

## III. Notice of termination

### 1. General

Ongoing continuing obligations (e.g. tenancy and lease agreements, employment con- **91** tracts, contracts of partnership, framework and supply agreements, authorised dealer or distribution contracts, commercial agency agreements, etc.) may not be rescinded but can be terminated. A recission would be impractical, as a return of rendered performances is often extremely complex and costly, since ongoing continuing obligations may have been running for years or even decades with a continuous exchange of contractual obligations, e.g. a residential tenant would have made monthly payments while the landlord would have supplied the use of a rental property. Therefore, ongoing continuing obligations may only be terminated in such a way that they end once the declaration of termination takes effect instead of having a retroactive effect (*ex nunc* effect instead of *ex tunc*). The law provides for different types of notice of termination: the extraordinary notice of termination, also commonly referred to as termination for cause (*außerordentliche Kündigung*) and termination with notice, also referred to as ordinary notice of termination (*ordentliche Kündigung*).

---

[57] If the parties reverse the purchase of an apartment or real estate, compensation for the use of the apartment/real estate for the time between the handover and return is assessed according to the average rent, see BGH V ZR 51/05, NJW 2006, 1582.

## 2. Types of termination

### a) Ordinary notice of termination

92 Ordinary notice of termination (*ordentliche Kündigung*) is commonly negotiated between the parties to a contract. Its conditions are usually inserted into the contract. This is particularly the case when the contract is supposed to run for an unlimited period of time. In some cases, the law also sets forth fallback or even mandatory rules on termination for cause and ordinary notice of termination. § 89 HGB regulates terms of ordinary notice of termination in commercial agency contracts that cannot be modified to the detriment of the agent.[58] These principles may also apply to distributorship agreements if specific conditions are fulfilled (→ Ch. 12 mn. 76). If the parties to a tenancy agreement have concluded their contract for an unlimited period of time, the landlord may only give ordinary notice of termination if he has a legitimate interest in termination (§ 573(1) and (2) BGB). In employment relationships, § 622 BGB specifies notice periods that are binding for the employer and that are intended to protect the employee. Pursuant to § 622(4) and (5) BGB, diverging contractual provisions are valid only under very limited circumstances (collective labour agreements or by individual agreement).

### b) Extraordinary notice of termination without notice period

93 § 314 BGB is the general rule when it comes to extraordinary notice of termination. For specific contracts, the law also provides specific rules on extraordinary notice of termination (e.g. § 89a HGB, § 543 BGB, § 626 BGB). However, the differences between these specific rules are minor. They follow the general principle of § 314 BGB while accounting for additional special features of the respective fields of law (tenancy, labour, commercial agency, etc.). § 314 BGB establishes the opportunity for either party of an ongoing continuing obligation to terminate the contract for cause (a compelling reason) without any notice period. This right of termination may not be excluded by agreement between the parties.[59]

### c) Good reason

94 An important or good reason (or cause) exists if the terminating party cannot reasonably be expected to continue the contractual relationship until the agreement ends or until the expiry of a notice period, taking into account all circumstances of the specific case and weighing the interests of both parties. The courts have developed this definition and established that, when assessing whether it is unacceptable for a party to continue the contractual relationship, one must also take into account the duration of the ongoing continuing obligation, including the possibility to terminate it with notice, the consequences of termination for the other party, the severity of a contractual violation (if any), and the behaviour of the parties.[60] If the compelling reason consists in the breach of a duty under the contract (which is not necessarily required for termination under § 314 BGB), the contract cannot be terminated until after the terminating party has sent a warning notice to the other party and such warning has not led to the mitigation of the underlying problem.

---

[58] BGH VII ZR 29/62, NJW 1964, 350; Oetker/Busche HGB § 89 mn. 24. However, an extension of the notice period that benefits the agent is permitted, KG 2 U 4731/96, MDR 1997, 1041.

[59] BGH VIII ZR 218/85, NJW 1986, 3134.

[60] BGH VIII ZR 312/79, NJW 1981, 1264 (relationship breakdown); OLG Frankfurt/Main 16 U 231/12, NJW-RR 2013, 1272 (suspicion of drug use).

#### d) Extraordinary termination with notice period

If the law does not set forth specific fallback rules (e.g. because the respective contract cannot be allocated to a specific contract type) the courts have developed an uncodified right to terminate an ongoing continuing obligation with an adequate notice period under specific circumstances.[61] The courts have established the requirement of a notice period by way of analogy to §§ 624 and 723 BGB.[62] This unwritten right to terminate the agreement extraordinarily is given if 95

1. the parties have concluded a contract for **unlimited ongoing obligations**,
2. **the right to terminate** the contractual relationship is **not foreseen in the contract,** and
3. the **parties did not exclude the right to terminate** the ongoing obligation ordinarily.[63]

Depending on the individual case and the interests of the parties, the courts have found a notice period of six months to be fair, just, and therefore adequate. However, such a notice period is not fixed. Instead, the interests of both parties must be weighed and the decision made on a case-by-case basis.[64] 96

### 3. Declaration of termination

#### a) Requirements

A declaration of termination does not necessarily have to contain the word 'termination' or phrase 'notice of termination'. Any behaviour by the declaring party that makes it clear for an objective recipient of the declaration that the declaring party wants to terminate the contractual relationship for the future is sufficient. The terminating party, however, is well-advised to formulate the declaration as clearly as possible to avoid dispute over the question of whether a declaration of termination was in fact made. Generally, the declaration of termination may not be subject to conditions. This restriction does not apply if the fulfilment of the condition lies in the discretion of the addressee. For example, if a declaration of termination has been issued in the event that the addressee does not hand over confidential documents – which he has taken from the employer – within one week, this declaration is valid even though it is subject to a condition. Moreover, an alternative declaration of termination may be validly declared (e.g. alternative ordinary termination applies if an extraordinary termination turns out to be invalid). 97

#### b) Pitfalls when declaring termination

Practice has shown that avoidable mistakes are often made when terminating commercial contracts and that such mistakes result in disputes between the parties as to (i) whether notices of termination are valid and (ii) whether notices of termination were given in a timely manner. In the case of ongoing continuing obligations that have a period of notice of a year or even longer, the mere uncertainty or possibility as to whether the notice of termination is invalid may establish material economic disadvantages for the party terminating the contract. 98

If notice of termination is given shortly before the expiry of the notice period, the terminating party is often confronted with an unpleasant surprise. For instance, notices of 99

---

[61] BGH III ZR 212/70, NJW 1972, 1128 (1129); BGH III ZR 145/05, NJW-RR 2006, 1427.

[62] BGH III ZR 145/05, NJW-RR 2006, 1427; OLG Munich 15 U 6473/94, NJW-RR 1996, 561 (563).

[63] The exclusion of the right to ordinarily terminate an ongoing continuing obligation may be invalid in general terms, see OLG Stuttgart, OLGZ 90, 249 (251). When such an exclusion is invalid, the termination with notice period will remain valid.

[64] Cf. BGH III ZR 212/70, NJW 1972, 1128 (1129–1130).

termination may be invalid if the recipient rejects the declaration for the lack of evidence of proper authorisation in accordance with § 174 BGB. This can spell disaster for a notice of termination that is given shortly or immediately before the expiry of the relevant time limit, since it is no longer possible in such a case to remedy the defect in due time.

**100** Likewise, the form in which the notice of termination is transmitted may harbour risks. For instance, notices of termination are often transmitted by registered letter with recorded delivery to 'be on the safe side'. However, if the postman does not find the recipient to accept delivery, the receipt thereof may not occur until after the last day of the notice of termination. Finally, notices of termination are frequently invalid because the applicable formal requirements are not satisfied when the notice of termination is given.

## 4. Form

**101** Statutory law does not usually specify a general requirement regarding the form of notice of termination of ongoing continuing obligations.[65] However, the parties can agree on the necessary form for a notice of termination (*gewillkürtes Formerfordernis*), e.g. written form, electronic form, or text form. Before giving notice of termination, the terminating party should therefore carefully examine the agreement to be terminated to be certain about the form, notice period, and possible causes for termination. §§ 126 et seqq. BGB help identify the specific formal requirements that need to be met in each individual case.[66] If no specific form is required, it is strongly recommended – for reasons of evidence – to make a declaration of termination in writing in any case. Moreover, the terminating party should send the declaration of termination by fax or email-scan in advance and ask for confirmation by the recipient.

## 5. Proper authorisation

### a) General

**102** If notice of termination is given by persons at the company who are authorised to represent the company and are registered as such in the commercial register (managing directors, management board members, registered managers, etc.), and if the manner of representation provided for in the commercial register (e.g. representation together with a second managing director or with a procurement officer) is adhered to, the notice of termination is not contestable in this regard. Problems may arise, however, if notice of termination is given by a 'mere' executive employee, a person with commercial power of attorney (*Handlungsbevollmächtigter*) or any another employee who is not entered into the commercial register as a representative of the company. In such a case the recipient is generally entitled to reject the notice of termination by means of a declaration to be made vis-à-vis the terminating person without delay (§ 174 BGB).

### b) Exclusion of the right to reject

**103** This right of rejection pursuant to § 174 BGB is excluded in the following cases only:

- The authorised representative giving notice of termination presents a power of attorney either in the **original** or as an executed copy in accordance with § 47 BeurKG.[67]

---

[65] An exception can be found in labour law, see § 623 BGB.
[66] For further details see Wagner/Mann, BB 2012, 2842 (2843).
[67] BGH III ZR 235/86, NJW 1988, 697.

- The authorisation of the person giving notice of termination to represent the company can be inferred from the **commercial register** (→ mn. 19) and any existing legal uncertainty can be eliminated by an inspection of the register.[68]
- The recipient of the notice of termination was **informed** about such authorisation by the person granting the authorisation (§ 174 sentence 2 BGB), because in this case, there is no justified doubt about representative not having valid authority to carry out such a declaration[69].
- The rejection of the notice of termination is **contrary to the principle of good faith** within the meaning of § 242 BGB. This is the case if (i) the recipient of the notice knew that the declarer was an authorised representative of the company from their contractual relationship,[70] (ii) the recipient of the notice of termination did not object to the declarer acting as a representative in the past, and (iii) it was clear to the recipient of the notice of termination, on account of the declarer actions in the past, that the declarer was also entitled to terminate the agreement.[71] This is typically the case if the declarer participated in the negotiation of the agreement or an amendment in the past, or if the entire performance of the contractual relationship was assigned to the declarer and he was therefore the sole contact person for the recipient in their contractual relationship. Yet, the reliance on this exception may lead to uncertainty regarding the validity of the declaration of termination.

#### c) Conditions of § 174 BGB

If the recipient rejects the declaration of termination due to § 174 BGB, such a rejection **104**
must occur promptly, i.e. without undue delay. If this condition is met, the rejection will result in the notice of termination being invalid. Such invalidity cannot be subsequently cured. The only remedy is to give a new notice of termination, which is not retroactive to the time of receipt of the first notice of termination, meaning that the new notice of termination may be given too late.

#### d) Rejecting the rejection

If the notice of termination has been declared by a lawyer or by another representative **105**
without presenting an original power of attorney and this has been rejected by the recipient's representative, who in turn does not have an original document proving power of attorney, the terminating party may still be able to save his declaration. The terminating party must have his original power of attorney and reject the rejection pursuant to § 174 BGB. A possible new rejection of the original notice of termination by the recipient of the notice would be unduly delayed and thus ineffective.

### 6. Transmission of notice of termination

The notice of termination becomes effective the moment it is received by the recipient. **106**
Any delays occurring in the transmission of the notice of termination are to the detriment of the party terminating the agreement. In the case of a dispute, the party terminating the agreement, additionally bears the burden of proving that the notice of termination was received in due time.[72] In particular, the following methods are possible when it comes

---

[68] See BAG 2 AZR 107/91, ZIP 1992, 497.
[69] In this case, the information must be given by an authorised representative of the company. As a consequence, this does not give the terminating party an advantage, Wagner/Mann, BB 2012, 2842 (2843).
[70] LG Aachen 5 S 411/77, NJW 1978, 1387.
[71] See MüKoBGB/Schubert BGB § 174 mn. 37.
[72] BGH ZR 204/75, NJW 1978, 886.

to transmitting a notice of termination. The advantages and disadvantages thereof are briefly presented in the following.

**a) Courier**

107 Probably the safest[73] – but also the most expensive – way of transmitting a notice of termination is delivery by hand or delivery by having the notice of termination placed in the mailbox by a courier. To prove, in a dispute, that the notice of termination was received by the recipient, the courier should be able to confirm that he (i) placed the actual notice of termination in the recipient's mailbox or (ii) personally handed it over to the recipient. The notice of termination should not be placed in an envelope until the courier is present to enable him to obtain knowledge of the content of the letter. It is also advisable for the courier to produce a brief note that includes the exact occurrences of the transmission, the exact time and date of these occurrences, and for the courier to sign such a note. A courier can also be an employee, a friend, family member, or any other third party.

**b) Registered letter**

108 Transmission of the notice of termination by registered letter is far less suitable for providing evidence of its receipt than is generally assumed. If the notice of termination is transmitted by registered letter, the person giving notice of termination is not able, in the case of a dispute, to provide adequate evidence that the recipient actually received the notice of termination. The certification note merely indicates that an unspecified letter was transmitted to the recipient and does not prove that the actual notice of termination was received. This may establish *prima facie* evidence of the receipt or may trigger a secondary burden of presentation on the recipient's part. In any case, residual risks will remain. It is therefore inadvisable to use a registered letter with recorded delivery for a notice of termination. For in this case – unlike the case of a registered letter being placed in the recipient's mailbox – an act of participation by the recipient is required. If the postman finds that the recipient is unavailable to accept the letter, he will merely leave a notification card. At this point in time, the notice of termination has not yet been received by the recipient. Only if the recipient picks up the registered letter at the local post office is the service performed, and this may be days or weeks later. In a worst-case scenario, the termination period might expire during this time.

**c) Ordinary letter**

109 Transmission of the notice of termination by an ordinary, unregistered letter is much less expensive. However, such a form of transmission is unsuitable in practice because it does not produce evidence of the notice of termination having been received by the recipient.[74] It may, however, be combined with an additional (previous) transmission by email depending on the likelihood of a future 'transmission dispute'.

**d) Email**

110 Regarding transmission by email, the discussion concerning transmission by an unregistered letter applies analogously. Here, too, it is not possible to provide full evidence of the notice of termination having been received. Even an automatically generated confirmation that the email was read is not sufficient for this purpose, because such confirmation,

---

[73] NK-BGB/Faust BGB § 130 mn. 90.

[74] A letter sent by post does not even constitute *prima facie* evidence for the reception of the notice of termination, see BGH II ZR 132/56, NJW 1957, 1230 (1231); LG Potsdam 11 S 233/99, NJW 2000, 3722.

being an automatic software product, is prone to error. Yet, transmission by email may also be combined with other forms of transmission.

#### e) Delivery by hand

111 The notice of termination is frequently handed to the recipient during a personal meeting in which the reasons underlying the termination are explained. In such a case, the notice of termination must be handed over in the presence of a witness. However, the corporate officers authorised to represent the company (managing directors, management board members, etc.) cannot be named by the company as witnesses according to the ZPO. It is therefore essential that at least one employee is present during such a talk who is not a member of the upper management team. This includes the person handing over the notice of termination.

## IV. Limitation

112 Claims are not enforceable forever. Legal certainty and legal concord require that an obligor has certainty as to whether or not the obligee will claim performance from him at some point in time. Moreover, evidence deteriorates over time, as witnesses might not recall the details of what actually happened and documents could disappear. Therefore, the BGB provides specific rules on limitation (*Verjährung*). Once a claim has lapsed (*verjährt*) it is not voided but can no longer be claimed by the obligee.[75] Therefore, limitation gives the obligor a right to refuse performance. This right to refuse performance must be exercised by the obligor. This means a judge would not apply limitation *ex officio*, if the obligor does not expressly raise this objection.

### 1. Definition of claim

113 Pursuant to § 194(1) BGB, only claims are subject to limitation. Claims are defined as the right to demand that another person performs or refrains from an act. For example, payment claims, injunctive relief, claims for restitution, or claims for recovery of property fall under § 194 BGB, whereas mere rights such as termination, rescission, revocation, or avoidance are not 'claims' within the meaning of § 194(1) BGB and are therefore not subject to limitation.[76]

### 2. Standard limitation period

114 Pursuant to § 195 BGB, the standard limitation period is three years, although certain claims lapse after 10 years (e.g. the transfer of ownership of land, § 196 BGB) or 30 years (e.g. claims that have been declared final and absolute, enforceable settlements or judgments, § 197 BGB). Moreover, sales law and other areas of law include specific limitation periods which prevail over the general standard limitation period (two years in sales law[77] and claims arising from a contract to produce a work[78]).

---

[75] For the consequences of this distinction, see Markesinis/Unberath/Johnston, p. 491.

[76] See OLG Stuttgart 5 U 108/06, NZG 2007, 239 (240); Jauernig/Mansel BGB § 194 mn. 2.

[77] In sales law, § 438 BGB stipulates that the limitation of claims for defects and therefore also the claim for performance is two years after the movable good was handed over (five years, if the purchased good is a building or shall be used for a building).

[78] § 634a(1) no. 1 BGB. For construction work, the limitation period is five years (§ 634a (I) no. 2 BGB).

### 3. Commencement of limitation

115 The commencement of limitation depends on whether the standard limitation or a specific limitation rule applies.

- The **standard limitation period** commences at the end of the year in which: (i) the claim arises and (ii) the obligee obtains knowledge of the circumstances that give rise to the claim and of the identity of the obligor, or would have obtained such knowledge had he not shown gross negligence. For example, if a party (the obligor) breaches its contractual duties in May 2020 and the obligee obtains knowledge of such breach in November 2020, the limitation period starts to run immediately after 31 December 2020 (at midnight). The claim would become statute-barred on 1 January 2024 (as the limitation period amounts to three full years: 2021, 2022, and 2023). If the obligee does not obtain knowledge in November 2020 but instead in January 2021, the limitation period starts to run immediately after 31 December 2021, as both elements – the existence of the claim and knowledge of the obligee – are required under § 199(1) BGB (standard limitation). In the latter case, the claim of the obligee against the obligor would become statute-barred on 1 January 2025 (as the limitation period amounts to three full years: 2022, 2023 and 2024).
- **Limitation** in **sales law** or in **claims arising from a contract to produce a work** commences upon delivery of the goods (sales law) pursuant to § 438(2) BGB or upon certified acceptance (*Abnahme*) pursuant to § 634a(2), 640 BGB (contract to produce a work). Specific limitation rules supersede the general standard limitation rule.
- **Claims for damages** based on injury to life, body, health, or liberty, notwithstanding the way they arose and notwithstanding knowledge or a grossly negligent lack of knowledge, become statute-barred 30 years from the date on which the act, breach of duty, or other event that caused the damage occurred (§ 199(2) BGB).
- **Maximum limitation period**: Irrespective of knowledge or a grossly negligent lack of knowledge on the part of the obligee, claims lapse 10 years after they arose (§ 199(3) no. 1 BGB). This maximum period does not commence at the end of the year but instead on the exact day on which the claim arose (e.g. the appearance of the damage, the conclusion of the contract, the breach of duty). This maximum period does not apply to damages based on injury to life, body, health or liberty, as § 199(2) BGB provides a 30-year limitation period in such cases.

### 4. Suspension and recommencement

116 The obligee may take measures to stop limitation of the claim. This may be done by suspension (*Hemmung*) pursuant to §§ 203 to 211 BGB or by recommencement (*Neubeginn*) pursuant to § 212 BGB.

#### a) Suspension

117 In this case, the suspended time period is not included in the calculation of the limitation period, meaning that the suspension period is added to the limitation period. The limitation period is suspended when:

- **serious negotiations** between the obligor and the obligee are in progress with respect to the claim (suspension is in effect until one party refuses to continue the negotiations) (§ 203 BGB);
- an **action is brought** for performance or for a declaration of the existence of the claim (§ 204(1) no. 1 BGB);

- a **payment order** (*Mahnbescheid*) in summary proceedings for recovery is served (§ 204(1) no. 3 BGB);
- an **application for conciliation** is filed with a conciliation body established or recognised by the state justice administration authority (§ 204(1) no. 4 BGB);
- the **set-off** of a claim in a legal action is asserted (§ 204(1) no. 5 BGB);
- an **application for evidence** to be taken in independent proceedings (*selbstständiges Beweisverfahren*) is served (§ 204(1) no. 7 BGB);
- a **claim in insolvency proceedings** or in proceedings for the distribution of assets under maritime law is filed (§ 204(1) no. 10 BGB);
- an **arbitration proceeding** is started (§ 204(1) no. 11 BGB);
- the parties have **agreed on a standstill** (*Stillhalteabkommen*) giving the obligor a right to refuse performance (§ 205 BGB).

#### b) Recommencement

Unlike suspension, recommencement leads to a complete restart of the entire limitation period. The limitation period recommences, for instance, if the obligor acknowledges the claim towards the obligee by part payment, by payment of interest, by providing security, or in another way. When carrying out the described acts, the obligor, however, must be aware of the existence of the obligation.[79] **118**

### 5. Deviating agreement

Limitation may in principle be subject to party agreement and amendment. Before or after a claim has arisen, parties may extend or shorten the limitation period or agree on a deviating commencement date. However, in consumer contracts the statutory rules on limitation are mandatory and binding. An agreement that deviates to the detriment of the consumer is invalid.[80] Term review is less restrictive in b2b contracts.[81] However, the limits of § 309 no. 8(b)(ff) BGB must be adhered to in standard terms and conditions. Whether a contractual agreement between the parties that deviates from the statutory provisions on limitation is permissible in b2b contracts will therefore depend on the circumstances of the individual case. **119**

## G. Contracts in the digital age

Businesses and governmental agencies are increasingly eliminating physical medium in favour of the digital. This has significantly transformed the way businesses communicate and undertake day-to-day activities. The impact of the digital transformation on the legal landscape is appropriately large. This section tracts the implications of the increasing digitisation on the conclusion of contracts. In particular, some of the possibilities of concluding a contract online will be described and the legality of such a conclusion discussed. **120**

Recently, many services that facilitate the conclusion of a contract online have emerged (for example, DocuSign, Yousign, eSignature, Dropbox Sign). These services allow their users to send, receive, and sign documents electronically. Usually, a person who has an **121**

[79] Cf. BGH IX ZR 159/95, NJW 1997, 516 (518).
[80] Graf v. Westphalen/Thüsing VertrR/AGB-Klauselwerke/Graf von Westphalen Verjährungsklauseln mn. 1 et seqq.
[81] Cf. BGH VII ZR 15/12, NJW 2013, 525.

account with one of these companies drafts a contract in which he determines who the recipient is and where he is to sign. The recipient receives the contract electronically and can sign and return it. The original sender then receives the concluded contract.

122 Different companies offer slightly different services. In most of them, certain metadata are collected and made visible to the contractual parties. For example, one can often see when the contract is signed and sent, when the contract is viewed by the recipient, the verification of the mobile number that the recipient has used (if applicable), when the contract is signed, the IP-addresses of the signatories, and the time when the contract is concluded. These services often allow the parties to use a signature on file that has been saved by the users or to sign by hand (for example, on a touch screen device).

123 For contracts without form requirement (→ mn. 45), their conclusion in electronic form is permitted. In trade relations, the corresponding declarations of intent to a contract are often expressed by the signatures of the parties and these services provide a way to do so online. The main advantage of these services is that they provide evidence on the conclusion of the contract. If there is any dispute between the parties about whether a contract has been concluded, the party that needs to prove the facts can point to the metadata which are attached to the contract. For example, if the party disputing the validity of the contract claims that it was not him who signed it, the other party can point out that the mobile number and/or the IP-address corresponds to those of the disputing party. The anonymity of the internet and the possibility of impersonation make these services helpful in dispelling doubt of the signatories' identities.

124 For contracts with a written form requirement, § 126(3) BGB allows the form to be replaced by the electronic form pursuant to § 126a BGB, if it is not specifically forbidden by statute. For example, the declaration of suretyship cannot be made in electronic form, § 766 sentence 2 BGB. To make use of the electronic form, certain technical requirements need to be fulfilled. The most important (and cumbersome) one is the qualified electronic signature. Such a signature is created by a qualified electronic signature device and based on a qualified certificate for electronic signatures (Article 3 no. 12 Regulation (EU) 910/2014). The qualified electronic signature device needs to fulfil the technical specifications in Annex II Regulation (EU) 910/2014, while the qualified certificate for electronic signatures can only be issued by trust service providers authorised by different national governments. In Germany, the list of trust service providers is maintained by the Federal Network Agency (*Bundesnetzagentur*).[82] The list does not include most private companies that currently provide electronic signature services.

125 As briefly discussed above (→ mn. 46), the use of the electronic form as pursuant to § 126a BGB remains limited because of the high cost and inconvenience associated with making a qualified electronic signature. The inconvenience of the written form is seen as the lesser of two evils in comparison to the electronic form. For this reason, it has not enjoyed widespread adoption.

---

[82] https://www.bundesnetzagentur.de/cln_121/EVD/DE/Uebersicht_eVD/start.html.

# Chapter 2
# Standard terms and conditions

**Bibliography:** Auer-Reinsdorff/Conrad, Handbuch IT und Datenschutzrecht, 3rd edn, Munich 2019; Graf von Westphalen, 'Das faktische Ende von Preisanpassungsklauseln', MDR 2008, 424; Grüneberg (ed.), Bürgerliches Gesetzbuch: BGB, 82nd edn, Munich 2023; Hopt (ed.), Handelsgesetzbuch: HGB, 42nd edn, Munich 2023; Mann, 'Die Einbeziehung von AGB in Verträgen zwischen Unternehmern', BB 2017, 2179; Mann, Vertriebsrecht in Handel und Industrie, Munich 2017; Martinek/Semler/Flohr, Vertriebsrecht, 4th edn, Munich 2016; Münchener Kommentar BGB, 9th edn, Munich 2021; Ohlendorf/Salamon, 'Die Aufrechterhaltung unwirksamer Formulararbeitsbedingungen – das Verhältnis des Verbots geltungserhaltender Reduktion zur ergänzenden Vertragsauslegung im Arbeitsrecht', RdA 2006, 281.

## A. Introduction

1 The law on standard terms and conditions (*Allgemeine Geschäftsbedingungen*) is ubiquitous in German contract and commercial **practices.** It must be taken into account when drafting and negotiating a contract, as the applicability of the law of standard terms and conditions is determined during this stage. Standard terms and conditions are commonly used not only in consumer contracts but also – at least to the same extent – in commercial relations between entrepreneurs. There are virtually no dealings between a supplier and manufacturer or between a seller and (commercial) customer that do not involve standard terms and conditions. The importance of terms and conditions should not be underestimated. The European Council Directive 93/13/EEC of 5th April 1993 on unfair terms in consumer contracts was not only considered a milestone in harmonising the contract laws of the EU Member States but also in advancing regulation of unfair terms in contracts concluded between a seller or supplier and a consumer. However, German law contains a review of standard terms and conditions (test of reasonableness) that goes far beyond what is established under the European Directive. In Germany, the law on standard terms and conditions is applied not only to consumer contracts but also to contracts between entrepreneurs (§ 310(1) sentence 2 BGB).

## B. The German test of reasonableness

2 German law establishes a system under which contract clauses (terms) are reviewed according to whether they constitute an unreasonable disadvantage (*unangemessene Benachteiligung*) for the other party. This review is called the test of reasonableness. The general rule is that if a standard term constitutes an unreasonable disadvantage for the other party, such term is void and can therefore not be applied.

3 The law on standard terms and conditions is incorporated in the BGB in §§ 305 to 310, which define the scope of application of standard terms and conditions. Once a

contractual clause is considered a standard clause, it is subject to the review according to §§ 307, 308 and 309 BGB. To evaluate whether a clause in a contract is considered an unreasonable disadvantage, German law establishes a non-exhaustive list of prohibited terms (§§ 308 and 309 BGB). Moreover, § 307 BGB serves two functions. First, it gives examples of cases that fall under the term unreasonable disadvantage (§ 307(2) BGB). Second, § 307(1) BGB serves as a general rule for cases where §§ 308 and 309 BGB are not applicable (e.g. b2b cases).

## C. Scope of application

4 § 305 BGB stipulates that standard terms are (i) contract terms, (ii) pre-formulated, (iii) intended for repeated use that (iv) one party to the contract (the user) imposes on the other party upon entering into the contract.

### I. Standard contract terms

5 This definition makes clear that not only the typical small-print documents that are commonly attached to a contract when concluding the transaction constitute standard terms. Framework agreements or other comprehensive contractual documents used repeatedly with one or several contracting parties are also standard terms in the meaning of § 305 BGB. It is even sufficient that repeated use of specific contractual terms is intended. Therefore, the first use of a newly drafted document may be subject to the test of reasonableness if the user intends to use the contract clauses at least three times.[1] Furthermore, it is important to note that each individual contract clause may be subject to the test of reasonableness if pre-formulated and used repeatedly; this does not only apply to the entire agreement. How long the contract is, what typeface or font is used, and what form the contract has is irrelevant (§ 305(1) sentence 2 BGB).

### II. Pre-formulation

6 Contract clauses are pre-formulated if the respective clause is ready to use prior to the signing of the contract. It is not necessary that the clauses are written down or handed over to the other party. It is sufficient if the clauses or the terms and conditions are visibly posted in the salesroom. Clauses are pre-formulated if, for instance, the director of a sales company asks his sales personnel or distributors to learn certain contract clauses by heart and to write them in the contract by hand or to use them when reaching an oral agreement with a customer.[2] It is not necessary that the party using the standard terms has drafted the clauses itself.[3] Clauses and terms drafted by a trade association, legal counsel or any third party also fulfil the requirement of 'pre-formulation' if imposed by the user on the other party.

7 Contract terms do not become standard business terms if they have been negotiated in detail between the parties (§ 305(1) sentence 3 BGB). Therefore, one strategy for avoiding

[1] BeckOK BGB/Becker BGB § 305 mn. 25.
[2] BGH VIII ZR 204/98, NJW 1999, 2180 (2181); OLG Frankfurt/Main 23 U 47/99, NJW-RR 2001, 55.
[3] BT-Drs. 7/3919, 16.

the statutory test of reasonableness is to negotiate each individual contract clause with the other party. However, the conditions under which courts acknowledge such a strategy are rather narrow and not easy to meet (→ mn. 20 et seqq.). Courts have determined that the condition of pre-formulation exists even in cases in which certain clauses are not used all the time or for all contracts of the user, but only from time to time,[4] or the specific formulation is changed but the central content of the clause remains.[5]

## III. Intended for repeated use

Contracts drafted only for one specific case are not subject to the test of reasonableness. 8
However, as soon as specific contract clauses or a draft contract is used a third time, the intention for repeated use is assumed. Even in cases in which a negotiated draft has not been signed but was later used (in part) to contract with another party, the risk of the test of reasonableness arises. The test of reasonableness applies regardless of whether a party intends to use specific terms with one or several parties. If the user has the intention to use contract clauses repeatedly, the first use of such a clause already triggers the test of reasonableness.[6] This applies when legal departments draft specific clauses or text modules which are used either in specific situations or when entering into contracts with specific categories of contract partners (suppliers, customers, distributors, commercial agents, sub-contractors and the like). Even cases in which a party uses pre-formulated terms that were drafted by a third party for repeated use, but the user itself does not intend to use such terms repeatedly, triggers the test of reasonableness.[7] This practice can be criticised for two reasons: first, the necessary intention to use terms repeatedly (see § 305(1) BGB) is not present with respect to the user in the latter case. Second, such a broad application of the test of reasonableness undermines the freedom of contract outside the influence and control of the user, as the user might not even know that the third party (a lawyer, notary, or an association) drafted the terms and conditions for repeated use.

## IV. Imposing standard terms

Standard terms are subject to the test of reasonableness pursuant to § 305 et seqq. 9
BGB only when they are imposed on the other party by the user. This is the case as soon as the user of the standard terms requires that the specific contract provisions apply to the contractual relationship (*Einbeziehungsangebot*). The test of reasonableness applies irrespective of whether the imposing party (user) is the economically stronger party. Standard terms are still considered to be imposed even if the user asks the other party to make amendments and change proposals, or if the user offers different alternatives (e.g. a contractual term of either three or five years or a warranty period of either 12 or 15 months). Contract terms must be individually negotiated not to be regarded as imposed standard business terms (→ mn. 20 et seqq.).

[4] BGH VIII ZR 204/98, NJW 1999, 2180 (2181) (use of specific clause in 15 % of all contracts of the user shall be sufficient).
[5] OLG Düsseldorf 6 U 283/95, NZG 1998, 353, OLG Dresden 8 U 3612/97, BB 1999, 228.
[6] BGH VII ZR 31/03, NJW 2004, 1454 (1455); Grüneberg/Grüneberg BGB § 305 mn. 9.
[7] BGH V ZR 217/89, NJW 1991, 843.

### V. The test of reasonableness among entrepreneurs

10 § 310(1) sentences 2 and 3 BGB stipulate that in contracts between entrepreneurs (b2b) or where legal persons under public law are involved, only a limited test of reasonableness applies (limited application of § 308 and no application of § 309 BGB). Such limited monitoring needs to take into account the practices and customs that apply in business dealings. However, this does not mean that no test of reasonableness applies. In contrast, under the general rule of § 307 BGB the legal assessment of the non-exhaustive lists of §§ 308 and 309 BGB has a very strong indicative effect and leads to a comprehensive application and a full test of reasonableness in b2b situations. Outside the scope of §§ 305 et seqq. BGB, courts may monitor contract terms only based on the lack of good faith (§ 242 BGB), the violation of public policy (§ 138 BGB), and the violation against statutory prohibitions (§ 134 BGB).

11 To what extent term control applies in b2b contracts is therefore less a question of the scope of §§ 307 et seqq. BGB than a question of whether standard terms and conditions were properly inserted or included in the contract and therefore have become part of the parties' contractual agreement. While in business to consumer (b2c) contracts § 305(2) BGB provides strict conditions for the user of standard terms, these conditions are less stringent in b2b relations. According to the principle of offer and acceptance, it is necessary that the contract partners agree on specific standard terms. Such agreement may be made by implied behaviour or explicit declaration.

## D. Conflicting standard terms and conditions

12 Which standard terms apply where both parties to a contract claim that their standard terms and conditions are part of the contract is a matter of high practical importance. The party making the offer generally attaches its standard terms and conditions. The other party generally attaches – or at least refers to – its own standard terms and conditions when either declaring acceptance or delivering the purchased goods. In these cases, the standard terms and conditions of the parties are valid only to the extent that they do not conflict with each other.[8]

13 The problem of conflicting standard terms and conditions can be avoided in commercial relations. The parties may agree on standard terms and conditions of one of the parties in the framework agreement. If the parties agree on the standard terms and conditions of one party, the other party cannot negate the full application of the so-chosen standard terms and conditions by attaching its own standard terms or referring to them after the framework agreement has been signed.[9] By signing a framework agreement that settles on the standard terms and conditions of one party, the other party waives its rights to apply its own standard terms.

---

[8] BGH VIII ZR 122/90, NJW 1991, 1604 (1606).

[9] BGH VIII ZR 232/78, NJW 1979, 2199 (2200); Martinek/Semler/Flohr VertriebsR-HdB/Budde § 39 mn. 58.

## E. Content that can be subject to the test of reasonableness

Service and work descriptions,[10] specifications and price agreements[11] (if they are easy to understand and therefore transparent) are not subject to the test of reasonableness. Likewise, the description of the parties' main performance is not governed by §§ 305 et seqq. BGB. The test of reasonableness only applies to contract terms that deviate from statutory legal provisions. **14**

## F. Typical standard terms in commercial contracts

Although §§ 308 and 309 BGB provide a non-exhaustive list of prohibited terms, the law on standard terms and conditions has been significantly influenced and developed by case law. Without knowledge of the respective case law, it is almost impossible to assess whether certain standard clauses are in line with the law on standard terms and conditions. The following common clauses are often found in framework agreements, general terms and conditions, purchase contracts or distributor and commercial agency agreements and will be briefly discussed below: **15**

- **Written form clauses** (*Schriftformklausel*) that require written form for any contract amendment or require that supplemental agreements must be made in writing are void in standard terms even if they are 'qualified' written form clauses. Standard terms may not prevail over individual agreements that are made later.[12] However, qualified written form clauses are valid when individually agreed upon.[13]
- **Complete exclusion of proper notice of termination** may be invalid in standard terms (depending on the specific type of contract).[14]
- **Exclusion of termination for good cause** is invalid according to § 314 BGB.[15] Even in individual agreements, the exclusion of termination for good cause (extraordinary notice of termination) may, at the most, be excluded for a limited period and only if there is a particular important reason for this exclusion.[16]
- **Prohibition of assignment** (*Abtretungsverbot*) is generally valid in standard terms, as the user's interest in a convenient and opportune execution of the contract deserves protection.[17] This interest may be jeopardised when the creditor/obligee assigns his obligation to a third party without knowledge of the obligor. However, according to § 354a HGB, a prohibition of assignment is invalid if (i) two merchants agree on (ii) the prohibition of assignment for outstanding debts (not goods). This rule aims to facilitate financing for small and medium-sized companies.
- **Exclusion or limitation of liability** for damage due to intentional behaviour or resulting from a grossly negligent breach is invalid in standard terms pursuant to §§ 276(3)

---

[10] BGH IV ZR 121/00, NJW 2001, 2014 (2016); BGH VIII ZR 404/12, NJW 2014, 2269.
[11] BGH III ZR 199/01, NJW 2002, 2386.
[12] BGH XII ZR 312/02, NJW 2006, 138; BAG 9 AZR 382/07, NJW 2009, 316.
[13] BGH VIII ZR 97/74, NJW 1976, 1395; OLG Düsseldorf 24 U 195/10, NJOZ 2012, 533.
[14] LG Kassel 4 O 802/93, NJW-RR 1995, 269 (tenancy agreement); BGH VII ZR 365/98, NJW 1999, 3261 (3262) (construction contract).
[15] BGH VIII ZR 218/85, NJW 1986, 3134.
[16] BGH VIII ZR 47/72, WM 1973, 694 et seqq.; cf. MüKoBGB/Gaier BGB § 314 mn. 7.
[17] BGH VII ZR 51/05, NJW 2006, 3486.

and 309 no. 7(b) BGB. This applies not only to a complete exclusion but also to any limitation of the scope of liability or to the exclusion of certain damages (e.g. direct or indirect).[18]

- Any exclusion or **limitation of liability for damage from injury to life, body, or health** is invalid in standard terms pursuant to § 309 no. 7(a) BGB.
- **Exclusion of liability for any category of negligence** may be invalid in standard terms if the limitation also applies to the core obligation (*Kardinalpflicht*) of the user (e.g. in purchase or distribution contracts, the duty of the seller to deliver defect-free goods) and the amount provided for compensation will presumably not cover the damage.[19] Yet, in such cases it is possible to limit the liability to the 'typically foreseeable damage'.[20]
- **Price adjustment clauses** (*Preisanpassungsklausel*) are generally invalid in standard terms when they provide the user with a unilateral right to adjust the price in his sole discretion.[21] The courts tend to take a less restrictive view on price adjustment clauses in b2b contracts. Unfortunately, whether a clause represents an unreasonable disadvantage pursuant to § 307 BGB is determined on a case-by-case basis. Price adjustment clauses in standard terms are likely to be valid if (i) the calculation basis for the price adjustment (including the calculation method) is described, (ii) the price adjustment in either direction is foreseen (increase and decrease), and (iii) a right for the other party to terminate the contract is secured in cases in which the price adjustment constitutes an unacceptable hardship.[22] For certain industrial sectors (banking, energy) or areas of law (tenancy, labour), further or different specific requirements need to be taken into account.
- **Limitation of warranty** by the seller is invalid in standard purchase contracts where the statutory warranty period (two years for transferable goods, § 438(1) no. 3 BGB) is limited to less than 12 months (§ 309 no. 8(b)(ff) BGB).
- The **extension of warranty** by the purchaser (e.g. an OEM contracting with its suppliers) is invalid in standard terms if the warranty is extended to a period of ten years but valid if the warranty is extended to a period of three years.[23]
- A **registered letter requirement** in standard terms that establishes the obligation to make declarations (e.g. termination of the contract) by registered letter does not render a declaration that was only made in writing invalid. A registered letter requirement is intended to secure the receipt of a declaration only, leaving the content and validity of the declaration untouched if it is not adhered to.[24]
- **Modification clauses** (*Änderungsklausel*), which stipulate that the user's current and frequently amended version of standard terms shall govern the contractual relationship, are only valid if the revised or amended version becomes part of the contractual relationship. This requires party agreement (at least implicitly).[25] Party agreement may be assumed where (i) the user makes the amended version accessible to the contract partner, (ii) the user highlights the changes in the amended standard terms, and (iii)

[18] See Grüneberg/Grüneberg BGB § 309 mn. 44.
[19] BGH I ZR 58/03, NJW-RR 2006, 267 (269).
[20] BGH I ZR 58/03, NJW-RR 2006, 267 (269). The BGH has dispelled concerns about this practice giving rise to problems regarding the clarity of such clauses, VIII ZR 337/11, NJW 2013, 291 (296).
[21] BGH III ZR 195/84, NJW 1986, 1803 (1804); cf. Graf von Westphalen, MDR 2008, 424.
[22] In individual cases a court might find that not all the described elements need to be fulfilled in b2b cases, cf. Grüneberg/Grüneberg BGB § 309 mn. 9.
[23] BGH VIII ZR 16/05, NJW 2006, 47, (48), (50).
[24] BGH XII ZR 214/00, NJW 2004, 1320.
[25] Cf. OLG Stuttgart 9 U 216/93, WM 1994, 626 (630).

the contract partner continues the contractual relationship without objecting to the user's change.
- The **exclusion of the buyer's duty to inspect and give notice of defects** with respect to incoming goods according to § 377 HGB is valid in standard terms only under very limited circumstances, where the incoming inspection – as it is commonly required under German law (and CISG) – is replaced by an inspection by the seller when delivering the goods.[26] Such a shift from incoming inspection to a distribution inspection is commonly agreed on in quality assurance agreements between the supplier and OEM in the automotive sector. However, an easing of the duty to inspect and give notice of defects with respect to incoming goods within two weeks after delivery may be validly agreed on in standard terms unless such defects are hidden. An exclusion of the buyer's duty to inspect is invalid for hidden defects.
- **Confidentiality clauses** (*Vertraulichkeitsvereimbarung*) are generally valid if they exclude certain information that the recipient should be able to disclose such as common knowledge or information that he obtained prior to the contractual relationship.[27]
- **Non-competition clauses** (*Wettbewerbsverbotsklausel*) are invalid if they unduly limit the recipient's ability to work for a competitor for a long period of time after the contractual relationship has ended.
- **Payment clauses** (*Zahlungsklausel*) regulate the modality and time of payment for the parties.
- **Contractual penalty clauses** (*Vertragsstrafenklausel*) regulate the penalty of the parties in case of a breach of duty. The validity of such clauses is regulated in principle in §§ 305 et seqq. BGB and in rules that govern specific contract types such as § 75c HGB.
- The validity of **choice-of-law clauses** (*Rechtswahlklausel*) depends on several factors. In a b2b context, if the parties choose to apply German law to govern the contract, these clauses are generally valid as long as they are not so surprising and unusual that the other party should not have to expect to encounter them, § 305c(1) BGB. In b2c contracts, any choice of law that deviates from that of the habitual residence of the consumer is valid only in so far as it does not weaken the protection that the consumer is entitled to (Article 6 Rome I Regulation).
- **Jurisdiction clauses** (*Gerichtsstandsklausel*) may be validly agreed on between merchants, § 38 ZPO. However, the choice of jurisdiction may be invalid if both parties have a common jurisdiction and the user chooses one elsewhere,[28] or if it has no connection to the content of the contract or to the seat of the user.[29]

## G. Legal consequences of unfair standard terms

According to § 307(1) BGB, provisions in standard terms are ineffective if they unreasonably disadvantage the other party to the contract. § 306(1) BGB makes clear that if a standard business term, in whole or in part, has not become part of the contract or is ineffective, the remainder of the contract nevertheless remains effective. However, when a part of an individual standard term is invalid, the entire standard term is generally null and void. Courts are not willing to reduce unfair terms to such extent so that they are 16

[26] Hopt/Hopt HGB § 377 mn. 59.
[27] Auer-Reinsdorff/Conrad IT- und DatenschutzR-HdB/Thalhofer/Zdanowiecki § 19, mn. 15.
[28] OLG Cologne 24 U 44/89, ZIP 1989, 1068.
[29] LG Constance 3 HO 31/83, BB 1983, 1372.

considered fair and balanced. The courts have repeatedly confirmed that they do not carry out a validity preserving reduction (*Verbot geltungserhaltender Reduktion*).[30] If courts handled this differently and reduced imbalanced terms to a fair scope, term users would be encouraged to design and use standard terms and conditions that are highly advantageous to themselves – but at the same time disadvantageous and unfair to the other party in the hope that the courts will correct the terms to what is legally acceptable. Nonetheless, courts can uphold a term that contains an unfair provision if the term still retains its meaning after the unfair provision is deleted. This is the case if the clause without the imbalanced provision has a self-contained, logical meaning. This method of upholding a clause is described as the 'blue pencil test'.[31] Given this approach, it is advisable to avoid linked and intertwined provisions and instead to insert self-contained paragraphs with short and clear sentences when drafting standard terms.

## H. Carrying out the test of reasonableness

**17** §§ 307, 308 and 309 BGB stipulate the conditions under which a contract term is an unreasonable or unfair disadvantage. A clause confers an unfair advantage on the user if it (i) is not compatible with essential principles of the statutory provision from which it deviates, or (ii) limits essential rights or duties inherent in the nature of the contract to such an extent that fulfilment of the purpose of the contract is jeopardised, or (iii) is not clear and comprehensible (non-transparent). The general clause of § 307 BGB is understood to be the core of the test of reasonableness. §§ 308 and 309 BGB contain a non-exhaustive list of examples of which clauses/terms are regularly considered to be an unfair disadvantage or are prohibited in standard terms and conditions, without giving the judge the possibility to evaluate the clause.

**18** To assess whether a certain contract clause withstands the test of reasonableness, the following steps need to be carried out:

1. is the contract clause a standard term pursuant to § 305 BGB (*Definition*)?
   If so,
2. did the standard term become part of the contract (*Einbeziehungskontrolle*)?
   If so,
3. does the standard term have content that may be subject to the test of reasonableness (*kontrollfähiger Inhalt*)?
   If so,
4. does the standard term constitute an unreasonable or unfair disadvantage according to § 309 BGB, § 308 BGB or § 307 BGB (*Inhaltskontrolle*)?
   If so, the respective clause is void.

**19** If the answer to any of the previous questions (i–iii) is 'no', the test of reasonableness does not apply or, as the case may be, the respective clause withstands the test of reasonableness. In such a case, the respective clause is generally valid (if it does not violate other statutory requirements, e.g. §§ 125, 134, 138, 242 BGB).

[30] BGH VIII ZR 269/98, NJW 2000, 1110.
[31] See Ohlendorf/Salamon, RdA 2006, 281 (282).

# I. Circumvention of the test of reasonableness

The strict law of standard terms and conditions provokes the question of whether the test of reasonableness can be circumvented. This is no easy task. The test of reasonableness does not apply if a contractual term is **individually negotiated**. Negotiation within the meaning of § 305(1) sentence 3 BGB requires the willingness of the user to **seriously present for discussion** (*ernsthaftes Zur-Disposition-stellen*) each individual contractual term.[32] In this regard, the user must give the other party the opportunity to fully safeguard his/her interests.[33] The standard for fulfilling such 'serious presentation for discussion' is high. It is not even fulfilled in the following cases: (i) express or implied declared consent to a contract or to specific terms by the other party,[34] (ii) special reference by the user to the risks of the contract or term,[35] (iii) invitation by the user to the other party to make amendments or change proposals,[36] (iv) provision of two or more alternatives to the other party,[37] (v) signed declaration by the other party saying that the contract/term has been negotiated in detail,[38] or (vi) the use of contract forms with placeholders or gaps to be individually filled in by the other party.[39] 20

Yet this does not mean that there is no escape from the applicability of the test of reasonableness where the parties have actually negotiated the contract clauses. Whether a court, in the case of a dispute, considers a clause to have been individually negotiated depends on the individual case, the knowledge of the parties, and the significance and volume of the specific transaction. In routine business cases, the standard for individual negotiation will be significantly higher than in high-volume contracts, which are rarely concluded by the user (SPA, real estate contract, commercial premises agreement, framework agreement and the like). Moreover, in b2b contracts the standard of individual negotiation is lower than in b2c contracts, as the need for protection of the other party is lower when it has business experience. As indications of individual negotiation, courts have accepted the fact that (i) amendments and changes to the original draft were inserted belatedly,[40] (ii) comprehensive correspondence was exchanged, or (iii) the parties frequently met for discussions.[41] Therefore, it is advisable for the user to discuss contract terms with the other party in detail, to produce minutes of such contract negotiations, and to exchange contract drafts (in markup). In case of dispute, such measures provide expedient arguments for claiming individual negotiation of contract clauses. Such arguments are essential for the user, as it carries the burden of prove that a contract clause was individually negotiated.[42] 21

---

[32] BGH VII ZR 192/01, NJW 2002, 2388 (2389); BGH VII ZR 9/97, NJW 1998, 3488 (3489).

[33] BGH III ZR 437/04, NJW 2005, 2543 (2544); BGH VIII ZR 27/04, NJW 2005, 1574 (1575).

[34] OLG Schleswig 7 U 83/99, MDR 2001, 262 (263).

[35] BGH VII ZR 128/91, NJW 1992, 2759.

[36] BGH III ZR 84/86, NJW 1987, 2011.

[37] BGH IV ZR 16/95, NJW 1996, 1676.

[38] BGH IV ZR 135/75, WM 1977, 15; BGH IV ZR 197/75, NJW 1977, 624.

[39] BGH XI ZR 77/91, NJW 1992, 503 (but individually negotiated when the other party may, at its sole discretion, fill the gaps and the gaps regulate substantial and not only minor issues).

[40] BGH XII ZR 129/90, NJW 1992, 2283 (2285).

[41] OLG Brandenburg 5 U 69/96, VIZ 1997, 375 (377).

[42] BGH V ZR 6/97, NJW 1998, 2600 (2601).

## J. How do standard terms and conditions become part of the party's agreement?

22 General terms and conditions are only subject to the test of reasonableness if they have been included in the contract between both parties. In other words, the parties need to agree that the standard terms of one party shall govern or at least additionally govern the contractual relationship. If the terms are incorporated into the physical contract, which is concluded by two signatures, they are included in the contract without problems and are consequently part of it. This is different, for example, in the case of contracts that are concluded orally or by implied conduct. In these cases, an explicit reference to the user's terms is required. The contracting party must in this case indicate that it agrees to the terms' inclusion. Exceptionally, a notice on the business premises may also be sufficient (especially in mass market transactions). However, the notice must be displayed in such a way that it cannot be overlooked.

23 The question of whether terms are included in a contract is of high relevance in transactions between entrepreneurs, particularly when contracts are concluded quickly or by a one-sided request of the buyer (in so far as the latter is permitted by commercial practice or special circumstances, such as just-in-time-production). In principle, the inclusion of terms in b2b transactions requires an inclusion agreement, but the requirements are lower than in b2c cases. In b2b transactions, the **user** needs to give opportunity to the contractual partner **to reasonably take note** of the standard terms. This requires at the least a correct indication of where the contractual partner can view the terms. A physical submission of the terms on paper is generally not required. In practice, it is often difficult to determine if terms are effectively included in the contract. For this reason, important practical cases in the following section will give the reader an idea of how to ensure proper inclusion of general terms and conditions.

24 For those who want to avoid doubts about whether terms are effectively included in the contract, a reference to the terms should be placed in the text of the contract, however, not below the signature bar, but above it.[43] Printing the terms on the back of the corresponding documents can also avoid doubt, although this does not replace the necessary reference to the inclusion of the terms in the contract document itself.

## K. Inclusion of standard terms and conditions in b2b contracts in practice

25 The following scenarios often appear in practice. They illustrate the challenges that appear in practice when it comes to the question of properly inserting standard terms. Moreover, the illustrations below intend to give guidance on typical practical scenarios:

26 **Order:** if the buyer wishes to base the order on his standard terms, he must indicate this in the order. The contract should also contain a clear and unambiguous reference to where the contractual partner can view the terms, at best, with the reference that the applicable terms are printed on the back of the contract or are enclosed. The printing of the terms on the reverse side of the contract without reference to its inclusion is not sufficient.

[43] Mann, mn. 141.

**Order confirmation:** if reference is made to the standard terms of the confirming party for the first time in an order confirmation (acceptance), this is a rejection of the offer made by the ordering party combined with a new offer by the confirming party (§ 150(2) BGB). A conclusion of the contract with the terms included then requires that the buyer accepts the modified order confirmation, whereas the reception of the modified order confirmation without objection is usually not sufficient.[44] However, a tacit acceptance of the standard terms and therefore an inclusion agreement can be assumed if the buyer accepts the contractual performance offered to him without objection.[45] 27

**Subsequent insertion of standard terms:** if no reference was made to the standard terms when the contract was concluded, it is generally insufficient to deliver or refer to the terms after the contract has been concluded. For example, a reference to the terms for the first time in the delivery note or on the invoice is not sufficient. This may be different if the note or invoice is delivered with the order and the buyer accepts everything together without objection. If a recipient of such a note wants to avoid having the seller's terms being included, he should object to the terms in order confirmations, invoices, or delivery notes (for reasons of evidence in writing or by email).[46] 28

**Sending of standard terms without comment**: if standard terms are sent without comment, they can only be effectively included in the contract if it is clear that the recipient agrees to the validity of the terms (e.g. through an affirmative reply, possibly also through the acceptance of the service without objection). No reaction of the contract partner results in the standard terms not being included in principle. 29

**Reference to standard terms in delivery or transport note for the first time**: this is likely insufficient for lawfully including the standard terms in the contract, especially because logistics employees or accountants who receive the delivery or transport notes usually do not have the authority (i.e. power of attorney) to amend contracts.[47] 30

**Commercial letter of confirmation:** an inclusion agreement between the parties by making a corresponding reference to the standard terms in a commercial letter of confirmation is possible if the letter is valid.[48] Anyone who receives a confirmation letter in the context of a supply relationship should check it carefully and object if it contains terms for the first time (the recipient should do so in writing or by email so that the objection can be proven in court). 31

**Conclusion of contracts via the internet**: the inclusion of standard terms is also possible by modern means of communication such as email, SMS, WhatsApp, or online ordering portals. According to the general principles, the standard term's user must provide for a reasonable possibility for the contractual partner to take note of the terms. In practice, this is often achieved by a so-called 'clickwrap', where the contractual partner must click on a button on an internet page to indicate consent to the terms.[49] This is a permissible and effective way to conclude an inclusion agreement. 32

**Inclusion of standard terms in a framework agreement:** general terms and conditions can be included relatively easily in a framework agreement. The user needs to give opportunity to the contractual partner to reasonably take note of the standard terms, i.e. by submitting it to the contract partner, or by including them in an annex to the contract. 33

**Extension clauses:** extension clauses are contractual clauses that stipulate the standard terms of one party shall apply to all future contracts between the parties. Such clauses 34

---

[44] BGH X ZR 42/99, NJW-RR 2001, 484, (485).

[45] The reception is in this case interpreted as the confirmation of the changed offer: BGH IX ZR 122/99, NJW-RR 2000, 1154 (1155).

[46] Mann, BB 2017, 2179.

[47] BGH I ZR 138/89, NJW-RR 1991, 570 (571); BGH V ZR 262/90, NJW 1992, 1099 (1100).

[48] BGH VIII ZR 146/77, NJW 1978, 2243 (2244); OLG Karlsruhe 4 U 61/92, DZWiR 1994, 70.

[49] Mann, mn. 151.

can be easily concluded in a framework contract, for example, if the parties agree that the standard terms of one party shall apply to all individual contracts to be concluded in the future. However, in conventional individual purchase contracts that are not concluded under an existing framework agreement or contracts for work and services, such extension clauses are unexpected pursuant to § 305c(1) BGB and therefore do not become part of the contract.[50] The reason lies in the nature of individual purchase contracts or contracts for work and services being geared towards a one-time exchange of services.

35 **Inclusion of future amendments to terms and conditions:** the validity of provisions (e.g. in a framework agreement) that certain standard terms shall apply in the future 'in their respective valid version' (so-called dynamic reference) is disputed. In any case, it will be necessary for the user to communicate its respective new version of the term to the other contracting party.

36 **Conflicting standard terms:** a frequently encountered case in practice is that each party wants to apply its own standard terms. This happens when the terms of respective parties are attached to both the offer and the order confirmation. The question of whether and which terms apply in these cases depends on the individual case and on the following circumstances:

- If only one party has validly (!) included its standard terms, these shall apply. The standard terms of the other contracting party, which has not effectively included its terms, do not apply.
- If both parties have validly included their standard terms, both standard terms shall apply in so far as they coincide ('congruence doctrine'). Provisions that contradict each other shall not become part of the contract. If this results in regulatory gaps, statutory provisions and eventually interpretation shall fill these gaps.
- The above does not apply if both or one version of the standard terms contain a defence clause. Defence clauses in standard terms stipulate that the contract only contains terms of the user while excluding the terms of the other party. A defence clause excludes not only contradictory but all other clauses of the other party's terms from the contract.[51] In the case that both parties' standard terms contain a defence clause, neither party's standard terms apply.

37 **Standard terms in cross-border contracts:** to incorporate standard terms in cross-border contracts, the terms of the user must be understood by the contracting party. Otherwise, the standard terms do not become a part of the contract. To ensure that the other party can understand the terms, it is advisable to write them in the native language of the foreign contracting party.[52] The same applies if the notice of the terms and the terms themselves are in the language of negotiation. The prevailing opinion deems it sufficient for the notice and the text of the standard terms to be drafted and presented in a world language (i.e. English) in the b2b sector.[53] This is not the case if the contracting party has indicated that it does not speak the language in question or if this is evident from the circumstances.

38 **Inclusion of standard terms under the UN Convention on Contracts for the International Sale of Goods (CISG):** if the CISG is applicable to a contract (with cross-border elements), it is not sufficient to merely provide the contracting party with the possibility to reasonably take note of the standard terms. The user needs to send them to the contracting party or otherwise make them specifically accessible.[54] The CISG thus sets a higher

[50] Mann, BB 2017, 2181.
[51] BGH X ZR 42/99, NJW-RR 2001, 484.
[52] BGH VII ZR 302/82, NJW 1983, 1489.
[53] OLG Hamburg 11 U 32/79, NJW 1980, 1233.
[54] BGH VIII ZR 60/01, NJW 2002, 370 (371).

standard for the inclusion of terms than German law, which allows for an appropriate reference to the source.

It is advisable to ensure that standard terms are validly included and contain a defence clause. Although the application of these terms cannot be guaranteed, it will in any case preclude the possibility that the terms of the other party is imposed on the contract. **39**

The following is a possible formulation for such terms: 'These Terms and Conditions of Sale/Purchase shall apply exclusively. Differing or conflicting terms and conditions shall neither be recognised nor become part of the contract unless they are expressly agreed upon. The parties agree that the general terms and conditions of the contracting party shall not apply even if they are referred to or handed over in the course of the business relationship (under this framework agreement).' **40**

## L. Pros and cons of the test of reasonableness

For a lawyer coming from less regulated jurisdictions (e.g. the US or UK) the law of standard terms and conditions appears to be a cumbersome, time-consuming and costly monstrosity. This view is understandable and to some extent true, yet it does not paint the full picture. In effect, the law on standard terms and conditions provides a **just balance** between the interests of contracting parties, thereby ensuring that contracts are not negotiated to the sole disadvantage of the economically weaker party. The law on standard terms and conditions also provides a basis for **legal certainty** as numerous court decisions have created a close net of case law adding to the already dense statutory provisions of §§ 308 and 309 BGB. Parties deciding to negotiate and conclude their contracts under German law are consequently rewarded with a comparably **high degree of predictability** that no common law jurisdiction – and hardly any other civil law jurisdiction – can provide. **41**

# Chapter 3
# Contracts in corporate crisis and insolvency

**Bibliography:** Braun (ed.), Insolvenzordnung: InsO, 9th edn, Munich 2022; Runkel (ed.), Anwaltshandbuch Insolvenzrecht, 2nd edn, Cologne 2008; Henssler/Strohn (eds), Gesellschaftsrecht, 5th edn, Munich 2021; Mann, 'Das Finanzmarktstabilisierungsgesetz: Eine kritische Analyse' DZWIR 2008, 496; Münchener Kommentar zu Insolvenzordnung: InsO, 4th edn, Munich 2019; Nerlich/Römermann, Insolvenzordnung (InsO), 46th edn, Munich 2022; Uhlenbruck (ed.), Insolvenzordnung: InsO, 15th edn, Munich 2019.

## A. Introduction

1 Correct payment of claims by its obligors is crucial for every organisation. Therefore, every organisation should be aware of imminent illiquidity or pending insolvency of its clients (obligors). Once insolvency proceedings are opened for an obligor, the creditor must consider how its interests can be best protected. There is no general answer to this question. The necessary steps to take depend on the status of the obligor's solvency. Beginning with a brief overview of insolvency proceedings, the following remarks will provide an overview of the basis of German insolvency law, which helps protect the rights and interests of creditors in an ongoing business relationship with an illiquid obligor.

## B. General synopsis of insolvency proceedings

### I. Filing for insolvency

#### 1. Obligation to file

2 Under German insolvency law, insolvency proceedings are neither initiated by the insolvency court *ex officio* nor by any governmental bodies or state agencies. The illiquid person himself or one of his creditors can file a request for the opening of insolvency proceedings. The managing directors (*Geschäftsführer*) of a German limited liability company (*GmbH*) or the members of the management board (*Vorstand*) of a German stock corporation (*Aktiengesellschaft*) are under a statutory obligation to file for the opening of insolvency proceedings if the company is insolvent, § 15a InsO (*Insolvenzordnung* – Insolvency Code).[1]

[1] Persons considered to be '*de facto* managing directors' (*faktischer Geschäftsführer*) – i.e. they act like a managing director even though they have never been formally appointed – are subject to the same obligations as appointed managing directors, see BGH II ZR 235/03, NZI 2006, 63 et seqq. Shareholders of a limited liability company generally also have a duty to file a request for insolvency if they have positive knowledge of the insolvency of the organisation. Such duty also applies to the supervisory board of a stock corporation (at least subsequently to the directors), see MüKoInsO/Klöhn InsO § 15a mn. 93.

## 2. Time period

A company is insolvent if it is illiquid (*zahlungsunfähig*) pursuant to § 17 InsO and/or overindebted (*überschuldet*) pursuant to § 19 InsO. Pursuant to § 15a(1) sentence 1 InsO, the managing directors must file a request for insolvency without undue delay, but at the latest three weeks after the company has become illiquid or six weeks after the company has become overindebted (§ 15a(1) sentence 2 InsO). These time periods are maximum periods. The insolvency petition has to be filed immediately if (i) it is either obvious at the beginning of this period or (ii) it becomes obvious at any time before the expiry of such period that there is no realistic chance of saving the insolvency (i.e. the overindebtedness and/or illiquidity) before the expiry of the time period.[2] German courts have determined that the maximum time period begins to run on the day the managing director(s) of the company/the board know(s), or could have known that the company is insolvent (*Erkennbarkeit der Insolvenzreife*). There is a presumption that the managing directors/the management board are at fault if they fail to obtain such knowledge of the company's insolvency, provided that it was in fact apparent to the managing directors that the company is insolvent.[3] 3

## 3. Signs of a corporate crisis

If there are signs that a company is in crisis, the managing directors/board members and the *de facto* managing directors of the company are under the obligation to evaluate whether the company is insolvent. A sign of such crisis exists if (i) the commercial balance sheet of the respective company shows a deficit that is not covered by shareholders' equity (*nicht durch Eigenkapital gedeckter Fehlbetrag*) or (ii) the company loses money endangering the existence of the company as a going concern. Practice has shown that managing directors often do not have the expertise to make such an evaluation. This results in the obligation to obtain adequate advice from an expert (usually an auditor or lawyer).[4] From the time the company has become insolvent and the managing directors knew, or could have known, of such insolvency (i.e. at the beginning of the time period), the managing directors/board are generally prohibited from making any payments to third parties unless (i) such payments do not reduce the assets of the potential future insolvency estate or (ii) such payments are required in order to maintain the possibility of restructuring the business. This usually leads to a change in the business behaviour of illiquid organisations that may be noticed by suppliers and other creditors. To combat this, the legislator conceived protective shield proceedings (*Schutzschirmverfahren*). § 270b InsO allows for companies to prepare for an insolvency without the risk of enforcement measures being initiated by individual creditors. This means that the companies themselves, under the supervision of an administrator, are allowed to administer their businesses and assets. Finally, in principle, any creditor of the company has the right (not the obligation) to file a request for the opening of insolvency proceedings (§§ 13(1) sentence 2, 14(1) sentence 1, 15(1) InsO). However, the creditor must provide sufficient evidence to trigger insolvency proceedings successfully. 4

[2] BGH II ZR 119/10, NZG 2012, 464 (465).

[3] BGH IX ZR 123/04, NJW 2005, 3062 (3064).

[4] Cf. BGH II ZR 171/10, DStR 2012, 1286 (1287); if adequate advice has been obtained and the expert concludes that company is not insolvent, a culpable breach of the obligation to file a request for insolvency is excluded, see BGH II ZR 48/06, NJW 2007, 2118.

## II. Reasons to file a request for insolvency

5 German law provides three reasons to file for insolvency: (i) imminent illiquidity, (ii) overindebtedness, and (iii) illiquidity. Only the last two reasons (overindebtedness and illiquidity) trigger the obligation to file for insolvency, whereas in the case of imminent illiquidity only the management can file for insolvency, but it is not obliged to do so.

### 1. Imminent illiquidity

6 When a company is not expected to be able to meet its payment obligations on their respective due dates in the future, the company is threatened by illiquidity (§ 18(2) InsO). In the case of imminent illiquidity, only the company itself (not the creditors) may file a request for insolvency (§ 18(1) InsO).

### 2. Illiquidity

7 Pursuant to § 17(2) InsO, a company is illiquid as soon as it is unable to fulfil its payment obligations that have come due. Essentially, illiquidity is to be assumed if the company ceases to make payments. German law, however, distinguishes between a temporary liquidity squeeze (*Zahlungsstockung*) and illiquidity (*Zahlungsunfähigkeit*). There is no obligation to file for insolvency in the mere case of a temporary liquidity crunch.[5]

### 3. Overindebtedness

8 A company is overindebted if its assets no longer cover its existing payment obligations, unless it is more likely than not – considering the circumstances – that the enterprise will continue to exist (§ 19(2) InsO). Conversely, this means that a company is not overindebted if it has a positive continuation prognosis (*positive Fortführungsprognose*), even if the value of the assets of the company (valued at going concern) is less than the liabilities of the company.[6] In other words, if the company has a positive continuation prognosis, it is not required to compare its assets and liabilities in an overindebtedness balance sheet.[7] If the company is seen to be able to fulfil its due payment obligations in the future, a positive continuation prognosis exists. To determine whether this is the case, a liquidity plan for this period must be drawn up and it must show that the continuation of the company appears likely.[8] Due to differing court practices, the legislator has decided to fix this period in law and determined that 12 months are sufficient.[9]

## III. Legal consequences of a breach of the obligation to file a request for insolvency

9 A violation of the duty to file a request for insolvency is called an insolvency delay (*Insolvenzverschleppung*). An insolvency delay may have both criminal and civil law

---

[5] BGH IX ZR 123/04, NJW 2005, 3062.

[6] See § 19(2) sentence 1 InsO (based on Article 5 of the Financial Market Stability Act (*Finanzmarktstabilisierungsgesetz* – FMStG); cf. Mann, DZWIR 2008, 496 (501)).

[7] For details, see Henssler/Strohn GesR/Arnold InsO§ 19 mn. 1 et seqq.

[8] BGH II ZR 269/91, NJW 1992, 2891 (2894).

[9] Braun/Salm-Hoogstraeten InsO § 19 mn. 7.

consequences for the managing directors of the company, the management board, and/or the members of the supervisory board.

### 1. Civil law sanctions

An omission or unduly delayed filing of a request for insolvency triggers liability on **10**
the part of the managing directors pursuant to § 43(1) GmbHG and § 15b(4) InsO or the management board of a stock corporation (§ 92 AktG and § 15b(4) InsO). Further liability may be triggered based on § 823(2) BGB and § 15a InsO.

### 2. Criminal law sanctions

Directors, officers, members of the supervisory board, and *de facto* managing direc- **11**
tors failing to file a request for the opening of insolvency proceedings in the event of the company's insolvency can be punished with up to three years' imprisonment or a fine pursuant to § 15a (4 to 6) InsO. If the perpetrator was guilty of negligence only, the penalty is a fine or imprisonment for up to one year. The StGB provides further sanctions for crimes that are often committed in connection with imminent insolvency or insolvency itself (§§ 266 and 283 et seqq. StGB).

## IV. Preliminary insolvency proceedings

After a company has filed a request for insolvency proceedings to be opened, it must **12**
be verified whether the remaining assets will cover the costs of the proceedings. During this time the responsible court must take all measures necessary to avoid any deterioration to the financial status of the creditors. The choice of available measures lies in the discretion of the court.

### 1. Preliminary insolvency administrator

Usually, the court that has jurisdiction over the filed request appoints a preliminary in- **13**
solvency administrator (*vorläufiger Insolvenzverwalter*) and grants him powers depending on the specific features of the case. Courts often appoint a 'weak' preliminary insolvency administrator (*schwacher vorläufiger Insolvenzverwalter*). This means that the debtor's assets are not vested in him and he therefore has no power to create new debts, especially debts that can become claims against the insolvency estate (*Masseverbindlichkeiten*). It is a widespread misconception that the written request of a preliminary insolvency administrator generally constitutes a secure basis for a supplier to deliver goods to the illiquid customer without further means of security. This is only the case when the preliminary insolvency administrator is a 'strong' (*starker vorläufiger Insolvenzverwalter*) and not a 'weak' preliminary insolvency administrator. A strong preliminary insolvency administrator has the power to establish claims against the insolvency estate pursuant to § 55(1) no. 2 InsO.[10]

---

[10] Cf. Nerlich/Römermann/Mönning InsO § 22 mn. 38–48.

### 2. Obligations of the weak insolvency administrator

14 If the insolvency court orders a 'weak' preliminary insolvency administrator, the day-to-day management will essentially remain with the debtor. He will, however, be subject to certain restrictions. The duty of the preliminary insolvency administrator is to safeguard and preserve the property of the insolvent company (the 'debtor') and to assess whether the debtor's net assets is sufficient to cover the costs of the insolvency proceedings. If the preliminary insolvency administrator finds that the remaining assets do not even cover the costs of the insolvency proceedings, they will not be opened pursuant to § 26 InsO.

### 3. Insolvency payments

15 The preliminary insolvency proceeding provides certain liquidity benefits. Three months prior to the opening of the insolvency proceeding, certain funds (provided by the Federal Employment Agency (*Bundesagentur für Arbeit*) and, ultimately, by contributions from employers) finance a large portion of the salaries of the debtor's employees (*Insolvenzgeld*). The preliminary insolvency administrators usually take advantage of this and in so doing, 'delay' the opening of the final insolvency proceedings. The time between the preliminary insolvency proceeding and the opening of the insolvency proceeding is therefore almost always three months. With respect to managing directors of a GmbH, German courts have generally objected to defining them as 'employees' from a labour law perspective. Being statutory representatives of the company, they assume the function of an employer instead of an employee.[11]

### 4. Supplier risks

16 During the preliminary insolvency proceeding it is essential for creditors of the debtor to continue to supply goods (or to give credit) to the debtor (→ mn. 29 et seqq.). However, it may be advisable for third parties (other creditors, suppliers, etc.) to provide financing or to supply goods to the debtor only if the preliminary insolvency administrator *and* the insolvency court give their consent. In such a case, the creditors/suppliers become 'creditors of the insolvency estate' (*Massegläubiger*). This means that the resulting liabilities will have a higher rank than other liabilities of the debtor that were entered into prior to the opening of the preliminary insolvency proceedings. However, the higher rank will not affect the existing security rights of the other creditors, which means that a default risk still remains.

## V. Opening of insolvency proceedings

### 1. Insolvency administrator's competence

17 Unless the insolvency court has issued an order for self-administration (*Eigenverwaltung*),[12] the right to manage the business and to dispose of assets of the insolvent company will rest with the insolvency administrator upon the opening of the insolvency proceedings (§ 80 InsO). In corporate groups, the insolvency administrator can exercise any shareholder right with respect to the debtor's shareholdings in other companies.[13]

[11] LSG Baden-Württemberg L 7 AL 1433/05, NJOZ 2007, 4137; however, there are exceptions: BGH IX ZR 39/02, BB 2003, 650.

[12] §§ 270 InsO et seqq.

[13] OLG Munich 31 Wx 154/10, NJW-RR 2010, 1715.

Claims have to be filed for registration with the insolvency administrator even if a court has already rendered a final judgment on a specific claim of a creditor against the insolvent company (§ 87 InsO).

### 2. Insolvency administrator's option of performance

German insolvency law contains several provisions dealing with the effect of insolvency proceedings on mutual contracts (*gegenseitige Verträge*) in general (§§ 103 et seqq. InsO), as well as on rent, lease, and loan agreements (§§ 108 to 112 InsO), retention of title (*Eigentumsvorbehalte*, § 107 InsO) or service contracts (§§ 108, 113 et seqq. InsO). These provisions are mandatory, and agreements to circumvent them are invalid (§ 119 InsO). The insolvency administrator has the option of performance (*Erfüllungswahlrecht*) with respect to all mutual contracts unless they are subject to specific rules under the InsO. Examples of such mutual contracts are sales contracts, franchising agreements, construction contracts, energy supply contracts, licence agreements, transportation contracts and the like.[14] Accordingly, the insolvency administrator has the right to decide whether to continue a mutual contract which, at the time the insolvency proceedings are opened, has not been fully performed by either the insolvent debtor or the respective creditor. Only if the creditor and/or the debtor have already fully complied with their obligations under a contract does the insolvency administrator have no option of performance. If the insolvency administrator chooses not to continue a contract, the creditor/supplier has a claim for damages against the debtor (if damage occurs due to non-performance). Such a claim, however, is a general insolvency claim which is only awarded with the insolvency dividend (§ 103(2) sentence 1 InsO). If the insolvency administrator chooses to continue the agreement, the creditor's claims against the debtor would be a preferred debt. **18**

## VI. Right to contest and annul previous transactions

The insolvency administrator's main task is to secure and maintain the assets of the insolvent company and to dispose of all assets (i) in the best possible way and (ii) equally among all creditors. The insolvency administrator has the right of annulment (*Insolvenzanfechtung*) which enables him to rescind legal transactions that are disadvantageous to the creditors and to claw back any assets received by the respective creditor as a result of any such transactions.[15] In practice, insolvency administrators often try to claw back assets/payments from third parties (in particular, shareholders of limited liability companies).[16] In practice, the last three months prior to the filing for insolvency are commonly a sensitive period. Payments that were made in this period, and which the creditor was entitled to receive, may be annulled if the debtor was illiquid at that point in time and the creditor knew about such illiquidity (§ 130(1) no. 1 InsO).[17] In the case of successful annulment, any asset that was removed from the debtor's property must be returned to **19**

---

[14] For a more extensive list, see Dahl, in: Runkel, § 8 mn. 16.

[15] See §§ 129 et seqq. InsO and § 143 InsO.

[16] The time periods are stipulated in §§ 130 et seqq. InsO (with the maximum period being ten years if the intention of disadvantaging the creditors (*Gläubigerbenachteiligung*) and corresponding knowledge of the respective other party are given).

[17] Knowledge is deemed to be given where the debtor is in arrears with payments for months (BGH IX ZR 142/98, NJW 2000, 211 (212)); however, the request for a payment extension due to a short-term liquidity shortage is not sufficient, cf. MüKoInsO/Kayser InsO § 130 mn. 39.

the insolvency administrator (§ 143(1) sentence 1 InsO) with the result that the recipient's claim against the debtor will be revived.

## VII. Treatment of claims in insolvency proceedings

20 There are various categories of claims under German insolvency law. The ranking and satisfaction of claims of the debtor's creditors are set forth in §§ 38, 39, 47 et seqq. and 55 et seqq. InsO. The costs of the insolvency proceedings are deducted (court fees for the insolvency proceedings, remuneration and expenses of the preliminary insolvency administrator, the insolvency administrator, and the members of the creditors' committee) before any claim can be satisfied. The claims of the debtor's various creditors are then ranked as follows:

### 1. Separation and preferential rights

21 Claims of creditors who have either a right to separation (*Aussonderungsrechte*) – e.g. where suppliers have retention of title rights (§§ 47 et seqq. InsO) – or a preferential right (*Absonderungsrechte*) – e.g. if a creditor was granted security by the debtor (§§ 49 et seqq. InsO) – have the highest rank. When a separation or preferential right of specific creditors exists, those specific assets are not available to the other creditors who are not beneficiaries of that specific security.

### 2. Claims against the insolvency estate

22 With the (remaining) assets of the debtor (after the removal of the assets according to the separation and preferential rights), the insolvency administrator must first fully satisfy the creditors of the insolvency estate (*Massegläubiger*) (§ 53 InsO). For instance, liabilities resulting from acts of the insolvency administrator are regarded as insolvency estate liabilities. If a preliminary insolvency administrator is appointed, he may establish claims against the insolvency estate only if he is a 'strong' preliminary insolvency administrator. Claims from mutual contracts that have not yet been fully performed also fall under this category if the insolvency administrator elected to incur such obligations. In short, apart from separation and preferential rights, which have higher ranks, all liabilities incurred by the insolvency administrator after the opening of the insolvency proceeding will generally rank higher than all liabilities of debtors that were incurred prior to the opening of insolvency proceedings (including liabilities entered into during preliminary insolvency proceedings). The insolvency administrator might be personally liable for such claims pursuant to § 61 InsO if the (remaining) assets of the debtor are not sufficient to cover these claims of the insolvency estate. As a result, there is a very high probability that liabilities incurred by the insolvency administrator after the opening of insolvency proceedings will be fully satisfied.

### 3. General insolvency claims

23 Subsequently, all other claims, referred to as 'insolvency claims' (*Insolvenzforderungen*), will be satisfied if and to the extent that any assets remain (§ 174 et seqq. InsO). Each insolvency creditor will thus be entitled to the respective dividend, i.e. the percentage of recovery (*Quote*), based on the remaining assets. In practice, this dividend often has a very low value (around 2 to 4 % of the original claim) or is even close to zero.

### 4. Subordinated creditors

Claims of subordinated creditors of the insolvency proceedings (*nachrangige Insolvenzgläubiger*) will be satisfied only after the other claims of insolvency creditors (including the insolvency claims) have been fully satisfied (§ 39(1) InsO).[18] Consequently, subordinated claims will usually not be satisfied at all. 24

## VIII. Creditors' participation in the insolvency proceeding

German insolvency law provides diverse opportunities and rights for the debtor's creditors to participate in the insolvency proceedings and to secure their rights and interests. 25

### 1. Registrations of claims

Creditors alleging to have a claim against the debtor may apply for registration of their claims with the insolvency administrator (and not with the insolvency court) (§ 174 InsO). Claims filed by creditors for registration will then be discussed in a verification meeting (*Prüfungstermin*) (§ 176 InsO). Every creditor, as well as the insolvency administrator, has the right to dispute and reject any claim filed by another creditor. If the insolvency administrator contests a filed claim, the creditor of this claim can institute legal proceedings for registration of the claim (*Feststellung des Anspruchs zur Insolvenztabelle*). Such a complaint is directed at the judicial declaration of the respective alleged claim (§ 179 InsO). Registration of the claims is a condition for taking part in the distribution of the debtor's remaining assets and therefore regularly constitutes the only possibility for creditors, at least in part, to realise their claims. 26

### 2. Creditors' meeting

The creditors may also participate in the insolvency proceeding through the creditors' meeting (*Gläubigerversammlung*), which is organised by the responsible insolvency court (§§ 74 et seqq. InsO) and attended by the insolvency administrator. In the first creditors' meeting, which is held after the opening of the insolvency proceedings, the insolvency administrator reports on the debtor's financial status. He describes the prospects of continuing the business operations of the debtor, including the chances of carrying out the restructuring under an insolvency plan (§ 156 InsO). Based on this report, the creditors will then decide whether the business operations of the debtor shall continue or be closed down (§ 157 InsO). In the second creditors' meeting, the claims filed for registration are discussed by the present creditors (§ 176 InsO). The insolvency administrator then compiles a register (*Schlussverzeichnis*) listing all claims and the relevant insolvency dividend for each claim.[19] In the final creditors' meeting, the register is discussed by the creditors and the insolvency administrator.[20] 27

---

[18] For further details, see MüKoInsO/Ehricke/Behme InsO § 39 mn. 10–70.

[19] Cf. Uhlenbruck/Wegener InsO § 188 mn. 4 et seqq. with useful commentary on claims the insolvency administrator must consider.

[20] The creditors may raise objections against the register, which will be decided upon by the insolvency court, § 197(3) InsO.

### 3. Creditors' committee

28 For the creditors, it is common practice to establish a creditors' committee (*Gläubigerausschuss*) (§ 68 InsO). This creditors' committee is usually comprised of a representative of the debtor's employees and further representatives of the main unsecured and secured creditors (§ 67(2) InsO), which are usually the financing banks. The members are commonly elected in the first creditors' meeting. The insolvency court, however, has the power to appoint a creditors' committee prior to the first creditors' meeting to support and supervise the insolvency administrator in the performance of his tasks.

## C. Protective measures of creditors

29 When a supplier's customer is insolvent or close to insolvency, the supplier must make use of all available opportunities to secure outstanding payments incurred by the purchase contract. In so far as goods have already been supplied and payment for the supply is due, the supplier may demand either payment or return of the delivered goods. The latter, however, requires that the supplier and customer have agreed on a valid retention of title. In such a case, the supplier has a right to separation (*Aussonderungsrecht*) pursuant to § 47 InsO which he can enforce. If no such retention of title exists, the supplier may only register its claims after the insolvency proceedings have been opened. As practice has shown, creditors commonly only receive a small fraction of the registered claim (around 2 to 4 %).

30 For the supplier's future deliveries, the relevant question is whether and, if so, how future payment claims may be secured apart from a retention of title agreement. There is no general answer to this question. The answer depends on both the status of the insolvency proceedings (threat of illiquidity, preliminary insolvency proceedings, or insolvency proceedings in progress) as well as on the contract type and the content of the contract under which the supply is made. The following offers a brief overview of the protective measures creditors can take once a creditor/supplier realises that his customer may be in financial difficulties. The question of which specific measure to take must be evaluated on a case-by-case basis.

## I. Retention of title

31 The most common measure for securing payment resulting from the supply of goods is to agree on a retention of title. Retention of title means that the customer may gain ownership of the delivered good only after the purchase price has been fully paid. The supplier may demand return of the delivered good, if full payment has not been made by the customer (or the insolvency administrator). If the insolvency administrator decides not to return the good but to pay, the supplier's payment claims are claims against the insolvency estate (*Masseverbindlichkeit*) pursuant to § 55(1) no. 2 InsO, which do not belong to general insolvency claims. Consequently, the supplier will receive preferred and likely full payment (and not only a small percentage). The courts have accepted modifications of the simple retention of title clause, such as overall or extended retention of title clauses. This gives the supplier a broader range of possibilities for securing its payment claims against the customer. After the customer has filed for insolvency, the retention of title right should be asserted and re-asserted once the insolvency proceeding has been opened. If the customer rejects a retention of title clause, the parties may conclude a commercial

credit insurance agreement. In practice, it is important for a supplier to ensure that a valid retention of title is contractually agreed on with the customer.

## II. Privileged cash transaction

As mentioned above (→ mn. 19), insolvency administrators often try to claw back payments that were made by the customer to the supplier, and in so doing, contest transactions that were made shortly (three months or less) before insolvency was filed (§§ 129 InsO et seqq.). To reduce the risk of such a contestation by the insolvency administrator, the supplier should carry out privileged cash transactions (*Bargeschäft*) pursuant to § 142 InsO. This requires (i) that only a short time has elapsed between performance and payment (e.g. money transfer within 14 days after delivery) as well as (ii) the equivalence of performance and payment. In any case, a supplier is well-advised to conclude transactions on a cash basis once he learns that the customer is or might be close to becoming illiquid. 32

## III. Prepayment

A relatively simple measure for the supplier to secure payment is to demand payment from the customer prior to delivery (*Vorauszahlung*). This is possible when no delivery commitment of the supplier exists (e.g. in framework supply agreements without a strict duty of the supplier to deliver). In such a case, the supplier may require prepayment as a contractual condition prior to the conclusion of each individual purchase contract. However, the supplier may not agree to switch to prepayment if the parties have agreed on an instalment or apportioned contract providing for an ongoing obligation of the supplier to deliver goods to the customer. In any case, prepayment in itself is not an efficient device for securing payment by an illiquid customer as it does not mitigate the risk of annulment by the insolvency administrator. Moreover, if the supplier unilaterally changes the purchase conditions of the contract to prepayment, the equivalence of performance which is required according to § 142 InsO can be affected. Hence, prepayment should be agreed on between supplier and customer on a bilateral basis, and prepayment should be combined with the conditions stipulated under § 142 InsO to trigger the benefits of a privileged cash transaction. 33

## IV. Individual court authorisation

When a 'weak' preliminary insolvency administrator requests ongoing supply to keep the customer's business going, the supplier's payment claim for the supply of goods to the customer is not automatically protected. In the absence of an individual agreement that requires the consent of (i) the preliminary insolvency administrator and (ii) the insolvency court, the payment claim of the supplier only constitutes a general insolvency claim. Therefore, if a 'weak' preliminary insolvency administrator requests ongoing supply, the safest way for the supplier to secure payment of the delivered goods is to ask for either (i) an individual court authorisation or (ii) an individual personal guarantee from the preliminary insolvency administrator. In the absence of such court authorisation or guarantee, the supplier can only secure payment by carrying out a privileged cash transaction. This, however, is still risky for the supplier if it turns out that the conditions of § 142 InsO were not met. 34

# Chapter 4
# International contract law

**Bibliography:** Ferrari/Kieninger/Mankowski, Internationales Vertragsrecht, 3rd edn, Munich 2018; Kondring, 'Flucht vor dem deutschen AGB-Recht bei Inlandsverträgen', RIW 2010, 184; Kröll/Mistelis/Perales Viscasillas, UN Convention on Contracts for the International Sales of Goods (CISG), 2nd edn, Munich 2018; McGuire, 'Grenzen der Rechtswahlfreiheit im Schiedsverfahrensrecht? – Über das Verhältnis zwischen der Rom-I-VO und § 1051 ZPO', SchiedsVZ 2011, 257; Münchener Kommentar zum Bürgerlichen Gesetzbuch, 8th edn, Munich 2019; Ostendorf, 'Wirksame Wahl ausländischen Rechts auch bei fehlendem Auslandsbezug im Fall einer Schiedsgerichtsvereinbarung und ausländischem Schiedsort?', SchiedsVZ, 2010, 234; Pfeiffer, 'Die Abwahl des deutschen AGB-Rechts in Inlandsfällen bei Vereinbarung eines Schiedsverfahrens', NJW 2012, 1169; Rauscher (ed.), Europäisches Zivilprozess- und Kollisionsrecht, 5th edn, Cologne 2020; Rützel/Wegen/Wilske, Commercial Dispute Resolution in Germany, 2nd edn, Munich 2016; Steinbrück/Lieberknecht, 'Grenzüberschreitende Zivilverfahren nach dem Brexit', EuZW 2021, 520; Wegen/Barth/Wexler-Uhlich, International Arbitration in Germany, Munich 2022.

## A. Introduction

1 International contract law governs the legal relationships between parties to contracts in cross-border cases. There is no international contract law as such, even though the United Nations Convention on Contracts for the International Sale of Goods (also called CISG or the Vienna Convention) may be regarded as a unified international law, one that only applies to the sale of goods.

2 For all other cases where neither the CISG nor other harmonised law (international convention) applies, the applicable law in international cross-border transactions are determined by rules in private international law (*internationales Privatrecht*), also called conflict of laws. Conflict of laws is composed of national and international legal norms which identify the national substantive rules that apply in a particular cross-border case and subsequently tell the parties 'who is right and who is wrong'.

## B. Sources of law

### I. United Nations Convention on Contracts for the International Sale of Goods (CISG)

3 The CISG is a uniform international convention governing the sale of goods. Pursuant to Article 1(1) CISG, the convention automatically applies to contracts of sale of goods between parties whose places of business are in different States (internationality) when (i) both States are Contracting States to the convention; or (ii) the rules of private international law lead to the application of the law of a Contracting State.

## 1. Scope of application

The CISG only applies to contracts for the sale of goods and mixed contracts with a predominant sales contract element. 4

### a) Sale of goods

A contract for the sale of goods is basically a contract according to which goods are exchanged and the corresponding payment is made. More precisely, a sales contract under the CISG is one according to which the seller is bound (i) to deliver the goods, (ii) to transfer the property of the goods sold, and (iii) the buyer is obliged to pay the purchase price and to accept the goods. Goods are defined as physical and movable things. Machines, products of all sorts, standard software (if it is on a data medium), gas, or water do fall within the scope of the CISG. The sale of rights (e.g. licences and IP) as well as of real estate does not fall under the CISG.[1] Moreover, Article 2 CISG contains further exceptions to the application of the Convention. Pursuant to Article 2 CISG, the sale of goods for personal, family or household use, stocks, shares, investment securities, negotiable instruments or money, ships, vessels, hovercraft, aircraft, or electricity do not fall under the CISG. The same applies to the sale of goods by auction. In dispute is whether distribution agreements fall under the CISG. Most national courts have determined that the CISG does not apply to distribution agreements, as they focus on the organisation of the distribution of goods (including marketing, warehousing, advertising, customer services) rather than the transfer of property and the delivery of goods. However, the individual sales contracts concluded under the distribution agreement are commonly governed by the CISG. 5

### b) Internationality

When assessing whether an international situation is given – necessary for the application of the CISG – neither the nationality of the parties nor the civil or commercial character of the parties is taken into consideration.[2] Decisive is only the **place of business** of the **contract partners**, which must be located in different CISG contracting states. If it is neither expressly visible nor evident from the circumstances that an international situation is given, the CISG is not applicable.[3] 6

### c) CISG not suspended

Once the criteria described above are fulfilled, the CISG applies automatically without the parties having to agree on this and without any need for recourse to private international law rules. This results in a worldwide and frequent application of the CISG, as more than 90 states have so far ratified the CISG, amongst them the most important industrial nations, including China, all of North America, and almost all of Europe (the United Kingdom is a notable exception). This, however, does not restrict the rights of the parties to expressly exclude the application of the CISG pursuant to Article 6 CISG. In this case, the clear and unambiguous (implicit or explicit) declarations of the parties to exclude the application of the CISG are required. A choice of law clause determining that German law shall govern the business relationship between the parties leads to the application of the CISG, as the CISG is a part of the German legal system. Therefore, when the parties want 7

---

[1] With helpful overview and further reference, MüKoBGB/Huber CISG Art. 1 mn. 19–23.

[2] See Article 1(3) CISG, Kröll/Mistelis/Perales Viscasillas CISG/Mistelis CISG Art. 1 mn. 44: 'diversity of place of business, not diversity of citizenship, is relevant to establish internationality'.

[3] For questions of proof, see Ferrari IntVertragsR/Saenger UN-Kaufrechts-Übereinkommen Art. 1 mn. 27.

to apply German substantive law and exclude the CISG, a clear phrasing of the parties' intention is necessary.

## 2. Scope of CISG regulation

8 The CISG does not provide a fully self-contained and comprehensive legal framework for the sale of goods.

### a) Regulated issues

9 The CISG regulates issues that most often arise in disputes over the sale of goods such as the formation of the contract (including, for example, the effectiveness of offer and acceptance), party obligations, delivery of the goods (place of delivery, shipping arrangements, time for delivery, documents relating to the goods), breach of contract and consequences (remedies and damage compensation), payment of the purchase price, distribution of the risk, preservation of the goods, and avoidance of the contract.

### b) Unregulated issues

10 Pursuant to Article 4b CISG, the ownership of the goods, which from a German perspective is important for the validity of a retention of title, is not governed by the CISG. Moreover, the CISG does not apply to the liability of the seller for death or personal injury caused by the goods to any person (Article 5 CISG), the effectiveness of the contract (including term review, Article 4a CISG), limitation, product liability, or offset. These issues are still governed by national law which is determined in accordance with the conflict of law rules (→ mn. 21 et seqq.).

## 3. Differences between German sales law and CISG

11 Whereas German sales law follows the rather technical approach of the BGB, the CISG pursues a more practical approach. In addition to the formation of the contract, the obligations of the parties and the corresponding remedies, the CISG governs typical problems that arise in connection with the sale of goods. These are the preservation of the goods (deposit in a warehouse of a third person or sale to a third party), impediment exempting a party from having to pay damages or specific rules referring to the avoidance of the contract. The following non-exhaustive list shows the main differences between the BGB and the CISG:

| Subject | BGB | CISG |
|---|---|---|
| Offer and acceptance | Offer and acceptance need to fully coincide. Otherwise, an acceptance with additions, restrictions or other alterations is a rejection combined with a new offer. | CISG differentiates between material and immaterial alteration (Article 19(2) CISG). An acceptance containing immaterial alterations results in the conclusion of the contract, whereas a material alteration (with different price, quality, or quantity) results in a new offer. |
| Revocability of offer | An offer is binding on the offeror once it is received by the other party (§§ 130(1), 145 BGB). | An offer may be revoked even after receipt by the other party, unless the offer is accepted (Articles 15, 16 CISG). |

| Subject | BGB | CISG |
|---|---|---|
| General Terms and Conditions | Reference to the general terms and conditions is sufficient between entrepreneurial parties. | According to Article 24 CISG, the party imposing/involving its general terms and conditions must deliver the text of the general terms and conditions (by post, fax or as an email attachment). The standard under the CISG is therefore more stringent than under the BGB. |
| Delivery | If no agreement regarding the delivery date was reached, performance is immediately due (§ 271 BGB). | If no individual agreement exists, delivery of the goods must be made within a reasonable time after the conclusion of the contract (Article 33(c) CISG). |
| Supplementary performance | The seller has the right to and obligation of secondary performance (including repair or replacement) (§ 439 BGB). | The buyer may demand compensation for damage without notice (Articles 46, 37 CISG). There is no explicit right for supplementary or secondary performance of the seller. |
| Limitation of liability | Generally comprehensive liability for all damages (unless legally limited). | Article 74 sentence 2 CISG provides a statutory limitation of liability according to which damages may not exceed the loss which the party in breach foresaw or ought to have foreseen at the time of the conclusion of the contract. |

## II. EU Directive on Contracts for the Supply of Digital Content and Digital Services

Although the attempt by the European Commission to introduce a common sales law 12
has not borne fruit, successful attempts have been made to at least partially unify sales law in the EU. One of these attempts is the Directive (EU) 2019/770 on contracts for the supply of digital content and digital services. This Directive does not apply directly to commercial contracts, but all EU Member States have ratified it and made its content a part of their national laws. As a result, contracts involving digital content, digital services, or products containing digital content, even if concluded under German law, will be similarly governed as contracts concluded under the law of any other EU Member State.

## III. Incoterms 2020

### 1. Definition

Incoterms (International Commercial Terms) are worldwide, acknowledged unified 13
contract and supply terms that establish a standardised handling of sales relationships for the parties of domestic or international sales contracts. They do so by regulating the

allocation of costs and risks between the parties to a sales contract. Incoterms enable the parties to quickly agree on important sales conditions and, in so doing, to avoid misunderstandings and costly disputes.

### 2. Origin

14 Incoterms have been issued by the International Chamber of Commerce in Paris since 1936. The current version of Incoterms 2020 has been in effect since 1 January 2020. There are currently 11 Incoterms rules.

### 3. Scope

15 The Incoterms' scope of regulation is limited. First, there is no automatic application of Incoterms. The parties must agree that Incoterms shall govern their contractual relationship. Second, legal issues such as the formation of contracts, the transfer of property, payment terms, or the legal consequences of defects or other non-contractual performance are not regulated in Incoterms. Therefore, Incoterms can never replace a purchase agreement. A description of the Incoterm rules, including a description of the seller's obligations under each respective rule, can be found on the national websites of the International Chamber of Commerce.[4]

### 4. Classification

16 The Incoterms can be classified in two ways: the first classification can be made according to the type of transport. There are Incoterm rules which may be applied to any sort of transport (by land, by ship, by air), these are: EXW, FCA, CPT, CIP, DAP, DPU, DDP. In addition to these Incoterm rules, there are rules that are suitable for navigation (sea or inland) only, such as FAS, FOB, CFR and CIF. The second classification is made according to the type of delivery that is common in trade. According to such differentiation, the 11 Incoterm rules are divided into four groups which are labelled according to the first letter of each Incoterm rule:

- Group E: departure terms (EXW)
- Group F: dispatch terms where main carriage is not paid by the seller (FCA, FAS, FOB)
- Group C: dispatch terms where main carriage is paid by the seller (CFR, CIF, CPT, CIP)
- Group D: arrival terms (DAP, DPU, DDP)

17 The seller's obligations increase from group to group. Whereas the obligation of the seller is the lowest pursuant to Incoterms 2020 EXW, the most comprehensive obligations of the seller are found under Incoterms 2020 DDP.

## C. Determining the applicable law

18 In cases where no harmonised international law (e.g. the CISG) applies, the parties determine the substantive law according to international or national conflict of laws rules. Every developed national legal system provides for conflict of laws rules (also private international law) which assist in the determination of the applicable substantive law.

[4] See http://www.iccgermany.de.

However, to determine the applicable substantive law, one must first identify the relevant conflict of laws rules. It is internationally acknowledged that the courts which decide (or would have to decide) on a dispute apply their own conflict of laws rules, i.e. the law of the state where the court is located (*lex fori* principle). Therefore, the applicable law is determined by a two-step test. In a first step, one must determine which court would have jurisdiction over the matter (in case of dispute). Frequently, this will be the courts of the defendant's seat. Once the place of jurisdiction has been established, the law of the state where the court is located determines what conflict of laws rules apply to determine the substantive law.

## I. Step 1: identifying the jurisdiction

When the parties have agreed on a **valid jurisdiction clause**, the competent court can 19
be easily identified in the contract. In the absence of a valid jurisdiction agreement, the parties must identify the competent court according to **national civil procedure law**. For example, a German party that wants to identify where it could bring a claim against a business partner (e.g. a business partner seated in Austin, Texas) applies the ZPO. Pursuant to §§ 12, 17 ZPO, the courts at the seat of the defendant, in this case, the courts in Austin, Texas, would have jurisdiction over the case.

When international treaties or **harmonised international law** provide specific rules on 20
the jurisdiction in civil matters, such legal rules have priority. The European Parliament and the European Council promulgated the Regulation No 1215/2012 on Jurisdiction and the Recognition and Enforcement of Judgments in Civil and Commercial Matters of 12 December 2012 (Brussels Ia Regulation). The Brussels Ia Regulation governs questions of international jurisdiction in civil and commercial matters if the **defendant** has its **seat in an EU Member State.**[5] Pursuant to Article 4(1) Brussels Ia Regulation, persons with seats in a Member State shall be sued in the courts of that Member State, whatever their nationality. Article 7 Brussels Ia Regulation establishes special jurisdiction deviating from the general principle in Article 4 Brussels Ia Regulation. Pursuant to Article 7(1) Brussels Ia Regulation, a person domiciled in a Member State may – in matters relating to a contract – be sued in the courts of the Member State where the **place of performance of the obligation** in question lies. In the case of the sale of goods, the place of performance of the obligation is the place where, under the contract, the goods are to be delivered to the buyer.[6] Parties to a contract must be aware that any contractual agreement about the place of performance of the obligation also acts as a jurisdiction clause and may justify the possibility of being sued in the courts of this place.

## II. Step 2: determining the applicable substantive law

### 1. Rome I Regulation

Once the jurisdiction is identified, the law of the state in which the court is seated (*lex* 21
*fori*) provides the conflict of laws rules that determine the substantive law. In Germany, the Introductory Act to the Civil Code (*Einführungsgesetz zum Bürgerlichen Gesetzbuche* – EGBGB) contains the national conflict of laws rules. However, European legal acts

---

5 This is the general principle of the Brussels Ia Regulation. For an overview of how to apply the Brussels Ia Regulation, see Rauscher/Mankowski EuGVVO Introduction to Article 4 mn. 1 et seqq.

6 See e.g. BGH VIII ZR 135/08, NJW 2010, 3452.

have largely replaced the EGBGB in its conflict of laws provisions. This is true for contract and commercial matters (Rome I Regulation[7]), for non-contractual obligations such as e.g. torts (Rome II Regulation[8]), and for certain family-law matters (Rome III Regulation[9]). If disputes about commercial contracts arise and German courts have jurisdiction, the Rome I Regulation will very likely determine the applicable (substantive) law. The scope of application of the Rome I Regulation is wide. In general, the Rome I Regulation is applicable when

1. a cross-border conflict between the parties exists,
2. this conflict has its basis on a contractual obligation,
3. this contractual obligation is of civil or commercial nature, and
4. the application is not expressly excluded pursuant to Article 1(2) Rome I Regulation.

### 2. Choice of law

22 Article 3 Rome I Regulation stipulates that the parties are free to choose the law that shall govern their contractual relationship. However, if all other elements relevant to the situation are located in a Member State different from the state which law the parties have chosen, it will not be possible to derogate from the mandatory legal rules of that Member State (→ mn. 25).

23 In the **absence of a choice of law**, Article 4 Rome I Regulation helps determine the governing law for specific contractual situations. As an example, a contract for the sale of goods is governed by the law of the state where the seller has his habitual residence. A contract for the provision of services is governed by the law of the state where the service provider has its habitual residence.[10] Distribution contracts (including commercial agency agreements as well as distributorship agreements[11]) are governed by the law of the state where the distributor or the agent has his habitual residence. The Rome I Regulation establishes specific connecting factors (*Anknüpfungspunkte*) for contracts of carriage, consumer contracts, insurance contracts, and individual employment contracts.

## III. Freedom of choice of law and its limitations

### 1. General principle

24 Article 3(1) of the Rome I Regulation recognises the principle of party autonomy and allows for the parties to generally choose the national law applicable to their contract by mutual (explicit or tacit) agreement. They can select the law applicable to the whole or to parts of the contract. A specific connection, relationship, or proximity of the contract to the country whose law has been chosen is not required. Therefore, the parties are generally allowed to agree on the application of an entirely 'neutral' law. However, while

[7] Regulation (EC) No 593/2008 of the European Parliament and of the Council of 17th June 2008 on the law applicable to contractual obligations applies to all EU Member States except Denmark.

[8] Regulation (EC) No 864/2007 of the European Parliament and of the Council of 11 July 2007 on the law applicable to non-contractual obligations applies to all EU Member States except Denmark.

[9] Council Regulation (EU) No 1259/2010 of 20 December 2010 implementing enhanced cooperation in the area of the law applicable to divorce and legal separation.

[10] See e.g. BGH XI ZR 9/11, RIW 2012, 566.

[11] See MüKoBGB/Wendland Rom I-VO Art. 3 mn. 239. The individual purchase orders delivered under the distributorship agreement are, however, to be determined according to the residence of the seller, Article 4(1)(a) Rome I Regulation.

this freedom of choice constitutes the general principle, it is subjected to the limitations discussed below.

## 2. Limitation pursuant to Article 3(3) Rome I Regulation

25 Article 3(3) Rome I Regulation contains such a limitation, which mandate that if all other elements relevant to the situation at the time of the choice are located in a country other than the country whose law has been chosen, the choice made by the parties shall not exclude the application of the **mandatory provisions** of the **law of that other country**, which cannot be derogated from by agreement. In other words: the parties may agree on the choice of another national law even if the contract is exclusively connected to one country. However, in these instances the choice of law is restricted to non-mandatory provisions of the law of the country to which the contract is exclusively connected.[12] A German and a Swiss party are, for example, generally free to choose English law as the applicable law to their contract. Only if the contract relates exclusively to one country (e.g. two contract parties seated and concluding the contract in Germany) is it not possible to derogate from the mandatory provisions of that country.

## 3. Limitation pursuant to Article 3(4) Rome I Regulation

26 A second limitation can be found in Article 3(4) Rome I Regulation, which stipulates that if all other elements relevant to the situation at the time of the choice are located in one or more EU Member States, the parties' choice of law other than that of an EU Member State shall not prejudice the application of provisions of EU law, which cannot be derogated from by agreement. In other words, mandatory rules of European Union law remain applicable, even if the parties chose a third country's law (e.g. Brazilian law), if the contract relates exclusively to one or more EU Member States.

## 4. Limitation pursuant to Article 9(2) Rome I Regulation

27 Further limitations to the parties' choice of law can be found in Article 9(2) Rome I Regulation (overriding mandatory rules, *Eingriffsnormen*) and Article 21 Rome I Regulation (incompatibility with the public policy of the forum). Article 9 Rome I Regulation defines a special connecting factor that governs situations in which overriding principles of a state (e.g. protection of competition, sanctions, embargoes) require the application of specific national rules protecting supra-individual interests irrespective of the applicable national law.

## 5. Exclusion of restraints in arbitration

28 If the parties agree to bring their (actual or future) dispute to arbitration and the seat of the arbitration is in Germany, German procedural law is applicable. Pursuant to § 1051(1) ZPO, the arbitral tribunal must decide on the dispute in accordance with the statutory **provisions** that the parties have designated as applicable. The choice of the substantive law may differ from the choice of law permissible under Article 3 Rome I Regulation. An arbitral tribunal is not bound by the mandatory provisions of a legal system in the way state courts are. Hence, the arbitral tribunal may help the parties designate individually

---

[12] Cf. MüKoBGB/Martiny Rom I-VO Art. 3 mn. 87. Relevant elements include the place of establishment of a party, the place of performance, the place of the property, or the place of the conclusion of the contract.

defined provisions as exclusively applicable. Commentators therefore consider it possible – even for parties to a domestic dispute – to circumvent mandatory provisions of their national law by transferring the power of dispute settlement to an arbitral tribunal when making the choice of law for their contract.[13]

## D. Brexit woes

29 The exit of the UK from the European Union (Brexit) has dramatically and negatively affected trade between the two entities. However, because of its proximity and historical ties to Europe, the UK remains an important trading partner to many European states. Brexit's effects on trade are dwarfed by the immense legal repercussions on cross-border contracts. The following is a short presentation on the legal challenges due to Brexit and recommendations on how businesses in Germany can best meet them.

### I. Anti-suit injunction

30 If a litigation is brought forward between a British and a European company, the competent court that should hear the resulting litigation should first be established. Brexit has no effect on the application of the Brussels Ia Regulation in Germany. If the Brussels Ia Regulation stipulates that a German court is competent to hear the case, this court has jurisdiction. However, British courts are known to use an instrument called the anti-suit injunction, forbidden by the European Court of Justice, that has now been revived.[14] For example, a court in Edinburgh can issue an interim injunction to prevent a party from filing a case in a foreign court. A party that goes against this injunction and brings forward a suit elsewhere can be sanctioned with a contempt of court ruling (with possible imprisonment).

### II. *Forum non conveniens*

31 As it is no longer a part of British law, the Brussels Ia Regulation can no longer establish the competence of a British court. Even if British courts are supposed to be competent according to British law, the courts have known to deploy a doctrine called *forum non conveniens*, which stipulates that if the case does not have sufficient connection to the UK, its courts are not competent to hear the case. This doctrine, also rejected by the European Court of Justice for being incompatible with European law, has also seen a revival after Brexit.[15]

---

[13] See Pfeiffer, NJW 2012, 1169; McGuire, SchiedsVZ 2011, 257; Ostendorf, SchiedsVZ, 2010, 234; Kondring, RIW 2010, 184 (189).

[14] Steinbrück/Lieberknecht, EuZW 2021, 517 (520).

[15] Steinbrück/Lieberknecht, EuZW 2021, 517 (520).

## III. Contractual agreement on the choice of court

For a business, these eccentricities in the British legal system present significant uncertainty regarding the competence of a court. This uncertainty can be somewhat mitigated by the contractual parties by agreeing that the national court of a certain country is competent. The Hague Choice of Court Convention, to which the EU (and therefore also Germany) and the UK (since 2021) are members, allows for contractual parties to agree on a choice of court in the Member States if the following conditions are met: (i) the parties have made a choice of court agreement, (ii) the application of the Convention is not excluded in Article 2 (it is most notably not applicable for contracts involving consumers), and (iii) the agreement between the parties was made in writing or any other mode of communication that renders the information accessible for subsequent reference (such as email). 32

## IV. Applicable substantive law

The determination of the applicable law for a contract is less complicated. For a dispute in German courts stemming from a contract between a German and a British company, the Rome I Regulation is still applicable, providing that the dispute lies in the scope of the regulation. If the dispute is heard in a British court, the applicable law is determined according to British international private law rules. Since the UK is no longer a part of the EU, the Rome I Regulation formally does not apply. However, British international private law for contracts is largely identical to the Rome I Regulation, given the desire of the British government to preserve legal certainty after Brexit. The CISG is not applicable since the UK is not a signatory state to the Convention. 33

## V. Recommendations

For businesses in Germany dealing with British companies, all these changes present unnecessary complications when designing contracts that govern the relationship between the parties. To mitigate these complications, a clear and unambiguous recommendation can be made in favour of (i) arbitration in Germany, the UK, or certain third states, and (ii) the choice that German law is applicable to the contract. 34

- In particular after Brexit, there are several advantages to agreeing on an arbitral tribunal to settle disputes. Because the Brussels Ia Regulation is no longer in force in the UK and it is from the perspective of Member States considered a third state, the cross-border enforcement of a court decision requires a complex exequatur procedure (*Exequaturverfahren*).[16] For example, a court decision from Frankfurt cannot be enforced immediately in London. It is necessary to go to a national court in Britain to declare the enforceability of the decision, which can be costly and time-consuming. The parties also run the risk that the British court may quash the decision from Frankfurt. In contrast, the New York Convention enables a decision from an arbitral tribunal from Germany to be enforced in the UK relatively easily.[17] An agreement on arbitration thus ensures that the uncertainty of the British legal system does not additionally burden

[16] Wegen/Barth/Wexler-Uhlich Ch. 11 mn. 1.
[17] Rützel/Wegen/Wilske, p. 189.

the parties if dispute arises. The parties need to make sure that the place of arbitration lies in a Member State of the New York Convention (→ Ch. 5 mn. 10).
- The parties should also agree on the applicability of German substantive law to govern the contract. The reasons are outlined in the following.

## E. Made in Germany: reasons for the choice of German law

35 German law is widely known for its balanced and fair approach. It provides a just balance between the interests of the parties. For entrepreneurs, German law constitutes a genuine competitive advantage, as it is predictable, affordable, and enforceable. Judgments are usually enforced swiftly and effectively. Although German contract law restricts the freedom of contract more than other legal systems do (e.g. English law or many US state laws), these restrictions also allow for the predictability and legal certainty treasured by many entrepreneurs.

### I. Predictability

36 The law on standard terms and conditions may seem to be a cumbersome feature of German contract law. Admittedly, term review in b2b cases may at times go beyond what is helpful in business relations. However, with their decisions over the years, German courts have accumulated many judgments that provide a high degree of predictability that no common-law jurisdiction and hardly any other civil law jurisdiction in the world can provide. The choice is clear: parties should unreservedly negotiate and conclude their contract under German law.

### II. Default rules

37 Unlike in many other jurisdictions, German civil law provides default rules that help find a fair and just solution in situations where parties have failed to reach a contractual agreement. This applies to all fields of German civil law such as, for example, warranty in sales or construction law, termination, damage compensation.

### III. Low costs

38 A larger scope of freedom of contract – provided by other legal systems – usually favours large enterprises, leaving small and medium-sized enterprises behind. This is often accompanied with considerable lawyer's fees and contracts that are ultimately disadvantageous for them. Moreover, contract design under German law is more cost-effective than in common-law jurisdictions, where hardly any default rule exists and the time needed to produce agreements, including drafting and negotiating, is significantly more extensive.

## IV. Efficient law enforcement

The German court system and the rules on civil procedure, as well as the rules on lawyer's remuneration ensure efficient law enforcement at a reasonable price. A first instance judgment takes between six and twelve months on average. Complex commercial cases may, however, take longer in individual cases, depending on whether comprehensive evidence must be considered by the court and several oral hearings are required. **39**

# Chapter 5
# Dispute settlement

**Bibliography:** Leisinger, Vertraulichkeit in internationalen Schiedsverfahren, Baden-Baden 2012; Mann, 'Der Schutz unternehmensinterner Anwaltskorrespondenz im transatlantischen Rechtsvergleich', ZVglRWiss 100 (2011), 302; Mann, 'Zur kollektiven Durchsetzung von Ansprüchen geschädigter Kapitalanleger mittels BGB-. Gesellschaften', ZIP 2011, 2393; Mann, 'Kollektive Rechtsdurchsetzung und das Rechtsdienstleistungsgesetz: Der BGH schafft Klarheit', DStR 2013, 765; Rützel/Wegen/Wilske, Commercial Dispute Resolution in Germany, 2nd edn, Munich 2016; Schultze-Moderow/Steinle/Muchow, 'Die neue Sammelklage – Ein Balanceakt zwischen Verbraucher- und Unternehmensinteressen', BB 2023, 72; Wegen/Barth/Wexler-Uhlich, International Arbitration in Germany, Munich 2022.

## A. Litigation vs arbitration

1 For legally unexperienced parties, the question of whether future disputes shall be settled by a court or an arbitral tribunal (*Schiedsgericht*) appears to be of minor importance. The differences between arbitration (*Schiedsverfahren*) and litigation (*Prozessführung vor staatlichen Gerichten*) may, however, significantly influence the outcome of a case. Therefore, when entering into a (commercial) contract, it is strongly recommended to seek legal advice with regard to whether a (future) dispute shall be settled before a state court or an arbitral tribunal. The following aspects need to be taken into consideration in this connection.

### I. Litigation

2 Litigation is the traditional form of formalised dispute resolution before competent national courts. Usually, the courts at the residential seat of a party (or seat of a company) will have jurisdiction over a claim brought against this party. However, the courts will only have jurisdiction in the absence of a valid agreement between the disputing parties that refer the dispute to settlement by arbitration or other means of alternative dispute resolution and thereby excluding court litigation. The advantages of litigation mainly stem from the institutional framework of the national court system. These are (i) the availability of an appeals system, (ii) the existence of rules on multi-party disputes, and (iii) the greater powers of national courts compared to arbitral tribunals.

#### 1. Appeals system

3 An advantage of litigation is that it contains an appeals mechanism common to almost all national court systems. Factual or legal errors as well as misinterpretation can be made by both judges and arbitrators, no matter how experienced. The ability to request a 'second look' by an appellate court (*Berufungsgericht*) available in national court

systems is an important procedural safeguard that does not exist in arbitration, where even an obviously wrong decision will remain enforceable and a challenge of the arbitral judgment is possible only under extremely narrow circumstances. The system of appeals also provides for increased legal certainty regarding the outcome of a dispute, since lower courts usually base their decisions on prior similar decisions rendered by higher national courts. In contrast, arbitration lacks such a system of precedents, which may in practice lead to conflicting judgments.

### 2. Multi-party disputes

In addition, national court systems usually have well-established rules on consolidation of claims (§ 260 ZPO, *Klagehäufung*), joinder (§§ 59, 60 ZPO, *Streitgenossenschaft*), and third-party intervention (§ 66 ZPO et seqq., *Nebenintervention*) at their disposal and can thus easily entertain multi-party disputes.[1] For instance, liability owed to the opposing contracting party may be directly traced down the chain of contracts to sub-contractors that were responsible for the complaints if the latter are joined to the original proceedings. In contrast, because of the consent-based nature of arbitration, arbitral tribunals cannot usually order the consolidation of claims or joinders to the proceedings if multiple parties are involved. 4

### 3. More comprehensive powers of judges to conduct the proceedings

The power of judges is generally greater than the power of arbitrators, which can make the proceedings more effective. For example, the power to require attendance of witnesses under penalty of fine or imprisonment and the power to enforce a decision by the attachment of a bank account or the sequestration of assets are instruments of national courts not available to private arbitrators. 5

## II. Arbitration

Arbitration is a form of alternative dispute resolution frequently used in the settlement of commercial disputes instead of litigation. Rather than a judge deciding on a case in a court room, an arbitral tribunal consists of one or more party-appointed arbitrators that will decide on the issues in dispute and render an enforceable and binding decision on the parties. The parties can either mutually agree upon arbitration (i) after a dispute has arisen, or more commonly, (ii) at the time of entering into a particular contract (with regard to all future disputes arising out of or in connection with that contract). Arbitration is frequently the dispute resolution means of choice for companies for a variety of reasons, including confidentiality, neutrality, efficiency and enforceability, as well as flexibility, each discussed below. 6

### 1. Confidentiality

Although this is has been criticised,[2] an important advantage of arbitration over litigation is that arbitration is essentially a private process that may remain confidential if 7

---

[1] For multi-party disputes under German law and collective claim enforcement, see Mann, DStR 2013, 765; Mann, ZIP 2011, 2393.

[2] Wegen/Barth/Wexler-Uhlich Ch. 1 mn. 38.

the parties so wish. This stands in contrast with the publicity that necessarily goes along with national court proceedings. Confidentiality may be particularly relevant in sensitive or high-profile cases or where allegations of poor performance are made.[3] Confidentiality may better help the parties maintain a cooperative business relationship despite their current dispute.

## 2. Neutrality of forum

8 Neutrality may be the crucial factor when deciding to refer disputes to arbitration instead of litigation. This is the case when the parties enter into international agreements and either party is faced with the potential risk of being sued in the courts of the other party's country. The fear of being faced with a corrupt court system is pervasive in developing countries or underdeveloped judicial systems of newly industrialised countries. Therefore, the neutrality offered by an arbitral tribunal composed of one or more party-appointed arbitrators of diverse nationalities can be an attractive alternative to national court proceedings, ensuring a fair hearing in a neutral forum under the law chosen by the parties. Moreover, the parties are free to choose the language, place, and venue of arbitration, affording the opportunity for the parties to choose a neutral forum. A German and a Chinese company may, for example, choose a Swiss arbitrator to decide on their dispute under the laws of Switzerland in a hearing held in accordance with the rules of the Singapore International Arbitration Centre.

## 3. Efficiency of arbitration and enforceability of arbitral awards

9 The alleged time and cost efficiency of arbitration is one of its most frequently cited advantages over litigation. Arbitral disputes are often more quickly resolved than disputes filed before a national court. While national courts tend to be overloaded, arbitral tribunals can commence their work as soon as one party submits a request for arbitration and the tribunal is appointed. Unlike a national court judgment, the final award issued by the tribunal does not constitute the first step on a ladder of appeals, but is instead the final, binding, and essentially incontestable decision of the tribunal. The opportunities to appeal or annul an arbitral award on its merits are severely limited. Notwithstanding these contributing factors, the argument that arbitrations are more time and cost efficient does not hold true in its entirety. In fact, arbitration may in certain cases take a longer time and/or be more expensive than litigation. This will depend on whether one of the parties appeals the arbitral award to the national court system. As a rule of thumb, arbitration is quicker than litigation, unless one party appeals. In particular, the costs to the parties are not bound by rules of the national courts. Costs incurred by an arbitration can be high and include the arbitrators' fees, administrative fees of the arbitral institution, tenancy fees for the hearing venue, and fees incurred for the taking of evidence.[4]

10 However, unlike a national court judgment, an award does not need to be first recognised by foreign courts before it can be enforced. The international enforceability of an arbitral award is governed by international treaties. The most important one is the New York Convention[5], which, with more than 170 contracting parties, covers most cross-border commercial disputes in the world. Because of this, an arbitral award is directly enforceable in various national legal systems.

---

[3] See Leisinger, pp. 37 et seqq.

[4] Rützel/Wegen/Wilske, p. 174.

[5] Convention on the Recognition and Enforcement of Foreign Arbitral Awards (1958). The text is available on https://www.newyorkconvention.org/11165/web/files/original/1/5/15432.pdf.

### 4. Flexibility

An additional advantage of arbitration over litigation is the degree of autonomy and flexibility that arbitration gives the parties in resolving their dispute. Arbitration also permits the parties to select the arbitrators who shall adjudicate the dispute. This ensures that the decision-makers are suitably experienced and competent, thereby being able to find a sound solution to the conflict. Furthermore, arbitration allows the parties to choose the language in which the arbitral proceedings will be conducted. Lastly, parties also have the choice of (i) whether to conduct their arbitration under the rules of a recognised arbitral institution (such as, for example, the International Chamber of Commerce, the London Court of Arbitration, the American Arbitration Association, the Stockholm Chamber of Commerce, or the DIS) that will assist the tribunal in the administration of the case, or (ii) to initiate arbitration on an ad hoc basis. While ad hoc arbitration offers the parties the greatest amount of flexibility, it is advisable to agree on institutional rules to provide a framework for the proceedings and to minimise potential court interventions, for example, because of the violation of due process. 11

## III. Litigation or arbitration?

### 1. Considerations

Considering the respective advantages and disadvantages of arbitration and litigation, the decision on which dispute resolution mechanism should be chosen depends on the particularities of the individual dispute. 12

- If the dispute arises from an international transaction, the balance shifts firmly in favour of arbitration because of the neutrality of the forum and the ready enforceability of the award in different national legal systems. Arbitral awards are enforceable in more than 170 states (amounting to approximately 95 % of the German foreign trade volume).
- The decision is more difficult in purely domestic disputes. Here, advantages stemming from the more institutionalised nature of national courts compete with the greater confidentiality and flexibility of arbitration and the better expertise of the appointed arbitrators. In disputes between company shareholders – at least in Germany – arbitral tribunals sometimes tend to be more sympathetic to the minority shareholders. For complex M&A disputes, arbitration is the method of choice.
- For merely domestic commercial (not corporate) disputes, it is often cheaper to agree on litigation instead of arbitration, unless the parties have a specific interest in confidentiality.

### 2. Arbitration clause

In any case, if the parties decide to choose arbitration by inserting an arbitration clause in their contract, it is necessary to ensure the validity of the clause. An unclear arbitration clause that can be interpreted in many ways may be found invalid and will commonly lead to a result not originally intended by the parties. If the parties decide to choose institutional arbitration as their means of dispute settlement, it is advisable to use standard arbitration clauses in contracts which may be found on the websites of these institutions. 13

### 3. Jurisdiction clause

#### a) Domestic business relationships

14 In domestic cases, jurisdiction clauses are generally invalid when they are agreed on between non-merchants or between a merchant and a non-merchant (§ 38(1) ZPO). However, two merchants may validly choose a venue for their disputes. In standard terms, the test of reasonableness may, however, lead to the invalidity of a jurisdiction clause (i) if both parties have a common jurisdiction and the user chooses a jurisdiction elsewhere,[6] (ii) the parties choose a jurisdiction that has no connection to the content of the contract or to the seat of the user,[7] or (iii) the jurisdiction clause establishes the competence of a foreign court in a case that has no foreign connections.[8] Otherwise, a jurisdiction clause when a non-merchant is involved can also be valid, as long as it is agreed upon after the emergence of the dispute, the clause is explicit, and made in writing (§ 38(3) no. 1 ZPO).

#### b) Cross-border business relationships

15 In cross-border cases, the validity of jurisdiction clauses is not dependent on the ZPO. If a clause establishes the jurisdiction of a national court in an EU Member State, the Brussels Ia Regulation is applicable. Article 25 Brussels Ia Regulation governs the validity of jurisdiction clauses, according to which a clause is valid if it does not go against the substantive law of the Member State and it adheres to certain form requirements, according to which the clause must be made (i) in writing, (ii) orally with written confirmation, (iii) in a form that the parties have established between themselves, or (iv) a form that is widely used in international trade or commerce that the parties ought to be aware of (Article 25(1)(a)–(c) Brussels Ia Regulation). Furthermore, any communication by electronic means that provides a durable record of the agreement is considered equivalent to 'writing', so that email can be used for this purpose.[9] If a clause establishes the jurisdiction of a national court outside the European Union, its validity is determined by national law or international conventions. For instance, the validity of a jurisdiction clause in favour of litigation in a London court is governed by the Hague Convention. Due to the aforementioned disadvantages involving the enforcement of a decision from a British court after Brexit, such a clause in a contract involving a German company is strongly discouraged.

## B. Collective redress

16 For companies, it is important to know what behaviours can lead to them to become liable for their products and services so that they can avoid them. In case a commercial dispute does arise, it is equally important to have insights into several important aspects of German procedure law to minimise the possible damage that can result from such disputes.

17 The US is generally friendly to plaintiffs. A person damaged by products can often litigate with other plaintiffs in class-action lawsuits, which sinks the cost of litigation for each person significantly. US procedural law allows for lawyers to charge contingent fees, which are payable only if a lawsuit is successful or results in a favourable settlement. The

[6] OLG Cologne 24 U 44/89, ZIP 1989, 1068.
[7] LG Constance 3 HO 31/83, BB 1983, 1372.
[8] OLG Düsseldorf 6 U 139/87, NJW-RR 1988, 1260 (1261).
[9] BeckOK ZPO/Gaier Brüssel Ia-VO Art. 25 mn. 46.1.

courts can award punitive damage, which can be very lucrative for some plaintiffs but also catastrophic for some defendants. The legal instrument of pre-trial discovery gives the plaintiff extensive powers to request evidence from often tight-lipped conglomerates. These features of the US system make it very attractive for plaintiffs to file suit there[10].

Although the German legal system does not currently embrace all these features, some of them have been adopted on a limited basis. As a rule, if a similar product defect has caused multiple incidents of damage, each injured person must bring an individual claim against the producer/manufacturer of the defective product. Before 2018, there were only a few possibilities for collective redress in Germany.[11] To manage the flood of lawsuits by consumers against Volkswagen on the heels of the diesel scandal, the German legislator introduced the Model Declaratory Action (*Musterfeststellungsklage*) in 2018, regulated in §§ 606 et seqq. ZPO. These rules allowed for suits of different plaintiffs who are consumers to be bundled in a model action. The courts could declare their decisions on different aspects of the suit that the plaintiffs have in common with each other. After these aspects are decided by the courts in the sample declaratory judgment, the plaintiffs must split up again and continue to sue for damage individually. 18

The possibility to sue for damage collectively is provided for in a new law at the order of the European Union's Directive 2020/1828, which allows for collective redress in suits brought by consumers.[12] This 'New Deal for Consumers' can offer relief to those damaged by malfeasance in cases in which many people are affected.[13] 19

However, both cases (the Model Declaratory Action and the new rules spurred on by the Directive) are limited in that the plaintiffs must be consumers. Although these rules make litigation more attractive in Germany for consumers, the wide-ranging legal instruments available to US plaintiffs are not available in Germany to the same extent. For companies, this is good news. Since the damage from individual lawsuits are limited, the predictability of the damage award gives businesses an advantage. 20

For companies that only have b2b business relationships, the following possibilities of a customer drawing another party into a lawsuit should be considered. The parties of a conflict are free to agree on the binding character of a model proceeding or may agree that a prior or future court decision not only has effect *inter partes* but also *inter omnes* (i.e. between multiple or several parties). Such an individual party agreement, however, is quite rare in practice. Under narrow circumstances it may, however, be possible to collect damage claims by professional claimants in respect of which the requirements of the Legal Services Act (*Rechtsdienstleistungsgesetz* – RDG) are met. This makes sense when the qualifying conditions of all individual cases are similar, and the facts of the cases are comparable; e.g. due to a similar product defect causing multiple incidents of damage. The professional claimants may then collectively enforce the assigned and bundled damage claims via a litigation vehicle, which is commonly a BGB company or a limited liability company.[14] 21

---

[10] Mann, ZVglRWiss 100 (2011), 302, 313.

[11] Collective redress is sanctioned by the Capital Markets Model Case Act (*Gesetz über Musterverfahren in kapitalmarktrechtlichen Streitigkeiten* – KapMuG), whose scope is limited to damages incurred in capital markets; although the claims of different parties can be assigned to one person, thereby allowing this person to bundle these claims into one court case, the Legal Services Act (*Rechtsdienstleistungsgesetz* – RDG) limits this bundling by making certain assignments illegal and therefore ineffective; and the Act for Injunctive Relief (*Unterlassungsklagegesetz* – UKlaG), which allows for collective suits for injunctive relief in very limited cases.

[12] Transposed into German law via the Consumer Rights Enforcement Act (*Verbraucherrechtedurchsetzungsgesetz* – VDuG), which repealed §§ 606 et seqq. ZPO.

[13] Schultze-Moderow/Steinle/Muchow, BB 2023, 72.

[14] See Mann, DStR 2013, 765; Mann, ZIP 2011, 2393.

# Chapter 6
# Purchase agreement

**Bibliography:** Grüneberg (ed.), Bürgerliches Gesetzbuch: BGB, 82nd edn, Munich 2023; Mann, Vertriebsrecht in Handel und Industrie, Munich 2017; Mann/Baisch, 'Internationale Lieferbeziehungen und Zulieferernominierung: Rechtliche Aspekte und AuslegungsfragenInhalt', ZVglWiss 120 (2021), 246; Münchener Kommentar zum Bürgerlichen Gesetzbuch, 8th edn, Munich 2019; Peusquens, 'Die zivilrechtliche Bedeutung des § 14 Abs. 1 S. 1 UStG', NJW 74, 683.

## A. Introduction

1 The most important type of contract in international commerce is the purchase/sales agreement. It may appear in different forms, e.g. as a consumer sales contract, a commercial purchase agreement or, in corporate law, an asset or share purchase agreement. The special features of sales law are regulated in §§ 433 et seqq. BGB. For international purchase agreements, the CISG provides rules that may apply if its application has not been excluded (→ Ch. 4 mn. 7).

## B. Basic principles

### I. Essential content

2 Like any other contract, the purchase agreement requires two corresponding and valid declarations of intent, which are offer and acceptance. The parties must reach an agreement about the essential content of the contract (*essentialia negotii*) which is (i) the identity of the buyer and seller, (ii) the goods sold, and (iii) the purchase price (→ Ch. 1 mn. 8).

### II. Form

3 Purchase agreements do not require a specific form. This, however, is not the case for the sale of real estate (§ 311b(1) sentence 1 BGB). The prescribed notarial recording is necessary for any type of contracts that directly or indirectly obliges a party to transfer or acquire a plot of land, irrespective of whether this is a pre-contract, a cancellation agreement, or a subcontract.

## III. Object of the purchase agreement

4 Goods as well as rights (§ 453 BGB) may be the object of a purchase agreement, although not every disposal of goods or rights constitutes a purchase agreement.

- A **licence agreement**, for instance, is not aimed at a final and exclusive disposal of rights but is instead intended to permit the use of know-how or an intellectual property right (patent, registered design, or trademark right) for a limited period. The licensor (*Lizenzgeber*) remains the owner of the property right. If the licensor/seller intends to dispose of the property right irrevocably to the other party, a sale/purchase of a right occurs.
- In **distributor** or **authorised dealer agreements**, the principal is obliged to supply the distributor with goods. The distributor promotes, advertises, and resells the goods. The distributorship agreement is a framework agreement *sui generis*, whereas the individual transactions conducted thereunder are purchase contracts. The same applies to **franchise agreements**.
- In **tenancy agreements**, the landlord rents the apartment or house to the tenant for a definite or indefinite period. However, there is no change in ownership of the apartment or house. The same applies to **lease agreements**, e.g. car leasing, although in finance lease agreements, strong elements of sales law may apply.
- In **construction contracts** and **contracts to produce a work** (§§ 631 et seqq. BGB) the contractor is obliged to produce the promised work, and the customer is obliged to pay the agreed remuneration. The core obligation of such contracts is the establishment of a specific work (e.g. a house or a factory) for the customer and not (only) the delivery and transfer of ownership of a certain good.
- In the case of a **gift** (§ 516 BGB), the giver (*Schenker*) enriches the receiver (*Beschenkter*) by giving him assets free of charge without any payment obligation.
- The **exchange** (*Tausch*) differs from sales in that instead of a purchase price, the parties perform their obligations by disposing of certain goods (exchange of two goods).

## IV. Special types of sale

5 The BGB regulates the ordinary purchase agreement in §§ 433 to 453 BGB and provides specific rules on special types of purchase agreements such as purchase on approval (§ 454 BGB, *Kauf auf Probe*), repurchase (§ 456 BGB, *Wiederkauf*), pre-emption (§ 463 BGB, *Vorkauf*), and purchase of consumer goods (§§ 474 et seqq. BGB, *Verbrauchsgüterkauf*). These specific types of sales play only a minor role in commerce, whereas the provisions on commercial transactions in §§ 343 et seqq. HGB set forth specific rules on purchase agreements relevant to trade.

## V. Specific provisions of commercial law

6 §§ 343 et seqq. HGB contain specific provisions for commercial transactions amongst merchants, including special provisions for the sale of goods in trade. §§ 343 et seqq. HGB contain general rules on commercial practices (§ 346 HGB), including the commercial letter of confirmation (*Kaufmännisches Bestätigungsschreiben*), rules on contractual penalties (§ 348 HGB, *Vertragsstrafe*), rules on suretyship (§§ 349, 350 HGB, *Bürgschaft*), rules on the effectiveness of the assignment of monetary claims (§ 354a HGB), rules on

the conclusion of contracts (§ 362 HGB), or commercial right of retention (§ 369 HGB, *kaufmännisches Zurückbehaltungsrecht*). §§ 373 et seqq. HGB establish specific rules regarding commercial purchase agreements. These rules supplement those of general sales law (§§ 433 et seqq. BGB). One provision with high practical relevance is the buyer's duty to examine the purchased goods and to object to defects (§ 377 HGB, → mn. 21 et seqq.).

# C. Rights and obligations

## I. Seller

7 The seller's main obligations are defined in § 433(1) BGB. Pursuant to § 433(1) sentence 1 BGB, the seller is obliged to hand over and to provide ownership of the sold good to the buyer. § 433(1) sentence 2 BGB substantiates the seller's obligation by clarifying that he must provide the purchased item to the buyer free from material and legal defects.

### 1. Handing over the purchased item

#### a) Place and time of performance

8 Where and when the seller must hand over the purchased item can be agreed on by the parties. In the absence of a party agreement, § 269 BGB stipulates that the seller must hand over the purchased item at his residence. Often, the parties to a purchase contract agree that the seller must transport the goods to the buyer's or a third party's residence or seat (e.g. to a manufacturing plant or a shop). If the parties have not agreed on a specific time of performance, § 271(1) BGB stipulates that the buyer may demand performance by the seller immediately and the seller must transfer ownership of the purchased item to the buyer immediately. In practice, the place and time of performance are commonly regulated either in the purchase agreement or in the standard terms and conditions of one of the parties. Also, both seller and buyer normally use sub-contractors and subsidiaries to fulfil their obligations.

#### b) Costs

9 In the absence of an individual party agreement, § 448 BGB provides for a splitting of the costs arising from the transfer of the purchased item. Pursuant to § 448(1) BGB, the seller bears the costs of delivery (e.g. storage, transport), whereas the buyer bears the costs of acceptance (e.g. costs of an incoming inspection) and of shipping the good to a place other than the place of performance. These provisions are default rules only and may be amended or changed by party agreement, which usually happens in trade. In international commercial relations, parties usually agree on the application of Incoterms regulating the allocation of costs and risks among the parties (→ Ch. 4 mn. 13 et seqq.).

### 2. Providing ownership

10 The seller must provide ownership of the purchased item to the buyer. This usually happens by effectively handing over the purchased goods (e.g. loading pallets onto a truck or – depending on the contractual agreement – unloading it on the buyer's premises). If the parties agreed on a retention of title clause, the seller of the good, pursuant to § 449(1)

BGB, is obligated to provide ownership only under the condition that the purchase price is paid in full. Retention of title clauses play an important role in commercial contracts, as they give the seller the opportunity to secure his payment claim (even in the case of the buyer's insolvency) until the buyer has made full payment (→ Ch. 3 mn. 31). If the purchase item is not a physical object but a right, the seller must assign the right to the buyer and enable him to use such a right.

### 3. Absence of defects

#### a) Free from defects

The seller must provide the purchased item to the buyer free from defects (§ 433(1) sentence 2 BGB). In practice, this obligation of the seller is often breached. A breach of this duty triggers the buyer's warranty claims stipulated in §§ 437 et seqq. BGB. The purchased item is free from defects if, upon the handover of the good, the purchased item 11

1. is of the **agreed quality,** or
2. to the extent that the quality has not been agreed on, the purchase item is **suitable for the intended use** according to the contract, or
3. is suitable for the **customary use** and its quality is usual in goods of the same kind, and
4. includes the agreed upon **accessories** as well as the instructions to assemble and install the good.

#### b) Party agreement

The parties' individual agreement regarding quality and absence of defects is decisive when it comes to the question of whether a purchased item is defective or not (subjective indication). If the parties, for instance, stipulate in the contract that the sold piece of land is free from contamination or the delivered products fulfil certain durability criteria and/or are free from certain toxic substances, such party agreements primarily determine whether a purchased item is free from defect. 12

#### c) Suitability for intended use

In most sales situations as well as in trade, the parties often do not specifically define criteria for the absence of defects. In such cases, the purchased item is free from defects if it is suitable for the intended use under the contract (§ 434(2) sentence 1 no. 2 BGB). The suitability may be derived from the circumstances of the case and the intended purpose of the sale. A defect is present, for instance, if the sold food has expired, a painting bought by an art gallery turns out to be a forgery, or a second-hand item is provided even though it is apparent from the circumstances that the buyer needs a new item. 13

#### d) Suitability for customary use

If the parties have not agreed on certain criteria for the absence of defects and what is suitable for the intended use under the contract, the question of whether a purchased item is defective depends on whether it (i) is suitable for the customary use (§ 434(3) sentence 1 no. 1 BGB) and (ii) is of the quality that is usual in goods of the same kind, (§ 434(3) sentence 1 no. 2 BGB). This objective catch-all definition helps determine, in all remaining cases, whether a purchased item is free from defects. Quality in this respect includes characteristics that the buyer can expect from the public statements on the good that are made by the seller, the producer, his sub-contractors, or his assistants. Such public statements include, in particular, advertising (e.g. TV, catalogue, oral promotion 14 at sales events), description of the good (e.g. fuel consumption claims by manufacturer or distributor in car sales), or inscriptions on the good. If the seller was not aware of the statement and had no duty to be aware of it, if the seller corrected the public statement, or if the public statement did not influence the buyer's decision to purchase the good, the buyer may not rely on such a statement. A material defect is also present if the agreed installation by the seller or his sub-contractors has been carried out improperly. In addition, a material defect exists if the installation instructions are defective (incomplete or incomprehensible), unless the good has already been installed without any error. Where the seller has delivered a different good or a lesser amount of the purchased products, this also constitutes a defect pursuant to § 434 (3) sentence 2, (5) BGB.

#### e) Burden of proof

15 The seller must furnish proof that the sold item is free from defects up until the passing of the risk (handover of the good). If the buyer refuses to accept the good, the seller has to prove that the item is defect free. Once the buyer has accepted the purchased item and a defect occurs thereafter, he has to prove that the purchased item (i) is defective, and (ii) was already defective when it was handed over (or at least the cause of the defect already existed at the passing of the risk).[1] There is a reversal of the burden of proof in the sale of consumer goods, whereby it is presumed that the purchased item was already defective when it was handed over if, up to a year after the date of the passing of the risk (handover), a defect occurs (§ 477 BGB). § 477 BGB, however, does not apply to commercial purchase contracts.

## II. Buyer

### 1. Payment and acceptance of the delivery

16 Pursuant to § 433(2) BGB, the buyer's main obligations are to pay the seller the agreed purchase price and to accept delivery of the purchased item.

#### a) Purchase price

17 Usually the parties explicitly agree on a defined purchase price. If the parties have either failed to specify the purchase price or to determine a standard for calculation, the price must be determined by the seller (§ 316 BGB). If the determined price was not appropriate, the seller's decision may be replaced by one of the courts (§ 315(3) BGB). If the parties see a necessity to adjust the prices, they may agree on a price renegotiation clause. A renegotiation clause obligates the parties to reconvene and renegotiate the prices in good faith. An automatic adjustment of prices can be effected by a valid price adjustment clause (→ Ch. 2 mn. 15).

#### b) Mode of payment

18 Generally, the buyer must hand over the money to the seller at the seller's residence. In trade, however, the parties almost always deviate from this antiquated payment method. The payment is often the content of an implied agreement, whereby the seller simply specifies his bank account (in letters, earlier invoices, or in the written contract) when corresponding with the buyer to indicate where the money is to be transferred.

---

[1] BGH VIII ZR 43/05, NJW 2006, 434 (435).

#### c) Problem in invoice

If a seller produces a faulty invoice, the buyer may be unsure as to whether he has an obligation to pay it. The buyer has a right to receive the correct invoice, including the corresponding VAT.[2] If this was not received by the buyer, he has the right to withhold payment pending a correct invoice pursuant to § 273(1) BGB.[3] In this case, the buyer should point to the error in the current invoice and let the seller know that payment is being withheld until the correct one is produced. 19

#### d) Acceptance of delivery

The seller physically hands over the purchased item to the buyer or a third designated party. The place of acceptance corresponds to the place of performance of the purchased item's transfer. 20

### 2. Examination of goods and objection to defects

If a sale is a commercial transaction for both parties, § 377 HGB establishes an obligation on the part of the commercial buyer to examine the purchased item without undue delay after delivery and to promptly object to defects. If the buyer fails to examine the delivered products and to object to defects, he risks forfeiting his warranty rights (§ 377(3) HGB). The conditions of § 377 HGB are as follows: 21

#### a) Scope of application

The buyer's obligation to examine the delivered products applies only to movable goods (e.g. the supply of manufactured parts, food, medical products, commodities, etc.). Hence, § 377 HGB does not apply to corporate share acquisitions, to sales of real estate, or to contracts to produce a work (§ 631 BGB). 22

#### b) Prompt examination

Upon delivery of the purchased item (or batch), the buyer is obliged to promptly examine the goods. Such examination must be carried out without undue delay following delivery of the goods. Delivery of the goods took place when the complete shipment (*Warenlieferung*) is handed over to the buyer and he has the opportunity to examine the goods. If the seller is obliged to dispatch the goods to the buyer's residence, delivery is complete when the seller (or his freight carrier) has handed over the goods at the buyer's residence. In contrast, if the buyer is obliged to pick up the goods at the seller's residence, delivery is complete when the seller has handed over the goods to the buyer (or the freight carrier) at the seller's residence.[4] 23

#### c) Timeline

The commercial buyer must examine the purchased item promptly. The determination of promptness depends on the special features of each individual case (e.g. industrial sector, size of organisation, type of product). The period for easily perishable groceries is shorter than the period for complex machinery. The time period varies from 24 hours to 24

---

[2] FG Hamburg, 3 V 247/13, BeckRS 2014, 94908.

[3] Peusquens, NJW 74, 683.

[4] To see how this works in a third-party deal (*Streckengeschäft*), see BGH VIII ZR 245/76, NJW 1978, 2394.

up to two months.[5] As a rule of thumb, commentators consider one week to be an adequate time period for the examination of industrial goods.

#### d) Extent of examination

25 The examination must be appropriate according to the individual case. Costs, technical capacities, visible damage to the goods, expenditure of time, necessity of experts, or likelihood of the goods being defective are relevant factors. Control samples may be admissible if large volumes of goods are sold and control samples are adequate and meaningful.[6] For example, the examination of groceries requires a visual examination and an assessment of smell and taste. It may be necessary to defrost control samples. Machines must be started and – in the case of complex machines – tested over a period. Commercial customs must also be considered. In case the buyer is unable to effectively examine the purchased good, he must employ an expert to do so.[7]

#### e) Objection to defects

26 If the buyer becomes aware of a defect, he must object and immediately notify the seller. The buyer must describe the defect(s) as precisely as possible. General statements like 'goods are not merchantable', 'goods do not work', or 'goods are of bad quality' are insufficient. A specific form, however, is not required. For reasons of evidence, the buyer is well-advised to notify the seller of the defect by email. The time period within which to notify the seller is shorter than the time period for examining the purchased goods. It amounts to one to two days[8] – but may even be shorter, for instance, if the purchased good is an easily perishable grocery item. As a rule, the time period begins once a defect becomes obvious.

- If the defect was **apparent**, i.e. the defect was visible or easily recognisable by properly examining the purchased item, the time period for notification begins as soon as the examination was or should have been completed.
- If the defect was **hidden**, i.e. the defect was not recognisable by properly examining the purchased item and did not otherwise become apparent, notice must be given promptly (within one to two days) following the discovery of the defect.

#### f) Legal consequences of omission

27 If the buyer fails to notify the seller of a defect, the goods are deemed to be free of defects. If the defect was hidden, this legal consequence applies once the hidden defect became apparent and the buyer still failed to notify the seller thereof. This fictional approval has severe consequences regarding the buyer's warranty claims stipulated in § 437 BGB and will be discussed below. Such claims are excluded if the buyer approves the delivered goods as provided for in the agreement. Therefore, if the buyer fails to examine the goods and object to defects pursuant to § 377 HGB, he forfeits his warranty claims. Such forfeiture also applies to consequential damages (*Mangelfolgeschäden*) but not the buyer's tortious claims, if any exists.[9]

---

[5] For the latter, see OLG Düsseldorf 22 U 46/98, NJW-RR 1999, 1714 (ventilator system).
[6] BGH VIII ZR 194/75, NJW 1977, 1150 (1151).
[7] Cf. BGH VIII ZR 164/73, NJW 1975, 2011 (2012).
[8] BGH VIII ZR 152/84, NJW-RR 1986, 52 (53) (trout).
[9] BGH VI ZR 344/87, NJW 1989, 707 (709).

#### g) Contractual alteration

The parties may generally alter the obligations set out in § 377 HGB. There are no restrictions on the alteration or exclusion of § 377 HGB if the parties agree on them by way of an individual agreement. This is different, however, if the parties make such alterations in standard terms and conditions: 28

- The parties may agree that the seller must be notified by the buyer in writing.
- The parties may agree on a specific deadline within which the buyer must object to defects, if such a fixed time period is appropriate (e.g. two weeks) and hidden defects are excluded from such an agreement.[10]
- The parties may not agree on a tightening of the duty to object to hidden defects (e.g. objection only upon delivery), as this would effectively exclude the buyer's warranty rights for defects that are not recognisable at first sight.
- A complete exclusion of the buyer's obligation to examine the goods and object to defects (§ 377 HGB) might be admissible in cases in which (i) the buyer's duty to examine the quality of the goods is shifted to the seller (e.g. by way of a quality assurance agreement) and (ii) a legitimate interest in such a shift is given (e.g. just-in-time production) (→ Ch. 8 mn. 6).

## D. Buyer's claim for rectification of defective goods

§ 437 BGB establishes the buyer's claims when the seller delivers a defective good. If the thing is defective, the buyer may, pursuant to § 437 BGB: 29

- demand cure (repair or replacement) (§ 439 BGB),
- rescind the agreement (§§ 440, 323 BGB),
- reduce the purchase price (§ 441 BGB), or
- demand damage compensation or expenditure reimbursement (*Aufwendungsersatz*),

provided that the requirements of the respective provisions are met, unless otherwise specified.

### I. Rectification of defects

If the seller hands over a defective good, the buyer may initially demand repair (*Nachbesserung*) or replacement (*Nachlieferung*). Pursuant to § 439(3) BGB, the seller may refuse to provide the kind of rectification (cure) chosen by the buyer if this cure is possible only at his disproportionate expense. This is the case, for instance, if the travel and transport expenses to the buyer's residence are higher than the value of the purchased item.[11] Otherwise, the seller must bear all expenses required for the purpose of rectification (cure of defect), in particular in transport, workmen's travel, work, and materials costs (§ 439(2) BGB). The buyer can generally determine if he demands repair or replacement (§ 439(1) BGB). The parties may – even in standard terms – deviate from this principle and agree on a clause granting the seller the right to determine that he either repairs or replaces the defective good. However, other restrictions of the buyer's right to rectify a defect in standard terms are admissible only to a very limited extent as stipulated in § 309 no. 8 30

[10] Cf. BGH III ZR 141/90, NJW 1992, 575 (576).
[11] Grüneberg/Weidenkaff BGB § 439 mn. 16a.

b) BGB. According to this, a provision in standard terms stipulating that the seller does not have to rectify the defect (but only make a refund) is invalid. Contract clauses in standard terms stipulating that the seller must only repair or replace the product, thereby excluding the buyer's right to rescind the agreement or reduce the purchase price where the rectification has failed are also invalid.

## II. No self-remedy

31 Sales law does not give the buyer a right to repair the defect by himself and to claim the corresponding costs from the seller.[12] The seller's right to have a second chance to rectify a defective good cannot be compromised in this way.

## III. Rescission

32 If the buyer has set an appropriate time limit for the rectification of the defect which then expires without effect, the seller has refused to cure the defect, or the rectification has failed (e.g. after the second unsuccessful repair attempt), the buyer may rescind the purchase agreement. The following conditions must be fulfilled: (i) a valid purchase agreement exists, (ii) a defective good is delivered, (iii) the time limit for the rectification has expired without effect, and (iv) the buyer has declared that he exercises his right of rescission. The effects of rescission are stipulated in §§ 346 et seqq. BGB. Pursuant to § 325 BGB, the buyer's right to demand damages is not excluded by rescission.

## IV. Price reduction

33 Alternatively, if the buyer has set an appropriate time limit for the rectification of the defect, which expires without effect, the seller has refused to cure the defect, or the rectification has failed, the buyer may reduce the purchase price pursuant to § 441 BGB. Once the buyer has declared the reduction of the purchase price, the seller's payment claim is reduced accordingly. The reduced price is determined by estimation (if necessary, by an expert). If the buyer has already made full payment, he may demand the excess amount (the difference between the full and reduced price) from the seller pursuant to § 441(4) sentence 1 BGB. Pursuant to § 325 BGB, the buyer's right to demand damages is not excluded in the case of reduction.

## V. Exclusion

34 The buyer's rights arising from a defect are excluded if he has knowledge of the defect during the conclusion of the contract. If the buyer obtains knowledge between the conclusion of the contract and the delivery of the purchased item, the buyer's rights are not excluded unless such behaviour of the buyer constitutes an implied agreement to alter the composition or quality of the good. In commercial practice, if the buyer disregards his obligation to examine the delivered good and object to defects, this can lead to an exclusion of the buyer's claims pursuant to § 377 HGB.

[12] BGH VIII ZR 126/05, NJW 2006, 988.

### VI. Limitation

Contrary to the standard limitation period of three years (§ 195 BGB), sales law provides for special limitation periods regarding the buyer's claims for rectification (cure) of defects. The limitation period for movable goods (e.g. the supply of parts, medical products, commodities, etc.) is only two years (§ 438(1) no. 3 BGB). For a building or goods that are used for a building, the limitation period is five years (§ 438(1) no. 2 BGB). These special limitation periods only apply to the buyer's claims arising from § 437 BGB (e.g. repair, replacement, rescission, reduction) and not to (i) the buyer's claim to hand over the purchased item, (ii) a claim resulting from a representation or an independent guarantee (§ 443 BGB), or (iii) claims for damage compensation arising from tort (§§ 823 et seqq. BGB). Pursuant to § 438(2) BGB, the limitation period of the buyer's warranty claims commences upon delivery of the good and not at the year's end. A reduction of such a limitation period is valid to a minimum of one year only. When reducing the limitation period, the parties must ensure that mandatory law, in particular mandatory liability, is not subject to such a reduction. For instance, § 309 no. 7 BGB (no limitation of liability for damage resulting in death, personal injury or health, or damage caused by wilful or grossly negligent conduct) prevents such a reduction from being valid.[13] On the flip side, an extension of the limitation period from two to ten years is considered invalid, whereas an extension of the limitation period up to three years is found by the courts to be acceptable.[14] 35

## E. Deviating agreement from the statutory warranty regime

In commercial practice, a deviating or simpler contractual agreement regarding buyer's warranty claim is frequently necessary. Especially, when large volumes of small items are sold, the need for flat rate accounting systems, lump-sum payments (e.g. EUR 50 for every defect), or rebate systems are indispensable. The parties may in principle deviate from the warranty system of the BGB. Lump-sum payments or rebate systems may fulfil this requirement unless they provide inappropriate compensation. The appropriateness can only be assessed on a case-by-case basis. Relevant cases regularly seen in practice are discussed below. 36

### I. Lump sum payments for damages

In practice, to simplify matters and, above all, to save time, especially in continuous supply relationships for the industrial production of goods, the parties often agree to dispense with the rectification of defects from the outset. Instead, the seller grants the buyer the right to claim lump-sum compensation for damages and expenses. 37

However, this agreement, which is common in practice, is permissible only under certain conditions.[15] Firstly, the lump sums and the actual expenses incurred must be equivalent. A 'global' equivalence (also calculative equivalence) is sufficient.[16] This means 38

[13] BGH VIII ZR 3/06, NJW 2007, 674 (675).
[14] BGH VIII ZR 16/05, NJW 2006, 47 (48), (50).
[15] BGH VIII ZR 123/95, NJW-Spezial 2010, 361.
[16] MüKoBGB/Lorenz BGB § 478 mn. 20.

that the lump sum does not have to correspond exactly to the actual expenses incurred in every warranty case (which is not possible anyway), but appropriate deviations are acceptable. In this respect, a value derived from experiences and averages may be used.

39 In an agreement on lump sum payments, the supplier must be allowed to prove that a reduction in value has not occurred or that the reduction is significantly lower than the stated lump sum pursuant to § 309 no. 5 BGB. The buyer must also be allowed to prove that a higher damage has occurred in an individual case. The omission of these clauses may mean that the agreement of lump sum payment for damages is void.

40 To speedily rectify defects, lump sum agreements can be advantageous for both parties in ongoing business relations. However, 'profit mark-ups' should be avoided. The lump sum should be based on realistic empirical values and make it possible to prove higher/lower damages in individual cases.

## II. Additional checks and controls

41 The question of whether the buyer has the right to demand additional tests, inspections, and delivery of a product from the seller is not regulated by law. This becomes relevant if deliveries have been defective in the past. According to the law governing defects and damage of goods, the buyer has no right to additional inspections. For this reason, it is advisable to regulate this contractually, for example, in a quality assurance agreement.

42 If there is no contractual regulation, the buyer can in certain cases charge the seller for the costs of additional inspections. According to § 448 BGB, this charge is permitted only if a product is actually defective. The costs of additional examinations are then damage caused by the initial defect. Otherwise, the costs of the examination are considered handover costs pursuant to § 448 BGB, which must be borne by the buyer.[17]

43 In industries related to security or in just-in-time delivery relationships, in which high quality standards and possibly a zero tolerance for defect exist, a quality assurance agreement should be concluded, among other topics, in order to contractually regulate outgoing inspections and quality standards.

## III. Rejection of future deliveries

44 Also relevant in practice is the question of whether the buyer may reject future (defect-free) deliveries and services if defects in supplier parts have been ascertained in the past. The problem arises especially in successive deliveries or in continuous supply relationships. A right of rejection can be agreed upon contractually. Otherwise, a distinction must be made according to the type of contract.

45 In successive delivery contracts (*Sukzessivliefervertrag*), which is an agreement to deliver a certain quantity of products fixed from the outset that are called off in instalments, the buyer can only withdraw from the entire successive delivery contract if he is no longer interested in the remaining partial performance due to the defect of one batch. A loss of interest may exist if the software developed for the buyer's purposes is missing when ordering a computer system or if essential parts of a machine are missing.[18] Mere annoyance is insufficient.

---

[17] BeckOK BGB/Faust BGB § 448 mn. 7.

[18] BGH VIII ZR 56/89, NJW 1990, 3011; BGH VII ZR 183/70, MDR 1973, 402.

In long-term or framework supply contracts, the buyer can simply discontinue the product call-off. However, if the framework contract provides for the obligation to call off products,[19] the buyer can only withdraw from future deliveries by terminating the framework supply contract itself. In such a case, an extraordinary reason for termination according to § 314 BGB is necessary. It must be unreasonable to expect the terminating party to adhere to the framework agreement. 46

## IV. Self-remedy of defects

According to the law governing defects and damage of goods, the seller has the right to make a second tender in the event of a defect. This means that the seller must be given a chance to try again if the good is defective. The parties may, however, agree to deviate from this legal provision. Whether this is also possible in general terms and conditions has not been conclusively clarified. Since the strict law on general terms and conditions only applies to a limited extent in contractual relationships between entrepreneurs, in cases where there is an understandable interest for the buyer to perform or remedy the defect himself, the arguments favour allowing for such contractual agreements even in general terms and conditions.[20] 47

# F. Guarantee

The seller's liability may be supplemented and/or extended by granting the buyer a guarantee. § 443 BGB contains fragmentary regulations on guarantees granted to the buyer by the seller or any other third party (e.g. the manufacturer). A guarantee can be independent or dependent. It may be granted in written form or orally during the contractual negotiations. The differentiation between a dependent and independent guarantee has significant practical implications, as independent guarantees do not fall under the warranty regime of the BGB. As a result, claims arising from an independent guarantee do not become time-barred two years after the handover of the purchased item but instead has the standard limitation period of three years. Moreover, the obligation to examine the goods and report defects pursuant to § 377 HGB do not apply if the seller has granted an independent guarantee. Whether the seller has granted an independent guarantee (i.e. he is seen to be responsible for a certain success regardless of negligence or fault and beyond the mere lack of defects) or simply a dependent guarantee (extension of warranty established by statutory law) is subject to interpretation. However, not every agreement on composition and quality of the purchased item constitutes a guarantee. A guarantee requires that the guarantor agrees to be responsible for a certain success (e.g. lifespan, durability, quality) beyond his statutory warranty obligations. Descriptions of technical data (e.g. DIN standards) do not commonly constitute a guarantee.[21] 48

---

[19] Mann/Baisch, ZVglWiss 120 (2021), 246.

[20] The Federal Court of Justice has, however, expressed critical views on this, see BGH VIII ZR 16/05, NJW 2006, 47; Mann, mn. 306.

[21] BGH VIII ZR 35/80, NJW 1981, 1501.

# G. Entrepreneurial recourse in the supply chain

49 Products are commonly not sold directly from the manufacturer to the consumer but instead sold and resold in a supply chain that involves several intermediaries. The supply or distribution chain is often consisted of the following actors: supplier (manufacturer) to entrepreneur (distributor) to entrepreneur (retailer or final seller) to consumer.

50 If a defect occurs, a buyer – irrespective of whether he is an entrepreneur, authorised dealer, distributor, or consumer – generally has the warranty claims stipulated in § 437 BGB against his seller. Such warranty rights exist irrespective of whether a consumer is involved or not. § 445a BGB provides additional rules on the entrepreneurial recourse with regard to the buyer's warranty rights and reimbursement of expenses that the buyer incurred vis-à-vis his customer when a consumer is involved.

## I. General principle

51 Recourse for defects can occur in each corresponding contractual relationship. Yet, in cases in which the last buyer in the supply chain is a consumer, the final seller (often the retailer or authorised dealer) bears the burden of higher consumer protection and the consumer's corresponding legal advantages (e.g. a reversal of burden of proof), even if the defect has not been caused by the final seller. Therefore, § 445a BGB establishes relief for the buyers in the supply chain vis-à-vis their corresponding sellers, **when a consumer is the buyer of the product** at the end of the supply chain.

### 1. No requirement to set a time limit

52 § 445a(2) BGB stipulates that if the seller was under the obligation to take back the sold item because of a defect, or if the consumer had reduced the purchase price legitimately, it is **not necessary** for him **to set an adequate time limit** that would otherwise be necessary to enforce the rights set out in § 437 BGB vis-à-vis the seller. Hence, if a consumer legitimately rescinds the purchase agreement due to a defect in the good, the final seller (retailer) may rescind the purchase agreement with his supplier without setting a time limit. Likewise, a buyer may demand from his supplier reimbursement of expenses that he had to bear in relation to the consumer under § 439(2) BGB. However, the purchased item must have been defective at the passing of the risk (handover of the good to the buyer) in each respective purchase relationship. If a defect occurs later (after the passing of the risk), the buyer does not have the warranty rights stipulated in § 437 BGB, nor can he assert his rights according to § 445a BGB.

### 2. Reversal of burden of proof

53 Moreover, pursuant to § 478(1) BGB, the buyer may assert the reversal of the burden of proof (*Beweislastumkehr*) stipulated in § 477(1) BGB when claiming recourse from his seller or supplier. § 477 BGB stipulates to the advantage of consumers that if a defect occurs within a year of the passing of the risk, it is presumed that the purchased item was already defective at the passing of the risk. As this presumption only applies to consumers, the final seller would be disadvantaged as he would be under the obligation to prove the defectiveness of the purchased item vis-à-vis his seller/supplier when claiming his warran-

ty rights, whereas the consumer was not under the obligation to do so. §§ 478(1), 445a(1) BGB establish that the relief set out in § 477 BGB applies to the relationship between all sellers of the supply chain and their suppliers if (i) the final buyer was a consumer and (ii) the conditions of § 437 BGB are met. In these cases, the period begins when the risk passes to the consumer, not to the respective buyer.

## II. Limited scope of application

The scope of § 445a(1) BGB is rather limited. The special provision only apply when its strict conditions are met. 54

- It is not applicable if the final buyer is not a consumer but an industrial customer.[22]
- It is only applicable to new products (no second-hand goods).
- It is not applicable to sub-contractor relationships when a sub-contractor supplies components that make up a product but not the finished product itself.
- It is not applicable in cases in which the seller is not obliged to cure the defective good pursuant to § 437 BGB. If the seller rectifies the defect for reasons of goodwill or customer care, § 445a(1) BGB does not apply.

## III. Limitation

The warranty rights provided in § 437 BGB generally become statute-barred two years after delivery of the purchased item. The supply and resale of goods may, however, take considerable time in the supply chain until a defect has been identified by the consumer. This is particularly true when a distributor or retailer stores the goods for some time. § 445b(2) BGB therefore stipulates that warranty claims become statute-barred, at the earliest, two months after the date on which the entrepreneur has satisfied the warranty claims of the consumer. This allows the entrepreneur to have recourse in cases where the commencement of the limitation period vis-à-vis the consumer, on the one hand, and vis-à-vis the seller (supplier), on the other hand, deviate significantly. 55

## IV. Entrepreneurial recourse for digital products

Directive (EU) 2019/770 on contracts for the supply of digital content and digital services obliged the German legislator to regulate contracts on digital products. §§ 327 to 327u BGB came into effect in 2022 and govern digital products and products that have digital components. While most of the regulations govern consumer contracts, § 327u BGB gives the entrepreneur the right for recourse against his own supplier due to a defect if a consumer is at the end of the supply chain. Additionally, the entrepreneur must reimburse his buyer for expenditures caused by the defect. The liability does not require fault on the part of the supplier.[23] 56

---

[22] BGH VIII ZR 16/05, NJW 2006, 47 (50).

[23] While the regulations are applicable for all contract types (for example, for rental contracts for products that contain digital elements), it plays an important role in purchase contracts.

# Chapter 7
# Product liability

**Bibliography:** Foerste/Graf v. Westphalen, Produkthaftungshandbuch, 3rd edn, Munich 2012; Geimer/Schütze (eds), Europäisches Zivilverfahrensrecht, 4th edn, Munich 2020; Leible/Lehmann, 'Die neue EG-Verordnung über das auf außervertragliche Schuldverhältnisse anzuwendende Recht ("Rom II")', RIW 2007, 721; Lenz, Produkthaftung, 2nd edn, Munich 2022; Münchener Kommentar zum Bürgerlichen Gesetzbuch, 8th edn, Munich 2019; Thomas/Putzo, Zivilprozessordnung: ZPO, 34th edn, Munich 2013; Wagner, 'Product Liability' in: Kaplan/Fowler/Castley (eds), Getting the deal through, 2014; Wagner/Mann, 'Kurzkommentar zu BGH, Urt. v. 5.2.2013 – VI ZR 1/12' EWiR 2013, 525.

## A. Sources of law

1 The manufacturing of products and their sale may result in liability for damages resulting from their use or from accidents caused by them. There are several ways in which the manufacturer of a product can become liable under German law. Product liability law in Germany is connected to all areas of German law, i.e. civil, administrative, and criminal law. Whereas civil law describes the conditions under which an injured person may claim compensation, administrative law aims to protect the consumer and other persons who come into contact with the manufactured products. Hence, administrative legislation such as the Product Safety Act (*Produktsicherheitsgesetz* – ProdSG), the Pharmaceuticals Act (*Arzneimittelgesetz* – AMG), or the Medicinal Devices Act (*Medizinproduktegesetz* – MPG) aim to ensure the safe use of products by establishing requirements for their use and certification.

2 In contrast, if damage and/or injury occur, criminal law may establish sanctions or punishments for the persons responsible. Unlike many other jurisdictions (e.g. US, England, France, Belgium), Germany only imposes criminal sanctions on natural persons (not organisations) (→ Ch. 1 mn. 28). The board of directors is responsible for establishing internal control systems that ensure sufficient reporting and compliance. If internal reporting fails, the directors may be subject to criminal sanction (e.g. for bodily injury caused by negligence or negligent homicide). Yet, criminal sanctions may only be imposed if it is proven that an act or omission of the persons in charge has caused the injury or death of a person. This may be the case, when (i) a product has been launched that does not adhere to current safety standards, (ii) the construction of, fabrication of, or instructions for how to use a product has been faulty, (iii) a necessary product recall was not carried out[1], (iv) products have been distributed in which defects have been detected, (v) necessary warnings or safety instructions have not been given,[2] (vi) wrongful choice or insufficient monitoring of employees has occurred, or (vii) wrongful organisation and compliance has caused damage, injury, or death.[3] Whether and to what extent employees may also

[1] Cf. Wagner, pp. 72, 75.
[2] BGH VI ZR 112/88, NJW 1989, 1542.
[3] BGH 5 StR 394/08, NJW 2009, 3173 (3175).

be subject to criminal prosecution in product liability cases has not yet been sufficiently clarified and is therefore subject to a case-by-case analysis.[4] The following considerations deal with the civil law sanctions of product liability.

# B. Civil product liability

German civil law provides three main statutory sources under which a person who suffered injury or incurred damage may claim compensation. First, the Product Liability Act (*Produkthaftungsgesetz* – ProdHaftG) establishes strict liability (*Gefährdungshaftung*) on the manufacturer of a defective product. The ProdHaftG implements the EU Product Liability Directive 85/374/EEC into national law. When applying the ProdHaftG, the rulings of European bodies, in particular judgments of the European Court of Justice, must be considered. Second, § 823 BGB establishes tort liability where a culpable (at least negligent) act or omission has caused damage. Third, sales law may impose liability on the product seller by requiring him to rectify a product defect or to replace a defective product (→ Ch. 6 mn. 29 et seqq.). The conditions and basic differences between the ProdHaftG and the traditional tort regime (§ 823 BGB) are discussed in the following. 3

## I. Conditions and legal consequences of the Product Liability Act

### 1. Conditions

The ProdHaftG is mandatory statutory law. Liability under the ProdHaftG may neither be excluded nor restricted in advance (§ 14 ProdHaftG). § 1 ProdHaftG establishes the manufacturer's duty to compensate damage if a defective product has caused property damage, personal injury, or the death of a person. No contractual relationship is required. The liability triggered by the ProdHaftG does not require culpability. Therefore, even in cases in which the manufacturer has not acted negligently, liability under the ProdHaftG will be triggered if a defective product has caused damage. In the case of damage to property, liability under the ProdHaftG is triggered only if (i) an object other than the defective product is damaged, (ii) this object is normally intended for private use or consumption, and (iii) it has actually been used by the injured party primarily for this purpose. 4

### 2. Capping

The compensation is of monetary character (cash payment). The maximum payment is capped at a sum of EUR 85 million. Pursuant to § 8 ProdHaftG, the injured person may additionally claim compensation for pain and suffering resulting from damage to his body or health. 5

### 3. Definition of product

Product within the meaning of the ProdHaftG includes any moveable object, even if it forms a part of another moveable object or a part of an immovable object. Electricity is also considered a product and may therefore also trigger liability. Unlike tort claims, the 6

[4] Cf. Lenz Produkthaftung/Lenz § 2 mn. 47.

ProdHaftG does not compensate for nuclear damage or damage resulting from pharmaceutical products (§ 15 ProdHaftG).[5]

## 4. Defect

7 The decisive condition for liability under the ProdHaftG is the occurrence of a product defect. A product may be defective due to its construction, its fabrication, or erroneous instructions. § 3 ProdHaftG stipulates that a product is defective if it does not provide the degree of safety that can justifiably be expected, regarding all circumstances, in particular (i) its presentation, (ii) its use that can be reasonably expected, and (iii) the time when it was put into circulation. The safety standard of a product or a product category determines whether a defect exists. For instance, the safety standard that is reasonably expected from a cardiac stimulator is different from that of garden furniture. Likewise, the safety standard that is reasonably expected from toys is different from that of a textbook. A product cannot be considered defective for the sole reason that an improved product was subsequently put into circulation.

8 It is contentiously debated whether a defect exists when it cannot be identified definitively but a significant **suspicion of a product defect** remains.[6] Generally, the suspicion of a defect does not constitute a defect itself. If the claimant is not able to prove that a product has a defect, he cannot successfully claim damage compensation and will therefore lose his claim. One must bear in mind, however, that for certain product categories even the reasonable suspicion of a product defect is not acceptable. In such cases (e.g. when the defect of the product inevitably results in death), facts supporting a strong suspicion may be sufficient for assuming a product defect according to § 3 ProdHaftG.

## 5. Potential defendant

9 The potential defendant of a liability claim under the ProdHaftG is the manufacturer. However, the term 'manufacturer' has a broad meaning. Pursuant to § 4(1) ProdHaftG, a manufacturer is a person who has manufactured the final product, a basic substance, or a component part of the product. The 'quasi-producer' is also subject to liability under § 4(1) sentence 2 ProdHaftG. A quasi-producer is a person who attaches his name, trademark, or any other distinctive mark to the product. This is practiced widely by major retailers, mail order companies, large fashion companies, as well as companies in the automotive sector. The 'quasi-manufacturer' is separately liable along with the manufacturer.

10 Moreover, pursuant to § 4(2) ProdHaftG, an **importer** may also be subject to liability under the ProdHaftG. This is the case if a person, within the scope of his commercial activity, imports products into the European Economic Community with the intention to sell, rent, or distribute them in any other way. However, a private person importing goods into the European Economic Community for private use (e.g. furniture from China, medicine from the US, or wine from South Africa) is not considered an importer. In contrast, a commercial re-importer is considered an importer pursuant to § 4(2) ProdHaftG. For instance, if a German manufacturer exports cars to Brazil and a distributor re-imports them back into Germany, the distributor is liable for defects of the car pursuant to §§ 1, 4(2) ProdHaftG. The application of § 4(2) ProdHaftG is not limited to final products but also applies to the import (or re-import) of basic substances or component parts.

[5] BeckOK/Förster BGB § 15 ProdhaftG mn. 10.

[6] See the conflicting judgments in almost identical cases: OLG Frankfurt/Main 22 U 89/101, MPR 2012, 169 (rejecting damage compensation) and OLG Düsseldorf 15 U 25/11 (granting damage compensation).

## 6. Supplier liability

Pursuant to § 4(3) ProdHaftG, every supplier (including distributors, authorised dealers, and the like) is treated as the manufacturer of the product if the actual manufacturer cannot be ascertained. The supplier, however, may name the manufacturer or the person supplying him with the product within one month of being asked the relevant question about the identity of the manufacturer. If the importer of a product cannot be ascertained or found, even if the manufacturer of the product is known, each supplier is liable as if it is the manufacturer. 11

## 7. Limitation period

Pursuant to § 12 ProdHaftG, claims under the ProdHaftG become statute-barred three years from the time when the claimant knew or could have known of the damage and who the producer is. The limitation period for claims under the ProdHaftG is similar in length to the standard limitation period of § 195 BGB. However, the limitation period of claims incurred pursuant to the ProdHaftG does not commence at the end of the year but instead on the day the claimant obtained knowledge (or could have obtained knowledge) of the damage and who the producer is. 12

## 8. Defendant's arguments to protect himself

Pursuant to § 1(2) ProdHaftG, the defendant may successfully defend himself by raising the objections discussed below. Generally, the defendant (manufacturer) has to prove the facts on which his objection is based.[7] In particular, the defendant may claim 13

- that he did not put the product into circulation (§ 1(2) no. 1 ProdHaftG);
- that the product was not yet defective when it was put into circulation (§ 1(2) no. 2 ProdHaftG);
- that the product was not produced for commercial use (§ 1(2) no. 3 ProdHaftG);
- that the defect was a result of a mandatory legal provision which had to be complied with at the time the product was launched (§ 1(2) no. 4 ProdHaftG);
- that the product was compliant with the scientific and technical 'state of the art' at the time of the product launch and that the defect could therefore not have been recognised (§ 1(2) no. 5 ProdHaftG).

§ 1(3) ProdHaftG contains further objections that the manufacturer may raise to defend against a claim. § 1(3) ProdHaftG establishes an exclusion of liability for component suppliers and other sub-contractors supplying parts or components to the manufacturer. Generally, a component supplier or sub-contractor is jointly (together with the manufacturer) liable for the defective end product. His liability is excluded, however, if the defect was caused 14

- by a defective part, component, or basic substance that was not delivered by the supplier;
- by the construction of the product into which the delivered part was inserted; or
- by the instruction of the maker of the product.

Pursuant to § 6(1) ProdHaftG, the defendant may reduce his liability by successfully claiming that the damage was caused (or partially caused) by (i) improper handling of the product,[8] (ii) non-compliance with the instruction or warning given by the manufac- 15

[7] § 1(4) sentence 1 ProdHaftG; see also BGH VI ZR 107/08, NJW 2009, 2952 (2955).
[8] LG Stuttgart 26 O 466/10, NJW-RR 2012, 1169 (1171).

turer, (iii) improper storage or handling of the product, or (iv) use of the product despite a warning or product recall.[9]

### 9. No exclusion of liability

16 Pursuant to § 14 ProdHaftG, the manufacturer's liability under the ProdHaftG cannot be excluded or limited in advance. Therefore, an agreement excluding the manufacturer's liability under the ProdHaftG prior to the time at which the damage occurs is void. In addition, under the ProdHaftG the defendant may not successfully exclude or limit his liability by objecting that he or his auxiliary persons did not act culpably. Liability under the ProdHaftG is not dependent on a culpable act or omission by the manufacturer. It is a widespread misconception that a manufacturer's liability shall be excluded if he obtains well-known seals of approval or certifications (such as the CE label or the GS mark). In the same vein, a CE label or the fulfilment of other administrative requirements (ISO rules) does not automatically release the manufacturer from liability under the ProdHaftG.[10] Consequently, a manufacturer could only be released from liability if a defect was unavoidable and could not be identified at the time the product was put on the market (§ 1(2) no. 5 ProdHaftG).

## II. Producer liability

### 1. General

17 In addition to the liability from the ProdHaftG, producers can also incur tortious liability. Stipulated in § 823(1) BGB, this is called 'producer liability'. It establishes a claim for certain negligent (or even intentional) acts or omissions that have caused personal injury, death, or property damage. Under certain circumstances, damages for pain and suffering (§ 253(2) BGB) may also be compensated for. However, German law does not provide for punitive damages.[11] A tortious claim based on § 823(1) BGB requires the following conditions: (i) unlawful behaviour or fault (ii) that was culpable (intentional or negligent), has (iii) caused a (iv) violation of a protected right or interest, and (v) this in turn has caused (vi) damage. As a rule, the claimant has to furnish proof of all facts on which his application is based. Therefore, if the defendant contests the facts, the claimant must provide evidence for all the conditions set out above. The most important ones are discussed in the following.

### 2. Producer's unlawful behaviour

18 The producer's liability pursuant to § 823(1) BGB requires unlawful behaviour on the part of the producer. Generally, in product liability cases there is no active misconduct on the part of a producer. A producer may, however, breach his duty of care (*Sorgfaltspflicht*) by failing to abide by necessary safety measures before producing defective products and putting them on the market, which may trigger liability pursuant to § 823(1) BGB. The producer of a product must therefore ensure that (i) the construction of a product is safe and secure, (ii) the fabrication (production) process is free of mistakes and the product are free of defects, (iii) sufficient instruction on the sound handling of the product is pro-

[9] See Lenz Produkthaftung/Lenz § 3 mn. 420.
[10] BGH VI ZR 1/12, NJW 2013, 1302 mn. 9.
[11] BVerfG 1 BvR 1279/94, NJW 1995, 649 (650).

vided, and (iv) the product is sufficiently monitored and observed even after the product launch. Not only can the latter duty result in the producer's obligation to issue a public warning, it can also oblige the producer to recall an entire product category in case the danger to life and health cannot be prevented otherwise.

The quality of the duty of care varies and depends on the function of the product and 19 the aptitude of the potential user. For instance, when a product is produced for use by common consumers, it must meet higher safety standards than a product for experienced industrial users. Consequently, safety applications must meet a higher standard if unexperienced users (e.g. children) have the opportunity to come into contact with potentially dangerous products (water boiler, lawn mower, sharp kitchen equipment, etc.), whereas a mere warning may be sufficient if only well-equipped and well-trained personnel operate a product (e.g. machines for industrial use).[12]

### 3. Violation of a protected right or interest

§ 823(1) BGB protects, among other things, life, body, health, and property of another 20 person. However, a violation of another's property means that the integrity of property is physically violated (e.g. destruction, loss). Mere financial damages are generally not compensated by § 823(1) BGB. Compensation for the loss of production, loss of earnings, or other financial losses may be claimed under § 823(2) BGB[13], § 826 BGB, or under very narrowly defined circumstances pursuant to § 823(1) BGB only.[14]

### 4. Culpability and damage

Generally, the claimant must prove that the defendant's unlawful behaviour was cul- 21 pable. Culpability includes intentional as well as negligent behaviour (§ 276(1) BGB). In producer liability cases, however, the claimant usually has no insight into the internal construction and fabrication (production) processes and is therefore not able to provide evidence for a culpable omission by the producer. The courts have therefore developed a reversal of the burden of proof in cases where (i) a product defect has occurred and (ii) it is beyond the claimant's sphere and insight to establish whether the producer acted culpably.[15] This shift of the burden of proof applies in particular to construction errors (*Konstruktionsfehler*) and errors concerning the production process (*Fabrikationsfehler*). In the case of instruction errors (*Instruktionsfehler*) for wrong or incomplete product information or insufficient monitoring, it is usually easier for the injured claimant to provide evidence as no internal processes are in dispute. However, even for instruction errors – where it would be easier for the claimant to furnish evidence of an error – the courts still apply the shift of the burden of proof.[16]

#### a) Practical guidance regarding culpability

The producer's liability may be excluded if he can successfully prove that a defective 22 product was an outlier (*Ausreißer*) and therefore unavoidable. However, the producer bears the burden of proof for such an allegation and this is not an easy task. The producer must prove that he has undertaken all necessary due diligence and reasonable organisa-

[12] Wagner/Mann, EWiR 2013, 525 (526).

[13] In particular, if a breach of a protective law (*Schutzgesetz*) occurs. For further details, see Foerste/Graf v. Westphalen ProdHaft-HdB/Foerste § 21 mn. 138.

[14] BGH VI ZR 270/80, NJW 1983, 812 (813).

[15] BGH VI ZR 171/91, NJW 1992, 1039 (1040).

[16] BGH VI ZR 212/66, NJW 1969, 269 (274).

tional precautions to avoid a defective product being put on the market. In this regard, quality assurance agreements can be of material significance in showing the producer's organisational effort and diligence (→ Ch. 8 mn. 7).[17] If the producer has obtained a seal or certificate (such as the CE label or the GS mark) or has observed DIN or ISO standards, the risk of a culpable behaviour is lowered but not excluded.

#### b) Damage and causation

23 The claimant (injured person) must prove that the damage was incurred and that the producer's unlawful behaviour has caused the damage.

### 5. Practical advice

24 If an injured person claims compensation for damage and he has the choice between either § 1 ProdHaftG or § 823 BGB, the claim will most likely be based on the ProdHaftG. Not only are the conditions less stringent, the burden of proof is also lower. If the injured claimant, for instance, bases his claim on tort, he needs to furnish evidence to demonstrate that (i) the product has caused the damage, and (ii) the product was put into circulation by the manufacturer. Moreover, the defendant in a tort claim may successfully prove that a defective product was an unavoidable outlier and his action was therefore not culpable. This opportunity is excluded when a claimant bases his claim on § 1 ProdHaftG.

## III. Contractual liability

25 Contractual liability completes the product liability regime under German civil law. Contractual liability first and foremost refers to the warranty claims by the purchaser of a defective product pursuant to § 437 BGB. Such claims are not only aimed at the rectification and replacement of the defective product sold, they are also useful if a defective product has violated the physical integrity of the purchaser or damaged other objects of the purchaser. In such cases, the purchaser could have his damages compensated pursuant to §§ 437 no. 3, 280(1) BGB. Damage to or defects of the purchased product itself can only be compensated in accordance with the requirements stipulated in § 437 BGB.

# C. Product recall

## I. Manufacturer's general obligations

### 1. General information

26 Product recalls are becoming increasingly important in international commerce. This stems from the fact that production processes are becoming more complex, safety regulations are increasing, market surveillance is being enhanced, and producers are implementing quality assurance and other control systems that make it easier to identify defective products. Since the beginning of the 1990s, courts and academics have steadily attempted to develop product recall law. There is still no law governing the conditions

---

[17] BeckRS 2010, 5571.

and legal consequences of a product recall despite the occasional calls for a Product Recall Act. Some laws merely mention or define product recall, such as § 2 no. 24 ProdSG (*Produktsicherheitsgesetz* – Product Safety Act).[18] The details of the legal obligation to recall a defective product are therefore in dispute, although it is clear that under certain conditions an obligation to recall defective products does exist.

## 2. Basic legal requirements of the Product Safety Act

Pursuant to § 6 ProdSG, a manufacturer, his authorised representative, and the importer must take appropriate measures to prevent potential risks associated with consumer products that they have brought to the market. Whether the manufacturer must, as a last resort, recall a defective product is subject to careful consideration. Generally, the manufacturer is under the obligation to consider whether there is a danger to life and limb of users or third parties. The greater the likelihood of physical injury, the more likely it is that the manufacturer is required to withdraw the product from the market. Pursuant to § 6 ProdSG, the manufacturer, his authorised representative, and the importer shall immediately inform the responsible market surveillance authorities if a consumer product that they brought to the market constitutes a risk to the safety and health of persons. Moreover, the manufacturer is obliged to inform the market surveillance authority about the measures taken to prevent the risks. 27

## 3. Careful consideration

Manufacturers often agree to recall defective products voluntarily to avoid liability and to protect the reputation of the brand name. The Federal Court of Justice has made clear, however, that there is no general obligation on the part of a manufacturer to recall a product in the case of a defect.[19] On the other hand, if a duty to recall a defective product exists and damage occurs due to the fact that the defective product was not recalled (in due time), the manufacturer may be liable for damages. Hence, careful consideration is warranted when deciding between avoiding high costs of recall, on the one hand, and taking a liability risk, on the other. If a manufacturer recalls a defective product and then tries to take recourse for the costs of the recall from the sub-contractor who delivered the defective component, such a claim against the component supplier may be successful only if the manufacturer was actually under the obligation to recall a product or product category. If the manufacturer voluntarily recalls or refits the defective products for reasons of fairness or customer care, the manufacturer does not have a claim for recourse against the component supplier.[20] As a result, careful consideration is necessary to assess whether no action, a product warning, or a product recall, including refit, should be carried out on a case-by-case basis. The following circumstances speak in favour of a product recall: (i) the public or bystanders are endangered by the defective product, (ii) the product poses a dangerous threat to life or health of the public, (iii) there is a high probability that damage will occur, or (iv) there is a high probability that a warning is insufficient or that the addressee will defy or disregard a warning. 28

---

[18] § 2 no. 24 ProdSG: 'Recall shall mean any measure aimed at achieving the return of a product that has already been made available to the end user.'

[19] BGH VI ZR 170/07, NJW 2009, 1080 (1081), (1082).

[20] BGH VI ZR 170/07, NJW 2009, 1080 (1082).

### 4. Types of product recalls

29 A product recall is commonly aimed at the return of a product that has already been made available to the market. Mere product warnings or product replacements ('refits') may also be considered a special form of product recall, although – in the case of warnings – they are not necessarily aimed at the return of the product.

## II. Claim to recall a product

30 An individual claim for a product recall only exists under very narrow circumstances. In so far as the defective product itself is concerned, no such claim exists. The buyer of a defective product is limited to the warranty claims stipulated in §§ 437 et seqq. BGB. However, an individual may have the right to demand the recall of a product if it significantly endangers other legally protected rights, such as life or limb.[21] In such cases, a claim to refit may be derived from §§ 823(1), 249 sentence 1 BGB.

## III. Officially ordered recall

31 A product recall may also be ordered by the responsible authorities to prevent imminent danger that stems from a defective product. The legal basis for such officially ordered recalls can be found in § 40(2) sentence 2 no. 2 German Food and Feed Code (*Lebensmittel- und Futtermittelgesetzbuch* – LFGB), in § 69(1) sentence 2 AMG, or in § 24(3) sentence 2 nos. 1, 8 Law on Epizootic Diseases (*Tierseuchengesetz* – TierSG). As the legislative process becomes more detailed in this field of law it is likely that officially ordered recalls and general market surveillance measures (such as warnings) will become more common in the future.

## IV. Recall management

32 Manufacturers are well-advised to implement an internal recall system before a recall event occurs. This includes sufficient monitoring of the products marketed by the manufacturer or its distributors, as well as the implementation of product quality control systems.

### 1. Implementing quality control

33 The implementation of quality control systems ensures that certain quality standards are met (→ Ch. 8 mn. 1). The conclusion of quality assurance agreements may also help lower tort liability if the manufacturer, as the defendant of a tort claim, successfully proves that a defective product was an unavoidable outlier and that his action was therefore not culpable. This standard of proof is difficult to meet. Sufficient proof, however, can be provided if the manufacturer has ensured that his contractor and the contractor's other sub-contractors have observed specific quality standards. A self-contained 'web'

[21] See BGH VI ZR 254/09, VersR 2010, 1666; OLG Hamm 21 U 163/08, VersR 2011, 637 (639) (the latter with doubtful reasoning).

of quality assurance agreements concluded with contractors and their sub-contractors may be sufficient.

### 2. Ensuring traceability

It is highly recommended that the manufacturer affix serial numbers or other signs (type designation or batch numbers) to enable the traceability of defective products. This recommendation applies irrespectively of whether the manufacturer produces end products or parts for end products. If a manufacturer is able to trace its defective products, it can – if necessary – carry out a 'silent recall' (by contacting customers in a targeted manner) and thereby avoiding negative public reporting. 34

### 3. Monitoring

The following measures help sufficiently monitor the market and avoid sudden product recalls, which usually gives an enterprise several serious problems: 35

- Centralised collection of consumer complaints.
- Examination of returns and identification of potential weak points and defects.
- Forwarding of complaints/identified weak points to the respective operating departments (development, construction, production), including the supply chain and possibly the distribution system.
- Eliminating weak links in the respective operating departments.

### 4. Recall team

Once a product defect is discovered, a well-functioning recall team may help handle the situation in an efficient manner. Therefore, it is strongly recommended that necessary structures be set up prior to the occurrence of a product defect. An interdisciplinary team consisting of employees from different organisational divisions can help handle the unfamiliar and often confusing situation in which the enterprise may suddenly find itself in. Practice has shown that a recall team should include representatives from the following divisions: construction, design, production, quality management, purchasing, sales, distribution, marketing, public relations, inventory control, and legal. Furthermore, a roadmap and an emergency plan may help describe and determine the tasks of the team members and their responsibilities (procedures, drafting of minutes, correspondence with authorities and press, reporting etc.). 36

## V. Practical instructions

An international product recall is particularly challenging for both the manufacturer and the advising legal counsel. This stems from the fact that (i) laws of different jurisdictions may apply or at least influence an international product liability case and (ii) these different legal regimes may impose differing legal requirements. If, for instance, a German car manufacturer sells defective cars in Germany but also delivers them to the US and Kenya, a public warning may be sufficient in Kenya, while a product recall is required in Germany and the US. Since product safety law is commonly public administrative law and it can vary significantly from country to country, the regimes of each jurisdiction need to be considered when assessing the need for a product recall. In contrast, civil claims for 37 recourse are still determined by national law. Which jurisdiction's laws are applicable in a cross-border civil claim is determined by the Rome II Regulation. The manufacturer may limit its liability risks by taking out a product liability insurance policy that covers the costs of a product recall and/or the defence against unjustified claims for compensation.

## D. After discovering a product defect

38 After discovering a product defect, there are many steps that a producer must take in quick succession to ensure that the resulting damage is kept to a minimum and product hazards are kept as low as possible.

### I. Fact finding

39 It is vital for companies to find out all the facts relating to the product defect as fast and as accurately as possible. The probability and the degree of damage that can be caused by the defect must be ascertained. This may include communications with the design, manufacturing, technical support, legal, and other departments. A formal report about the defect may need to be commissioned.

### II. Risk assessment

40 EU law stipulates that before any product comes into the market, a risk assessment must be undertaken. The German legislator has implemented the EU Directive in § 3 ProdSG. Even though a product in the market has already undergone this initial step, a new risk assessment must take place because of the new knowledge of defect.

41 The Commission's guidelines for the management of the European Union Rapid Information System 'RAPEX' serve as an important tool to carry out such an assessment. The guidelines establish risk assessment methods, streamline the processes for the notification mechanism, and defines what the parties must do after such a notification. This tool thus provides a uniform assessment method in the EU that is accepted by all Member States.

### III. Contact with regulator

42 After the discovery of a new product defect, the competent authority must be informed of the precise defect and how this may constitute a product hazard without undue delay. The company then enters into correspondence with the competent authority to negotiate the next steps. As a rule, the company will suggest what measures are to be taken, based on the results of the risk analysis from the RAPEX-guidelines. For example, if the impact of the product defect is small – it only affects a small percentage of the products and the effects from the defect are minor – the company may suggest a notification of the public through specific channels and a change in manufacturing process that eliminates the defect. However, if the defect potentially causes severe damage to many people, a product recall may be necessary. Depending on whether the suggestion from the company is

sufficient to protect the public from the defect, the competent authority may accept the company's plan or order another course of action.

# E. Conflict of laws

In the case of a product recall, the administrative laws of all states to which the product was delivered must be taken into account when assessing whether a product recall needs to be carried out. However, when assessing whether an individual claim for compensation arising from § 1 ProdHaftG or § 823(1) BGB exists, the conflict of laws rules help determine the applicable law. In product liability cases with no foreign element, German law applies. However, in cases with cross-border elements, the applicable law has to be first determined according to the conflict of laws rules. **43**

## I. General concept

From a German perspective, the Rome II Regulation[22] determines the applicable law in all cases of non-contractual obligations, including tort. As a rule, Article 4(1) Rome II Regulation stipulates that the law of the country in which the damage occurs shall be applicable. For instance, if a company with seat in Germany pours chemicals in the Rhine River and damages crops in the Netherlands, Dutch law is applicable to determine the possible civil claims that may arise. For cases of product liability, more specific rules in the Rome II Regulation apply. However, Article 4(2) Rome II Regulation stipulates that if the person claimed to be liable and the person sustaining damage both have their habitual residence (*gewöhnlicher Aufenthalt*) in the same country at the time when the damage occurs, the law of that country shall apply. For instance, if the product of a manufacturer that has its registered office in Germany damages an Italian person who also has his habitual residence in Germany, German law would be applicable. **44**

## II. Determining the applicable law

### 1. Seven-step test

The Rome II Regulation provides specific connecting factors for international product liability cases. Article 5 Rome II Regulation establishes a seven-step cascade process to determine the applicable law to a product liability case, i.e. when a party, the claimant, was (allegedly) damaged by another party, the defendant. The seven-step test is applied in the following order: **45**

- **Step 1**: If the parties have made a valid choice of law, such law chosen by the parties is applicable. Pursuant to Article 14 Rome II Regulation, the injured party and the party causing the damage are free to make a **choice of law** by means of an agreement entered into **after** the event giving rise to the **damage has occurred**. If no valid choice of law was made, step 2 applies.

[22] Regulation (EC) No 864/2007 of the European Parliament and of the Council of 11 July 2007 on the law applicable to non-contractual obligations applies to all EU Member States except Denmark.

- **Step 2**: Article 4(2) Rome II Regulation stipulates that if the person claimed to be liable and the person sustaining damage both have their **habitual residence** (*gewöhnlicher Aufenthalt*) in the **same country** at the time when the damage occurs, the law of that country shall apply. For a company, its place of central administration is considered its habitual residence, Article 23(1) Rome II Regulation. For instance, if the product of a manufacturer that has its administration centre in Germany damages an Italian person in Italy who has his habitual residence in Germany, Article 4(2) Rome II Regulation stipulates that German law governs this case. If the parties do not have a common habitual residence, step 3 applies.
- **Step 3**: Article 5(1)(a) Rome II Regulation determines that the law of the country applies in which the person sustaining the damage (i) had his or her **habitual residence** where the damage occurred, if (ii) the **product was marketed** (*in Verkehr gebracht*) in that state. A product is marketed (or put into circulation) when it is taken out of the manufacturing process operated by the producer and enters a marketing process in the form in which it is offered to the public in order to be used or consumed.[23] Damage refers to the primary damage sustained by the claimant (e.g. an injury, a burning, or a violation of property) and not subsequent damage, such as the loss of income. If a French consumer, for instance, buys a car imported by a French distributor, French law applies even if the car was originally manufactured in Germany. If the conditions of Article 5(1)(a) are not fulfilled, step 4 applies.
- **Step 4**: Article 5(1)(b) Rome II Regulation stipulates that the law of the country applies (i) in which the **product was acquired**, if (ii) the **product was marketed** in that country. If the conditions of Article 5(1)(b) are not fulfilled, step 5 applies.
- **Step 5**: Article 5(1)(c) Rome II Regulation stipulates that the law of the country applies (i) in which the **primary damage occurred**, if (ii) the **product was marketed** in that country. If, for instance, a Chinese tourist is injured in Greece due to defective diving gear sold in Greece by a German distributor, the Greek law determines the aggrieved party's (*Geschädigter*) claims. Then, step 6 applies.
- **Step 6**: Article 5(1) sentence 2 Rome II Regulation stipulates that the applicable law shall be of the state in which the **person claimed to be liable** (commonly the defendant) is **habitually resident** if he or she could not reasonably foresee the marketing of the product, or a product of the same type, in the country the law of that is applicable under Article 5(1)(a), (b) or (c). This requirement of predictability applies as an additional element to steps 3 to 5. Consequently, the requirement of the defendant's (manufacturer or producer) habitual residence is aimed at lowering the defendant's liability risk. Moreover, such foreseeable liability makes it easier for a producer or manufacturer to find insurance at adequate cost. For example, if a product was marketed in a state without the verifiable consent or knowledge of the defendant, it is generally not reasonably foreseeable for the defendant to be liable in that jurisdiction pursuant to Article 5 Rome II Regulation.[24] The burden of proof rests with the defendant claiming such an exception. If a German citizen who has his habitual residence in Germany buys a motor bike in Spain, and such motor bike was produced in Poland and then imported to Spain without the consent and knowledge of the Polish producer, the law of Poland is applicable pursuant to Article 5(1) sentence 2 Rome II Regulation, as Polish law is of the state in which the person claimed to be liable (defendant) is habitually resident.
- **Step 7**: If it is clear from all circumstances of the case that the tort/delict is manifestly **more closely connected** with a state other than that identified in steps 3 to 6, the law of that other, more closely connected state shall apply pursuant to Article 5(2) Rome II

[23] ECJ 9.2.2006 case C-127/04, ECLI:EU:C:2006:93 para. 32 – *Declan O'Byrne v Sanofi Pasteur MSD Ltd.*
[24] Cf. Leible/Lehmann, RIW 2007, 721 (728); MüKoBGB/Junker Rom II-VO Art. 5 mn. 44.

Regulation. This escape clause (*Ausweichklausel*) applies, in particular, in cases where a contractual relationship between the parties exists that is closely connected to the tort/delict in question (e.g. claimant and defendant have concluded a purchase contract on the defective product). In the case of bystanders, step 7 does not normally provide a closer connection than the law identified pursuant to steps 3 to 6.

### 2. *Loi uniforme*

The Rome II Regulation is universally applicable (*loi uniforme*). Therefore, the Rome II Regulation may lead to the application of the law of a non-Member State (e.g. Chinese or US law), which nonetheless applies. 46

## III. Rules on safety and conduct

It is difficult for a producer to assess what legal requirements (e.g. DIN, ISO, CE, GS standard) his products must fulfil. The Rome II Regulation does not provide helpful guidance on this topic. Article 17 Rome II Regulation stipulates that the rules of safety and conduct that were in force at the place and time of the event giving rise to the liability shall be taken into account as a matter of fact and to the appropriate extent. Effectively, this may lead to the additional application of safety rules. If, for instance, Article 4 or Article 5 Rome II Regulation leads to the application of German law, but the damage occurred due to an accident in the US, a judge may additionally take into consideration the safety regulations of the US that were in force at the time of the accident. Similarly, if an accident has caused damage in Germany, but the law applicable to the case is Chinese law, German safety rules must be taken into consideration pursuant to Article 17 Rome II Regulation. Such 'additional' application of safety rules applies, in particular, when a judge has to determine if a product is defective pursuant to § 3 ProdHaftG.[25] In such cases, one must assess whether a product provides the degree of safety that can justifiably be expected. 47

## IV. Multiple liability and recourse

If an injured person has a claim against several debtors who are liable for the same claim, and one of the debtors (debtor 1) has already satisfied the claim in whole or in part, the question of that debtor's right to demand compensation from the other debtors (e.g. debtors 2, 3 and 4) is – pursuant to Article 20 Rome II Regulation – governed by the law under which the **injured person has claimed damage compensation** from debtor 1. This rule of recourse is significant particularly in supply chains (between a sub-contractor and its OEMs or in multi-level sub-contractor relationships) whereby several debtors are liable for a defective product. 48

[25] See Foerste/Graf v. Westphalen ProdHaft-HdB/Wilde § 100 mn. 30.

## F. Jurisdiction

49 The question of what court has jurisdiction over a product liability case is different from the question of what law is applicable to a specific case. For instance, a German court may have jurisdiction over a case but is obliged to apply French, Swiss, or Chinese law. If both parties are entrepreneurs, they are free to agree on a specific jurisdiction or a competent court – even prior to the occurrence of a conflict and irrespective of their nationality or residence.[26] In the absence of a valid jurisdiction agreement, as may most likely be the case in product liability matters, the parties must identify the competent court in accordance with national or European civil procedure law. For domestic disputes in Germany, the ZPO determines the competent court. In international civil and commercial matters, however, the Brussels Ia Regulation and the Lugano Convention on Jurisdiction and the Enforcement of Judgments in Civil and Commercial Matters of 16 September 1988 (*Luganer Übereinkommen*) prevail over the ZPO. This is true in cases where the defendant is domiciled in an EU Member State (Article 4(1) Brussels Ia Regulation) or in Iceland, Norway, or Switzerland (Article 2(1) Lugano Convention).[27] **Nationality** is **not decisive** when it comes to the application of the **Brussels Ia Regulation** and the **Lugano Convention**. In international product liability cases, Article 7 Brussels Ia Regulation establishes special jurisdiction. Pursuant to Article 7 Brussels Ia Regulation, a person domiciled in one Member State may, in another Member State, be sued

- in matters relating to a contract, in the courts for the **place of performance** of the obligation in question (Article 7 no. 1(a));
- in matters relating to tort, delict, or quasi-delict, in the courts for the place where the **harmful event occurred** or may occur (Article 7 no. 2).

50 The application of Article 7 no. 2 Brussels Ia Regulation is not limited to culpable misbehaviour but instead extends to strict liability and therefore all kinds of compensatory civil product liability cases arising due to defective products.[28] Notwithstanding the apparently clear wording, the claimant has the opportunity to sue the defendant either in the courts of the place where the damage occurred (*Erfolgsort*) or in the courts of the place where the injuring action was carried out (*Handlungsort*).[29] This may offer several places of jurisdiction in cases where the occurrence of damage and the causal action appear to be in different places (*Distanzdelikt*) or where damage in multiple places occur (*Streudelikt*). If, for instance, a defective product was produced and put into circulation in Barcelona but injures the buyer in Stuttgart, he may claim compensation from the manufacturer either in the courts of Barcelona or Stuttgart.

---

[26] See § 38 ZPO; Article 25(1), Article 7 Brussels Ia Regulation.

[27] This is the general principle regarding the application of the Brussels Ia Regulation. For a helpful overview of how to apply the Brussels Ia Regulation, see, Thomas/Putzo/Hüßtege EuGVVO, Article 2 mn. 2.

[28] See Geimer/Schütze EuZivilVerfR/Geimer EuGVVO Art. 55 mn. 211; Lenz Produkthaftung/Lenz § 6 mn. 29.

[29] ECJ 16.7.2009 case C-189/08, ECLI:EU:C:2009:475 para. 23 – *Zuid-Chemie BV v Philippo's Mineralenfabriek NV/SA*.

# Chapter 8
# Quality assurance agreement

**Bibliography:** Hopt (ed.), Handelsgesetzbuch: HGB, 42nd edn, Munich 2023; Lehmann, 'Allgemeine Geschäftsbedingungen, unangemessene Benachteiligung, Allgemeines (Just-in-Time-Delivery)', BB 1990, 1849; Lenz, Produkthaftung, 2nd edn, Munich 2022.

## A. Introduction

1 Quality assurance agreements (also called quality management agreements) aim at securing and increasing the quality of the delivered products. They commonly contain phrases stating that the manufacturer (buyer) pursues a zero-defect strategy and that the quality assurance agreement aims to make a fundamental contribution to such zero-fault production. The significance and number of quality assurance agreements have increased remarkably in recent years. This stems from several factors. First, OEMs try to implement lean production processes, thereby avoiding costs for the storage of components and spare parts. Such just-in-time production requires that the delivered goods have close to 'zero defect', as even a small mistake may lead to a production breakdown resulting in severe production losses. Second, OEMs using quality assurance agreements lower their liability risk by shifting the legal responsibility for defects onto the suppliers and sub-contractors (→ mn. 6).

## B. Definition

### I. General

2 Quality assurance agreements consist of rules that a manufacturer arranges with his component supplier; often, the component supplier makes similar agreements with his own component suppliers. Quality assurance agreements regulate the standard of quality of the delivered products, the supplier's obligation to implement and maintain a quality management system, procedures for initial sampling, warranty issues, regulation on incoming and distribution inspection, and/or logistical issues. Quality assurance agreements were first used in industrial production (in particular, in the automotive and pharmaceuticals industries) but are now increasing in commercial trade too.

### II. Term review

3 Provisions on quality assurance may be agreed on within supply agreements, standard terms and conditions, or other special contracts. However, they are commonly concluded

as a separate agreement/document. Whether or not provisions constitute a quality assurance agreement does not depend on how the agreement is designated but instead on its content. If the provisions are (i) pre-formulated, (ii) intended for repeated use, and (iii) not negotiated in detail, the provisions of a quality assurance agreement are considered standard terms and conditions pursuant to §§ 305 et seqq. BGB. In practice, the provisions of quality assurance agreements are regularly subject to term review.

### III. Avoiding overlapping regulation

4 The user of a quality assurance agreement is well-advised to avoid overlapping regulation. It is frequently the case that a manufacturer concludes a framework supply agreement, standard terms and conditions, a confidentiality agreement, as well as an agreement on quality assurance. Each of these contracts has its own justification. If the framework supply agreement and/or the standard terms and conditions govern the warranty regime between the manufacturer and its supplier, the parties need to ensure that the quality assurance agreement does not contain deviating provisions on warranty. If it contains warranty provisions, they must be similar to those used in the standard terms and conditions and/or the framework supply agreement.

## C. Main legal issues

### I. Exclusion of the duty to object to defects

5 Generally, a commercial buyer is under the obligation to examine the purchased item immediately after delivery and to promptly object to defects, § 377 HGB. However, OEMs – in particular in the automotive sector – try to waive their duty to inspect by shifting and imposing that obligation onto the component supplier, thereby transforming the incoming inspection into a distribution inspection (*Warenausgangsprüfung*) of the component supplier. It is acknowledged that the incoming inspection stipulated in § 377 HGB may be amended by mutual party agreement. This is generally possible either by individual agreement or by using standard terms and conditions.

6 There is dispute, however, as to whether the transformation of the incoming inspection into a distribution inspection is legally valid under German commercial law. The Federal Court of Justice has repeatedly made clear that a complete exclusion of the buyer's duty to inspect incoming goods is not possible in standard terms and conditions (which quality assurance agreements regularly are).[1] But the Federal Court of Justice has not yet expressly ruled on the question of whether the buyer's obligation to inspect incoming goods may be validly shifted to the seller (component supplier) if there is a legitimate interest, such as just-in-time production.[2] There is an increasing need for just-in-time production or other forms of fabrication in modern production systems in specific industries, such as automotive, construction, or pharmaceuticals. Such modern fabrication does not have much in common with the traditional commercial transactions that the German legislator originally intended to regulate in § 377 HGB. Accordingly, there are a large number of

[1] Cf. BGH VIII ZR 149/90, NJW 1991, 2633 (2634).
[2] For an in-depth discussion, see Lenz Produkthaftung/Lenz § 3 mn. 123–125.

legal scholars who welcome the possibility to transform the buyer's incoming inspection into a distribution inspection of the supplier.[3] However, courts have so far not confirmed this legal view.[4] To increase the likelihood of a valid agreement, it is recommended that the exclusion of an incoming inspection should not cover apparent defects.

## II. Minimising product liability risks

7 OEMs and other industrial buyers also use quality assurance agreements to minimise their product liability risk. Other than the ProdHaftG, the liability for tort (§ 823 BGB) requires an unlawful (and therefore culpable) behaviour on the part of the producer or its vicarious agents (*Erfüllungsgehilfen*). The producer's liability may be excluded if he can successfully prove that a defective product was an outlier (*Ausreißer*). The producer, however, bears the burden of proof for such an assertion. The producer might successfully prove that the behaviour was not culpable if he can show that he has undertaken all reasonable care and diligence to avoid product defects. It can be a clear indication – or even evidence – of such an assertion if the producer is able to show that he has implemented a functional and effective quality management system ensuring good quality of the products and avoiding product defects. In practice, the producer (OEM or buyer) will therefore submit all the quality assurance agreements entered into with his sub-component suppliers. To prove that the quality management system is a self-contained and fully functional system, the buyer (OEM) should show that he has obliged all his suppliers to conclude similar quality assurance agreements with their own suppliers.

# D. Typical content

8 It can be difficult to define the proper content of a quality assurance agreement and at the same time avoid conflicting or overlapping regulations. Therefore, it may help to precisely define the typical content of quality assurance agreements. They commonly contain provisions on the following subjects:

- **Definition of technical and/or organisational measures** to ensure high quality and possibly zero defects (description of product and quality requirements, description of production processes, controls, responsibilities, and corresponding documentation).
- **Replacement of incoming inspection by a distribution inspection** onto the seller (component supplier). Whether the buyer's waiver of his obligation to inspect incoming goods pursuant to § 377(1) HGB is valid must be assessed on a case-by-case basis. It will largely depend on the scope of the waiver (the exclusion of incoming inspection for apparent and obvious defects is not recommended) as well as on the buyer's reason for this shift in responsibilities (more justifiable in complex just-in-time production).
- **Implementation of a quality management system** pursuant to ISO 9000 et seqq. ISO is a private international organisation for standardisation that provides voluntary international standards on different kinds of subjects such as quality management (ISO 9001), environmental management (ISO 14000), social responsibility (ISO 26000), risk

[3] Cf. Lenz Produkthaftung/Lenz § 3 mn. 124; Hopt/Leyens HGB § 377 mn. 59; Lehmann, BB 1990, 1849.
[4] See LG Wuppertal 14 O 70/00, BeckRS 2006, 10926.

management (ISO 31000), and others. ISO also provides sector-specific standards for certain industries.
- **Transfer and protection of know-how**, sample of tools or initial sampling (*Erstbemusterung*).
- Supplier's duty to implement **labels or marks** (such as, for instance, a CE label or GS mark).
- Rules on the **allocation of liability**, including indemnity clauses and/or a **product recall scenario** (obligations to cooperate and costs). Rules allocating the entire liability risk to the supplier could constitute an unfair disadvantage to the supplier and might therefore be invalid pursuant to § 307(1) and (2) BGB.
- Buyer's right to carry out **audits** at the supplier's branch or production facility.
- Supplier's obligation to provide **adequate insurance** in case of product liability and/or product recall.
- Provisions on the **traceability** of the supplied products or components. This aims to identify the buyers and consumers in case of a product defect. Excessive obligations on traceability may, however, constitute an unfair disadvantage to the component supplier and might therefore be invalid. This is the case, for instance, if the component supplier delivers screws or other bulk commodities and the manufacturer requires that each individual screw (or other bulk products) be marked.
- **Contractual penalty**.
- **Quality managers** (names, tasks, and responsibilities).
- **Term and termination**.
- **Choice of law** and **jurisdiction clause** (it is recommended to settle on the law and jurisdiction that already govern all other agreements between the parties, such as, for example, the framework supply agreement and/or the standard terms and conditions).

# Chapter 9
# Confidentiality agreement

**Bibliography**: Grüneberg (ed.), Bürgerliches Gesetzbuch: BGB, 82nd edn, Munich 2023; Hengstler, Die Geheimhaltungsvereinbarung, Frankfurt 2011; Krapfl/Mann, 'Die Grenzen der Urkundenvorlage durch eine Partei' in: Festschrift Schütze, Munich 2014.

## A. Introduction

1 Although the origins of confidentiality or non-disclosure agreements (NDA) can be found in the Anglo-American legal tradition, confidentiality agreements are widely used in Germany. German OEMs and subcontractors have an understandable interest in protecting their know-how. Therefore, confidentiality agreements are commonly concluded either during or prior to the negotiation of a contract (especially when it is unavoidable for the parties to disclose confidential information to proceed with negotiations) or as a supplement to the main contract when one of the parties has a special need to protect confidential information throughout the entire contractual relationship.

## B. Statutory parameters

2 German law provides protection for certain types of information, such as trade secrets, pursuant to § 4 GeschGehG (*Gesetz zum Schutz von Geschäftsgeheimnisse* – Act on the Protection of Trade Secrets), which prohibits the attainment and communication of trade secrets by unauthorised parties. Trade secrets are defined as information (i) which is not generally known or readily accessible to persons in the circles that normally handle that type of information, and is therefore of commercial value, (ii) which is the subject of confidentiality measures imposed by its rightful owner, and (iii) whose owner has a legitimate interest in confidentiality (§ 2 no. 1 GeschGehG). Further confidentiality obligations may stem from the Data Protection Act (*Bundesdatenschutzgesetz* – BDSG), the General Data Protection Regulation[1] (*Datenschutz-Grundverordnung* – DSGVO), or § 203 StGB. Finally, certain types of contracts establish a non-disclosure obligation as a secondary obligation.[2] If at least one party of a contract wants to establish comprehensive protection for a certain type of information, data, or know-how, the parties are well-advised to conclude a confidentiality agreement.

[1] Regulation (EU) 2016/679 of the European Parliament and of the Council of 27 April 2016 on the protection of natural persons with regard to the processing of personal data and on the free movement of such data.

[2] Cf. Grüneberg/Grüneberg BGB § 280 mn. 28b (purchase contract under certain conditions).

# C. Typical content

## I. Definition

3 German statutory law does not provide a general definition of confidential information, although the GeschGehG gives at least some guidance. What information the parties want to protect and therefore define as confidential information is subject to individual agreement. In fact, one of the core functions of confidentiality agreements is to precisely define the confidential information in order to avoid dispute about its extent and to define the purpose of the cooperation for which the confidentiality obligation or NDA is concluded. As the purpose of the cooperation often defines the extent to which the confidential information may be used by the recipient, this definition is of great importance. It is advisable to make clear that it is of no relevance whether the confidential information is disclosed orally, electronically, in embodied or other form. The state of the confidential information or its form of data storage is also irrelevant. The following definition is commonly used:

> 'Confidential Information' is all information of a Party or information of a business enterprise affiliated with it within the meaning of §§ 15 et seqq. of the Stock Corporation Act (Aktiengesetz (AktG)) ('Holder') which the other Party ('Recipient') receives directly or indirectly, in a written, spoken, or any other manner, or obtains knowledge thereof in any other way and which (i) have commercial value, and (ii) is either marked as confidential by the Holder in its reasonable discretion or where a legitimate interest of the Holder in keeping it confidential arises either from the nature of the information or the disclosure. In particular, the following shall be deemed to be Confidential Information: (i) business secrets, know-how, products and product ideas, recipes, product composition, pricing structures and strategies, business connections, business strategies, business plans, financial information and financial planning, personnel matters, sales information including information on customers and distribution channels, digitally embodied information ('Data'); (ii) technical information (e.g., manufacturing processes), inventions, drawings, drafts, sketches, plans, descriptions, specifications, results of measurements, calculations, experience, procedures, patterns, source code, program code; (iii) the existence and content of this confidentiality agreement as well as of the business relationship.

## II. Extent of non-disclosure obligation

4 A well-defined confidentiality agreement should, moreover, describe the extent to which a party or the parties shall maintain confidentiality. This usually includes a general prohibition to disclose confidential information to any third party. However, the party obligated not to disclose confidential information (information recipient) likely has a legitimate interest in disclosing certain information to certain third parties, such as employees or subcontractors, who have a necessity to know certain confidential information or parts thereof to fulfil their contractual obligations. These persons must be defined in the confidentiality agreement. The parties should also clarify in the NDA that obligations under data protection regulations going beyond that scope as well as mandatory provisions of the GeschGehG remain unaffected.

## III. Exceptions

Additionally, it is advisable to define circumstances under which confidential information is no longer deemed to be confidential. Since confidentiality agreements are usually pre-formulated standard terms and designed for repeated use, they are commonly subject to the test of reasonableness pursuant to §§ 305 et seqq. BGB. Hence, the provisions of the confidentiality agreement may not constitute an unfair disadvantage to the other party (§ 307 BGB). An agreement that does not specify exceptions very likely constitutes an unfair disadvantage and will therefore be void. The information recipient might, for instance, become subject to a statutory obligation to disclose confidential information, e.g. if a court (§ 142 ZPO) or governmental administrative authority legitimately requires disclosure.[3] It might constitute an unfair disadvantage if the information recipient was forced to violate a statutory obligation to comply with the confidentiality agreement, thereby rendering parts of the agreement invalid. The following exceptions are therefore commonly inserted into a non-disclosure agreement. Under these circumstances, no confidentiality obligation on the part of the information recipient exists: 5

- Confidential information has become public without violation of the confidentiality agreement.
- Confidential information was already legitimately known to the information recipient at the time it was disclosed.
- Confidential information was lawfully disclosed to the information recipient by a third party and the aforementioned third party was not subject to any obligation to maintain confidentiality vis-à-vis the information provider.
- Confidential information was developed independently.
- The information recipient is obliged by mandatory law or by an enforceable court order or by any other public administrative authority to disclose the confidential information.

## IV. Storage of confidential information

Depending on the need for protection and the sensitivity of the confidential information, the parties may agree on defined storage procedures for the confidential information. In any case, it makes sense to oblige the information recipient to securely protect and store the confidential information (e.g. written documents) and any copies made thereof (and, if necessary, in burglary-proof containers such as safes, etc.). In so far as the confidential information exists in electronic form, the parties may agree (i) that the information recipient must store it in a protective system that complies with the latest state-of-the-art systems (e.g. using secure passwords, changed regularly, etc.) and (ii) that data must be protected from unauthorised external access (e.g. via the internet, via spyware), obliging the recipient to exercise the same degree of care as in its own affairs. 6

## V. Return of confidential information

The parties may also agree on rules regulating the return of confidential information upon the termination of the contractual relationship. Usually, the information recipient is automatically obliged to return all confidential information and all reproductions in 7

[3] With regard to § 142 ZPO, see Krapfl/Mann, pp. 279 et seqq.

physical form upon termination or at the written request of the information provider. Should such return be technically impossible, for example because the confidential information exists in electronic form only, the parties may agree that the information recipient must delete the confidential information completely, which he shall confirm with the information provider (in written form). However, it must be given the recipient the right to keep backup copies to comply with legal requirements, in particular legal storage obligations, if any.

## VI. Contractual penalty

8 A party aiming to protect its confidential information usually has a strong interest in penalising unauthorised disclosure of confidential information. It can do so by establishing a contractual penalty on the party breaching the confidentiality agreement. A contractual penalty clause not only supports the enforcement of the confidentiality obligation, it also facilitates the enforcement of damage compensation. In fact, a contractual penalty is generally not required to claim compensation if the information recipient is in breach of its confidentiality obligation. However, in practice, it is nearly impossible for the information provider to prove that a violation of the confidentiality obligation by the information recipient has caused damage. Given that the information provider bears the burden of proof regarding all elements of a compensation claim against the information recipient (including the damage), the information provider will regularly insist on a contractual penalty clause. If a contractual penalty clause is subject to term review according to § 307 BGB (which is generally the case), it must fulfil two requirements: first, such a clause must determine a fair and appropriate amount to be paid in the case of a violation of the confidentiality agreement. The question of appropriateness depends on (i) the type of agreement and the value of the goods in question, (ii) the importance of the non-disclosure for the information provider, and/or (iii) the value of the confidential information. Second, a contractual penalty clause must establish a penalty payment only if the confidentiality obligation has been violated culpably.[4]

[4] Cf. Hengstler, p. 20.

# Chapter 10
# Framework and supply agreement

## A. Types of framework and supply agreements

A framework or supply agreement concluded between a supplier and a buyer is generally aimed at a continuous and consolidated cooperation between the parties. Unlike authorised dealer or distribution relationships, it constitutes a rather loose form of integration and cooperation between the parties. However, this might be different if the buyer has additional obligations on exclusivity, marketing, or reporting. In such cases, a framework or supply agreement may in fact be a distributorship or franchise agreement, thereby triggering the legal consequences of these types of agreements. 1

When a supply agreement defines a specific number of products to be sold from the supplier (seller) to the buyer, such framework or supply agreement may in fact be a contract for delivery by instalments (*Sukzessivlieferungsvertrag*) providing apportioned delivery of products whose quantity is defined. In this case, the supply agreement is considered a purchase contract triggering the legal regime of §§ 433 et seqq. BGB. In most cases, however, the parties to a framework or supply agreement merely intend to regulate the legal framework of their supply cooperation and not establish any specific purchase requirements. In such cases, the framework or supply agreement is a business management contract (*Geschäftsbesorgungsvertrag*) pursuant to § 675 BGB. 2

This distinction is not only of theoretical but also of practical importance, as it determines the legal consequences, for instance, of the termination of the agreement (rescission or notice of termination) and the rights and duties of the parties. 3

## B. General content

A framework or supply agreement determines the obligations of the parties in an abstract manner and with regard to future purchase agreements that the parties intend to conclude under the framework or supply agreement. The supplier declares that he is ready and willing to supply, and the buyer agrees to obtain products (or a certain number of products) under the framework or supply agreement. A framework or supply agreement does not normally establish a specific delivery obligation on the part of the supplier or a corresponding payment obligation on the part of the buyer. In contrast, the parties usually define only the essential details of their cooperation, which are, for instance, (i) the quantity of products generally provided by the supplier, (ii) the product type, (iii) the order process (release order or order confirmation), (iv) payment terms, (v) minimum purchase requirements (and/or order forecast), (vi) promotional activities to be carried out by the buyer, if any, (vii) quality and warranty, (viii) conditions of sale and delivery, (ix) retention of title, (x) term and termination, and (xi) miscellaneous aspects such as choice of law and jurisdiction. 4

# C. Specific legal problems

## I. Exclusivity

### 1. Exclusive purchase obligation

5 Exclusivity in supply agreements may have several meanings. It may oblige the buyer to meet its demand for the contract products or services by purchasing exclusively from the supplier for a certain period of time. This type of exclusivity is called an exclusive purchase obligation (*Alleinbezugsverpflichtung*). Pursuant to Article 1(1)(f) Commission Regulation 2022/720 of 10 May 2022 on categories of vertical agreements and concerted practices (Vertical Block Exemption Regulation, Vertical-BER 2022/720), an exclusive purchase obligation is exempted and therefore permitted without timely restraints as long as it obliges the buyer to purchase no more than 80 % of its overall volume from the supplier (calculated according to the purchase volume of the previous year). If such a threshold is exceeded, an exclusive purchase obligation is permitted only for a maximum duration of five years (Article 5(1)(a) Vertical-BER 2022/720) or where the exclusive purchase obligation is tacitly renewable beyond a period of five years if the buyer can effectively renegotiate or terminate the vertical agreement containing the obligation.[1]

### 2. Exclusive supply obligation

6 More common in framework and supply agreements is an exclusive supply obligation (*Alleinbelieferungsverpflichtung*) of the supplier. Under an exclusive supply obligation, the supplier agrees to sell its products to one buyer only. This effectively excludes the buyer's competitors. An exclusive purchase right is permitted if neither the supplier's nor the buyer's market share exceeds 30 %. If a market share exceeds 30 % or an exclusive purchase right is combined with an exclusive distribution right (*Alleinvertriebsrecht*), further conditions must be considered when assessing the permissibility of such restraints (→ Ch. 12 mn. 12).

## II. Order process

7 The parties are well-advised to precisely define the order process. There are several ways to do so. Typically, the parties wish to avoid binding obligations arising from the framework or supply agreement itself. The purchase of products is commonly governed by additional and individual purchase contracts concluded under the framework or supply agreement. However, it should be noted that an arbitrary rejection of orders by the supplier is likely to be legally impermissible even if the parties have not agreed on release orders or binding delivery quantities under the framework agreement.

8 The conclusion of such purchase contracts may either be carried out (i) by means of the buyer's purchase orders and the supplier's corresponding order confirmations, or (ii) by means of mere release orders (*Produktabrufe*) of the buyer not requiring order confirmation from the supplier. Whereas in the first case the supplier is still in a position to reject a purchase order (e.g. in case of a production bottleneck), the second alternative (release order) obliges the supplier to deliver the requested products without giving him an oppor-

---

[1] Guidelines on Vertical Restraints mn. 248.

tunity to reject the buyer's demand. In particular, buyers with significant market power (e.g. large OEMs) or manufacturers with just-in-time production occasionally require a release order system and impose the corresponding contractual requirements on their suppliers. In such cases, the supplier should include a maximum delivery commitment and/or exclude the liability for loss of production. Otherwise, the buyer could theoretically request any product amount irrespective of the supplier's production capacity. In any case, a minimum or maximum purchase requirement and a binding or non-binding (rolling) forecast help the supplier provide sufficient production capacity.

## III. Application of §§ 84 et seqq. HGB by analogy

In common framework or supply agreements, the parties' cooperation regularly involves the supply of goods only. The supplier und the buyer generally have a mere seller-purchaser relationship. The buyer usually does not fulfil tasks comparable to those of a commercial agent. Consequently, there is usually no reason for an analogous application of the rules on commercial agents involving, in particular, the commercial agent's claim for termination compensation (§ 89b HGB) and notice periods protecting the commercial agent (§ 89 HGB). In some cases, however, in which the framework or supply agreement establishes obligations on the buyer that are comparable to those of a commercial agent, the said rules of the HGB may apply. This may be the case if the buyer is under the contractual (or factual) obligation to market and advertise the products in a defined territory, to report to the supplier, and to transfer customer data to the supplier. The designation of the agreement is of no relevance. Therefore, if the buyer is under the written or non-written obligation to provide the aforementioned services, the risk of an analogous application of §§ 84 et seqq. HGB is heightened. 9

## IV. Termination

### 1. Types of termination

Framework and supply agreements are normally ongoing continuing obligations. If the parties have defined a fixed runtime, the agreement ends upon the specified point in time. Generally, in the case of a fixed runtime, no right to ordinary notice of termination exists, unless the parties have so agreed. If the parties have (i) concluded an ongoing obligation with no end date, (ii) no right to ordinarily terminate the contractual relationship exists, and (iii) the parties did not exclude such a right, the courts have developed a non-written right to terminate an ongoing continuing obligation with an adequate notice period.[2] Depending on the individual case, especially the interests of the parties, courts have found a notice period of around six months to be fair, just, and therefore adequate (decided on a case-by-case basis) (→ Ch. 1 mn. 97). 10

### 2. Extraordinary notice of termination

In any case, either party to a framework or supply agreement has the right to extraordinarily terminate the continuing obligation for cause, without a notice period, pursuant to 11

[2] Cf. BGH III ZR 145/05, NJW-RR 2006, 1427; OLG Munich 15 U 6473/94, NJW-RR 1996, 561 (563) (analogous to § 624 and § 723 BGB).

§ 314 BGB (non-excludable right). § 314 BGB requires a compelling reason. Such a cause is given if the terminating party cannot reasonably be expected to continue the contractual relationship until the agreed upon end or until the expiry of a notice period, taking into account all circumstances of the specific case and weighing the interests of both parties.

### 3. Compelling reason

12 The courts have developed a definition and established that when assessing whether it is unacceptable for a party to be expected to continue the contractual relationship, one has to take into account (i) the runtime of the continuing obligation, (ii) including the right to terminate the relationship ordinarily, (iii) the consequences of termination for the other party, (iv) the severity of a contractual violation (if any), and (v) the parties' behaviour. If the compelling reason consists in the breach of a duty under the contract (which is not necessarily required for the termination under § 314 BGB), the contract may not be terminated unless the terminating party has sent a warning notice to the other party and such warning has not mitigated the violation. The parties may contractually define specific cases that grant one or both parties the right to terminate the framework or supply agreement for cause. Typically defined cases are change of control in the respective companies or certain breaches of contract, such as the violation of the minimum purchase requirement. The following cases commonly constitute a compelling reason in § 314 BGB: (i) breach of the framework or supply agreement (defects, delay) that is not of a minor nature; (ii) non-performance by the other party; (iii) continual and ongoing late payments (outstanding debts); (iv) or criminal offence by one of the parties. To be on the safe side, it is advisable to send a warning notice to the party that is in breach of the contract unless such warning can clearly be dispensed with pursuant to §§ 323(2), 314(2) BGB.

## V. Order of application

13 The conclusion of a framework or supply agreement may mark the starting point of a comprehensive cooperation between the parties. Often, one or both parties feel the need to govern further issues in addition to the mere supply of products. In addition to the framework or supply agreement, the parties frequently conclude a confidentiality agreement and/or a quality assurance agreement. Moreover, one of the parties might try to include its standard terms and conditions to govern further details of the supply. This heightens the risk of creating double or conflicting regulations. The parties should therefore make sure they clearly define the order of application of the said contractual documents. This may be done by simply naming all contractual documents and defining the order of application. The following formulation is recommended:

> 'In case of conflict between this framework agreement and other agreements concluded between the parties, the following documents shall apply in descending order:
> - This framework agreement;
> - The confidentiality agreement;
> - The quality assurance agreement;
> - The supplier's [buyer's] standard terms and conditions.'

# Chapter 11
# Commercial agency agreement

**Bibliography:** Alber et al., Beck'sches Steuer- und Bilanzrechtslexikon, 64th edn, Munich 2023; Ebenroth/Boujong/Joost, Handelsgesetzbuch: HGB, 4th edn, Munich 2020; Hopt (ed.), Handelsgesetzbuch: HGB, 42nd edn, Munich 2023; Kieninger, 'Informations-, Aufklärungs- und Beratungspflichten beim Abschluß von Versicherungsverträgen', AcP 199 (1999), 190; Lingemann/von Steinau-Steinrück/Mengel, Employment & Labor Law in Germany, 3rd edn, Munich 2012; Malec/von Bodungen, 'Die neue Vertikal-GVO und ihre Auswirkungen auf die Gestaltung von Liefer- und Vertriebsverträgen', BB 2010, 2383; Mann, 'Die vertriebsrechtliche Aufhebungs- und Vergleichsvereinbarung', ZVertriebsR 2017, 25; Martinek/Semler/Flohr, Vertriebsrecht, 4th edn, Munich 2016; Münchener Kommentar zum Handelsgesetzbuch: HGB, 5th edn, Munich 2021; Schaub, Arbeitsrechts-Handbuch, 19th edn, Munich 2021; Staub, Handelsgesetzbuch HGB (Band 2/2), 6th edn, Berlin 2021; Mäger/Mäger, Europäisches Kartellrecht, 2nd edn, Baden-Baden 2011.

## A. Definition

Pursuant to § 84 HGB, a commercial agent is someone who, as a self-employed businessperson, is regularly authorised to solicit business for another entrepreneur (the principal) or who enters into transactions in the principal's name. An independent person is essentially free to structure the activities to be undertaken as well as his work schedule and working time. Therefore, an employee is not a commercial agent, as an employee is not free to determine his work schedule and working time. An employee is dependent on instructions given by the employer, whereas a commercial agent is not. 1

### I. Distinction from other forms of distribution and employment contracts

#### 1. Commission broker

Like the commercial agent, the commission broker solicits contracts concerning the purchase and sale of goods, securities, or other commercial matters for other persons. Unlike the commercial agent, the commission broker is not authorised to do so by contractual relationship on a regular basis but rather at his discretion. 2

#### 2. Distributor

The distributor acts in his own name and for his own account whereas the commercial agent does not conclude contracts with the customers but only solicits the opportunity for the principal to conclude contracts with the customers. The distributor also bears the risks and costs of warehousing, transport, and pricing, which the commercial agent does not. 3

### 3. Franchising

4 Just like a distributor the franchisee is under the obligation to purchase products from the principal (franchisor). However, the franchisee concludes contracts not only in his own name but also for his own account and usually also licences a specific business model from the franchisor.

### 4. Employee

5 At times it can be difficult to differentiate between a commercial agent and an employee. When a person works dependently (*persönlich abhängig*), he is in fact an employee even if he is called a commercial agent, freelancer, or independent contractor. A person is dependent on the employer if he is closely integrated into the employer's (principal's) organisation and is subject to the employer's (principal's) directives.[1] Elements that suggest an employment relationship are: (i) regular (monthly) payments instead of profit-related remuneration, (ii) permission of the contract partner to use the principal's premises and equipment, (iii) the principal's right to give instructions, (iv) social dependence on the principal due to the agent/employee not having another source of income, and (v) continued payment of wages in case of illness. In the case of a dispute, the mere fact that the parties agreed that the 'commercial agent' will not be subject to the principal's instructions may not be sufficient to prove that the elements of agency are fulfilled. The mere description of an agreement as a 'commercial agency agreement' or 'freelance-agreement' is irrelevant. Instead, how the parties actually perform their contractual relationship is decisive.

## II. Pseudo-independence

6 If it turns out that the commercial agent was in fact not an independent merchant but instead a pseudo-independent person (also called pseudo self-employed person, *scheinselbstständig*), this may have severe consequences, particularly for the principal. A pseudo-independent person is legally an employee under labour laws and the social security laws on the date on which pseudo-independence was ascertained. This aims to prevent a circumvention of employees' protection rules (e.g. termination, vacation entitlement, claims to continuation of remuneration in case of illness, claims to social insurance, etc.). The employee may also need to be added to the company pension plan. Pseudo-independence can also lead to serious financial burdens for the company retroactively. Pursuant to § 25 SGB IV (*Sozialgesetzbuch* – Social Security Code), the employer may be subject to pay social insurance contributions for the current year as well as for the past four years. If the respective amount cannot be deducted from the employee's next three remuneration payments, the employer's payment obligation is comprised of both the employer's and the employee's contributions pursuant to § 28g SGB IV. Any agreements made in derogation of the social insurance contribution provisions to the detriment of the employee are null and void, pursuant to § 32 SGB I. Furthermore, the tax authority may compel the employer to make up for unpaid withholding taxes and wrongfully deducted value added taxes incurred. The employee may also have to pay a higher amount of value added tax retroactively.[2]

---

[1] Cf. BAG 9 AZR 102/20, NZA 2021, 552; Schaub ArbR-HdB/Vogelsang § 11 mn. 3.
[2] For a detailed discussion on this topic, see Lingemann/von Steinau-Steinrück/Mengel, p. 78.

### III. Form requirements

Commercial agency agreements do not have to comply with a specific form. Therefore, the parties may establish a contractual relationship by implied behaviour, orally, in written form, or by notarial acknowledgment. For reasons of evidence, § 85 HGB stipulates that either party may demand that the terms of the contract, as well as any subsequent amendment thereof, to be written in a document signed by the other party. 7

## B. Types of commercial agency

The law provides for different types of commercial agents, such as an agent who is authorised to contract (*Abschlussvertreter*) or an agent who is authorised to solicit business (*Vermittlungsvertreter*). An agent who is authorised to contract is not a distributor, as the distributor contracts in his own name and for his own account, whereas an agent who is authorised to contract concludes a contract in the name of the principal and for the principal's account. A commercial agent may be active for the seller or the buyer. A commercial agent may also engage sub-agents. In such a case, the sub-agent's claims for commission or compensation are directed at the main commercial agent and not the principal, unless the parties agree otherwise. 8

District agency (*Bezirksvertretung*) is governed by § 87(2) HGB. If the principal appoints his commercial agent as a district agent, he has a commission claim for all businesses carried out in the district (e.g. by the principal or the principal's distributors) unless the parties agree otherwise.[3] District agency must be distinguished from exclusive agency (*Alleinvertretung*). Exclusive agency means that neither the principal nor any other agent or salesperson is active in the commercial agent's territory. If the exclusivity has been violated, the commercial agent may claim damage compensation for lost profit.[4] 9

Commercial agents may be natural persons as well as corporate bodies. There is no limitation regarding the activity carried out by the commercial agent. Commercial agency is widespread in the sale of goods, particularly in the automotive, pharmaceuticals, and fashion sectors. Moreover, travel agencies or the leaseholders of gasoline stations are usually commercial agents. 10

## C. Rights and obligations

A commercial agency agreement is an ongoing continuing obligation, as it establishes not only a singular duty to exchange or solicit goods but also stipulates continuing obligations of the parties for an indefinite or long period of time. 11

[3] BGH I ZR 136/76, BB 1978, 1136.

[4] BGH I ZR 143/74, BB 1975, 1409. The violation of exclusivity may also constitute an important reason to terminate the contract pursuant to § 89a HGB.

## I. Commercial agent

### 1. Main obligation

12 Pursuant to § 86 HGB, a commercial agent is obliged to make efforts toward the solicitation or conclusion of business transactions (often purchase contracts). In connection herewith, he must act in the best interest of the principal. § 86 HGB only gives indefinite contours to the commercial agent's duties, which have been further developed by the courts (→ mn. 14). A commercial agent has the duty to canvass new customers and to care for existing customers. This means that a commercial agent is under the obligation to act vis-à-vis customers and potential customers in a way that encourages them to buy the principal's products or services. How a commercial agent carries out such obligations lies within the agent's own discretion. However, the parties are free to describe and substantiate the commercial agent's duties and to oblige him to visit the customers regularly and physically in the territory within a reasonable period of time.[5] A commercial agent has to fulfil his duties with the care of a prudent merchant. This standard, however, is hard to evaluate. The parties are therefore well-advised to define the obligations of the commercial agent as precisely as possible in the commercial agency agreement. Otherwise, it will be difficult for the principal to take action against the agent, such as terminating his contract, for a breach of his duties under § 86 HGB.

13 There is no duty on the part of a commercial agent to promote the products of the principal if such promotion goes beyond the solicitation or conclusion of specific business transactions. However, the parties are free to amend or expand the commercial agent's duties (e.g. duty to attend trade fairs, duty to provide a web presence or to place ads in magazines). There is no general duty on the part of the commercial agent to generate a certain turnover unless the parties have agreed to a specific sales volume. The commercial agent does not have the obligation to carry out warehousing for the principal.

### 2. Secondary obligations

14 A commercial agent must protect the interests of the principal when carrying out his business. The duty to protect the principal's interest not only applies when performing his main obligation. Courts and legal scholars have derived multiple secondary obligations from the commercial agent's duty to protect the principal's interests:

- **Solvency check**: a commercial agent must check the creditworthiness of customers and report the result to the principal. This applies particularly to new customers.[6]
- **Secure principal's benefits**: a commercial agent has the duty to arrange business in the most beneficial way for the principal.[7]
- **Product information:** a commercial agent must inform the customers about the products in a comprehensive manner.[8]
- **Subordinate own interests**: the commercial agent must subordinate his own commission interests, if any, to the interests of the principal.
- **Prevent damages**: the commercial agent must prevent the principal from incurring damage[9] or any other detriment.[10]

---

[5] OLG Munich 21 U 1608/02, NJW-RR 2003, 401 (402).
[6] RG I 323/86, RGZ 18, 112.
[7] BeckOGK/Bieder HGB § 86 mn. 35–36.
[8] Kieninger, AcP 199 (1999), 190.
[9] Ebenroth/Boujong/Joost/Strohn/Löwisch HGB § 86 mn. 11.
[10] BGH VII ZR 254/62, NJW 1964, 1621 (1622).

- **Market observation**: the commercial agent has the duty to monitor and observe the market for the solicitation or conclusion of business transactions.[11]
- **Non-competition**: the commercial agent has the duty to avoid competition with the principal.[12] Generally, the commercial agent may operate for other principals as long as (i) this activity does not constitute any competition (same or similar products in the same market) and (ii) the agent is not a single-firm agent (*Einfirmenvertreter*). The agent may not conclude contracts with customers in his own name and for his own account; entice away (*abwerben*) employees from the principal; perform competing activities as an agent, undercover agent, employee, distributor, or in any other manner; counsel any of the principal's competitors; or criticise the principal's products while complimenting products of competitors.
- **Confidentiality**: during the runtime of the commercial agency agreement and even thereafter (§ 90 HGB), the commercial agent is under the obligation not to disclose trade secrets of the principal to any third party or use them for his own benefit without the principal's prior consent.
- **Obligation to inform**: the commercial agent shall give the principal all necessary information on his business activities relating to the contract. This means the commercial agent must inform the principal immediately of every solicitation and every conclusion of a transaction. The duty to inform the principal includes the following: (i) all significant activities in the territory, (ii) content of customer lists made by the agent, (iii) details about customer requests,[13] (iv) *status quo*/progress report of (future) acquisitions, (v) customers' breach of contract, or (vi) perceptions about the competitive environment.

## II. Principal

The principal's main obligations towards the commercial agent are (i) commission payment pursuant to § 87 HGB and (ii) payment of the termination compensation according to § 89b HGB. There are multiple secondary obligations of the principal that are either contained in § 86a HGB or have been developed by the courts. 15

### 1. Commission payment

The commercial agent's commission claim is regulated in §§ 87 to 87d HGB. The principal's duty to pay commission to the commercial agent is the principal's main obligation. § 87 HGB covers commission entitlement. § 87a HGB states the additional conditions that must be fulfilled in order to trigger the commercial agent's commission claim. § 87b HGB specifies how the commission amount is to be determined unless the parties have agreed on a different calculation (which is usually the case). § 87c HGB prescribes rules for the accounting of the commission payments. 16

#### a) Commercial agent's commission entitlement

§ 87 HGB specifies the conditions under which the commercial agent is entitled to a commission. 17

---

[11] MüKoHGB/Ströbl HGB § 86 mn. 45.
[12] BeckOGK/Bieder HGB § 86 mn. 40–54; BGH VII ZB 45/12, NJW-RR 2013, 1511.
[13] OLG Cologne 2 U 63/70, BB 1971, 543.

18 **aa) Transaction solicited by the commercial agent.** The commission pursuant to § 87 HGB is a performance-based remuneration. It is incurred when a transaction has been solicited by the commercial agent through his or her activities. However, the parties may agree on an alternative remuneration system and change the conditions set out in § 87 HGB, as this legal standard is not mandatory.[14] The parties may, for instance, agree on (i) fixed remuneration of the commercial agent, (ii) bonus-related remuneration, or (iii) a contingent commission. Generally, the parties are well-advised to precisely define the prerequisites for the commercial agent's commission claim in the contract to avoid future disputes. In the absence of such a contractual definition, the statutory parameters apply.

19 **bb) Concurrently causal.** It is necessary that the commercial agent's activity was causal for the conclusion of the contract between the principal and the customer. In this regard, it is sufficient that the solicitation by the commercial agent is concurrently causal (*mitursächlich*). This is the case when a customer who was originally acquired by the commercial agent places subsequent orders. Nonetheless, negligible activity of the commercial agent (mere translation or written support) or purchase orders for his own use are not considered concurrently causative. Generally, the principal is free to decide whether he will enter into a transaction solicited by the commercial agent. However, the principal may not reject the conclusion of transactions solicited by the commercial agent arbitrarily.

20 **cc) District agency commission.** If the principal has appointed the commercial agent as an exclusive agent for a specific district or clientele, he may be regarded as a district agent pursuant to § 87(2) HGB. In such a case, the commercial agent has a commission claim for all transactions that were performed with customers in a specific district or with certain clientele, irrespective of whether he has contributed to the conclusion of the contract by a causal act. In most cases, the principal wants to avoid this legal consequence, as he would have to pay commission to the commercial agent even if customers from the territory buy from the principal directly. The principal therefore needs to ensure that an appropriate clause is inserted in the commercial agency agreement which makes clear that a causal act of the commercial agent is necessary for the commercial agent's commission claim.

#### b) Further conditions for the commercial agent's commission claim

21 Pursuant to § 87a(1) HGB the commercial agent has a right to commission as soon as, and in so far as, the principal has performed the transaction, which means that – in the absence of a deviating contractual agreement – the commercial agent's commission claim is due once the principal delivers the order to the customer. However, the parties are free to deviate from this statutory specification. It is common for parties to agree that the commercial agent's commission claim shall not arise until the customer (as the third party, § 87a(1) sentence 3 HGB) has made payment to the principal.[15]

22 **aa) Reasonable advance.** Irrespective of any deviating individual party agreement, the commercial agent, upon performance of the transaction by the principal, has in any event a right to a reasonable advance due no later than the last day of the following month,

[14] Hopt/Hopt HGB § 87 mn. 48.
[15] BeckOK/Lehmann HGB § 87a mn. 6; BGH I ZR 6/89, NJW-RR 1991, 155 (156).

§ 87a(1) sentence 2 HGB. This provision is intended to secure the agent's liquidity. It is mandatory law.

**bb) Customer's non-performance.** If the third party (usually the customer) does not perform, the commercial agent does not have a commercial claim. In such a case, amounts already received by the commercial agent are to be returned. However, the principal must first attempt to enforce its payment claim against the customer in court, if this is deemed reasonable. 23

**cc) Principal's non-performance.** The commercial agent also has a right to commission if the principal does not perform the transaction, performs only partially, or does not perform according to the contract with the customer (§ 87a(3) HGB). § 87a(3) HGB is mandatory law and may not be derogated from by party agreement to the detriment of the commercial agent. This rule requires that the principal has concluded the contract with the customer that was solicited by the commercial agent and subsequently does not perform the contract. In such a case, the commercial agent retains its commission claim. This covers cases where the non-performance of the principal falls within his own responsibility, such as (i) production downtimes, (ii) product defects, (iii) delays, (iv) too many incoming orders, (v) calculation errors, (vi) labour deficit, (vii) supply difficulties, or (viii) loss of the principal's goodwill. If the customer, however, exercises his contractual right to withdraw from the contract with the principal, the commercial agent has no commission claim.[16] In exceptional cases, where a customer threatens to cancel the entire business relationship and the principal consequently cancels the purchase order even though he neither has a contractual nor a statutory obligation to do so, the commercial agent might lose its commission.[17] Generally, the commercial agent has no commission claim in the event of the principal's non-performance due to reasons beyond the latter's control (such as cases of *force majeure*). 24

**dd) Due date of commission.** Pursuant to § 87c(1) HGB, the principal shall provide a monthly commission statement to the commercial agent indicating the transactions entitling the commercial agent to a commission. The commission for the accounting period (*Abrechnungszeitraum*) is due at the end of the next month. For example, the commission for an accounting period that runs from 15 June to 15 July is due on 30 August. The due date generally corresponds to the principal's obligation to make an advance payment pursuant to § 87a(1) sentence 2 HGB. However, the principal may, by mutual agreement of the parties, extend the accounting period to a maximum of three months. In such a case, the commercial agent's claim for an advance payment is not affected and is still due at the end of the last day of the following month. 25

### c) Amount of commission

**aa) Commission rate.** Negotiating the commission rate is usually one of the most important points for the parties to an agency agreement. In the rare case that the commission rate or the amount of commission is not specified, the customary rate is imposed. The customary commission of the industrial sector in the district of the commercial agent is used to determine the 'customary rate'. The commercial agent claiming the commission must substantiate the amount and the method of calculation used.[18] An authorised expert opinion will often be necessary to determine the 'customary rate'. To avoid these complications, it is essential to explicitly agree on a commission rate. 26

---

[16] Cf. BGH I ZR 6/89, NJW-RR 1991, 155 (156).
[17] BAG 3 AZR 241/66, NJW 1967, 846.
[18] OLG Hamm, 26.10.2009 – I-18 U 212/08.

The commission rates granted to commercial agents depend on the industrial sector. Typically, the higher the value and price of the product, the lower the commission rate (e.g. 2 % to 6 % for large and expensive industrial goods; up to 40 % for low-value products and consumable durables).

27 **bb) Calculation of commission.** Pursuant to § 87b(2) HGB, the commission is to be calculated based on the amount that the third party or the principal is obliged to pay. Deductions for cash payment cannot be made; the same applies to miscellaneous costs, such as freight, packaging, customs duties and taxes, unless the miscellaneous costs have been itemised separately in the invoice sent to the third party. This provision, however, is a default rule only and may be changed by party agreement. The parties are free to mutually agree on a deviating commission rate and calculation method prior to the beginning of their contractual relationship or at any other time.

28 **cc) No unilateral commission reduction.** The principal is well-advised to choose and fix the commission rate with caution, as a unilateral commission reduction is void. Of course, the parties may – even through implicit behaviour – amend the commission rate at any time. This must be done bilaterally and – for reasons of evidence – preferably in written form (or by email). The courts have made clear that the commercial agent's acceptance of reduced commission invoices in past years does not constitute an acknowledgment or implied agreement about the commission rate.[19] Likewise, a contractual provision granting the principal the right to reduce the commission rate unilaterally is invalid in standard terms and conditions. On the other hand, a renegotiation clause stipulating that the parties shall renegotiate the commission rate after a certain period of time does not guarantee that both parties will actually agree on a new rate. Therefore, the parties may agree on sliding commission rates, e.g. rates depending on the duration of the agency relationship (establishing a reduction or increase every year) or on the turnover created by the commercial agent.

**d) Loss of the commission claim**

29 In practice, the entitlement of a commercial agent to a commission payment is regularly questioned in the following cases: when the principal (i) as a goodwill gesture, takes back goods that have already been delivered, (ii) does not carry out transactions because of shortages in supplies caused by subcontractors' failure to deliver, (iii) has customers that unilaterally cancel their orders for goods, or (iv) has customers that return the goods based on an agreement with the principal.

30 Generally, the principal is free to decide whether a transaction solicited by the commercial agent is in fact concluded by the former. Pursuant to § 87(1) HGB, the commercial agent acquires a prospective entitlement (*Anwartschaft*) to commission only if the principal concludes a purchase contract with its customer that has been solicited by the commercial agent. This prospective entitlement to commission becomes a commission claim of the commercial agent if the principal has performed the transaction (§ 87a(1) sentence 1 HGB). The commercial agent generally has a right to a commission payment even if the principal will not perform the transaction in whole or in part, or not as it was concluded (§ 87a(3) sentence 1 HGB). However, there is no right to a commission when the principal does not perform the transaction for reasons for which he is not responsible (§ 87a(3) sentence 2 HGB). That being said, the commercial agent has a commission claim against the principal for example if (i) the principal, as a gesture of goodwill, takes back

[19] See BGH VIII ZR 293/94, NJW 1996, 588; abandonment of the decision by the BGH VII ZR 120/63, NJW 1965, 1136.

goods that have already been delivered to the customer, (ii) the principal does not carry out transactions because of shortages in supplies caused by his own or subcontractors' failure to deliver, or (iii) the principal and the customer subsequently agree to cancel the order. Where the customer, however, returns the goods on the basis of a contractual right to rescind the agreement with the principal, no commission payment is due.[20]

#### e) Invoicing and book excerpt

**aa) Regular invoicing.** The principal has the obligation to provide the commercial agent with regular commission statements. § 87c(1) sentence 1 HGB stipulates that the accounting period for such statements shall be monthly. However, the parties may, by mutual agreement, extend the accounting period to a maximum of three months. 31

**bb) Content of book excerpt.** The commercial agent may require an excerpt from the books concerning all transactions for which he has a claim to commission pursuant to § 87 HGB. This shall give the commercial agent the opportunity to verify the principal's invoicing and to enforce its commission claim. The excerpt must include the purchase order, order number and date, order size with an exact indication of the type of goods, number of goods, individual price, and overall value. Moreover, the excerpt must specify the date and scope of delivery, date of the customer invoice, invoice number, and amount. Furthermore, the name of the customer, including the address or, alternatively, the customer number, is required. The excerpt must contain cancellations, returns, and non-performed orders, in each case specifying the reasons.[21] 32

**cc) Form.** The excerpt must be transparent and clearly arranged. Copies of purchase orders or bills of delivery are not sufficient. Monthly invoices, however, may constitute a book excerpt pursuant to § 87c(2) HGB if the principal provides all necessary and additional information when preparing the monthly invoices.[22] 33

### 2. Secondary obligations

#### a) Provision of material

The principal shall provide the commercial agent with all materials that are necessary for the performance of his duties, such as samples, drawings, price lists, advertising material, and terms and conditions of business. The list in § 86a(1) HGB is non-exhaustive. However, the obligation under § 86a HGB does not include general office equipment such as tables, paper, printer, pens, suitcases, car, mobile phone, computer, and software. The material must be provided and transported to the commercial agent free of charge. Any deviating agreement is invalid.[23] With the termination of the contractual relationship, the commercial agent has to give back all materials to the principal at the principal's expense. The commercial agent is liable for any damage to the samples. 34

#### b) Duty to inform

Pursuant to § 86a(2) HGB, the principal shall keep the commercial agent informed. In particular, the principal shall inform the commercial agent promptly of the acceptance or rejection of a transaction solicited by the commercial agent or in case a transaction was concluded by him without authority. Moreover, the principal must inform the commercial 35

---

[20] Cf. BGH I ZR 6/89, NJW-RR 1991, 155 (156).

[21] For detailed discussion and further reference, see OLG Munich 7 U 5369/09, VersR 2010, 1367.

[22] Cf. BGH I ZR 32/89, NJW-RR 1991, 156 (159); BGH I ZR 171/79, WM 1982, 152.

[23] OLG Munich 7 U 6158/98, BB 1999, 2320; Hopt/Hopt HGB § 86a mn. 18.

agent of any non-completion of a transaction solicited or concluded by him, including the reasons therefor. He shall inform the commercial agent promptly if he (the principal) desires, or will likely be able, to conclude transactions only on a significantly reduced scale in comparison to what the agent could expect under normal circumstances. Courts and legal scholars have assumed an obligation on the part of the principal to inform the commercial agent about the following situations: status of fabrication; supply availability; modification of products,[24] prices and terms of delivery; strategic changes that affect the agent's business (territory);[25] closure or transfer of a company or plant section;[26] suspension of delivery to certain customers;[27] as well as future changes of the contractual relationship (including extension or termination).[28]

#### c) Fiduciary duty and duty to care

36 The principal is not allowed to harm the agent by acquiring a plant section with competitive products, poaching regular customers, poaching sub-agents, or forwarding the agent's customer lists to other commercial agents or distributors in the territory.[29] However, if no further obligations are explicitly or implicitly agreed upon (e.g. exclusive agency), the principal is generally free to compete with the commercial agent by carrying out direct sales or by appointing further commercial agents for the territory. The principal may not harm the commercial agent by systematically rejecting transactions solicited by the agent or by constraining the agent's activity.

#### d) Duties by party agreement

37 Apart from the obligations stipulated in § 86a HGB, the parties are free to create further obligations on the part of the principal, e.g. marketing and advertising obligations, provided that they do not (i) violate the law of standard terms and conditions, (ii) violate statutory prohibitions (§ 134 BGB), (iii) violate public policy (§ 138(1) BGB), or (iii) create a grossly disproportionate and unduly obtained bargain (§ 138(2) BGB).

## D. Drafting

### I. Typical content

38 The parties to a commercial agency agreement are well-advised to define the following in their contract as minimum content:

- territory
- exclusivity, if applicable
- products to be procured by the agent
- obligations of the parties, in particular, the extent of the agent's marketing and advertising duties
- commission, in particular, rates, due date, requirements to be met for a commission payment, cancellation of commission, commission statement

---

[24] BeckOGK/Bieder HGB § 86a mn. 64; BGH II ZR 52/56, NJW 1958 219.
[25] BGH I ZR 126/85, NJW-RR 1987, 873.
[26] BGH VII ZR 93/73, NJW 1974, 795; BGH I ZR 126/85, NJW-RR 1987, 873.
[27] BGH VII ZR 40/65, NJW 1968, 394.
[28] BGH II ZR 130/58, DB 1960, 636 (637).
[29] With a helpful overview, Hopt/Hopt HGB § 86a mn.17.

- competition
- term and termination
- termination compensation (possible exclusion or upfront payment)
- return of samples
- miscellaneous (confidentiality, severability, choice of law, jurisdiction, or arbitration clauses)

## II. Do's and don'ts

- Do not conclude oral agency agreements, as this might lead to problems in terms of evidence and result in costly disputes. 39
- Do not agree on a right of either party to unilaterally change the contract (e.g. commission rates, products, territory), as this might be invalid in standard terms and conditions and therefore cause dispute.
- Do precisely define the exclusivity if the commercial agent is appointed exclusively in the territory. The parties must regulate whether the exclusivity includes the principal's right to direct sales in the territory. Otherwise, the commercial agent may claim damage compensation if the principal has breached the agent's alleged exclusivity by carrying out direct sales in the territory.
- Do precisely define the existing customer base in the contractual territory at the time of the conclusion of the commercial agency agreement (in an annex to the agency agreement) to avoid dispute over the customer base and the solicitation of new customers within the meaning of § 89b HGB.
- Do regulate each topic only once in the agency agreement to avoid double regulation, conflicting rules, and costly disputes.
- Do be careful when drafting the choice of law clause (e.g. a choice of 'European law' is not possible) as well as the jurisdiction or arbitration clause to avoid vagueness in a possible dispute settlement process.

# E. Competition law

The regulations set out in the contract between the principal and the commercial agent may at times restrain competition, violating Article 101 Treaty on the Functioning of the European Union (TFEU). This European regulation prohibits agreements that may affect trade between EU Member States and have as their object or effect the prevention, restriction, or distortion of competition within the internal market. In general, commercial agents fall outside the scope of Article 101 TFEU. They are considered an extended arm of the principal and therefore do not act on a different level in the production or distribution chain. However, this is only true for sales intermediaries who act as commercial agents. If the parties conclude a commercial agency agreement but in fact exercise their contractual relationship as a distributor relationship, Article 101(1) TFEU applies to this contractual relationship.[30] Whether an intermediary is actually a commercial agent is determined by the financial and commercial risks material to the definition of an agency agreement.[31] 40

[30] Originally, the commission distinguished between genuine (echte) and false (unechte) commercial agents, see Mäger/Mäger, Ch IV mn. 98.
[31] Guidelines on Vertical Restraints mn. 30.

With regard to the three criteria described below, the commercial agent must not bear any – or may only bear insignificant – risks in relation to the agreement concluded. Otherwise, Article 101 TFEU applies to the contractual relationship (regarding restraints, possible exemptions, and all other legal consequences).[32]

- Firstly, there are **contract-specific risks** that are directly related to the contracts concluded and/or negotiated by the commercial agent on behalf of the principal, such as financing of goods, payment risks, and risk of loss when transporting or storing the goods.
- Secondly, there are **risks related to market-specific investments**. These are investments specifically required for the type of activity for which the commercial agent has been appointed by the principal. These investments are required to enable the agent to conclude and/or negotiate this type of contract. An example is the purchase of specific repair tools or clothing with logos.[33]
- Thirdly, there are **risks related to other activities undertaken on the same product market**, to the extent that the principal requires the commercial agent to undertake such activities at his own risk – and not as an agent on behalf of the principal. This criterion is relevant if the commercial agent also acts as a distributor for certain types of products in the same market (e.g. fashion, gas, automotive).

# F. Termination

41 Commercial agency agreements are either concluded for a definite or an indefinite period of time. In the first case, the commercial agency agreement usually ends when this period elapses, while in the latter the agreement ends by (ordinary or extraordinary) notice of termination. Moreover, commercial agency agreements may be terminated because of a resolutive condition (*auflösende Bedingung*), by cancellation agreement, or with the commercial agent's death (if the agent is not a company). Insolvency of the commercial agent does not automatically result in the termination of the agency agreement unless this constitutes a contractual right of termination for the principal. §§ 89 and 89a HGB provide statutory rules on the notice of termination of agency agreements.

## I. Ordinary notice of termination

### 1. Staggered notice periods

42 § 89 HGB stipulates that if a contractual agency relationship was entered into for an indefinite period, it may be terminated with prior notice of one month during the first year, two months during the second year, and three months in the third through the fifth years. After five years, the contractual relationship may be terminated with prior notice of six months. Absent any agreement to the contrary, termination is effective only at the end of a calendar month. These staggered notice periods are intended to establish a fair and just balance between the interests of the parties, which is prompt termination on the one hand (principal) and a socially acceptable retention period on the other (commercial agent).

[32] Guidelines on Vertical Restraints mn. 30–32.
[33] Malec/von Bodungen, BB 2010, 2383 (2384). These are called 'sunk costs'.

### 2. Equality of notice periods

The notice periods established pursuant to § 89(1) sentences 1 and 2 HGB may be extended by party agreement. However, the periods may not be shorter for the principal than for the commercial agent, § 89(2) sentence 1 HGB. If a shorter period for the principal is agreed upon, the period agreed upon for the commercial agent applies instead (§ 89(2) sentence 2 HGB). **43**

### 3. Indefinite period of time

§ 89 HGB only applies to commercial agency agreements that have been concluded for an indefinite period of time. Agency agreements concluded with an end date are not subject to the parameters of § 89 HGB. A probation period for the commercial agent does not constitute a time limit unless the agency agreement does not regulate the future of the agency agreement after the probation period. Agency agreements stipulating the end of the contract once the agent has reached a certain age (e.g. 65 years) are considered to be concluded for an indefinite period of time as well.[34] Likewise, consecutive or 'chain' agreements, which are prolonged annually, are considered to be agreements without a time period.[35] A contractual agency relationship of definite duration which, upon expiration, is extended by both parties (implicitly or explicitly) shall be deemed to be extended indefinitely pursuant to § 89(3) sentence 1 HGB. For calculation of the notice periods under § 89(1) sentences 1 and 2 HGB, the total duration of the relationship shall be decisive. **44**

### 4. Deviating agreement

The notice periods established under § 89(1) sentences 1 and 2 HGB may be **extended** by contractual agreement. If the parties agree on a notice period longer than those provided in § 89(1) sentences 1 and 2 HGB, it may not be shorter for the principal than for the commercial agent. If a shorter period for the principal is agreed upon, the period for the commercial agent applies to the principal too. **No reduction** of the notice periods (not even to the advantage of the commercial agent) is possible. In the case of invalid party agreement, the statutory notice periods according to § 89(1) sentences 1 and 2 HGB apply. All aforementioned principles also apply if the parties agree on a probation period.[36] **45**

### 5. Notice of termination pursuant to § 624 BGB

In cases where the parties have concluded a commercial agency agreement for a period of time longer than five years, courts have applied § 624 BGB by analogy, thereby granting the agent the right to terminate the agency agreement with a notice period of six months.[37] In such cases, § 89(1) HGB does not provide a right for the agent to exit the commercial agency agreement because § 89(1) HGB requires the commercial agency agreement to be concluded for an indefinite period. Pursuant to § 624 BGB, a party obliged to personally perform services shall, however, not be bound for a longer period than five years without recourse to terminate the service agreement. Hence, in cases where the commercial agent is obliged to personally perform the services, he might have a right to terminate once the agency agreement has exceeded a period of five years. However, this right does not apply **46**

---

[34] BGH VII ZR 125/66, VersR 1969, 445.
[35] BGH VIII ZR 61/95, NJW 1996, 848 (849).
[36] BGH VII ZR 29/62, NJW 1964, 350.
[37] OLG Hamm 18 U 205/77, BB 1978, 1335.

to an agent who is also the owner of a large agency, to an agent organised in the legal form of a company, to an agent who has sub-agents, or to an agent whose main duty is not of a service character.

## II. Extraordinary notice of termination without notice period

47 The commercial agency relationship can be terminated without observance of a notice period by either party for cause, § 89a(1) HGB. This right to termination cannot be excluded or limited.

### 1. Important reason

48 § 89a HGB establishes the opportunity for either party of a commercial agency relationship to terminate the contract for an important reason (compelling reason, cause) without a notice period. An important reason is given when the terminating party cannot reasonably be expected to continue the contractual relationship until the agreed upon end or until the expiry of a notice period (§ 89a HGB), taking into account all circumstances of the specific case and weighing the interests of both parties.[38] The courts have provided such a definition and established that, when assessing whether it is untenable for a party to continue the contractual relationship, one must also consider the uninterrupted run time of the continuing obligation, the consequences of termination for the other party, the severity of a contractual violation (if any), the behaviour of the parties (including a possible toleration of any infringements). Consequently, minor contractual violations that generally do not harm the trust of the other party can rarely constitute an important reason. Multiple minor contractual violations or other reasons may not, individually, constitute an important reason pursuant to § 89a(1) HGB, but they may do so collectively.[39] To assess whether specific circumstances constitute an important reason, one must balance all specific circumstances of each individual case. Thus, no general conclusions can be drawn. However, courts have acknowledged several circumstances as important reasons.[40]

49 These are important reasons for the agent:

- Baseless and **random refusal of orders** by the principal;
- **Repeated wrongful warnings** of the principal;
- Repeated **refusal to invoice or issuance of confusing invoices** by the principal;
- **Poaching of customers** by the principal with the intention to carry out direct sales with customers;
- **Appointment of other commercial agents** despite exclusivity;
- **Unilateral commission reduction** by the principal;
- Slow and irregular **commission payment**;
- **Wrongful partial termination** by the principal;
- **Direct sales by the principal** despite exclusivity granted to the agent, if the exclusivity under the agency agreement excludes the principal's direct sales.

50 The following constitutes important reasons for the principal:

- **Poaching of the principal's employees** by the agent;
- Agent's threat to **divulge or disclose trade secrets** or internal matters;
- Agent's **inaction** or **lack of effort**;

---

[38] BGH I ZR 39/79, MDR 1981, 906.

[39] Cf. OLG Saarbrücken 1 U 593/00-131, NJW-RR 2002, 542 (543).

[40] For further reference and a useful case-based overview, see Staub/Emde HGB § 89a mn. 27.

- Agent has spread **untrue information about the product**;
- Repeated **solicitation of illiquid customers** by the agent;
- Simulated **incapacity to work** by the agent;
- **Misappropriation of sample collection** by the agent;
- **Sexual harassment** of the principal, its employees, or customers by the agent;
- **Long-term alcohol misuse** by the agent;
- **Criminal allegations** of agent vis-á-vis customers;
- **False statement of expenses** by the agent;
- **Violation of minimum turnover** agreement by the agent, only if the violation is caused by the agent's lack of effort (and not on market situation, recession);
- Severe **violation of the agent's reporting duty** or customer visit reports;
- **Customer complaints** about the agent, only if complaints refer to the agent's breach of the agency agreement;
- **Impoliteness of the agent**, only if the impoliteness constitutes an insult;
- **Long-term sickness** of the agent, if the agent is prevented from working;
- Revocation of the agent's **driver's licence,** if the agent is prevented from working;
- **Inappropriate behaviour** by the agent might constitute an important reason;
- **Multiple representation** by the agent, only if the prohibition of competition is violated by the commercial agent.

The lack of success of the agent does not constitute an important reason for the principal, as his obligation is to perform to his best effort only. **51**

Generally, the burden of proof lies with the party who wants to terminate the contract. Therefore, the party claiming the important reason must furnish proof of all circumstances establishing the important reason. **52**

## 2. Warning letter

If the important reason consists in the breach of a contractual duty under the agency agreement, and therefore trust in the other party's capacity, conduct, or performance – and not its integrity – is concerned, the agreement may not be terminated until the terminating party has sent a warning letter to the other party and such warning has not mitigated the problem.[41] In such a letter, the warning party must set a time limit for the addressee. Only if the contractual obligations were violated in a particularly serious manner or it is certain that a warning will not produce any results can a warning be dispensed with. **53**

## 3. Declaration of termination

The declaration of termination is subject to interpretation. Any behaviour of the declaring party that makes clear to an objective recipient of the declaration that the declaring party wants to terminate the contractual relationship for the future is sufficient. In practice, it is often unclear whether an important reason for an extraordinary notice of termination without notice period is actually given, as the courts have wide discretion in this respect. Therefore, the declaring party may, alternatively, declare an ordinary notice of termination in the event that the extraordinary notice of termination is found to be invalid. Even if the declaring party did not issue an ordinary notice of termination alternatively, the extraordinary notice of termination may be reinterpreted as an ordinary notice with effect for the next possible date. Such reinterpretation is possible if it is appar- **54**

[41] BGH VIII ZR 159/07, NZG 2009, 310 (312).

ent that the terminating party would have intended to terminate the agency agreement ordinarily had it known that the extraordinary notice was invalid.[42]

### 4. Declaration within an adequate time

55 Once the terminating party has obtained knowledge of circumstances that constitute an important reason, the declaration of termination must be made within adequate time. There is no fixed time period. What is considered adequate time depends on the circumstances of the case. The declaring party must have time to clarify the facts and obtain definite knowledge of all necessary circumstances that constitute an important reason. As a rule of thumb, two weeks seem to be an appropriate time once definite knowledge of the necessary facts is obtained.[43]

### 5. Damage compensation

#### a) Wrongful termination

56 If termination has been **wrongfully declared**, such termination is invalid and the declaring party must compensate the other party for damage if the declaring party has ceased to fulfil its contractual obligations, which usually is the case after the declaration of termination has been made. For the commercial agent, the compensatory damage is usually lost profit (e.g. lost commission payments). The principal, however, may also lose profit due to an agent's non-performance or a necessary reorganisation of his (the principal's) business. Hence, a wrongfully terminated agency agreement constitutes an important reason for the other party to extraordinarily terminate the agency agreement itself, at least if the first extraordinary termination is accompanied by non-performance of the commercial agency agreement.

#### b) Lawful termination

57 However, in the case of **valid extraordinary termination** due to behaviour for which the terminated party is responsible, that terminated party is obliged to compensate the other party for damages arising from the termination of the contractual relationship. For example, if the commercial agent lawfully terminates the agency agreement extraordinarily, the principal must compensate for the commercial agent's damage. When calculating such damage (e.g. lost commission), one must regard the contractual relationship as if the parties had performed their contractual duties as per the agreement. In the example described above, a principal is well-advised to ordinarily terminate the agreement to reduce the compensation payable to the commercial agent.

#### c) No protection of the agent's investments

58 Neither statutory law nor the courts have acknowledged a commercial agent's compensation claim for non-amortised investments (e.g. acquisition of a car, computer, telephone, hiring employees, etc.) made by the commercial agent to fulfil his obligations under the commercial agency agreement. So far, some commentators have advocated for an investment claim on the part of the commercial agent.[44]

---

[42] Hopt/Hopt HGB § 89a mn. 5.

[43] A declaration made after two months is deemed to be too late, cf. BGH VIII ZR 157/92, NJW 1994, 722 (723).

[44] For an overview, Martinek/Semler/Habermeier/Flohr VertriebsR-HdB/Flohr/Pohl § 18 mn. 25.

## III. Partial notice of termination

In principle, a partial notice of termination of commercial agency agreements is not permitted, as such notice is deemed to disadvantage the commercial agent, leaving him without protection.[45] Therefore, the principal may not alter the content of the contract by, for instance, terminating parts of the contractual territory, parts of the product portfolio, parts of the customer base (exclusion of certain customers) or parts of the remuneration (commission rates). If the principal intends to partially change the agency agreement, he must (i) terminate the entire agreement and (ii) offer continuance on the basis of an amended agency agreement. However, this entails risks (→ mn. 65 et seqq.). The parties to a commercial agency agreement may not validly agree on the possibility for one of the parties to partially terminate the commercial agency agreement if the agreement is subject to the test of reasonableness (§ 307 BGB),[46] which is normally the case. However, partial notice of termination is rightly permitted if an agency agreement consists of separable parts and the partial notice of termination does not materially change the content of the agency agreement itself. In such a case, the commercial agent must receive appropriate compensation. 59

## IV. Notice of termination with option to continue

Notice of termination with an option to continue (*Änderungskündigung*) typically consists of an unconditional ordinary notice of termination combined with an offer to conclude a new agreement with (partially) changed content.[47] Such a notice of termination with an option to continue may be a useful device for changing the existing agency agreement. However, it is not without risks: First, the commercial agent has a claim for termination compensation (*Ausgleichsanspruch*) pursuant to § 89b HGB once the existing agency agreement is terminated. Second, the commercial agent is free to accept or reject the offered continuance of the agency relationship. There is no guarantee for the principal that the commercial agent will accept his offer. Thus, the termination with an option to continue is advisable in cases in which the principal will presumably have no difficulties in finding an alternative new commercial agent. When concluding the new agency agreement, the principal is in any case well-advised to list all existing customers in the territory that he has supplied to date in an annex to the new agency agreement. This might lower the risk of dispute over a future termination compensation (and the payable amount) once the new agency agreement is terminated. 60

## V. Cancellation agreement

The parties to a commercial agency agreement may at any time terminate their commercial agency relationship by concluding a cancellation agreement. Such an agreement has no prescribed form and may even be concluded by implied behaviour. At times, a principal may wish to collectively renew one or all agency agreements with some or all commercial agents (e.g. due to internal compliance requirements). In such cases, a bilateral cancellation agreement combined with the conclusion of the new agency agreement is 61

45 BGH I ZR 248/89, NJW-RR 1992, 481 (482); BGH I ZR 175/75, WM 1977, 589 (590).
46 BGH VIII ZR 125/98, NJW 2000, 515 (516).
47 BGH VIII ZR 125/98, NJW 2000, 515 (517).

the approach with the fewest downsides and risks, provided that the commercial agent is willing to consent thereto. It should be noted that the cancellation of an agency agreement also triggers the agent's claim for termination compensation.[48] But the parties are free to determine the content of the cancellation agreement and may, under the conditions described below, waive the commercial agent's claim for termination compensation.

62 When negotiating a cancellation agreement, the commercial agent may be willing to waive its claim for termination compensation if he in turn receives a certain fixed amount as overall compensation for the cancellation. Such an agreement is generally possible. However, pursuant to § 89b(4) sentence 1 HGB, the claim for termination compensation cannot be excluded **in advance** and the regulation is mandatory.[49] This regulation protects the commercial agent from being pressured into waiving his claim for compensation in the hopes of concluding the commercial agency agreement. Although the commercial agent may negotiate the exclusion of the termination compensation before the agency agreement ends, such a waiver may, however, only become effective at the time when the commercial agency agreement ends.[50] To dispel any doubt: in a cancellation agreement signed at the end of January and stipulating that the commercial agency relationship ends at the beginning of February, the waiver of termination compensation signed with the cancellation agreement is considered to be 'in advance' and therefore invalid. In contrast, a formulation stipulating that the 'commercial agency relationship ends with immediate effect' (with signature) allows the exclusion of the termination compensation, as the termination of the commercial agency agreement and the exclusion of the commercial agent's claim for termination compensation coincide.[51]

63 The Federal Court of Justice has also acknowledged the validity of an exclusion shortly before the termination of the agency agreement, if the commercial agent has ceased acting for the principal by common agreement.[52] As this refers to a special and exceptional case, it is not advisable to conclude cancellation agreements with such a structure unless absolutely unavoidable.

## VI. No legal form requirement

64 The termination of a commercial agency agreement is not restricted to a certain form, i.e. the declaration of termination may be made in writing, per email, or even orally. For reasons of evidence, it is advisable to give notice of termination by email in advance and then by post. Moreover, the particularities of § 174 BGB and the corresponding pitfalls may also cause problems when terminating commercial agency agreements (→ Ch. 1 mn. 102 et seqq.). Therefore, an authorised person should never give notice of termination orally.

[48] BGH VII ZR 48/67, NJW 1969, 1023.
[49] Mann, ZVertriebsR 2017, 25 (27).
[50] BGH VIII ZR 261/95, NJW 1996, 2867 (2868); BGH VII ZR 102/66, NJW 1969, 504.
[51] For a detailed discussion on termination and compensation agreement for commercial agents, see Mann, ZVertriebsR 2017, 25 et seqq.
[52] BGH VII ZR 141/68, NJW 1971, 465 et seqq.

# G. Post-contractual matters

The termination of a commercial agency agreement may cause problems for the parties. These include invoicing of the commercial agent's outstanding commission claims, his post-contractual competition prohibition, or the return of samples or other items. **65**

## I. Post-contractual commission claims

Under specific circumstances, the commercial agent may have commission claims for the solicitation of transactions even if such transactions were concluded after the termination of the contractual agency relationship. This type of commission is called a backlog commission (*Überhangprovision*). § 87(3) HGB regulates two scenarios that trigger the commercial agent's backlog commission claim: **66**

- The principal or the commercial agent has received a customer's purchase order prior to the termination of the commercial agency agreement and the purchase order would have triggered a compensation claim pursuant to § 87(1) or (2) HGB; or
- The commercial agent (i) **solicited, initiated, or prepared** the transaction in such a way that (ii) the **conclusion of** the **transaction** between the customer and the principal was (iii) **predominantly caused** by the commercial agent's activity, and the transaction was (iv) concluded in a **reasonable time after the termination** of the commercial agency agreement. The element 'reasonable time' must be assessed according to the products solicited by the commercial agent. For daily consumer goods, 'reasonable time' is shorter than for seasonal goods (e.g. fashion). For large and specialised goods (e.g. construction of a sprinkler), courts have considered 24 months from the termination of the commercial agency agreement to be 'reasonable time' pursuant to § 87(3) no. 1 HGB.[53] Re-orders and follow-up orders do not fall under § 87(3) no. 1 HGB and, consequently, do not trigger post-contractual commission claims of the commercial agent.

## II. Post-contractual prohibition of competition

Pursuant to § 90 HGB, the commercial agent is obliged not to disclose trade secrets of the principal to any third party or to use them for his own benefit without the principal's prior consent. This duty of confidentiality also applies after termination of the agency agreement without any time restrictions. However, the commercial agent's duty to not compete with the principal ends with the termination of the commercial agency agreement. This is not true if the parties have agreed on a post-contractual prohibition of competition (*nachvertragliches Wettbewerbsverbot*) pursuant to § 90a HGB. § 90a HGB sets forth narrow conditions under which a post-contractual prohibition of competition may be agreed upon between the principal and the commercial agent. **67**

### 1. Duration

Pursuant to § 90a HGB, a commercial agent may be restricted in his commercial activity for only two years following the termination of the contractual relationship. The **68**

[53] MüKoHGB/Ströbl HGB § 87 mn. 122.

parties may agree on a period shorter than two years. However, the time limit may not be prolonged or postponed. A party agreement exceeding the two-year limit does not result in the complete invalidity of the commercial agent's competition prohibition but automatically reduces the time limit to two years.[54] A *de facto* extension of the commercial agent's competition prohibition may, however, be achieved if the parties jointly agree on a renewal after two years' time. The limitations of § 90a HGB apply only prior to or during an ongoing commercial agency relationship. Therefore, a jointly concluded competition prohibition may be agreed upon between the parties without constraints.

### 2. Content

69 Pursuant to § 90a(1) sentence 2 HGB, a post-contractual prohibition of competition may only cover the geographical area (territory) or group of customers assigned to the commercial agent and may only refer to the type of business for which the commercial agent was responsible for soliciting transactions. Any agreement constraining the commercial agent's activity once the agency agreement is terminated is a post-contractual prohibition of competition. For example:

- automatic continuation of the statutory prohibition of competition after the agency agreement has been terminated,
- commercial agent's obligation to refund payments in the case of post-contractual competition,
- prohibition on the commercial agent from using information about the customers, or
- prohibition on the commercial agent from enticing customers to switch to another supplier or from providing assistance to this end.

70 The commercial agent's future status is irrelevant. He might be constrained in a future position as a self-employed commercial agent, as a shareholder of a company (which itself is the agent), or as an employee. A suspension (*Suspendierung*) of the commercial agent for the time until the agency agreement is terminated does not constitute a competition prohibition, as such suspension is not post-contractual. The legal consequences of § 90a HGB are therefore not triggered if the commercial agent is suspended from his activity.

### 3. Form

71 A post-contractual prohibition of competition requires two corresponding declarations of intent — offer and acceptance. Such an agreement might well be made through standard terms and conditions. The principal and the commercial agent normally regulate a post-contractual prohibition of competition in their commercial agency agreement. A post-contractual prohibition of competition must be in writing, and the document containing the conditions agreed upon must be signed by the principal and delivered to the commercial agent. Violations of the written form requirement may be remedied. If the parties fail to remedy a violation of the written form requirement, such a prohibition is invalid.[55]

---

[54] MüKoHGB/Ströbl HGB § 90a mn. 35; Ebenroth/Boujong/Joost/Strohn/Löwisch HGB § 90a mn. 32; BGH VII ZR 56/11, NJW 2013, 2027.

[55] Cf. Ebenroth/Boujong/Joost/Strohn/Löwisch HGB§ 90a mn. 23.

## 4. Reasonable non-competition compensation

The principal is obligated to pay reasonable compensation (*Karenzentschädigung*) to the commercial agent for the duration of the prohibition of competition (§ 90a(1) sentence 3 HGB). Such payment is intended to compensate the commercial agent for his loss of income due to the prohibition on competition. The compensation is due even if the commercial agent never intended to compete with the principal, or the principal mistakenly thought the prohibition of competition would not trigger any compensation. The compensation is due at once unless the parties agree on payment by instalments (e.g. monthly). The principal must pay 'reasonable compensation'. What is considered reasonable must be assessed on a case-by-case basis and may be examined by the courts. One must consider the commercial agent's disadvantages that arise from the prohibition of competition and the monthly remuneration that the commercial agent has earned. Savings, expenditures, or the commercial agent's post-contractual income is not considered when assessing the reasonableness.[56] If the parties have agreed on a specific amount, such amount is – as minimum compensation – generally binding. However, the principal can furnish proof that the agreed compensation is unreasonably high due to circumstances that arose after the conclusion of the prohibition of competition. Unreasonable compensation agreed upon between the parties is invalid.[57] Non-payment by the principal does not release the commercial agent from the prohibition of competition. In the case of non-payment by the principal, the commercial agent must sue the principal for payment. 72

## 5. Elimination of the prohibition of competition

A breach of either the post-contractual prohibition of competition or the obligation to pay compensation does not generally result in the cessation of other obligations. 73

- If the principal does not pay the agreed upon compensation, the commercial agent must sue the principal for payment while still being bound by the post-contractual prohibition of competition.
- If the commercial agent wrongfully acts as a competitor of the principal, the commercial agent loses his compensation claim for this period for his wrongful action. Moreover, the principal may successfully claim damages if the commercial agent is in breach of his post-contractual prohibition of competition. In addition, the principal may have a right to rescind the agreed upon prohibition.

### a) Waiver of competition prohibition

The principal may waive the prohibition of competition until the end of the contractual relationship with the effect that he will be free from the obligation to pay compensation (§ 90a(2) HGB). The declaration of waiver must be made to the commercial agent in writing. At the end of six months after the declaration, the principal is released from his obligation to pay compensation. Objections by the commercial agent have no effect if the waiver was validly made. If a post-contractual prohibition of competition was agreed upon but the principal intends to avoid any payment, he must make the declaration of waiver with six months' prior notice to the end of the commercial agency agreement. Otherwise, partial compensation payment must be made until the expiration of the six-month period. The unilateral declaration of waiver can only be made before the commercial agency 74

---

[56] BGH VII ZR 2/74, NJW 1975, 388 (389).

[57] In such cases the court must determine the reasonable compensation, cf. BAG 5 AZR 278/63, NJW 1964, 1641 (1643).

agreement ends. Once it is terminated, the principal may not unilaterally decouple itself from the competition prohibition and its corresponding payment obligation.

#### b) Cancellation agreement

75 The parties may at any time (prior to or after the termination of the commercial agency agreement, e.g. when concluding a cancellation agreement) mutually agree on the post-contractual prohibition of competition and the corresponding compensation payment.

#### c) Notice of termination

76 If one party terminates the commercial agency agreement for an important reason due to culpable (mis)conduct of the other party, the terminating party may – pursuant to § 90a(3) HGB – declare that it is not bound by the agreement prohibiting competition. Such declaration must be made in writing and within one month after giving notice of the termination of the commercial agency agreement. In a typical case, the principal terminates the commercial agency agreement due to culpable misbehaviour of the commercial agent. In such a case, the principal may want to avoid the compensation payment. The principal may do so by making a written declaration within one month after the termination of the agency agreement stating that the prohibition of competition shall not apply. In such a case, the commercial agent is not bound by the prohibition and may therefore compete with the principal.

#### d) Closure of business or death

77 If the commercial agent dies or closes his business, the prohibition on competition and the principal's obligation to compensate the agent ceases. The mere incapacity to work does not eliminate the commercial agent's claim for reasonable compensation.[58]

## III. Return of sample collection

78 Sample collections, advertising material, and all other goods belonging to the principal must be returned to the principal upon termination of the commercial agency agreement. This also applies to the principal's spare parts and warehouse stock, if any, which are in the commercial agent's possession at the time of the termination of the commercial agency agreement. Difficulties may arise in cases where the principal supports the commercial agent by setting up pieces of exhibition furniture in the commercial agent's sales rooms (ornamental covers, clothes rails, kitchens, etc.). The principal may have lost ownership by way of mandatory German property law. To avoid uncertainty about the extent of the commercial agent's obligations to return goods or his duty to compensate the principal in case the agent became the owner of such goods, the parties are well-advised to explicitly set out the commercial agent's return obligations and their extent in the commercial agency agreement.

[58] In the case of insolvency of the principal or the agent, see Staub/Emde HGB § 90a mn. 60–67.

## IV. Return of customer addresses

Pursuant to § 667 BGB, the commercial agent is under the obligation to hand over to the principal all customer lists showing the contact details of all customers, irrespective of whether they are existing or new customers. Despite this obligation, the commercial agent may contact the customers and compete with the principal unless the parties have validly agreed on a post-contractual competition prohibition.[59] If the commercial agent uses the customer data after the termination of the commercial agency relationship, this does not eliminate the commercial agent's claim for termination compensation pursuant to § 89b HGB (but may reduce it). However, pursuant to § 90 HGB, the commercial agent may not give the customer data to third parties (in particular, the principal's competitors).[60] **79**

## V. Claim for continued supply

Under very rare and exceptional circumstances the commercial agent has a claim against the principal for continued supply of goods (in particular, spare parts) pursuant to §§ 19 et seqq. GWB. Courts have stated that a commercial agent who – in addition to soliciting transactions – provides after-sales service in his own name and for his own account may have a claim against the principal for continued supply with spare parts for a reasonable transitional period after the termination of the commercial agency agreement.[61] **80**

## VI. Limitation

### 1. General

Claims arising from or in connection with the commercial agency relationship are subject to limitation according to §§ 195 et seqq. BGB and, consequently, lapse three years after the end of the year in which: (i) the claim arose and (ii) the obligee obtains knowledge of the circumstances giving rise to the claim and of the identity of the obligor, or would have obtained such knowledge if he had not shown gross negligence. As an example, for all monthly commission claims due in the period from January to December 2022, limitation starts to run on 1 January 2023. After three years' time (i.e. at the end of 31 December 2025), the commission claims for the year 2022 lapse, meaning that on 1 January 2026 the commercial agent's commission claims would become statute-barred. **81**

### 2. Claim for book excerpt

Limitation of the commercial agent's claims for information pursuant to § 87c HGB does not start at the time when the commercial agent first had the opportunity to request the information but rather at the end of the year in which the commercial agent actually demanded such information (e.g. a book excerpt or inspection of the principal's books).[62] **82**

---

[59] Cf. BGH I ZR 28/06, NJW 2009, 1420; with further reference, Martinek/Semler/Habermeier/Flohr VertriebsR-HdB/Semler § 23 mn. 16.

[60] OLG Koblenz 6 U 604/86, NJW-RR 1987, 95 (98).

[61] BGH KZR 3/88, NJW-RR 1989, 1310; OLG Frankfurt/Main 6 U (Kart) 197/88, WuW 1991, 623.

[62] BGH I ZR 7/77, NJW 1979, 764.

### 3. Agent's misapprehension

83 Courts have considered claims of the commercial agent not to be statute-barred if the commercial agent had no knowledge of the fact that the respective contractual agreement (e.g. a reduction of commission, a limitation period of six months) was invalid due to mandatory law.[63] This legal assessment is wrong and must be rejected. The commercial agent can easily avoid any misapprehension about the existence of a claim by simply seeking legal advice. The commercial agent is responsible for assessing whether regulations in the commercial agency agreement are valid or violate mandatory law. An avoidable legal misapprehension may therefore not constitute an excuse for the commercial agent.[64] Moreover, the approach taken by the Higher Regional Court of Karlsruhe severely undermines the law of limitation.

# H. Claim for termination compensation

## I. Basic principles

84 The commercial agent may claim reasonable compensation from the principal upon the termination of the commercial agency relationship pursuant to § 89b HGB (termination compensation). The commercial agent's claim for termination compensation is not compensation for damage but instead contractual compensation for the advantages to the principal from the customer base built up by the agent.[65] As a future claim, the commercial agent's claim for termination compensation may be assigned, pledged, or expropriated even before the end of the commercial agency relationship.[66]

85 The following persons, among others, are entitled to termination compensation: sub-agents, incorporated agencies, commercial agents who are authorised to contract, those who are authorised to solicit business, district agents, exclusive and non-exclusive agents, and the commercial agent's successors. Distributors[67], commission agents, insurance agents, franchisees, and licensees can, under certain (additional) conditions, also have a claim for termination compensation. In contrast, part-time commercial agents (§ 92b HGB), non-self-employed agents, sales employees or lessees are not entitled to claim termination compensation. The legal form in which the commercial agent organises his agency (e.g. freelancer, GmbH, non-incorporated company) is of no relevance for the question of whether he has a claim for termination compensation against the principal.

## II. Conditions

86 The claim for termination compensation is triggered only when the following five conditions are fulfilled, whereby the first four are discussed in the following:

- The commercial agency agreement has to be terminated,
- the commercial agent has solicited new customers or materially expanded the business relations with existing customers,

[63] OLG Karlsruhe 8 U 64/73, BB 1974, 904.

[64] For the strict approach of German courts in legal misapprehension in capital investment law, see – as a comparison – BGH II ZR 224/91, NJW 1992, 3296.

[65] BeckOK/Lehmann HGB vor § 89b.

[66] OLG Hamm 14 W 179/78, BB 1979, 1579 (1580).

[67] BGH I ZR 146/80, NJW 1982, 2819.

- the principal retains substantial advantages from the business relations with the new customers,
- the payment of certain termination compensation is just and equitable, and
- the claim for termination compensation was made within one year after the termination of the commercial agency relationship.

## 1. Termination

The commercial agent's claim for termination compensation requires the termination of the commercial agency agreement. The reason for termination is of no relevance. Therefore, notice of termination[68], partial termination, expiration of the agreement (even after a probation period), termination by mutual cancellation agreement, and termination due to insolvency of the principal all fall under § 89b HGB. The expiration of a consecutive or 'chain' agreement does not constitute a termination if upon expiration of the agreement a new agreement is concluded and the entire business relationship appears as one unified contractual agreement. 87

## 2. Solicitation of new customers or material expansion of existing business relations

The purpose of a claim for termination compensation is to compensate the commercial agent's efforts in building up a client base. Therefore, only business with new clients (solicited by the commercial agent) and business with existing customers with whom the commercial agent significantly expanded the business relations are considered when calculating the termination compensation. 88

## 3. New customer

New customers are those who did not have a business relationship with the principal before the commercial agency agreement was concluded. If a customer has ordered products with the principal and later, due to the commercial agent's solicitation, orders other products, this person is considered a new customer.[69] If the commercial agent solicits largely independent subsidiaries of a company group, and the group or other subsidiaries of the group already order products from the principal, the independent subsidiary will most likely be considered a new customer. Regular customers of the commercial agent that he transfers to the principal are, from the principal's perspective, new customers if there was no prior business relationship between such customers and the principal. A mere change of the customer's name, corporate setting, or legal form does not make an existing customer new. To avoid dispute about which customers are solicited by the commercial agent and are therefore new, it is advisable to name all existing customers in an annex to the commercial agency agreement when concluding the contract. 89

## 4. Material expansion of existing business relations

Solicitation of new customers also includes the material expansion of business relations with existing customers, which corresponds economically to the acquisition of a new customer. Courts have acknowledged a material expansion in cases where the turnover with 90

---

[68] This generally includes extraordinary and ordinary notice of termination → 40 et seqq.
[69] BGH VIII ZR 354/97, NJW 1999, 2668 (2670).

an existing customer was doubled (an increase of 100 %).[70] This is rightly considered to be the minimum necessary, as the law requires a *material* expansion that corresponds economically to the acquisition of a new customer. The commercial agent bears the burden of proof when it comes to demonstrating that an expansion of the business relations (e.g. the turnover) was caused by him. However, since a mere turnover increase in the territory is generally an indication of the commercial agent's causal activity, it will ultimately be the principal who must substantially demonstrate that external circumstances – and not the commercial agent – have caused the turnover increase.[71]

### 5. Soliciting by the agent

91 The commercial agent's activity must be causal for soliciting the new customer or for the expansion of the business relationship. A customer from the commercial agent's contractual territory who orders products on the recommendation of a third party, due to the principal's internet presence, or to a unique market position, is not considered to have been solicited by the commercial agent. This is true even in cases where a customer – who has only decided to buy on the recommendation of a third party – contacts the commercial agent to complete the purchase order.[72] Concurrent causality (*Mitursächlichkeit*) is sufficient.[73] In cases where the customer had knowledge of the principal's product but was ultimately convinced by the commercial agent to place an order, the commercial agent's activity is considered causal. If the commercial agent successfully prevents an existing customer from buying from the principal's competitor, such customer is neither a new customer nor is such activity of the commercial agent itself an expansion of business relations.

### 6. Principal's substantial advantages

92 The commercial agent has a claim for compensation only if the principal is able to gain substantial advantages from the customer base solicited by the commercial agent. This is the case only if the principal can use and develop the client base after termination of the commercial agency relationship.

#### a) Regular customers

93 **aa) Principal's future gains.** When calculating the termination compensation, only regular customers are considered as the principal will presumably not draw future profits from one-time customers or customers who have occasionally ordered products. Courts consider customers to be regular only if their buying behaviour is reasonably continuous (e.g. multiple refuelling stops at the petrol station during a calendar quarter, repeated orders at regular intervals).[74] The continuity naturally depends on the type of contract products and is consequently assessed on a case-by-case basis. As an example, order intervals are normally lower in the car industry (two-time car purchase required[75]) than in the pharmaceuticals industry. A customer who has ordered only once prior to the termination of the commercial agency relationship cannot automatically be excluded from the calculation if he could become a regular customer in the future. In such a

---

[70] BGH VII ZR 23/70, NJW 1971, 1611; BGH VIII ZR 354/97, NJW 1999, 2668 (2670).
[71] Cf. BGH VII ZR 23/70, NJW 1971, 1611.
[72] OLG Karlsruhe 2 U 144/58, BB 1960, 381.
[73] BGH VIII ZR 322/09, NJW 2011, 1143 (1144).
[74] BGH VIII ZR 194/06, BB 2007, 2475.
[75] BGH VIII ZR 272/95, NJW 1997, 1503.

case, the commercial agent must provide sufficiently concrete indications of subsequent transactions. On the other hand, there are also industries where no second order can usually be expected and therefore the principal has no substantial future advantage (prefabricated houses, windows, encyclopaedias, gravestones, large farm machinery).[76]

**bb) Use of the customer base.** Whether the principal makes use of the customer base is irrelevant. It is sufficient if the principal is potentially able to make use of the customer base built up by the commercial agent. 94

#### b) Churn rate

The principal must compensate the commercial agent for regular customers only in so far as they were newly solicited by the commercial agent and the principal can therefore do business with them in the future. It is common even for regular customers to change their supplier from time to time. Therefore, a deduction has to be made for regular customers migrating to competitors in the future. This deduction does not require a forecast, as the migration of regular customers during the years prior to the termination of the commercial agency relationship indicates the rate that must be deducted for future customer migration, also known as the 'churn rate'. If the recent contractual years provide no indication, the churn rate is subject to the court's discretion and assessment. Courts have determined that a churn rate of 20 % is appropriate for each contractual year that the principal will presumably benefit from the customer base.[77] A party claiming a different churn rate must present and furnish proof of indicators that demonstrate a lower or higher migration of regular customers. For example: if the commercial agent's commissions with regular customers during the last contractual year amounted to EUR 100,000, a churn rate of 20 % for the first forecast year would amount to EUR 20,000, thereby reducing the fictive commission to EUR 80,000; for a second forecast year, the reduction would amount to EUR 16,000 (20 % of EUR 80,000); and for a third forecast year, it would amount to EUR 12,800 (20 % of EUR 64,000) and so forth.[78] 95

#### c) Agent's administrative activity

The commercial agent may merely claim termination compensation for the formation of a customer base and the principal's economic advantages associated with the chance to use such customer base in the future. However, this is the result of the commercial agent's soliciting and promotional activity only, and not of administrative activities, warehousing, or debt collection. Consequently, commissions or other payments which the commercial agent has received from the principal for administrative activities, or extra payments for office equipment, etc. are excluded when calculating the termination compensation.[79] 96

#### d) No substantial advantage

The courts have acknowledged further cases that exclude or significantly reduce the commercial agent's compensation claim. This might be the case if the principal's factory was shut down due to insolvency[80] or even voluntarily in case the principal decides to 97

---

[76] For a detailed overview, see Staub/Emde HGB § 89b mn. 82.

[77] BGH VIII ZR 13/05, NJW-RR 2009, 824 (827–828).

[78] BGH VIII ZR 58/00, NJW-RR 2002, 1548 (1553).

[79] BGH I ZR 79/82, NJW 1985, 860 (861); BGH VII ZR 36/71, NJW 1972, 1662; BGH II ZR 81/57, NJW 1959, 1430.

[80] For a discussion of exceptions, see Staub/Emde HGB § 89b mn. 104–106.

discontinue his business activities or parts thereof.[81] In such cases where neither the principal nor any third person continues to use the customer base, no substantial advantage exists. This is not the case, however, if the principal sells his company and as a result may have achieved a higher selling price due to the expanded customer base. If the commercial agent successfully entices customers after termination of the commercial agency agreement, no substantial advantage for the principal exists.[82] No substantial or reduced advantages of the principal remain in cases in which customers migrate to competitors just because the commercial agent quits his job.

#### e) Forecast

98 At the time of termination, the principal's advantages have not yet materialised and therefore cannot be precisely denoted. As the principal's advantages are commonly realised in the future, a forecast of transactions with the new customers solicited by the commercial agent is necessary. When making such a forecast, the crucial question is how long and to what extent the principal may benefit from the relationship with the new customers. The length of the forecast period depends on how long the business relations with the new customers will presumably last. This in turn depends on the order intervals of the new customers. There is no general answer to the question of how frequently customers order products. Therefore, the courts must use a case-by-case approach, taking into account (i) the special features of the respective industrial sector, (ii) the market, as well as (iii) the competitive conditions, (iv) customer fluctuation, and (v) the type of commercial activity.[83] Long-lasting industrial products (e.g. pallet transporters or cars) commonly have far longer order intervals than, for instance, consumable goods (e.g. medical or cosmetic products, calculators, office equipment). Courts have determined an average period of two years to be an appropriate length. However, pursuant to § 287 ZPO, courts have broad discretion and may find significantly shorter or longer periods to be appropriate. The following catalogue provides an overview of how long the business relationship is expected to last in specific industrial sectors and products:

- Fashion agency: 3 years[84]
- Frozen food: 3 years[85]
- Radio advertising and general advertising agency: 3–4 years[86]
- Petrol station and related shops: 4 years[87]
- Software products: 4 years[88]
- Building society: 4 years[89]
- Newspaper and journals agency: 4 years[90]
- Electronic household appliances (refrigerator, vacuum cleaner, washing machine): 5 years[91]

---

[81] BGH II ZR 99/58, NJW 1959, 1964. Regarding partial discontinuation cf. OLG Munich 7 U 5042/95, NJW-RR 1996, 991 (993).
[82] OLG Celle 11 U 185/58, BB 1959, 1151.
[83] BGH I ZR 173/91, NJW-RR 1993, 221.
[84] OLG Munich 7 U 5118/00, NJOZ 2002, 617.
[85] OLG Düsseldorf 16 U 47/11, BB 2013, 788.
[86] OLG Munich 7 U 7270/93 (four years: radio advertising); OLG Munich 7 U 3617/97, OLGR 1998, 170 (three years: general advertising).
[87] BGH VIII ZR 150/96, ZIP 1997, 1832 (gas); BGH VIII ZR 108/09, NJW-RR 2010, 1550 (shop).
[88] BGH VIII ZR 13/05, BB 2008, 2594.
[89] BGH VII ZR 36/71, NJW 1972, 1664 (1666); OLG Celle 11 U 193/01, VersR 2002, 976.
[90] BGH VII ZR 3/71, DB 1973, 1740.
[91] BGH I ZR 104/82, NJW 1985, 859; BGH VIII ZR 94/93, NJW 1994, 1350.

- Motorbikes: 5 years[92]
- Industrial flooring: 5 years[93]
- Insurance agency: 6 years[94]
- Cars: 5–8 years[95]
- Pallet transporter: 13 years[96]
- Lottery agency: 20 years[97]

## 7. Equitableness

### a) Definition and identification

The commercial agent's claim for termination compensation does not apply if such compensation is not equitable. In most cases, however, equitableness (*Billigkeit*) does not eliminate the claim for termination compensation but instead reduces it. Equitableness may be comprehensively reviewed by the courts. A judge must fully determine and define all possible factors of equitableness in each individual case and, in a second step, appraise all applicable factors. In a third step, all evaluated factors must be balanced. An extensive number of court decisions make it possible to create case groups which can serve as a basis for a future court decision. **99**

### b) Case law

The following factors help provide an overview.[98] **100**

The following are irrelevant to the determination of equitableness: **101**

- **Direct sales** of the principal
- Termination compensation **claimed by successor**
- **Duration** of business relationship
- Offered but rejected **replacement contract** for the commercial agent
- Additional **income opportunity** for the commercial agent
- **Lack of success** of the commercial agent, if there is no simultaneous breach of contract
- Commercial agent's **state of health**
- Commercial agent's **maintenance obligations** or his family status
- **Principal's advertising**

These factors are relevant to the determination of equitableness and can lead to a reduction or increase in termination compensation: **102**

- **Malicious behaviour** of the commercial agent during the contractual relationship (reduction)
- **Culpable breach of contract** by the commercial agent or his employees (reduction)
- **Insufficient customer visits** by the commercial agent (reduction)
- **Careless and negligent behaviour** of the commercial agent (reduction)
- **Inactivity** or reduced activity of commercial agent or his employees (reduction)
- **Business activity that competes with the principal** by the commercial agent prior to or after termination (reduction)

---

92 OLG Cologne 19 U 169/09.
93 BGH VIII ZR 322/09, DB 2011, 173 (174).
94 OLG Hamm 18 U 148/05.
95 Five years: BGH VIII ZR 17/09, NJW 2011, 3438 and BGH ZR 188/85, NJW-RR 1988, 42 (45); six to eight years possible: BGH VIII ZR 173/04, NJW-RR 2006, 1328.
96 BGH I ZR 142/89, NJW-RR 1991, 1050.
97 BGH I ZR 130/73, WM 1975, 931.
98 With helpful overview and further reference, see Staub/Emde HGB § 89b mn. 162.

- Superior, **unusually high commission** rates or other significantly favourable contract provisions for the commercial agent (reduction)
- **Commercial agent's request for termination** of the contractual relationship (reduction)
- **Pull effect**/attraction of trademark[99] (reduction of up to 30 % in the case of strong trademarks, depending on public recognition and awareness level)

#### c) Comprehensive overall assessment

103 All aspects of equitableness are to be balanced in an overall assessment that either increases or reduces the amount of the commercial agent's compensation. The aspects of equitableness regularly reduce the compensation that stems from the pull effect of the principal's trademarks.[100]

#### d) Point in time

104 Whether specific circumstances constitute considerable factors is to be determined by means of a forecast at the time of termination of the commercial agency agreement. It is unclear whether factors occurring after the termination (e.g. collusion or threat by one party) are to be considered when assessing equitableness. In any case, developments after termination of the commercial agency agreement may help prove or refute the parties' allegations (e.g. development of sales figures, customers buying behaviour, etc.).

#### e) Burden of proof

105 The party asserting either an increase (commercial agent) or a reduction (principal) of the termination compensation due to reasons of equitableness must demonstrate and prove any asserted factors.

## III. Calculation of termination compensation

106 The termination compensation is calculated in two steps: First, the gross adjustment (*Rohausgleich*) is derived from the commission that the commercial agent is forecasted to lose pursuant to § 89b(1) HGB and, second, the result is capped (*Obergrenze*) by taking into account the average of the annual commission or other annual remuneration over the last five years of the commercial agent's activity (§ 89b(2) HGB). The cap pursuant to § 89b(2) HGB is merely intended to limit the amount of the commercial agent's claim for termination compensation. The law stipulates that the cap applies only if it is below the compensation calculated pursuant to the commercial agent's commission losses (§ 89b(1) HGB). However, the parties are free to agree on foregoing the calculation method of § 89b(1) HGB altogether and only depending on the far simpler method of § 89b(2) HGB, which often happens in practice.

---

[99] For strong trademarks in the car industry, the courts have accepted significant deductions of up to 30%. Mitsubishi: 20% (BGH VIII ZR 173/04, NJW-RR 2006, 1328 (1331)); Renault: 10 to 25% (BGH VIII ZR 272/95, NJW 1997, 1503), Fiat/Lancia: 10% (BGH VIII ZR 141/95, NJW 1996, 2298); Peugeot: 15% (OLG Saarbrücken 1 U 924/01-211, NJW-RR 2003, 900). Well-known fashion brands like BOSS or ESCADA also have a pull effect (OLG Munich 7 U 5118/00, NJOZ 2002, 617 (625)). This must also apply to the pharma industry and well-known brands and product names (e.g. ASPIRIN); the toy industry (e.g. LEGO, Playmobil, Ravensburger); the food industry (e.g. Ritter Sport, Kinderschokolade, Nutella) and many other industries, including smaller ones.

[100] BeckOK/Lehmann HGB § 89b mn. 67; MüKoHGB/Ströbl HGB § 89b mn. 131.

## 1. Calculation pursuant to the forecasted commission losses

The legislators did a rather poor job when constructing and revising § 89b HGB, as the wording is clumsily structured and it is not possible for a layperson to derive the calculation method by reading § 89b(1) HGB alone. To ameliorate this situation, the courts have developed calculation methods that give the parties a rough idea of what amount will be due as termination compensation. Even with these methods, it is not possible for the parties to predict what the courts will award, since the calculation according to the forecasted commission losses gives the courts wide discretion, in particular regarding the assessment of equitableness. **107**

The calculation pursuant to § 89b(1) HGB (gross adjustment) follows the following steps: **108**

1. **Basis for calculation**: the commercial agent's assumed commission losses are the starting point for the calculation of the gross adjustment pursuant to § 89b(1) HGB. When assessing the commercial agent's commission losses, the last contractual year indicates what losses he might suffer in the future. Therefore, all commissions or other remuneration he has received for soliciting new customers or expanding business with existing customers in the last contractual year are summed up. Remuneration that the commercial agent has received during the last contractual year for administrative activity as well as warehousing commissions, collection commissions, or extra payments for office equipment are not counted.
2. **Forecast of future commissions**: based on the commercial agent's commissions in the last contractual year, one must estimate the period in which the principal may presumably derive future economic advantages from the customers solicited by the commercial agent. This requires a forecast which – depending on the industrial sector and the contract products – is typically between two to three years. The number of years covered by the forecast is then added up.
3. **Deduction of churn rate**: the termination compensation is intended to compensate the commercial agent's future commission claims in so far as the principal may have substantial advantages from customers solicited by the commercial agent. Since customers tend to leave a supplier after a period of time, a churn rate must be deducted when calculating the principal's substantial advantages. A churn rate of 20 % is common and has been acknowledged by the courts. However, higher and lower churn rates may be claimed by the parties, if verifiable.
4. **Interest discount**: the calculated intermediate total is then discounted for interest as the commercial agent's forecasted commission losses will only be incurred in the future.
5. **No remaining substantial advantages for the principal**: the commercial agent has a claim for termination compensation only and in so far as the principal can profit from substantial advantages from the customers solicited by the commercial agent. Therefore, full or partial deductions must be made in cases where (i) neither the principal nor a potential buyer of the principal's business can use the customer base due to a factory shutdown, (ii) the commercial agent successfully entices customers away from the principal after termination, or (iii) customers migrate to competitors due to the commercial agent's terminated activity.
6. **Equitableness**: Due to reasons of equitableness, the commercial agent's claim for termination compensation is typically reduced, particularly in cases where the commercial agent has breached the contract, was lazy, or the principal's trademarks have a strong pull effect.

### 2. Calculation example

| | | |
|---|---|---|
| 1. | Agent's commissions during the last 12 months: | EUR 400,000 |
| | ./. Deduction for one-time customers 10 % (EUR 40,000): | EUR 360,000 |
| 2. and 3. | forecast of future commissions (three years) taking into account a churn rate of 20 %: | |
| | • 2023: 360,000 ./. 20 % (EUR 72,000) | EUR 288,000 |
| | • 2024: 288,000 ./. 20 % (EUR 57,600) | EUR 230,400 |
| | • 2025: 230,400 ./. 20 % (EUR 46,080) | EUR 184,320 |
| | | EUR 702,720 |
| 4. | ./. Interest of 5 % discounted over three years (EUR 100,225.44): | EUR 602,494.56 |
| 5. | ./. Deduction of 15 % for loss of principal's substantial advantages (EUR 90,374.18): | EUR 512,120.37 |
| 6. | Deduction of 20 % for reasons of equitableness (EUR 102,424.07): | **EUR 409,696.29** |

### 3. Calculation pursuant to the cap

109 Pursuant to § 89b(2) HGB, the commercial agent's claim for termination compensation may amount to no more than the average of the annual commission or other annual remuneration over the last five years of the commercial agent's activity. If the contractual relationship has been shorter than five years, the average during the period of activity applies.

110 The cap is only applicable if the termination compensation calculated based on § 89b(1) HGB exceeds it.[101] The calculation pursuant to § 89b(2) HGB is relatively simple. Other than the calculation of the gross adjustment, it is not subject to equitableness. The cap is simply calculated by determining the average of the commission payments made by the principal to the commercial agent during the last five years (or fewer, if the contractual relationship did not last for five years).

111 When calculating the cap, all remuneration components must be considered. Contrary to § 89b(1) HGB, the calculation also includes the principal's payment to the commercial agent for administrative activity, warehousing commissions, commissions for debt collection or other services, as well as other extra payments to the agent (e.g. allowances for office equipment). The calculation pursuant to § 89b(2) HGB is made based on the principal's gross payments (*Bruttozahlungen*) made to the commercial agent. This means that taxes and T&E expenses (if any) are not deducted. As the cap limits the commercial agent's claim for termination compensation, the burden of proof lies with the principal.

## IV. Exclusion of the agent's claim for termination compensation

112 When drafting or negotiating commercial agency agreements, the parties will from time to time want to exclude the commercial agent's claim for termination compensation. Pursuant to § 89b(4) sentence 1 HGB, the commercial agent's claim for termination compensation is binding and cannot be excluded in advance. Therefore, it is virtually impossible for the principal to exclude the commercial agent's claim for termination

[101] BGH VIII ZR 221/97, NJW 1999, 946 (948).

compensation when concluding the commercial agency agreement. However, the law itself specifies some situations in which the commercial agent does not have a claim for termination compensation. These situations are discussed in the following.

## 1. Termination from the commercial agent

### a) Notice of termination

Pursuant to § 89b(3) no. 1 HGB, no claim for termination compensation shall exist if the commercial agent has terminated the contractual relationship, unless (i) the actions of the principal constituted sufficient grounds therefor, or (ii) the commercial agent cannot be expected to continue his activities due to his age or health. Whether the commercial agent's notice of termination was ordinary or extraordinary is irrelevant. Yet, if he terminates the commercial agency agreement for an important reason, his claim for termination compensation will in most cases be preserved. **113**

### b) Sufficient grounds

If the principal's action constitutes sufficient grounds for the commercial agent to terminate the agency agreement, the latter will still have a claim for termination compensation. This regulation balances the interests of both parties. The commercial agent usually has sufficient grounds to terminate the commercial agency relationship if his right to give notice of termination stems from an important reason. However, 'sufficient grounds' and an 'important reason' pursuant to § 89a HGB are not necessarily congruent. The behaviour of the principal may constitute sufficient grounds for the commercial agent's termination but, at the same time, not be severe enough to constitute an important reason. Yet an illegal or culpable behaviour of the principal is not always necessary to establish sufficient grounds. In any case, any important reason that results from a culpable action of the principal constitutes sufficient grounds. Courts have considered the following to be sufficient: **114**

- restriction on production that potentially endangers the commercial agent's economic existence;[102]
- product diversification by the principal resulting in a conflict of interest for the commercial agent due to the commercial agent's distribution of competing products;[103]
- temporary but illegal non-payment of commissions by the principal;[104]
- direct sales by the principal in violation of the commercial agency agreement.[105]

### c) Agent's health or age

Even if the commercial agent terminated the contract, he does not lose his claim for termination compensation if the continuation of the commercial agency agreement cannot reasonably be expected from him due to his age or sickness. When the commercial agent reaches the age of retirement, it is generally considered unreasonable for him to continue his work.[106] Sickness may constitute unreasonableness if the commercial agent's state of health obstructs his job for a longer period of time and temporary personnel cannot stop **115**

---

[102] BGH I ZR 138/74, NJW 1976, 671.
[103] BGH I ZR 51/85, NJW 1987, 778.
[104] BGH I ZR 185/87, NJW-RR 1989, 862.
[105] BGH VIII ZR 47/92, NJW-RR 1993, 678.
[106] Hopt/Hopt HGB § 89b mn. 61.

such obstructions.[107] In such cases, the commercial agent may terminate the commercial agency relationship without losing his claim for termination compensation.

## 2. Legitimate notice of termination by the principal

116 Pursuant to § 89b(3) no. 2 HGB, the commercial agent does not have a claim to termination compensation if the principal has terminated the contractual relationship for an important reason based on the culpable conduct of the commercial agent. Whether the commercial agent's culpable conduct results in an extraordinary or ordinary termination is irrelevant. § 89b(3) no. 2 HGB also applies in cases in which the principal does not extend a consecutive or 'chain' agreement even though this was originally intended.

117 The important reason under § 89b(3) no. 2 HGB must be based on the culpable conduct of the commercial agent. Therefore, an effective notice of termination for an important reason does not necessarily result in the commercial agent's loss of his claim for termination compensation. The requirements of § 89b(3) no. 2 HGB are thus narrower than those in § 89a HGB, as the latter do not require culpable behaviour of the commercial agent in all cases. Courts have acknowledged the following important reasons as sufficient within the meaning of § 89b(3) no. 2 HGB: insult of the principal; document or signature fraud; the commercial agent's competitive action in violation of the agency agreement; the commercial agent's unjustified notice of termination followed by a notice of termination by the principal. Insufficient is a decrease in turnover or the commercial agent's insolvency.[108]

## 3. Shift of principal's obligation to a third party

118 Pursuant to § 89b(3) no. 3 HGB, the commercial agent shall not have a claim to termination compensation if an agreement between the principal and the commercial agent stipulates that a third party will assume the rights and obligations of the commercial agent. Such an agreement, however, cannot be made prior to the termination of the contractual relationship. This provision applies in cases where the commercial agent sells his agency to a third person (another agent). § 89b(3) no. 3 HGB is intended to avoid a situation in which the commercial agent receives two overlapping payments: one from the principal for compensation and another one from the buyer of his agency. It only has minor practical significance.

## 4. Exclusion for agencies based outside of Europe

### a) Activity outside Europe

119 Pursuant to § 92c(1) HGB, the parties may exclude the commercial agent's claim for termination compensation in cases where the commercial agent is not contractually obliged to carry out his activities for the principal in the European Union or other contracting states of the European Economic Area Agreement. Such exclusion may be agreed prior to the termination of the commercial agency agreement as well as in standard terms and conditions.[109] Relevant is only the place where the commercial agent must carry out his activities. For example, if the commercial agent must carry out his business in China, Switzerland or England, the parties may – irrespective of their nationalities or the seat of their companies – exclude the commercial agent's claim for termination compensation.

---

[107] Cf. BGH I ZR 150/91, NJW-RR 1993, 996.
[108] With helpful overview Staub/Emde HGB § 89b mn. 232.
[109] OLG Munich 23 U 4416/01, NJW-RR 2003, 471 (472).

The claim for termination compensation may even be excluded if the law of the state where the commercial agent is contractually obliged to carry out his activities provides for termination compensation or a similar compensation claim.[110]

#### b) Determining the place

120 The main contractual obligation of the commercial agent, as defined in the commercial agreement, determines the place where he must carry out his activities. However, such obligations usually consist of soliciting and/or the conclusion of purchase contracts. If the parties have defined a contractual territory or district, the commercial agent must also carry out his main activity in this territory. Minor or secondary obligations that are fulfilled in the territory of the European Union or other contracting states of the European Economic Area Agreement will not prevent the applicability of § 92c(1) HGB.[111]

#### c) Express or implied amendment

121 Subsequent changes to the commercial agency agreement may render § 92c(1) HGB inapplicable from the point in time when the change has been agreed or occurs. This is the case where the parties – by explicit or implicit behaviour – expand the contractual territory and the 'new' territory includes a state within the European Union or another contracting state of the European Economic Area Agreement.

### 5. Choice of law

#### a) Free choice of law

122 A principal may try to exclude the commercial agent's claim for termination compensation by derogating from these provisions in German law and instead choosing the law of a jurisdiction that does not provide for termination compensation. Despite the principle that the parties to a contract are generally free to choose the national law applicable to their contract (Article 3(1) Rome I Regulation), such freedom is severely limited when it comes to excluding the commercial agent's claim for termination compensation. Article 3(3) Rome I Regulation limits the parties' free choice of law, in particular for domestic cases (where two parties based in Germany conclude a commercial agency agreement).

#### b) Constraints under the Rome I Regulation

123 Pursuant to Article 3(3) Rome I Regulation, the parties may not derogate from mandatory law, such as the commercial agent's claim for termination compensation, if all other elements relevant to the situation at the time of the choice of law are located in a country other than the country whose law has been chosen. The same applies to mandatory European law if all elements relevant to the situation at the time are in the European Union, Article 3(4) Rome I Regulation. Therefore, if the principal and the commercial agent are both located in Germany, the means for choosing foreign law to govern the commercial agent's claim for termination compensation are limited. However, Article 3 Rome I Regulation allows the parties to derogate from provisions of mandatory law (including the commercial agent's claim for termination compensation) in cases where some elements relevant to the situation are located in a state whose law does not provide for termination compensation or a similar compensation claim. With questionable reasons, the European

[110] OLG Munich 7 U 5609/01, NJW-RR 2003, 201.
[111] OLG Munich 23 U 4416/01, NJW-RR 2003, 471 (472).

Court of Justice – with its *Ingmar* decision in 2000 – extended the application of mandatory agency law to situations in which a connection to a third country was actually given and the law of such country was chosen by the parties.

### c) *Ingmar* decision

124 In this case, the commercial agent, Ingmar GB Ltd, a company established in the United Kingdom (at the time of the contract conclusion, still a part of the European Union), claimed payment of termination compensation by the principal, Eaton Leonard Technologies Inc., a company with seat in California. When concluding the commercial agency agreement in 1989, the parties chose the law of the State of California, which does not regulate claims of the commercial agent for termination compensation. In contrast, UK law provides such a claim based on Articles 17 to 19 of the Council Directive 86/653/EEC of 18 December 1986 on the coordination of the laws of the Member States relating to self-employed commercial agents. Despite the derogation from provisions of UK law, the European Court of Justice still applied mandatory EU law in this case and stated:

> It must therefore be held that it is essential for the Community legal order that a principal established in a non-member country, whose commercial agent carries on his activity within the Community, cannot evade those provisions by the simple expedient of a choice-of-law clause. The purpose served by the provisions in question requires that they be applied where the situation is closely connected with the Community, in particular where the commercial agent carries on his activity in the territory of a Member State, irrespective of the law by which the parties intended the contract to be governed.
> In the light of those considerations, the answer to the question must be that Articles 17 and 18 of the Directive […] must be applied where the commercial agent carried on his activity in a Member State although the principal is established in a non-member country and a clause of the contract stipulates that the contract is to be governed by the law of that country.[112]

125 It is clear from this decision that the European Court of Justice regards Articles 17 to 19 of the Council Directive 86/653/EEC as overriding mandatory provisions within the meaning of Article 9(1) of the Rome I Regulation (previously the Rome Convention from 1980). This is questionable, as the commercial agent's claim for termination compensation can hardly be considered a provision that is regarded by a country as crucial for safeguarding its public interests, such as its political, social, or economic organisation, justifying its application to any situation falling within their scope, irrespective of the law chosen by the parties. Regardless of what the correct interpretation is, the decision from the European Court of Justice is binding and presents a protective interpretation in favour of commercial agents, which in turn should be considered when drafting commercial agency agreements. The European Court of Justice has since confirmed this legal opinion in *Unamar*.[113]

## 6. Contractual exclusion after termination

126 Pursuant to § 89b(4) sentence 1 HGB, the commercial agent's claim for termination compensation may not be excluded in advance, even if it was agreed upon only a few days before the termination of the commercial agency agreement comes into effect.[114] However, this does not prevent the parties from excluding the commercial agent's claim for termination compensation after the commercial agency agreement has been terminated.

---

[112] ECJ 9.11.2000 case C-381/98, ECLI:EU:C:2000:605 para. 25–26 – *Igmar GB v Eaton Leonard Technologies Ltd.*

[113] Ebenroth/Boujong/Joost/Strohn/Kindler HGB § 92c mn. 16.

[114] BGH VII ZR 141/68, NJW 1971, 465; Mann, ZVertriebsR 2017, 25 (26).

This also includes an exclusion of such claim by agreement at the time of termination of the commercial agency agreement.[115]

### 7. Upfront payment

#### a) Definition and conditions

127 One possibility for the principal to ease his payment burden vis-á-vis the commercial agent's claim for termination compensation is to agree with the latter on an upfront payment. An upfront payment is made by the commercial agent to the principal as remuneration for the allocation of the contractual territory when entering into the commercial agency agreement. However, the commercial agent will often only agree to an upfront payment if he does not have to incur any out-of-pocket costs. This requires the following legal construct: First, the parties defer the payment until the commercial agency agreement is effectively terminated and the commercial agent's claim for termination compensation actually arises. Second, the parties agree to set off the principal's claim for the upfront payment against the commercial agent's claim for termination compensation. Third, the parties agree that (i) where the principal's claim for an upfront payment exceeds the commercial agent's claim for termination compensation or (ii) no such claim arises, the principal will waive his claim for the upfront payment in so far as it is covered by the termination compensation.[116]

#### b) Remaining legal uncertainty

128 Even if the parties agree on an upfront payment as described, disputes over termination compensation can still arise. The courts have generally confirmed the possibility to agree on an upfront payment.[117] The Federal Court of Justice has, however, determined that the amount of an upfront payment must be appropriate.[118] The question of how to determine appropriateness is in dispute, and the courts have offered differing solutions. The Higher Regional Court of Düsseldorf has determined that it is generally possible to agree on an upfront payment amounting to an average annual commission.[119] In contrast, the Higher Regional Court of Celle has considered such an agreement to be void, since in such a case, the commercial agent would have to work an entire year without effectively having income.[120] Therefore, it is not possible to make a general statement about what is considered appropriate. Instead, the specific circumstances of each individual case are decisive. The parties to a contract must assess whether, in their individual case, the commercial agent's consideration is appropriate relative to the agreed upon upfront payment. The question of appropriateness will largely depend on the commercial agent's consideration for his upfront payment. An agreement to an upfront payment is invalid in cases where no customer base is provided to the commercial agent. In the following cases, the risk of an upfront payment agreement being found invalid may be lowered (but not excluded):

- a long-term and/or fixed-term contract;[121]
- the district was well-run before its disposal to the commercial agent;

---

115 BGH VIII ZR 261/95, NJW 1996, 2867 (2868); BGH VII ZR 102/66, NJW 1969, 504; Mann, ZVertriebsR 2017, 25 (27).
116 For a discussion on how to design such a construct, see Mann, ZVertriebsR 2017, 25 (28).
117 Even in standard terms and conditions, cf. BGH VIII ZR 23/92, NJW-RR 1993, 375.
118 BGH I ZR 14/81, NJW 1983, 1727 (1728).
119 OLG Düsseldorf 16 U 86/99.
120 OLG Celle 11 U 90/01; OLG Celle 11 U 61/00.
121 OLG Düsseldorf 16 U 66/02; Westphal, MDR 2005, 421 (423).

- agreement pursuant to which the customers already acquired at the time of the agreement will be considered new customers.[122]

#### c) Execution of an upfront payment

129 There are different ways to execute an upfront payment. If the parties have not agreed to set off the upfront payment against the future claim for termination compensation, the commercial agent either has to make a full payment or pay by instalment. Alternatively, the parties may defer the upfront payment until the commercial agent's claim for termination compensation arises. Once this happens, the principal may offset his claim for an upfront payment against the commercial agent's claim for termination compensation.[123]

## V. Preclusive period and limitation

### 1. Preclusive period

130 To avoid preclusion of his claim, the commercial agent must assert the claim for termination compensation within one year from the termination of the agency agreement (§ 89b(4) sentence 2 HGB). § 89b(4) sentence 2 HGB neither requires a specific form[124] nor requires that the commercial agent file a lawsuit within one year after termination. The receipt of the commercial agent's declaration by the principal is decisive for determining compliance with the deadline. If the commercial agent decides to claim for termination compensation by filing a suit, the one-year period is preserved if the statement of claim is (i) submitted to the court before the one-year period has expired and (ii) the court quickly forwards the statement of claim to the principal.[125]

### 2. Limitation

131 Once the commercial agent has, in due time, asserted his claim for termination compensation, such claim is subject to the regular limitation period of three years (§ 195 BGB). This limitation period starts at the end of the calendar year in which the commercial agent's claim for termination compensation arose and he has knowledge (or would have obtained such knowledge had he not shown gross negligence) of such claim. Of practical importance is what happens in cases where the commercial agency agreement terminates with effect as of 31 December (at midnight). In such cases, the commercial agent's claim for termination compensation lapses effectively after four years and not three years as his claim for termination compensation does not arise before 1 January of the following year. Pursuant to § 89b(1) sentence 1 HGB, the commercial agent's claim arises *after expiration* of the contractual relationship and not during the termination. The statutory limitation period (not the preclusive period) with regard to the commercial agent's claim for termination compensation may be reduced by mutual agreement.[126]

---

[122] OLG Munich 7 U 3915/96, NJW-RR 1997, 986.
[123] For a discussion of upfront payments in tax and accounting, Staub/Emde HGB § 89b mn. 366.
[124] BGH VII ZR 125/68, NJW 1970, 1002 (1003).
[125] See § 167 ZPO; BGH VII ZR 125/68 NJW 1970, 1002 (1003), (1004).
[126] BGH I ZR 175/88, NJW-RR 1991, 35 (36).

## VI. Accounting

Pursuant to German accounting standards, the principal can make provisions (*Rückstellungen*) regarding the commercial agent's claim for termination compensation only if the commercial agency relationship has been terminated or its termination is imminent.[127] 132

[127] BFH I R 39, 40/70, NJW 1972, 78; for further details, see BeStLex/Hottmann Ausgleichsanspruch (Handelsvertreter) mn. 1–17.

# Chapter 12
# Distributorship agreement

**Bibliography:** Bechtold/Denzel, 'Weiterverkaufs- und Verwendungsbeschränkungen in Vertikalverträgen', WuW 2008, 1272; Emde, 'Handelsvertreterrecht – Relevante Vorschriften bei nationalen und internationalen Verträgen', MDR 2002, 190; Hopt (ed.), Handelsgesetzbuch: HGB, 42nd edn, Munich 2023; Immenga/Mestmäcker (eds), EU-Wettbewerbsrecht, 6th edn, Munich 2019; Kocher, 'Analoge Anwendung des Handelsvertreterrechts auf Vertragshändler in Europa', RIW 2003, 512; Martinek/Semler/Flohr (eds), Vertriebsrecht, 4th edn, Munich 2016; Niebling, 'Die aktuelle Entwicklung im Vertriebsrecht', WRP 2010, 81; Liebscher/Flohr/Petsche (eds), Handbuch der EU-Gruppenfreistellungsverordnungen, 3rd edn, Munich 2023; Schultze et al., Der Vertragshändlervertrag, 5th edn, Munich 2016; T. Mäger/S. Mäger, Europäisches Kartellrecht, 2nd edn, Munich 2011; Wiedemann, Kartellrecht, 4th edn, Munich 2020.

## A. Introduction

### I. Significance

1 The distributor is an important element for international trade relations and plays a key role in the supply chain. Whereas the commercial agent acts on behalf of and for the account of the principal, the distributor buys and resells in his own name and for his own account. He – and not the principal – bears the entrepreneurial risk for his activities and is therefore well-advised to precisely calculate such risks, in particular those regarding the depreciation of his assets. However, a distributor also has significant opportunities, as he is in a position to determine the reselling price and may therefore earn significantly more than what a commercial agent can expect from his commission payments.

### II. Definition

2 The law of distributorship is not codified. The distributor is a creation of practical necessity and has been developed by practice and by the courts. The Federal Court of Justice has defined a distributor relationship as a framework contract *sui generis* concluded for a certain period in accordance with which one of the parties is obliged to distribute products of the other party in his own name and for his own account, and whereby the retailer (distributor) is integrated into the sales organisation of the manufacturer (supplier or principal).[1] Modern trade has given rise to different types of distributor relationships. Although these relationships can differ from case to case, certain special types have emerged. The following types should be noted:

- **Specialist dealers**: specialist dealers (*Fachhändler*) are common for electronic, cosmetic, or fashion retailers. Strong trademarks (e.g. exclusive watches) are often distributed by specialist dealers in selective distribution systems.

[1] BGH VIII ZR 255/68, NJW 1971, 29 (30).

- **Exclusive distributorships**: exclusive distributorship agreements (*Alleinvertriebsverträge*) are usually found in wholesale trade.
- **Retailers in the automotive sector**.

Distributor relationships must be distinguished from **mere supply relationships** in which the buyer is not – or only slightly – integrated into the suppliers' distribution or sales system. **Sub- and OEM agreements** also contain elements of the purchase and resale of products. However, unlike distributorship agreements, these types of agreements stipulate that the OEM processes the purchased product and resells a different reconstructed product. In these cases, the originally delivered product has been completely overhauled and is therefore no longer identifiable for the end customer. Moreover, distributor relationships also need to be distinguished from **franchise agreements**. In franchise relationships the franchisor (*Franchisegeber*) not only sells products to the franchisee (*Franchisenehmer*), he also renders services to him for which he, the franchisee, has to remunerate the franchisor in return (→ Ch. 14 mn. 1 et seqq.). 3

It is important to know that the mere labelling of an agreement is irrelevant. Where the parties label their contract a distributorship agreement but stipulate in the agreement that the 'distributor' shall not have the right to buy and resell products in his own name and for his own account, but may instead solicit purchase contracts for the principal only, the parties have in fact concluded a commercial agency agreement and not a distributorship agreement. 4

## III. Legal framework

Neither the HGB nor any other law provide a self-contained set of rules that specifically and exclusively describe and govern distributor relationships. Distributorship agreements are framework contracts under which individual purchase agreements are concluded. These two levels must be distinguished from each other. Whereas the distributorship agreement is a mixed contract *sui generis*, the individual purchase agreements concluded thereunder are governed by sales law. The framework contract or individual provisions therein may be subject to provisions of commercial agency law if specific conditions are met. However, if this is the case, commercial agency law is not applicable in its entirety but instead with regard to specific legal issues such as, for instance, the notice of termination, the distributor's claim for termination compensation, or the parties' obligations.[2] In addition to the said legal provisions, the law on standard terms and conditions as well as certain rules of German and European competition law might apply additionally in distributor relationships. This makes the distributorship law complex and therefore often confusing for non-experts. 5

# B. Formation

There are no form requirements to the conclusion of a distributorship agreement. The parties may therefore establish a contractual relationship by implied behaviour, orally, in written form, or in any other form. The parties are well-advised to conclude a written distributorship agreement and to precisely define the obligations of the parties for reasons 6

[2] BGH II ZR 73/57, NJW 1959, 144 (145).

of clarity and evidence. This applies in particular to the main content such as the contract products, territory, terms of delivery, prices and discounts, sales volume targets, or any minimum purchase requirements. Where the parties have failed to determine their obligations precisely, such lack of clarity is eliminated through interpretation, which in turn gives rise to the threat of dispute and litigation.

## C. Content

7 Although no written or explicit agreement is necessary to establish a distributor relationship between the principal and the distributor, it is advisable for the parties to precisely define and stipulate the parties' obligations and the (core) content of the distributor relationship. This applies in particular to the contractual territory, contract products (including order process and exclusivity) and prices (and/or the distributor's discounts).

### I. Territory

8 The principal commonly appoints the distributor for a well-defined contractual territory (e.g. defined by postcodes, state, or country). Where the principal appoints the distributor for a specific contractual territory, this does not mean that the principal may not appoint other distributors for the same territory. This is only the case if the principal grants exclusivity to the distributor. A change to the contractual territory after the conclusion of the distributorship agreement is only possible by mutual agreement of both parties. In particular, the principal cannot change the content of the distributorship agreement (the contractual territory) by partial notice of termination. A one-sided contractual right to alter the territory by the principal is only valid if agreed upon individually. In standard terms, such a clause is valid only if the parties (i) have defined justified reasons for the contractual change and (ii) the interests of the distributor are adequately taken into consideration and protected.[3]

### II. Contract products

9 For reasons of clarity, the parties are well-advised to define the contract products precisely. This is usually contained in an annex to the distributorship agreement. The parties commonly list the product names including technical terms, if any, as well as the sales price for each product. Moreover, the parties need to make sure that they define a procedure for how to subsequently insert (new) products into the agreement. Practice has shown that distributorship agreements are normally concluded for a longer period of time. However, short product life cycles, new products, or product modifications often give rise to the need to amend the product list. This can be managed in different ways:

- The parties may agree on a global distribution clause, meaning that the distributor is obliged to distribute all current and future products of the principal. However, the principal should carefully consider whether such a global distribution clause actually reflects his interests, as he may not foresee all product changes, developments, and

[3] BGH VIII ZR 125/98, NJW 2000, 515 (516); BGH VIII ZR 195/82, NJW 1984, 1182.

inventions in his business and may therefore want to segment the distribution of his products at a later date.

- The parties may, by individually agreed upon contracts, decide that the principal has the right to unilaterally change or amend the contract products distributed by the distributor. In standard terms, however, the parties must observe § 308 no. 4 BGB. Pursuant to § 308 no. 4 BGB, an agreement according to which the user (here, the principal) has the right to modify the promised performance or deviate from it is void. The modification may only be regarded as valid where the deviation or modification can reasonably be expected of the other party (the distributor). Whether a reservation clause in standard terms is valid depends on whether the interests of both parties are considered and balanced.
- The principal may not unilaterally change the distributorship agreement by partially terminating the agreement and thereby deleting products or product groups from it.

## III. Order process

To avoid dispute, the principal is well-advised to not agree on a strict delivery obligation (*Belieferungspflicht*) but instead to reserve the right to accept or reject the distributor's individual purchase orders. 10

If the production of the contract products is no longer profitable, the principal is generally free to cease production. The principal is not obliged to produce or distribute products merely out of consideration for the distributor.[4] If the principal arbitrarily reduces or stops his production without objective justification, the distributor could have a claim for continued delivery. 11

## IV. Exclusivity

The principal often grants an exclusive distribution right to the distributor. In such a case, the parties should precisely define what an exclusive distribution right means, as the term exclusivity may have different meanings: 12

- The **principal is obliged to not supply** other distributors or intermediaries within the territory.
- The **principal is obliged to not carry out direct sales** to end customers within the contractual territory.
- The **distributor is obliged** to **cover its entire demand** for contract products by buying them from the principal alone, which is called an exclusive purchasing obligation (*Alleinbezugspflicht*).
- The **principal is obliged** to take measures to **protect the distributor** from competition within the contractual territory.

If the parties fail to precisely define what exclusivity means in the context of their contract, one must interpret the true intention of the parties when using the term. The Federal Court of Justice has determined that '*exclusive distribution right*', in the absence of a more detailed definition, means that during the term of the distributorship agreement, only the distributor is supplied with the contract products by the principal. The principal therefore cannot sell the contract products to third parties within the contractual territo- 13

[4] BGH II ZR 189/57, BB 1959, 864.

ry. At the same time, the principal generally has the duty to not actively carry out direct sales within the contractual territory.[5]

## V. Distributor's obligations

14 The rights and duties of the distributor are not stipulated by law. Commercial agency law may close this gap to a limited extent only. The distributor's main obligations, however, can be derived from the common fiduciary duty and have been further developed by the courts.

### 1. Fiduciary duty

15 The conclusion of a distributorship agreement usually leads to a mutual dependence of the parties. The distributor is often integrated into the sales organisation of the principal and the principal in turn is dependent on the distributor's sales efforts. The distributor may, however, resell the principal's products only if he is sufficiently supplied by the principal. From this mutual dependence stems each party's obligation to cooperate with the other party in a trusting manner and to consider the other party's interests. The more the distributor is integrated into the sales organisation of the principal, the greater the distributor's obligation to protect the principal's interests. Although courts have developed and defined distributor's duties quite precisely, the parties are well-advised to define their respective obligations to avoid costly legal disputes.

### 2. Sales promotion

16 One of the distributor's main obligations is to sustainably ensure the distribution of the contract products by actively promoting them. It is not sufficient to merely wait for opportunities to sell them. A part of the distributor's sales promotion responsibilities is to identify the customer's needs, advertise the contract products in the territory, attend trade fairs, and be available at the principal's stand. In the absence of a deviating contractual agreement, the distributor must bear all costs that are incurred by its sales promotion. Although these obligations of the distributor are acknowledged, the principal should nonetheless insist on a precise definition of the distributor's sales obligations (including a minimum purchase requirement, if intended) and to make reference to the advertising measures and trade fair visits.

### 3. Acting in his own name

17 The distributor is under the duty to act in his own name and for his own account.

### 4. Maintaining the legal form

18 The distributor's general fiduciary duty obliges him to not change his legal form after the conclusion of the distributorship agreement without the principal's consent. Otherwise, the distributor could alter his liability towards the principal, e.g. from unlimited

[5] See BGH VIII ZR 116/67, BB 1970, 99 (100).

liability to limited liability. If the distributor violates this obligation, the principal has the right to terminate the contractual relationship extraordinarily without notice.[6]

### 5. Report and protection of trade secrets

Regarding the protection of trade secrets and the duty to report to the principal, the general rules as described with respect to commercial agency agreements apply (→ Ch. 11 mn. 14). Again, the principal should ensure that these obligations are precisely defined in the distributorship agreement. 19

## VI. Principal's obligations

### 1. Fiduciary obligation

The close contractual relationship and the mutual trust between the parties give rise to the principal's obligation to protect the interests of the distributor. The extent of the principal's consideration depends, in particular, on the degree of the distributor's integration into the principal's sales organisation (distributor's marketing obligations, exclusive or non-exclusive distribution rights, distributor's exclusive purchasing obligations, etc.). 20

### 2. Obligation to to inform

The principal must inform the distributor about supply difficulties, production bottlenecks, modifications of the contract products, changes of retail prices, quality problems, or application errors. The principal's obligation to keep the distributor informed may, in specific cases, even be extended to the pre-contractual negotiation stage. This is the case where certain circumstances are highly important for the distributor's decision to conclude the distributorship agreement (e.g. expiration of licenses).[7] If the principal violates his duty to inform, the distributor might claim compensation, e.g. if the distributor is unable to fulfil the supply obligations that are incumbent upon him vis-à-vis his customers. 21

### 3. Obligation to provide advertising material

The principal must supply the distributor with merchandising material such as catalogues, brochures, advertising material, or service manuals. This obligation is also derived from the general fiduciary duty of the principal. If the parties have failed to agree on the costs, they must be borne by the distributor,[8] unless the parties have agreed that such materials shall remain the principal's property. 22

### 4. Equal treatment

Under certain conditions (especially pursuant to §§ 19 et seqq. GWB), the principal may be under the obligation to treat his distributors equally if he has appointed several competing distributors within a territory. However, the duty to treat distributors equally also restricts the principal's entrepreneurial freedom. This duty is therefore present only 23

---

[6] BGH VIII ZR 214/75, NJW 1978, 416.
[7] OLG Düsseldorf 16 U 14/00; OLGR 2001, 339.
[8] Schultze et al., mn. 238–241.

in very few cases.[9] For example, the principal may validly agree on a preferential position for one of his distributors by agreeing on a fixed delivery commitment exclusively with him.

### 5. Termination compensation

24 Under certain conditions, the principal may have to pay termination compensation to the distributor upon the termination of the distributorship agreement in an analogous application of § 89b HGB (→ Ch. 11 mn. 83 et seqq.).

### 6. Supply

25 The distributor's main obligation is to promote, buy, and resell contract products. However, the distributor can only successfully buy and sell the principal's products when he is accordingly supplied with the desired number of ordered products by the principal. When concluding the distributorship agreement, the parties regularly neglect to negotiate the obligation of the principal to supply products, as both the principal and the distributor usually intend to sell and resell as many products as possible. In practice, however, it may be difficult for the principal to supply the distributor due to a shortage of material, a change in production, or a strike.

#### a) Reduced supply obligation

26 If the parties determine that the principal is free to accept the distributor's purchase orders, there is no duty to supply the distributor. However, the principal may not reject the distributor's orders arbitrarily.[10] Whether the principal's rejection is arbitrary can only be answered on a case-by-case basis. As a rule, an exclusive purchase obligation of the distributor combined with a minimum purchase requirement creates a relatively strict duty of the principal to supply the distributor on a regular basis and to show such distributor preference in relation to other distributors.[11]

#### b) Contract design

27 In any case, the parties should define as precisely as possible all circumstances that might lead to supply difficulties. However, the principal may not entirely exclude his liability for properly supplying the distributor in standard distributorship agreements.

- A clause pursuant to which the principal may withdraw from originally accepted purchase orders is void according to § 307(2) no. 1 BGB.[12]
- The parties may validly agree on a clause stipulating that the principal reserves the right to supply the distributor according to his supply capacity or 'while stocks last'.[13]
- The principal may not exclude his liability for supply delays in standard terms. Delivery in due time is one of the principal's core obligations and may therefore not be excluded in standard terms.[14]

---

9 BGH KZR 2/90, NJW 1992, 1827 (1828 et seqq.); BGH I ZR 115/81, BB 1984, 166.
10 BGH VIII ZR 189/57, NJW 1958, 1138.
11 BGH VIII ZR 86/71, BB 1972, 193.
12 BGH VIII ZR 214/83, NJW 1985, 623.
13 BGH VIII ZR 165/92, NJW 1994, 1060.
14 Schultze et al., mn. 297.

### c) Allocation in case of supply difficulties

In case of supply difficulties, the principal must treat his distributors equally by allocating the remaining products either *pro rata* amongst his distributors or according to the sequence of incoming orders.[15] The principal may (or even must) deviate from the equal treatment of his distributors if there are objective reasons for doing so, e.g. an agreement of minimum purchase requirements with and/or an exclusive purchase obligation to a distributor. **28**

### d) Spare part distribution

The supply of spare parts can give rise to complications in distributor relationships. In particular, one question is whether the distributor has the right to obtain spare parts for the contract products under the distributorship agreement even if the parties did not explicitly regulate this issue. There is no general answer to this question; the answer is subject to interpretation and is largely dependent on the industrial sector and the product type in question. If spare parts are commonly sold via separate distribution channels (e.g. special service repair shops), the distributor has no right to obtain spare parts in the absence of a corresponding contractual agreement, since he can easily do so in the market. Whether the principal has the obligation to deliver spare parts to the distributor is therefore determined by the specific distributorship agreement and is subject to interpretation.[16] **29**

### e) Defective products

Another question is often raised: whether the distributor has a claim against the principal for the supply of spare parts in case the contract product is defective. There is no explicit rule of law stipulating such a supply obligation of the principal. In most cases, however, the principal will be happy to supply spare parts instead of repairing the defective product himself. In cases where the principal refuses to deliver spare parts, the distributor has a claim against the principal for delivery of products free of defect and can demand repair or subsequent delivery from the principal pursuant to §§ 437 no. 1 and 439 BGB. The parties may of course agree otherwise. **30**

### f) Post-contractual supply of spare parts

The principal's obligation to supply products and spare parts to the distributor generally ceases upon termination of the distributorship agreement. There might, however, be a competition law obligation to supply spare parts to the distributor pursuant to Article 102 TFEU in exceptional cases in which, for instance, the principal has a dominant market position with regard to spare parts.[17] Even if a principal has no dominant position on the market for spare parts, it may be obliged by German competition law in §§ 18 et seqq. GWB to further supply the distributor for a certain period of time, if the distributor is dependent in a way that sufficient and reasonable possibilities for switching to third party suppliers do not exist. If the distributor has ordered spare parts and the principal has accepted such purchase orders prior to the termination, the principal is obliged to carry out such accepted orders even after termination of the distributorship agreement (unless the distributorship agreement was terminated for an important reason). **31**

---

[15] OLG Munich 7 U 1805/83, WM 1985, 362.
[16] Cf. LG Cologne 83 O 26/97, NJW-RR 1999, 1285; for details, see Schultze et al., mn. 327–329.
[17] See ECJ 31.5.1979 C-22/78, ECLI:EU:C:1979:138 – *Hugin v Commission*.

## VII. Distributor's remuneration

32 Unlike a commercial agent, the distributor does not receive commission payments from the principal. The distributor's remuneration consists of different components, such as (i) the distributor's right to use the principal's trademarks, (ii) discounts on the product list price, and (iii) reimbursement of expenses or corresponding allowances (the latter is rather rare).

### 1. Right to use trademarks

33 It is common for the principal to partly remunerate the distributor by granting him the right to use his trademark. In such a case, the distributor can benefit from the pull effect that a strong trademark may have, thereby attracting potential customers.

### 2. List-price discount

34 The main remuneration component is the gross margin, the difference between the distributor's purchase price and his resale price to the (end) customer. The distributor is normally granted a discount on the principal's list price. This difference minus the distributor's costs for administration, warehousing, marketing, logistics, and other overhead constitutes the distributor's net income. The distributor may unilaterally influence his net income, as he is generally free to determine the resale price.

### 3. Reimbursement of expenses

35 The principal may grant the distributor allowances for certain services such as marketing, warehousing, or the keeping of a repair shop. If the parties have not agreed on allowances or on reimbursement of expenses such as travel costs, telephone and other communication costs, use and maintenance of vehicles, rents or salaries, the principal is not under the obligation to reimburse these expenses or services.

## VIII. Typical content

36 The parties to a distributorship agreement are well-advised to define the following in their agreement (as minimum content):

- contractual territory
- exclusivity, if any
- products to be distributed by the distributor (minimum purchase requirement, if any) and prices
- payment conditions including due dates
- obligations of the parties, in particular, extent of the distributor's marketing and advertising duties
- retention of title
- warranty and liability, including product liability
- competition
- term and termination
- termination compensation (possibly exclusion or upfront payment)
- return of sample collection

- miscellaneous (confidentiality, severability clause, choice of law, jurisdiction or arbitration clause)

# D. Subsidiary and supplemental agreements

## I. Warehousing agreement

In practice, the principal often requires that the distributor ensure his delivery capacity by maintaining a warehouse of his own. This can be done by keeping a consignment stock warehouse (*Konsignationswarenlager*) or a self-owned warehouse (*Eigenlager*). Whereas the products in a self-owned warehouse are owned by the distributor, a consignment stock is located in the vicinity of, or possibly even on, the distributor's premises. The goods, however, remain the property of the principal until the distributor removes them from the warehouse. Maintaining a consignment stock warehouse frequently involves high costs for the principal, whereas in a self-owned warehouse, the liquidity risk remains with the distributor. A consignment stock warehouse agreement ends automatically once the distributorship agreement is terminated.[18] However, the parties can and should expressly stipulate the term and termination options of the warehousing agreement. **37**

## II. Agreement to maintain a service and repair shop

In specific industrial sectors, such as automotive, electronics, or machine-building industries, the principal has a strong interest in supplying end customers with sufficient repair services. Therefore, the principal often requires the distributor to maintain a service and repair shop, which also includes the obligation to train employee, maintain uniform appearance, and/or use original spare parts exclusively. The principal may require that the distributor only use the principal's original spare parts, as the manufacturing principal usually has – for reasons of safety and quality – a legitimate interest in his products being used for the operation of his equipment only.[19] **38**

However, Article 5(a) Vertical-BER 461/2010 prohibits a manufacturer of motor vehicles from restricting the sales of spare parts for motor vehicles by members of a selective distribution system to independent repairers which use those parts for the repair and maintenance of motor vehicles. Without this prohibition, independent repairers could be fully excluded from using a principal's spare parts, thereby lowering the competitive pressure on the manufacturer to the disadvantage of the consumers. A corresponding agreement between the manufacturer and a supplier of spare parts is void. **39**

It is strongly recommended to explicitly regulate the future of the service and repair agreement upon termination of the distributorship agreement. It makes sense to regulate the distributorship agreement and the service and repair agreement together. The future of the service and repair shop largely depends on how closely both agreements were connected with each other. If the parties fail to regulate the consequences of termination of the distributorship agreement or the service and repair agreement, the letter agreement may be terminated. If it becomes apparent that the distributor relationship was the sole **40**

---

[18] Cf. Martinek/Semler/Habermeier/Flohr VertriebsR-HdB/Manderla § 25 mn. 33.

[19] Article 5(1)(a) and Article 1(1)(f) Commission Regulation (EU) 2022/720 (also the vertical block exemption 2022/720) need to be considered.

basis for the repair shop, the parties may have a claim for cancellation of the service and repair agreement upon the termination of the distributorship agreement pursuant to § 313(1), (3) BGB.

## E. Competition law

41 The principal usually has an interest in coordinating its distributors by assigning them specific territories, sectors, or customer groups. An entrepreneur is generally free to determine and coordinate its distribution channels. Yet, if the principal's coordination of its distribution channels contains restraints of competition, these agreements between the principal and the distributor may be prohibited and therefore void. The exact consequence depends on the severity of the restraints and the market strength of the parties (principal and distributor). Because of this, competition law is briefly discussed below in so far as vertical restraints are concerned. Moreover, particular scenarios referring to the business cooperation between the principal (also referred to as supplier or manufacturer here) and its distributors will be depicted.

### I. No restraint of competition

42 Article 101(1) TFEU stipulates that all agreements that may affect trade between EU Member States and have as their object or effect the prevention, restriction, or distortion of competition within the internal market are prohibited. This covers horizontal competition restraints (referring to agreements between competitors at the same economic level) as well as vertical competition restraints (referring to agreements between companies each of which operates at different levels of the production or distribution chain).[20] Therefore, the relationship between the principal and the distributor is generally governed by Article 101(1) TFEU, as agreements between them may constitute a vertical restraint of competition. Pursuant to Article 101(2) TFEU, an agreement containing a restraint of competition is generally void unless it is exempted according to Article 101(3) TFEU. An exemption may apply when the conditions of a group exemption regulation (block exemption) are fulfilled. If no block exemption (*Gruppenfreistellung*) applies, Article 101(3) TFEU may still lead to an exemption on a case-by-case basis (*Einzelfreistellung*).

43 The effects doctrine (*Auswirkungsprinzip*) ensures that European competition law only applies to restraints of competition within the European market (internal market). Therefore, if the agreement of a German principal with its Chinese distributor concerning its Chinese territory contains restraints of competition, these restraints are governed by European competition law only in so far as the restraints influence the internal European market. For instance, price maintenance agreements is not restrained by European competition law if there is no effect on the internal market. However, if – by agreement between the principal and the distributor – a third country's competitor is prevented from entering the European market, there is an effect on the internal market and European competition law applies.[21]

---

[20] Article 1(1)(a) Commission Regulation (EU) 2022/720.

[21] See Immenga/Mestmäcker/Rehbinder IntWbR mn. 31–32.

## II. Legal consequences

### 1. Invalidity

Any agreement prohibited pursuant to Article 101(1) TFEU shall be automatically void unless it is exempted by one of the BER or exempted on an individual basis pursuant to Article 101(3) TFEU. The invalidity, however, only applies to such provisions of an agreement that either (i) violate Article 101(1) TFEU or (ii) are inseparably linked to such provisions. If a separable agreement remains, whether the remainder of the agreement still constitutes a valid contract is subject to national law. In German law, § 139 BGB stipulates that a legal transaction (i.e. an agreement) is void if only a part of it is invalid, unless it is to be assumed that it would have been undertaken even without the invalid part. § 139 BGB is applicable only if doubts exist about the intention of the parties. If the agreement between the principal and the distributor contains a severability clause or a replacement clause, it is regularly assumed that the parties wanted to adhere to the contract in the event that a separable part of it is void. There is generally no severability for hardcore restrictions.[22] 44

### 2. Fines

A violation of Article 101(1) TFEU (either intentionally or negligently) gives the European Commission the right to impose fines on companies or associations of companies pursuant to Article 23 Council Regulation (EC) No 1/2003.[23] In exercising its power to impose such fines, the European Commission enjoys a wide margin of discretion within the limits set by Council Regulation (EC) No 1/2003. The European Commission has issued guidelines on the method of setting fines (2006/C 210/02) that help apply them in a consistent manner. The Commission takes into consideration both the gravity and the duration (number of years) of the infringement. The basic amount is calculated as a percentage of the value of the sales connected with the infringement and multiplied by the number of years the infringement has been taking place. The basic amount calculated may then be adjusted by the Commission downwards if it finds that there are mitigating circumstances (e.g. negligence, marginal participation, cooperation with investigators, termination of infringement), or upwards in the event of exacerbating circumstances (e.g. re-offending, refusal to cooperate, role of leader). The maximum fine for each firm shall not exceed 10 % of the company's total turnover in the preceding business year.[24] In recent years, the European Commission has imposed individual fines of up to almost EUR 500 million on individual companies or corporate groups for violating Article 101 TFEU. 45

### 3. Prohibition order

Pursuant to Article 7 Council Regulation (EC) No 1/2003, the European Commission may require a company to bring infringements of Article 101 TFEU to an end. For this purpose, it may impose on companies any behavioural or structural remedies (prohibition orders are common), including corresponding interim measures (Article 8). Furthermore, the European Commission may, by decision, render commitments of companies 'binding' to bring infringements of Article 101 TFEU to an end (Article 9). 46

---

[22] Guidelines on Vertical Restraints mn. 7.

[23] The TFEU and European directives use the misleading term 'undertakings' to describe 'companies'. For the sake of clarity, the latter is used in this book.

[24] See Guidelines on the method of setting fines imposed pursuant to Article 23(2)(a) of Regulation No 1/2003 (2006/C 210/02) in particular mn. 19, 27 et seqq. and 32.

### 4. Cartel damages claims

47 In addition to fines, a cartel infringement may also trigger civil law actions if damages are incurred. This might be the case where e.g. competitors have collusively agreed on a cartel and therefore raised the market price of certain goods. Purchasers, indirect purchasers and even competitors might claim compensation, injunctive relief, or restitution in such cases.[25]

## III. Appreciable effect and *De Minimis* Notice

48 Restraints of competition that are not appreciable (*spürbar*) do not fall under Article 101(1) TFEU and are therefore not prohibited. The European Commission Notice on agreements of minor importance which do not appreciably restrict competition (*De Minimis* Notice 2001/C 368/07) defines, with the help of market share thresholds, what is not considered an appreciable restriction of competition (*Bagatellbekanntmachung*) under Article 101 TFEU. This negative definition does not imply that agreements between companies which exceed the thresholds will automatically restrict competition. However, it creates a safe harbour for enterprises below the thresholds (particularly important for small and medium-sized enterprises). For vertical agreements (i.e. agreements between non-competitors), the market share held by each party (i.e. the principal and the distributor) may not exceed 15 % in any of the relevant markets to benefit from the *De Minimis* Notice. However, this does not apply to the hardcore restrictions, as they always have an appreciable effect on competition.[26] These hardcore restrictions include those listed in Article 4 Vertical-BER 2022/720.[27]

## IV. Block exemption regulations

49 Pursuant to Article 101(2) TFEU, any agreement or decision restricting competition within the EU according to Article 101(1) TFEU is void. However, an agreement can be exempted either by a BER or by an individual exemption pursuant to Article 101(3) TFEU. Regarding the relationship between the principal and the distributor, the block exemption regulations (*Gruppenfreistellungsverordnungen*) and, in particular, Commission Regulation No 2022/720 of 10 May 2022 on categories of vertical agreements and concerted practices (the Vertical-BER 2022/720) are important.

### 1. System of block exemptions

50 The Vertical-BER 2022/720 applies to vertical agreements unless the subject matter of such a vertical agreement falls within the scope of any other BER. This means, if another BER more precisely regulates the subject matter of a vertical agreement, such a block exemption applies. Other block exemptions that can possibly apply are the BER on technology transfer agreements (No. 316/2014) and the BER on research and development agreements (No. 2023/1066). The BER on vertical agreements and concerted practices in the motor vehicle sector (No. 461/2010) has expired in so far as the purchase, sale or resale

[25] For details, Wiedemann KartellR-HdB § 50 mn. 35 et seqq.

[26] See ECJ 30.6.1966 case 56-65, ECLI:EU:C:1966:38, *Société Technique Minière (L.T.M.) v Maschinenbau Ulm GmbH (M.B.U).*

[27] See footnote 3 of the De Minimis Notice.

of new motor vehicles is concerned, Article 3 Commission Regulation No. 461/2010. In its place, the Vertical-BER 2022/720 applies to vertical agreements relating to the purchase, sale or resale of new motor vehicles. The Vertical-BER 461/2010, however, is still applicable to agreements of the automotive aftermarket (purchase, sale or resale of spare parts, repair and maintenance services for motor vehicles), if both the conditions of Regulation 461/2010 and Regulation 2022/720 are met.[28]

## 2. Scope of application of Vertical-BER

Article 2(1) Vertical-BER 2022/720 provides a general exemption for vertical restraints: 51
Article 101(1) TFEU shall not apply to any vertical agreement containing vertical restraints. However, Vertical-BER 2022/720 limits the scope of this general exemption in the following ways:

### a) Market share threshold

Pursuant to Article 3(1) Vertical-BER 2022/720, the exemption established in Article 2 52
shall apply if (i) the market share held by the supplier (principal) does not exceed 30 % of the relevant market on which it sells the contract products or services and (ii) the market share held by the buyer (distributor) does not exceed 30 % of the relevant market on which it purchases the contract goods or services either.

### b) Hardcore restrictions

The exemption established in Article 2 Vertical-BER 2022/720 shall not apply to agree- 53
ments containing hardcore restrictions (so-called blacklisted clauses, *schwarze Klauseln*). Such hardcore restrictions are (i) certain agreements regulating the resale price (*Preisbindungsklauseln*), (ii) territory or customer protection (*Gebiets- und Kundenschutz*) in certain cases, (iii) restriction of active or passive sales in certain cases, (iv) restriction of cross-supplies (*Querlieferungsverbot*) between distributors within a selective distribution system, (v) the prevention of the effective use of the internet by the buyer or its customers to sell the contract goods or services, and (vi) certain spare part distribution restrictions. If there are one or more hardcore restrictions, the benefit of the Vertical-BER 2022/720 is inapplicable for the entire vertical agreement. A severability clause in an agreement with hardcore restriction is invalid.[29]

### c) Excluded restrictions

Article 5 Vertical-BER 2022/720 lists non-compete obligations (including purchase ob- 54
ligations) that are not covered by the general exemption of Article 2 (so-called grey listed clauses, *graue Klauseln*). If a vertical agreement between the principal and the distributor violates Article 5 Vertical-BER 2022/720, the benefit of the BER is lost only in relation to the part of the vertical agreement which does not comply with the conditions set out in Article 5. The rule of severability therefore applies in these cases.[30]

### d) Withdrawal and inapplicability

The presumption of legality conferred by the Vertical-BER 2022/720 can be withdrawn 55
by the European Commission. The conditions of Article 101(3) TFEU may, for example,

---

[28] See Regulation No. 2023/822 that extends the application of Regulation No. 416/2010 until 31 May 2028.
[29] Guidelines on Vertical Restraints mn. 7.
[30] Guidelines on Vertical Restraints mn. 246.

not be fulfilled if access to the relevant market or competition therein is significantly restricted by the cumulative effect of parallel networks of similar vertical agreements practiced by competing suppliers or buyers. This is sometimes the case when suppliers exercise purely selective distribution.[31] Where parallel networks of similar vertical restraints cover more than 50 % of a relevant market, the European Commission shall have the right to declare that the Vertical-BER 2022/720 does not apply to vertical agreements containing specific restraints relating to that market.

#### e) Vertical agreements outside the scope

56 If the market share threshold is exceeded or the Vertical-BER 2022/720 does not apply for any other reason, a restraint of competition may be exempted only on a case-by-case basis pursuant to Article 101(3) TFEU.

## V. Examples

57 The following situations are of practical relevance in contractual relationships between a principal and its distributors (intermediaries).

### 1. Exclusive purchase obligation

58 An exclusive purchase obligation (*Alleinbezugsverpflichtung*) is an obligation of the distributor to meet its demand for a specific product, product group, or service for a certain period of time by purchasing exclusively from the manufacturer (principal). It is related to single branding. Such an exclusive purchase obligation falls under the non-compete obligation (*Wettbewerbsverbot*) of Article 1(1)(f) Vertical-BER 2022/720. An exclusive purchase obligation impedes market access of competitors and could therefore be problematic from a competition law perspective. An exclusive purchase obligation that obliges the distributor to purchase more than 80 % of its overall volume from the principal is permissible for a duration of five years only (Article 5(1)(a) Vertical-BER 2022/720). A purchase obligation that obliges the distributor to purchase from the principal 80 % or less of its overall volume is permissible irrespective of the duration.

### 2. Exclusive distribution right

59 An exclusive distribution right (*Alleinvertriebsrecht*) is given where the supplier (principal) agrees to appoint only one distributor for resale in a particular territory. At the same time, the distributor is usually limited in its *active* selling into other (also exclusively allocated) territories. Exclusive distribution is permitted when neither the supplier's nor the buyer's market share exceeds 30 %, even if combined with other non-hardcore vertical restraints, such as e.g. a non-compete obligation limited to five years, quantity forcing, or exclusive purchasing.[32] Pursuant to Article 4(a)(i) Vertical-BER 2022/720, the distributor's restrictions of active sales may be exempted if the principal reserves the excluded territory or customer group for himself or assigns it exclusively to a maximum of five other exclusive distributors. The principal must therefore be aware that the exclusivity to one distributor may affect agreements with other distributors and vice versa. The BER remains even if the principal – in addition to the exclusive distributor – reserves the right

[31] Guidelines on Vertical Restraints mn. 260.
[32] Guidelines on Vertical Restraints mn. 120.

to carry out direct sales in the territory. *Passive* sales (i.e. customers approach the distributor on their own initiative) including online sales may not be restrained.[33]

### 3. Resale price maintenance

Whereas retail prices may not be subject to arrangements, this prohibition does not **60**
apply to a cap of the distributor's maximum resale price, as such a cap is favourable for the customers. This, however, is true only if the maximum price maintenance agreement is not the consequence of pressure by the principal and is therefore effectively a fixed price.

### 4. Non-compete for the distributor

Pursuant to Article 5(1)(a) Vertical-BER 2022/720, any direct or indirect non-compete **61**
obligation of the distributor may only be exempted for a maximum duration of five years. Such non-compete obligation includes exclusive purchase obligations, buyer's purchase commitments (exceeding 80 %), obligations causing the buyer not to manufacture, sell, or resell products or services that compete with the contract products or services. This principle also applies to post-contractual non-compete obligations. An indefinite term of the contract or an evergreen clause exceeds the period of five years stipulated pursuant to Article 5(1)(a) Vertical-BER 2022/720. However, the parties may well conclude a non-compete obligation of up to five years with the parties being obliged to renegotiate the agreement thereafter. The party under the non-compete obligation must have the opportunity to decide whether it wants to extend the agreement. A mere right to give notice of termination is not sufficient, as in such a case an active behaviour of the party would be necessary to exit the contract.

### 5. Non-compete for the principal

A non-compete obligation at the expense of the principal (manufacturer) is not restrict- **62**
ed by the Vertical-BER 2022/720. It is exempted pursuant to Article 2(1) Vertical-BER 2022/720 (with the exception of Article 4(f)).

### 6. Online distribution

A distributor is generally free to advertise and sell its products online. A contractual **63**
prohibition to sell products online is forbidden, as the European Commission considers online distribution to be passive sales (running of homepage).[34] A provision stating that not more than 40 % of the distributor's turnover may be attained by online sales is also not permitted. However, restrictions on a distributor's online sale activities may be exempted, if the restrictions in place do not prevent the *effective* use of the internet by the distributor for selling the products.[35] A dual pricing scheme (i.e. an agreement that the distributor shall pay a higher price for products intended to be resold by the distributor online than

---

[33] Cf. Guidelines on Vertical Restraints mn. 122, which also applies to online sales. For the very limited exceptions (new product introduction, ban on sale of dangerous substances to certain customers for reasons of safety or health), see mn. 180.

[34] Guidelines on Vertical Restraints mn. 203, 222, 229, 240. Online sales are considered active sales only when online advertising is aimed exclusively at a certain territory or a certain customer group (territory-based banners), e.g. paying a search engine or online advertisement provider to have advertisements displayed specifically to users in a particular territory (mn. 214).

[35] See Article 4(e) Vertical-BER regulation 2022/720.

for products intended to be resold offline) can be exempted, subject to its effect.[36] The principal may also require that the distributor sells a certain amount of products (in value or volume) offline to ensure an efficient operation of its shops (physical points of sales) without limiting the online sales of the distributor.[37] Moreover, the principal may require that its distributor fulfils certain quality standards for an online shop or for advertising and promotion in general.[38] He may also require that his distributors keep one or more offline retail stores. Consequently, the principal is not obliged to sell his products to mere online dealers, unless he has relative market power or a dominant position. Time restrictions on the distributor for selling the products online are generally not permissible either. Only in cases where a distributor is the first to sell a new brand or the first to sell an existing brand in a new market can a temporary ban on online sales for up to two years be imposed with regard to other distributors. This is intended to help the distributor redeem its investment.

## 7. Resale price maintenance

64 Resale price maintenance agreements, i.e. agreements which directly or indirectly fix distributor's selling price or selling price range, are prohibited hardcore restrictions pursuant to Article 4(a) Vertical-BER 2022/720 and may be exempted only under extremely rare circumstances (efficiency defence argument) and only pursuant to Article 101(3) TFEU.[39] The practice of recommending a resale price to a reseller (distributor) or requiring the distributor to respect a maximum resale price is permitted if the market share of each of the parties to the agreement (principal and distributor) does not exceed the 30 % threshold. This is true only in cases where the recommended resale price does not amount to a minimum or fixed sale price because of pressure from or incentives offered by either of the parties.[40]

## 8. Restrictions on use

65 Restrictions on use are requirements by the principal on the use of the delivered products. Two scenarios are conceivable: (i) A prohibition on the distributor from processing the purchased products (*Weiterverarbeitungsverbot*) and (ii) an obligation of the distributor to process the purchased products (*Weiterverarbeitungsgebot*). A prohibition from processing the purchased product is a mere prohibition of usage between parties on different levels of the production or distribution chain and therefore exempted pursuant to Article 2(1) Vertical-BER 2022/720. In particular, a prohibition from processing is not a hardcore restriction, as it leaves the 'reselling act' of the distributor – regulated by Article 4(a) Vertical-BER 2022/720 – untouched. Whether an obligation to process the purchased product is permissible is still unclear. It is possible, however, that such an agreement can be considered a hardcore restriction pursuant to Article 4(a) Vertical-BER 2022/720, as such an obligation to process is directly connected with the distributor's right to resell the purchased product (no right to resell if not processed).[41]

[36] Guidelines on Vertical Restraints mn. 209.
[37] Guidelines on Vertical Restraints mn. 208(e).
[38] Guidelines on Vertical Restraints mn. 235.
[39] Guidelines on Vertical Restraints mn. 185, 197, 201.
[40] Article 4(a) Vertical-BER 2022/720; Guidelines on Vertical Restraints mn. 188. For the assessment of maximum or recommended prices above the market share threshold of 30 %, see mn. 198–201.
[41] Cf. Bechtold/Denzel, WuW 2008, 1272 (1280).

## 9. Selective distribution

In selective distribution systems, (i) the supplier (principal) undertakes to sell the contract products or services, either directly or indirectly, only to distributors selected on the basis of specified criteria and (ii) these distributors undertake not to sell such goods or services to unauthorised distributors within the territory reserved by the supplier to operate that system (Article 1(1)(g) Vertical-BER 2022/720). Brand-name products such as cars, cosmetics, jewellery, or electronics are commonly distributed through specialist dealers in selective distribution systems. A distinction must be made between purely **qualitative** and **quantitative** selective distribution. Purely **qualitative** selective distribution selects dealers only based on objective criteria, for example, training of sales personnel, the service provided at the point of sale, a certain range of the products being sold, appropriate shop premises, or a specific way of presenting the products at the point of sale. Purely **qualitative** selective distribution is generally considered to fall outside the scope of Article 101(1) TFEU for pro-competitive effects outweighing anti-competitive effects, provided that three conditions are satisfied: (i) The nature of the product in question must necessitate a selective distribution system, for example, to preserve its quality and ensure its proper use. (ii) Resellers must be chosen on the basis of objective criteria of a qualitative nature that are defined uniformly for all potential resellers and are not applied in a discriminatory manner. (iii) The criteria may not exceed what is necessary to ensure that the product is correctly sold and used.[42] Therefore, if these criteria are met, it is – in the absence of another restraint of competition – not necessary to check whether the specific distribution system is exempted from Article 101(1) TFEU. Quantitative selective distribution systems and qualitative distribution systems that do not fulfil the conditions defined by the European Court of Justice (*qualifizierte Fachhandelsbindung*) are a restraint of competition pursuant to Article 101(1) TFEU and, consequently, are admissible only when exempted by Vertical-BER 2022/720. Generally, these selective distribution systems are exempted by Vertical-BER 2022/720 as long as the respective market shares of the supplier and the buyer do not exceed 30 %. This is true even if selective distribution is combined with other non-hardcore vertical restraints, such as non-compete obligations. 66

- Pursuant to Article 4(c)(iii) Vertical-BER 2022/720, the restriction of active or passive sales to end users by members of a selective distribution system operating at the retail level is a hardcore restriction and therefore not permitted. The standard in selective distribution systems is thus stricter than it generally is in common distribution relationships in which the right of active sales may be exclusively assigned to one distributor. Yet, it is possible to prohibit wholesale dealers from supplying directly to end customers (*Sprunglieferungsverbot*).[43] The supplier may also reserve the right to supply end customers in addition to the authorised dealers.
- Pursuant to Article 4(c)(ii) Vertical-BER 2022/720, the restriction of cross-supplies (*Querlieferungsverbot*) between distributors within a selective distribution system (including between distributors operating at different levels of trade) is a hardcore restriction and not permitted.
- Article 5(1)(c) Vertical-BER 2022/720 stipulates that the supplier may not impose an obligation causing the authorised dealers, either directly or indirectly, to not sell the

[42] ECJ 25.10.1977 case C-26/76, ECLI:EU:C:1977:167 p. 1905 – *Metro v Commission*, GRURInt 1978, 254 (256); Guidelines on Vertical Restraints mn. 147–152. In Germany, such type of qualitative selective distribution is often referred to as *einfache Fachhandelsbindung*. It must be distinguished from *qualifizierte Fachhandelsbindung* where the manufacturer (principal) requires minimum or maximum sales from the distributor in addition to qualitative criteria such as qualified personnel, appropriate shop premises, or a certain presentation of the products. For such differentiation, see Mäger/Mäger, Ch IV mn. 160.

[43] Article 4(c)(iii) Vertical-BER 2022/720.

brands of particular competing suppliers. Such a condition aims to avoid the creation of a selective club of brands by the leading suppliers.[44]

67 In nos. 153 et seqq. of the Guidelines on Vertical Restraints, guidance is provided for the assessment of selective distribution in individual cases that are (i) either not covered by Vertical-BER 2022/720 or (ii) cumulative effects resulting from parallel networks of selective distribution become noticeable.

## 10. Subcontracting agreements

68 Subcontracting agreements (*Zulieferverträge*) do not fall under Article 101(1) TFEU, provided that the contractor's (principal's) technology, know-how, patents, industrial designs, or equipment is necessary to enable the subcontractor to produce the products (extended workbench).[45] A subcontracting agreement is given when a contractor (entrepreneur) provides technology or equipment to a subcontractor to produce certain products (exclusively) for the contractor.[46] In such cases, where the subcontractor's manufactured products deviate from the common products available in the market, the entrepreneur has a legitimate interest in the subcontractor only manufacturing the specialised products for him. Moreover, in such a case, where the subcontractor manufactures or sells individual and non-exchangeable products, the contractor is not deemed a competitor. Other restrictions imposed on the subcontractor – such as the obligation not to conduct or exploit its own research and development or not to produce for third parties in general – may trigger the applicability of Article 101(1), (2) TFEU. For the relationship between the principal and the distributor, the subcontracting exception is of minor relevance, as neither the principal nor the distributor/reseller commonly manufactures specific products for the other party.

## 11. Tying

69 Tying refers to situations in which customers who purchase a product (the tying product) are also required to purchase a distinct product (the tied product) from the same supplier or someone designated by it. Tying may constitute an abuse within the meaning of Article 102 TFEU, but may also constitute a vertical restraint falling under Article 101 TFEU if it results in a single branding obligation for the tied product.[47]

## 12. Upfront access payment

70 Upfront access payments or pay-to-stay fees are payments made by the principal to the distributor at the beginning of a relevant period (often upon the commencement of the contractual relationship) to gain access to the distributor's distribution network (shelf space, advertising, or promotion campaigns). It must be distinguished from the distributor's upfront payment to the principal for the allocation of the contractual territory and the corresponding client base (→ Ch. 11 mn. 126 et seq.). Upfront access payments are exempted under Vertical-BER 2022/720 when neither the principal's nor distributor's market share exceeds 30 %.[48]

---

[44] Guidelines on Vertical Restraints mn. 159: such an obligation is unlikely to be exempt pursuant to Article 101(3) TFEU if the five largest suppliers (principals) have 50 % or more of the market share unless none of the suppliers imposing such an obligation is among the five largest suppliers on the market.

[45] Cf. Commission notice of 18 December 1978 concerning the assessment of certain subcontracting agreements.

[46] Guidelines on Vertical Restraints mn. 47.

[47] Guidelines on Vertical Restraints mn. 389 et seqq.

[48] Guidelines on Vertical Restraints mn. 7.

# F. Term and termination

## I. Term of the distributorship agreement

The parties to a distributorship agreement may, in principle, freely determine the term of the contractual relationship. For contracts in specific industrial sectors (e.g. car industry), an extremely long or an extremely short contract term may, however, constitute an unreasonable disadvantage to the distributor and therefore be void pursuant to § 307(1), (2) BGB. This might be the case if the distributor has to undertake considerable investments in order to distribute the principal's products. The more extensive the distributor's investments are, the longer the term of the distributorship agreement should be. This gives the distributor the chance to amortise his investments. 71

Where a court determines that the term of a distributorship agreement is too long or too short due to a violation of § 307 BGB, the distributor relationship is deemed to be concluded for an unlimited period of time. In such a case, it can be terminated with an appropriate notice period, which will often be the notice periods stipulated in § 89 HGB.[49] 72

Where the duration is excessive, the term of a distributorship agreement may, in exceptional cases, constitute a violation of public policy pursuant to § 138(1) BGB and therefore be void. However, this is only the case if the excessive duration restricts the distributor's economic freedom and his freedom of choice in an unacceptable manner. A duration exceeding 20 years has been considered invalid in beer supply agreements.[50] However, whether the concrete term of a distributorship agreement is inappropriate and therefore void must be assessed on a case-by-case basis and will depend on the circumstances of the individual case. There is no general or sector-related approach that provides guidance. There are considerable doubts as to whether a term of more than 20 years would be considered too long for the distribution of cars, trucks, or other long-lasting industrial goods. The term requirements for the exemption of vertical restraints regarding distributorship agreements in the automotive sector (BER 1400/2002) have expired and therefore cannot provide any guidance on a mandatory minimum duration of distributorship agreements. 73

## II. Consecutive or 'chain' agreements and probation time

Consecutive or 'chain' agreements, which are prolonged periodically, are considered agreements for an indefinite period of time if they have identical or at least similar content.[51] Moreover, a contractual distributor relationship of a definite duration which, upon expiration, is extended by both parties (implicitly or explicitly), shall be deemed to be extended indefinitely. The total duration of the relationship is decisive for calculating the notice periods under § 89(1) sentences 1 and 2 HGB. A probation period for the distributor does not constitute a limitation in terms of time if the distributorship agreement is continued after the probation period has expired. 74

---

[49] Schultze et al., mn. 579.

[50] BGH VIII ZR 14/71, NJW 1972, 1459 (20 years); LG Cologne 22 O 369/91, NJW-RR 1994, 242 (10 years).

[51] BGH VIII ZR 95/01, NJW 2003, 98 (99), (100); BGH VIII ZR 354/97, NJW 1999, 2668.

## III. Ordinary notice of termination

75 Generally, the parties are free to determine the term of the distributorship agreement as well as the provisions for termination and the notice periods. However, there are specific restrictions on the parties' freedom to define the notice periods for ordinary termination that need to be considered when concluding a distributorship agreement.

### 1. Analogous application of § 89 HGB

76 If certain conditions are met, the courts apply the notice periods established for commercial agency agreements in § 89 HGB to distributorship agreements by analogy.[52] For the analogous application of § 89 HGB, the courts require that the distributor renders activities similar to those of a commercial agent. However, this standard is not especially high: it is sufficient that the distributor performs activities which are essentially similar to those of a commercial agent. This is the case if the distributor has for example agreed to a minimum purchase requirement, has supervisory or marketing obligations, or is obliged to check the liquidity of potential customers.[53] However, a distributor often has significantly greater expenditures than a commercial agent, since the former has to establish a distribution system. Therefore, the periods set out in § 89 HGB might even be too short in certain cases. Regardless, the parties must adhere to the equality requirements of § 89(3) HGB when negotiating the notice periods. Pursuant to § 89 HGB, the notice periods stipulated in § 89(1) HGB may not be shorter for the principal than for the distributor. If a shorter period for the principal than for the distributor is agreed upon, the shorter period also applies to the distributor.

### 2. Termination pursuant to § 624 BGB

77 In cases where the parties have agreed on a distributorship agreement not for an indefinite period, but for longer than five years, § 624 BGB may grant the distributor the right to terminate the distributorship agreement with a notice period of approximately six months (notice period depending on the individual case at hand). Pursuant to § 624 BGB, a party obliged to personally perform services shall, however, not be bound for a period longer than five years without recourse to terminate the service agreement. Hence, in cases where the distributor is obliged to predominantly perform the services personally, he might have a right to terminate once the distributorship agreement has exceeded a period of five years. However, this right does not apply to a distributor who is the owner of a large company, to a distributor who has sub-agents or sub-distributors, or if the main duty of the distributor is not to provide a service.

### 3. Prohibition of unfair obstruction

78 Pursuant to §§ 18 et seqq. GWB, a principal with a dominant market position (e.g. large automotive manufacturers) may neither directly or indirectly hinder the distributor in an unfair manner in business activities that are usually open to similar companies (other distributors), nor may such principal directly or indirectly treat the distributor differently from similar companies without any objective justification. In exceptional cases, this statutory obligation of the principal may render a contractually agreed upon (short)

[52] BGH VII ZR 202/60, NJW 1962, 1107.
[53] BGH VIII ZR 95/01, NJW 2003, 98 (99).

notice period void and lead to a longer notice period (e.g. two years). However, this is only possible in the rare case where a notice period is found to be so short that it constitutes unjustified discrimination or an abuse of market power.[54]

### 4. Term review

Pursuant to § 307(1) BGB, provisions in standard business terms are ineffective if they unreasonably disadvantage the other party of the contract. According to § 307(2) BGB, an unreasonable disadvantage exists if (i) the provision is not compatible with essential principles of the statutory provision from which it deviates, or if (ii) it limits essential rights or duties inherent in the nature of the contract to such an extent that fulfilment of the purpose of the contract is jeopardised. As most distributorship agreements are standardised contracts, this test of reasonableness generally applies. An unreasonable disadvantage can be seen in a situation where the distributor was obliged to create a costly distribution system and, due to the termination, the distributor had no chance to amortise such an investment. Moreover, an unreasonable disadvantage might occur where the reorganisation of the distributor's distribution system requires a considerable amount of time. § 307 BGB is especially important to notice periods in the automotive sector. Commentators assume that the notice period for ordinary termination of distributorship agreements in the automotive sector is one year pursuant to § 307 BGB.[55] However, this has not yet been determined by the courts. **79**

## IV. Extraordinary notice of termination

### 1. Conditions

Distributorship agreements may be terminated – like other continuing obligations – extraordinarily for cause. Pursuant to § 89a HGB, which applies by analogy, a distributor relationship may be terminated by either party without observance of a noticed period for an important reason (cause or good reason). An important reason is given if the terminating party cannot reasonably be expected to continue the contractual relationship until the agreed upon end or until the expiry of a notice period, thereby taking into account all circumstances of the specific case and weighing the interests of both parties.[56] Whether conditions for an important reason are present depends on the facts of an individual case. Yet, the courts have acknowledged the following circumstances as important reasons for termination by the **principal**: **80**

- The authorised dealer has stopped the operation of the repair shop (automotive sector);[57]
- Insolvency of the distributor;[58]
- Violation of the distributor's accounting and payment obligations when reselling the products from a consignment warehouse;
- Consistent gross negligence or intentional disregard of distribution obligations;

---

[54] See OLG Düsseldorf VI-U (Kart) 1/08, GRUR-RR 2009, 109 (111).

[55] Cf. Niebling, WRP 2010, 81 (84); Liebscher/Flohr/Petsche Gruppenfreistellungs-VO-HdB/Schlenger/Hinrichs/Blazejak § 14 mn. 57.

[56] The principles described in the context of commercial agents apply accordingly → Ch. 11 mn. 47 et seqq.

[57] BGH VIII ZR 360/86, NJW-RR 1988, 1077.

[58] OLG Munich 7 U 5350/05, ZIP 2006, 1916.

- Violation of confidentiality obligations;
- Unauthorised removal of product labels placed by the principal;
- Manipulation of invoices or fraudulent behaviour in connection with the distributor's business activities.

For termination by the **distributor**, the following circumstances are acknowledged as important reasons:

- Appointment of other distributors even though the principal has granted exclusivity to the distributor;
- Direct sales by the principal even though he had granted exclusivity to the distributor, and such exclusivity also excluded the principal's right to carry out direct sales in the territory;[59]
- Arbitrary rejection of purchase orders;
- Arbitrary obstruction of the distributor's activity, in particular, unilateral downsizing of the contractual territory by the principal.

### 2. Practical remarks

**81** The parties may agree on certain important reasons when concluding the distributorship agreement.[60] This helps avoid uncertainty about whether the behaviour of a party actually fulfils the conditions of an important reason. It also reduces the risk of dispute about whether an extraordinary notice of termination is given. The parties are in any case well-advised to make clear that the agreed and listed important reasons shall not prevent the subsidiary application of statutory law. This is usually done by using the phrase 'in particular' when listing the important reasons in the distributorship agreement. If the parties agree on specific important reasons by contract, they need to ensure that the interests of both parties are adequately considered. Otherwise, an important reason agreed by the parties may be invalid due to unfair discrimination of one of the parties pursuant to § 307 BGB.

## G. Investment compensation

**82** Commentators repeatedly acknowledge the distributor's claim for investment compensation when (i) the distributor has incurred considerable expenses in setting up his sales organisation and (ii) has had no opportunity to amortise these investments due to an early termination. However, there is neither a statutory provision establishing such a claim for the distributor, nor is there a legal judgment awarding investment compensation to the distributor due to an early termination of the distributorship relationship. In contrast, the Higher Regional Court of Munich explicitly rejected such a claim of a distributor.[61] Yet, this does not mean that a court will reject any distributor's claim for investment compensation in the future. In rare cases where (i) a distributor incurs extremely high expenses in setting up his sales organisation, (ii) such investment is irreversible and cannot be used for other purposes, and (iii) the distributor's investments have not yet been amortised, the distributor might have a claim for compensation of his investments.

---

[59] BGH VIII ZR 47/92, NJW-RR 1993, 678 (682).
[60] BGH I ZR 117/90, NJW-RR 1992, 1059.
[61] OLG Munich U (K) 2843/91, NJW-RR 1995, 1137 (1139).

# H. Post-contractual matters

## I. Legal situation between declaration of termination and cessation of business

Once the declaration of termination has been made, the question arises of whether and, if so, to what extent the principal is obliged to supply the distributor with the contract products until the actual end of the contractual relationship. On one hand, the principal has a legitimate interest in the distributor ceasing its sale of contract products once the contractual relationship has ended. On the other hand, it is the principal's obligation to supply the distributor with products for as long as the contractual relationship is still running. Between the declaration of an ordinary notice of termination and cessation of business, the principal is therefore obliged to accept the distributor's purchase orders in so far as these products may – in the ordinary course of business and considering the distributor's existing stock – be sold by the distributor during the remaining term of the distributor relationship.[62] **83**

To ensure a smooth transfer of business, either party may contact possible successors even before the actual end of the business relationship and even if the distributor was granted an exclusive right to sell the products in the territory. This includes the principal's right to familiarise the new distributor with the contractual territory. However, where the principal makes (public) announcements that the distributor relationship with the previous distributor has been terminated, this might trigger compensation claims of the distributor in cases where the principal's announcement damages the commercial activities of the distributor. **84**

## II. Post-contractual supply obligation

Upon termination of the distributorship agreement, the principal's obligation to supply products to the distributor ceases. However, if the distributor has ordered products and the principal has accepted such purchase orders prior to the termination, the principal is obliged to fill such accepted orders. This may not be the case if the principal has terminated the distributorship agreement without notice for an important reason. Depending on the individual important reason, the principal might not be under the obligation to fill the distributor's purchase orders in such cases even if they were accepted by him prior to the termination.[63] **85**

## III. Return of remaining stock and spare parts

Upon termination of a distributorship agreement, the fate of the remaining stock and spare parts that the distributor has not yet been able to sell must be regulated. Statutory law does not provide any guidance in this question. However, courts have defined the rights and obligations of the parties regarding the return of the remaining stock. The principles discussed below provide a rough overview of the obligations of the parties to a **86**

[62] Cf. OLG Frankfurt/Main 5 U 127/95, BeckRS 2016, 16324.

[63] With regard to post-contractual supply of spare parts → mn. 31 et seqq.

distributor relationship concerning such stock. The parties are in any case well-advised to explicitly regulate a buy-back procedure in their contract, as courts might reach different conclusions depending on the particular features of the case.

### 1. Principal's obligation to buy back remaining stock

87 After termination of the distributorship agreement, the principal is generally not under an obligation to buy back delivered products that remain with the distributor. This is not the case, however, if the distributor is under the contractual obligation to maintain a warehouse. However, in such a case, the principal's buy-back obligation extends only to the remaining stock that (i) the distributor has built up in the ordinary course of business, (ii) the distributor has obtained from the principal or third parties appointed by the principal,[64] (iii) is undamaged, in original packaging, and has not been used. Usually, the principal is entitled to buy back the remaining stock at a discount of 10 % (exceptions are possible) unless the termination falls within his sole responsibility (in which case the principal would have to make full payment). The distributor must request that the principal take back the products within an appropriate period (e.g. six months) after termination. The parties may validly agree that the distributor bears the costs of returning the remaining stock.

### 2. Principal's right to buy back remaining stock

88 Independent of whether the distributor has asked the principal to buy back remaining stock, the principal may have the right to demand its return from the distributor. There is often a legitimate interest of the principal in buying back the remaining stock, as the distributor could dump such stock, thereby disturbing the price of the product in the market. However, such a right of the principal exists only if the parties have agreed on a corresponding contractual clause. To protect the interests of both parties, they are well-advised to agree on the principal's right to buy back remaining stock. It is also advisable to agree on the buy-back price. The parties may therefore agree that the principal (i) pays the full sales price as the buy-back price and that (ii) he raises such a claim within three months from the end of the contractual relationship.[65]

## IV. Return of advertising material

89 Upon termination of the distributorship agreement, the distributor must return sample collections, advertising material, and all other goods belonging to the principal such as repair manuals, drawings, plans, list of items, and customer lists, if originally provided by the principal.

## V. Post-contractual non-compete obligation

90 A post-contractual non-compete obligation may be agreed upon between the principal and the distributor in very limited circumstances only. Pursuant to Article 5(1)(a) Verti-

[64] This may not apply to the motor vehicle sector due to the prohibition of the restriction of cross-supplies, see BGH VIII ZR 121/04, NJW-RR 2005, 1496 (1503).

[65] Schultze et al., mn. 732.

cal-BER 2022/720, any direct or indirect obligation causing the buyer, after termination of the agreement, not to manufacture, purchase, sell or resell goods or services is considered a post-contractual non-compete obligation. Pursuant to Article 5(3) Vertical-BER 2022/720, such a post-contractual non-compete obligation may only be agreed upon for a period of one year after termination of the agreement, if (i) the obligation relates to goods or services that compete with the contract products or services, (ii) the obligation is limited to the contractual territory, and (iii) the obligation is indispensable to protect know-how transferred by the supplier to the buyer. If such conditions are fulfilled, the additional requirements of § 90a HGB must still be observed, in particular, the written form requirement and the principal's obligation to provide reasonable non-compete compensation to the distributor (→ Ch. 11 mn. 71).

## VI. Protection of business and trade secrets

During the term of the distributorship agreement and even thereafter, the distributor 91 is under the obligation not to disclose trade secrets of the principal to any third party or to use them for his own benefit without the principal's prior consent. § 90 HGB applies to distributors by analogy. If a distributor violates such obligation, the principal may claim damage compensation if damage occurs. It is usually difficult for the principal to prove that a violation of the distributor's confidentiality obligation has caused measurable damage. The principal is therefore well-advised to insist on a contractual penalty when negotiating the distributorship agreement (→ Ch. 9 mn. 8).

# I. Claim for termination compensation

There is no law establishing termination compensation for the distributor upon the 92 termination of the distributor relationship. Under certain conditions, however, courts regularly apply § 89b HGB by analogy, thereby granting the distributor compensation for the setup of the customer base, which the principal may use after termination of the distributor relationship. Therefore, a distributor has a claim against the principal for termination compensation where (i) § 89b HGB is applicable by analogy and (ii) the conditions of § 89b HGB are met.

## I. Analogous application of § 89b HGB

In its rulings, the Federal Court of Justice consistently applies § 89b HGB to distrib- 93 utors when two requirements are met. First, the distributor must be integrated into the principal's sales organisation in such a way that the distributor, in economic terms, is required to perform tasks that are comparable to those of a commercial agent to a substantial extent.[66] This requirement is deemed to be satisfied if the terms and conditions of the legal relationship between the distributor and the principal are such that the relationship is not limited to a mere seller-purchaser relationship but integrates the distributor into the principal's sales organisation. Second, the analogous application of § 89b HGB requires

[66] Cf. BGH VIII ZR 41/93, NJW 1994, 657 (658); BGH II ZR 73/57, NJW 1959, 144 (145).

that the distributor be obliged to transfer its customer data to the principal to enable the latter to benefit from the advantages of the customer base immediately and upon the termination of the distributor relationship.[67]

## 1. Integration into the principal's sales organisation

94 The distributor is deemed to be integrated into the principal's sales organisation if the distributor is contractually required to make the same efforts as a commercial agent to sell the principal's products and, in other respects, is subject to obligations and commitments typical for a commercial agent.[68] In the course of its consistent practice, the Federal Court of Justice has developed criteria that indicate whether the distributor is integrated into the principal's sales organisation.[69]

95 In particular, these criteria exist if the principal (i) grants the distributor an exclusive distribution right, (ii) imposes a prohibition of competition on the distributor, (iii) imposes an obligation to promote sales, (iv) trains the distributor's sales staff, (v) imposes a minimum purchase volume on the distributor, (vi) obliges the distributor to maintain a stock of goods and spare parts, (vii) obliges the distributor to provide customer services, (viii) obliges the distributor to advertise, (ix) imposes reporting and notification duties, or (x) reserves monitoring and supervisory powers over the distributor. The analogous application of § 89b HGB does not require all or even most of these criteria to be satisfied. Instead, based on the overall appearance of its commitments and obligations, the distributor must be integrated into the principal's sales organisation in a way comparable to a commercial agent.[70] For example, an obligation to provide information and to report may be sufficient to justify the assumption that the distributor is integrated into the principal's sales organisation.[71] In contrast, it is uncertain that an exclusive distribution right, a prohibition of competition, and the distributor's contractual duty to promote sales are sufficient for assuming an integration of the distributor into the principal's sales organisation even if imposed on the distributor collectively. In the final analysis, the specific features of each individual case are decisive.

## 2. Transfer of customer data to the principal

### a) Contractual obligation

96 In addition to the distributor's integration into the principal's sales organisation, the analogous application of § 89b HGB requires a contractual obligation of the distributor to transfer his customer data to the principal.

- The Federal Court of Justice, however, has ruled that an explicit contractual duty to transfer the client base is not necessary to trigger the claim for termination compensation according to § 89b HGB. A contractual duty to transfer client data exists where the distributor has the obligation to forward marketing reports that contain client data and enable the principal to use such data to identify the clients.[72]
- In particular, the obligation to provide customer data does not need to be explicit in the contractual agreement. Rather, it is sufficient that such obligation to provide customer

[67] BGH VIII ZR 41/93, NJW 1994, 657 (658); BGH VIII ZR 41/93, NJW 1994, 657 (658).
[68] BGH VIII ZR 352/04, NJW-RR 2007, 1327 (1328).
[69] BGH VIII ZR 19/99, NJW 2000, 1413.
[70] See BGH I ZR 51/90, NJW-RR 1992, 421; BGH I ZR 146/80, NJW 1982, 2819 (2820).
[71] Cf. BGH I ZR 51/90, NJW-RR 1992, 421; BGH VIII ZR 47/92, NJW-RR 1993, 678 (680).
[72] BGH VIII ZR 172/92, NJW-RR 1994, 99 (100).

data follows indirectly from the contractual agreements (e.g. distributor's duty to allow inspection of his accounts, distributor's duty to provide sales reports).[73]

- Likewise, it is sufficient if the distributor is under the obligation to furnish information that makes it possible for the principal to identify the customers (e.g. copy of registration card for initial registration of cars).[74]
- On the other hand, for the analogous application of § 89b HGB, it is not sufficient for the distributor to supply information on individual (important) customers when specifically requested by the principal. The Federal Court of Justice has determined that where the distributor may refuse to answer specific requests of the principal without violating his duties, a contractual obligation to transfer customer data cannot be assumed.[75]
- Similarly, § 89b HGB is not applicable by analogy where no contractual obligation exists, and the distributor has transferred customer data only due to economic incentives (e.g. promised discounts by the principal).[76]
- Where the distributor is under the contractual obligation to transfer customer data to a third party only, an analogous application of § 89b HGB is also excluded, even if such third party (e.g. a marketing service provider) uses the customer data for advertising services on behalf of the principal. The service provider, however, must be under the obligation not to disclose the customer data to the principal at any time.[77]
- For the application of § 89b HGB, it is not relevant whether the distributor's obligation to transfer customer data originated upon termination of the distributorship agreement or already existed during the contractual relationship by virtue of the permanent transfer of information to the principal (e.g. through marketing reports, customer lists or the like).[78]
- The obligation to provide such data may also be established by the parties' conduct (e.g. an implicit agreement), meaning that the obligation may also follow implicitly from the way in which the distributorship agreement is performed in practice.[79]
- For the application of § 89b HGB, it is of no relevance whether the principal actually uses the customer data. It is sufficient that the principal could potentially use the data.[80]
- For the application of § 89b HGB, it is of no relevance whether the transfer of customer data is made to the principal's advantage only or lies in the interests of both parties.[81]
- For the application of § 89b HGB, the specific purpose of the transfer of customer data is also irrelevant (supervision of the distributor, sales promotion, actual use of customer data after the termination of the distributorship agreement).[82]

**b) Scope of data transfer**

An actual transfer of all customer data from the distributor is not necessary. A complete or even almost complete transmission of customer data to the principal is – regardless of the form in which it takes place – virtually impossible, because individual customers may object to their data being transferred, the data of the distributor may be 97

[73] BGH I ZR 59/79, NJW 1981, 1961 (1962).
[74] BGH I ZR 146/80, NJW 1982, 2819 (2820).
[75] BGH VIII ZR 41/93, NJW 1994, 657 (658).
[76] BGH VIII ZR 41/93, NJW 1994, 657 (658).
[77] BGH VIII ZR 283/96, NJW-RR 1998, 390 (391).
[78] BGH I ZR 185/75, NJW 1977, 896.
[79] BGH VIII ZR 172/92, NJW-RR 1994, 99 (100).
[80] BGH I ZR 86/82, NJW 1984, 2102 (2103).
[81] BGH VIII ZR 172/92, NJW-RR 1994, 99 (100).
[82] BGH I ZR 146/80, NJW 1982, 2819 (2820).

erroneous or incomplete, customer addresses may change, etc. Instead, required and sufficient are that (i) the contractual agreement between the principal and the distributor is aimed at a transmission of customer data that is as complete as possible and (ii) that the method chosen for achieving this goal is not unsuitable.[83] If the parties have transmitted customer data in a certain way over a longer period of time (e.g. quarterly manuals, annual reports), this chosen method is not unsuitable. In contrast, occasional requests regarding certain individual customers are – by themselves – not a suitable method; but they could be suitable in connection with other measures of transferring customer data. However, it is still not clear what percentage of the overall customer data actually need to be transferred to the principal in order to trigger the analogous application of § 89b HGB. 58 % is likely insufficient, at least if all customers generate approximately the same turnover.[84] However, if the distributor transfers data of only a few customers to the principal but these customers make up almost all of the distributor's turnover (e.g. 75 % or more), even a percentage below 58 % of all customers might be sufficient to trigger the analogous application of § 89b HGB. Therefore, the scope of data transfer must be determined by both the number of customers and the turnover made by them.

## II. Conditions of § 89b HGB

98 Besides the requirements for the analogous application of § 89b HGB, the distributor's claim for termination compensation exists only when the conditions of § 89b HGB itself are fulfilled in addition. These are: (i) the distributorship agreement must be terminated; (ii) the distributor has solicited new customers or materially expanded the business relations with existing customers; (iii) the principal retains substantial advantages from the business relations with the new customers; (iv) the payment of the termination compensation is just and equitable; and (v) the claim for termination compensation was raised by the distributor within one year of the termination of the distributor relationship. The discussion on the commercial agent's termination compensation apply (→ Ch. 11 mn. 83 et seqq.).

### 1. Gross margin

99 The distributor's termination compensation is calculated based on the distributor's gross margin and not commission payments. The reason is that a distributor normally does not receive commission payments from the principal but generates his profit with the margin from the difference between the purchase price and sales price, as the latter is usually higher.[85] Instead of commission payments during the last contractual year, the starting point for the calculation is the distributor's relevant margin that he has realised with regular customers in the last year of the contractual agreement.

### 2. Deductions not typical for dealers

100 Certain amounts must then be deducted from the calculated gross margin, because only that portion of the distributor's gross margin may be applied for the purpose of determining the distributor's compensation that relate to the activity of a commercial

[83] BGH VIII ZR 172/92, NJW-RR 1994, 99 (101).
[84] Cf. OLG Schleswig 5 U 59/12 with questionable reasoning.
[85] BGH VIII ZR 173/04, NJW-RR 2006, 1328 (1330).

agent. Therefore, any remuneration components that are not related to advertising and are typically incurred by distributors or dealers must be deducted from the distributor's turnover for the last year of the contractual agreement.[86] This includes remuneration components for price fluctuation, warehousing, or credit risks as well as the costs for logistics, delivery, repair shop, insurance policies, costs for buildings, electricity, IT, administration, and related wages. Regarding all further calculations such as deduction of churn rate, prognosis of future commissions, interest discount, equitableness, and capping pursuant to § 89b(2) HGB, the principles discussed with regard to the commercial agent's termination compensation apply (→ 11 mn. 105 et seqq.).

## III. Exclusion of distributor's claim for termination compensation

### 1. Exclusion by agreement

If § 89b HGB is applicable by analogy, such application also extends to § 89b(4) HGB, according to which the parties to a distributorship agreement may not validly exclude the distributor's claim for termination compensation in advance.[87] Only if the distributor carries out his activity outside the territory of the European Union and the other contracting states of the European Economic Area Agreement does § 92c(1) HGB establish the possibility to exclude the claim for termination compensation in advance. Numerous commentators support the view that the exclusion of the distributor's claim for termination compensation may even be ruled out in all cases where the distributor carries out its activity outside Germany (and not only outside the EU/EEA). As the mandatory character of the EU Directive on Commercial Agents does not include distributors, there are good arguments to support these commentators' view. However, courts have rejected such a broad exclusion of the termination compensation in advance.[88] **101**

### 2. Choice of law

By choosing an applicable law that does not provide for termination compensation for distributors, the parties have a more useful tool to circumvent the distributor's claim for termination compensation. The constraints established under the Rome I Regulation (in particular, Article 3(3)) and the *Ingmar* decision do not apply to distributorship agreements in the same way as they do to commercial agency agreements, since the distributor law is not considered mandatory law.[89] **102**

### 3. Further options

For further (rather limited) possibilities to circumvent the termination compensation see → Ch. 11 mn. 111 et seqq. With regard to the preclusive period and limitation of the distributor's claim → Ch. 11 mn. 129 et seqq. **103**

---

[86] BGH I ZR 188/85, NJW-RR 1988, 42 (44); BGH VIII ZR 141/95, NJW 1996, 2298 (2300).

[87] BGH I ZR 62/83, WM 1986, 392 (393).

[88] See OLG Schleswig 5 U 59/12.

[89] Cf. Emde, MDR 2002, 190 (196); Kocher, RIW 2003, 512 (515), (518); Schultze et al., mn. 996; Hopt/Hopt HGB § 92c mn. 10 et seqq.

# Chapter 13
# Commission agency agreement

## A. Definition

1 Pursuant to § 383 HGB, a commission agent (*Kommissionsagent*) is a person who professionally undertakes to buy or sell goods or securities in his own name but for the principal's account. The commission agent may – in his own name – act as a purchaser (purchase commission) or seller (sales commission) of the principal's goods. The commission agency agreement is a special type of service contract pursuant to § 675 BGB. It is explicitly regulated in §§ 383 et seqq. HGB. Such statutory law provides fallback rules for the parties. For securities trading, special laws such as the Securities Deposit Act (*Depotgesetz* – DepotG) or the Securities Exchange Act (*Börsengesetz* – BörsG) provide further rules for commission agency.

2 Regarding the trading of goods and commodities, the significance of commission agency has decreased during recent years. Goods are commonly distributed by commercial agents or distributors. However, due to the upsurge in securities trading, commission agency law has become more prominent. In the trading of goods, the legal concept of commission agency is still common in specialised markets such as art, second-hand vehicles, antiques, or industrial instruments. This is also true for consignment stock contracts for exported goods.

## B. Contractual relations

3 Commission agency establishes three contractual relationships. The first and most important one exists between the commission agent and the principal. This contractual relationship is called the commission agency agreement (*Kommissionsvertrag*). It governs the rights and obligations of the commission agent and the principal (e.g. the commission agent's claim for commission payment; the commission agent's claim for reimbursement of expenditures; details about direction and guidance; liability of the commission agent, etc.).

4 Further contractual relationships exist between the commission agent and the third party (which is either a buyer or a seller, depending on the type of commission agency). This contractual relationship is called an accomplishment agreement (*Ausführungsvertrag*). As the commission agent buys or sells goods or securities in his own name, the commission agent – and not the principal – is a party to the accomplishment agreement.

5 The third contractual relationship is between the commission agent and his principal. It is called a process agreement (*Abwicklungsgeschäft*) and governs the transfer of property, claims, or money from the commission agent to the principal.

# C. Differentiation from other contract types

It is characteristic for the commission agent to act in his own name but for the principal's account. This distinguishes commission agency from other forms of distribution. 6

- **Agency**: unlike a customary agent (§§ 164 BGB et seqq.), the commission agent acts in his own name and not in the name of the principal. Moreover, the commission agent receives a commission and acts professionally.
- **Commercial agency**: unlike the commission agent, the commercial agent does not conclude contracts with a third party but instead creates the opportunity for the principal to conclude contracts with a third party, the customer. In contrast, the commission agent concludes contracts with third parties in his own name.
- **Franchising**: the franchisee is integrated into the franchisor's organisation and is usually under the obligation to purchase products from the franchisor. Moreover, the franchisee concludes contracts not only in his own name but also for his own account.
- **Distributor**: unlike the commission agent, the distributor acts for his own account. Moreover, distributors are often integrated into the principal's sales organisation. The distributor also bears the risks and costs of warehousing, transport, and pricing, which the commission agent usually does not.
- **Employee**: it may be difficult to differentiate between an employee and a commission agent at times. This is particularly true if the principal has imposed certain restrictions on the commission agent regarding the latter's job responsibilities or working times. Whether the commission agent will be considered an independent merchant instead of an employee largely depends on the degree of his independence and his room to manoeuvre. The commission agent's independence is normally guaranteed if he also acts for other principals or has additional sources of income. However, the commission agent is in need of social protection if he only acts for the principal and the contract is concluded for an unlimited period of time.[1]

# D. Rights and obligations

The parties to a commission agency agreement may determine the rights and obligations of the parties by mutual consent. However, statutory law provides fallback rules and defines the rights and obligations of the parties in §§ 383 HGB et seqq. Accordingly, the commission agent's most important rights are the following: 7

- Claim for commission (§ 396(1) HGB);
- Claim for reimbursement of expenditures (§ 396(1) HGB);
- Lien (*Pfandrecht*) on the principal's commission goods (§§ 397(1), 398 HGB);
- Commission agent's right to self-substitution (*Selbsteintritt*) (§ 400 HGB).

The principal's rights are the following: 8

- Claim against the commission agent to protect the principal's interests and follow his instructions (§ 384 HGB);

---

[1] Cf. BAG 5 AZB 3/97, NJW 1998, 701; for the differentiation between employee and freelancer → Ch. 11 mn. 5..

- Claim against the commission agent to receive all necessary information (§ 384(2) HGB);
- Claim to receive anything obtained by the commission agent from the business commissioned (e.g. property, claims, or money) (§ 384(2) HGB);
- Claim to receive the name/identity of the third party (purchaser or seller) with whom the purchase agreement (accomplishment agreement) was concluded.

## E. Typical content

9 A commission agency agreement typically contains provisions on the following topics:
- Object of the commission agreement (e.g. the sale of goods or securities)
- Insurance of the goods
- Transport expenditures
- Principal's instructions (price, payment terms)
- Transfer of money or goods to the principal
- Conclusion of the accomplishment agreement(s) and corresponding information;
- Commission
- Liability for the goods (if any)
- Reimbursement for expenditures
- Terms of the agreement, including termination
- Miscellaneous (jurisdiction clause, choice of law, severability clause)

# Chapter 14
# Franchise agreement

**Bibliography**: Münchener Kommentar zum Handelsgesetzbuch: HGB, 5th edn, Munich 2021.

## A. Introduction

Franchising is a special form of distribution. The network of franchise systems is steadily growing not only in Germany, but in almost all western industrialised countries. Franchise systems are primarily found in the service industry (e.g. cleaners, IT sector, car wash), in consumer trade and fashion (e.g. *OBI* and other do-it-yourself stores), as well as in the catering (e.g. *Subway*, *McDonald's*) and hotel industry (e.g. *Novotel*, *Hilton*, or *Sheraton*). Franchising was initially developed in the US only for products and trade names and was first introduced by *Coca-Cola* for its operations in bottling and distribution. In the middle of the 20th century, product franchising became less popular in favour of franchising for an entire business, also called business format franchising (*Betriebs-Franchising*). The result of this change is that the contractual obligations are not limited to a single product but instead encompass the entire business of the franchisee. Business franchising has significantly influenced and developed the form of franchising as we know it today. 1

In simple terms, franchise agreements contain licences of intellectual property rights relating to trademarks and know-how for the use and distribution of goods or services by the franchisee. In addition to the licence of intellectual property rights, the franchisor usually provides the franchisee with commercial, marketing-related, or technical assistance (e.g. advertising, training, financing assistance) during the term of the franchise agreement. The licence and the assistance are integral components of the business concept being franchised. The franchisor is generally paid a (one-time and/or monthly) franchise fee by the franchisee for the use of the business concept. Monthly franchise fees are usually equivalent to two to seven percent of the franchisee's monthly turnover. If the franchising is not a mere service franchise, the franchisee may be obliged to obtain the franchisor's products and store fittings and distribute them (exclusively) in his own name and for his own account. The franchisee is usually in a significantly weaker position than the franchisor. This may at times result in the law protecting the franchisee, for example by imposing certain disclosure obligations upon the franchisor[1] or application of legal provisions of the HGB to protect the franchisee.[2] Typically, the franchise agreement constitutes standard terms and conditions, which results in a term review to protect the weaker party, here the franchisee. 2

---

1 See OLG Munich 6 U 5495/92, NJW 1994, 667.

2 Courts have, for instance, applied § 89b HGB by analogy to franchise agreements if specific (narrow) requirements are met, see OLG Munich 7 U 5730/01, BB 2002, 2521 (2523); LG Frankfurt/Main 3-08 O 28/99, EWiR 2004, 69; Cf. also BGH I ZR 3/09, GRUR 2010, 1107 (1108), (1109).

## B. Differentiation from other contract types

3 Although franchising is distinct from other forms of distribution, it may at times have common characteristics with authorised dealership (distributorship), commercial agency, or licence agreement. The differences from other forms of distribution are discussed below:

- **Authorised dealer**: the integration of a franchisee is usually stronger than that of a distributor or authorised dealer. The franchisee is obliged to use not only the franchisor's trademark and products but also his marketing and advertising strategy. For this reason, the parties to a franchise agreement usually compile a franchise handbook describing the features of the cooperation (business processes, presentation of goods, sale of goods, advertising, trainings, etc.). Unlike the distributor or authorised dealer, the franchisee normally pays a regular royalty or franchise fee. The franchisor has far-reaching control rights vis-á-vis the franchisee.
- **Commercial and commission agency**: unlike the commercial agent, the franchisee acts for his own account and provides services or products in his own name, thereby bearing the full entrepreneurial risk.
- **Licence agreements**: a franchisee not only uses the franchisor's trademark and business concept; he is also under the obligation to distribute products and services. The franchisor has strong control rights, which is atypical in mere licence agreements.

## C. Types of franchising and its regulation

4 Unlike in the US, where a crisis in franchising has led to a codification of franchise regulation (franchise law) with the aim of protecting the weaker franchisee, no such explicit law exists in Germany. However, there are many court decisions providing legal certainty for the franchisor and the franchisee. Parties entering into a franchise agreement will find that their contractual relationship is governed by law from disparate areas such as sales law, licencing law, agency law, tenancy law, and/or business management law (*Geschäftsbesorgungsrecht*). Therefore, franchise agreements are combined contracts under German law and do not have predetermined content. The nucleus of the legal elements governing the franchise agreement is determined by the parties' individual contractual arrangements.

5 The categories of franchising practiced today are the following:

- **Product and service franchise** refers to a franchise system where manufacturers allow retailers to distribute products or services and to use names and trademarks developed and manufactured by the franchisor.
- **Manufacturing franchise** refers to a franchise system where the franchisor allows a manufacturer (franchisee) to produce and sell products itself using the name and trademark of the franchisor.
- **Business format franchise** refers to a franchise system where the franchisor provides the franchisee with an established business concept, including name and trademark. Product, service, and manufacturing franchises may also operate as a business format franchise.

## D. Benefits of franchising

Franchising helps the franchisor spread and build up his trademark with the help of a network following his business concept. The franchisor's required investment is marginal, as the franchisee bears the entrepreneurial risk. Franchising may therefore enable the franchisor to establish, with limited investments, a uniform network for the distribution of his products. The franchisor makes use of the franchisee's entrepreneurial energy, his willingness to invest his local and/or regional know-how, and his motivation to expand his own business. 6

On the other hand, the franchisee benefits from the franchisor's high level of recognition and visibility in the market. The franchisee normally receives support from the franchisor in terms of know-how, marketing, and/or formation of the enterprise. The franchisee may make use of a well-tested business concept. As a result, the insolvency rate of franchise startups is significantly below average. 7

To avoid fraud in franchising, national and international franchise associations have developed codes of ethics, codes of conduct, and recommended practice guides. 8

## E. Typical content

It is impossible to define in abstract the necessary content of a franchise agreement. This stems from the fact that franchise systems differ from one another depending on the type of franchise and the individual needs of the parties. However, there are specific issues that typically require regulation between the parties. These include: 9

- Description of subject matter of the franchise
- Contract products or services (definitions, minimum purchase requirements, order procedures, and merchandise management)
- Contractual territory
- Exclusivity or non-exclusivity
- IP (e.g. licences) and know-how
- Supply and warehousing
- Duties of the franchisor (training concept, marketing, and advertising concept)
- Franchise handbook
- Duties of the franchisee
- Consideration (licence payment, franchise fee, entrance fee)
- Franchisor's right to monitor and control
- Franchisee's duty to report
- Parties' duty to confidentiality
- Restraint on competition
- Contractual penalty
- Term
- Termination
- Post-contractual matters (including termination compensation or its exclusion and/or post-contractual prohibition of competition)
- Quality management and certification
- Miscellaneous (written form clause, choice of law, jurisdiction or arbitration clause, severability clause)

# F. Specific legal problems

## I. Form requirements

10 Generally, there is no specific form requirement for the conclusion of franchise agreements, although in practice the parties usually sign written contracts. However, §§ 510(1), 513 BGB may impose a written form requirement on the parties if the franchisee is a start-up entrepreneur entering into a franchise agreement containing delivery by instalments (*Ratenlieferungen*) and the franchisee's payment obligation does not exceed EUR 75,000.

## II. Pre-contractual information

11 Prior to entering into a franchise agreement, the parties find themselves in a pre-contractual relationship of trust (*vorvertragliches Vertrauensverhältnis*) that triggers duties of care pursuant to § 311(2) no. 1 BGB.

### 1. Franchisor's duty to inform

12 During negotiations, the franchisor must act in good faith, with loyalty and fairness, providing the prospective franchisee with all the information necessary to or useful in deciding on whether to enter into the franchise agreement. In a pre-contractual franchise relationship, the requirements regarding disclosure of information by the franchisor to the franchisee are particularly high. This stems from the fact that the franchisee is usually less experienced in business matters than the franchisor. Moreover, franchisees are often founders of new businesses, thereby accepting a considerably high commercial risk. According to case law and the principles of the German Franchise Association (*Deutscher Franchiseverband*), the franchisor must disclose, in particular, (i) the prospects of success of the business concept, (ii) the functioning of the concept, including the services of the franchisor, (iii) information about discounts, (iv) information about the required labour and capital investments, (v) the practical experience made with the franchisor's pilot projects and other average franchises,[3] and (vi) true key performance parameters.[4] The extent of information to be disclosed to the franchisee depends on the individual needs of the franchisee[5] that are typically derived from the franchisee's knowledge, his former activities (startup entrepreneur or former manager) and the complexity of the franchise. However, the franchisor is not the franchisee's startup consultant and is therefore not under the obligation to inform the franchisee about general risks of freelancing.[6]

### 2. Franchisee's duty to inform

13 The franchisee is obliged to fully inform the franchisor about his professional and personal skills, his business experiences, and his financial status.

---

[3] OLG Frankfurt/Main 22 U 181/08, ZVertriebsR 2012, 51.
[4] For further details, see OLG Düsseldorf I-22 U 62/13, NJOZ 2014, 1622.
[5] See OLG Schleswig 1 W 27/07, NJW-RR 2009, 64 (65).
[6] OLG Düsseldorf I-22 U 62/13, NJOZ 2014, 1622 (1623).

### 3. Practical advice

If a party breaches its pre-contractual duty to inform by supplying incorrect or incomplete information, it may be liable to the other party for the incurred damage according to the legal concept of *culpa in contrahendo* (§§ 311(2), (3), 241(2), 280 BGB). Moreover, the franchise agreement may be void pursuant to §§ 142(1), 123(1) BGB. To avoid liability, the parties are well-advised to draft and sign a document or record showing the extent of information that the parties have disclosed to each other. If the franchisee claims insufficient or incorrect disclosure of information by the franchisor, the franchisor has to provide evidence of proper disclosure of information to the franchisee.[7] This is hardly possible without documentation. **14**

## III. Employee Status

It is of great importance for the franchisor that the franchisee is an independent freelancer and not the franchisor's employee, as this might trigger payment obligations from the franchisor. If the franchisee is a pseudo-freelancer, he will be legally deemed an employee under employment and social security law as of the date on which the pseudo-freelancing was ascertained. In such a case, the employee may also need to be added to the company pension plan, which would lead to serious financial burdens for the franchisor retroactively, as the franchisor would be liable to pay social insurance contributions (→ Ch. 11 mn. 5). **15**

Hence, the distinction between a franchisee and an employee is of high practical relevance. If a person's work is dependent on his superior, such a person is in fact an employee even if he is called a franchisor. A person is dependent on the employer if he is closely integrated into the employer's organisation and is subject to the employer's instructions, thereby being in need of protection comparable to that of an employee. German courts have considered a franchisee to be an employee when the following criteria are fulfilled: (i) the franchisee had no other source of income, (ii) the franchisee owed his full working time to the franchise, (iii) the franchisee was not under the obligation to hire employees, (iv) the franchise handbook issued precise and detailed instructions on how to carry out the franchise business, leaving no room for entrepreneurial initiatives, and (v) the franchisee's revenues were channelled into the franchisor's bank account, who then transferred the margin to the franchisee.[8] Therefore, if the franchisor wants to avoid employer liability, he needs to ensure that the franchisee acts as an independent person that is not closely integrated into his (the franchisor's) organisation. **16**

## IV. Competition law in franchise agreements

Competition law plays an important role in franchise agreements. This stems from the fact that, in addition to the provision of the business concept and the licensing of trademarks and know-how, franchise agreements usually contain a combination of different vertical restraints concerning the products being distributed, especially selective distribution and/or non-compete obligations and/or exclusive distribution or weaker forms thereof (e.g. territorial delineations, exclusive purchase obligations, exclusive distribution rights, etc). Hence, franchise agreements often contain provisions that typically would **17**

---

[7] OLG Munich 8 U 2207/87, BB 1988, 865.
[8] Cf. BGII VIII ZB 12/98, NJW 1999, 218 (220); BAG 5 AZB 29/96, NJW 1997, 2973 (2974).

restrict competition and would usually be prohibited pursuant to Article 101(1) TFEU, § 1 GWB. The parties are therefore well-advised to precisely and comprehensively ensure that the provisions agreed upon in the franchise agreement are in line with German and European (and perhaps even other) competition laws.

### 1. European Commission's Guidance on Franchise Agreements

18 Given the special characteristics of franchising, restraints that are strictly necessary for the functioning of franchising systems are considered to fall outside the scope of Article 101(1) TFEU.[9] Hence they do not require an exemption. Restraints in franchise agreements are permitted, if they are necessary to protect the franchisor's intellectual property rights or to maintain the common identity and reputation of the franchise network, e.g.:

- an obligation of the franchisee not to engage, directly or indirectly, in any similar business;
- an obligation of the franchisee not to acquire financial interests in the capital of a competing company that would give the franchisee the power to influence the economic conduct of such a company;
- an obligation of the franchisee not to disclose the know-how provided by the franchisor to third parties as long as this know-how is not in the public domain;
- an obligation of the franchisee to communicate to the franchisor any experience gained in exploiting the franchise and to grant the franchisor (and other franchisees) a non-exclusive licence for the know-how resulting from that experience;
- an obligation of the franchisee to inform the franchisor of infringements of licenced intellectual property rights, to take legal action against infringers or to assist the franchisor in any legal actions against violators;
- an obligation of the franchisee not to use know-how licenced by the franchisor for purposes other than the operation of the franchise; and
- an obligation of the franchisee not to assign the rights and obligations under the franchise agreement without the franchisor's consent.

19 In addition, if non-compete obligation on the goods or services purchased by the franchisee is deemed necessary and falls outside the scope of Article 101(1) TFEU, the duration of the non-compete obligation is irrelevant, as long as it does not exceed the duration of the franchise agreement itself.[10]

### 2. Vertical-BER

20 If an agreement between the franchisor and the franchisee leads to the prevention, restriction, or distortion of competition and is not deemed necessary for protecting the franchisor's intellectual property rights or to maintaining the franchise network, such a restraint of competition may be exempted. This means that the negative legal consequences stipulated in Article 101(2) TFEU do not apply. For franchise agreements, the Vertical-BER 2022/720 is of particular significance. If the respective market shares of the franchisor and the franchisee do not exceed 30 %, the exemption provided in Article 2 Vertical-BER 2022/720 generally applies to franchise agreements in the same way as it applies to other vertical restraints on the purchase, sale, and resale of goods and services. Vertical restraints contained in franchise agreements will be assessed using the principles applicable to the distribution system that most closely corresponds to the particular

[9] Guidelines on Vertical Restraints mn. 166.
[10] Guidelines on Vertical Restraints mn. 166.

franchise agreement. A franchise agreement that results in a closed network, i.e. the franchisees are prohibited from selling to non-franchisees, will be assessed under the principles applicable to selective distribution systems.[11] A franchise agreement that does not create a closed network but grants territorial exclusivity and protection from active sales by other franchisees will be assessed under the principles applicable to exclusive distribution.[12] The licensing of intellectual property rights is typically exempted as well, if certain conditions are met (Article 2(3) Vertical-BER 2022/720).[13]

### 3. Individual exemption

The exemption for franchise agreements may go even further. If a franchise agreement does not meet the conditions of the Vertical-BER, it may benefit from an individual exemption according to Article 101(3)TFEU, as Guidelines on Vertical Restraints explain (No. 168): the more important the transfer of know-how is, the more likely it is that the restraints of competition create efficiencies and/or are indispensable for protecting the franchisor's know-how. This increases the likelihood of an individual exemption pursuant to the case-by-case application provided in Article 101(3)TFEU. 21

## V. Franchising and consumer protection

Under German law, the franchisee has a right of revocation (*Widerrufsrecht*) pursuant to the consumer protection regulation in §§ 355, 510(1) BGB if the franchisee is a consumer (§ 13 BGB) or start-up entrepreneur (§ 513 BGB). A franchisee is usually not a consumer, as he carries out the franchise business as a commercial activity and normally concludes the franchise agreement as part of this commercial activities.[14] However, § 513 BGB establishes that the right of revocation and the written form requirement also apply to start-up entrepreneurs (i) if a consumer loan (*Verbraucherdarlehen*), a postponement of payment, or other financing assistance was granted to the start-up entrepreneur (franchisee) for taking up a trade or self-employed occupation, or (ii) a start-up entrepreneur (franchisee) enters into a contract for delivery by instalments (*Ratenlieferungsvertrag*) to take up a trade or self-employed occupation. The consumer protection applies only if – in the case of a consumer loan – the net loan does not exceed EUR 75,000; and – in the case of a delivery by instalment – the cash price does not exceed EUR 75,000. In practice, the franchisor must check whether the franchisee's payment obligation resulting from the franchise agreement exceeds EUR 75,000. This is typically the case if the franchisee has to pay an entrance fee to the franchisor to enter into the franchise system. Future obligations (e.g. the franchisee's payment obligations for the purchase of the franchisor's products) are not taken into consideration when assessing the cash price. 22

A violation of the franchisor's obligation to notify the franchisee of his right of revocation – if the franchisee has such a right – may have severe consequences for the franchisor. Pursuant to § 355(3) BGB, the franchisee may have an unlimited right to revoke the franchise agreement where the franchisor's notification was either wrong (in form or content) or was omitted entirely. This gives the franchisee effectively the right to cancel the franchise agreement at any time and without cause. Therefore, if the conditions described above are met (or even if doubt about the fulfilment of the said conditions exists), 23

[11] Guidelines on Vertical Restraints mn. 167.
[12] Guidelines on Vertical Restraints mn. 167.
[13] Guidelines on Vertical Restraints mn. 71 et seqq.
[14] Cf. BGH III ZB 36/04, NJW 2005, 1273 (1774).

the franchisor is well-advised to instruct or notify the franchisee in the form described in § 356(3) BGB.

### VI. Franchise agreements as standard terms and conditions

24 Franchise agreements are typically contract terms that are pre-formulated and intended for repeated use, which the franchisor imposes on the franchisee upon entering into the agreement.[15] If these requirements are fulfilled (which is normally the case), the provisions of the franchise agreements are subject to the test of reasonableness. Specific provisions of the franchise agreement may effectively be void if a provision constitutes an unfair disadvantage to the franchisee. To avoid the risk of invalidity, the franchisor is well-advised to only use contractual terms that are compatible with the essential principles of the statutory provision. This means that the franchisor should only use such contract clauses that are fair and well-balanced (legal advice will be necessary). This also applies to the franchise agreement's annexes and particularly to the franchise handbook and the obligations listed therein.

## G. Termination

### I. Ordinary and extraordinary notice of termination

25 Franchise agreements are ongoing continuing obligations. They may therefore be terminated for cause without notice (§ 89a HGB and § 314 BGB) or ordinarily with notice (→ Ch. 1 mn. 92 et seqq.).

#### 1. Notice period

26 If the parties (i) have failed to agree on notice periods for ordinary notice of termination or (ii) such notice periods agreed on between the parties are void due to the test of reasonableness (§§ 305 et seqq. BGB – unfair disadvantage), the parties' right to terminate the franchise agreement ordinarily is not automatically excluded. The right to terminate a franchise agreement by giving ordinary notice stems from the ability of a party to terminate any ongoing continuing obligation (§§ 542(1), 620(2), 723(1) BGB). However, the determination of the proper notice period in such cases remains problematic.

#### 2. Distribution-based franchising

27 With regard to franchise agreements that are dominated by the distribution of products, the notice periods stipulated in § 89 HGB apply.[16] Pursuant to § 89(1) HGB, franchise agreements of an indefinite duration may be terminated with prior notice of one month during the first year (if the parties have not agreed on a startup or probation period), two months during the second year, and three months in the third through the fifth year. After five years, the franchise agreement may be terminated with prior notice of six months.

[15] Cf. OLG Munich 7 U 5730/01, BB 2002, 2521 (2522).
[16] BGH VIII ZR 59/01, NJW-RR 2002, 1554 (1555).

## II. Franchisee's termination compensation

28 So far there are only a few judgments from German courts expressly granting or rejecting a claim for termination compensation from franchisors (→ mn. 2). It is apparent, however, that in certain franchising constellations the dependency of the franchisee is comparable to that of a commercial agent. This may be the case, in particular, if the franchisee is integrated into the franchisor's sales organisation in such a way that the franchisee, in economic terms, is required to perform tasks which are comparable to those of a commercial agent to a substantial extent and the franchisee is obliged to transfer his customer data or significant parts thereof to the franchisor in order to enable the latter to benefit from the advantages of the customer base immediately after the termination of the franchise agreement. The Federal Court of Justice has determined that a trademark licensee may, under the described conditions, have a claim for termination compensation against the trademark licensor pursuant to § 89b HGB by analogy.[17] Such an application of § 89b HGB is also acknowledged for distributors under the said conditions.[18] Although the Federal Court of Justice has not yet clarified whether a franchisee has a claim for termination compensation upon the termination of the franchise agreement,[19] there is a considerable likelihood that the highest German civil court will award such a claim if the conditions for an analogous application of § 89b HGB are fulfilled.[20]

## III. Post-contractual prohibition of competition

29 According to § 90a HGB, an agreement in which a commercial agent is restricted in his commercial activity following termination of the contractual relationship (post-contractual prohibition of competition) (i) must be made in writing, (ii) may run for no longer than two years following the termination of the contractual relationship, (iii) may cover only the geographical area or group of customers assigned to the commercial agent, and (iv) may only refer to the type of business in which the commercial agent was responsible for soliciting transactions. As recompense the principal is obliged to pay a reasonable compensation to the commercial agent for the duration of the prohibition of competition.

30 The Federal Court of Justice has ruled that § 90a HGB is applicable to franchise agreements by analogy if the franchisee's position in the given case is comparable to that of a commercial agent. However, there is no general analogous application of § 90a HGB (nor of any other provision of the HGB) to franchise agreements.[21]

---

17 BGH I ZR 3/09, GRUR 2010, 1107.
18 BGH VIII ZR 352/04, NJW-RR 2007, 1327.
19 MüKoHGB/Ströbl HGB § 89b mn. 28.
20 BGH VII ZR 109/13, NJW 2015, 945 (946).
21 BGH I ZR 209/84, NJW-RR 1987, 612.

# Chapter 15
# Transport and freight agreement

**Bibliography:** Ebenroth/Boujong/Joost/Strohn, HGB/Reuschle, 4th edn, Munich 2020; Höra/Schubach (eds), Münchener Anwaltshandbuch, Versicherungsrecht, 5th edn, Munich 2022; Herber, 'Neue Entwicklungen im Recht des Multimodaltransports', TranspR 2006, 435; Hopt (ed.), Handelsgesetzbuch: HGB, 42nd edn, Munich 2023; Mankowski, 'Neues aus Europa zum Internationalen Privatrecht der Transportverträge: Art. 5 Rom I-VO', TranspR 2008, 339; Münchener Kommentar zum Handelsgesetzbuch: HGB, 5th edn, Munich 2021; Prölss/Martin (eds), Versicherungsvertragsgesetz, 31st edn, Munich 2021.

## A. Introduction

1 Freight and forwarding laws regulate how goods are organised for transport and who is liable – and to what extent – for damages to the goods. As a rule, freight or forwarding agreements often accompany purchase agreements. The purchase agreement or provisions in purchase law simply stipulate when risk passes from one party to another, i.e. who is liable at what point for any deterioration in or for the loss of the goods. The BGB stipulates in § 269 that the buyer can collect the goods at the seller's premises (obligation to be performed at the debtor's place of business).[1] However, the parties can agree to deviate from this provision, which happens often. In practice, parties usually agree that the seller will send the goods to the buyer. The seller is then obliged to hand the goods over to the transport company (e.g. a carrier or forwarding agent) specified to carry out the shipment.[2]

2 Transport law is regulated in §§ 407 et seqq. HGB. These paragraphs contain certain mandatory provisions that either cannot be waived or can only be deviated from subject to specific formal requirements. §§ 407 et seqq. HGB govern freight agreements (*Frachtvertrag*), while §§ 453 et seqq. HGB govern forwarding agreements (*Speditionsvertrag*). The freight carrier (*Frachtführer*) undertakes to carry the goods to their destination and to deliver them at the destination to the receiver. A freight agreement is therefore a contract to produce a work (*Werkvertrag*).

3 The forwarding agent (*Spediteur*), in contrast, organises the shipment of the goods. The forwarding agreement is a subcategory of the business management contract (*Geschäftsbesorgungsvertrag*). It can also contain carrier obligations if the forwarding agent is, in addition to organising the shipment, also under the obligation to carry out (at least a part of) the shipment itself.[3] The forwarding agreement is therefore often more extensive than the freight agreement, since the forwarding agent is entrusted with the organisation – i.e. overall handling – of a shipment (and often a large number of shipments) and frequently also carries out carrier services.

---

[1] Article 31(a) CISG contains a similar provision.

[2] Cf. § 447(1) BGB and Article 31(a), 67 CISG. The handover of the goods also marks the passing of the risk.

[3] If the forwarding agent substitutes itself for the third party (*Selbsteintritt*, self-substitution), the forwarding agent is liable as a freight carrier (*Obhutshaftung*, custodial liability) (§ 458 HGB).

## B. Content of the agreement

The purchase agreement does not, as a rule, stipulate any transport obligation or lay down the details pertaining to the transport. These are typically regulated in a transport agreement (i.e. a freight or forwarding agreement) that covers aspects such as (i) the place of delivery, (ii) the time of delivery, (iii) documentation, (iv) the means of transport, (v) safety obligations, and (vi) liability. A transport agreement is often accompanied by an insurance contract, which is intended to reduce the risks associated with liability and damages. The following contracts must be distinguished from each another: purchase agreemet, transport agreement, and transport insurance contract. 4

## C. The transport process

A typical combined transport chain often consists of the following links: 5
- Transport of the goods to the transshipment terminal by truck (pre-carriage)
- Transshipment in the source terminal (*Quellenterminal*) and loading onto a different means of transport
- Transport by rail, sea, or inland waterway to the target terminal (main carriage)
- Transshipment in the target terminal
- Transport to the receiver by truck (on-carriage)

A sequence of different modes of transport during the main carriage is also conceiv- 6
able, for example carriage by sea from the source terminal to an interim terminal, and then carriage by rail to the target terminal.

## D. Liability

The liability of the freight carrier and that of the forwarding agent are largely similar. 7
The provisions governing forwarding activities are related to the provisions governing freight activities. The freight carrier's liability arises from § 425 HGB and that of the forwarding agent from § 461 HGB. The most typical situations involving liability are briefly discussed below.

### I. Damage to goods

Pursuant to § 461(1) HGB, the forwarding agent is liable for the damage that arises from 8
the loss of or damage to goods in its custody, similar to the liability of a freight carrier defined by law. They both have custodial liability regardless of fault. The forwarding agent is deemed to have custody of the goods if they are in his safekeeping. Auxiliary parties (the forwarding agent's own employees/sub-forwarding agents) may also hold the goods in safekeeping on behalf of the forwarding agent. The custody phase starts as soon as the forwarding agent acquires possession of the goods and ends as soon as it relinquishes

possession. Only forwarding agents that act purely in an organisational capacity without any possession of the goods (*Schreibtischspediteur*) do not have any custodial liability.

## II. Other breaches of duty

9 The forwarding agent is liable for (other) breaches of duty (such as delay) subject to the principle of presumed fault (*vermutetes Verschulden*) (§ 461(2) HGB). This gives the forwarding agent the opportunity to exculpate himself from liability pursuant to §§ 461(2), 454 HGB. Exculpation, however, requires that neither the forwarding agent nor one of its vicarious agents was negligent in causing the damage. This negative proof is very difficult for the forwarding agent to provide.[4]

## III. Deviating agreements

10 §§ 466, 449 HGB stipulate to what extent it is possible to deviate from the provisions on liability applicable to the forwarding agent and the freight carrier. Pursuant to § 466(2) sentence 1 HGB, it is only possible for a forwarding agent to deviate from such provisions if the deviating clauses have been negotiated in detail. This means that the user must present the respective provisions for serious discussion. Unlike in the case of the law governing standard terms and conditions, these detailed negotiations do not fail because a deviating liability provision has been agreed upon or are identical in a number of similar agreements (i.e. framework agreements). The requirements are therefore less stringent than in standard terms and conditions. § 466(2) sentence 2 HGB provides a way for the parties to limit liability by deviating from legal provisions in a specific corridor.

## IV. Extent of liability

11 The liability provisions applicable to the forwarding agent and the freight carrier are essentially based on the weight of the goods shipped (§§ 431, 461 HGB). According to these provisions, the compensation to be paid due to loss of or damage to the entire shipment is limited to an amount of 8.33 accounting units for each kilogram of the gross weight of the shipment. According to § 431(4) HGB, accounting unit means the special drawing right (*Sonderziehungsrecht* – SZR) of the International Monetary Fund published on its website. A special drawing right is currently equal to around EUR 1.23. This means that the liability pursuant to § 431(1) HGB is limited to around EUR 10.25 per kilogram.

## V. When the limitation of liability does not apply

### 1. Vicarious liability

12 § 428 sentence 1 HGB regulates the so-called vicarious liability. According to this, the freight carrier is liable for the acts and omissions of his employees to the same extent as for his own acts and omissions as when the employees act to fulfil their duties. § 428 HGB is an imputation rule and applies to liability in the following cases, among others:

[4] For further reference, see MüKoHGB/Bydlinski/Valder HGB § 461 mn. 17.

- Liability for damage to goods and for delay (§ 425 HGB)
- Liability for damage caused through loss of or damage to the documents handed over to the freight carrier or their incorrect use (§ 413(2) HGB)
- Violations of the obligations laid down in §§ 408 et seqq. HGB

This imputation of liability also applies to the acts and omissions of other persons used by the freight carrier to carry out the shipment (§ 428 sentence 2 HGB). For example, the freight carrier is liable for damage caused by its independent sub-carriers and any vicarious agents used by them as well as any sub-carriers commissioned by said independent sub-carriers. If § 428 HGB is not applicable, the general attribution rule stipulated in § 278 BGB applies. 13

## 2. Liability for intentional acts or omissions

### a) Intentional acts or omissions

§ 435 HGB stipulates that the exemptions from and limitations of liability in §§ 407 et seqq. HGB and the freight agreement do not apply if loss or damage is caused by an act or an omission by the freight carrier or a person referred to in § 428 HGB (this covers both the freight carrier's employees and subcontractors) with the intent to cause damage or recklessly and in the knowledge that damage would probably occur. The reason is that the liability privileges granted to the freight carrier specifically relate to risks typical in freight and forwarding agreements. If the freight carrier acts intentionally or recklessly, these liability privileges cease to apply, i.e. all limitations of liability laid down in the law governing freight agreements or in the freight agreement itself are subject to the condition that the freight carrier does not act intentionally or with deliberate recklessness.[5] As a result, the limitations of and exemptions from liability do not apply if the freight carrier itself, one of its employees or another person brought in by the freight carrier, pursuant to § 428 HGB, acted either intentionally or recklessly and in the knowledge that loss or damage was likely to occur. While it is the auxiliary person himself who must be considered when determining whether an act was committed intentionally or recklessly, the freight carrier must – even if he is not at fault in this regard per se – allow the subjective element of fault to be imputed to him because he chose to make use of this person. 14

### b) Evidence

The injured party bears the burden of proof.[6] The evidence to be furnished by the injured party indicating fault pursuant to § 435 HGB may arise from the nature and extent of the damage to the goods.[7] The burden of proof cannot be reversed. However, if the injured customer claims damages from the freight carrier, the latter is obliged to provide information on all the facts and circumstances arising from his area of operations, including (i) how the transport was organised, (ii) the possible causes of the damage, (iii) how the damage occurred, and (iv) the safety measures taken. The freight carrier therefore has a secondary burden of presentation in this regard.[8] 15

---

[5] Cf. also Article 29(2) sentence 1 CMR.

[6] BGH I ZR 55/01, NJW-RR 2004, 395; Hopt/Merkt HGB § 435 mn. 1.

[7] BGH I ZR 176/03, TranspR 2006, 393.

[8] BGH I ZR 74/05, NJW 2008, 920; BGH I ZR 275/00, TranspR 2004, 175; BGH I ZR 176/03, NJW-RR 2007, 34; for examples of qualified fault (*qualifiziertes Verschulden*), see Hopt/Merkt HGB § 435 mn. 3.

## E. Other mandatory provisions in transport law

16 In addition to the provisions of the HGB, there are numerous other rules and regulations in transport law that must be observed by the parties.

### I. CMR

17 Such mandatory provisions in transport law can be found in Article 41 of the Convention on the Contract for the International Carriage of Goods by Road (CMR). The CMR applies to every contract that regulates (i) the carriage of goods by road (ii) in vehicles (iii) for reward, if (iv) the place of taking over of the goods and the one designated for delivery are in two different countries, of which (v) at least one is a contracting country (Article 1 CMR). Article 17 CMR regulates the question of liability. Liability under the CMR is to a large extent defined as strict liability.

### II. German Forwarding Agents Standard Terms and Conditions

18 The German Forwarding Agents Standard Terms and Conditions (*Allgemeine Deutsche Spediteurbedingungen* – ADSp) are model terms and conditions that the parties can include as part of the freight or forwarding agreement. They are not mandatory, but are merely non-binding recommendations developed by bodies such as the Association of German Chambers of Commerce and Industry (*Deutsche Industrie- und Handelskammer* – DIHK) and others. They have more authority than other rules and regulations because, as is clear from the preamble, they were agreed upon by stakeholders with various economic interests, namely traders, industry specialists, and the forwarding sector. The ADSp is therefore generally well-balanced. They must be agreed on by the parties to be included in a contractual relationship. ADSp 22, 23, 24 contain liability provisions that deviate from the HGB in that they are more favourable to forwarding agents. Although the provisions are subject to the test of reasonableness,[9] the ADSp is a structure negotiated by participants from different stakeholders. As a result, its well-balanced regulations are generally commensurate with existing law, as can be seen by the number of court decisions upholding their validity.[10]

## F. Multimodal transport

19 The rise in container shipping means that carriage very often takes place based on a uniform freight agreement by different means of transport. Typically, the multimodal freight carrier retains custody of the goods even if it transfers direct possession of the goods to sub-carriers. The sub-carriers shipping the goods usually do not have any control during shipment, especially when it comes to transloading from one means of transport to another, since the responsibility for transloading the goods lies with the multimodal

[9] Hopt/Merkt HGB preliminary note to ADSp mn. 5.
[10] BGH, NJW 1995, 1490; NJW 1995, 3117; NJW 1982, 1820.

freight carrier. This creates considerable problems when it comes to determining which provisions are decisive in terms of liability for damages. The provisions on multimodal transport resolve these problems.

## I. Provisions of German law in general

In 1998, German legislator codified the principles developed by the Federal Court of Justice on multimodal transport in §§ 452 et seqq. HGB. Multimodal transport is a transport chain consisting of several links, in which the carriage of persons or goods is carried out using two or more different modes of transport. This is also known as combined transport and is the opposite of direct transport (unimodal transport). § 452 HGB stipulates that multimodal transport exists in cases where 20

1. the shipment of goods is carried out by different means of transport,
2. different legal provisions would apply to the different fare stages (hypothetical sections) of the route, and
3. the shipment is based on a uniform freight agreement.

## II. Specific requirements

### 1. Uniform freight agreement

A uniform freight agreement does not exist in the case of so-called fractional transport (*gebrochene Beförderung*), which is when separate agreements are concluded for individual sections of a route.[11] A forwarding based on a uniform freight agreement may also fall under § 452 HGB if carried out by different means of transport.[12] A forwarding agent acting on a fixed-cost basis (§ 459 HGB) is liable pursuant to § 452 HGB if the carriage takes place using different means of transport (and the other requirements have also been fulfilled). However, a uniform freight agreement does not exist if the freight carrier only undertakes to transport the goods over one section of the route and hires other freight carriers in the name of the sender or in its own name for the account of the sender to transport the goods over the subsequent sections of the route (§ 453 HGB).[13] 21

### 2. Different means of transport

The transport of the goods must be carried out consecutively using at least two means of transport that are different from one another in technical terms. Transloading is required for this (no piggyback transport), since the means of transport is decisive (rail and road transport are multimodal). Different means of transport are, for example, transport by air, road, sea, inland waterway, and rail. It is not sufficient if a different means of transport is used for a small section during transloading, e.g. moving a container from ship A to ship B at a port using a fork-lift truck. In this case, the transport is considered the same modality. If, however, the same type of transport is used in a multi-functional manner (e.g. ships as inland waterway and seagoing vessels or amphibious craft in the water and on land), whether the means of transport are in fact different depends on how 22

---

[11] BGH I ZR 127/85, TranspR 1987, 447.

[12] Hopt/Merkt HGB § 452 mn. 4.

[13] Cf. MüKoHGB/Herber/Pötschke HGB § 452 mn. 16.

the respective modes of transport are used and what the sections of the route are like.[14] A carriage from Cologne to Rotterdam by ship (inland waterway) and then transloading into a consecutive shipment from Rotterdam to New York City also by ship (sea) constitutes different means of transport.

### 3. Application of legal provisions to hypothetical sections of the route

23 This criterion presupposes that different laws would apply to at least two of the means of transport (sections of the route) if the parties had concluded separate agreements for the individual sections of the route instead of a uniform freight agreement. The legal relationships that actually exist or would theoretically exist between the multimodal carrier and any sub-carrier do not matter; only the relationship between the parties to the multimodal agreement is decisive (*e.g.* the forwarding agent and the seller of the goods).[15]

## III. Legal consequences

24 If the requirements for multimodal transport are met, the rights and obligations of the parties to the agreement arise from §§ 407 et seqq. HGB (unless international conventions have priority). This also applies to multimodal transport that includes a leg at sea, even though unimodal maritime carriage is, as such, subject to the mandatory provisions in §§ 476 et seqq. HGB. Consequently, agreements pursuant to which all the sections of the route would – if they were independently linked – be governed by different legal provisions could also be subject to the general freight law provisions in §§ 407 et seqq. HGB. Examples include (i) the carriage of goods involving an international section by air followed by cross-border road transport or (ii) the carriage of goods involving an international section by inland waterway and a subsequent section by sea (with trans-loading).[16]

25 The rights and obligations of the parties to the agreement in §§ 407 et seqq. HGB are for the most part optional. The parties can therefore adjust these in line with their requirements. Standard terms and conditions can also be used, if these do not affect the liability for damage to goods and for delays. Any deviating provisions affecting these areas must satisfy the specific formal requirements of §§ 449(2), 452d(2) HGB. The provisions of §§ 407 et seqq. HGB apply in any case to transport within Germany by car, truck, airplane, train, or inland waterway vessel.

## IV. Liability provisions for multimodal transport according to European and national law

26 Should there be any loss, damage, or delay in delivery in a multimodal transport, the applicable national law must first be determined.

[14] Ebenroth/Boujong/Joost/Strohn/Reuschle HGB § 452 mn. 15.
[15] BGH I ZR 151/04, NJW-RR 2008, 840.
[16] MüKoHGB/Herber/Pötschke HGB § 452 mn. 38.

## 1. Applicable law

The applicable law for the contract is determined by Articles 3 and 5 Rome I Regulation. Article 3 Rome I Regulation allows the parties to choose which country's substantive law is applicable. If no such choice was made, Article 5 Rome I Regulation states that the law of the habitual residence of the carrier comes into effect. If German law governs the contract, a distinction must then be made as to whether the place where the damage occurred is known or unknown. 27

## 2. Known place of damage

If the place of damage is known, § 452a HGB applies. Effectively, the provisions under the law governing the section of carriage where the damage occurred apply (e.g. international transport law convention, freight or forwarding law, merchant shipping law, CMR, foreign substantive law, etc.).[17] Thus, the liability rules that would apply to a (hypothetically concluded individual) contract of carriage for this section of carriage are applicable (§ 452a sentence 1 HGB). The specific law of the hypothetically concluded individual contract is not determined by § 452a HGB but instead in accordance with general private international law. From the perspective of the German *lex fori*, Articles 3 and 5 Rome I Regulation are again applicable for this section only.[18] If a choice of law is made for a uniform freight agreement, the chosen law is decisive.[19] 28

## 3. Unknown place of damage

If, on the other hand, the place of damage is unknown, general freight law set forth in §§ 407 et seqq. HGB applies. This is the more common case in practice, since the majority of transports are carried out by means of containers. If, for example, German law is applicable for a contract in which a container laden with glass windows were transported from Stuttgart to Antwerp, loaded onto a seagoing vessel there and then transported to Morocco, and it became apparent upon unloading that a number of the window panes were broken, whether the damage occurred during the transport by land or sea cannot be determined in usual circumstances. For this reason, general freight law applies (§§ 452, 407 et seqq. HGB). 29

## 4. Order of application

For purposes of practical application, the procedure is as follows: If German law is applicable and different means of transport are used and the transported goods are damaged or lost, one must examine (i) whether §§ 452 et seqq. HGB are applicable (i.e. a case of multimodal transport) and, if so, (ii) whether the place of damage is known. 30

## 5. No overriding international conventions

A differentiation between a known and an unknown place of damage is only necessary if the liability in the case of multimodal transport is not governed by overriding international conventions. If international conventions provide rules in the case at hand, these rules take precedence. Currently, international conventions contain special provisions 31

---

17 For an overview, see MüKoHGB/Herber/Pötschke HGB § 452a mn. 21–39.

18 Cf. Mankowski, TranspR 2008, 341.

19 OLG Hamburg 6 U 178/03, TranspR 2004, 402 (403); Herber, TranspR 2006, 435 (436 et seqq.).

with respect to a multimodal carriage only for specific issues, for example the provisions in Article 2(1) CMR (international carriage of goods by road); Article 38 Convention concerning International Carriage by Rail 1999 (CIM); Article 18(3) and Article 31 Warsaw Convention; Article 18(3) and Article 38 Montreal Convention. These provisions take precedence.

## V. Notice of damage; limitation period

32 In the event of a claim, notice of damage must be given in due time and in the correct form. According to § 452b(1) HGB, the notice of damage is sufficient if it complies with the legal provisions that apply to a hypothetical contract for the last section of the carriage. The limitation period for loss, damage, or delay in delivery begins with the delivery of the goods to the receiver. The delivery that ends the last section of the carriage is decisive. The delivery to the contractually agreed upon final receiver and not the occurrence of the damage triggers the start of the limitation period, § 452b(2), sentence 2 HGB. This is true even if the place and time of the actual damage is known.

# G. Maritime law and liability

33 Maritime law and the corresponding liability provisions are regulated in §§ 481 et seqq. HGB. They are not discussed in this book.

# H. Transport insurance

34 The term transport insurance mainly covers two types of insurance. The (actual) goods transport insurance (*Warentransportversicherung*) and freight forwarders liability insurance (*Verkehrshaftungsversicherung*). The purpose of transport insurances is to make risks – that can be exorbitant – predictable in exchange for payment of an insurance premium, and in so doing, allow for a reliable price calculation for the goods and the carriage. Should the goods be damaged during transport, the forwarding agent or freight carrier is liable vis-à-vis the customer for the goods in his custody. Therefore, in order to cover their statutory liability, freight carriers or forwarding agents almost always conclude freight forwarders liability insurance policies. If the parties apply the ADSp, the forwarding agent or freight carrier is obliged to provide insurance. However, since the liability of a forwarding agent or freight carrier is limited, it can make sense for the customer to also obtain goods transport insurance – either on its own or through the freight carrier. This makes sense especially if the goods are valuable and the extent of potential damage is great.

# I. Goods transport insurance

## 1. Insurance beneficiary

Goods transport insurance protects against damage and loss of the transported goods. The beneficiary is the policyholder – i.e. depending on the delivery, the buyer or the seller of the goods, and not the freight carrier or the forwarding agent. The legal basis of goods transport insurance is an insurance contract entered into under private law pursuant to §§ 130 to 141 VVG (*Versicherungsvertragsgesetz* – Insurance Contracts Act) that is often concluded with the content of the model terms and conditions of the German Insurance Association.[20] Thus, the actual goods being transferred – and not the conduct of the carrier – are insured. The conditions of the DTV Cargo 2000/2008 are only focused on the risks posing a threat to the goods being transported. Neither the means of transport nor the third-party liability of the transport staff are insured.[21] 35

## 2. Insurance coverage

The insurance generally covers the goods 'from door to door', i.e. from their removal in the scope of the carriage until their arrival, including discharge, unless otherwise agreed upon. Regarding the extent of the coverage, a distinction must be made between 'full coverage' and 'limited coverage'. Limited coverage only includes protection against certain risks, whereas full coverage includes all damage regardless of the risk from which they arose. The individually insured risks can also be inferred from the model terms and conditions of the DTV Cargo 2000/2008. Since the 'limited coverage' only covers the risks explicitly referred to in section 2.1. DTV Cargo 2000/2008 (transport accident, collapse of storage facilities, fire, lightning, explosions, natural disasters, goods jettisoned, washed overboard or sacrificed, discharge at a port of distress and total loss of entire shipments during loading, transloading or unloading of a means of transport), this insurance form is not very common in practice.[22] In addition, the insured party also bears the burden of proof for the cause of the damage. In particular, if valuable goods are being transported, the comprehensive full coverage has become popular as an 'all-risk' coverage. It generally covers all damage regardless of cause. 36

## 3. Practical advice

In general, each insurance contract should be individually agreed upon since the level of transport risk can vary depending on the goods, transport route, means of transport, packaging, etc. In principle, all the goods can be insured; one should make sure that all the insured goods are specified in the insurance contract – at least in general terms. Otherwise, gaps in coverage are possible. The exact description of the insured goods is necessary to avoid dispute about whether the damage is covered by the insurance. 37

# II. Freight forwarders liability insurance

A freight carrier, forwarding agent, or warehouse keeper (*Lagerhalter*) usually concludes a freight forwarders liability insurance policy to protect itself from its statutory 38

[20] See DTV cargo insurance conditions 2000 in the version of 2008 (DTV Cargo 2000/2008).
[21] Prölss/Martin/Koller VVG § 130 mn. 2–2d.
[22] Cf. MAH VersR/Gercke/Gerhard § 11 mn. 52.

liability. Pursuant to §§ 425 et seqq. HGB, a freight carrier generally has custodial liability regardless of fault for all goods in its custody. In the case of a forwarding agent, a distinction must be made: On one hand, he has custodial liability regardless of fault pursuant to § 461(1) HGB if he carries out the shipment himself (forwarding agent's right to contract with himself, § 458 HGB). On the other hand, if the objects are not in his custody, a forwarding agent is liable only for breaches of duty that fall within his responsibility (e.g. if he only handles organisational tasks, such as selecting the freight carrier), § 461(2) HGB. Liability of a warehouse keeper is less strict than that of a freight carrier or forwarding agent. A warehouse keeper is only liable for presumed fault, § 475 HGB.

**39** Freight forwarders liability insurance is third-party liability insurance in the sense of §§ 100 et seqq. VVG. However, according to §§ 113 et seqq. VVG, insurance is only compulsory for certain freight carriers, namely those who carry goods using a truck with a permissible total weight of more than 3.5 tons pursuant to §§ 7a, 1(1) Act on Road Haulage of Goods (*Güterkraftverkehrsgesetz* – GüKG) or those who carry goods via air pursuant to § 4 Act Implementing the Montreal Convention (*Durchführungsgesetz zum Montrealer Übereinkommen* – MontÜG).[23] The ADSp also oblige the forwarding agent or freight carrier to take out a freight forwarders liability insurance policy, ADSp 29. Otherwise, the forwarding agent is prohibited from invoking the provisions of the ADSp that are more favourable for him. The model terms and conditions of the DTV (DTV-VHV 2003/2011) have also gained acceptance in practice with respect to freight forwarders liability insurance.

## I. International transport law

**40** The question of the applicable law is often important since goods are frequently transported around the world. Private international law of the forum state (*lex fori*) is decisive when determining the relevant law. However, international treaties supersede national law and therefore also the private international law of the court called upon to hear the matter. This applies to the CMR, among others.

[23] MAH VersR/Gercke/Gerhard § 11 mn. 177.

# Chapter 16
# Warehousing agreement

**Bibliography:** Ebenroth/Boujong/Joost, Handelsgesetzbuch: HGB, 4th edn, Munich 2020; Hopt (ed.), Handelsgesetzbuch: HGB, 42nd edn, Munich 2023; Lommatzsch, Transportrecht, Stuttgart 2012.

## A. Introduction

After distribution and transport, goods often need to be stored in a warehouse before they are processed and/or sold. Warehousing goods not only provides security of supply, it also increases efficiency. In Germany, the law relating to warehousing is contained in §§ 467 et seqq. HGB. Pursuant to § 475h HGB, large parts of warehousing legislation are not mandatory. In practice, standard terms and conditions or ADSp are often used in the warehousing industry. 1

A warehousing contract (*Lagervertrag*) creates a long-term legal relationship that involves the performance of continuing obligations. In addition to the specific rules contained in §§ 467 to 475h HGB, the provisions of §§ 688 et seqq. BGB relating to contracts on safekeeping (*Verwahrungsvertrag*) also apply on a subsidiary basis. Warehousing is more than just safekeeping, however. The main subject matter of a warehousing contract is the warehousing and storage of goods by a commercial warehouse keeper, whose responsibility is to safeguard the goods against all conceivable dangers. Warehousing contracts are distinct from logistics or transport contracts. Logistics contracts are a hybrid form of contract for services that generally go beyond pure warehousing and include further services such as commissioning and packaging goods. Transport contracts solely concern the transport of goods from one place to another. 2

## B. Parties' obligations

### I. Storing party

The obligations of the storing party (i.e. the party wishing to have goods stored in the warehouse, *Einlagerer*) are set out in §§ 467(2), 474, and 468 HGB. The storing party's main obligation is to pay the agreed upon fees, but it must also reimburse the warehouse keeper for disbursements (*Aufwendungen*) incurred – that are legitimately considered to be necessary – for the warehousing of the goods.[1] Costs that are necessary to perform the duty of care for the goods are not disbursements pursuant to § 474 HGB. These costs are already covered by the fees paid by the storing party. Under § 468 HGB the storing party also has extensive obligations to provide information to the warehouse keeper and to 3

[1] This includes insurance costs, see Ebenroth/Boujong/Joost/Strohn/Heublein HGB § 474 mn. 4.

secure the goods (information about dangers, packaging, labelling obligations, and duty of disclosure). This is due to the warehouse keeper often not having detailed information about the goods in question (that can heighten risk) and frequently not being able to tell from the packaging exactly what goods he has in storage.

### II. Warehouse keeper

4 The warehouse keeper's job is to warehouse (*lagern*) and take custody (*aufbewahren*) of the goods. Warehousing is defined as the placing of goods in premises intended and designed for this purpose for a defined period. Taking custody, on the other hand, means that the warehouse keeper takes the goods into his custody (*Obhut*).[2] Simply renting out warehouse facilities does not constitute custody.[3] Custody includes the warehouse keeper's obligation to keep the goods properly, to check them regularly, and to notify the storing party about any changes in the goods,[4] which includes taking receipt of the goods. It is also the warehouse keeper's obligation to protect the goods against dangers, although this does not mean that the warehouse keeper has to constantly take preventive measures. At the request of the storing party, the warehouse keeper must insure the goods (§ 472 HGB). Yet, pursuant to § 474 HGB, the warehouse keeper can demand reimbursement of the insurance costs. The warehouse keeper must also secure the storing party's claims for damages. This means that the warehouse keeper must point out visible damage when taking receipt of the goods, inform the storing party without delay, and, in cases of special urgency, call in an expert to examine the damage. The storing party can demand the return of the warehoused goods at any time (§ 473(1) HGB). § 472(2) HGB stipulates that the warehouse keeper may only subcontract the warehousing services if the storing party expressly agrees thereto.

## C. Special form of warehousing: consignment stock warehouse contract

### I. Definition

5 A consignment stock warehouse (*Konsignationswarenlager*) is a warehouse of a supplier or service provider located in the vicinity of, or possibly even on, the customer's (purchaser's) premises. The goods remain the property of the supplier (storing party) until such time as the customer removes them from the warehouse. The removal of the goods from the warehouse marks the time of delivery and transfer of title to the customer.

### II. Advantages

6 Maintaining a consignment stock warehouse frequently involves high costs for the storing party. However, the storing party (usually the seller) in a long-term supply re-

---

[2] LG Munich 3 HK O 9954/05, TranspR 2007, 82.
[3] Hopt/Merkt HGB § 467 mn. 4.
[4] BGH I ZR 90/50, MDR 1951, 669.

lationship may be able to secure the customer's loyalty because it is cheaper and easier for the latter to take goods from the consignment stock warehouse than to look around for another supplier. For the customer (warehouse keeper), having a consignment stock warehouse nearby has the advantage that it gives him a high level of security in terms of supply and that the goods only have to be transported over a very short distance, or no distance at all. Also, since the goods are only billed upon removal from the warehouse, the customer has less capital tied up in stock.

### III. Other forms of warehousing

In business, factory supply storage centres (*Vorratslager*), transshipment warehouses (*Umschlagslager*), and distribution centres (*Auslieferungslager*) are also important types of warehouses. 7

## D. Warehouse warrant

A warehouse warrant (*Lagerschein*) is a document issued by the warehouse keeper in which he undertakes to hand over the stored goods to the persons or categories of persons who present the warrant. If sold, the warehouse warrant has the function of a security paper.[5] 8

## E. Warehouse keeper's liability

### I. Liability for presumed fault

The liability of the warehouse keeper and its staff for loss or damage to the goods kept in the warehouse is regulated in § 475 HGB. This liability is a duty of care liability for presumed fault on the part of the warehouse keeper from the time he takes receipt of the goods to when they leave the warehouse. The warehouse keeper cannot escape liability by storing the goods with a third party (§ 475, sentence 2 HGB). The warehouse keeper is not liable only if he can show that even using the due care of a prudent merchant would not have prevented the damage. 9

### II. Compensation for loss of profit

Unlike in the law governing freight, the warehouse keeper must also compensate for pecuniary damage, which includes lost profit. This can result in significant risks on the part of the warehouse keeper, particularly in case of the loss or destruction of goods that are destined for use in production, for example, after the warehousing contract expired. In this case, compensation for loss of production must be paid. 10

[5] For details, see Lommatzsch, mn. 305–306.

## III. Deviating agreement

11 The warehouse keeper's liability is not capped by law. The parties may, however, agree on deviating provisions by mutual agreement (including standard terms and conditions). Therefore, from the warehouse keeper's perspective, it is advisable to agree on a liability cap in his favour and/or to take out insurance to cover the risks. This is often done by agreeing on the ADSp.[6]

## IV. Limitation

12 As a rule, the warehouse keeper's liability becomes statute-barred after one year (§ 475a HGB).

# F. Important content

13 The following points should be covered in a warehousing contract:

- Nature, characteristics of goods (suitability for storage, weight, hazardous substances), quantity of goods
- Instructions on special treatment (humidity, heat, stacking, storeroom conditions)
- Delivery intervals and periods
- Length of storage
- Type of packaging (pallet, cage, cardboard box)
- Warehouse opening times
- Warehousing insurance
- Warehouse keeper's liability
- Warehouse warrants
- Warehouse receipt (confirmation of receipt of goods by the warehouse keeper)
- Warehousing fees
- Miscellaneous (choice of law, jurisdiction, or arbitration clause)

---

[6] Cf. MüKoHGB/Hesse HGB § 475 mn. 20.

# Chapter 17
# Supply Chains Due Diligence Act

**Bibliography:** Gehling/Ott (eds), LkSG Kommentar, Cologne 2022; Hembach, 'Das LkSG und seine Umsetzung – ein Überblick', LMuR 2023, 15; Passas/Holtz, 'Die Gestaltung von LkSG-Compliance-Klauseln in Lieferbeziehungen', BB 2023, 387.

## A. Introduction

The Act on Corporate Due Diligence to Prevent Human Rights Violations in Supply Chains or, in short, the Supply Chain Due Diligence Act (*Lieferkettensorgfaltspflichtengesetz* – LkSG) came into force on 1 January 2023. From this date onwards, companies based in Germany with at least 3,000 employees are obliged to avoid and counteract human rights violations or environmental violations in their supply chains. This obligation is extended from 1 January 2024 to apply to all companies seated in Germany with at least 1,000 employees. For brevity, this text will only refer to companies with more than 1,000 employees. 1

The purpose of the LkSG is to strengthen compliance with human rights and environmental concerns in supply chains. Even though the LkSG primarily addresses human rights and environmental obligations of German companies with more than 1,000 employees, this does not mean that suppliers in the supply chain with employees less than 1,000 could ignore the LkSG. On the contrary, the requirements of the law will have an impact on many different facets of running a business, including sales, marketing, controlling, import/export, and other areas. The LkSG is not only relevant for companies with more than 1,000 employees, but also for their direct and indirect suppliers, even if they have fewer than 1,000 employees. 2

## B. Obligations imposed by the LkSG in a nutshell

Companies with more than 1,000 employees are obliged to determine the human rights and environmental risks of their direct suppliers by means of a risk analysis (§ 5 LkSG). If a company identifies such risks in its analysis, it must immediately take appropriate preventive measures vis-à-vis their direct suppliers (§ 6(1), (4) LkSG). The LkSG lists various preventive measures by way of example and also sets out requirements for the drafting of contracts between companies and their direct suppliers: 3

- Under § 6(4) no. 2 of the LkSG, companies with 1,000 employees are required to obtain contractual assurances from their direct suppliers that the direct supplier 'complies with human rights and environmental expectations and adequately addresses them along the supply chain.'

- According to § 6(4) no. 4 LkSG, companies with 1,000 employees are obliged to agree on appropriate contractual control mechanisms with their direct suppliers as well as their risk-based implementation in order to verify compliance with the human rights strategy at the direct supplier.
- Pursuant to § 6(5) LkSG, these companies must assess the effectiveness of its preventive measures once a year or on an ad hoc basis if the company expects its risk situation to significantly expand.
- Under § 7(3)LkSG, a company that falls under the scope of the law may even be required to terminate a business relationship under certain circumstances.

4 The LkSG thus not only sets out requirements for the contractual relationship between the company and its direct supplier, it also affects the internal governance and controlling mechanisms of a company.

## C. Definition of the relevant risks

5 If the risk analysis reveals human rights or environmental risks with regard to a direct supplier, the company must ensure that its direct supplier will comply with the human rights and environmental requirements established. The definition of a human rights risk can be found in § 2(2) LkSG; it is a condition in which there is a sufficient probability of a violation of a listed prohibition. This includes the prohibition of disregarding occupational protections, of disregarding freedom to join trade unions, of unequal treatment in employment, or not paying a fair wage, among others. An environmental risk is defined in § 2(3) LkSG. It is as a condition in which a sufficient probability of a violation mentioned in the law exists. The law largely references existing international conventions as a basis, most prominently, the 1989 Basel Convention on the Control of Cross-Border Movements of Hazardous Wastes and their Disposal.

## D. Contract design when concluding new contracts

6 For contracts newly concluded by the company and the direct supplier after the LkSG has come into force, the following must be observed.

### I. Contractual assurance of the direct supplier

7 To ensure that the direct supplier is adequately obliged, two different contractual agreements are recommended. First, the direct supplier itself must commit to complying with human rights and environmental standards discussed above (→ mn. 5). Second, it must also ensure that its own suppliers comply with these standards by means of corresponding contractual agreements (§ 6(4) no. 2 LkSG).

8 In practice, this contractual agreement is likely to be regularly implemented by the company drafting a supplier code (code of conduct) in which it formulates risk-specific human rights and environmental expectations of the supply chain, i.e. its suppliers. Its direct supplier will itself need to comply with the code of conduct and pass it on to its own suppliers (sub-suppliers or indirect suppliers of the company).

## II. Do's and don'ts in practice

The contractual agreement between the company and its direct supplier should be designed in such a way that the company is entitled to subsequently adapt the supplier code or the human rights and environmental obligations of the direct supplier if this is necessary due to a new risk assessment (the risk analyses must be carried out at least once a year or on an ad hoc basis if the company is expecting a significantly changed or expanded risk position according to § 5(4) LkSG). 9

These codes will likely be imposed by a company on its direct suppliers and are therefore considered general terms and conditions. It is advisable for companies to embed such a code in their framework agreements with their direct suppliers. The regulations stipulated in these agreements will then apply to all subsequent supply agreements. In so doing, a company can avoid the problem of its direct supplier rejecting its general terms and conditions when delivering a component. The code agreed on in the framework agreement has priority and cannot be invalidated by subsequent declarations by the direct supplier.[1] 10

Conversely, it might be challenging for a supplier with multiple buyers to not get caught in a complex situation where the supplier is confronted with diverse supplier codices of its multiple customers. For example, if a supplier has several buyers, each with more than 1,000 employees, the supplier may have a strong interest in not agreeing to different supplier codes with each buyer, as this would otherwise oblige him to comply with different supplier codes with its upstream supplier or suppliers. It may therefore be advantageous for the direct supplier to formulate a risk-specific supplier code with human rights-related and environmental expectations himself and to agree on it with his customers. Whether this will succeed in practice is ultimately a question of negotiating strength. 11

## III. Contractual control mechanisms of the company

As mentioned, the LkSG requires companies to establish contractual control mechanisms in their direct suppliers (§ 6(4) no. 4 LkSG). Companies must therefore contractually ensure that they have the right to monitor compliance with respect to their direct suppliers. This could include obligations of self-assessment, visits or quick checks on site, internal monitoring through the company, external monitoring through a third party, or the use of a recognised certification or audit system (see § 6(4) no. 4 LkSG).[2] 12

## IV. Indemnification for violation of human rights-related or environmental obligations

Although it is not required by the LkSG, it is recommended for companies to agree on an indemnity with the direct supplier. Such a contractual regulation would ensure that the direct supplier would have to indemnify the company against all obligations and damages resulting from the direct supplier's violation of its contractual human rights-related or environmental obligations. It should be noted that such indemnifications are disadvantageous for direct suppliers, as they become liable to the company for indemnification (regardless of fault), if they have violated their human rights obligations or environmental 13

[1] See Passas/Holtz, BB 2023, 387 et seqq. for a discussion on how these codes can be structured.
[2] LkSG Kommentar/Ott, 2022, § 6 mn. 150.

obligations. For that reason, it will remain a matter of negotiations strength, whether the company succeeds in imposing an indemnity obligation on its suppler.

## E. Contract design for existing contracts

**14** Continuing supply contracts between affected companies and their direct suppliers that will continue after 1 January must be adapted by the company to the new legal landscape created by the LkSG. To do this, the company must agree with the direct supplier on the assurances (→ mn. 7) and audit rights (→ mn. 12). If the company does not have a contractual or a legal right to unilaterally change the contract, which is usually the case, the company's only option is to negotiate a contract change with the immediate supplier. If the immediate supplier refuses, the company would have to terminate the business relationship and, if desired and possible, enter into a new amended contract with the direct supplier.

## F. Risk analysis

**15** As mentioned above (→ mn. 3), companies that fall under the scope of the LkSG must regularly undergo risk analysis for itself and its direct suppliers. If any company structures its supply relationships in a way that circumvents this rule, any indirect supplier will be treated as a direct supplier in terms of risk analysis (§ 5(1) sentence 2 LkSG).

**16** For the risk analysis, a company must start with gathering information from internal (its own departments) and external sources (its direct supplier, indirect supplier, or even newspapers or articles). Appropriate measures must be taken to gather information, which means that a company may not feign ignorance.[3] In practice, the information gathering of a supplier is often outsourced to companies or service providers that specialise in this. After doing, so the company will have to evaluate the scale and the possibility of this risk being realised. There is no standardised way to evaluate risk, which depends on the branch and sector of the business. For example, a company that produces toxic chemicals has to be more diligent about its environmental risks because of the damage to the environment in case of contamination. Which countries the company operates in and the structure of the supply chain may also have an impact on the method of risk analysis.[4] In general, the likelihood of this risk being realised and the severity of the violation need to be taken into account. The Federal Office for Economic Affairs and Export Control (*Bundesamt für Wirtschaft und Ausfuhrkontrolle*) has developed criterium that can help companies with the risk analysis.[5]

[3] LkSG Kommentar/Ott, 2022, § 5 mn. 8.
[4] LkSG Kommentar/Ott, 2022, § 5 mn. 9.
[5] Hembach, LMuR 2023, 15.

# G. After the identification of a risk

If a relevant risk or a violation of a prohibition has been identified, remedial action must be taken to end the risk or the violation. If it cannot be ended in the foreseeable future, a plan to end or minimise the risk of the violation with a concrete timeline must be made and executed without delay. The LkSG gives some examples of remedial actions that can be put into such a plan, including the temporary suspension of the business relationship during the efforts to end the risk or the violation, § 7(2) sentence 3 no. 3 LkSG. 17

The company may even have to end its business relationship with its direct supplier, if the violation is very serious, the plan to remediate the situation did not have an effect after the planned timeline, and the company has no other less severe means that could ameliorate the violation (§ 7(3)LkSG). From the company's perspective, it is therefore advisable to agree on extraordinary grounds for termination in the contract with the direct supplier in the event that the direct supplier violates its human rights related or environmental obligations. 18

# PART II
# RELEVANT STATUTORY MATERIALS

## A. Excerpts from the Commercial Code (*Handelsgesetzbuch*)

### Erstes Buch
### Handelsstand

### Erster Abschnitt
### Kaufleute (§§ 1–7)

#### § 1
#### [Istkaufmann]

(1) Kaufmann im Sinne dieses Gesetzbuchs ist, wer ein Handelsgewerbe betreibt.

(2) Handelsgewerbe ist jeder Gewerbebetrieb, es sei denn, dass das Unternehmen nach Art oder Umfang einen in kaufmännischer Weise eingerichteten Geschäftsbetrieb nicht erfordert.

#### § 2
#### [Kannkaufmann]

Ein gewerbliches Unternehmen, dessen Gewerbebetrieb nicht schon nach § 1 Abs. 2 Handelsgewerbe ist, gilt als Handelsgewerbe im Sinne dieses Gesetzbuchs, wenn die Firma des Unternehmens in das Handelsregister eingetragen ist. Der Unternehmer ist berechtigt, aber nicht verpflichtet, die Eintragung nach den für die Eintragung kaufmännischer Firmen geltenden Vorschriften herbeizuführen. Ist die Eintragung erfolgt, so findet eine Löschung der Firma auch auf Antrag des Unternehmers statt, sofern nicht die Voraussetzung des § 1 Abs. 2 eingetreten ist.

#### § 3
#### [Land- und Fortwirtschaft; Kannkaufmann]

(1) Auf den Betrieb der Land- und Forstwirtschaft finden die Vorschriften des § 1 keine Anwendung.

### Book One
### Trading status

### Part One
### Merchants (§§ 1–7)

#### § 1
#### [Merchant by legal definition]

(1) A merchant within the meaning of this Code is one who conducts a business.

(2) A business is every commercial operation unless the enterprise by type and volume does not require a commercially organised business operation.

#### § 2
#### [Business operations by voluntary registration]

A business enterprise whose operation is not already defined as a business pursuant to § 1(2) is deemed to be a business within the meaning of this Code if the firm name of the enterprise has been registered in the Commercial Register. The entrepreneur is entitled, but not obligated, to register pursuant to the provisions applicable to the registration of commercial firms. If the firm name has been registered, the firm name shall also be deleted from the Commercial Register upon application of the entrepreneur unless the requirement of § 1(2) has been fulfilled in the meantime.

#### § 3
#### [Agriculture and forestry; merchant by voluntary registration]

(1) The provisions of § 1 do not apply to an agricultural or forestry operation.

(2) Für ein land- oder forstwirtschaftliches Unternehmen, das nach Art und Umfang einen in kaufmännischer Weise eingerichteten Geschäftsbetrieb erfordert, gilt § 2 mit der Maßgabe, dass nach Eintragung in das Handelsregister eine Löschung der Firma nur nach den allgemeinen Vorschriften stattfindet, welche für die Löschung kaufmännischer Firmen gelten.

(3) Ist mit dem Betrieb der Land- oder Forstwirtschaft ein Unternehmen verbunden, das nur ein Nebengewerbe des land- oder forstwirtschaftlichen Unternehmens darstellt, so finden auf das im Nebengewerbe betriebene Unternehmen die Vorschriften der Absätze 1 und 2 entsprechende Anwendung.

(2) § 2 applies to agricultural or forestry enterprises which by type and volume require a commercially organised business operation, with the provision that after registration in the Commercial Register, deletion of the firm name can be only effected pursuant to the provisions generally applicable to the deletion of commercial firm names.

(3) If such an agricultural or forestry operation has a related enterprise representing only a business ancillary to the agricultural or forestry operation, the provisions of subsections 1 and 2 will apply analogously to that enterprise.

**§ 4**
*(aufgehoben)*

**§ 4**
*(repealed)*

**§ 5**
**[Kaufmann kraft Eintragung]**

Ist eine Firma im Handelsregister eingetragen, so kann gegenüber demjenigen, welcher sich auf die Eintragung beruft, nicht geltend gemacht werden, dass das unter der Firma betriebene Gewerbe kein Handelsgewerbe sei.

**§ 5**
**[Merchant by registration]**

Where a firm name is registered in the Commercial Register, it may not be asserted against those who claim reliance on the registration that the operation carried out under the firm name is not a commercial business.

**§ 6**
**[Handelsgesellschaften; Formkaufmann]**

(1) Die in betreff der Kaufleute gegebenen Vorschriften finden auch auf die Handelsgesellschaften Anwendung.

(2) Die Rechte und Pflichten eines Vereins, dem das Gesetz ohne Rücksicht auf den Gegenstand des Unternehmens die Eigenschaft eines Kaufmanns beilegt, bleiben unberührt, auch wenn die Voraussetzungen des § 1 Abs. 2 nicht vorliegen.

**§ 6**
**[Commercial companies and partnerships; merchant by form of organisation]**

(1) The provisions applicable to merchants also apply to commercial companies and partnerships.

(2) The rights and duties of an association to which the law attributes merchant status irrespective of the purpose of the enterprise, are not affected even if the requirements of § 1(2) are not fulfilled.

**§ 7**
**[Kaufmannseigenschaft und öffentliches Recht]**

Durch die Vorschriften des öffentlichen Rechtes, nach welchen die Befugnis zum Gewerbebetrieb ausgeschlossen oder von gewissen Voraussetzungen abhängig gemacht ist, wird die Anwendung der die Kaufleute betreffenden Vorschriften dieses Gesetzbuchs nicht berührt.

**§ 7**
**[Merchant status and public law]**

The provisions of this Code applying to merchants will not be affected by public law provisions pursuant to which the right to carry on a business operation can be denied or conditioned on certain preconditions.

**§§ 8–37a**
**[...]**

**§§ 8–37a**
**[...]**

**§§ 38–47b**
*(aufgehoben)*

**§§ 38–47b**
*(repealed)*

## Fünfter Abschnitt Prokura und Handlungsvollmacht (§§ 48–58)

### § 48 [Erteilung der Prokura; Gesamtprokura]

(1) Die Prokura kann nur von dem Inhaber des Handelsgeschäfts oder seinem gesetzlichen Vertreter und nur mittels ausdrücklicher Erklärung erteilt werden.

(2) Die Erteilung kann an mehrere Personen gemeinschaftlich erfolgen (Gesamtprokura).

### § 49 [Umfang der Prokura]

(1) Die Prokura ermächtigt zu allen Arten von gerichtlichen und außergerichtlichen Geschäften und Rechtshandlungen, die der Betrieb eines Handelsgewerbes mit sich bringt.

(2) Zur Veräußerung und Belastung von Grundstücken ist der Prokurist nur ermächtigt, wenn ihm diese Befugnis besonders erteilt ist.

### § 50 [Beschränkung des Umfangs]

(1) Eine Beschränkung des Umfangs der Prokura ist Dritten gegenüber unwirksam.

(2) Dies gilt insbesondere von der Beschränkung, dass die Prokura nur für gewisse Geschäfte oder gewisse Arten von Geschäften oder nur unter gewissen Umständen oder für eine gewisse Zeit oder an einzelnen Orten ausgeübt werden soll.

(3) Eine Beschränkung der Prokura auf den Betrieb einer von mehreren Niederlassungen des Geschäftsinhabers ist Dritten gegenüber nur wirksam, wenn die Niederlassungen unter verschiedenen Firmen betrieben werden. Eine Verschiedenheit der Firmen im Sinne dieser Vorschrift wird auch dadurch begründet, dass für eine Zweigniederlassung der Firma ein Zusatz beigefügt wird, der sie als Firma der Zweigniederlassung bezeichnet.

### § 51 [Zeichnung des Prokuristen]

Der Prokurist hat in der Weise zu zeichnen, dass er der Firma seinen Namen mit einem die Prokura andeutenden Zusatz beifügt.

## Part Five General Commercial authority (*Prokura*) and Commercial Power of Attorney (§§ 48–58)

### § 48 [Conferring the general commercial authority (*Prokura*), joint *Prokura*]

(1) The *Prokura* (general commercial authority) can be conferred only by the owner of the business or his legal representative and only by means of an express declaration.

(2) The *Prokura* can be conferred jointly on several persons (joint *Prokura*).

### § 49 [Scope of the *Prokura*]

(1) The *Prokura* constitutes authority to enter into every kind of judicial and non-judicial business and legal transaction related to the operation of a commercial business.

(2) The holder of the *Prokura* is authorised to transfer and encumber real property only where this power has been specifically conferred.

### § 50 [Limiting the scope of the *Prokura*]

(1) A limitation on the scope of the *Prokura* is ineffective as to third parties.

(2) This applies in particular to a limitation whereby the *Prokura* may only be exercised for certain transactions or kinds of transactions, only under certain circumstances, for a limited period of time or at certain specific locations.

(3) A limitation of the *Prokura* to the operation of one of several branches operated by the business owner is only effective as to third parties if the branches operate under different firm names. A firm name is different within the meaning of this provision where an addition is attached to the firm name which designates it as the firm name of the branch.

### § 51 [Signature of the *Prokura* holder]

The holder of the *Prokura* must sign in such a manner as to add to the firm name his own signature with an addition indicating his *Prokura*.

### § 52
### [Widerruflichkeit; Unübertragbarkeit; Tod des Inhabers]

(1) Die Prokura ist ohne Rücksicht auf das der Erteilung zugrunde liegende Rechtsverhältnis jederzeit widerruflich, unbeschadet des Anspruchs auf die vertragsmäßige Vergütung.

(2) Die Prokura ist nicht übertragbar.

(3) Die Prokura erlischt nicht durch den Tod des Inhabers des Handelsgeschäfts.

### § 52
### [Revocability; non-transferability; death of the business owner]

(1) The *Prokura* is revocable at any time regardless of the legal relationship underlying the conferral thereof, without prejudice to the right to contractual consideration.

(2) The *Prokura* is not transferable.

(3) The *Prokura* is not terminated upon the death of the owner of the commercial business.

### § 53
### [Anmeldung der Erteilung und des Erlöschens; Zeichnung des Prokuristen]

(1) Die Erteilung der Prokura ist von dem Inhaber des Handelsgeschäfts zur Eintragung in das Handelsregister anzumelden. Ist die Prokura als Gesamtprokura erteilt, so muss auch dies zur Eintragung angemeldet werden.

(2) Das Erlöschen der Prokura ist in gleicher Weise wie die Erteilung zur Eintragung anzumelden.

### § 53
### [Notice of the conferral of the *Prokura* and termination thereof; *Prokura* holder's specimen signature]

(1) The owner of the commercial business must file for registration of the conferral of the *Prokura* in the Commercial Register. Where the *Prokura* has been conferred as a joint *Prokura*, this must also be indicated in the registration.

(2) Termination of the *Prokura* is to be registered in the same manner as conferral thereof.

### § 54
### [Handlungsvollmacht]

(1) Ist jemand ohne Erteilung der Prokura zum Betrieb eines Handelsgewerbes oder zur Vornahme einer bestimmten zu einem Handelsgewerbe gehörigen Art von Geschäften oder zur Vornahme einzelner zu einem Handelsgewerbe gehöriger Geschäfte ermächtigt, so erstreckt sich die Vollmacht (Handlungsvollmacht) auf alle Geschäfte und Rechtshandlungen, die der Betrieb eines derartigen Handelsgewerbes oder die Vornahme derartiger Geschäfte gewöhnlich mit sich bringt.

(2) Zur Veräußerung oder Belastung von Grundstücken, zur Eingehung von Wechselverbindlichkeiten, zur Aufnahme von Darlehen und zur Prozessführung ist der Handlungsbevollmächtigte nur ermächtigt, wenn ihm eine solche Befugnis besonders erteilt ist.

(3) Sonstige Beschränkungen der Handlungsvollmacht braucht ein Dritter nur dann gegen sich gelten zu lassen, wenn er sie kannte oder kennen musste.

### § 54
### [Commercial power of attorney]

(1) Where any person is authorised, without conferral of a *Prokura*, to operate a commercial business, to undertake a certain kind of transaction relating to a business or to undertake individual transactions relating to a business, this power of attorney (commercial power of attorney) extends to all business and legal transactions which normally relate to the conduct of such business or the undertaking of such transactions.

(2) The holder of a commercial power of attorney is only authorised to transfer or encumber real property, to endorse or accept bills of exchange, to assume loans and conduct litigation if such authority has been specifically conferred on him.

(3) Other limitations of the commercial power of attorney are effective against a third party only where the third party knew or should have known thereof.

## § 55
## [Abschlussvertreter]

(1) Die Vorschriften des § 54 finden auch Anwendung auf Handlungsbevollmächtigte, die Handelsvertreter sind oder die als Handlungsgehilfen damit betraut sind, außerhalb des Betriebs des Prinzipals Geschäfte in dessen Namen abzuschließen.

(2) Die ihnen erteilte Vollmacht zum Abschluss von Geschäften bevollmächtigt sie nicht, abgeschlossene Verträge zu ändern, insbesondere Zahlungsfristen zu gewähren.

(3) Zur Annahme von Zahlungen sind sie nur berechtigt, wenn sie dazu bevollmächtigt sind.

(4) Sie gelten als ermächtigt, die Anzeige von Mängeln einer Ware, die Erklärung, dass eine Ware zur Verfügung gestellt werde, sowie ähnliche Erklärungen, durch die ein Dritter seine Rechte aus mangelhafter Leistung geltend macht oder sie vorbehält, entgegenzunehmen; sie können die dem Unternehmer (Prinzipal) zustehenden Rechte auf Sicherung des Beweises geltend machen.

## § 55
## [Agent authorised to transact business]

(1) The provisions of § 54 are also applicable to holders of a commercial power of attorney who are commercial agents or are entrusted as clerical employees with the transaction of business in the principal's name outside the premises of the principal's business.

(2) The power conferred on such persons to transact business does not authorise them to amend existing agreements, especially to extend periods for payment.

(3) Such persons are only authorised to accept payments if they have been specifically granted such power.

(4) Such persons are deemed to be authorised to accept notice of defective goods, statements that goods have been rejected as well as similar statements by which a third party asserts or reserves its rights arising from defective contractual performance; they can assert rights of the business owner (principal) to preserve the evidence.

## § 56
## [Angestellte in Laden oder Warenlager]

Wer in einem Laden oder in einem offenen Warenlager angestellt ist, gilt als ermächtigt zu Verkäufen und Empfangnahmen, die in einem derartigen Laden oder Warenlager gewöhnlich geschehen.

## § 56
## [Sales clerks or warehouse employees]

Any person who is employed in a store or warehouse open to the public is deemed to be authorised to sell and receive anything which is customary for such a business or warehouse.

## § 57
## [Zeichnung des Handlungsbevollmächtigten]

Der Handlungsbevollmächtigte hat sich bei der Zeichnung jedes eine Prokura andeutenden Zusatzes zu enthalten; er hat mit einem das Vollmachtsverhältnis ausdrückenden Zusatz zu zeichnen.

## § 57
## [Signature of holder of commercial power of attorney]

The holder of a commercial power of attorney must refrain from using with his signature an addition indicating a *Prokura*. He must sign with an addition which indicates the power of attorney.

## § 58
## [Unübertragbarkeit der Handlungsvollmacht]

Der Handlungsbevollmächtigte kann ohne Zustimmung des Inhabers des Handelsgeschäfts seine Handlungsvollmacht auf einen anderen nicht übertragen.

## § 58
## [Non-transferability of the commercial power of attorney]

The holder of a commercial power of attorney may not transfer his commercial power of attorney to another without the business owner's consent.

## §§ 59–83
[…]

## §§ 59–83
[…]

## Siebenter Abschnitt Handelsvertreter (§§ 84–92c)

### § 84 [Begriff des Handelsvertreters]

(1) Handelsvertreter ist, wer als selbständiger Gewerbetreibender ständig damit betraut ist, für einen anderen Unternehmer (Unternehmer) Geschäfte zu vermitteln oder in dessen Namen abzuschließen. Selbständig ist, wer im Wesentlichen frei seine Tätigkeit gestalten und seine Arbeitszeit bestimmen kann.

(2) Wer, ohne selbständig im Sinne des Absatzes 1 zu sein, ständig damit betraut ist, für einen Unternehmer Geschäfte zu vermitteln oder in dessen Namen abzuschließen, gilt als Angestellter.

(3) Der Unternehmer kann auch ein Handelsvertreter sein.

(4) Die Vorschriften dieses Abschnittes finden auch Anwendung, wenn das Unternehmen des Handelsvertreters nach Art oder Umfang einen in kaufmännischer Weise eingerichteten Geschäftsbetrieb nicht erfordert.

## Part Seven Commercial Agents (§§ 84–92c)

### § 84 [Definition of commercial agent]

(1) A commercial agent is one who, as an independent person engaged in business, is regularly authorised to solicit business for another entrepreneur (the 'principal') or to enter into transactions in the principal's name. A person is independent if he is essentially free to structure his activity and determine his hours of work.

(2) Any person who, without being independent within the meaning of subsection 1, is regularly authorised to solicit business for a principal or to enter into transactions in his name, is deemed to be an employee.

(3) The principal can also be a commercial agent.

(4) The provisions of this part also apply if the business of the commercial agent, based on its nature or scope, does not require a commercially organised business operation.

### § 85 [Vertragsurkunde]

Jeder Teil kann verlangen, dass der Inhalt des Vertrags sowie spätere Vereinbarungen zu dem Vertrag in eine vom anderen Teil unterzeichnete Urkunde aufgenommen werden. Dieser Anspruch kann nicht ausgeschlossen werden.

### § 85 [Contract documents]

Either party can demand that the terms of the contract, as well as any subsequent amendment thereof, be set out in a document signed by the other party. This right may not be excluded.

### § 86 [Pflichten des Handelsvertreters]

(1) Der Handelsvertreter hat sich um die Vermittlung oder den Abschluss von Geschäften zu bemühen; er hat hierbei das Interesse des Unternehmers wahrzunehmen.

(2) Er hat dem Unternehmer die erforderlichen Nachrichten zu geben, namentlich ihm von jeder Geschäftsvermittlung und von jedem Geschäftsabschluss unverzüglich Mitteilung zu machen.

(3) Er hat seine Pflichten mit der Sorgfalt eines ordentlichen Kaufmanns wahrzunehmen.

(4) Von den Absätzen 1 und 2 abweichende Vereinbarungen sind unwirksam.

### § 86 [Duties of the commercial agent]

(1) The commercial agent is obligated to make efforts toward the solicitation or conclusion of business transactions. In connection herewith he must act in the interest of the principal.

(2) He shall give the principal all necessary information, i.e. inform him immediately of every solicitation and conclusion of every transaction.

(3) He must fulfil his duties with the care of a prudent merchant.

(4) Any agreement contrary to subsections 1 and 2 hereof is void.

### § 86a [Pflichten des Unternehmers]

(1) Der Unternehmer hat dem Handelsvertreter die zur Ausübung seiner Tätigkeit erforderlichen Unterlagen, wie Muster, Zeichnungen, Preislisten, Werbedrucksachen, Geschäftsbedingungen, zur Verfügung zu stellen.

(2) Der Unternehmer hat dem Handelsvertreter die erforderlichen Nachrichten zu geben. Er hat ihm unverzüglich die Annahme oder Ablehnung eines vom Handelsvertreter vermittelten oder ohne Vertretungsmacht abgeschlossenen Geschäfts und die Nichtausführung eines von ihm vermittelten oder abgeschlossenen Geschäfts mitzuteilen. Er hat ihn unverzüglich zu unterrichten, wenn er Geschäfte voraussichtlich nur in erheblich geringerem Umfange abschließen kann oder will, als der Handelsvertreter unter gewöhnlichen Umständen erwarten konnte.

(3) Von den Absätzen 1 und 2 abweichende Vereinbarungen sind unwirksam.

### § 86a [Principal's duties]

(1) The principal shall provide the commercial agent with all materials which are necessary for the performance of his duties, such as samples, drawings, price lists, advertising material and terms and conditions of business.

(2) The principal shall keep the commercial agent generally informed. In particular, he shall inform him promptly of the acceptance or rejection of a transaction solicited by the commercial agent or a transaction concluded by the commercial agent without authority, and of the non-completion of a transaction solicited or concluded by him. He shall inform the commercial agent promptly if the principal intends, or will likely be able, to conclude transactions only on a significantly reduced scale in comparison to that which the commercial agent could expect under normal circumstances.

(3) Any agreement contrary to subsections 1 and 2 hereof is void.

### § 86b [Delkredereprovision]

(1) Verpflichtet sich ein Handelsvertreter, für die Erfüllung der Verbindlichkeit aus einem Geschäft einzustehen, so kann er eine besondere Vergütung (Delkredereprovision) beanspruchen; der Anspruch kann im Voraus nicht ausgeschlossen werden. Die Verpflichtung kann nur für ein bestimmtes Geschäft oder für solche Geschäfte mit bestimmten Dritten übernommen werden, die der Handelsvertreter vermittelt oder abschließt. Die Übernahme bedarf der Schriftform.

(2) Der Anspruch auf die Delkredereprovision entsteht mit dem Abschluss des Geschäfts.

(3) Absatz 1 gilt nicht, wenn der Unternehmer oder der Dritte seine Niederlassung oder beim Fehlen einer solchen seinen Wohnsitz im Ausland hat. Er gilt ferner nicht für Geschäfte, zu deren Abschluss und Ausführung der Handelsvertreter unbeschränkt bevollmächtigt ist.

### § 86b [*Del credere* commission]

(1) Where a commercial agent guarantees the fulfilment of the obligation arising from a transaction, he may demand special compensation (*del credere* commission). This right may not be excluded in advance. The obligation may only be undertaken for a specific transaction or for transactions with specific third parties which the commercial agent solicits or concludes. This undertaking must be in writing.

(2) The right to a *del credere* commission arises upon conclusion of the transaction.

(3) Subsection 1 does not apply if the principal or third party has his office or, failing such, his residence abroad. Furthermore, it does not apply to transactions for the conclusion and performance of which the commercial agent has unlimited authority.

## § 87
## [Provisionspflichtige Geschäfte]

(1) Der Handelsvertreter hat Anspruch auf Provision für alle während des Vertragsverhältnisses abgeschlossenen Geschäfte, die auf seine Tätigkeit zurückzuführen sind oder mit Dritten abgeschlossen werden, die er als Kunden für Geschäfte der gleichen Art geworben hat. Ein Anspruch auf Provision besteht für ihn nicht, wenn und soweit die Provision nach Absatz 3 dem ausgeschiedenen Handelsvertreter zusteht.

(2) Ist dem Handelsvertreter ein bestimmter Bezirk oder ein bestimmter Kundenkreis zugewiesen, so hat er Anspruch auf Provision auch für die Geschäfte, die ohne seine Mitwirkung mit Personen seines Bezirks oder seines Kundenkreises während des Vertragsverhältnisses abgeschlossen sind. Dies gilt nicht, wenn und soweit die Provision nach Absatz 3 dem ausgeschiedenen Handelsvertreter zusteht.

(3) Für ein Geschäft, das erst nach Beendigung des Vertragsverhältnisses abgeschlossen ist, hat der Handelsvertreter Anspruch auf Provision nur, wenn

1. er das Geschäft vermittelt hat oder es eingeleitet und so vorbereitet hat, dass der Abschluss überwiegend auf seine Tätigkeit zurückzuführen ist, und das Geschäft innerhalb einer angemessenen Frist nach Beendigung des Vertragsverhältnisses abgeschlossen worden ist oder
2. vor Beendigung des Vertragsverhältnisses das Angebot des Dritten zum Abschluss eines Geschäfts, für das der Handelsvertreter nach Absatz 1 Satz 1 oder Absatz 2 Satz 1 Anspruch auf Provision hat, dem Handelsvertreter oder dem Unternehmer zugegangen ist.

Der Anspruch auf Provision nach Satz 1 steht dem nachfolgenden Handelsvertreter anteilig zu, wenn wegen besonderer Umstände eine Teilung der Provision der Billigkeit entspricht.

(4) Neben dem Anspruch auf Provision für abgeschlossene Geschäfte hat der Handelsvertreter Anspruch auf Inkassoprovision für die von ihm auftragsgemäß eingezogenen Beträge.

## § 87
## [Transactions for which commission is due]

(1) The commercial agent has a right to commissions for all transactions concluded during the term of his contractual relationship which are to be attributed to his activity or which are concluded with third parties whom he has acquired as customers for similar business. He has no right to a commission if this is owed to the prior commercial agent pursuant to subsection 3.

(2) Where the commercial agent has been assigned to a specific district or a particular group of customers, he also has a right to commission for transactions concluded without his assistance with persons in his district or among his group of customers during the term of his contractual relationship. This does not apply if the commission is owed to the prior commercial agent pursuant to subsection 3.

(3) For transactions concluded after the termination of the contractual agency relationship, the commercial agent shall have a right to commission only if:

1. he solicited, initiated or prepared the transaction in such a way that conclusion thereof was predominantly due to his activity, and the transaction was concluded within a reasonable time after termination of the agency contract, or
2. prior to the termination of the agency contract, the offer of a third party to conclude a transaction for which the commercial agent has a claim for commission under subsection 1, sentence 1 or subsection 2, sentence 1 hereof has been received by the commercial agent or the principal.

Pursuant to sentence 1 the subsequent agent shall have a claim to a share of the commission when, due to special circumstances, fairness requires that the commission be split.

(4) In addition to the right to commission for transactions concluded, the commercial agent has a right to a collection commission for amounts collected by him pursuant to instructions.

### § 87a
### [Fälligkeit der Provision]

(1) Der Handelsvertreter hat Anspruch auf Provision, sobald und soweit der Unternehmer das Geschäft ausgeführt hat. Eine abweichende Vereinbarung kann getroffen werden, jedoch hat der Handelsvertreter mit der Ausführung des Geschäfts durch den Unternehmer Anspruch auf einen angemessenen Vorschuss, der spätestens am letzten Tag des folgenden Monats fällig ist. Unabhängig von einer Vereinbarung hat jedoch der Handelsvertreter Anspruch auf Provision, sobald und soweit der Dritte das Geschäft ausgeführt hat.

(2) Steht fest, dass der Dritte nicht leistet, so entfällt der Anspruch auf Provision; bereits empfangene Beträge sind zurückzugewähren.

(3) Der Handelsvertreter hat auch dann einen Anspruch auf Provision, wenn feststeht, dass der Unternehmer das Geschäft ganz oder teilweise nicht oder nicht so ausführt, wie es abgeschlossen worden ist. Der Anspruch entfällt im Falle der Nichtausführung, wenn und soweit diese auf Umständen beruht, die vom Unternehmer nicht zu vertreten sind.

(4) Der Anspruch auf Provision wird am letzten Tag des Monats fällig, in dem nach § 87c Abs. 1 über den Anspruch abzurechnen ist.

(5) Von Absatz 2 erster Halbsatz, Absätzen 3 und 4 abweichende, für den Handelsvertreter nachteilige Vereinbarungen sind unwirksam.

### § 87a
### [Due date of the commission]

(1) The commercial agent has a right to commission as soon as, and in so far as, the principal has performed the transaction. An agreement to the contrary may be made, but the commercial agent, upon performance of the transaction by the principal, has in any event a right to a reasonable advance due no later than the last day of the following month. Independent of any agreement, however, the commercial agent has a right to commission as soon as, and in so far as, the third party has performed the transaction.

(2) Where it has been determined that the third party will not perform, there is no right to commission. Amounts already received are to be returned.

(3) The commercial agent also has a right to commission when it is determined that the principal will not perform the transaction, will perform only partially, or will not perform in the manner agreed upon. No right to commission shall exist in the event of non-performance due to reasons beyond the principal's control.

(4) The commission is due on the last day of the month in which the claim is accounted for pursuant to § 87c(1).

(5) Agreements contrary to subsection 2, first half-sentence or subsections 3 and 4, to the disadvantage of the commercial agent, are void.

### § 87b
### [Höhe der Provision]

(1) Ist die Höhe der Provision nicht bestimmt, so ist der übliche Satz als vereinbart anzusehen.

(2) Die Provision ist von dem Entgelt zu berechnen, das der Dritte oder der Unternehmer zu leisten hat. Nachlässe bei Barzahlung sind nicht abzuziehen; dasselbe gilt für Nebenkosten, namentlich für Fracht, Verpackung, Zoll, Steuern, es sei denn, dass die Nebenkosten dem Dritten besonders in Rechnung gestellt sind. Die Umsatzsteuer, die lediglich auf Grund der steuerrechtlichen Vorschriften in der Rechnung gesondert ausgewiesen ist, gilt nicht als besonders in Rechnung gestellt.

### § 87b
### [Amount of the commission]

(1) Where the amount of commission is not specified, the customary rate is deemed to be agreed upon.

(2) Commission is to be calculated on the basis of the amount that the third party or the principal is obligated to pay. Discounts for cash payment are not to be made; the same applies to miscellaneous costs, such as freight, packaging, customs duties and taxes, unless the miscellaneous costs have been itemised separately in the invoice sent to the third party. Value-added tax which is itemised separately solely by reason of the tax law is deemed not to be separately itemised.

(3) Bei Gebrauchsüberlassungs- und Nutzungsverträgen von bestimmter Dauer ist die Provision vom Entgelt für die Vertragsdauer zu berechnen. Bei unbestimmter Dauer ist die Provision vom Entgelt bis zu dem Zeitpunkt zu berechnen, zu dem erstmals von dem Dritten gekündigt werden kann; der Handelsvertreter hat Anspruch auf weitere entsprechend berechnete Provisionen, wenn der Vertrag fortbesteht.

(3) With respect to rental and use agreements of specific duration, commission is to be calculated on the consideration received for the term of the contract. With respect to agreements of indefinite duration, commission is to be calculated on the consideration received up until the time when the third party can for the first time terminate the agreement; the commercial agent has a right to additional commission calculated accordingly if the contract continues in force.

### § 87c
### [Abrechnung über die Provision]

(1) Der Unternehmer hat über die Provision, auf die der Handelsvertreter Anspruch hat, monatlich abzurechnen; der Abrechnungszeitraum kann auf höchstens drei Monate erstreckt werden. Die Abrechnung hat unverzüglich, spätestens bis zum Ende des nächsten Monats, zu erfolgen.

(2) Der Handelsvertreter kann bei der Abrechnung einen Buchauszug über alle Geschäfte verlangen, für die ihm nach § 87 Provision gebührt.

(3) Der Handelsvertreter kann außerdem Mitteilung über alle Umstände verlangen, die für den Provisionsanspruch, seine Fälligkeit und seine Berechnung wesentlich sind.

(4) Wird der Buchauszug verweigert oder bestehen begründete Zweifel an der Richtigkeit oder Vollständigkeit der Abrechnung oder des Buchauszugs, so kann der Handelsvertreter verlangen, dass nach Wahl des Unternehmers entweder ihm oder einem von ihm zu bestimmenden Wirtschaftsprüfer oder vereidigten Buchsachverständigen Einsicht in die Geschäftsbücher oder die sonstigen Urkunden so weit gewährt wird, wie dies zur Feststellung der Richtigkeit oder Vollständigkeit der Abrechnung oder des Buchauszugs erforderlich ist.

(5) Diese Rechte des Handelsvertreters können nicht ausgeschlossen oder beschränkt werden.

### § 87c
### [Accounting for the commission]

(1) The principal shall account monthly for the commission to which the commercial agent is entitled. The accounting period can be extended to a maximum of three months. The accounting shall be made without delay, in any case not later than by the end of the following month.

(2) At the time of accounting, the commercial agent may demand an excerpt from the books concerning all transactions for which he has a claim to commission pursuant to § 87.

(3) In addition, the commercial agent may demand information regarding all matters which are material to a determination of the right to commission, its due date and amount.

(4) Where the excerpt from the books is withheld, or reasonable doubt exists as to the accuracy or completeness of the account or the excerpt, the commercial agent may demand that, at the principal's option, either he or an auditor or certified accountant designated by him shall be permitted to inspect the business books and other documents to the extent that is necessary to establish the accuracy or completeness of the accounting or excerpt.

(5) These rights of the commercial agent cannot be excluded or limited.

### § 87d
### [Ersatz von Aufwendungen]

Der Handelsvertreter kann den Ersatz seiner im regelmäßigen Geschäftsbetrieb entstandenen Aufwendungen nur verlangen, wenn dies handelsüblich ist.

### § 87d
### [Reimbursement of expenses]

The commercial agent may only demand reimbursement of his regular business expenses if this is customary within the trade.

### § 88
*(aufgehoben)*

### § 88
*(repealed)*

### § 88a
### [Zurückbehaltungsrecht]

(1) Der Handelsvertreter kann nicht im Voraus auf gesetzliche Zurückbehaltungsrechte verzichten.

(2) Nach Beendigung des Vertragsverhältnisses hat der Handelsvertreter ein nach allgemeinen Vorschriften bestehendes Zurückbehaltungsrecht an ihm zur Verfügung gestellten Unterlagen (§ 86a Abs. 1) nur wegen seiner fälligen Ansprüche auf Provision und Ersatz von Aufwendungen.

### § 88a
### [Legal right of retention]

(1) The commercial agent cannot waive his legal rights of retention in advance.

(2) After expiration of the contractual relationship the commercial agent has the right, pursuant to general provisions, to retain materials placed at his disposal (§ 86a(1)) only by reason of unpaid commissions or reimbursement of expenses owed to him.

### § 89
### [Kündigung des Vertrags]

(1) Ist das Vertragsverhältnis auf unbestimmte Zeit eingegangen, so kann es im ersten Jahr der Vertragsdauer mit einer Frist von einem Monat, im zweiten Jahr mit einer Frist von zwei Monaten und im dritten bis fünften Jahr mit einer Frist von drei Monaten gekündigt werden. Nach einer Vertragsdauer von fünf Jahren kann das Vertragsverhältnis mit einer Frist von sechs Monaten gekündigt werden. Die Kündigung ist nur für den Schluss eines Kalendermonats zulässig, sofern keine abweichende Vereinbarung getroffen ist.

(2) Die Kündigungsfristen nach Absatz 1 Satz 1 und 2 können durch Vereinbarung verlängert werden; die Frist darf für den Unternehmer nicht kürzer sein als für den Handelsvertreter. Bei Vereinbarung einer kürzeren Frist für den Unternehmer gilt die für den Handelsvertreter vereinbarte Frist.

(3) Ein für eine bestimmte Zeit eingegangenes Vertragsverhältnis, das nach Ablauf der vereinbarten Laufzeit von beiden Teilen fortgesetzt wird, gilt als auf unbestimmte Zeit verlängert. Für die Bestimmung der Kündigungsfristen nach Absatz 1 Satz 1 und 2 ist die Gesamtdauer des Vertragsverhältnisses maßgeblich.

### § 89
### [Termination of the agreement]

(1) If the contractual relationship is of indefinite duration, it may be terminated with prior notice of one month during the first year, two months during the second year and three months in the third through the fifth years. After a duration of five years, the contractual relationship may be terminated with prior notice of six months. Absent any agreement to the contrary, termination is effective only as of the end of a calendar month.

(2) The notice periods under subsection 1, sentences 1 and 2 may be extended by agreement; the period may not be shorter for the principal than for the commercial agent. If a shorter period for the principal is agreed upon, the period for the commercial agent shall apply instead.

(3) A contractual relationship of definite duration which, upon expiration, is extended by both parties shall be deemed to be extended indefinitely. For calculation of the termination notice periods under subsection 1, sentences 1 and 2, the total duration of the relationship shall be decisive.

### § 89a
### [Fristlose Kündigung]

(1) Das Vertragsverhältnis kann von jedem Teil aus wichtigem Grund ohne Einhaltung einer Kündigungsfrist gekündigt werden. Dieses Recht kann nicht ausgeschlossen oder beschränkt werden.

(2) Wird die Kündigung durch ein Verhalten veranlasst, das der andere Teil zu vertreten hat, so ist dieser zum Ersatz des durch die Aufhebung des Vertragsverhältnisses entstehenden Schadens verpflichtet.

### § 89a
### [Termination without observance of a notice period]

(1) The contractual relationship can be terminated without observance of a notice period by either party for cause. This right cannot be excluded or limited.

(2) Where termination results from conduct of the other party, that party is obligated to compensate for losses arising from the termination of the contractual relationship.

## § 89b
## [Ausgleichsanspruch]

(1) Der Handelsvertreter kann von dem Unternehmer nach Beendigung des Vertragsverhältnisses einen angemessenen Ausgleich verlangen, wenn und soweit

1. der Unternehmer aus der Geschäftsverbindung mit neuen Kunden, die der Handelsvertreter geworben hat, auch nach Beendigung des Vertragsverhältnisses erhebliche Vorteile hat und
2. die Zahlung eines Ausgleichs unter Berücksichtigung aller Umstände, insbesondere der dem Handelsvertreter aus Geschäften mit diesen Kunden entgehenden Provisionen, der Billigkeit entspricht.

Der Werbung eines neuen Kunden steht es gleich, wenn der Handelsvertreter die Geschäftsverbindung mit einem Kunden so wesentlich erweitert hat, dass dies wirtschaftlich der Werbung eines neuen Kunden entspricht.

(2) Der Ausgleich beträgt höchstens eine nach dem Durchschnitt der letzten fünf Jahre der Tätigkeit des Handelsvertreters berechnete Jahresprovision oder sonstige Jahresvergütung; bei kürzerer Dauer des Vertragsverhältnisses ist der Durchschnitt während der Dauer der Tätigkeit maßgebend.

(3) Der Anspruch besteht nicht, wenn

1. der Handelsvertreter das Vertragsverhältnis gekündigt hat, es sei denn, dass ein Verhalten des Unternehmers hierzu begründeten Anlass gegeben hat oder dem Handelsvertreter eine Fortsetzung seiner Tätigkeit wegen seines Alters oder wegen Krankheit nicht zugemutet werden kann, oder
2. der Unternehmer das Vertragsverhältnis gekündigt hat und für die Kündigung ein wichtiger Grund wegen schuldhaften Verhaltens des Handelsvertreters vorlag oder
3. auf Grund einer Vereinbarung zwischen dem Unternehmer und dem Handelsvertreter ein Dritter anstelle des Handelsvertreters in das Vertragsverhältnis eintritt; die Vereinbarung kann nicht vor Beendigung des Vertragsverhältnisses getroffen werden.

(4) Der Anspruch kann im Voraus nicht ausgeschlossen werden. Er ist innerhalb eines Jahres nach Beendigung des Vertragsverhältnisses geltend zu machen.

## § 89b
## [Claim for termination compensation]

(1) The commercial agent may, after expiration of the contractual relationship, demand from the principal reasonable compensation if and in so far as

1. the principal retains substantial advantages, after termination of the contractual relationship, from business relations with new customers solicited by the commercial agent, and
2. the payment of compensation is equitable after consideration of all the circumstances, in particular the commercial agent's lost commissions from transactions with these customers.

'Solicitation of new customers' shall also include the expansion of business relations with an existing customer to such an extent that this corresponds economically to the acquisition of a new customer.

(2) Compensation may amount to no more than the average of the annual commission or other annual remuneration over the last five years of the activity of the commercial agent; in the event that the contractual relationship has been shorter than five years, the average during the period of activity applies.

(3) No claim for compensation shall exist where:

1. the commercial agent has terminated the contractual relationship, unless the actions of the principal constituted sufficient grounds therefor, or the commercial agent cannot be expected to continue his activities by reason of his age or health, or
2. the principal has terminated the contractual relationship for cause relating to culpable conduct of the commercial agent, or
3. by reason of an agreement between the principal and the commercial agent, a third party assumes the rights and obligations of the commercial agent; such an agreement cannot be made prior to the termination of the contractual relationship.

(4) The compensation claim may not be excluded in advance. It must be asserted within one year after termination of the contractual relationship.

(5) Die Absätze 1, 3 und 4 gelten für Versicherungsvertreter mit der Maßgabe, dass an die Stelle der Geschäftsverbindung mit neuen Kunden, die der Handelsvertreter geworben hat, die Vermittlung neuer Versicherungsverträge durch den Versicherungsvertreter tritt und der Vermittlung eines Versicherungsvertrages es gleichsteht, wenn der Versicherungsvertreter einen bestehenden Versicherungsvertrag so wesentlich erweitert hat, dass dies wirtschaftlich der Vermittlung eines neuen Versicherungsvertrages entspricht. Der Ausgleich des Versicherungsvertreters beträgt abweichend von Absatz 2 höchstens drei Jahresprovisionen oder Jahresvergütungen. Die Vorschriften der Sätze 1 und 2 gelten sinngemäß für Bausparkassenvertreter.

(5) Subsections 1, 3 and 4 hereof shall apply to insurance agents in such a manner that the concept of business relationships with new customers solicited by the commercial agent shall be replaced by the concept of conclusion of new insurance contracts by the insurance agent, and expansion by the insurance agent of an existing insurance contract which corresponds economically to the conclusion of a new insurance contract shall be deemed to be the conclusion of a new insurance contract. Notwithstanding subsection 2 hereof, the compensation claim of an insurance agent shall equal, at a maximum, three years' worth of commissions or remuneration. Sentences 1 and 2 hereof shall apply analogously to agents of building and savings associations.

## § 90
## [Geschäfts- und Betriebsgeheimnisse]

Der Handelsvertreter darf Geschäfts- und Betriebsgeheimnisse, die ihm anvertraut oder als solche durch seine Tätigkeit für den Unternehmer bekanntgeworden sind, auch nach Beendigung des Vertragsverhältnisses nicht verwerten oder anderen mitteilen, soweit dies nach den gesamten Umständen der Berufsauffassung eines ordentlichen Kaufmanns widersprechen würde.

## § 90
## [Trade and business secrets]

The commercial agent may not, even after termination of the contractual relationship, utilise or divulge to others trade or business secrets which have been entrusted to him or which he has learned by reason of his activity for the principal in so far as, considering the overall circumstances, this would be contrary to the professional standards of a prudent merchant.

## § 90a
## [Wettbewerbsabrede]

(1) Eine Vereinbarung, die den Handelsvertreter nach Beendigung des Vertragsverhältnisses in seiner gewerblichen Tätigkeit beschränkt (Wettbewerbsabrede), bedarf der Schriftform und der Aushändigung einer vom Unternehmer unterzeichneten, die vereinbarten Bestimmungen enthaltenden Urkunde an den Handelsvertreter. Die Abrede kann nur für längstens zwei Jahre von der Beendigung des Vertragsverhältnisses an getroffen werden; sie darf sich nur auf den dem Handelsvertreter zugewiesenen Bezirk oder Kundenkreis und nur auf die Gegenstände erstrecken, hinsichtlich deren sich der Handelsvertreter um die Vermittlung oder den Abschluss von Geschäften für den Unternehmer zu bemühen hat. Der Unternehmer ist verpflichtet, dem Handelsvertreter für die Dauer der Wettbewerbsbeschränkung eine angemessene Entschädigung zu zahlen.

(2) Der Unternehmer kann bis zum Ende des Vertragsverhältnisses schriftlich auf die Wettbewerbsbeschränkung mit der Wirkung verzichten, dass er mit dem Ablauf von sechs Monaten seit der Erklärung von der Verpflichtung zur Zahlung der Entschädigung frei wird.

## § 90a
## [Agreement prohibiting competition]

(1) An agreement by which a commercial agent is restricted in his commercial activity following termination of the contractual relationship (agreement prohibiting competition) must be in writing, and the document containing the conditions agreed to must be signed by the principal and delivered to the commercial agent. The agreement may run for no longer than two years following the termination of the contractual relationship. The agreement may cover only the geographical area or group of customers assigned to the commercial agent and may only refer to the type of business in which the commercial agent was responsible for soliciting or concluding transactions. The principal is obligated to pay reasonable compensation to the commercial agent for the duration of the prohibition of competition.

(2) The principal may waive the prohibition of competition in writing up to the end of the contractual relationship with the effect that he will be free from the obligation to pay compensation as of the end of six months after the date of such declaration.

(3) Kündigt ein Teil das Vertragsverhältnis aus wichtigem Grund wegen schuldhaften Verhaltens des anderen Teils, kann er sich durch schriftliche Erklärung binnen einem Monat nach der Kündigung von der Wettbewerbsabrede lossagen.

(4) Abweichende für den Handelsvertreter nachteilige Vereinbarungen können nicht getroffen werden.

(3) Where one party terminates the contractual relationship for cause because of culpable conduct of the other party, he may, by a declaration in writing made within one month after such termination, declare that he is not bound by the prohibition of competition.

(4) Agreements deviating from these provisions to the disadvantage of the commercial agent cannot be made.

**§ 91**
**[Vollmachten des Handelsvertreters]**

(1) § 55 gilt auch für einen Handelsvertreter, der zum Abschluss von Geschäften von einem Unternehmer bevollmächtigt ist, der nicht Kaufmann ist.

(2) Ein Handelsvertreter gilt, auch wenn ihm keine Vollmacht zum Abschluss von Geschäften erteilt ist, als ermächtigt, die Anzeige von Mängeln einer Ware, die Erklärung, dass eine Ware zur Verfügung gestellt werde, sowie ähnliche Erklärungen, durch die ein Dritter seine Rechte aus mangelhafter Leistung geltend macht oder sich vorbehält, entgegenzunehmen; er kann die dem Unternehmer zustehenden Rechte auf Sicherung des Beweises geltend machen. Eine Beschränkung dieser Rechte braucht ein Dritter gegen sich nur gelten zu lassen, wenn er sie kannte oder kennen musste.

**§ 91**
**[Authority of the commercial agent]**

(1) § 55 also applies to a commercial agent who is authorised to conclude transactions for a principal who is not a merchant.

(2) Even if he is not authorised to conclude transactions, a commercial agent is deemed to have authority to accept notice of defective goods, the statement that rejected goods are being made available for collection, as well as similar statements by means of which a third party asserts or reserves rights arising from defective contractual performance; he may assert the principal's rights to preserve evidence. Limitation of this authority is deemed to be valid against a third party only where the third party knew or should have known thereof.

**§ 91a**
**[Mangel der Vertretungsmacht]**

(1) Hat ein Handelsvertreter, der nur mit der Vermittlung von Geschäften betraut ist, ein Geschäft im Namen des Unternehmers abgeschlossen, und war dem Dritten der Mangel an Vertretungsmacht nicht bekannt, so gilt das Geschäft als von dem Unternehmer genehmigt, wenn dieser nicht unverzüglich, nachdem er von dem Handelsvertreter oder dem Dritten über Abschluss und wesentlichen Inhalt benachrichtigt worden ist, dem Dritten gegenüber das Geschäft ablehnt.

(2) Das gleiche gilt, wenn ein Handelsvertreter, der mit dem Abschluss von Geschäften betraut ist, ein Geschäft im Namen des Unternehmers abgeschlossen hat, zu dessen Abschluss er nicht bevollmächtigt ist.

**§ 91a**
**[Lack of authority]**

(1) Where a commercial agent only authorised to solicit business has concluded a transaction in the principal's name, and the third party did not know of this lack of authority, the transaction will be regarded as approved by the principal if he fails to repudiate it without undue delay upon being informed by the commercial agent or third party of the conclusion of the agreement and its material terms.

(2) The same applies where a commercial agent authorised to enter into business transactions has concluded in the principal's name a transaction which he is not authorised to conclude.

**§ 92**
**[Versicherungs- und Bausparkassenvertreter]**

(1) Versicherungsvertreter ist, wer als Handelsvertreter damit betraut ist, Versicherungsverträge zu vermitteln oder abzuschließen.

**§ 92**
**[Insurance and building and loan association agents]**

(1) An insurance agent is one who, as a commercial agent, is authorised to solicit or conclude insurance contracts.

(2) Für das Vertragsverhältnis zwischen dem Versicherungsvertreter und dem Versicherer gelten die Vorschriften für das Vertragsverhältnis zwischen dem Handelsvertreter und dem Unternehmer vorbehaltlich der Absätze 3 und 4.

(3) In Abweichung von § 87 Abs. 1 Satz 1 hat ein Versicherungsvertreter Anspruch auf Provision nur für Geschäfte, die auf seine Tätigkeit zurückzuführen sind. § 87 Abs. 2 gilt nicht für Versicherungsvertreter.

(4) Der Versicherungsvertreter hat Anspruch auf Provision (§ 87a Abs. 1), sobald der Versicherungsnehmer die Prämie gezahlt hat, aus der sich die Provision nach dem Vertragsverhältnis berechnet.

(5) Die Vorschriften der Absätze 1 bis 4 gelten sinngemäß für Bausparkassenvertreter.

(2) The provisions applicable to the contractual relationship between the commercial agent and the principal apply, subject to subsections 3 and 4 hereof, to the contractual relationship between the insurance agent and the insurer.

(3) As an exception to § 87(1), sentence 1, an insurance agent has a right to commission only for transactions which are a result of his activity. § 87(2) does not apply to insurance agents.

(4) The insurance agent has a right to commission (§ 87a(1)) as soon as the insured has paid the premium on which the commission, according to the contractual relationship, is calculated.

(5) The provisions of subsections 1 through 4 apply analogously to building and loan association agents.

### § 92a
### [Mindestarbeitsbedingungen]

(1) Für das Vertragsverhältnis eines Handelsvertreters, der vertraglich nicht für weitere Unternehmer tätig werden darf oder dem dies nach Art und Umfang der von ihm verlangten Tätigkeit nicht möglich ist, kann das Bundesministerium der Justiz im Einvernehmen mit dem Bundesministerium für Wirtschaft und Technologie nach Anhörung von Verbänden der Handelsvertreter und der Unternehmer durch Rechtsverordnung, die nicht der Zustimmung des Bundesrates bedarf, die untere Grenze der vertraglichen Leistungen des Unternehmers festsetzen, um die notwendigen sozialen und wirtschaftlichen Bedürfnisse dieser Handelsvertreter oder einer bestimmten Gruppe von ihnen sicherzustellen. Die festgesetzten Leistungen können vertraglich nicht ausgeschlossen oder beschränkt werden.

(2) Absatz 1 gilt auch für das Vertragsverhältnis eines Versicherungsvertreters, der auf Grund eines Vertrags oder mehrerer Verträge damit betraut ist, Geschäfte für mehrere Versicherer zu vermitteln oder abzuschließen, die zu einem Versicherungskonzern oder zu einer zwischen ihnen bestehenden Organisationsgemeinschaft gehören, sofern die Beendigung des Vertragsverhältnisses mit einem dieser Versicherer im Zweifel auch die Beendigung des Vertragsverhältnisses mit den anderen Versicherern zur Folge haben würde. In diesem Falle kann durch Rechtsverordnung, die nicht der Zustimmung des Bundesrates bedarf, außerdem bestimmt werden, ob die festgesetzten Leistungen von allen Versicherern als Gesamtschuldnern oder anteilig oder nur von einem der Versicherer geschuldet werden und wie der Ausgleich unter ihnen zu erfolgen hat.

### § 92a
### [Minimum working conditions]

(1) For the contractual relationship of a commercial agent who is not permitted to represent other principals or for whom this is impossible because of the type and volume of business activity demanded of him, the Federal Ministry of Justice may, in agreement with the Federal Ministry of Economics and Technology, after a hearing with the commercial agent's and principal's representative associations, determine – by means of a statutory instrument – the minimum contractual duties of the principal in order to ensure that the requisite social and economic needs of these commercial agents or a particular group of commercial agents are provided for. Such a statutory instrument shall not require the consent of the Federal Council (*Bundesrat*). The duties thus determined may not be excluded or limited by party agreement.

(2) Subsection 1 also applies to the contractual relationship of an insurance agent who, by reason of one or more contracts, has been authorised to solicit or conclude business transactions for numerous insurers who belong to an insurance concern or an organisation common to all of them, to the extent that termination of the contractual relationship with one of these insurers could potentially also have the effect of terminating the contractual relationship with the other insurers. In this case it can be determined, by means of a statutory instrument which shall not require the consent of the Federal Council, whether the duties established are to be performed by all insurers jointly and severally or by only one insurer and how the compensation is to be apportioned among them.

## § 92b
## [Handelsvertreter im Nebenberuf]

(1) Auf einen Handelsvertreter im Nebenberuf sind §§ 89 und 89b nicht anzuwenden. Ist das Vertragsverhältnis auf unbestimmte Zeit eingegangen, so kann es mit einer Frist von einem Monat für den Schluss eines Kalendermonats gekündigt werden; wird eine andere Kündigungsfrist vereinbart, so muss sie für beide Teile gleich sein. Der Anspruch auf einen angemessenen Vorschuss nach § 87a Abs. 1 Satz 2 kann ausgeschlossen werden.

(2) Auf Absatz 1 kann sich nur der Unternehmer berufen, der den Handelsvertreter ausdrücklich als Handelsvertreter im Nebenberuf mit der Vermittlung oder dem Abschluss von Geschäften betraut hat.

(3) Ob ein Handelsvertreter nur als Handelsvertreter im Nebenberuf tätig ist, bestimmt sich nach der Verkehrsauffassung.

(4) Die Vorschriften der Absätze 1 bis 3 gelten sinngemäß für Versicherungsvertreter und für Bausparkassenvertreter.

## § 92b
## [Part-time commercial agent]

(1) §§ 89 and 89b are not applicable to a part-time commercial agent. Where the contractual relationship is for an indefinite period, it can be terminated as of the end of a calendar month on prior notice of one month. Where a different notice period is agreed to, it must be the same for both parties. The right to a reasonable advance pursuant to § 87a(1), sentence 2 can be excluded by agreement.

(2) Subsection 1 can only be asserted by a principal who has authorised the commercial agent to solicit or conclude business transactions expressly as a part-time commercial agent.

(3) Whether or not a commercial agent is active only as a part-time agent is determined by the prevailing public opinion.

(4) The provisions of subsections 1 through 3 apply analogously to insurance agents and building and loan association agents.

## § 92c
## [Handelsvertreter außerhalb der EG; Schifffahrtsvertreter]

(1) Hat der Handelsvertreter seine Tätigkeit für den Unternehmer nach dem Vertrag nicht innerhalb des Gebietes der Europäischen Gemeinschaft oder der anderen Vertragsstaaten des Abkommens über den Europäischen Wirtschaftsraum auszuüben, so kann hinsichtlich aller Vorschriften dieses Abschnittes etwas anderes vereinbart werden.

(2) Das gleiche gilt, wenn der Handelsvertreter mit der Vermittlung oder dem Abschluss von Geschäften betraut wird, die die Befrachtung, Abfertigung oder Ausrüstung von Schiffen oder die Buchung von Passagen auf Schiffen zum Gegenstand haben.

## § 92c
## [Commercial agent outside the EEC; shipping agent]

(1) Where the commercial agent is not contractually obligated to carry out his activities for the principal within the territory of the European Community or the other contracting states of the European Economic Area Agreement, all provisions of this part may be altered by agreement.

(2) The same applies if the commercial agent is authorised to solicit or conclude business transactions concerning the chartering, dispatch or equipping of vessels, or the booking of passages on ships.

## Achter Abschnitt Handelsmakler (§§ 93–104a)

### § 93 [Begriff]

(1) Wer gewerbsmäßig für andere Personen, ohne von ihnen auf Grund eines Vertragsverhältnisses ständig damit betraut zu sein, die Vermittlung von Verträgen über Anschaffung oder Veräußerung von Waren oder Wertpapieren, über Versicherungen, Güterbeförderungen, Schiffsmiete oder sonstige Gegenstände des Handelsverkehrs übernimmt, hat die Rechte und Pflichten eines Handelsmaklers.

(2) Auf die Vermittlung anderer als der bezeichneten Geschäfte, insbesondere auf die Vermittlung von Geschäften über unbewegliche Sachen, finden, auch wenn die Vermittlung durch einen Handelsmakler erfolgt, die Vorschriften dieses Abschnitts keine Anwendung.

(3) Die Vorschriften dieses Abschnittes finden auch Anwendung, wenn das Unternehmen des Handelsmaklers nach Art oder Umfang einen in kaufmännischer Weise eingerichteten Geschäftsbetrieb nicht erfordert.

### § 94 [Schlussnote]

(1) Der Handelsmakler hat, sofern nicht die Parteien ihm dies erlassen oder der Ortsgebrauch mit Rücksicht auf die Gattung der Ware davon entbindet, unverzüglich nach dem Abschluss des Geschäfts jeder Partei eine von ihm unterzeichnete Schlussnote zuzustellen, welche die Parteien, den Gegenstand und die Bedingungen des Geschäfts, insbesondere bei Verkäufen von Waren oder Wertpapieren deren Gattung und Menge sowie den Preis und die Zeit der Lieferung, enthält.

(2) Bei Geschäften, die nicht sofort erfüllt werden sollen, ist die Schlussnote den Parteien zu ihrer Unterschrift zuzustellen und jeder Partei die von der anderen unterschriebene Schlussnote zu übersenden.

(3) Verweigert eine Partei die Annahme oder Unterschrift der Schlussnote, so hat der Handelsmakler davon der anderen Partei unverzüglich Anzeige zu machen.

## Part Eight Commercial broker (§§ 93–104a)

### § 93 [Definition]

(1) Anyone who undertakes commercially the solicitation of contracts concerning the purchase and sale of goods or securities, insurance, shipping and forwarding of goods, marine charter or other commercial matters for other persons, without being authorised to do so on a regular basis by contractual relationship, has the rights and duties of a commercial broker.

(2) The provisions of this part do not apply to the solicitation of business other than the kind set forth above, especially the solicitation of business relating to immovable assets, even if the solicitation is effected through a commercial broker.

(3) The provisions of this part also apply if the business of the commercial broker, based on its nature or scope, does not require a commercially organised business operation

### § 94 [Memorandum of sale]

(1) The commercial broker must, unless released therefrom by the parties or by local custom with regard to the nature of the goods involved, supply each party, without undue delay following the conclusion of the transaction, with a memorandum of sale signed by him and setting forth the names of the parties, the subject and terms of the transaction, especially in the case of a sale of goods or securities, their type and quantity, as well as the price and date of delivery.

(2) In the case of transactions that are not to be performed immediately, the memorandum of sale is to be forwarded to the parties for signature and each party is to be sent the memorandum of sale signed by the other party.

(3) Where one party refuses to accept or sign the memorandum of sale, the commercial broker must notify the other party hereof without undue delay.

## § 95
## [Vorbehaltene Aufgabe]

(1) Nimmt eine Partei eine Schlussnote an, in der sich der Handelsmakler die Bezeichnung der anderen Partei vorbehalten hat, so ist sie an das Geschäft mit der Partei, welche ihr nachträglich bezeichnet wird, gebunden, es sei denn, dass gegen diese begründete Einwendungen zu erheben sind.

(2) Die Bezeichnung der anderen Partei hat innerhalb der ortsüblichen Frist, in Ermangelung einer solchen innerhalb einer den Umständen nach angemessenen Frist zu erfolgen.

(3) Unterbleibt die Bezeichnung oder sind gegen die bezeichnete Person oder Firma begründete Einwendungen zu erheben, so ist die Partei befugt, den Handelsmakler auf die Erfüllung des Geschäfts in Anspruch zu nehmen. Der Anspruch ist ausgeschlossen, wenn sich die Partei auf die Aufforderung des Handelsmaklers nicht unverzüglich darüber erklärt, ob sie Erfüllung verlange.

## § 95
## [Temporary reservation of disclosure of principal]

(1) Where one party accepts a memorandum of sale in which the commercial broker has not disclosed the identity of the other party, the party accepting is bound to the transaction with the other party, the identity of whom is to be disclosed later, unless justifiable objections are raised against the other party.

(2) The other party must be identified within the locally customary period and, in the absence thereof, within a period reasonable under the circumstances.

(3) Where identification is not made or where justifiable objections can be raised against the person or company identified, the party is entitled to demand that the commercial broker perform the contract. The right does not exist if the party does not, on request by the commercial broker, declare without undue delay whether it demands performance.

## § 96
## [Aufbewahrung von Proben]

Der Handelsmakler hat, sofern nicht die Parteien ihm dies erlassen oder der Ortsgebrauch mit Rücksicht auf die Gattung der Ware davon entbindet, von jeder durch seine Vermittlung nach Probe verkauften Ware die Probe, falls sie ihm übergeben ist, so lange aufzubewahren, bis die Ware ohne Einwendung gegen ihre Beschaffenheit angenommen oder das Geschäft in anderer Weise erledigt wird. Er hat die Probe durch ein Zeichen kenntlich zu machen.

## § 96
## [Storage of samples]

The commercial broker must, unless released therefrom by the parties or by local custom with respect to the nature of the goods, retain a sample of each piece of merchandise sold by sample by his solicitation, provided the sample has been given to him, until the merchandise is accepted without objection as to quality or the transaction has been concluded otherwise. He must identify the sample by marking.

## § 97
## [Keine Inkassovollmacht]

Der Handelsmakler gilt nicht als ermächtigt, eine Zahlung oder eine andere im Vertrage bedungene Leistung in Empfang zu nehmen.

## § 97
## [No collective authority]

The commercial broker is not deemed to be authorised to accept payment or any other contractually stipulated consideration.

## § 98
## [Haftung gegenüber beiden Parteien]

Der Handelsmakler haftet jeder der beiden Parteien für den durch sein Verschulden entstehenden Schaden.

## § 98
## [Liability with respect to both parties]

The commercial broker is liable to each of the two parties for damages arising through his fault.

### § 99
### [Lohnanspruch gegen beide Parteien]

Ist unter den Parteien nichts darüber vereinbart, wer den Maklerlohn bezahlen soll, so ist er in Ermangelung eines abweichenden Ortsgebrauchs von jeder Partei zur Hälfte zu entrichten.

### § 99
### [Compensation right against both parties]

Where it has not been agreed upon between the parties as to who should pay the broker's fee, in the absence of a contrary local custom, one-half is to be paid by each party.

### § 100
### [Tagebuch]

(1) Der Handelsmakler ist verpflichtet, ein Tagebuch zu führen und in dieses alle abgeschlossenen Geschäfte täglich einzutragen. Die Eintragungen sind nach der Zeitfolge zu bewirken; sie haben die in § 94 Abs. 1 bezeichneten Angaben zu enthalten. Das Eingetragene ist von dem Handelsmakler täglich zu unterzeichnen oder gemäß § 126a Abs. 1 des Bürgerlichen Gesetzbuchs elektronisch zu signieren.

(2) Die Vorschriften der §§ 239 und 257 über die Einrichtung und Aufbewahrung der Handelsbücher finden auf das Tagebuch des Handelsmaklers Anwendung.

### § 100
### [Broker's transaction book]

(1) The commercial broker is obligated to maintain a transaction book and, on a daily basis, to enter into such book all transactions concluded. Entries are to be made chronologically; they must include the information set forth in § 94(1). The entry is to be signed on a daily basis by the commercial broker or, pursuant to § 126a(1) of the Civil Code, to be signed electronically.

(2) The provisions of §§ 239 and 257 concerning the establishment and storage of commercial records apply to the commercial broker's transaction book.

### § 101
### [Auszüge aus dem Tagebuch]

Der Handelsmakler ist verpflichtet, den Parteien jederzeit auf Verlangen Auszüge aus dem Tagebuche zu geben, die von ihm unterzeichnet sind und alles enthalten, was von ihm in Ansehung des vermittelten Geschäfts eingetragen ist.

### § 101
### [Transaction book extracts]

The commercial broker is obligated to give to the parties, at any time on request, excerpts from the transaction book signed by him and containing everything entered by him with regard to the transaction negotiated.

### § 102
### [Vorlegung im Rechtsstreit]

Im Laufe eines Rechtsstreits kann das Gericht auch ohne Antrag einer Partei die Vorlegung des Tagebuchs anordnen, um es mit der Schlussnote, den Auszügen oder anderen Beweismitteln zu vergleichen.

### § 102
### [Production during litigation]

In the course of litigation, the court can, on its own motion, order the production of the transaction book in order to compare it with the memorandum of sale, the excerpts or other evidence.

### § 103
### [Ordnungswidrigkeiten]

(1) Ordnungswidrig handelt, wer als Handelsmakler

1. vorsätzlich oder fahrlässig ein Tagebuch über die abgeschlossenen Geschäfte zu führen unterlässt oder das Tagebuch in einer Weise führt, die dem § 100 Abs. 1 widerspricht oder
2. ein solches Tagebuch vor Ablauf der gesetzlichen Aufbewahrungsfrist vernichtet.

### § 103
### [Administrative offences]

(1) It shall be deemed an administrative offence if a commercial broker

1. intentionally or negligently fails to maintain a transaction book for the transactions concluded or maintains the transaction book in a manner inconsistent with § 100(1) or
2. destroys such a transaction book before expiration of the retention period required by law.

(2) Die Ordnungswidrigkeit kann mit einer Geldbuße bis zu fünftausend Euro geahndet werden.

(2) The administrative offence can be punished with a fine of up to five thousand euro.

### § 104
### [Krämermakler]

Auf Personen, welche die Vermittlung von Warengeschäften im Kleinverkehr besorgen, finden die Vorschriften über Schlussnoten und Tagebücher keine Anwendung. Auf Personen, welche die Vermittlung von Versicherungs- oder Bausparverträgen übernehmen, sind die Vorschriften über Tagebücher nicht anzuwenden.

### § 104
### [Petty broker]

The provisions concerning memoranda of sale and transaction books do not apply to persons who provide for the solicitation of merchandise transactions of small value. The provisions concerning transaction books do not apply to persons who solicit insurance or building savings contracts.

### § 104a
### Bußgeldvorschrift

(1) Ordnungswidrig handelt, wer vorsätzlich oder leichtfertig entgegen § 8b Abs. 3 Satz 1 Nr. 2 dort genannte Daten nicht, nicht richtig oder nicht vollständig übermittelt. Die Ordnungswidrigkeit kann mit einer Geldbuße bis zu zweihunderttausend Euro geahndet werden.

(2) Verwaltungsbehörde im Sinne des § 36 Abs. 1 Nr. 1 des Gesetzes über Ordnungswidrigkeiten ist die Bundesanstalt für Finanzdienstleistungsaufsicht.

### § 104a
### [Provision on administrative fines]

(1) It shall be deemed an administrative offence to intentionally or negligently fail to transfer the data mentioned in § 8b(3), sentence 1, no. 2, or transfer them incorrectly or incompletely. The administrative offence can be punished with a fine of up to two hundred thousand euro.

(2) An administrative authority within the meaning of § 36(1), no. 1 of the Administrative Offences Act is the (German) Federal Financial Supervisory Authority.

### §§ 105–177a
[...]

### §§ 178–229
*(aufgehoben)*

### §§ 230–342e
[...]

### §§ 105–177a
[...]

### §§ 178–229
*(repealed)*

### §§ 230–342e
[...]

# Viertes Buch
# Handelsgeschäfte

## Erster Abschnitt
## Allgemeine Vorschriften
## (§§ 343–362, 373–475h)

# Book Four
# Commercial Transactions

## Part One
## General Provisions
## (§§ 343–362, 373–475h)

### § 343
### [Begriff der Handelsgeschäfte]

(1) Handelsgeschäfte sind alle Geschäfte eines Kaufmanns, die zum Betriebe seines Handelsgewerbes gehören.

(2) (weggefallen)

### § 343
### [Definition of commercial transactions]

(1) Commercial transactions are all transactions of a merchant that relate to the operation of his business.

(2) (repealed)

### § 344
### [Vermutung für das Handelsgeschäft]

(1) Die von einem Kaufmanne vorgenommenen Rechtsgeschäfte gelten im Zweifel als zum Betriebe seines Handelsgewerbes gehörig.

(2) Die von einem Kaufmanne gezeichneten Schuldscheine gelten als im Betriebe seines Handelsgewerbes gezeichnet, sofern nicht aus der Urkunde sich das Gegenteil ergibt.

### § 344
### [Presumption of a commercial transaction]

(1) Legal transactions undertaken by a merchant are deemed, in case of doubt, to be related to the operation of his business.

(2) Promissory notes signed by a merchant are deemed to have been signed in the course of the operation of his business unless a contrary result follows from the document.

### § 345
### [Einseitige Handelsgeschäfte]

Auf ein Rechtsgeschäft, das für einen der beiden Teile ein Handelsgeschäft ist, kommen die Vorschriften über Handelsgeschäfte für beide Teile gleichmäßig zur Anwendung, soweit nicht aus diesen Vorschriften sich ein anderes ergibt.

### § 345
### [Unilateral commercial transactions]

The provisions concerning commercial transactions apply in the same manner for both parties to a legal transaction that is a commercial transaction for at least one of the two parties, to the extent that these provisions do not provide otherwise.

### § 346
### [Handelsbräuche]

Unter Kaufleuten ist in Ansehung der Bedeutung und Wirkung von Handlungen und Unterlassungen auf die im Handelsverkehre geltenden Gewohnheiten und Gebräuche Rücksicht zu nehmen.

### § 346
### [Commercial practices]

Among merchants, due consideration shall be given to prevailing commercial customs and usages in view of the meaning and effect of acts and omissions in the commercial intercourse.

### § 347
### [Sorgfaltspflicht]

(1) Wer aus einem Geschäfte, das auf seiner Seite ein Handelsgeschäft ist, einem anderen zur Sorgfalt verpflichtet ist, hat für die Sorgfalt eines ordentlichen Kaufmanns einzustehen.

(2) Unberührt bleiben die Vorschriften des Bürgerlichen Gesetzbuchs, nach welchen der Schuldner in bestimmten Fällen nur grobe Fahrlässigkeit zu vertreten oder nur für diejenige Sorgfalt einzustehen hat, welche er in eigenen Angelegenheiten anzuwenden pflegt.

### § 347
### [Duty of care]

(1) One who, by reason of a transaction that is for him a commercial transaction, is obligated to observe a certain standard of care with regard to another person, shall meet the standard of care of a prudent merchant.

(2) The provisions of the Civil Code, according to which the obligor in certain cases is only liable for gross negligence or only has to exercise the care he normally applies to his own affairs, remain unaffected.

### § 348
### [Vertragsstrafe]

Eine Vertragsstrafe, die von einem Kaufmann im Betriebe seines Handelsgewerbes versprochen ist, kann nicht auf Grund der Vorschriften des § 343 des Bürgerlichen Gesetzbuchs herabgesetzt werden.

### § 348
### [Contract penalty]

A contract penalty which a merchant has promised in the operation of his business cannot be reduced by reason of the provisions of § 343 of the Civil Code.

**§ 349**
**[Keine Einrede der Vorausklage]**

Dem Bürgen steht, wenn die Bürgschaft für ihn ein Handelsgeschäft ist, die Einrede der Vorausklage nicht zu. Das gleiche gilt unter der bezeichneten Voraussetzung für denjenigen, welcher aus einem Kreditauftrag als Bürge haftet.

**§ 349**
**[No defence by a guarantor that the creditor must first unsuccessfully try to execute his claim on the debtor]**

If the guaranty is a commercial transaction for the guarantor, he is not entitled to raise the defence that the creditor must first unsuccessfully try to execute his claim on the debtor. The same applies, under the conditions stated, to anyone who is liable as a guarantor under a financing agreement.

**§ 350**
**[Formfreiheit]**

Auf eine Bürgschaft, ein Schuldversprechen oder ein Schuldanerkenntnis finden, sofern die Bürgschaft auf der Seite des Bürgen, das Versprechen oder das Anerkenntnis auf der Seite des Schuldners ein Handelsgeschäft ist, die Formvorschriften des § 766 Satz 1 und 2, des § 780 und des § 781 Satz 1 und 2 des Bürgerlichen Gesetzbuchs keine Anwendung.

**§ 350**
**[Freedom from formal requirements]**

The formal requirements of § 766, sentences 1 and 2, § 780 and § 781, sentences 1 and 2 of the Civil Code do not apply to a guaranty, an admission of liability or a debt acknowledged to the extent that the guaranty, for the guarantor, or the admission of liability or debt acknowledgement, for the debtor, is a commercial transaction.

**§ 351**
*(aufgehoben)*

**§ 351**
*(repealed)*

**§ 352**
**[Gesetzlicher Zinssatz]**

(1) Die Höhe der gesetzlichen Zinsen, mit Ausnahme der Verzugszinsen, ist bei beiderseitigen Handelsgeschäften fünf vom Hundert für das Jahr. Das gleiche gilt, wenn für eine Schuld aus einem solchen Handelsgeschäfte Zinsen ohne Bestimmung des Zinsfußes versprochen sind.

(2) Ist in diesem Gesetzbuche die Verpflichtung zur Zahlung von Zinsen ohne Bestimmung der Höhe ausgesprochen, so sind darunter Zinsen zu fünf vom Hundert für das Jahr zu verstehen.

**§ 352**
**[Statutory interest rate]**

(1) Interest, with the exception of interest due as a consequence of default, is five per cent per annum for bilateral commercial transactions. The same applies if interest has been promised with respect to a debt relating to such a commercial transaction without specification of a rate of interest.

(2) Where an interest obligation is established by this Commercial Code without specification of the rate, interest of five per cent per annum shall be understood.

**§ 353**
**[Fälligkeitszinsen]**

Kaufleute untereinander sind berechtigt, für ihre Forderungen aus beiderseitigen Handelsgeschäften vom Tage der Fälligkeit an Zinsen zu fordern. Zinsen von Zinsen können auf Grund dieser Vorschrift nicht gefordert werden.

**§ 353**
**[Interest from the date due]**

Merchants are entitled, with respect to claims arising out of bilateral commercial transactions, to demand interest from one another beginning with the due date of the respective claims. Interest on interest may not be demanded by reason of this provision.

## § 354
## [Provision; Lagergeld; Zinsen]

(1) Wer in Ausübung seines Handelsgewerbes einem anderen Geschäfte besorgt oder Dienste leistet, kann dafür auch ohne Verabredung Provision und, wenn es sich um Aufbewahrung handelt, Lagergeld nach den an dem Orte üblichen Sätzen fordern.

(2) Für Darlehen, Vorschüsse, Auslagen und andere Verwendungen kann er vom Tage der Leistung an Zinsen berechnen.

## § 354
## [Commission; storage charges; interest]

(1) One who, in the conduct of his business, solicits or transacts business or renders services for another, may demand commission therefor even absent an express agreement. If such business or services consist of storage, he may demand storage charges at rates which are customary in the area.

(2) He may charge interest from the date of performance for loans, advances, expenses and other financial outlays.

## § 354a
## [Wirksamkeit der Abtretung einer Geldforderung]

(1) Ist die Abtretung einer Geldforderung durch Vereinbarung mit dem Schuldner gemäß § 399 des Bürgerlichen Gesetzbuchs ausgeschlossen und ist das Rechtsgeschäft, das diese Forderung begründet hat, für beide Teile ein Handelsgeschäft, oder ist der Schuldner eine juristische Person des öffentlichen Rechts oder ein öffentlich-rechtliches Sondervermögen, so ist die Abtretung gleichwohl wirksam. Der Schuldner kann jedoch mit befreiender Wirkung an den bisherigen Gläubiger leisten. Abweichende Vereinbarungen sind unwirksam.

(2) Absatz 1 ist nicht auf eine Forderung aus einem Darlehensvertrag anzuwenden, deren Gläubiger ein Kreditinstitut im Sinne des Kreditwesengesetzes ist.

## § 354a
## [Effectiveness of assignment of monetary claim]

(1) If the transfer of a monetary claim by agreement with the debtor pursuant to § 399 of the Civil Code is precluded and if the legal transaction underlying this claim is a commercial transaction for both parties, or if the debtor is a legal person under public law or a special fund under public law, then the transfer is effective despite the preclusion. The debtor can, however, render performance to the previous creditor with discharging effect. Deviating agreements are invalid.

(2) Subsection 1 does not apply to a claim arising from a loan agreement whose creditor is a credit institution within the meaning of the Banking Act.

## § 355
## [Laufende Rechnung, Kontokorrent]

(1) Steht jemand mit einem Kaufmanne derart in Geschäftsverbindung, dass die aus der Verbindung entspringenden beiderseitigen Ansprüche und Leistungen nebst Zinsen in Rechnung gestellt und in regelmäßigen Zeitabschnitten durch Verrechnung und Feststellung des für den einen oder anderen Teil sich ergebenden Überschusses ausgeglichen werden (laufende Rechnung, Kontokorrent), so kann derjenige, welchem bei dem Rechnungsabschluss ein Überschuss gebührt, von dem Tage des Abschlusses an Zinsen von dem Überschuss verlangen, auch soweit in der Rechnung Zinsen enthalten sind.

(2) Der Rechnungsabschluss geschieht jährlich einmal, sofern nicht ein anderes bestimmt ist.

## § 355
## [Current account]

(1) Where someone has a business relationship with a merchant such that bilateral claims and payments (along with interest) arising from the relationship are placed on account and balanced at regular intervals by charging, and determining the balance for, one or the other of the parties (current account), the person to whom a balance is due on the balance date, may demand interest on the balance due from the balance date even if interest is included in the account.

(2) Accounts shall be balanced annually, absent an agreement to the contrary.

(3) Die laufende Rechnung kann im Zweifel auch während der Dauer einer Rechnungsperiode jederzeit mit der Wirkung gekündigt werden, dass derjenige, welchem nach der Rechnung ein Überschuss gebührt, dessen Zahlung beanspruchen kann.

(3) In case of doubt, the current account may also be terminated at any time during the term of an accounting period with the effect that the person to whom a balance is due following balancing of the account may demand payment thereof.

**§ 356**
**[Sicherheiten]**

(1) Wird eine Forderung, die durch Pfand, Bürgschaft oder in anderer Weise gesichert ist, in die laufende Rechnung aufgenommen, so wird der Gläubiger durch die Anerkennung des Rechnungsabschlusses nicht gehindert, aus der Sicherheit insoweit Befriedigung zu suchen, als sein Guthaben aus der laufenden Rechnung und die Forderung sich decken.

(2) Haftet ein Dritter für eine in die laufende Rechnung aufgenommene Forderung als Gesamtschuldner, so findet auf die Geltendmachung der Forderung gegen ihn die Vorschrift des Absatzes 1 entsprechende Anwendung.

**§ 356**
**[Security interests]**

(1) Where an outstanding debt secured by pledge, guaranty or otherwise is included in the current account, the creditor is not, by acknowledgement of the account balance, hindered from seeking satisfaction of such debt out of the collateral to the extent that the debt does not exceed the balance due him on the current account.

(2) Where a third party is liable as joint debtor for a debt included in the current account, the provisions of subsection 1 apply analogously in the assertion of the debt against him.

**§ 357**
**[Pfändung des Saldos]**

Hat der Gläubiger eines Beteiligten die Pfändung und Überweisung des Anspruchs auf dasjenige erwirkt, was seinem Schuldner als Überschuss aus der laufenden Rechnung zukommt, so können dem Gläubiger gegenüber Schuldposten, die nach der Pfändung durch neue Geschäfte entstehen, nicht in Rechnung gestellt werden. Geschäfte, die auf Grund eines schon vor der Pfändung bestehenden Rechtes oder einer schon vor diesem Zeitpunkte bestehenden Verpflichtung des Drittschuldners vorgenommen werden, gelten nicht als neue Geschäfte im Sinne dieser Vorschrift.

**§ 357**
**[Execution on the account balance]**

Where a third-party creditor of one of the parties has executed on, and effected transfer to himself of, the balance of the current account due to his debtor, the creditor's claim cannot be reduced by debit items which arise from new transactions following such execution. Transactions which have been undertaken by reason of a right existing prior to the execution, or by reason of an obligation of the debtor existing before this point in time, are not considered to be new transactions within the meaning of this provision.

**§ 358**
**[Zeit der Leistung]**

Bei Handelsgeschäften kann die Leistung nur während der gewöhnlichen Geschäftszeit bewirkt und gefordert werden.

**§ 358**
**[Time of performance]**

Performance of commercial transactions may only be made and demanded during normal business hours.

**§ 359**
**[Vereinbarte Zeit der Leistung; „acht Tage']**

(1) Ist als Zeit der Leistung das Frühjahr oder der Herbst oder ein in ähnlicher Weise bestimmter Zeitpunkt vereinbart, so entscheidet im Zweifel der Handelsgebrauch des Ortes der Leistung.

**§ 359**
**[Agreed time for performance; 'eight days']**

(1) In case of doubt, local custom of the place of performance shall be determinative for the time of performance where the time agreed is 'spring', 'autumn' or a point in time defined in a similar manner.

(2) Ist eine Frist von acht Tagen vereinbart, so sind hierunter im Zweifel volle acht Tage zu verstehen.

(2) In case of doubt, eight full days are to be understood where a period of 'eight days' is agreed.

### § 360 [Gattungsschuld]

Wird eine nur der Gattung nach bestimmte Ware geschuldet, so ist Handelsgut mittlerer Art und Güte zu leisten.

### § 360 [Obligation to deliver merchandise specified only by generic characteristics]

Where merchandise specified only by the generic characteristics is to be provided, merchandise of average kind and quality shall be tendered.

### § 361 [Maß, Gewicht, Währung, Zeitrechnung und Entfernungen]

Maß, Gewicht, Währung, Zeitrechnung und Entfernungen, die an dem Orte gelten, wo der Vertrag erfüllt werden soll, sind im Zweifel als die vertragsmäßigen zu betrachten.

### § 361 [Measure, weight, currency, computation of time, distance]

Measure, weight, currency, computation of time and distance which are customary at the location where the contract is to be fulfilled are, in case of doubt, to be considered as contractually agreed upon.

### § 362 [Schweigen des Kaufmanns auf Anträge]

(1) Geht einem Kaufmanne, dessen Gewerbebetrieb die Besorgung von Geschäften für andere mit sich bringt, ein Antrag über die Besorgung solcher Geschäfte von jemand zu, mit dem er in Geschäftsverbindung steht, so ist er verpflichtet, unverzüglich zu antworten; sein Schweigen gilt als Annahme des Antrags. Das gleiche gilt, wenn einem Kaufmann ein Antrag über die Besorgung von Geschäften von jemand zugeht, dem gegenüber er sich zur Besorgung solcher Geschäfte erboten hat.

(2) Auch wenn der Kaufmann den Antrag ablehnt, hat er die mitgesendeten Waren auf Kosten des Antragstellers, soweit er für diese Kosten gedeckt ist und soweit es ohne Nachteil für ihn geschehen kann, einstweilen vor Schaden zu bewahren.

### § 362 [Silence of merchant as to offers]

(1) Where an offer is made to a merchant whose business includes solicitation or conclusion of business transactions for others, and such offer is from someone with whom the merchant has a business relationship and concerns solicitation or conclusion of such transactions on behalf of the offeror, the merchant is obligated to reply immediately; his silence will be deemed to be an acceptance of the offer. The same applies where the merchant receives an offer to conclude transactions from someone to whom he has offered his services in concluding such transactions.

(2) Even if the merchant rejects the offer, he is obligated temporarily to protect from damage the goods sent to him at the offeror's expense, in so far as he is covered for these expenses and in so far as it can be done without disadvantage to him.

### §§ 363–372 [...]

### §§ 363–372 [...]

### § 373 [Annahmeverzug des Käufers]

(1) Ist der Käufer mit der Annahme der Ware im Verzug, so kann der Verkäufer die Ware auf Gefahr und Kosten des Käufers in einem öffentlichen Lagerhaus oder sonst in sicherer Weise hinterlegen.

### § 373 [Default in taking delivery by the buyer]

(1) Where the buyer of goods is in default as regards taking delivery, the seller may deposit the goods at the buyer's risk and expense in a public warehouse or in some other secure manner.

(2) Er ist ferner befugt, nach vorgängiger Androhung die Ware öffentlich versteigern zu lassen; er kann, wenn die Ware einen Börsen- oder Marktpreis hat, nach vorgängiger Androhung den Verkauf auch aus freier Hand durch einen zu solchen Verkäufen öffentlich ermächtigten Handelsmakler oder durch eine zur öffentlichen Versteigerung befugte Person zum laufenden Preis bewirken. Ist die Ware dem Verderb ausgesetzt und Gefahr im Verzug, so bedarf es der vorgängigen Androhung nicht; dasselbe gilt, wenn die Androhung aus anderen Gründen untunlich ist.

(2) He is furthermore authorised after prior warning to have the goods sold at public auction; he may, if the goods have an exchange or market price, following prior warning, also have the sale conducted on the open market at the current price by a broker officially authorised to conduct such sales or by a public auctioneer. If the goods are perishable and there is risk in delay, prior warning is not required; the same applies if the warning is impracticable for other reasons.

(3) Der Selbsthilfeverkauf erfolgt für Rechnung des säumigen Käufers.

(3) The self-help sale is made for the account of the defaulting buyer.

(4) Der Verkäufer und der Käufer können bei der öffentlichen Versteigerung mitbieten.

(4) Both the seller and the buyer may bid at the public auction.

(5) Im Falle der öffentlichen Versteigerung hat der Verkäufer den Käufer von der Zeit und dem Ort der Versteigerung vorher zu benachrichtigen; von dem vollzogenen Verkauf hat er bei jeder Art des Verkaufs dem Käufer unverzüglich Nachricht zu geben. Im Falle der Unterlassung ist er zum Schadensersatz verpflichtet. Die Benachrichtigungen dürfen unterbleiben, wenn sie untunlich sind.

(5) In the event of a public auction, the seller must inform the buyer beforehand as to the time and place of the auction; he must immediately inform the buyer of the execution of any kind of sale. In the case of failure to do this, he is liable for damages. Notifications may be omitted if they are impracticable.

### § 374
### [Vorschriften des BGB über Annahmeverzug]

Durch die Vorschriften des § 373 werden die Befugnisse nicht berührt, welche dem Verkäufer nach dem Bürgerlichen Gesetzbuch zustehen, wenn der Käufer im Verzug der Annahme ist.

### § 374
### [Provisions of the Civil Code with respect to default in taking delivery]

The rights of the seller pursuant to the Civil Code where a buyer defaults in taking delivery will not be affected by the provisions of § 373.

### § 375
### [Bestimmungskauf]

(1) Ist bei dem Kauf einer beweglichen Sache dem Käufer die nähere Bestimmung über Form, Maß oder ähnliche Verhältnisse vorbehalten, so ist der Käufer verpflichtet, die vorbehaltene Bestimmung zu treffen.

(2) Ist der Käufer mit der Erfüllung dieser Verpflichtung im Verzug, so kann der Verkäufer die Bestimmung statt des Käufers vornehmen oder gemäß den §§ 280, 281 des Bürgerlichen Gesetzbuchs Schadensersatz statt der Leistung verlangen oder gemäß § 323 des Bürgerlichen Gesetzbuchs vom Vertrag zurücktreten. Im ersteren Falle hat der Verkäufer die von ihm getroffene Bestimmung dem Käufer mitzuteilen und ihm zugleich eine angemessene Frist zur Vornahme einer anderweitigen Bestimmung zu setzen. Wird eine solche innerhalb der Frist von dem Käufer nicht vorgenommen, so ist die von dem Verkäufer getroffene Bestimmung maßgebend.

### § 375
### [Sale where the buyer specifies the item]

(1) Where, with respect to the sale of tangible property, specific determinations are reserved to the buyer with respect to form, size or similar conditions, the buyer is obligated to make the determinations thus reserved.

(2) Where the buyer defaults in fulfilling this duty the seller may make the determination instead of the buyer, demand damages for non-performance pursuant to §§ 280, 281 of the Civil Code or rescind the contract pursuant to § 323 of the Civil Code. In the first case, the seller must inform the buyer of the determination made by him and at the same time set a reasonable period for him to make a contrary determination. Where a determination is not made by the buyer within the period, the determination made by the seller shall prevail.

### § 376
### [Fixhandelskauf]

(1) Ist bedungen, dass die Leistung des einen Teiles genau zu einer festbestimmten Zeit oder innerhalb einer festbestimmten Frist bewirkt werden soll, so kann der andere Teil, wenn die Leistung nicht zu der bestimmten Zeit oder nicht innerhalb der bestimmten Frist erfolgt, von dem Vertrag zurücktreten oder, falls der Schuldner im Verzug ist, statt der Erfüllung Schadensersatz wegen Nichterfüllung verlangen. Erfüllung kann er nur beanspruchen, wenn er sofort nach dem Ablauf der Zeit oder der Frist dem Gegner anzeigt, dass er auf Erfüllung bestehe.

(2) Wird Schadensersatz wegen Nichterfüllung verlangt und hat die Ware einen Börsen- oder Marktpreis, so kann der Unterschied des Kaufpreises und des Börsen- oder Marktpreises zur Zeit und am Ort der geschuldeten Leistung gefordert werden.

(3) Das Ergebnis eines anderweit vorgenommenen Verkaufs oder Kaufs kann, falls die Ware einen Börsen- oder Marktpreis hat, dem Ersatzanspruch nur zugrunde gelegt werden, wenn der Verkauf oder Kauf sofort nach dem Ablauf der bedungenen Leistungszeit oder Leistungsfrist bewirkt ist. Der Verkauf oder Kauf muss, wenn er nicht in öffentlicher Versteigerung geschieht, durch einen zu solchen Verkäufen oder Käufen öffentlich ermächtigten Handelsmakler oder eine zur öffentlichen Versteigerung befugte Person zum laufenden Preis erfolgen.

(4) Auf den Verkauf mittels öffentlicher Versteigerung findet die Vorschrift des § 373 Abs. 4 Anwendung. Von dem Verkauf oder Kauf hat der Gläubiger den Schuldner unverzüglich zu benachrichtigen; im Falle der Unterlassung ist er zum Schadensersatz verpflichtet.

### § 376
### [Sale to be performed at a fixed point in time]

(1) Where it is stipulated that performance by one of the parties should be effected at an exact time or within a specific period, the other party may rescind the contract if performance is not made at the exact time or within the period specified, or in the event that the debtor has defaulted, demand payment of damages for non-performance of the contract. He may only demand performance if he indicates to the other party, immediately following expiration of the time or the period, that he insists on performance.

(2) Where damages are demanded for non-performance and the goods have an exchange or market price, the difference between the purchase price and the exchange or market price at the time and place of the performance due can be demanded.

(3) The result of another sale or purchase can, in the case where the goods have an exchange or market price, only be taken as the basis for the damage claim if the sale or purchase is effected immediately after the performance time or performance deadline has elapsed. If it does not occur at a public auction, the sale or purchase must be carried out at the current price by a broker officially authorised to conduct such sales or by a public auctioneer.

(4) The provision of § 373(4) applies to the sale at public auction. The creditor must promptly notify the debtor of the sale or purchase; in case of failure to do this, he is liable for damages.

### § 377
### [Untersuchungs- und Rügepflicht]

(1) Ist der Kauf für beide Teile ein Handelsgeschäft, so hat der Käufer die Ware unverzüglich nach der Ablieferung durch den Verkäufer, soweit dies nach ordnungsmäßigem Geschäftsgang tunlich ist, zu untersuchen und, wenn sich ein Mangel zeigt, dem Verkäufer unverzüglich Anzeige zu machen.

(2) Unterlässt der Käufer die Anzeige, so gilt die Ware als genehmigt, es sei denn, dass es sich um einen Mangel handelt, der bei der Untersuchung nicht erkennbar war.

### § 377
### [Duty to examine and object to defects]

(1) Where the sale is a commercial transaction for both parties, the buyer must examine the goods promptly following delivery by the seller in so far as this is practicable in the proper course of business and, if a defect becomes apparent, promptly advise the seller.

(2) If the buyer fails to advise the seller, the goods are deemed to have been approved, unless there is a defect which was not apparent during the examination.

(3) Zeigt sich später ein solcher Mangel, so muss die Anzeige unverzüglich nach der Entdeckung gemacht werden; anderenfalls gilt die Ware auch in Ansehung dieses Mangels als genehmigt.

(4) Zur Erhaltung der Rechte des Käufers genügt die rechtzeitige Absendung der Anzeige.

(5) Hat der Verkäufer den Mangel arglistig verschwiegen, so kann er sich auf diese Vorschriften nicht berufen.

(3) Where such a defect becomes apparent at a later time, notice must be given promptly following the discovery; otherwise, the goods are to be deemed approved, also with regard to this defect.

(4) The timely dispatch of notice suffices to preserve the buyer's rights.

(5) Where the seller has maliciously concealed the defect, he may not assert these provisions.

**§ 378**
*(aufgehoben)*

**§ 378**
*(repealed)*

**§ 379**
**[Einstweilige Aufbewahrung; Notverkauf]**

(1) Ist der Kauf für beide Teile ein Handelsgeschäft, so ist der Käufer, wenn er die ihm von einem anderen Ort übersendete Ware beanstandet, verpflichtet, für ihre einstweilige Aufbewahrung zu sorgen.

(2) Er kann die Ware, wenn sie dem Verderb ausgesetzt und Gefahr im Verzug ist, unter Beobachtung der Vorschriften des § 373 verkaufen lassen.

**§ 379**
**[Temporary storage; forced sale]**

(1) Where the sale is a commercial transaction for both parties, a buyer who refuses to accept goods shipped to him from another location is obligated to provide temporary storage for them.

(2) He may have the goods sold, under observance of the provisions of § 373, if they are perishable and there is risk in delay.

**§ 380**
**[Taragewicht]**

(1) Ist der Kaufpreis nach dem Gewicht der Ware zu berechnen, so kommt das Gewicht der Verpackung (Taragewicht) in Abzug, wenn nicht aus dem Vertrag oder dem Handelsgebrauch des Ortes, an welchem der Verkäufer zu erfüllen hat, sich ein anderes ergibt.

(2) Ob und in welcher Höhe das Taragewicht nach einem bestimmten Ansatz oder Verhältnis statt nach genauer Ausmittelung abzuziehen ist, sowie, ob und wieviel als Gutgewicht zugunsten des Käufers zu berechnen ist oder als Vergütung für schadhafte oder unbrauchbare Teile (Refaktie) gefordert werden kann, bestimmt sich nach dem Vertrag oder dem Handelsgebrauch des Ortes, an welchem der Verkäufer zu erfüllen hat.

**§ 380**
**[Tare weight]**

(1) Where the purchase price is calculated according to the weight of the merchandise, the weight of the packaging (tare weight) is to be subtracted unless the contract or the trade custom of the place at which the seller is to perform provides otherwise.

(2) Whether and to what extent the tare weight is to be subtracted pursuant to a specific rate or ratio in lieu of an exact weight, as well as whether and how much is to be calculated as weight for the buyer's benefit or can be claimed as compensation for defective or useless parts (allowance for loss, breakage, shrinkage, etc.) shall be determined by the contract or the trade custom of the place at which the seller is obligated to perform.

**§ 381**
**[Kauf von Wertpapieren; Werklieferungsvertrag]**

(1) Die in diesem Abschnitt für den Kauf von Waren getroffenen Vorschriften gelten auch für den Kauf von Wertpapieren.

**§ 381**
**[Sale of securities; contract for work and materials]**

(1) The provisions set forth in this Part for the sale of goods also apply to the sale of securities.

(2) Sie finden auch auf einen Vertrag Anwendung, der die Lieferung herzustellender oder zu erzeugender beweglicher Sachen zum Gegenstand hat.

(2) They also apply to contracts that relate to the delivery of tangible goods due to be manufactured or made.

### § 382
*(aufgehoben)*

### § 382
*(repealed)*

## Dritter Abschnitt Kommissionsgeschäft

## Part Three Transactions on a Commission Basis

### § 383 [Kommissionär; Kommissionsvertrag]

(1) Kommissionär ist, wer es gewerbsmäßig übernimmt, Waren oder Wertpapiere für Rechnung eines anderen (des Kommittenten) in eigenem Namen zu kaufen oder zu verkaufen.

(2) Die Vorschriften dieses Abschnittes finden auch Anwendung, wenn das Unternehmen des Kommissionärs nach Art oder Umfang einen in kaufmännischer Weise eingerichteten Geschäftsbetrieb nicht erfordert und die Firma des Unternehmens nicht nach § 2 in das Handelsregister eingetragen ist. In diesem Fall finden in Ansehung des Kommissionsgeschäfts auch die Vorschriften des Ersten Abschnittes des Vierten Buches mit Ausnahme der §§ 348 bis 350 Anwendung.

### § 383 [Commission agent; contract concluded by a commission agent]

(1) A commission agent is one who professionally undertakes to buy and sell goods or securities in his own name for the account of another (principal).

(2) The provisions of this Part also apply where the enterprise of the commission agent, based on its nature or scope, does not require a commercially organised business operation and the firm name of the enterprise is not registered in the Commercial Register pursuant to § 2. In this case the provisions of the First Part of the Fourth Book, with the exception of §§ 348 to 350, also apply with respect to the commission business.

### § 384 [Pflichten des Kommissionärs]

(1) Der Kommissionär ist verpflichtet, das übernommene Geschäft mit der Sorgfalt eines ordentlichen Kaufmanns auszuführen; er hat hierbei das Interesse des Kommittenten wahrzunehmen und dessen Weisungen zu befolgen.

(2) Er hat dem Kommittenten die erforderlichen Nachrichten zu geben, insbesondere von der Ausführung der Kommission unverzüglich Anzeige zu machen; er ist verpflichtet, dem Kommittenten über das Geschäft Rechenschaft abzulegen und ihm dasjenige herauszugeben, was er aus der Geschäftsbesorgung erlangt hat.

(3) Der Kommissionär haftet dem Kommittenten für die Erfüllung des Geschäfts, wenn er ihm nicht zugleich mit der Anzeige von der Ausführung der Kommission den Dritten namhaft macht, mit dem er das Geschäft abgeschlossen hat.

### § 384 [Duties of the commission agent]

(1) The commission agent is obligated to carry out the transaction undertaken with the care of a prudent merchant; in so doing he must protect the principal's interests and follow his instructions.

(2) He must give the principal the necessary information, especially prompt notice as to the conclusion of the transaction; he is obligated to account to the principal for the transaction and deliver to him anything obtained from the business commissioned.

(3) The commission agent is liable to the principal for performance of the transaction if he does not, simultaneously with notice of conclusion of the transaction, name the third party with whom he concluded the transaction.

## § 385
## [Weisungen des Kommittenten]

(1) Handelt der Kommissionär nicht gemäß den Weisungen des Kommittenten, so ist er diesem zum Ersatz des Schadens verpflichtet; der Kommittent braucht das Geschäft nicht für seine Rechnung gelten zu lassen.

(2) Die Vorschriften des § 665 des Bürgerlichen Gesetzbuchs bleiben unberührt.

## § 385
## [Instructions of the principal]

(1) Where the commission agent does not act in accordance with the principal's instructions, he is liable to him for damages; the principal need not accept the transaction for his account.

(2) The provisions of § 665 of the Civil Code remain unaffected.

## § 386
## [Preisgrenzen]

(1) Hat der Kommissionär unter dem ihm gesetzten Preis verkauft oder hat er den ihm für den Einkauf gesetzten Preis überschritten, so muss der Kommittent, falls er das Geschäft als nicht für seine Rechnung abgeschlossen zurückweisen will, dies unverzüglich auf die Anzeige von der Ausführung des Geschäfts erklären; anderenfalls gilt die Abweichung von der Preisbestimmung als genehmigt.

(2) Erbietet sich der Kommissionär zugleich mit der Anzeige von der Ausführung des Geschäfts zur Deckung des Preisunterschieds, so ist der Kommittent zur Zurückweisung nicht berechtigt. Der Anspruch des Kommittenten auf den Ersatz eines den Preisunterschied übersteigenden Schadens bleibt unberührt.

## § 386
## [Buying and selling price limitations]

(1) Where the commission agent has sold for less than the price set for him or has exceeded the price set for the purchase, the principal, in the event he desires to reject the transaction as not having been concluded for his account, must give notice thereof promptly upon receiving notification of the conclusion of the transaction; otherwise, the deviation from the price stipulation is deemed to have been consented to.

(2) Where the commission agent, simultaneously with notice of conclusion of the transaction, offers to cover the price difference, the principal may not reject the transaction. The principal's right to damages which exceed the price difference remains unaffected.

## § 387
## [Vorteilhafterer Abschluss]

(1) Schließt der Kommissionär zu vorteilhafteren Bedingungen ab, als sie ihm von dem Kommittenten gesetzt worden sind, so kommt dies dem Kommittenten zustatten.

(2) Dies gilt insbesondere, wenn der Preis, für welchen der Kommissionär verkauft, den von dem Kommittenten bestimmten niedrigsten Preis übersteigt oder wenn der Preis, für welchen er einkauft, den von dem Kommittenten bestimmten höchsten Preis nicht erreicht.

## § 387
## [More profitable conclusion of business]

(1) Where the commission agent concludes the transaction on more favourable terms than were stipulated for him by the principal, the resulting benefit shall accrue to the principal.

(2) This applies particularly where the price at which the commission agent sold exceeded the lowest price specified by the principal or where the price at which he bought did not reach the highest price specified by the principal.

## § 388
## [Beschädigtes oder mangelhaftes Kommissionsgut]

(1) Befindet sich das Gut, welches dem Kommissionär zugesendet ist, bei der Ablieferung in einem beschädigten oder mangelhaften Zustand, der äußerlich erkennbar ist, so hat der Kommissionär die Rechte gegen den Frachtführer oder Schiffer zu wahren, für den Beweis des Zustands zu sorgen und dem Kommittenten unverzüglich Nachricht zu geben; im Falle der Unterlassung ist er zum Schadensersatz verpflichtet.

## § 388
## [Damaged or defective goods on commission]

(1) Where the goods sent to the commission agent are in a damaged or defective condition apparent at the time of delivery, the commission agent is obligated to reserve all rights against the freight carrier or shipper, make arrangements to preserve proof of the condition and notify the principal promptly; where he fails to do this, he is liable for damages.

(2) Ist das Gut dem Verderb ausgesetzt oder treten später Veränderungen an dem Gut ein, die dessen Entwertung befürchten lassen, und ist keine Zeit vorhanden, die Verfügung des Kommittenten einzuholen, oder ist der Kommittent in der Erteilung der Verfügung säumig, so kann der Kommissionär den Verkauf des Gutes nach Maßgabe der Vorschriften des § 373 bewirken.

(2) Where the goods are perishable or subsequent changes therein cause concern that they will depreciate and there is no time to obtain instructions from the principal, or the principal delays in responding with instructions, the commission agent may have the goods sold according to the provisions of § 373.

### § 389
### [Hinterlegung; Selbsthilfeverkauf]

Unterlässt der Kommittent über das Gut zu verfügen, obwohl er dazu nach Lage der Sache verpflichtet ist, so hat der Kommissionär die nach § 373 dem Verkäufer zustehenden Rechte.

### § 389
### [Deposit; self-help sale]

Where the principal fails to dispose of the merchandise although obligated to do so under the circumstances, the commission agent has the rights of a seller pursuant to § 373.

### § 390
### [Haftung des Kommissionärs für das Gut]

(1) Der Kommissionär ist für den Verlust und die Beschädigung des in seiner Verwahrung befindlichen Gutes verantwortlich, es sei denn, dass der Verlust oder die Beschädigung auf Umständen beruht, die durch die Sorgfalt eines ordentlichen Kaufmanns nicht abgewendet werden konnten.

(2) Der Kommissionär ist wegen der Unterlassung der Versicherung des Gutes nur verantwortlich, wenn er von dem Kommittenten angewiesen war, die Versicherung zu bewirken.

### § 390
### [The commission agent's liability for the goods]

(1) The commission agent is responsible for loss of and damage to goods in his custody unless the loss or damage is due to circumstances which could not have been avoided by use of the care of a prudent merchant.

(2) The commission agent is responsible for failure to insure the goods only if he was instructed by the principal to obtain the insurance.

### § 391
### [Untersuchungs- und Rügepflicht; Aufbewahrung; Notverkauf]

Ist eine Einkaufskommission erteilt, die für beide Teile ein Handelsgeschäft ist, so finden in Bezug auf die Verpflichtung des Kommittenten, das Gut zu untersuchen und dem Kommissionär von den entdeckten Mängeln Anzeige zu machen, sowie in Bezug auf die Sorge für die Aufbewahrung des beanstandeten Gutes und auf den Verkauf bei drohendem Verderb die für den Käufer geltenden Vorschriften der §§ 377 bis 379 entsprechende Anwendung. Der Anspruch des Kommittenten auf Abtretung der Rechte, die dem Kommissionär gegen den Dritten zustehen, von welchem er das Gut für Rechnung des Kommittenten gekauft hat, wird durch eine verspätete Anzeige des Mangels nicht berührt.

### § 391
### [Duty to examine and object; storage; forced sale]

Where the commission to purchase is a commercial transaction for both parties, the provisions of §§ 377 through 379 applicable to the buyer are analogously applicable to the principal's duty to examine the goods and give notice to the commission agent of defects discovered, as well as to the duty of storage for the rejected goods and the sale of perishable goods. The right of the principal to assignment of the rights of the commission agent against third parties from whom he bought the goods for the principal's account will not be affected by late notification of defects.

## § 392
## [Forderungen aus dem Kommissionsgeschäft]

(1) Forderungen aus einem Geschäft, das der Kommissionär abgeschlossen hat, kann der Kommittent dem Schuldner gegenüber erst nach der Abtretung geltend machen.

(2) Jedoch gelten solche Forderungen, auch wenn sie nicht abgetreten sind, im Verhältnis zwischen dem Kommittenten und dem Kommissionär oder dessen Gläubigern als Forderungen des Kommittenten.

## § 392
## [Claims arising from transactions on a commission basis]

(1) Claims arising from a transaction concluded by the commission agent may be asserted by the principal against the debtor only after assignment.

(2) However, even if they are not assigned, such claims are deemed to be claims of the principal in the relationship between the principal and the commission agent or his creditors.

## § 393
## [Vorschuss; Kredit]

(1) Wird von dem Kommissionär ohne Zustimmung des Kommittenten einem Dritten ein Vorschuss geleistet oder Kredit gewährt, so handelt der Kommissionär auf eigene Gefahr.

(2) Insoweit jedoch der Handelsgebrauch am Ort des Geschäfts die Stundung des Kaufpreises mit sich bringt, ist in Ermangelung einer anderen Bestimmung des Kommittenten auch der Kommissionär dazu berechtigt.

(3) Verkauft der Kommissionär unbefugt auf Kredit, so ist er verpflichtet, dem Kommittenten sofort als Schuldner des Kaufpreises die Zahlung zu leisten. Wäre beim Verkauf gegen bar der Preis geringer gewesen, so hat der Kommissionär nur den geringeren Preis und, wenn dieser niedriger ist als der ihm gesetzte Preis, auch den Unterschied nach § 386 zu vergüten.

## § 393
## [Advance; credit]

(1) Where an advance is paid or credit is given to a third party by the commission agent without the principal's consent, the commission agent acts at his own risk.

(2) To the extent, however, that commercial usage at the location of the transaction includes a grace period for payment of the purchase price, the commission agent is authorised to grant such extension in the absence of a contrary instruction by the principal.

(3) Where the commission agent sells on credit without authorisation, he is obligated, as the party liable for the purchase price, to pay the principal immediately. If the price for a cash sale would have been lower, the commission agent is obligated to pay only the lower price plus the difference pursuant to § 386 if the lower price is even lower than the price set by the principal.

## § 394
## [Delkredere]

(1) Der Kommissionär hat für die Erfüllung der Verbindlichkeit des Dritten, mit dem er das Geschäft für Rechnung des Kommittenten abschließt, einzustehen, wenn dies von ihm übernommen oder am Ort seiner Niederlassung Handelsgebrauch ist.

(2) Der Kommissionär, der für den Dritten einzustehen hat, ist dem Kommittenten für die Erfüllung im Zeitpunkt des Verfalls unmittelbar insoweit verhaftet, als die Erfüllung aus dem Vertragsverhältnis gefordert werden kann. Er kann eine besondere Vergütung (Delkredereprovision) beanspruchen.

## § 394
## [*Del credere* commission]

(1) The commission agent shall be responsible for performance by the third party with whom he concludes the transaction for the account of the principal if this is undertaken by him or is commercially customary at the location of his establishment.

(2) The commission agent who is responsible for third-party performance is directly liable to the principal for performance at the time of the breach in so far as performance can be demanded on the basis of the contractual relationship. He may demand special remuneration (*del credere* commission).

**§ 395**
**[Wechselindossament]**

Ein Kommissionär, der den Ankauf eines Wechsels übernimmt, ist verpflichtet, den Wechsel, wenn er ihn indossiert, in üblicher Weise und ohne Vorbehalt zu indossieren.

**§ 395**
**[Bill of exchange indorsement]**

A commission agent who undertakes to purchase a bill of exchange is obligated to indorse the same, if at all, in the customary manner and without reservation.

**§ 396**
**[Provision des Kommissionärs; Ersatz von Aufwendungen]**

(1) Der Kommissionär kann die Provision fordern, wenn das Geschäft zur Ausführung gekommen ist. Ist das Geschäft nicht zur Ausführung gekommen, so hat er gleichwohl den Anspruch auf die Auslieferungsprovision, sofern eine solche ortsgebräuchlich ist; auch kann er die Provision verlangen, wenn die Ausführung des von ihm abgeschlossenen Geschäfts nur aus einem in der Person des Kommittenten liegenden Grund unterblieben ist.

(2) Zu dem von dem Kommittenten für Aufwendungen des Kommissionärs nach den §§ 670 und 675 des Bürgerlichen Gesetzbuchs zu leistenden Ersatz gehört auch die Vergütung für die Benutzung der Lagerräume und der Beförderungsmittel des Kommissionärs.

**§ 396**
**[Commission agent's commission; reimbursement for expenditures]**

(1) The commission agent may demand the commission when the transaction has been performed. Where the transaction has not been performed, he nevertheless has the right to a delivery commission to the extent that this is customary within the area; he may also demand the commission if the performance of the transaction concluded by him does not take place solely because of a personal reason related to the principal.

(2) Included within the amount to be reimbursed by the principal for the commission agent's expenditures pursuant to §§ 670 and 675 of the Civil Code are expenditures for the use of the storage areas and the commission agent's means of transport.

**§ 397**
**Pfandrecht des Kommissionärs**

Der Kommissionär hat wegen der auf das Gut verwendeten Kosten, der Provision, der auf das Gut gegebenen Vorschüsse und Darlehen sowie der mit Rücksicht auf das Gut gezeichneten Wechsel oder in anderer Weise eingegangenen Verbindlichkeiten ein Pfandrecht an dem Kommissionsgut des Kommittenten oder eines Dritten, der dem Kauf oder Verkauf des Gutes zugestimmt hat. An dem Gut des Kommittenten hat der Kommissionär auch ein Pfandrecht wegen aller Forderungen aus laufender Rechnung in Kommissionsgeschäften. Das Pfandrecht nach den Sätzen 1 und 2 besteht jedoch nur am Kommissionsgut, das der Kommissionär im Besitz hat oder über das er mittels Konnossements, Ladescheins oder Lagerscheins verfügen kann.

**§ 397**
**Lien of the commission agent**

The commission agent shall have a lien on the commission goods of the principal or of a third party who consented to the purchase or sale of the goods, for costs applied to the goods, the commission, advances and loans given on the goods, as well as bills of exchange signed with respect to the goods, or obligations entered into in another way. The commission agent shall also have a lien on the principal's goods for all current account claims from commission transactions. The lien pursuant to sentences 1 and 2 only exists, however, on the commission goods that the commission agent has in his possession or which he can dispose of by means of a maritime bill of lading, a bill of lading or a warehouse receipt.

**§ 398**
**[Befriedigung aus eigenem Kommissionsgut]**

Der Kommissionär kann sich, auch wenn er Eigentümer des Kommissionsguts ist, für die in § 397 bezeichneten Ansprüche nach Maßgabe der für das Pfandrecht geltenden Vorschriften aus dem Gut befriedigen.

**§ 398**
**[Satisfaction from one's own commission goods]**

The commission agent may satisfy himself for the claims listed in § 397, according to the provisions applicable to liens, out of the goods, even if he is the legal owner of the commission goods.

**§ 399**
**[Befriedigung aus Forderungen]**

Aus den Forderungen, welche durch das für Rechnung des Kommittenten geschlossene Geschäft begründet sind, kann sich der Kommissionär für die in § 397 bezeichneten Ansprüche vor dem Kommittenten und dessen Gläubigern befriedigen.

**§ 399**
**[Satisfaction out of claims]**

The commission agent may satisfy himself ahead of the principal and the principal's creditors for the claims listed in § 397 out of claims (against third parties) arising from the transaction concluded for the principal's account.

**§ 400**
**[Selbsteintritt des Kommissionärs]**

(1) Die Kommission zum Einkauf oder zum Verkauf von Waren, die einen Börsen- oder Marktpreis haben, sowie von Wertpapieren, bei denen ein Börsen- oder Marktpreis amtlich festgestellt wird, kann, wenn der Kommittent nicht ein anderes bestimmt hat, von dem Kommissionär dadurch ausgeführt werden, dass er das Gut, welches er einkaufen soll, selbst als Verkäufer liefert oder das Gut, welches er verkaufen soll, selbst als Käufer übernimmt.

(2) Im Falle einer solchen Ausführung der Kommission beschränkt sich die Pflicht des Kommissionärs, Rechenschaft über die Abschließung des Kaufes oder Verkaufs abzulegen, auf den Nachweis, dass bei dem berechneten Preis der zur Zeit der Ausführung der Kommission bestehende Börsen- oder Marktpreis eingehalten ist. Als Zeit der Ausführung gilt der Zeitpunkt, in welchem der Kommissionär die Anzeige von der Ausführung zur Absendung an den Kommittenten abgegeben hat.

(3) Ist bei einer Kommission, die während der Börsen- oder Marktzeit auszuführen war, die Ausführungsanzeige erst nach dem Schluss der Börse oder des Marktes zur Absendung abgegeben, so darf der berechnete Preis für den Kommittenten nicht ungünstiger sein als der Preis, der am Schluss der Börse oder des Marktes bestand.

(4) Bei einer Kommission, die zu einem bestimmten Kurs (erster Kurs, Mittelkurs, letzter Kurs) ausgeführt werden soll, ist der Kommissionär ohne Rücksicht auf den Zeitpunkt der Absendung der Ausführungsanzeige berechtigt und verpflichtet, diesen Kurs dem Kommittenten in Rechnung zu stellen.

(5) Bei Wertpapieren und Waren, für welche der Börsen- oder Marktpreis amtlich festgestellt wird, kann der Kommissionär im Falle der Ausführung der Kommission durch Selbsteintritt dem Kommittenten keinen ungünstigeren Preis als den amtlich festgestellten in Rechnung stellen.

**§ 400**
**[Commission agent's right to self-substitution]**

(1) The commission to buy or sell goods that have an exchange or market price, as well as securities for which an exchange or market price is officially determined may be performed by the commission agent such that, where the principal has not otherwise instructed, he himself delivers as seller the goods which he is to buy or accepts as buyer the goods which he is to sell.

(2) Where the commission has been performed in such a manner, the commission agent's duty to account for the conclusion of the purchase or sale is limited to furnishing proof that, with respect to the price charged, the existing exchange or market price at the time of performance of the commission was adhered to. Time of performance is deemed to be the time at which the commission agent sent the notice of performance to the principal.

(3) Where the notice of performance of a commission which was to be performed during the time the exchange or market was open is not sent until after the close of the exchange or market, the price charged may not be less favourable for the principal than the price existing at the close of the exchange or market.

(4) With respect to a commission which was to be performed at a specific rate (opening rate, mean rate, closing rate), the commission agent is authorised and obligated to charge this rate to the principal without regard to the time at which the notice of performance was sent.

(5) With respect to securities and goods for which the exchange or market price is officially determined, the commission agent cannot, where he performs the commission by substituting himself for the third party he would otherwise deal with on the principal's behalf, charge the principal a price less favourable than the officially established price.

## § 401
## [Deckungsgeschäft]

(1) Auch im Falle der Ausführung der Kommission durch Selbsteintritt hat der Kommissionär, wenn er bei Anwendung pflichtmäßiger Sorgfalt die Kommission zu einem günstigeren als dem nach § 400 sich ergebenden Preise ausführen konnte, dem Kommittenten den günstigeren Preis zu berechnen.

(2) Hat der Kommissionär vor der Absendung der Ausführungsanzeige aus Anlass der erteilten Kommission an der Börse oder am Markt ein Geschäft mit einem Dritten abgeschlossen, so darf er dem Kommittenten keinen ungünstigeren als den hierbei vereinbarten Preis berechnen.

## § 401
## [Covering transactions]

(1) Even if the commission agent has performed the commission by self-substitution, he must charge the principal the more favourable price if by the exercise of due care he could have obtained a more favourable price than the one resulting from the application of § 400.

(2) Where the commission agent has, on the basis of the commission, concluded a transaction with a third party on the exchange or on the market before sending the notice of performance, he may not charge the principal a less advantageous price than the price agreed.

## § 402
## [Unabdingbarkeit]

Die Vorschriften des § 400 Abs. 2 bis 5 und des § 401 können nicht durch Vertrag zum Nachteil des Kommittenten abgeändert werden.

## § 402
## [Unalterable rights]

The provisions of § 400(2) through (5) and § 401 cannot be altered contractually to the principal's disadvantage.

## § 403
## [Provision bei Selbsteintritt]

Der Kommissionär, der das Gut selbst als Verkäufer liefert oder als Käufer übernimmt, ist zu der gewöhnlichen Provision berechtigt und kann die bei Kommissionsgeschäften sonst regelmäßig vorkommenden Kosten berechnen.

## § 403
## [Commission in case of commission agent's self-substitution]

The commission agent who has delivered goods himself as the seller or who has accepted goods as the buyer may charge the customary commission and the costs which regularly occur in conjunction with commission transactions.

## § 404
## [Gesetzliches Pfandrecht]

Die Vorschriften der §§ 397 und 398 finden auch im Falle der Ausführung der Kommission durch Selbsteintritt Anwendung.

## § 404
## [Statutory lien]

The provisions of §§ 397 and 398 also apply where the commission is performed by the commission agent substituting himself for the third party he would otherwise deal with on the principal's behalf.

## § 405
## [Ausführungsanzeige und Selbsteintritt; Widerruf der Kommission]

(1) Zeigt der Kommissionär die Ausführung der Kommission an, ohne ausdrücklich zu bemerken, dass er selbst eintreten wolle, so gilt dies als Erklärung, dass die Ausführung durch Abschluss des Geschäfts mit einem Dritten für Rechnung des Kommittenten erfolgt sei.

## § 405
## [Notice of performance and self-substitution; revocation of the commission]

(1) Where the commission agent gives notice of performance of the commission without expressly noting that he plans to carry out a self-substitution, this shall be deemed to be a statement that performance has been made through conclusion of the transaction with a third party for the principal's account.

(2) Eine Vereinbarung zwischen dem Kommittenten und dem Kommissionär, dass die Erklärung darüber, ob die Kommission durch Selbsteintritt oder durch Abschluss mit einem Dritten ausgeführt sei, später als am Tag der Ausführungsanzeige abgegeben werden dürfe, ist nichtig.

(3) Widerruft der Kommittent die Kommission und geht der Widerruf dem Kommissionär zu, bevor die Ausführungsanzeige zur Absendung abgegeben ist, so steht dem Kommissionär das Recht des Selbsteintritts nicht mehr zu.

(2) Any agreement between the principal and the commission agent, pursuant to which the statement specifying whether the commission carries out a self-substitution or by a transaction with a third party may be sent later than the date of the notice of completion, is void.

(3) In the event that the principal revokes the commission and the revocation reaches the commission agent before notice of performance has been sent, the commission agent is no longer entitled to carry out a self-substitution.

### § 406
### [Ähnliche Geschäfte]

(1) Die Vorschriften dieses Abschnitts kommen auch zur Anwendung, wenn ein Kommissionär im Betrieb seines Handelsgewerbes ein Geschäft anderer als der in § 383 bezeichneten Art für Rechnung eines anderen im eigenen Namen zu schließen übernimmt. Das gleiche gilt, wenn ein Kaufmann, der nicht Kommissionär ist, im Betrieb seines Handelsgewerbes ein Geschäft in der bezeichneten Weise zu schließen übernimmt.

(2) Als Einkaufs- und Verkaufskommission im Sinne dieses Abschnitts gilt auch eine Kommission, welche die Lieferung einer nicht vertretbaren beweglichen Sache, die aus einem von dem Unternehmer zu beschaffenden Stoff herzustellen ist, zum Gegenstand hat.

### § 406
### [Similar transactions]

(1) The provisions of this Part also apply if a commission agent agrees, within the context of the operation of his business, to conclude a transaction other than the type set out in § 383 in his own name for the account of another. The same applies if a merchant who is not a commission agent agrees to conclude a transaction within the operation of his business in the manner described.

(2) A commission which relates to the delivery of a non-fungible tangible good to be made out of material to be procured by the manufacturer is also deemed to be a buying and selling commission within the meaning of this Part.

## Vierter Abschnitt
## Frachtgeschäft

## Erster Unterabschnitt
## Allgemeine Vorschriften

### § 407
### Frachtvertrag

(1) Durch den Frachtvertrag wird der Frachtführer verpflichtet, das Gut zum Bestimmungsort zu befördern und dort an den Empfänger abzuliefern.

(2) Der Absender wird verpflichtet, die vereinbarte Fracht zu zahlen.

(3) Die Vorschriften dieses Unterabschnitts gelten, wenn

1. das Gut zu Lande, auf Binnengewässern oder mit Luftfahrzeugen befördert werden soll und
2. die Beförderung zum Betrieb eines gewerblichen Unternehmens gehört.

## Part Four
## Carrier Business

## First Subpart
## General Provisions

### § 407
### Freight agreement

(1) The freight agreement obligates the freight carrier to transport the goods to the place of destination and to deliver them there to the consignee.

(2) The shipper is obligated to pay the freight charges agreed upon.

(3) The provisions of this Subpart apply where

1. the goods are to be transported by land, on inland waterways or by aircraft and
2. the shipment is part of the operation of a commercial enterprise.

Erfordert das Unternehmen nach Art oder Umfang einen in kaufmännischer Weise eingerichteten Geschäftsbetrieb nicht und ist die Firma des Unternehmens auch nicht nach § 2 in das Handelsregister eingetragen, so sind in Ansehung des Frachtgeschäfts auch insoweit die Vorschriften des Ersten Abschnitts des Vierten Buches ergänzend anzuwenden; dies gilt jedoch nicht für die §§ 348 bis 350.

Where the enterprise, based on its nature or scope, does not require a commercially organised business operation and the firm name of the enterprise is not registered in the Commercial Register pursuant to § 2, the provisions of the First Part of the Fourth Book shall apply in a supplementary manner with respect to the freight business; this, however, does not apply to §§ 348 to 350.

## § 408
## Frachtbrief. Verordnungsermächtigung

(1) Der Frachtführer kann die Ausstellung eines Frachtbriefs mit folgenden Angaben verlangen:

1. Ort und Tag der Ausstellung;
2. Name und Anschrift des Absenders;
3. Name und Anschrift des Frachtführers;
4. Stelle und Tag der Übernahme des Gutes sowie die für die Ablieferung vorgesehene Stelle;
5. Name und Anschrift des Empfängers und eine etwaige Meldeadresse;
6. die übliche Bezeichnung der Art des Gutes und die Art der Verpackung, bei gefährlichen Gütern ihre nach den Gefahrgutvorschriften vorgesehene, sonst ihre allgemein anerkannte Bezeichnung;
7. Anzahl, Zeichen und Nummern der Frachtstücke;
8. das Rohgewicht oder die anders angegebene Menge des Gutes;
9. die bei Ablieferung geschuldete Fracht und die bis zur Ablieferung anfallenden Kosten sowie einen Vermerk über die Frachtzahlung;
10. den Betrag einer bei der Ablieferung des Gutes einzuziehenden Nachnahme;
11. Weisungen für die Zoll- und sonstige amtliche Behandlung des Gutes;
12. eine Vereinbarung über die Beförderung in offenem, nicht mit Planen gedecktem Fahrzeug oder auf Deck.

In den Frachtbrief können weitere Angaben eingetragen werden, die die Parteien für zweckmäßig halten.

(2) Der Frachtbrief wird in drei Originalausfertigungen ausgestellt, die vom Absender unterzeichnet werden. Der Absender kann verlangen, dass auch der Frachtführer den Frachtbrief unterzeichnet. Nachbildungen der eigenhändigen Unterschriften durch Druck oder Stempel genügen. Eine Ausfertigung ist für den Absender bestimmt, eine begleitet das Gut, eine behält der Frachtführer.

## § 408
## Waybill. Power to issue statutory instruments

(1) The carrier may require issuance of a waybill with the following data:

1. place and date of issuance;
2. name and address of the shipper;
3. name and address of the freight carrier;
4. place and date of acceptance of the goods as well as the place foreseen for delivery;
5. name and address of the consignee and any registered address;
6. the customary description of the type of goods and the type of packaging, in case of dangerous goods the description pursuant to the statutory provisions relating to dangerous goods or otherwise the generally accepted description;
7. quantity, identifying marks and numbers of the packages;
8. the gross weight or the other designated quantity of the goods;
9. the agreed freight charges and the costs which will be incurred up to the time of delivery as well as a notation concerning the payment of the freight charges;
10. the amount of any charges to be collected upon delivery of the goods;
11. instructions for the customs and other official handling of the goods;
12. an agreement concerning the shipment in open vehicles not covered by tarps or on deck.

Further data which the parties consider to be useful can be included in the waybill.

(2) The waybill shall be issued in three counterparts which are to be signed by the shipper. The shipper may require that the freight carrier also signs the waybill. Facsimiles of the signatures by print or stamp suffice. One counterpart is intended for the shipper, one accompanies the goods and one is retained by the freight carrier.

(3) Dem Frachtbrief gleichgestellt ist eine elektronische Aufzeichnung, die dieselben Funktionen erfüllt wie der Frachtbrief, sofern sichergestellt ist, dass die Authentizität und die Integrität der Aufzeichnung gewahrt bleiben (elektronischer Frachtbrief). Das Bundesministerium der Justiz wird ermächtigt, im Einvernehmen mit dem Bundesministerium des Innern durch Rechtsverordnung, die nicht der Zustimmung des Bundesrates bedarf, die Einzelheiten der Ausstellung, des Mitführens und der Vorlage eines elektronischen Frachtbriefs sowie des Verfahrens einer nachträglichen Eintragung in einen elektronischen Frachtbrief zu regeln.

An electronic record that fulfils the same functions as the waybill is equivalent to the waybill, provided that the authenticity and the integrity of the record are preserved (electronic waybill). The Federal Ministry of Justice is authorised, in agreement with the Federal Ministry of the Interior, to govern – by means of a statutory instrument which does not require the consent of the Federal Council – the details of the issuance, the carriage and the presentation of the electronic waybill as well as the process of a subsequent entry into an electronic waybill.

**§ 409**
**Beweiskraft des Frachtbriefs**

(1) Der von beiden Parteien unterzeichnete Frachtbrief dient bis zum Beweis des Gegenteils als Nachweis für Abschluss und Inhalt des Frachtvertrages sowie für die Übernahme des Gutes durch den Frachtführer.

(2) Der von beiden Parteien unterzeichnete Frachtbrief begründet ferner die Vermutung, dass das Gut und seine Verpackung bei der Übernahme durch den Frachtführer in äußerlich gutem Zustand waren und dass die Anzahl der Frachtstücke und ihre Zeichen und Nummern mit den Angaben im Frachtbrief übereinstimmen. Der Frachtbrief begründet diese Vermutung jedoch nicht, wenn der Frachtführer einen begründeten Vorbehalt in den Frachtbrief eingetragen hat; der Vorbehalt kann auch damit begründet werden, dass dem Frachtführer keine angemessenen Mittel zur Verfügung standen, die Richtigkeit der Angaben zu überprüfen.

(3) Ist das Rohgewicht oder die anders angegebene Menge des Gutes oder der Inhalt der Frachtstücke vom Frachtführer überprüft und das Ergebnis der Überprüfung in den von beiden Parteien unterzeichneten Frachtbrief eingetragen worden, so begründet dieser auch die Vermutung, dass Gewicht, Menge oder Inhalt mit den Angaben im Frachtbrief übereinstimmt. Der Frachtführer ist verpflichtet, Gewicht, Menge oder Inhalt zu überprüfen, wenn der Absender dies verlangt und dem Frachtführer angemessene Mittel zur Überprüfung zur Verfügung stehen; der Frachtführer hat Anspruch auf Ersatz seiner Aufwendungen für die Überprüfung.

**§ 409**
**Evidentiary value of the waybill**

(1) The waybill signed by both parties serves as evidence for the conclusion and contents of the freight agreement, as well as for the acceptance of the goods by the freight carrier, until the contrary has been proven.

(2) The waybill signed by both parties also establishes the presumption that the goods and their packaging were externally in good condition upon the acceptance by the freight carrier and that the quantity of packages and their identifying marks and numbers corresponded to the data in the waybill. The waybill, however, does not establish this presumption if the freight carrier entered a justified reservation in the waybill; the reservation can also be justified by the fact that the freight carrier did not have appropriate means available to check the correctness of the data.

(3) If the gross weight or the other designated quantity of the goods or the contents of the packages have been examined by the freight carrier and the result of the examination has been entered in the waybill signed by both parties, then this also establishes the presumption that weight, quantity or contents correspond to the data in the waybill. The freight carrier is obligated to examine weight, quantity or contents where the shipper so requests and the freight carrier has appropriate means for examination available; the freight carrier is entitled to reimbursement of his costs for the examination.

## § 410
## Gefährliches Gut

(1) Soll gefährliches Gut befördert werden, so hat der Absender dem Frachtführer rechtzeitig in Textform die genaue Art der Gefahr und, soweit erforderlich, zu ergreifende Vorsichtsmaßnahmen mitzuteilen.

(2) Der Frachtführer kann, sofern ihm nicht bei Übernahme des Gutes die Art der Gefahr bekannt war oder jedenfalls mitgeteilt worden ist,

1. gefährliches Gut ausladen, einlagern, zurückbefördern oder soweit erforderlich, vernichten oder unschädlich machen, ohne dem Absender deshalb ersatzpflichtig zu werden, und
2. vom Absender wegen dieser Maßnahmen Ersatz der erforderlichen Aufwendungen verlangen.

## § 410
## Dangerous goods

(1) Where dangerous goods are to be transported, the shipper shall inform the freight carrier in a timely manner and in writing or other legible form about the exact type of danger and, as far as necessary, the precautions to be taken.

(2) The freight carrier may, to the extent that the type of danger was unknown to him or in any case was not communicated to him upon acceptance of the goods

1. unload, place in storage, return or, to the extent necessary, destroy or render harmless the dangerous goods without becoming liable to the shipper for damages therefor, and
2. demand from the shipper reimbursement of the costs necessitated by these measures.

## § 411
## Verpackung. Kennzeichnung

Der Absender hat das Gut, soweit dessen Natur unter Berücksichtigung der vereinbarten Beförderung einer Verpackung erfordert, so zu verpacken, dass es vor Verlust und Beschädigung geschützt ist und dass auch dem Frachtführer keine Schäden entstehen. Soll das Gut in einem Container, auf einer Palette oder in oder auf einem sonstigen Lademittel, das zur Zusammenfassung von Frachtstücken verwendet wird, zur Beförderung übergeben werden, hat der Absender das Gut auch in oder auf dem Lademittel beförderungssicher zu stauen und zu sichern. Der Absender hat das Gut ferner, soweit dessen vertragsgemäße Behandlung dies erfordert, zu kennzeichnen.

## § 411
## Packaging. Labelling

To the extent that the nature of the goods requires packaging taking into consideration the agreed shipment, the shipper shall package the goods in such a manner that they are protected against loss and damage and also such that no damage is incurred by the freight carrier. Where the goods are to be handed over for shipment in a container, on a pallet or another load carrier that is used to combine freight pieces, the shipper shall stow and secure the goods also in or on (top of) the load carrier so that they can be safely transported. The shipper shall also label the goods to the extent that the agreed-upon handling requires this.

## § 412
## Verladen und Entladen. Verordnungsermächtigung

(1) Soweit sich aus den Umständen oder der Verkehrssitte nicht etwas anderes ergibt, hat der Absender das Gut beförderungssicher zu laden, zu stauen und zu befestigen (loading) sowie zu entladen. Der Frachtführer hat für die betriebssichere Verladung zu sorgen.

(2) Für die Lade- und Entladezeit, die sich mangels abweichender Vereinbarung nach einer den Umständen des Falles angemessenen Frist bemisst, kann keine besondere Vergütung erlangt werden.

## § 412
## Loading and unloading. Power to issue statutory instruments

(1) Unless the circumstances or customary practice indicate otherwise, the shipper shall load, stow, secure (off-load) as well as unload the goods so that they can be safely transported. The freight carrier is responsible for the safe loading.

(2) No special remuneration can be requested for the time of loading and unloading which, absent a deviating agreement, is determined according to a period reasonable for the circumstances of the case.

(3) Wartet der Frachtführer auf Grund vertraglicher Vereinbarung oder aus Gründen, die nicht seinem Risikobereich zuzurechnen sind, über die Lade- oder Entladezeit hinaus, so hat er Anspruch auf eine angemessene Vergütung (Standgeld).

(4) Das Bundesministerium der Justiz wird ermächtigt, im Einvernehmen mit dem Bundesministerium für Verkehr, Bau und Stadtentwicklung durch Rechtsverordnung, die nicht der Zustimmung des Bundesrates bedarf, für die Binnenschifffahrt unter Berücksichtigung der Art der zur Beförderung bestimmten Fahrzeuge, der Art und Menge der umzuschlagenden Güter, der beim Güterumschlag zur Verfügung stehenden technischen Mittel und der Erfordernisse eines beschleunigten Verkehrsablaufs die Voraussetzungen für den Beginn der Lade- und Entladezeit, deren Dauer sowie die Höhe des Standgeldes zu bestimmen.

(3) The freight carrier is entitled to reasonable remuneration (demurrage) if he waits beyond the time for loading or unloading on the basis of a contractual agreement or for reasons which are not attributable to his sphere of risks.

(4) The Federal Ministry of Justice is authorised, in agreement with the Federal Ministry of Transportation, Building and Urban Development, to determine – by means of a statutory instrument which does not require the consent of the Federal Council – the requirements for the commencement of the times for loading and unloading, their duration and the amount of demurrage for the inland waterway carriers, taking into consideration the types of vehicles designated for shipment, the kind and quantity of the goods to be transshipped, the technical means available for transshipping the goods and the requirements of expedited traffic operations.

## § 413
## Begleitpapiere

(1) Der Absender hat dem Frachtführer alle Urkunden zur Verfügung zu stellen und Auskünfte zu erteilen, die für eine amtliche Behandlung, insbesondere eine Zollabfertigung, vor der Ablieferung des Gutes erforderlich sind.

(2) Der Frachtführer ist für den Schaden verantwortlich, der durch Verlust oder Beschädigung der ihm übergebenen Urkunden oder durch deren unrichtige Verwendung verursacht worden ist, es sei denn, dass der Verlust, die Beschädigung oder die unrichtige Verwendung auf Umständen beruht, die der Frachtführer nicht vermeiden und deren Folgen er nicht abwenden konnte. Seine Haftung ist jedoch auf den Betrag begrenzt, der bei Verlust des Gutes zu zahlen wäre.

## § 413
## Documents accompanying the goods

(1) The shipper shall make documents available to the freight carrier and give him the information necessary for an official handling prior to delivery of the goods, especially a customs clearance.

(2) The freight carrier is responsible for the damage caused through loss of or damage to the documents handed over to him or their incorrect use unless the loss, the damage or the incorrect use is caused by circumstances which the freight carrier could not avoid and whose consequences he could not prevent. His liability, however, is limited to the amount which would have to be paid in case of loss of the goods.

## § 414
## Verschuldensunabhängige Haftung des Absenders in besonderen Fällen

(1) Der Absender hat, auch wenn ihn kein Verschulden trifft, dem Frachtführer Schäden und Aufwendungen zu ersetzen, die verursacht werden durch

1. ungenügende Verpackung oder Kennzeichnung,
2. Unrichtigkeit oder Unvollständigkeit der in den Frachtbrief aufgenommenen Angaben,
3. Unterlassen der Mitteilung über die Gefährlichkeit des Gutes oder
4. Fehlen, Unvollständigkeit oder Unrichtigkeit der in § 413 Abs. 1 genannten Urkunden oder Auskünfte.

## § 414
## Strict liability of the shipper in special cases

(1) The shipper, even if he is not at fault, has to reimburse the freight carrier for damage and expenditures which are caused by the following circumstances:

1. Insufficient packaging or labelling,
2. incorrectness or incompleteness of the details contained in the waybill,
3. omission of the information concerning the dangerous nature of the goods,
4. lack, incompleteness or incorrectness of the documents or information mentioned in § 413(1).

(2) Hat bei der Verursachung der Schäden oder Aufwendungen ein Verhalten des Frachtführers mitgewirkt, so hängen die Verpflichtung zum Ersatz sowie der Umfang des zu leistenden Ersatzes davon ab, inwieweit dieses Verhalten zu den Schäden und Aufwendungen beigetragen hat.

(2) Where conduct of the freight carrier contributed to the cause of the damage or expenditures, the obligation to pay damages and the amount of the damages to be paid depend on the extent to which this conduct has contributed to the damage and expenditures.

(3) Ist der Absender ein Verbraucher, so hat er dem Frachtführer Schäden und Aufwendungen nach den Absätzen 1 und 2 nur zu ersetzen, soweit ihn ein Verschulden trifft.

(3) If the shipper is a consumer, he only has to reimburse the freight carrier for damage and expenditures pursuant to subsections 1 and 2 to the extent that he is at fault.

## § 415
## Kündigung durch den Absender

(1) Der Absender kann den Frachtvertrag jederzeit kündigen.

(2) Kündigt der Absender, so kann der Frachtführer entweder

1. die vereinbarte Fracht, das etwaige Standgeld sowie zu ersetzende Aufwendungen unter Anrechnung dessen, was er infolge der Aufhebung des Vertrages an Aufwendungen erspart oder anderweitig erwirbt oder zu erwerben böswillig unterlässt, oder
2. ein Drittel der vereinbarten Fracht (Fautfracht)

verlangen. Beruht die Kündigung auf Gründen, die dem Risikobereich des Frachtführers zuzurechnen sind, so entfällt der Anspruch auf Fautfracht nach Satz 1 Nr. 2; in diesem Falle entfällt auch der Anspruch nach Satz 1 Nr. 1, soweit die Beförderung für den Absender nicht von Interesse ist.

(3) Wurde vor der Kündigung bereits Gut verladen, so kann der Frachtführer auf Kosten des Absenders Maßnahmen entsprechend § 419 Abs. 3 Satz 2 bis 4 ergreifen oder vom Absender verlangen, dass dieser das Gut unverzüglich entlädt. Der Frachtführer braucht das Entladen des Gutes nur zu dulden, soweit dies ohne Nachteile für seinen Betrieb und ohne Schäden für die Absender oder Empfänger anderer Sendungen möglich ist. Beruht die Kündigung auf Gründen, die dem Risikobereich des Frachtführers zuzurechnen sind, so ist abweichend von den Sätzen 1 und 2 der Frachtführer verpflichtet, das Gut, das bereits verladen wurde, unverzüglich auf eigene Kosten zu entladen.

## § 415
## Termination by the shipper

(1) The shipper can terminate the freight agreement at any time.

(2) In case of termination by the shipper, the freight carrier can request either

1. the agreed freight charges, demurrage, if any, as well as expenditures to be reimbursed taking into account the amounts he saves on expenditures due to the termination of the agreement, the amounts he otherwise earns or the amounts he maliciously neglects to earn, or
2. one-third of the agreed freight charges (dead freight).

If the termination is caused by reasons which are attributable to the sphere of risks of the freight carrier, the claim to dead freight pursuant to sentence 1, no. 2 is dropped; in this case, the claim pursuant to sentence 1, no. 1 is also dropped to the extent that the shipment is not of interest for the shipper.

(3) Where goods have already been loaded before the termination, the freight carrier can take measures according to § 419(3), sentences 2 to 4 at the expense of the shipper or he can request that the shipper unload the goods without undue delay. The freight carrier only has to tolerate the unloading of the goods to the extent that this is possible without disadvantages to his operations and without damages for the shippers or consignees of other shipments. If the termination is caused by reasons which are attributable to the sphere of risks of the freight carrier he is obligated, notwithstanding sentences 1 and 2, to unload goods which have already been loaded without undue delay at his own expense.

### § 416
### Anspruch auf Teilbeförderung

Wird das Gut nur teilweise verladen, so kann der Absender jederzeit verlangen, dass der Frachtführer mit der Beförderung des bereits verladenen Teils des Gutes beginnt. In diesem Fall gebührt dem Frachtführer die volle Fracht, das etwaige Standgeld sowie Ersatz der Aufwendungen, die ihm durch das Fehlen eines Teils des Gutes entstehen; von der vollen Fracht kommt jedoch die Fracht für dasjenige Gut in Abzug, welches der Frachtführer mit demselben Beförderungsmittel anstelle des nicht verladenen Gutes befördert. Der Frachtführer ist außerdem berechtigt, soweit ihm durch das Fehlen eines Teils des Gutes die Sicherheit für die volle Fracht entgeht, die Bestellung einer anderweitigen Sicherheit zu fordern. Beruht die Unvollständigkeit der Verladung auf Gründen, die dem Risikobereich des Frachtführers zuzurechnen sind, so steht diesem der Anspruch nach den Sätzen 2 und 3 nur insoweit zu, als tatsächlich Gut befördert wird.

### § 416
### Claim to partial shipment

If only part of the cargo agreed upon is loaded, the shipper can request at any time that the freight carrier start with the shipment of the part that is already loaded. In this case the freight carrier is entitled to the full freight charges, the demurrage, if any, as well as reimbursement of expenditures incurred by him due to the absence of part of the cargo; the freight charges for the goods which the carrier transports with the same means of shipment in place of the goods not loaded shall, however, be deducted from the full freight charges. The freight carrier is also entitled to request that other security be furnished to the extent that he does not obtain security for the full freight charges due to the incompleteness of the cargo. Where the incompleteness of the loading is caused by reasons which are attributable to the sphere of risks of the freight carrier, he is entitled to the claim pursuant to sentences 2 and 3 only to the extent that cargo is actually transported.

### § 417
### Rechte des Frachtführers bei Nichteinhaltung der Ladezeit

(1) Verlädt der Absender das Gut nicht innerhalb der Ladezeit oder stellt er, wenn ihm das Verladen nicht obliegt, das Gut nicht innerhalb der Ladezeit zur Verfügung, so kann ihm der Frachtführer eine angemessene Frist setzen, innerhalb derer das Gut verladen oder zur Verfügung gestellt werden soll.

(2) Wird bis zum Ablauf der nach Absatz 1 gesetzten Frist kein Gut verladen oder zur Verfügung gestellt oder ist offensichtlich, dass innerhalb dieser Frist kein Gut verladen oder zur Verfügung gestellt wird, so kann der Frachtführer den Vertrag kündigen und die Ansprüche nach § 415 Abs. 2 geltend machen.

(3) Wird das Gut bis zum Ablauf der nach Absatz 1 gesetzten Frist nur teilweise verladen oder zur Verfügung gestellt, so kann der Frachtführer mit der Beförderung des bereits verladenen Teils des Gutes beginnen und die Ansprüche nach § 416 Satz 2 und 3 geltend machen.

(4) Der Frachtführer kann die Rechte nach Absatz 2 oder 3 auch ohne Fristsetzung ausüben, wenn der Absender sich ernsthaft und endgültig weigert, das Gut zu verladen oder zur Verfügung zu stellen. Er kann ferner den Vertrag nach Absatz 2 auch ohne Fristsetzung kündigen, wenn besondere Umstände vorliegen, die ihm unter Abwägung der beiderseitigen Interessen die Fortsetzung des Vertragsverhältnisses unzumutbar machen.

### § 417
### Rights of the freight carrier in case of non-observance of the loading time

(1) If the shipper does not load the goods within the loading time or, where he is not obligated to load, he does not make the goods available within the loading time, the freight carrier can set a reasonable time limit within which the goods are to be loaded or made available.

(2) Where upon expiry of the time limit set pursuant to subsection 1 no cargo has been loaded or made available or where it is obvious that no goods will be loaded or made available within this time limit, the freight carrier may terminate the freight agreement and assert the claims pursuant to § 415(2).

(3) Where upon expiry of the time limit set pursuant to subsection 1 only part of the cargo agreed upon has been loaded or made available, the carrier may start with the shipment of the part of the cargo already loaded and assert the claims pursuant to § 416 sentences 2 and 3.

(4) The freight carrier can exercise the rights pursuant to subsections 2 or 3 even without a time limit if the shipper seriously and finally refuses to load the goods or make them available. Furthermore, in the event of special circumstances which, after weighing the interests of both parties, make the continuation of the contractual relationship unacceptable to him, he can also terminate the freight agreement pursuant to subsection 2 without a time limit.

(5) Dem Frachtführer stehen die Rechte nicht zu, wenn die Nichteinhaltung der Ladezeit auf Gründen beruht, die seinem Risikobereich zuzurechnen sind.

### § 418
### Nachträgliche Weisungen

(1) Der Absender ist berechtigt, über das Gut zu verfügen. Er kann insbesondere verlangen, dass der Frachtführer das Gut nicht weiterbefördert oder es an einem anderen Bestimmungsort, an einer anderen Ablieferungsstelle oder an einen anderen Empfänger abliefert. Der Frachtführer ist nur insoweit zur Befolgung solcher Weisungen verpflichtet, als deren Ausführung weder Nachteile für den Betrieb seines Unternehmens noch Schäden für die Absender oder Empfänger anderer Sendungen mit sich zu bringen droht. Er kann vom Absender Ersatz seiner durch die Ausführung der Weisung entstehenden Aufwendungen sowie eine angemessene Vergütung verlangen; der Frachtführer kann die Befolgung der Weisung von einem Vorschuss abhängig machen.

(2) Das Verfügungsrecht des Absenders erlischt nach Ankunft des Gutes an der Ablieferungsstelle. Von diesem Zeitpunkt an steht das Verfügungsrecht nach Absatz 1 dem Empfänger zu. Macht der Empfänger von diesem Recht Gebrauch, so hat er dem Frachtführer die entstehenden Mehraufwendungen zu ersetzen sowie eine angemessene Vergütung zu zahlen; der Frachtführer kann die Befolgung der Weisung von einem Vorschuss abhängig machen.

(3) Hat der Empfänger in Ausübung seines Verfügungsrechts die Ablieferung des Gutes an einen Dritten angeordnet, so ist dieser nicht berechtigt, seinerseits einen anderen Empfänger zu bestimmen.

(4) Ist ein Frachtbrief ausgestellt und von beiden Parteien unterzeichnet worden, so kann der Absender sein Verfügungsrecht nur gegen Vorlage der Absenderausfertigung des Frachtbriefs ausüben, sofern dies im Frachtbrief vorgeschrieben ist.

(5) Beabsichtigt der Frachtführer, eine ihm erteilte Weisung nicht zu befolgen, so hat er denjenigen, der die Weisung gegeben hat, unverzüglich zu benachrichtigen.

(5) The freight carrier is not entitled to the claims if the non-observance of the loading time is caused by reasons which are attributable to his sphere of risks.

### § 418
### Subsequent instructions

(1) The shipper is entitled to dispose of the goods. He can in particular request that the freight carrier discontinue to transport the goods or that he deliver them to another place of destination, another delivery point or to another consignee. The freight carrier is only obligated to follow such instructions to the extent that carrying them out does not threaten to bring about disadvantages for the operation of his enterprise or damage for the shippers or consignees of other shipments. He can request from the shipper reimbursement of his expenditures incurred in carrying out the instructions as well as reasonable remuneration. The freight carrier can make his compliance with the instructions conditional upon the payment of an advance.

(2) The shipper's right of disposition terminates when the goods have arrived at the point of delivery. From this time on, the right of disposition pursuant to subsection 1 belongs to the consignee. Where the consignee makes use of this right, he has to reimburse the freight carrier for any additional expenditures incurred and pay him reasonable remuneration; the freight carrier can make his compliance with the instructions conditional upon the payment of an advance.

(3) Where in exercising his right of disposition the consignee has instructed the freight carrier to deliver the goods to a third party, such third party is not entitled, on his part, to designate another consignee.

(4) Where a waybill has been issued and signed by both parties, the shipper can exercise his right of disposition only upon presentation of the shipper's counterpart of the waybill, to the extent that this has been required in the waybill.

(5) Where the freight carrier does not intend to comply with instructions issued to him, he shall without undue delay inform the party which has given the instructions.

(6) Ist die Ausübung des Verfügungsrechts von der Vorlage des Frachtbriefs abhängig gemacht worden und führt der Frachtführer eine Weisung aus, ohne sich die Absenderausfertigung des Frachtbriefs vorlegen zu lassen, so haftet er dem Berechtigten für den daraus entstehenden Schaden. Die Haftung ist auf den Betrag begrenzt, der bei Verlust des Gutes zu zahlen wäre.

(6) If the exercise of the right of disposition has been made contingent on the presentation of the waybill and the freight carrier follows instructions without having the shipper's counterpart of the waybill presented to him, he is liable to the entitled party for the damage resulting therefrom. Liability is limited to the amount which would be payable upon loss of the goods.

## § 419 Beförderungs- und Ablieferungshindernisse

(1) Wird nach Übernahme des Gutes erkennbar, dass die Beförderung oder Ablieferung nicht vertragsgemäß durchgeführt werden kann, so hat der Frachtführer Weisungen des nach § 418 oder § 446 Verfügungsberechtigten einzuholen. Ist der Empfänger verfügungsberechtigt und ist er nicht zu ermitteln oder verweigert er die Annahme des Gutes, so ist, wenn ein Ladeschein nicht ausgestellt ist, Verfügungsberechtigter nach Satz 1 der Absender; ist die Ausübung des Verfügungsrechts von der Vorlage eines Frachtbriefs abhängig gemacht worden, so bedarf es in diesem Fall der Vorlage des Frachtbriefs nicht. Der Frachtführer ist, wenn ihm Weisungen erteilt worden sind und das Hindernis nicht seinem Risikobereich zuzurechnen ist, berechtigt, Ansprüche nach § 418 Abs. 1 Satz 4 geltend zu machen.

(2) Tritt das Beförderungs- oder Ablieferungshindernis ein, nachdem der Empfänger auf Grund seiner Verfügungsbefugnis nach § 418 die Weisung erteilt hat, das Gut an einen Dritten abzuliefern, so nimmt bei der Anwendung des Absatzes 1 der Empfänger die Stelle des Absenders und der Dritte die des Empfängers ein.

(3) Kann der Frachtführer Weisungen, die er nach § 418 Abs. 1 Satz 3 befolgen müsste, innerhalb angemessener Zeit nicht erlangen, so hat er die Maßnahmen zu ergreifen, die im Interesse des Verfügungsberechtigten die besten zu sein scheinen. Er kann etwa das Gut entladen und verwahren, für Rechnung des nach § 418 oder § 446 Verfügungsberechtigten einem Dritten zur Verwahrung anvertrauen oder zurückbefördern; vertraut der Frachtführer das Gut einem Dritten an, so haftet er nur für die sorgfältige Auswahl des Dritten. Der Frachtführer kann das Gut auch gemäß § 373 Abs. 2 bis 4 verkaufen lassen, wenn es sich um verderbliche Ware handelt oder der Zustand des Gutes eine solche Maßnahme rechtfertigt oder wenn die andernfalls entstehenden Kosten in keinem angemessenen Verhältnis zum Wert des Gutes stehen. Unverwertbares Gut darf der Frachtführer vernichten. Nach dem Entladen des Gutes gilt die Beförderung als beendet.

## § 419 Hindrances to shipment and delivery

(1) The freight carrier shall ask for instructions from the party entitled to the right of disposition pursuant to § 418 or § 446 where, upon acceptance of the goods, it becomes apparent that the shipment or delivery cannot be carried out according to the freight agreement. If the consignee is entitled to the right of disposition and he cannot be located or refuses to accept the goods, then, if a bill of lading has not been issued, the party entitled to the right of disposition pursuant to sentence 1 is the shipper; where the exercise of the right of disposition has been made subject to presentation of a waybill, the presentation of the waybill in this case is not required. The freight carrier is entitled to assert claims pursuant to § 418(1), sentence 4 if instructions have been given to him and the hindrance is not attributable to his sphere of risks.

(2) Where the hindrance to shipment or delivery occurs after the consignee has given instructions, based on his right of disposition pursuant to § 418, to deliver the goods to a third party, the consignee replaces the shipper and the third party replaces the consignee in applying subsection 1.

(3) Where the freight carrier cannot, within a reasonable period of time, obtain instructions which he would have to follow pursuant to § 418(1), sentence 3, he shall take the measures which seem to be in the best interests of the party entitled to the right of disposition. He may, for example, unload the goods and store them, hand them over to a third party for safe keeping for the account of the party entitled to the right of disposition pursuant to § 418 or § 446, or return them; where the freight carrier hands over the goods to a third party, he is only liable for the careful selection of the third party. The freight carrier may also have the goods sold under § 373(2) to (4) if the goods are perishable, or if the condition of the goods justifies such a measure, or if the costs which would otherwise arise do not bear a reasonable relationship to the value of the goods. The freight carrier may destroy goods which are unsalable. Once the goods have been unloaded, the shipment is deemed to have been completed.

(4) Der Frachtführer hat wegen der nach Absatz 3 ergriffenen Maßnahmen Anspruch auf Ersatz der erforderlichen Aufwendungen und auf angemessene Vergütung, es sei denn, dass das Hindernis seinem Risikobereich zuzurechnen ist.

(4) The freight carrier is entitled to reimbursement of the necessary expenditures incurred in connection with the measures taken pursuant to subsection 3 and to reasonable remuneration unless the hindrance is attributable to his sphere of risks.

## § 420 Zahlung. Frachtberechnung

## § 420 Payment. Computation of freight charges

(1) Die Fracht ist bei Ablieferung des Gutes zu zahlen. Der Frachtführer hat über die Fracht hinaus einen Anspruch auf Ersatz von Aufwendungen, soweit diese für das Gut gemacht wurden und er sie den Umständen nach für erforderlich halten durfte.

(1) Freight charges are payable upon delivery of the goods. In addition to the freight charges, the freight carrier has a claim for reimbursement of his expenditures to the extent that these were made for the goods and he could deem them to be necessary according to the circumstances.

(2) Der Anspruch auf die Fracht entfällt, soweit die Beförderung unmöglich ist. Wird die Beförderung infolge eines Beförderungs- oder Ablieferungshindernisses vorzeitig beendet, so gebührt dem Frachtführer die anteilige Fracht für den zurückgelegten Teil der Beförderung, wenn diese für den Absender von Interesse ist.

(2) Where the shipment is impossible, there is no claim to the freight charges. Where the shipment is terminated prematurely because of a hindrance to shipment or delivery, the freight carrier is entitled to the pro rata freight charges for the part of the shipment which has been made if this part is of interest to the shipper.

(3) Abweichend von Absatz 2 behält der Frachtführer den Anspruch auf die Fracht, wenn die Beförderung aus Gründen unmöglich ist, die dem Risikobereich des Absenders zuzurechnen sind oder die zu einer Zeit eintreten, zu welcher der Absender im Verzug der Annahme ist. Der Frachtführer muss sich jedoch das, was er an Aufwendungen erspart oder anderweitig erwirbt oder zu erwerben böswillig unterlässt, anrechnen lassen.

(3) Notwithstanding subsection 2, the freight carrier shall retain the claim to the freight charges if the shipment is impossible due to reasons attributable to the sphere of risks of the freight carrier or if they occur at a time when the shipper defaults in taking delivery. However, the freight carrier must allow the deduction of the amounts he saves on expenditures, the amounts he earns otherwise or the amounts he maliciously neglects to earn.

(4) Tritt nach Beginn der Beförderung und vor Ankunft an der Ablieferungsstelle eine Verzögerung ein und beruht die Verzögerung auf Gründen, die dem Risikobereich des Absenders zuzurechnen sind, so gebührt dem Frachtführer neben der Fracht eine angemessene Vergütung.

(4) If, after the start of the shipment and before arrival at the point of delivery, a delay occurs and is caused by reasons which are attributable to the sphere of risks of the shipper, the freight carrier is entitled to reasonable remuneration in addition to the freight charges.

(5) Ist die Fracht nach Zahl, Gewicht oder anders angegebener Menge des Gutes vereinbart, so wird für die Berechnung der Fracht vermutet, dass Angaben hierzu im Frachtbrief oder Ladeschein zutreffen; dies gilt auch dann, wenn zu diesen Angaben ein Vorbehalt eingetragen ist, der damit begründet ist, dass keine angemessenen Mittel zur Verfügung standen, die Richtigkeit der Angaben zu überprüfen.

(5) If the freight charges have been agreed upon according to the number, weight or other designated quantity of the goods, it shall be presumed for the computation of the freight charges that the pertinent data in the waybill or the bill of lading are accurate. This also applies if, with respect to the data, a reservation has been entered which is justified by the fact that no reasonable means were available to check the correctness of the data.

## § 421 Rechte des Empfängers. Zahlungspflicht

(1) Nach Ankunft des Gutes an der Ablieferungsstelle ist der Empfänger berechtigt, vom Frachtführer zu verlangen, ihm das Gut gegen Erfüllung der Verpflichtungen aus dem Frachtvertrag abzuliefern. Ist das Gut beschädigt oder verspätet abgeliefert worden oder verlorengegangen, so kann der Empfänger die Ansprüche aus dem Frachtvertrag im eigenen Namen gegen den Frachtführer geltend machen; der Absender bleibt zur Geltendmachung dieser Ansprüche befugt. Dabei macht es keinen Unterschied, ob Empfänger oder Absender im eigenen oder fremden Interesse handeln.

(2) Der Empfänger, der sein Recht nach Absatz 1 Satz 1 geltend macht, hat die noch geschuldete Fracht bis zu dem Betrag zu zahlen, der aus dem Frachtbrief hervorgeht. Ist ein Frachtbrief nicht ausgestellt oder dem Empfänger nicht vorgelegt worden oder ergibt sich aus dem Frachtbrief nicht die Höhe der zu zahlenden Fracht, so hat der Empfänger die mit dem Absender vereinbarte Fracht zu zahlen, soweit diese nicht unangemessen ist.

(3) Der Empfänger, der sein Recht nach Absatz 1 Satz 1 geltend macht, hat ferner ein Standgeld oder eine Vergütung nach § 420 Absatz 4 zu zahlen, ein Standgeld wegen Überschreitung der Ladezeit und eine Vergütung nach § 420 Absatz 4 jedoch nur, wenn ihm der geschuldete Betrag bei Ablieferung des Gutes mitgeteilt worden ist.

(4) Der Absender bleibt zur Zahlung der nach dem Vertrag geschuldeten Beträge verpflichtet.

## § 421 Rights of the consignee. Payment obligation

(1) Upon arrival of the goods at the point of delivery the consignee is entitled to request that the freight carrier deliver the goods against performance of the obligations arising out of the freight agreement. If the goods have been damaged or delivered late or have been lost, the consignee may assert the claims arising out of the freight agreement in his own name against the freight carrier; the shipper remains entitled to assert these claims. It makes no difference whether the consignee or the shipper acts in his own or in a third party's interest.

(2) The consignee who asserts his rights pursuant to subsection 1, sentence 1 still has to pay the freight charges due up to the amount which results from the waybill. If a waybill has not been issued or has not been presented to the consignee, or if the amount of the freight charges payable is not shown on the waybill, the consignee shall pay the freight charges agreed with the shipper unless these are unreasonable.

(3) The consignee who asserts his rights pursuant to subsection 1, sentence 1 also has to pay demurrage or remuneration pursuant to § 420(4); he has to pay demurrage for exceeding the loading time and remuneration pursuant to § 420(4), however, only where he has been informed of the amount due upon delivery of the goods.

(4) The shipper remains obligated to pay the amounts due pursuant to the agreement.

## § 422 Nachnahme

(1) Haben die Parteien vereinbart, dass das Gut nur gegen Einziehung einer Nachnahme an den Empfänger abgeliefert werden darf, so ist anzunehmen, dass der Betrag in bar oder in Form eines gleichwertigen Zahlungsmittels einzuziehen ist.

(2) Das auf Grund der Einziehung Erlangte gilt im Verhältnis zu den Gläubigern des Frachtführers als auf den Absender übertragen.

(3) Wird das Gut dem Empfänger ohne Einziehung der Nachnahme abgeliefert, so haftet der Frachtführer, auch wenn ihn kein Verschulden trifft, dem Absender für den daraus entstehenden Schaden, jedoch nur bis zur Höhe des Betrages der Nachnahme.

## § 422 Cash due on delivery

(1) If the parties have agreed that the goods may be delivered to the consignee only against collection of payment, then it is presumed that the amount is to be collected in cash or in the form of an equivalent means of payment.

(2) In the relationship to the creditors of the freight carrier, the amount collected is deemed to have been transferred to the shipper.

(3) Where the goods are delivered to the consignee without collecting the payment, the freight carrier is liable to the shipper for the resulting damage even if he is not at fault, but only up to the amount of the payment to be collected.

## § 423
## Lieferfrist

Der Frachtführer ist verpflichtet, das Gut innerhalb der vereinbarten Frist oder mangels Vereinbarung innerhalb der Frist abzuliefern, die einem sorgfältigen Frachtführer unter Berücksichtigung der Umstände vernünftigerweise zuzubilligen ist (Lieferfrist).

## § 423
## Delivery period

The freight carrier is obligated to deliver the goods within the term agreed upon or, absent such agreement, within the time period which is to be reasonably granted to a careful freight carrier taking the circumstances into consideration (delivery period).

## § 424
## Verlustvermutung

(1) Der Anspruchsberechtigte kann das Gut als verloren betrachten, wenn es weder innerhalb der Lieferfrist noch innerhalb eines weiteren Zeitraums abgeliefert wird, der der Lieferfrist entspricht, mindestens aber zwanzig Tage, bei einer grenzüberschreitenden Beförderung dreißig Tage beträgt.

(2) Erhält der Anspruchsberechtigte eine Entschädigung für den Verlust des Gutes, so kann er bei deren Empfang verlangen, dass er unverzüglich benachrichtigt wird, wenn das Gut wiederaufgefunden wird.

(3) Der Anspruchsberechtigte kann innerhalb eines Monats nach Empfang der Benachrichtigung von dem Wiederauffinden des Gutes verlangen, dass ihm das Gut Zug um Zug gegen Erstattung der Entschädigung, gegebenenfalls abzüglich der in der Entschädigung enthaltenen Kosten, abgeliefert wird. Eine etwaige Pflicht zur Zahlung der Fracht sowie Ansprüche auf Schadenersatz bleiben unberührt.

(4) Wird das Gut nach Zahlung einer Entschädigung wiederaufgefunden und hat der Anspruchsberechtigte eine Benachrichtigung nicht verlangt oder macht er nach Benachrichtigung seinen Anspruch auf Ablieferung nicht geltend, so kann der Frachtführer über das Gut frei verfügen.

## § 424
## Presumption of loss

(1) The beneficiary can consider the goods to be lost if they are not delivered within the delivery period or within an additional period that is equal to the delivery period, but at least twenty days, or, in the case of a cross-border shipment, thirty days.

(2) If the beneficiary receives an indemnification for the loss of the goods, he can request upon its receipt that he be informed without undue delay if the goods reappear.

(3) The beneficiary may request, within one month after receipt of the notification of the goods having been found again, that the goods be delivered to him concurrently against reimbursement of the indemnification less the costs contained in the indemnification, if any. Any obligation to pay the freight charges as well as claims for payment of damages shall not be affected.

(4) Where the goods have been found after payment of an indemnification and where the beneficiary has not requested to be notified or where he does not assert his claim for delivery after notification, the freight carrier may freely dispose of the goods.

## § 425
## Haftung für Güter- und Verspätungsschäden. Schadensteilung

(1) Der Frachtführer haftet für den Schaden, der durch Verlust oder Beschädigung des Gutes in der Zeit von der Übernahme zur Beförderung bis zur Ablieferung oder durch Überschreitung der Lieferfrist entsteht.

(2) Hat bei der Entstehung des Schadens ein Verhalten des Absenders oder des Empfängers oder ein besonderer Mangel des Gutes mitgewirkt, so hängen die Verpflichtung zum Ersatz sowie der Umfang des zu leistenden Ersatzes davon ab, inwieweit diese Umstände zu dem Schaden beigetragen haben.

## § 425
## Liability for damages to goods and for delay. Apportionment of damages

(1) The freight carrier is liable for the damage which arises from loss of or damage to the goods from the time they are accepted for shipment until delivery, or from non-compliance with the delivery period.

(2) Where the conduct of the shipper or the consignee or a special defect of the goods has contributed to the cause of the damages, the obligation to pay damages and the amount of the damages to be paid depend on the extent to which these circumstances have contributed to the damage.

## § 426 Haftungsausschluss

Der Frachtführer ist von der Haftung befreit, soweit der Verlust, die Beschädigung oder die Überschreitung der Lieferfrist auf Umständen beruht, die der Frachtführer auch bei größter Sorgfalt nicht vermeiden und deren Folgen er nicht abwenden konnte.

## § 426 Exclusion of liability

The freight carrier is exempted from liability to the extent that the loss, the damage or the failure to comply with the delivery period is caused by circumstances which the freight carrier could not avoid even with the utmost care and whose consequences he could not prevent.

## § 427 Besondere Haftungsausschlussgründe

(1) Der Frachtführer ist von seiner Haftung befreit, soweit der Verlust, die Beschädigung oder die Überschreitung der Lieferfrist auf eine der folgenden Gefahren zurückzuführen ist:

1. vereinbarte oder der Übung entsprechende Verwendung von offenen, nicht mit Planen gedeckten Fahrzeugen oder Verladung auf Deck;
2. ungenügende Verpackung durch den Absender;
3. Behandeln, Verladen oder Entladen des Gutes durch den Absender oder den Empfänger;
4. natürliche Beschaffenheit des Gutes, die besonders leicht zu Schäden, insbesondere durch Bruch, Rost, inneren Verderb, Austrocknen, Auslaufen, normalen Schwund, führt;
5. ungenügende Kennzeichnung der Frachtstücke durch den Absender;
6. Beförderung lebender Tiere.

(2) Ist ein Schaden eingetreten, der nach den Umständen des Falles aus einer der in Absatz 1 bezeichneten Gefahren entstehen konnte, so wird vermutet, dass der Schaden aus dieser Gefahr entstanden ist. Diese Vermutung gilt im Falle des Absatzes 1 Nr. 1 nicht bei außergewöhnlich großem Verlust.

(3) Der Frachtführer kann sich auf Absatz 1 Nr. 1 nur berufen, soweit der Verlust, die Beschädigung oder die Überschreitung der Lieferfrist nicht darauf zurückzuführen ist, dass der Frachtführer besondere Weisungen des Absenders im Hinblick auf die Beförderung des Gutes nicht beachtet hat.

(4) Ist der Frachtführer nach dem Frachtvertrag verpflichtet, das Gut gegen die Einwirkung von Hitze, Kälte, Temperaturschwankungen, Luftfeuchtigkeit, Erschütterungen oder ähnlichen Einflüssen besonders zu schützen, so kann er sich auf Absatz 1 Nr. 4 nur berufen, wenn er alle ihm nach den Umständen obliegenden Maßnahmen, insbesondere hinsichtlich der Auswahl, Instandhaltung und Verwendung besonderer Einrichtungen, getroffen und besondere Weisungen beachtet hat.

## § 427 Special grounds for exclusion of liability

(1) The freight carrier is exempted from his liability to the extent that the loss, the damage or the failure to comply with the delivery period is attributable to one of the following risks:

1. Utilisation of open vehicles not covered by tarps or loading on deck as agreed upon or according to trade custom;
2. inadequate packaging by the shipper;
3. handling, loading or unloading of the goods by the shipper or the consignee;
4. natural condition of the goods which leads especially easily to damages, especially by breakage, rust, inner spoilage, drying up, leaking out, normal shrinkage;
5. insufficient labelling of the freight pieces by the shipper;
6. shipment of live animals.

(2) Where damage has occurred which, according to the circumstances of the case, could have arisen from a designated risk described in subsection 1, it shall be presumed that the damage has arisen from this risk. This presumption does not apply in case of subsection 1, no. 1 where the loss is extraordinarily large.

(3) The freight carrier can only rely on subsection 1, no. 1 to the extent that the loss, the damage or failure to comply with the delivery period is not attributable to the fact that the freight carrier has disregarded special instructions of the shipper with regard to the shipment of the goods.

(4) Where the freight carrier is obligated pursuant to the freight agreement to specially protect the goods against the effects of heat, cold, temperature fluctuations, humidity, vibrations or similar influences, he can only rely on subsection 1, no. 4 if he has taken all measures he was supposed to take under the circumstances, especially with regard to the selection, maintenance and use of special equipment and has followed special instructions.

(5) Der Frachtführer kann sich auf Absatz 1 Nr. 6 nur berufen, wenn er alle ihm nach den Umständen obliegenden Maßnahmen getroffen und besondere Weisungen beachtet hat.

(5) The freight carrier can only rely on subsection 1, no. 6 if he has taken all measures he was supposed to take under the circumstances and has followed special instructions.

## § 428
## Haftung für andere

Der Frachtführer hat Handlungen und Unterlassungen seiner Leute in gleichem Umfange zu vertreten wie eigene Handlungen und Unterlassungen, wenn die Leute in Ausübung ihrer Verrichtungen handeln. Gleiches gilt für Handlungen und Unterlassungen anderer Personen, deren er sich bei Ausführung der Beförderung bedient.

## § 428
## Liability for others

The freight carrier is liable for the acts and omissions of his employees to the same extent as for his own acts and omissions where the employees act in performance of their duties. The same applies to acts and omissions of other persons he uses in carrying out the shipment.

## § 429
## Wertersatz

(1) Hat der Frachtführer für gänzlichen oder teilweisen Verlust des Gutes Schadenersatz zu leisten, so ist der Wert am Ort und zur Zeit der Übernahme zur Beförderung zu ersetzen.

(2) Bei Beschädigung des Gutes ist der Unterschied zwischen dem Wert des unbeschädigten Gutes am Ort und zur Zeit der Übernahme zur Beförderung und dem Wert zu ersetzen, den das beschädigte Gut am Ort und zur Zeit der Übernahme gehabt hätte. Es wird vermutet, dass die zur Schadensminderung und Schadensbehebung aufzuwendenden Kosten dem nach Satz 1 zu ermittelnden Unterschiedsbetrag entsprechen.

(3) Der Wert des Gutes bestimmt sich nach dem Marktpreis, sonst nach dem gemeinen Wert von Gütern gleicher Art und Beschaffenheit. Ist das Gut unmittelbar vor Übernahme zur Beförderung verkauft worden, so wird vermutet, dass der in der Rechnung des Verkäufers ausgewiesene Kaufpreis abzüglich darin enthaltener Beförderungskosten der Marktpreis ist.

## § 429
## Compensation for lost value

(1) Where the freight carrier has to pay damages for the total or partial loss of the goods, the value at the place and at the time of acceptance for shipment must be compensated.

(2) Where the goods have been damaged, the difference between the value of the undamaged goods at the place and at the time of the acceptance for shipment and the value which the damaged goods would have had at the place and time of acceptance must be compensated. It is presumed that the costs incurred to minimise or repair the damage correspond to the difference in amounts to be computed according to sentence 1.

(3) The value of the goods is determined by the market price and otherwise the common value of goods of the same kind and condition. If the goods have been sold immediately before acceptance for shipment, it shall be presumed that the market price is the purchase price shown in the invoice of the seller less the costs of shipment contained therein.

## § 430
## Schadensfeststellungskosten

Bei Verlust oder Beschädigung des Gutes hat der Frachtführer über den nach § 429 zu leistenden Ersatz hinaus die Kosten der Feststellung des Schadens zu tragen.

## § 430
## Costs of determining the damage

Where goods have been lost or damaged, the freight carrier shall, in addition to the compensation to be paid pursuant to § 429, also bear the costs of determining the damage.

## § 431
## Haftungshöchstbetrag

(1) Die nach den §§ 429 und 430 zu leistende Entschädigung wegen Verlust oder Beschädigung ist auf einen Betrag von 8,33 Rechnungseinheiten für jedes Kilogramm des Rohgewichts des Gutes begrenzt.

## § 431
## Maximum liability

(1) The indemnification to be paid pursuant to §§ 429 and 430 because of loss of or damage to the shipment is limited to an amount of 8.33 accounting units for each kilogram of the gross weight of the shipment.

(2) Besteht das Gut aus mehreren Frachtstücken (Sendung) und sind nur einzelne Frachtstücke verloren oder beschädigt worden, so ist der Berechnung nach Absatz 1

1. die gesamte Sendung zu Grunde zu legen, wenn die gesamte Sendung entwertet ist, oder
2. der entwertete Teil der Sendung zu Grunde zu legen, wenn nur ein Teil der Sendung entwertet ist.

(3) Die Haftung des Frachtführers wegen Überschreitung der Lieferfrist ist auf den dreifachen Betrag der Fracht begrenzt.

(4) Die in den Absätzen 1 und 2 genannte Rechnungseinheit ist das Sonderziehungsrecht des Internationalen Währungsfond. Der Betrag wird in Euro entsprechend dem Wert des Euro gegenüber dem Sonderziehungsrecht am Tag der Übernahme des Gutes zur Beförderung oder an dem von den Parteien vereinbarten Tag umgerechnet. Der Wert des Euro gegenüber dem Sonderziehungsrecht wird nach der Berechnungsmethode ermittelt, die der Internationale Währungsfonds an dem betreffenden Tag für seine Operationen und Transaktionen anwendet.

(2) Where the freight consists of several freight pieces (shipment) and only individual freight pieces of the shipment have been lost or damaged, the computation pursuant to subsection 1 is based on

1. the total shipment if the total shipment has been devalued or
2. the devalued part of the shipment, if only part of the shipment has been devalued.

(3) The liability of the freight carrier for failure to comply with the delivery period is limited to three times the amount of the freight charges.

(4) The accounting unit mentioned in subsections 1 and 2 is the special drawing right of the International Monetary Fund. The amount will be converted into euro according to the value of the euro as compared to the special drawing right on the day of the acceptance of the goods for shipment or on the day agreed upon by the parties. The value of the euro as compared to the special drawing rights shall be determined pursuant to the conversion method that the International Monetary Fund uses for its operations and transactions on the relevant day.

### § 432
### Ersatz sonstiger Kosten

Haftet der Frachtführer wegen Verlust oder Beschädigung, so hat er über den nach den §§ 429 bis 431 zu leistenden Ersatz hinaus die Fracht, öffentliche Abgaben und sonstige Kosten aus Anlass der Beförderung des Gutes zu erstatten, im Fall der Beschädigung jedoch nur in dem nach § 429 Abs. 2 zu ermittelnden Wertverhältnis. Weiteren Schaden hat er nicht zu ersetzen.

### § 432
### Reimbursement of other costs

Where the freight carrier is liable due to loss or damage, he shall, in addition to the compensation payable pursuant to §§ 429 to 431, reimburse the freight charges, the public levies and other costs incurred in connection with the shipment of the goods, in the case of damage, however, only in proportion of the amount to be determined pursuant to § 429(2). He is not obligated to compensate further damage.

### § 433
### Haftungshöchstbetrag bei sonstigen Vermögensschäden

Haftet der Frachtführer wegen der Verletzung einer mit der Ausführung der Beförderung des Gutes zusammenhängenden vertraglichen Pflicht für Schäden, die nicht durch Verlust oder Beschädigung des Gutes oder durch Überschreitung der Lieferfrist entstehen, und handelt es sich um andere Schäden als Sach- oder Personenschäden, so ist auch in diesem Falle die Haftung begrenzt, und zwar auf das Dreifache des Betrages, der bei Verlust des Gutes zu zahlen wäre.

### § 433
### Maximum amount of liability in case of other pecuniary loss

Where the freight carrier, due to violation of a contractual duty connected with carrying out the shipment of goods, is liable for damage which does not arise out of loss of or damage to the goods or failure to comply with the delivery period, and where the damage is different from damage to property or persons, the liability is also limited, in this case to three times the amount which would be payable upon loss of the goods.

## § 434
## Außervertragliche Ansprüche

(1) Die in diesem Unterabschnitt und im Frachtvertrag vorgesehenen Haftungsbefreiungen und Haftungsbegrenzungen gelten auch für einen außervertraglichen Anspruch des Absenders oder des Empfängers gegen den Frachtführer wegen Verlust oder Beschädigung des Gutes oder wegen Überschreitung der Lieferfrist.

(2) Der Frachtführer kann auch gegenüber außervertraglichen Ansprüchen Dritter wegen Verlust oder Beschädigung des Gutes die Einwendungen nach Absatz 1 geltend machen. Die Einwendungen können jedoch nicht geltend gemacht werden, wenn

1. sie auf eine Vereinbarung gestützt werden, die von den in § 449 Absatz 1 Satz 1 genannten Vorschriften zu Lasten des Absenders abweicht,
2. der Dritte der Beförderung nicht zugestimmt hat und der Frachtführer die fehlende Befugnis des Absenders, das Gut zu versenden, kannte oder infolge grober Fahrlässigkeit nicht kannte oder
3. das Gut vor Übernahme zur Beförderung dem Dritten oder einer Person, die von diesem ihr Recht zum Besitz ableitet, abhandengekommen ist.

Satz 2 Nummer 1 gilt jedoch nicht für eine nach § 449 zulässige Vereinbarung über die Begrenzung der vom Frachtführer zu leistenden Entschädigung wegen Verlust oder Beschädigung des Gutes auf einen niedrigeren als den gesetzlich vorgesehenen Betrag, wenn dieser den Betrag von 2 Rechnungseinheiten nicht unterschreitet.

## § 434
## Non-contractual claims

(1) The exemptions from and limitations of liability provided for in this Subpart and in the freight agreement also apply to non-contractual claims of the shipper or the consignee against the freight carrier due to loss of or damage to the goods or due to failure to comply with the delivery period.

(2) The freight carrier can also assert the objections pursuant to subsection 1 against non-contractual claims of third parties due to loss of or damage to the goods. The objections, however, cannot be asserted where

1. they are based on an agreement deviating from the provisions mentioned in § 449(1), sentence 1 at the expense of the shipper,
2. the third party has not consented to the shipment and the freight carrier was aware – or negligently unaware – of the lack of authority of the shipper to ship the goods;
3. the goods have been lost prior to acceptance for shipment by the third party or a person who derives his right to possess the goods from the third party.

However, sentence 2, no. 1 does not apply to an agreement permitted under § 449 on the limitation of the indemnification, due to loss of or damage to the goods, payable by the freight carrier to an amount lower than the amount required by law if this amount does not fall below the amount of 2 accounting units.

## § 435
## Wegfall der Haftungsbefreiungen und -begrenzungen

Die in diesem Unterabschnitt und im Frachtvertrag vorgesehenen Haftungsbefreiungen und Haftungsbegrenzungen gelten nicht, wenn der Schaden auf eine Handlung oder Unterlassung zurückzuführen ist, die der Frachtführer oder eine in § 428 genannte Person vorsätzlich oder leichtfertig und in dem Bewusstsein, dass ein Schaden mit Wahrscheinlichkeit eintreten werde, begangen hat.

## § 435
## Loss of exemptions from and limitations of liability

The exemptions from and limitations of liability provided for in this Subpart and in the freight agreement do not apply if the damage is caused by an act or an omission which the freight carrier or a person mentioned in § 428 has wilfully or recklessly committed with the knowledge that damage would likely occur.

### § 436
### Haftung der Leute

Werden Ansprüche aus außervertraglicher Haftung wegen Verlust oder Beschädigung des Gutes oder wegen Überschreitung der Lieferfrist gegen einen der Leute des Frachtführers erhoben, so kann sich auch jener auf die in diesem Unterabschnitt und im Frachtvertrag vorgesehenen Haftungsbefreiungen und -begrenzungen berufen. Dies gilt nicht, wenn er vorsätzlich oder leichtfertig und in dem Bewusstsein, dass ein Schaden mit Wahrscheinlichkeit eintreten werde, gehandelt hat.

### § 436
### Liability of auxiliary persons

Where claims are asserted against an auxiliary person of the freight carrier based on non-contractual liability due to loss of or damage to the goods or due to failure to comply with the delivery period, such auxiliary person can also invoke the exemptions from and limitations of liability provided for in this Subpart and with the freight agreement. This does not apply if he has acted wilfully or recklessly and with the knowledge that damage would probably occur.

### § 437
### Ausführender Frachtführer

(1) Wird die Beförderung ganz oder teilweise durch einen Dritten ausgeführt (ausführender Frachtführer), so haftet dieser für den Schaden, der durch Verlust oder Beschädigung des Gutes oder durch Überschreitung der Lieferfrist während der durch ihn ausgeführten Beförderung entsteht, so, als wäre er der Frachtführer. Vertragliche Vereinbarungen mit dem Absender oder Empfänger, durch die der Frachtführer seine Haftung erweitert, wirken gegen den ausführenden Frachtführer nur, soweit er ihnen schriftlich zugestimmt hat.

(2) Der ausführende Frachtführer kann alle Einwendungen und Einreden geltend machen, die dem Frachtführer aus dem Frachtvertrag zustehen.

(3) Frachtführer und ausführender Frachtführer haften als Gesamtschuldner.

(4) Werden die Leute des ausführenden Frachtführers in Anspruch genommen, so gilt für diese § 436 entsprechend.

### § 437
### Acting freight carrier

(1) Where the shipment is carried out totally or partially by a third party (acting freight carrier), this acting freight carrier is liable in the same way as the freight carrier for the damage which arises out of loss of or damage to the goods or failure to comply with the delivery period during the shipment carried out by him. Contractual agreements with the shipper or the consignee by means of which the freight carrier extends his liability are effective against the acting freight carrier only to the extent that he has consented to these in writing.

(2) The acting freight carrier can assert all the objections and defences that the freight carrier could assert based on the freight agreement.

(3) The freight carrier and acting freight carrier are jointly and severally liable.

(4) Where claims are asserted against employees of the acting freight carrier, § 436 applies to them analogously.

### § 438
### Schadensanzeige

(1) Ist ein Verlust oder eine Beschädigung des Gutes äußerlich erkennbar und zeigt der Empfänger oder der Absender dem Frachtführer Verlust oder Beschädigung nicht spätestens bei Ablieferung des Gutes an, so wird vermutet, dass das Gut vollständig und unbeschädigt abgeliefert worden ist. Die Anzeige muss den Verlust oder die Beschädigung hinreichend deutlich kennzeichnen.

(2) Die Vermutung nach Absatz 1 gilt auch, wenn der Verlust oder die Beschädigung äußerlich nicht erkennbar war und nicht innerhalb von sieben Tagen nach Ablieferung angezeigt worden ist.

### § 438
### Notification of damage

(1) If loss or damage to the goods is externally visible and the consignee or the shipper does not notify the freight carrier of the loss or damage by the time of delivery of the goods at the latest, it shall be presumed that the goods have been delivered in full and in an undamaged condition. The notification must indicate the loss or damage with adequate clarity.

(2) The presumption pursuant to subsection 1 shall also apply where the loss or the damage was not externally visible and notice has not been given within seven days after delivery.

(3) Ansprüche wegen Überschreitung der Lieferfrist erlöschen, wenn der Empfänger dem Frachtführer die Überschreitung der Lieferfrist nicht innerhalb von einundzwanzig Tagen nach Ablieferung anzeigt.

(4) Eine Schadensanzeige nach Ablieferung ist in Textform zu erstatten. Zur Wahrung der Frist genügt die rechtzeitige Absendung.

(5) Werden Verlust, Beschädigung oder Überschreitung der Lieferfrist bei Ablieferung angezeigt, so genügt die Anzeige gegenüber demjenigen, der das Gut abliefert.

(3) Claims due to non-compliance with the delivery period expire where the consignee does not notify the freight carrier of such non-compliance within twenty-one days after delivery.

(4) Notification of damage after delivery shall be made in writing. Timely dispatch is sufficient to comply with the time limit.

(5) Where notice of loss, damage or non-compliance with the delivery period is given upon delivery, the notification is sufficient if it is given to the party delivering the goods.

## § 439
## Verjährung

(1) Ansprüche aus einer Beförderung, die den Vorschriften dieses Unterabschnitts unterliegt, verjähren in einem Jahr. Bei Vorsatz oder bei einem dem Vorsatz nach § 435 gleichstehenden Verschulden beträgt die Verjährungsfrist drei Jahre.

(2) Die Verjährung beginnt mit Ablauf des Tages, an dem das Gut abgeliefert wurde. Ist das Gut nicht abgeliefert worden, beginnt die Verjährung mit dem Ablauf des Tages, an dem das Gut hätte abgeliefert werden müssen. Abweichend von den Sätzen 1 und 2 beginnt die Verjährung von Rückgriffsansprüchen mit dem Tag des Eintritts der Rechtskraft des Urteils gegen den Rückgriffsgläubiger oder, wenn kein rechtskräftiges Urteil vorliegt, mit dem Tag, an dem der Rückgriffsgläubiger den Anspruch befriedigt hat, es sei denn, der Rückgriffsschuldner wurde nicht innerhalb von drei Monaten, nachdem der Rückgriffsgläubiger Kenntnis von dem Schaden und der Person des Rückgriffsschuldners erlangt hat, über diesen Schaden unterrichtet.

(3) Die Verjährung eines Anspruchs gegen den Frachtführer wird auch durch eine Erklärung des Absenders oder Empfängers, mit der dieser Ersatzansprüche erhebt, bis zu dem Zeitpunkt gehemmt, in dem der Frachtführer die Erfüllung des Anspruchs ablehnt. Die Erhebung der Ansprüche sowie die Ablehnung bedürfen der Textform. Eine weitere Erklärung, die denselben Ersatzanspruch zum Gegenstand hat, hemmt die Verjährung nicht erneut.

(4) Die Verjährung von Schadensersatzansprüchen wegen Verlust oder Beschädigung des Gutes oder wegen Überschreitung der Lieferfrist kann nur durch Vereinbarung, die im Einzelnen ausgehandelt ist, auch wenn sie für eine Mehrzahl von gleichartigen Verträgen zwischen denselben Vertragsparteien getroffen ist, erleichtert oder erschwert werden.

## § 439
## Limitation

(1) Claims resulting from a shipment that is subject to the provisions of this Subpart prescribe within one year. In the case of wilfulness or fault equivalent to wilfulness pursuant to § 435, the limitation period is three years.

(2) The limitation period begins to run upon expiry of the day on which the goods were delivered. If the goods have not been delivered, the limitation period begins to run upon expiry of the day on which the goods should have been delivered. Notwithstanding sentences 1 and 2, the limitation for recourse claims begins to run on the day the judgment against the recourse creditor becomes final or, where there is no final judgment, on the day on which the recourse creditor has paid the claim unless the recourse debtor has not been informed about the damage within three months after the recourse creditor became aware of the damage and of the identity of the recourse debtor.

(3) The limitation for a claim against the freight carrier shall also be suspended by a declaration of the shipper or the consignee by means of which one of the latter asserts claims for damages until such point in time as the freight carrier refuses to pay the claim. The raising of the claims as well as the rejection must be in text form. A further declaration dealing with the same claim does not suspend limitation anew.

(4) The limitation for claims for damages due to loss of or damage to the goods, or due to failure to comply with the delivery period, can only be facilitated or impeded by an agreement negotiated in detail, even if it applies to a number of similar contracts between the same parties.

## §440
## Pfandrecht des Frachtführers

(1) Der Frachtführer hat für alle Forderungen aus dem Frachtvertrag ein Pfandrecht an dem ihm zur Beförderung übergebenen Gut des Absenders oder eines Dritten, der der Beförderung des Gutes zugestimmt hat. An dem Gut des Absenders hat der Frachtführer auch ein Pfandrecht für alle unbestrittenen Forderungen aus anderen mit dem Absender abgeschlossenen Fracht-, Seefracht-, Speditions- und Lagerverträgen. Das Pfandrecht nach den Sätzen 1 und 2 erstreckt sich auf die Begleitpapiere.

(2) Das Pfandrecht besteht, solange der Frachtführer das Gut in seinem Besitz hat, insbesondere solange er mittels Konnossements, Ladescheins oder Lagerscheins darüber verfügen kann.

(3) Das Pfandrecht besteht auch nach der Ablieferung fort, wenn der Frachtführer es innerhalb von drei Tagen nach der Ablieferung gerichtlich geltend macht und das Gut noch im Besitz des Empfängers ist.

(4) Die in §1234 Abs. 1 des Bürgerlichen Gesetzbuchs bezeichnete Androhung des Pfandverkaufs sowie die in den §§1237 und 1241 des Bürgerlichen Gesetzbuchs vorgesehenen Benachrichtigungen sind an den nach §418 oder §446 verfügungsberechtigten Empfänger zu richten. Ist dieser nicht zu ermitteln oder verweigert er die Annahme des Gutes, so haben die Androhung und die Benachrichtigung gegenüber dem Absender zu erfolgen.

## §440
## Lien of the freight carrier

(1) For all claims arising out of the freight agreement, the freight carrier shall have a lien on the goods of the shipper or a third party consenting to the shipment of the goods that have been handed over to him. The freight carrier shall also have a lien on the goods of the shipper for all undisputed claims arising out of other freight, maritime shipping, forwarding and warehouse contracts concluded with the shipper. The lien pursuant to sentences 1 and 2 also extends to the accompanying documents.

(2) The lien exists as long as the freight carrier has the goods in his possession, especially as long as he can dispose of them by means of a maritime bill of lading, a bill of lading or warehouse receipt.

(3) The lien continues to exist even after delivery if the freight carrier has asserted the lien in court within three days after delivery of the goods and the goods are still in the consignee's possession.

(4) The warning of a sale of pledged property described in §1234(1) of the Civil Code, as well as the notice provided for in §§1237 and 1241 of the Civil Code, are to be addressed to the consignee entitled to the right of disposition pursuant to §418 or §446. Where he cannot be located or refuses to accept the goods, the warning and notice must be given to the shipper.

## §441
## Nachfolgender Frachtführer

(1) Hat im Falle der Beförderung durch mehrere Frachtführer der letzte bei der Ablieferung die Forderungen der vorhergehenden Frachtführer einzuziehen, so hat er die Rechte der vorhergehenden Frachtführer, insbesondere auch das Pfandrecht, auszuüben. Das Pfandrecht jedes vorhergehenden Frachtführers bleibt so lange bestehen wie das Pfandrecht des letzten Frachtführers.

(2) Wird ein vorhergehender Frachtführer von einem nachgehenden befriedigt, so gehen Forderung und Pfandrecht des ersteren auf den letzteren über.

(3) Die Absätze 1 und 2 gelten auch für die Forderungen und Rechte eines Spediteurs, der an der Beförderung mitgewirkt hat.

## §441
## Subsequent freight carrier

(1) Where, in case of shipment by more than one freight carrier, the last freight carrier has to collect the claims of the prior freight carriers upon delivery, he shall exercise the rights of the prior freight carriers and in particular the lien. The lien of each prior freight carrier continues to exist as long as the lien of the last freight carrier.

(2) Where a preceding freight carrier is paid by a subsequent freight carrier, his claim and lien are transferred to the latter.

(3) Subsections 1 and 2 also apply to the claims and rights of a forwarding agent who has been involved in the shipment.

### § 442
### Rang mehrerer Pfandrechte

(1) Bestehen an demselben Gut mehrere nach den §§ 397, 440, 464, 475b und 495 begründete Pfandrechte, so geht unter denjenigen Pfandrechten, die durch die Versendung oder durch die Beförderung des Gutes entstanden sind, das später entstandene dem früher entstandenen vor.

(2) Diese Pfandrechte haben Vorrang vor dem nicht aus der Versendung entstandenen Pfandrecht des Kommissionärs und des Lagerhalters sowie vor dem Pfandrecht des Spediteurs, des Frachtführers und des Verfrachters für Vorschüsse.

### § 442
### Priority among multiple liens

(1) Where more than one lien exists on the same goods by reason of §§ 397, 440, 464, 475b and 495, among the liens existing by reason of the forwarding or shipment of the goods, the later lien has priority over the earlier lien.

(2) These liens have priority over the liens of the commission agent and warehouse keeper not arising from the forwarding of the goods, as well as over the lien of the forwarding agent, the freight carrier and the charterer for advances.

### § 443
### Ladeschein. Verordnungsermächtigung

(1) Über die Verpflichtung zur Ablieferung des Gutes kann von dem Frachtführer ein Ladeschein ausgestellt werden, der die in § 408 Abs. 1 genannten Angaben enthalten soll. Der Ladeschein ist vom Frachtführer zu unterzeichnen; eine Nachbildung der eigenhändigen Unterschrift durch Druck oder durch Stempel genügt.

(2) Ist der Ladeschein an Order gestellt, so soll er den Namen desjenigen enthalten, an dessen Order das Gut abgeliefert werden soll. Wird der Name nicht angegeben, so ist der Ladeschein als an Order des Absenders gestellt anzusehen.

(3) Dem Ladeschein gleichgestellt ist eine elektronische Aufzeichnung, die dieselben Funktionen erfüllt wie der Ladeschein, sofern sichergestellt ist, dass die Authentizität und die Integrität der Aufzeichnung gewahrt bleiben (elektronischer Ladeschein). Das Bundesministerium der Justiz wird ermächtigt, im Einvernehmen mit dem Bundesministerium des Innern durch Rechtsverordnung, die nicht der Zustimmung des Bundesrates bedarf, die Einzelheiten der Ausstellung, Vorlage, Rückgabe und Übertragung eines elektronischen Ladescheins sowie die Einzelheiten des Verfahrens einer nachträglichen Eintragung in einen elektronischen Ladeschein zu regeln.

### § 443
### Bill of lading. Power to issue statutory instruments

(1) A bill of lading, which should contain the data mentioned in § 408(1), may be issued by the freight carrier with respect to the obligation for delivery of the goods. The bill of lading shall be signed by the freight carrier; a facsimile of the signature by print or by stamp is sufficient.

(2) If the bill of lading is issued to order, it shall contain the name of the party to whose order the goods are to be delivered. If the name is not mentioned, the bill of lading is to be deemed to have been issued to the order of the shipper.

(3) An electronic record that fulfils the same functions as the bill of lading is equivalent to the bill of lading provided that the authenticity and the integrity of the record are preserved (electronic bill of lading). The Federal Ministry of Justice is authorised, in agreement with the Federal Ministry of the Interior, to govern – by means of a statutory instrument which does not require the consent of the Federal Council – the details of the issuance, presentation, return and transfer of the electronic bill of lading as well as the process of a subsequent entry into an electronic bill of lading.

### § 444
### Wirkung des Ladescheins. Legitimation

(1) Der Ladeschein begründet die Vermutung, dass der Frachtführer das Gut so übernommen hat, wie es im Ladeschein beschrieben ist; § 409 Absatz 2 und 3 Satz 1 gilt entsprechend.

### § 444
### Effect of the bill of lading. Legitimation

(1) The bill of lading establishes the presumption that the freight carrier has accepted the goods as described in the warehouse receipt; § 409(2) and (3), sentence 1 applies accordingly.

(2) Gegenüber einem im Ladeschein benannten Empfänger, an den der Ladeschein begeben wurde, kann der Frachtführer die Vermutung nach Absatz 1 nicht widerlegen, es sei denn, dem Empfänger war im Zeitpunkt der Begebung des Ladescheins bekannt oder infolge grober Fahrlässigkeit unbekannt, dass die Angaben im Ladeschein unrichtig sind. Gleiches gilt gegenüber einem Dritten, dem der Ladeschein übertragen wurde. Die Sätze 1 und 2 gelten nicht, wenn der aus dem Ladeschein Berechtigte den ausführenden Frachtführer nach § 437 in Anspruch nimmt und der Ladeschein weder vom ausführenden Frachtführer noch von einem für ihn zur Zeichnung von Ladescheinen Befugten ausgestellt wurde.

(2) The freight carrier cannot refute the presumption pursuant to subsection 1 vis-à-vis a consignee designated in the bill of lading to whom the bill of lading was issued unless the consignee knew at the time of the issuance that the data provided in the bill of lading were inaccurate or, due to gross negligence, did not know this. The same applies with respect to a third party to whom the bill of lading was transferred. Sentences 1 and 2 do not apply if the rightful holder of the bill of lading asserts claims against the acting freight carrier pursuant to § 437 and the bill of lading was not issued by the acting freight carrier or by a person authorised to sign bills of lading for him.

(3) Die im Ladeschein verbrieften frachtvertraglichen Ansprüche können nur von dem aus dem Ladeschein Berechtigten geltend gemacht werden. Zugunsten des legitimierten Besitzers des Ladescheins wird vermutet, dass er der aus dem Ladeschein Berechtigte ist. Legitimierter Besitzer des Ladescheins ist, wer einen Ladeschein besitzt, der

1. auf den Inhaber lautet,
2. an Order lautet und den Besitzer als Empfänger benennt oder durch eine ununterbrochene Reihe von Indossamenten ausweist oder
3. auf den Namen des Besitzers lautet.

(3) The claims out of the freight agreement as documented by the bill of lading can only be asserted by the rightful holder of the bill of lading. It shall be presumed for the benefit of the legitimate holder of the bill of lading that he is the rightful holder based on the bill of lading. A legitimate holder of the bill of lading is anyone who holds a bill of lading that

1. is made out to the owner,
2. is issued to order and names the holder as the consignee or designates him as such by means of an uninterrupted chain of indorsements or
3. is made out in the name of the holder.

## § 445
## Ablieferung gegen Rückgabe des Ladescheins

(1) Nach Ankunft des Gutes an der Ablieferungsstelle ist der legitimierte Besitzer des Ladescheins berechtigt, vom Frachtführer die Ablieferung des Gutes zu verlangen. Macht er von diesem Recht Gebrauch, ist er entsprechend § 421 Absatz 2 und 3 zur Zahlung der Fracht und einer sonstigen Vergütung verpflichtet.

(2) Der Frachtführer ist zur Ablieferung des Gutes nur gegen Rückgabe des Ladescheins, auf dem die Ablieferung bescheinigt ist, und gegen Leistung der noch ausstehenden, nach § 421 Absatz 2 und 3 geschuldeten Zahlungen verpflichtet. Er darf das Gut jedoch nicht dem legitimierten Besitzer des Ladescheins abliefern, wenn ihm bekannt oder infolge grober Fahrlässigkeit unbekannt ist, dass der legitimierte Besitzer des Ladescheins nicht der aus dem Ladeschein Berechtigte ist.

## § 445
## Delivery against return of the bill of lading

(1) Upon arrival of the goods at the point of delivery, the legitimate holder of the bill of lading is entitled to request that the freight carrier deliver the goods. Where he makes use of this right he is obligated to pay the freight and other remuneration in accordance with § 421(2) and (3).

(2) The freight carrier is only obligated to deliver the goods against return of the bill of lading on which the delivery is acknowledged, and against performance of the outstanding payments owed pursuant to § 421(2) and (3). However, he may not deliver the goods to the legitimate holder of the bill of lading if he knows that the legitimate holder of the bill of lading is not the rightful holder of the bill of lading or if, due to gross negligence, he does not know this.

(3) Liefert der Frachtführer das Gut einem anderen als dem legitimierten Besitzer des Ladescheins oder, im Falle des Absatzes 2 Satz 2, einem anderen als dem aus dem Ladeschein Berechtigten ab, haftet er für den Schaden, der dem aus dem Ladeschein Berechtigten daraus entsteht. Die Haftung ist auf den Betrag begrenzt, der bei Verlust des Gutes zu zahlen wäre.

(3) Where the freight carrier delivers the goods to a person other than the legitimate holder of the bill of lading or, in the case of subsection 2, sentence 2, to a person other than the rightful holder of the bill of lading, he is liable for any resulting damage incurred by the rightful holder of the bill of lading. The liability is limited to the amount which would be payable upon loss of the goods.

**§ 446**
**Befolgung von Weisungen**

(1) Das Verfügungsrecht nach den §§ 418 und 419 steht, wenn ein Ladeschein ausgestellt worden ist, ausschließlich dem legitimierten Besitzer des Ladescheins zu. Der Frachtführer darf Weisungen nur gegen Vorlage des Ladescheins ausführen. Weisungen des legitimierten Besitzers des Ladescheins darf er jedoch nicht ausführen, wenn ihm bekannt oder infolge grober Fahrlässigkeit unbekannt ist, dass der legitimierte Besitzer des Ladescheins nicht der aus dem Ladeschein Berechtigte ist.

(2) Befolgt der Frachtführer Weisungen, ohne sich den Ladeschein vorlegen zu lassen, haftet er dem aus dem Ladeschein Berechtigten für den Schaden, der diesem daraus entsteht. Die Haftung ist auf den Betrag begrenzt, der bei Verlust des Gutes zu zahlen wäre.

**§ 446**
**Compliance with instructions**

(1) Where a bill of lading has been issued, only the legitimate holder of the bill of lading is entitled to the right of disposition pursuant to §§ 418 and 419. The freight carrier may carry out instructions only upon presentation of the bill of lading. He may not, however, carry out instructions of the legitimate holder of the bill of lading if he knows that the legitimate holder of the bill of lading is not the rightful holder of the bill of lading or if, due to gross negligence, he does not know this.

Where the freight carrier follows instructions without having the bill of lading presented to him, he is liable for any resulting damage incurred by the rightful holder of the bill of lading for this reason. The liability is limited to the amount which would be payable upon loss of the goods.

**§ 447**
**Einwendungen**

(1) Dem aus dem Ladeschein Berechtigten kann der Frachtführer nur solche Einwendungen entgegensetzen, die die Gültigkeit der Erklärungen im Ladeschein betreffen oder sich aus dem Inhalt des Ladescheins ergeben oder dem Frachtführer unmittelbar gegenüber dem aus dem Ladeschein Berechtigten zustehen. Eine Vereinbarung, auf die im Ladeschein lediglich verwiesen wird, ist nicht Inhalt des Ladescheins.

(2) Wird ein ausführender Frachtführer nach § 437 von dem aus dem Ladeschein Berechtigten in Anspruch genommen, kann auch der ausführende Frachtführer die Einwendungen nach Absatz 1 geltend machen.

**§ 447**
**Objections**

(1) The freight carrier can only raise objections against the rightful holder of the bill of lading that concern the validity of the declarations made in the bill of lading or that result from the content of the bill of lading or that the freight carrier is directly entitled to vis-à-vis the rightful holder of the bill of lading. An agreement to which the bill of lading merely makes reference is not content of the bill of lading.

(2) Where claims are asserted by the rightful holder of the bill of lading against an acting freight carrier pursuant to § 437, the acting freight carrier can also raise objections pursuant to subsection 1.

**§ 448**
**Traditionswirkung des Ladescheins**

Die Begebung des Ladescheins an den darin benannten Empfänger hat, sofern der Frachtführer das Gut im Besitz hat, für den Erwerb von Rechten an dem Gut dieselben Wirkungen wie die Übergabe des Gutes. Gleiches gilt für die Übertragung des Ladescheins an Dritte.

**§ 448**
**Effect of delivery of bill of lading**

The issuance of the bill of lading to the consignee designated therein has, if the goods are in possession of the freight carrier, the same effect with respect to the acquisition of rights in the goods as the delivery of the goods. The same applies to the transfer of the bill of lading to a third party.

## § 449
## Abweichende Vereinbarungen über die Haftung

(1) Soweit der Frachtvertrag nicht die Beförderung von Briefen oder briefähnlichen Sendungen zum Gegenstand hat, kann von den Haftungsvorschriften in § 413 Absatz 2, den §§ 414, 418 Absatz 6, § 422 Absatz 3, den §§ 425 bis 438, 445 Absatz 3 und § 446 Absatz 2 nur durch Vereinbarung abgewichen werden, die im Einzelnen ausgehandelt wird, auch wenn sie für eine Mehrzahl von gleichartigen Verträgen zwischen denselben Vertragsparteien getroffen wird. Der Frachtführer kann sich jedoch auf eine Bestimmung im Ladeschein, die von den in Satz 1 genannten Vorschriften zu Lasten des aus dem Ladeschein Berechtigten abweicht, nicht gegenüber einem im Ladeschein benannten Empfänger, an den der Ladeschein begeben wurde, sowie gegenüber einem Dritten, dem der Ladeschein übertragen wurde, berufen.

(2) Abweichend von Absatz 1 kann die vom Frachtführer zu leistende Entschädigung wegen Verlust oder Beschädigung des Gutes auch durch vorformulierte Vertragsbedingungen auf einen anderen als den in § 431 Absatz 1 und 2 vorgesehenen Betrag begrenzt werden, wenn dieser Betrag

1. zwischen 2 und 40 Rechnungseinheiten liegt und der Verwender der vorformulierten Vertragsbedingungen seinen Vertragspartner in geeigneter Weise darauf hinweist, dass diese einen anderen als den gesetzlich vorgesehenen Betrag vorsehen, oder
2. für den Verwender der vorformulierten Vertragsbedingungen ungünstiger ist als der in § 431 Absatz 1 und 2 vorgesehene Betrag.

Ferner kann abweichend von Absatz 1 durch vorformulierte Vertragsbedingungen die vom Absender nach § 414 zu leistende Entschädigung der Höhe nach beschränkt werden.

(3) Ist der Absender ein Verbraucher, so kann in keinem Fall zu seinem Nachteil von den in Absatz 1 Satz 1 genannten Vorschriften abgewichen werden, es sei denn, der Frachtvertrag hat die Beförderung von Briefen oder briefähnlichen Sendungen zum Gegenstand.

(4) Unterliegt der Frachtvertrag ausländischem Recht, so sind die Absätze 1 bis 3 gleichwohl anzuwenden, wenn nach dem Vertrag sowohl der Ort der Übernahme als auch der Ort der Ablieferung des Gutes im Inland liegen.

## § 449
## Deviating agreements on liability

(1) Unless the subject of the freight agreement is not the shipment of letters or letter-like consignments, one may deviate from the liability provisions in § 413(2), §§ 414, 418(6), § 422(3), §§ 425 to 438, 445(3) and § 446(2) only by an agreement which has been negotiated in detail even if it applies to a number of similar contracts between the same parties. The freight carrier, however, cannot assert a provision in the bill of lading that deviates from the provisions mentioned in sentence 1 at the expense of the rightful holder of the bill of lading vis-à-vis a consignee designated in the bill of lading to whom the inland bill of lading was handed over or vis-à-vis a third party to whom the bill of lading was transferred.

(2) Notwithstanding subsection 1, the indemnification to be paid by the freight carrier because of loss of or damage to the goods may also be limited to an amount other than the amount provided for in § 431(1) and (2) by means of pre-formulated contractual provisions, provided that this amount

1. is between 2 and 40 accounting units and the user of the pre-formulated contractual provisions has duly pointed out to his contractual partner that they specify an amount different from that provided for by law, or
2. is less advantageous to the user of the pre-formulated contractual provisions than the amount provided for in § 431(1) and (2).

Furthermore, notwithstanding subsection 1, the amount of the indemnification to be paid by the shipper pursuant to § 414 may be limited by means of pre-formulated contractual provisions.

(3) Where the shipper is a consumer, the provisions mentioned in subsection 1, sentence 1 cannot, under any circumstances, be deviated from to his detriment unless the subject of the freight agreement is the shipment of letters or letter-like consignments.

(4) If the freight agreement is subject to foreign law, subsections 1 to 3 are still applicable if, according to the agreement, the place of acceptance and the place for delivery of the goods are in Germany.

### §450
### Anwendung von Seefrachtrecht

Hat der Frachtvertrag die Beförderung des Gutes ohne Umladung sowohl auf Binnen- als auch auf Seegewässern zum Gegenstand, so ist auf den Vertrag Seefrachtrecht anzuwenden, wenn

1. ein Konnossement ausgestellt ist oder
2. die auf Seegewässern zurückzulegende Strecke die größere ist.

### §450
### Application of maritime shipping law

Where the freight agreement deals with the shipment of the goods without transhipment by both inland waterways and sea, maritime shipping law shall apply to the contract where

1. a maritime bill of lading has been issued; or
2. the distance to be covered by sea is the longer one.

### §§451–451h
[...]

### §§451–451h
[...]

### §452
### Frachtvertrag über eine Beförderung mit verschiedenartigen Beförderungsmitteln

Wird die Beförderung des Gutes auf Grund eines einheitlichen Frachtvertrags mit verschiedenartigen Beförderungsmitteln durchgeführt und wären, wenn über jeden Teil der Beförderung mit jeweils einem Beförderungsmittel (Teilstrecke) zwischen den Vertragsparteien ein gesonderter Vertrag abgeschlossen worden wäre, mindestens zwei dieser Verträge verschiedenen Rechtsvorschriften unterworfen, so sind auf den Vertrag die Vorschriften des Ersten Unterabschnitts anzuwenden, soweit die folgenden besonderen Vorschriften oder anzuwendende internationale Übereinkommen nichts anderes bestimmen. Dies gilt auch dann, wenn ein Teil der Beförderung über See durchgeführt wird.

### §452
### Freight agreement pertaining to a shipment by different means of transportation

Where, based on a uniform freight agreement, the shipment of the goods is carried out by different means of transportation and where, if a separate agreement had been made between the parties pertaining to each part of the shipment with one means of transportation (partial route), at least two of these agreements would have been subject to different legal regulations, the provisions of the First Subpart are to be applied to the agreement to the extent that the following special provisions or applicable international conventions do not provide otherwise. This also applies if a part of the shipment is carried out on sea.

### §452a
### Bekannter Schadensort

Steht fest, dass der Verlust, die Beschädigung oder das Ereignis, das zu einer Überschreitung der Lieferfrist geführt hat, auf einer bestimmten Teilstrecke eingetreten ist, so bestimmt sich die Haftung des Frachtführers abweichend von den Vorschriften des Ersten Unterabschnitts nach den Rechtsvorschriften, die auf einen Vertrag über eine Beförderung auf dieser Teilstrecke anzuwenden wären. Der Beweis dafür, dass der Verlust, die Beschädigung oder das zu einer Überschreitung der Lieferfrist führende Ereignis auf einer bestimmten Teilstrecke eingetreten ist, obliegt demjenigen, der dies behauptet.

### §452a
### Identified place where damage occurred

Where it is certain that the loss, the damage or the incident which led to non-compliance with the delivery period has occurred on a particular partial route, the liability of the freight carrier is determined, notwithstanding the provisions of the First Subpart, in accordance with the legal regulations that would be applicable to a contract pertaining to a shipment on this partial route. The proof showing that the loss, the damage or the event resulting in non-compliance with the delivery period occurred on a particular partial route must be furnished by the person who asserts this.

**§ 452b**
**Schadensanzeige. Verjährung**

(1) § 438 ist unabhängig davon anzuwenden, ob der Schadensort unbekannt ist, bekannt ist oder später bekannt wird. Die für die Schadensanzeige vorgeschriebene Form und Frist ist auch gewahrt, wenn die Vorschriften eingehalten werden, die auf einen Vertrag über eine Beförderung auf der letzten Teilstrecke anzuwenden wären.

(2) Für den Beginn der Verjährung des Anspruchs wegen Verlust, Beschädigung oder Überschreitung der Lieferfrist ist, wenn auf den Ablieferungszeitpunkt abzustellen ist, der Zeitpunkt der Ablieferung an den Empfänger maßgebend. Der Anspruch verjährt auch bei bekanntem Schadensort frühestens nach Maßgabe des § 439.

**§ 452b**
**Notification of damage. Limitation**

(1) § 438 shall be applied regardless of whether the place where the damage occurred is unknown, known or becomes known later. The form and time limit prescribed for the notification of damage shall also be deemed to have been complied with where the provisions which would have applied to a freight agreement covering the last partial route are complied with.

(2) If the point in time of delivery is to be taken as the basis when determining the beginning of the limitation period pertaining to claims for losses, damage or failure to comply with the delivery period, the point in time of delivery to the consignee is decisive. The claim prescribes at the earliest in accordance with § 439, even if the place where the damage occurred is known.

**§ 452c**
**Umzugsvertrag über eine Beförderung mit verschiedenartigen Beförderungsmitteln**

Hat der Frachtvertrag die Beförderung von Umzugsgut mit verschiedenartigen Beförderungsmitteln zum Gegenstand, so sind auf den Vertrag die Vorschriften des Zweiten Unterabschnitts anzuwenden. § 452a ist nur anzuwenden, soweit für die Teilstrecke, auf der der Schaden eingetreten ist, Bestimmungen eines für die Bundesrepublik Deutschland verbindlichen internationalen Übereinkommens gelten.

**§ 452c**
**Relocation agreement pertaining to shipment by different means of transportation**

Where the freight agreement provides for the shipment of goods of relocation with different means of transportation, the provisions of the Second Subpart apply. § 452a applies only to the extent that provisions of an international convention binding for the Federal Republic of Germany apply to the partial route where the damage occurred.

**§ 452d**
**Abweichende Vereinbarungen**

(1) Von der Regelung des § 452b Abs. 2 Satz 1 kann nur durch Vereinbarung abgewichen werden, die im Einzelnen ausgehandelt ist, auch wenn diese für eine Mehrzahl von gleichartigen Verträgen zwischen denselben Vertragsparteien getroffen ist. Von den übrigen Regelungen dieses Unterabschnitts kann nur insoweit durch vertragliche Vereinbarung abgewichen werden, als die darin in Bezug genommenen Vorschriften abweichende Vereinbarungen zulassen.

(2) Abweichend von Absatz 1 kann jedoch auch durch vorformulierte Vertragsbedingungen vereinbart werden, dass sich die Haftung bei bekanntem Schadensort (§ 452a)

1. unabhängig davon, auf welcher Teilstrecke der Schaden eintreten wird, oder
2. für den Fall des Schadenseintritts auf einer in der Vereinbarung genannten Teilstrecke

**§ 452d**
**Deviating agreements**

(1) One may deviate from the provisions of § 452b(2), sentence 1 only by an agreement which has been negotiated in detail, even if such agreement applies to a number of similar contracts between the same parties. One may deviate from the other provisions of this Subpart by contractual agreements only to the extent that the pertinent provisions permit deviating agreements.

(2) Notwithstanding subsection 1, it can be agreed, however, also by means of pre-formulated contractual provisions that the liability, in the event that the place of damage is known (§ 452a), is determined by the provisions of the First Subpart

1. irrespective of on which partial route the damage occurred, or
2. if the damage occurred on a partial route mentioned in the agreement.

nach den Vorschriften des Ersten Unterabschnitts bestimmt.

(3) Vereinbarungen, die die Anwendung der für eine Teilstrecke zwingend geltenden Bestimmungen eines für die Bundesrepublik Deutschland verbindlichen internationalen Übereinkommens ausschließen, sind unwirksam.

(3) Agreements that exclude the applicability of provisions of an international convention binding for the Federal Republic of Germany which are mandatory for a partial route are invalid.

## Fünfter Abschnitt Speditionsgeschäft

## Part Five Forwarding business

### § 453 Speditionsvertrag

(1) Durch den Speditionsvertrag wird der Spediteur verpflichtet, die Versendung des Gutes zu besorgen.

(2) Der Versender wird verpflichtet, die vereinbarte Vergütung zu zahlen.

(3) Die Vorschriften dieses Abschnitts gelten nur, wenn die Besorgung der Versendung zum Betrieb eines gewerblichen Unternehmens gehört. Erfordert das Unternehmen nach Art oder Umfang einen in kaufmännischer Weise eingerichteten Geschäftsbetrieb nicht und ist die Firma des Unternehmens auch nicht nach § 2 in das Handelsregister eingetragen, so sind in Ansehung des Speditionsgeschäfts auch insoweit die Vorschriften des Ersten Abschnitts des Vierten Buches ergänzend anzuwenden; dies gilt jedoch nicht für die §§ 348 bis 350.

### § 453 Forwarding agreement

(1) The forwarding agreement obligates the forwarding agent to handle the shipment of the goods.

(2) The shipper is obligated to pay the agreed remuneration.

(3) The provisions of this part apply only if the handling of the shipment is part of the operation of a commercial enterprise. Where the nature or scope of the enterprise does not require a commercially organised business operation and where the name of the enterprise is neither registered in the Commercial Register pursuant to § 2, the provisions of the First Part of the Fourth Book are to be applied in a supplementary manner with respect to the forwarding business; this does not apply, however, to §§ 348 to 350.

### § 454 Besorgung der Versendung

(1) Die Pflicht, die Versendung zu besorgen, umfasst die Organisation der Beförderung, insbesondere

1. die Bestimmung des Beförderungsmittels und des Beförderungsweges,
2. die Auswahl ausführender Unternehmer, den Abschluss der für die Versendung erforderlichen Fracht-, Lager- und Speditionsverträge sowie die Erteilung von Informationen und Weisungen an die ausführenden Unternehmer und
3. die Sicherung von Schadensersatzansprüchen des Versenders.

(2) Zu den Pflichten des Spediteurs zählt ferner die Ausführung sonstiger vereinbarter auf die Beförderung bezogener Leistungen wie die Versicherung und Verpackung des Gutes, seine Kennzeichnung und die Zollbehandlung. Der Spediteur schuldet jedoch nur den Abschluss der zur Erbringung dieser Leistungen erforderlichen Verträge, wenn sich dies aus der Vereinbarung ergibt.

### § 454 Handling the shipment

(1) The obligation to handle the shipment includes the organisation of the shipment, in particular

1. the determination of the means of shipment and the route of shipment,
2. the selection of enterprises to carry out the shipment, the conclusion of the freight, warehouse and forwarding contracts necessary for the shipment as well as the giving of information and instructions to the enterprises carrying out the shipment, and
3. securing the shipper's claims for damages.

(2) The obligations of the forwarding agent also include the carrying out of other services agreed upon and pertaining to the shipment, such as the insurance and packaging of the goods, their labelling and customs handling. The forwarding agent is, however, only obligated to conclude the contracts necessary to procure these services where this follows from the forwarding agreement.

(3) Der Spediteur schließt die erforderlichen Verträge im eigenen Namen oder, sofern er hierzu bevollmächtigt ist, im Namen des Versenders ab.

(4) Der Spediteur hat bei Erfüllung seiner Pflichten das Interesse des Versenders wahrzunehmen und dessen Weisungen zu befolgen.

### § 455
### Behandlung des Gutes, Begleitpapiere, Mitteilungs- und Auskunftspflichten

(1) Der Versender ist verpflichtet, das Gut, soweit erforderlich, zu verpacken und zu kennzeichnen und Urkunden zur Verfügung zu stellen sowie alle Auskünfte zu erteilen, deren der Spediteur zur Erfüllung seiner Pflichten bedarf. Soll gefährliches Gut versendet werden, so hat der Versender dem Spediteur rechtzeitig in Textform die genaue Art der Gefahr und, soweit erforderlich, zu ergreifende Vorsichtsmaßnahmen mitzuteilen.

(2) Der Versender hat, auch wenn ihn kein Verschulden trifft, dem Spediteur Schäden und Aufwendungen zu ersetzen, die verursacht werden durch

1. ungenügende Verpackung oder Kennzeichnung,
2. Unterlassen der Mitteilung über die Gefährlichkeit des Gutes oder
3. Fehlen, Unvollständigkeit oder Unrichtigkeit der Urkunden oder Auskünfte, die für eine amtliche Behandlung des Gutes erforderlich sind.

§ 414 Absatz 2 ist entsprechend anzuwenden.

(3) Ist der Versender ein Verbraucher, so hat er dem Spediteur Schäden und Aufwendungen nach Absatz 2 nur zu ersetzen, soweit ihn ein Verschulden trifft.

### § 456
### Fälligkeit der Vergütung

Die Vergütung ist zu zahlen, wenn das Gut dem Frachtführer oder Verfrachter übergeben worden ist.

### § 457
### Forderungen des Versenders

Der Versender kann Forderungen aus einem Vertrag, den der Spediteur für Rechnung des Versenders im eigenen Namen abgeschlossen hat, erst nach der Abtretung geltend machen. Solche Forderungen sowie das in Erfüllung solcher Forderungen Erlangte gelten jedoch im Verhältnis zu den Gläubigern des Spediteurs als auf den Versender übertragen.

(3) The forwarding agent concludes the necessary contracts in his own name or, to the extent he has been authorised to do so, in the name of the shipper.

(4) The forwarding agent shall, in fulfilling his duties, protect the interests of the shipper and follow his instructions.

### § 455
### Handling of goods; accompanying documents; duties to notify and inform

(1) The shipper shall, to the extent that necessary, package and label the goods, make documents available and provide all the information which the forwarding agent needs to discharge his duties. Where dangerous goods are to be shipped, the shipper shall inform the forwarding agent – in a timely manner and in text form about the specific kind of danger and, if necessary, the precautions to be taken.

(2) The shipper shall, even if he is not at fault, reimburse the forwarding agent for damages and expenditures which are caused by the following circumstances:

1. insufficient packaging or labelling,
2. failure to disclose the dangerous nature of the goods, or
3. lack, incompleteness or incorrectness of the documents or information required for official handling of the goods.

§ 414(2) applies accordingly.

(3) Where the shipper is a consumer, he shall reimburse the forwarding agent for damages and expenditures pursuant to subsection 2 only to the extent that he is at fault.

### § 456
### Due date of the remuneration

The remuneration is due when the goods have been handed over to the freight carrier or the charterer.

### § 457
### Claims of the shipper

The shipper can assert claims arising out of an agreement which the forwarding agent has concluded in his own name for the account of the shipper only after it has been assigned to him. However, in relation to the creditors of the forwarding agent, such claims as well as what has been obtained in fulfilment of such claims are deemed to have been transferred to the shipper.

## § 458
## Selbsteintritt

Der Spediteur ist befugt, die Beförderung des Gutes durch Selbsteintritt auszuführen. Macht er von dieser Befugnis Gebrauch, so hat er hinsichtlich der Beförderung die Rechte und Pflichten eines Frachtführers oder Verfrachters. In diesem Fall kann er neben der Vergütung für seine Tätigkeit als Spediteur die gewöhnliche Fracht verlangen.

## § 458
## The forwarding agent's right to self-substitution

The forwarding agent is authorised to carry out the shipment by way of self-substitution. If he makes use of this right, he has the rights and obligations of a freight carrier or charterer with respect to the shipment. In this case he can claim the normal freight charges in addition to the remuneration for his activity as forwarding agent.

## § 459
## Spedition zu festen Kosten

Soweit als Vergütung ein bestimmter Betrag vereinbart ist, der Kosten für die Beförderung einschließt, hat der Spediteur hinsichtlich der Beförderung die Rechte und Pflichten eines Frachtführers oder Verfrachters. In diesem Fall hat er Anspruch auf Ersatz seiner Aufwendungen nur, soweit dies üblich ist.

## § 459
## Forwarding at fixed costs

To the extent that a fixed amount which includes the cost of the shipment has been agreed upon as remuneration, the forwarding agent has the rights and obligations of a freight carrier or a charterer with respect to the shipment. In this case he has a claim for reimbursement of his expenditures only to the extent that this is customary.

## § 460
## Sammelladung

(1) Der Spediteur ist befugt, die Versendung des Gutes zusammen mit Gut eines anderen Versenders auf Grund eines für seine Rechnung über eine Sammelladung geschlossenen Frachtvertrages zu bewirken.

(2) Macht der Spediteur von dieser Befugnis Gebrauch, so hat er hinsichtlich der Beförderung in Sammelladung die Rechte und Pflichten eines Frachtführers oder Verfrachters. In diesem Fall kann der Spediteur eine den Umständen nach angemessene Vergütung verlangen, höchstens aber die für die Beförderung des einzelnen Gutes gewöhnliche Fracht.

## § 460
## Consolidated consignment

(1) The forwarding agent is authorised to effect the shipping of the goods together with goods of another shipper based on a forwarding agreement concerning a consolidated consignment concluded for his account.

(2) Where the forwarding agent makes use of this authorisation, he shall have the rights and duties of a freight carrier or charterer with respect to the shipping as a consolidated consignment. In this case the forwarding agent may claim remuneration reasonable according to the circumstances, but not more than the customary freight charges for the shipping of the individual goods.

## § 461
## Haftung des Spediteurs

(1) Der Spediteur haftet für den Schaden, der durch Verlust oder Beschädigung des in seiner Obhut befindlichen Gutes entsteht. Die §§ 426, 427, 429, 430, 431 Abs. 1, 2 und 4, die §§ 432, 434 bis 436 sind entsprechend anzuwenden.

(2) Für Schaden, der nicht durch Verlust oder Beschädigung des in der Obhut des Spediteurs befindlichen Gutes entstanden ist, haftet der Spediteur, wenn er eine ihm nach § 454 obliegende Pflicht verletzt. Von dieser Haftung ist er befreit, wenn der Schaden durch die Sorgfalt eines ordentlichen Kaufmanns nicht abgewendet werden konnte.

## § 461
## Liability of the forwarding agent

(1) The forwarding agent is liable for the damage which arises from loss of or damage to goods in his custody. §§ 426, 427, 429, 430, 431(1), (2) and (4), §§ 432, 434 to 436 apply analogously.

(2) The forwarding agent is liable for damage which has not arisen from loss of or damage to the goods in the custody of the forwarding agent if he violates a duty incumbent on him pursuant to § 454. He is exempted from this liability if the damage could not have been averted by exercising the care of a prudent merchant.

(3) Hat bei der Entstehung des Schadens ein Verhalten des Versenders oder ein besonderer Mangel des Gutes mitgewirkt, so hängen die Verpflichtung zum Ersatz sowie der Umfang des zu leistenden Ersatzes davon ab, inwieweit diese Umstände zu dem Schaden beigetragen haben.

(3) If conduct on the part of the shipper or a special defect of the goods has contributed to the occurrence of the damage, the obligation to pay damages as well as the amount of the damages to be paid depend on the extent to which these circumstances have contributed to the damage.

**§ 462**
**Haftung für andere**

Der Spediteur hat Handlungen und Unterlassungen seiner Leute in gleichem Umfang zu vertreten wie eigene Handlungen und Unterlassungen, wenn die Leute in Ausübung ihrer Verrichtungen handeln. Gleiches gilt für Handlungen und Unterlassungen anderer Personen, deren er sich bei Erfüllung seiner Pflicht, die Versendung zu besorgen, bedient.

**§ 462**
**Liability for others**

The forwarding agent is liable for the acts and omissions of his auxiliary persons to the same extent as for his own acts and omissions provided the auxiliary persons act in performance of their duties. The same applies for acts and omissions of other persons whose services he uses to fulfil his duty to carry out the shipment.

**§ 463**
**Verjährung**

Auf die Verjährung der Ansprüche aus einer Leistung, die den Vorschriften dieses Abschnitts unterliegt, ist § 439 entsprechend anzuwenden.

**§ 463**
**Statute of limitations**

§ 439 applies analogously to the limitation for claims arising from a service which is subject to the provisions of this Part.

**§ 464**
**Pfandrecht des Spediteurs**

Der Spediteur hat für alle Forderungen aus dem Speditionsvertrag ein Pfandrecht an dem ihm zur Versendung übergebenen Gut des Versenders oder eines Dritten, der der Versendung des Gutes zugestimmt hat. An dem Gut des Versenders hat der Spediteur auch ein Pfandrecht für alle unbestrittenen Forderungen aus anderen mit dem Versender abgeschlossenen Speditions-, Fracht-, Seefracht- und Lagerverträgen. § 440 Absatz 1 Satz 3 und Absatz 2 bis 4 ist entsprechend anzuwenden.

**§ 464**
**Lien of the forwarding agent**

The forwarding agent shall have a lien on the goods of the shipper or a third party consenting to the shipment of the goods that have been handed over to him for all claims arising out of the forwarding agency agreement. The forwarding agent shall also have a lien on the goods of the shipper for all undisputed claims arising out of other forwarding agency, freight, maritime shipping and warehouse agreements concluded with the shipper. § 440(1), sentence 3 and (2) to (4) apply analogously.

**§ 465**
**Nachfolgender Spediteur**

(1) Wirkt an einer Beförderung neben dem Frachtführer auch ein Spediteur mit und hat dieser die Ablieferung zu bewirken, so ist auf den Spediteur § 441 Absatz 1 entsprechend anzuwenden.

(2) Wird ein vorhergehender Frachtführer oder Spediteur von einem nachfolgenden Spediteur befriedigt, so gehen Forderung und Pfandrecht des ersteren auf den letzteren über.

**§ 465**
**Subsequent forwarding agent**

(1) If, in addition to the freight carrier, a forwarding agent is also involved in the shipment and he is responsible for the delivery, § 441(1) shall apply analogously to the forwarding agent.

(2) If a preceding freight carrier or forwarding agent is paid by a subsequent forwarding agent, the claim and lien of the former are transferred to the latter.

## § 466
## Abweichende Vereinbarungen über die Haftung

(1) Soweit der Speditionsvertrag nicht die Versendung von Briefen oder briefähnlichen Sendungen zum Gegenstand hat, kann von den Haftungsvorschriften in § 455 Absatz 2 und 3, § 461 Absatz 1 sowie in den §§ 462 und 463 nur durch Vereinbarung abgewichen werden, die im Einzelnen ausgehandelt wird, auch wenn sie für eine Mehrzahl von gleichartigen Verträgen zwischen denselben Vertragsparteien getroffen wird.

(2) Abweichend von Absatz 1 kann die vom Spediteur zu leistende Entschädigung wegen Verlust oder Beschädigung des Gutes auch durch vorformulierte Vertragsbedingungen auf einen anderen als den in § 431 Absatz 1 und 2 vorgesehenen Betrag begrenzt werden, wenn dieser Betrag

1. zwischen 2 und 40 Rechnungseinheiten liegt und der Verwender der vorformulierten Vertragsbedingungen seinen Vertragspartner in geeigneter Weise darauf hinweist, dass diese einen anderen als den gesetzlich vorgesehenen Betrag vorsehen, oder
2. für den Verwender der vorformulierten Vertragsbedingungen ungünstiger ist als der in § 431 Absatz 1 und 2 vorgesehene Betrag.

Ferner kann durch vorformulierte Vertragsbedingungen die vom Versender nach § 455 Absatz 2 oder 3 zu leistende Entschädigung der Höhe nach beschränkt werden.

(3) Von § 458 Satz 2, § 459 Satz 1 und § 460 Absatz 2 Satz 1 kann nur insoweit durch vertragliche Vereinbarung abgewichen werden, als die darin in Bezug genommenen Vorschriften abweichende Vereinbarungen zulassen.

(4) Ist der Versender ein Verbraucher, so kann in keinem Fall zu seinem Nachteil von den in Absatz 1 genannten Vorschriften abgewichen werden, es sei denn, der Speditionsvertrag hat die Beförderung von Briefen oder briefähnlichen Sendungen zum Gegenstand.

(5) Unterliegt der Speditionsvertrag ausländischem Recht, so sind die Absätze 1 bis 4 gleichwohl anzuwenden, wenn nach dem Vertrag sowohl der Ort der Übernahme als auch der Ort der Ablieferung des Gutes im Inland liegen.

## § 466
## Deviating agreements on liability

(1) Unless the subject of the forwarding agreement is the shipment of letters or letter-like consignments, one may deviate from the liability provisions in § 455(2) and (3), § 461(1) as well as in §§ 462 and 463 only by an agreement which has been negotiated in detail, even if it applies to a number of similar contracts between the same parties.

(2) Notwithstanding subsection 1, the indemnification to be paid by the forwarding agent because of loss of or damage to the goods may, however, be limited to an amount other than the amount provided for in § 431(1) and (2) by pre-formulated contractual provisions, provided that this amount

1. is between 2 and 40 accounting units and the user of the pre-formulated contractual provisions has duly pointed out to his contractual partner that they specify an amount different from that provided for by law, or
2. is less favourable for the user of the pre-formulated contractual provisions than the amount provided for in § 431(1) and (2).

Furthermore, the indemnification to be paid by the shipper pursuant to § 455(2) or (3) may be limited in its amount by pre-formulated contractual provisions.

(3) One may deviate from § 458 sentence 2, § 459 sentence 1 and § 460(2), sentence 1 by contractual agreement only to the extent that the provisions referred to therein permit deviating agreements.

(4) Where the shipper is a consumer, the provisions referred to in subsection 1 cannot, under any circumstances, be deviated from to his detriment unless the subject of the forwarding agreement is the shipment of letters or letter-like consignments.

(5) If the forwarding agreement is subject to foreign law, subsections 1 to 4 shall nevertheless apply if, according to the agreement, the place of acceptance of the goods and the place of delivery of the goods are in Germany.

## Sechster Abschnitt
## Lagergeschäft

### § 467
### Lagergeschäft

(1) Durch den Lagervertrag wird der Lagerhalter verpflichtet, das Gut zu lagern und aufzubewahren.

(2) Der Einlagerer wird verpflichtet, die vereinbarte Vergütung zu zahlen.

(3) Die Vorschriften dieses Abschnitts gelten nur, wenn die Lagerung und Aufbewahrung zum Betrieb eines gewerblichen Unternehmens gehören. Erfordert das Unternehmen nach Art oder Umfang einen in kaufmännischer Weise eingerichteten Geschäftsbetrieb nicht und ist die Firma des Unternehmens auch nicht nach § 2 in das Handelsregister eingetragen, so sind in Ansehung des Lagergeschäfts auch insoweit die Vorschriften des Ersten Abschnitts des Vierten Buches ergänzend anzuwenden; dies gilt jedoch nicht für die §§ 348 bis 350.

### § 468
### Behandlung des Gutes, Begleitpapiere, Mitteilungs- und Auskunftspflichten

(1) Der Einlagerer ist verpflichtet, dem Lagerhalter, wenn gefährliches Gut eingelagert werden soll, rechtzeitig in Textform die genaue Art der Gefahr und, soweit erforderlich, zu ergreifende Vorsichtsmaßnahmen mitzuteilen. Er hat ferner das Gut, soweit erforderlich, zu verpacken und zu kennzeichnen und Urkunden zur Verfügung zu stellen sowie alle Auskünfte zu erteilen, die der Lagerhalter zur Erfüllung seiner Pflichten benötigt.

(2) Ist der Einlagerer ein Verbraucher, so ist abweichend von Absatz 1

1. der Lagerhalter verpflichtet, das Gut, soweit erforderlich, zu verpacken und zu kennzeichnen,
2. der Einlagerer lediglich verpflichtet, den Lagerhalter über die von dem Gut ausgehende Gefahr allgemein zu unterrichten; die Unterrichtung bedarf keiner Form.

Der Lagerhalter hat in diesem Falle den Einlagerer über dessen Pflicht nach Satz 1 Nr. 2 sowie über die von ihm zu beachtenden Verwaltungsvorschriften über eine amtliche Behandlung des Gutes zu unterrichten.

## Part Six
## Warehousing

### § 467
### Warehousing agreement

(1) The warehousing agreement obligates the warehouse keeper to warehouse and store the goods.

(2) The person storing the goods is obligated to pay the agreed remuneration.

(3) The provisions of this part apply only if warehousing and storage are part of the operation of a commercial enterprise. Where the nature or scope of the business do not require a commercially organised business operation and where the firm name is neither registered in the Commercial Register pursuant to § 2, the provisions of the First Part of the Fourth Book are to be applied in a supplementary manner with respect to the warehousing business; this does not apply, however, to §§ 348 to 350.

### § 468
### Handling of the goods; accompanying documents; duties to notify and inform

(1) Where dangerous goods are to be warehoused, the person storing the goods shall inform the warehouse keeper in a timely manner and in text form about the specific kind of danger and, if necessary, the precautions to be taken. He shall also, to the extent necessary, package and label the goods, make documents available and provide all the information the warehouse keeper needs in order to discharge his duties.

(2) Where the person storing the goods is a consumer, contrary to subsection 1

1. the warehouse keeper is obligated, to the extent necessary, to package and label the goods,
2. the person storing the goods is merely obligated to advise the warehouse keeper about the danger emanating from the goods in a general manner; the information does not have to be in any special form.

The warehouse keeper shall in this case advise the person storing the goods about the latter's duty according to sentence 1, no. 2 as well as about the administrative regulations pertaining to official handling of the goods to be complied with by him.

(3) Der Einlagerer hat, auch wenn ihn kein Verschulden trifft, dem Lagerhalter Schäden und Aufwendungen zu ersetzen, die verursacht werden durch

1. ungenügende Verpackung oder Kennzeichnung,
2. Unterlassen der Mitteilung über die Gefährlichkeit des Gutes oder
3. Fehlen, Unvollständigkeit oder Unrichtigkeit der in § 413 Abs. 1 genannten Urkunden oder Auskünfte.

§ 414 Absatz 2 ist entsprechend anzuwenden.

(4) Ist der Einlagerer ein Verbraucher, so hat er dem Lagerhalter Schäden und Aufwendungen nach Absatz 3 nur zu ersetzen, soweit ihn ein Verschulden trifft.

(3) The person storing the goods shall – even if he is not at fault – reimburse the warehouse keeper for damages and expenditures that are caused by

1. insufficient packaging or labelling,
2. failure to disclose the dangerous nature of the goods, or
3. lack, incompleteness or incorrectness of the documents or information mentioned in § 413(1).

§ 414(2) applies analogously.

(4) Where the person storing the goods is a consumer, he shall reimburse the warehouse keeper for damages and expenditures pursuant to subsection 3 only to the extent that he is at fault.

## § 469
## Sammellagerung

(1) Der Lagerhalter ist nur berechtigt, vertretbare Sachen mit anderen Sachen gleicher Art und Güte zu vermischen, wenn die beteiligten Einlagerer ausdrücklich einverstanden sind.

(2) Ist der Lagerhalter berechtigt, Gut zu vermischen, so steht vom Zeitpunkt der Einlagerung ab den Eigentümern der eingelagerten Sachen Miteigentum nach Bruchteilen zu.

(3) Der Lagerhalter kann jedem Einlagerer den ihm gebührenden Anteil ausliefern, ohne dass er hierzu der Genehmigung der übrigen Beteiligten bedarf.

## § 469
## Collective storage

(1)The warehouse keeper is entitled to mingle fungible goods with goods of the same kind and quality only where the participating persons storing goods have expressly permitted him to do so.

(2) Where the warehouse keeper is entitled to mingle goods, the owners of the warehoused goods, from the point in time of the warehousing onwards, will be fractional co-owners.

(3) The warehouse keeper can deliver to each person storing goods the share due to him without needing the consent of the other participants therefor.

## § 470
## Empfang des Gutes

Befindet sich Gut, das dem Lagerhalter zugesandt ist, beim Empfang in einem beschädigten oder mangelhaften Zustand, der äußerlich erkennbar ist, so hat der Lagerhalter Schadenersatzansprüche des Einlagerers zu sichern und dem Einlagerer unverzüglich Nachricht zu geben.

## § 470
## Receipt of the goods

If, upon receipt, the goods that have been sent to the warehouse keeper are in a damaged or defective condition that is externally visible, the warehouse keeper shall secure claims for damages of the person storing the goods and notify the person storing the goods without undue delay.

## § 471
## Erhaltung des Gutes

(1) Der Lagerhalter hat dem Einlagerer die Besichtigung des Gutes, die Entnahme von Proben und die zur Erhaltung des Gutes notwendigen Handlungen während der Geschäftsstunden zu gestatten. Er ist jedoch berechtigt und im Falle der Sammellagerung auch verpflichtet, die zur Erhaltung des Gutes erforderlichen Arbeiten selbst vorzunehmen.

## § 471
## Maintenance of the goods

(1) The warehouse keeper must permit the person storing the goods, during business hours, to inspect the goods, to take samples and to perform acts necessary for the maintenance of the goods. He is, however, entitled and, in case of collective storage, also obligated to perform the work necessary for the maintenance of the goods himself.

(2) Sind nach dem Empfang Veränderungen an dem Gut entstanden oder zu befürchten, die den Verlust oder die Beschädigung des Gutes oder Schäden des Lagerhalters erwarten lassen, so hat der Lagerhalter dies dem Einlagerer oder, wenn ein Lagerschein ausgestellt ist, dem letzten ihm bekannt gewordenen legitimierten Besitzer des Scheins unverzüglich anzuzeigen und dessen Weisungen einzuholen. Kann der Lagerhalter innerhalb angemessener Zeit Weisungen nicht erlangen, so hat er die angemessen erscheinenden Maßnahmen zu ergreifen. Er kann insbesondere das Gut gemäß § 373 verkaufen lassen; macht er von dieser Befugnis Gebrauch, so hat der Lagerhalter, wenn ein Lagerschein ausgestellt ist, die in § 373 Abs. 3 vorgesehene Androhung des Verkaufs sowie die in Absatz 5 derselben Vorschriften vorgesehenen Benachrichtigungen an den letzten ihm bekannt gewordenen legitimierten Besitzer des Lagerscheins zu richten.

(2) If, after receipt, changes to the goods have occurred or are to be feared which are likely to lead to the loss of or damage to the goods or damages of the warehouse keeper, the warehouse keeper shall, without undue delay, notify the person storing the goods, or if a warehouse receipt has been issued, the last legitimate holder of the receipt known to him, about the situation and ask for his instructions. If the warehouse keeper cannot obtain instructions within a reasonable period of time, he shall take such measures as seem to be reasonable. In particular, he can have the goods sold according to § 373; if he makes use of this right, the warehouse keeper shall, if a warehouse receipt has been issued, direct the notice of sale provided for in § 373(3) as well as the notification provided for in subsection 5 of the same provision to the last legitimate holder of the warehouse receipt known to him.

## § 472
## Versicherung, Einlagerung bei einem Dritten

(1) Der Lagerhalter ist verpflichtet, das Gut auf Verlangen des Einlagerers zu versichern. Ist der Einlagerer ein Verbraucher, so hat ihn der Lagerhalter auf die Möglichkeit hinzuweisen, das Gut zu versichern.

(2) Der Lagerhalter ist nur berechtigt, das Gut bei einem Dritten einzulagern, wenn der Einlagerer ihm dies ausdrücklich gestattet hat.

## § 472
## Insurance, storage with a third party

(1) The warehouse keeper is obligated to insure the goods upon request of the person storing the goods. Where the person storing the goods is a consumer, the warehouse keeper shall advise him about the possibility to insure the goods.

(2) The warehouse keeper is only entitled to store the goods with a third party if the person storing the goods has expressly permitted him to do so.

## § 473
## Dauer der Lagerung

(1) Der Einlagerer kann das Gut jederzeit herausverlangen. Ist der Lagervertrag auf unbestimmte Zeit geschlossen, so kann er den Vertrag jedoch nur unter Einhaltung einer Kündigungsfrist von einem Monat kündigen, es sei denn, es liegt ein wichtiger Grund vor, der zur Kündigung des Vertrags ohne Einhaltung der Kündigungsfrist berechtigt.

(2) Der Lagerhalter kann die Rücknahme des Gutes nach Ablauf der vereinbarten Lagerzeit oder bei Einlagerung auf unbestimmte Zeit nach Kündigung des Vertrags unter Einhaltung einer Kündigungsfrist von einem Monat verlangen. Liegt ein wichtiger Grund vor, so kann der Lagerhalter auch vor Ablauf der Lagerzeit und ohne Einhaltung einer Kündigungsfrist die Rücknahme des Gutes verlangen.

## § 473
## Duration of the warehousing

(1) The person storing the goods can demand delivery of the goods at any time. If the warehousing agreement has been concluded for an indefinite period of time, he can terminate the contract only by giving one month's notice unless there is cause that would entitle termination of the contract without notice period.

(2) The warehouse keeper may demand that the goods be taken back upon expiration of the storage period agreed upon, or in case of storage for an indefinite period of time, after the contract has been terminated on one month's notice. Where there is cause, the warehouse keeper can demand that the goods be taken back before the storage time has expired and without notice period.

(3) Ist ein Lagerschein ausgestellt, so sind die Kündigung und das Rücknahmeverlangen an den letzten dem Lagerhalter bekannt gewordenen legitimierten Besitzer des Lagerscheins zu richten.

(3) If a warehouse receipt has been issued, the notice of termination and the demand to take back the goods are to be addressed to the last legitimate holder of the warehouse receipt known to the warehouse keeper.

### § 474
### Aufwendungsersatz

Der Lagerhalter hat Anspruch auf Ersatz seiner für das Gut gemachten Aufwendungen, soweit er sie den Umständen nach für erforderlich halten durfte.

### § 474
### Reimbursement of expenditures

The warehouse keeper is entitled to reimbursement of his expenditures incurred for the goods to the extent that it was reasonable for him to regard them as necessary according to the circumstances.

### § 475
### Haftung für Verlust oder Beschädigung

Der Lagerhalter haftet für den Schaden, der durch Verlust oder Beschädigung des Gutes in der Zeit von der Übernahme zur Lagerung bis zur Auslieferung entsteht, es sei denn, dass der Schaden durch die Sorgfalt eines ordentlichen Kaufmanns nicht abgewendet werden konnte. Dies gilt auch dann, wenn der Lagerhalter gemäß § 472 Abs. 2 das Gut bei einem Dritten einlagert.

### § 475
### Liability for loss or damage

The warehouse keeper is liable for any damage that arises from loss of or damage to the goods from the time they are accepted for warehousing until delivery unless the damage could not have been averted by exercising the care of a prudent merchant. This also applies where the warehouse keeper stores the goods with a third party in accordance with § 472(2).

### § 475a
### Verjährung

Auf die Verjährung von Ansprüchen aus einer Lagerung, die den Vorschriften dieses Abschnitts unterliegt, findet § 439 entsprechende Anwendung. Im Falle des gänzlichen Verlusts beginnt die Verjährung mit Ablauf des Tages, an dem der Lagerhalter dem Einlagerer oder, wenn ein Lagerschein ausgestellt ist, dem letzten ihm bekannt gewordenen legitimierten Besitzer des Lagerscheins den Verlust anzeigt.

### § 475a
### Limitation

§ 439 applies analogously to the limitation of claims arising from warehousing that is subject to the provisions of this Part. In the case of a total loss, the limitation period commences upon expiration of the day on which the warehouse keeper gives notice of loss to the person storing the goods or, if a warehouse receipt has been issued, the last legitimate holder of the warehouse receipt known to him.

### § 475b
### Pfandrecht des Lagerhalters

(1) Der Lagerhalter hat für alle Forderungen aus dem Lagervertrag ein Pfandrecht an dem ihm zur Lagerung übergebenen Gut des Einlagerers oder eines Dritten, der der Lagerung zugestimmt hat. An dem Gut des Einlagerers hat der Lagerhalter auch ein Pfandrecht für alle unbestrittenen Forderungen aus anderen mit dem Einlagerer abgeschlossenen Lager-, Fracht-, Seefracht- und Speditionsverträgen. Das Pfandrecht erstreckt sich auch auf die Forderung aus einer Versicherung sowie auf die Begleitpapiere.

### § 475b
### Lien of the warehouse keeper

(1) For all claims arising out of the warehousing agreement, the warehouse keeper shall have a lien on the goods of the person storing the goods or of a third party consenting to the warehousing of the goods. The warehouse keeper also has a lien on the goods of the person storing the goods for all undisputed claims arising out of other warehousing, freight, maritime shipping and forwarding agent agreements concluded with the person storing the goods. The lien also extends to a claim out of an insurance contract and to the accompanying documents.

(2) Ist ein Orderlagerschein durch Indossament übertragen worden, so besteht das Pfandrecht dem legitimierten Besitzer des Lagerscheins gegenüber nur wegen der Vergütungen und Aufwendungen, die aus dem Lagerschein ersichtlich sind oder ihm bei Erwerb des Lagerscheins bekannt oder infolge grober Fahrlässigkeit unbekannt waren.

(3) Das Pfandrecht besteht, solange der Lagerhalter das Gut in seinem Besitz hat, insbesondere solange er mittels Konnossements, Ladescheins oder Lagerscheins darüber verfügen kann.

(2) Where a negotiable warehouse receipt has been transferred by indorsement, the lien exists vis-à-vis the legitimate holder of the warehouse receipt only with respect to remuneration and expenditures which are obvious from the warehouse receipt or were known to him upon acquiring the warehouse receipt or were unknown as a result of gross negligence.

(3) The lien exists as long as the warehouse keeper has the goods in his possession, in particular as long as he can dispose of them by means of an (inland) bill of lading or warehouse receipt.

## § 475c
## Lagerschein. Verordnungsermächtigung

(1) Über die Verpflichtung zur Auslieferung des Gutes kann von dem Lagerhalter, nachdem er das Gut erhalten hat, ein Lagerschein ausgestellt werden, der die folgenden Angaben enthalten soll:

1. Ort und Tag der Ausstellung des Lagerscheins;
2. Name und Anschrift des Einlagerers;
3. Name und Anschrift des Lagerhalters;
4. Ort und Tag der Einlagerung;
5. die übliche Bezeichnung der Art des Gutes und die Art der Verpackung, bei gefährlichen Gütern ihre nach den Gefahrgutvorschriften vorgesehene, sonst ihr allgemein anerkannte Bezeichnung;
6. Anzahl, Zeichen und Nummern der Packstücke;
7. Rohgewicht oder die anders angegebene Menge des Gutes;
8. im Falle der Sammellagerung einen Vermerk hierüber.

(2) In den Lagerschein können weiter Angaben eingetragen werden, die der Lagerhalter für zweckmäßig hält.

(3) Der Lagerschein ist vom Lagerhalter zu unterzeichnen. Eine Nachbildung der eigenhändigen Unterschrift durch Druck oder Stempel genügt.

## § 475c
## Warehouse receipt. Power to issue statutory instruments

(1) The warehouse keeper may issue a warehouse receipt pertaining to his obligation to deliver the goods after he has received them; the warehouse receipt shall contain the following data:

1. place and day of issuance of the warehouse receipt;
2. name and address of the person storing the goods;
3. name and address of the warehouse keeper;
4. place and day of the warehousing;
5. the customary description of the type of goods and the type of packaging, in the case of dangerous goods the description pursuant to the provisions relating to dangerous goods or otherwise the generally accepted description;
6. quantity, identifying marks and numbers of the packages;
7. gross weight or other designated quantity of the goods;
8. in the case of collective storage, a note as to this.

(2) Further data which the warehouse keeper considers to be useful can be entered in the warehouse receipt.

(3) The warehouse receipt shall be signed by the warehouse keeper. A facsimile of the signature by print or stamp is sufficient.

(4) Dem Lagerschein gleichgestellt ist eine elektronische Aufzeichnung, die dieselben Funktionen erfüllt wie der Lagerschein, sofern sichergestellt ist, dass die Authentizität und die Integrität der Aufzeichnung gewahrt bleiben (elektronischer Lagerschein). Das Bundesministerium der Justiz wird ermächtigt, im Einvernehmen mit dem Bundesministerium des Innern durch Rechtsverordnung, die nicht der Zustimmung des Bundesrates bedarf, die Einzelheiten der Ausstellung, Vorlage, Rückgabe und Übertragung eines elektronischen Lagerscheins sowie die Einzelheiten des Verfahrens über nachträgliche Eintragungen in einen elektronischen Lagerschein zu regeln.

(4) An electronic record that fulfils the same functions as the warehouse receipt is equivalent to the warehouse receipt provided that the authenticity and the integrity of the record are preserved (electronic warehouse receipt). The Federal Ministry of Justice is authorised, in agreement with the Federal Ministry of the Interior, to govern – by means of a statutory instrument which does not require the consent of the Federal Council – the details of the issuance, presentation, return and transfer of the electronic warehouse receipt as well as the process relating to subsequent entries into an electronic warehouse receipt.

### § 475d
### Wirkung des Lagerscheins. Legitimation

(1) Der Lagerschein begründet die Vermutung, dass das Gut und seine Verpackung in Bezug auf den äußerlich erkennbaren Zustand sowie auf Anzahl, Zeichen und Nummern der Packstücke wie im Lagerschein beschrieben übernommen worden sind. Ist das Rohgewicht oder die anders angegebene Menge des Gutes oder der Inhalt vom Lagerhalter überprüft und das Ergebnis der Überprüfung in den Lagerschein eingetragen worden, so begründet dieser auch die Vermutung, dass Gewicht, Menge oder Inhalt mit den Angaben im Lagerschein übereinstimmt.

(2) Wird der Lagerschein an eine Person begeben, die darin als zum Empfang des Gutes berechtigt benannt ist, kann der Lagerhalter ihr gegenüber die Vermutung nach Absatz 1 nicht widerlegen, es sei denn, der Person war im Zeitpunkt der Begebung des Lagerscheins bekannt oder infolge grober Fahrlässigkeit unbekannt, dass die Angaben im Lagerschein unrichtig sind. Gleiches gilt gegenüber einem Dritten, dem der Lagerschein übertragen wird.

(3) Die im Lagerschein verbrieften lagervertraglichen Ansprüche können nur von dem aus dem Lagerschein Berechtigten geltend gemacht werden. Zugunsten des legitimierten Besitzers des Lagerscheins wird vermutet, dass er der aus dem Lagerschein Berechtigte ist. Legitimierter Besitzer des Lagerscheins ist, wer einen Lagerschein besitzt, der

1. auf den Inhaber lautet,
2. an Order lautet und den Besitzer als denjenigen, der zum Empfang des Gutes berechtigt ist, benennt oder durch eine ununterbrochene Reihe von Indossamenten ausweist oder
3. auf den Namen des Besitzers lautet.

### § 475d
### Effect of the warehouse receipt. Legitimation

(1) The warehouse receipt establishes the presumption that the goods and their packaging with respect to their apparent condition as well as the quantity, identifying marks and numbers of the packages have been accepted as described in the warehouse receipt. If the gross weight or other designated quantity of the goods or the contents have been inspected by the warehouse keeper and the result of the inspection has been entered in the warehouse receipt, the warehouse receipt also establishes the presumption that weight, quantity or contents are in conformity with the data in the warehouse receipt.

(2) Where the warehouse receipt is issued to a person designated therein as being entitled to receive the goods, the warehouse keeper cannot refute the presumption pursuant to subsection 1 as to this person, unless the person knew at the time of the issuance of the warehouse receipt that the data in the warehouse receipt were inaccurate or did not know this as a result of gross negligence. The same applies to a third party to whom the warehouse receipt is transferred.

(3) The claims out of the warehouse agreement as documented by the warehouse receipt can only be asserted by the rightful holder of the warehouse receipt. It shall be presumed for the benefit of the legitimate holder of the warehouse receipt that he is the rightful holder based on the warehouse receipt. A legitimate holder of the warehouse receipt is anyone who owns a warehouse receipt that

1. is made out to the owner,
2. is issued to order and names the holder as being authorised to accept delivery of the goods, or that designates him as such by means of an uninterrupted succession of indorsements or
3. is made out in the name of the holder.

## § 475e Auslieferung gegen Rückgabe des Lagerscheins

(1) Der legitimierte Besitzer des Lagerscheins ist berechtigt, vom Lagerhalter die Auslieferung des Gutes zu verlangen.

(2) Ist ein Lagerschein ausgestellt, so ist der Lagerhalter zur Auslieferung des Gutes nur gegen Rückgabe des Lagerscheins, auf dem die Auslieferung bescheinigt ist, verpflichtet. Der Lagerhalter ist nicht verpflichtet, die Echtheit der Indossamente zu prüfen. Er darf das Gut jedoch nicht dem legitimierten Besitzer des Lagerscheins ausliefern, wenn ihm bekannt oder infolge grober Fahrlässigkeit unbekannt ist, dass der legitimierte Besitzer des Lagerscheins nicht der aus dem Lagerschein Berechtigte ist.

(3) Die Auslieferung eines Teils des Gutes erfolgt gegen Abschreibung auf dem Lagerschein. Der Abschreibungsvermerk ist vom Lagerhalter zu unterschreiben.

(4) Der Lagerhalter haftet dem aus dem Lagerschein Berechtigten für den Schaden, der daraus entsteht, dass er das Gut ausgeliefert hat, ohne sich den Lagerschein zurückgeben zu lassen oder ohne einen Abschreibungsvermerk einzutragen.

## § 475e Delivery against return of the warehouse receipt

(1) The legitimate holder of the warehouse receipt is entitled to request that the warehouse keeper delivers the goods.

(2) Where a warehouse receipt has been issued, the warehouse keeper is obligated to deliver the goods only against return of the warehouse receipt on which the delivery is acknowledged. The warehouse keeper is not obligated to examine the authenticity of the indorsement. However, he may not deliver the goods to the legitimate holder of the warehouse receipt if he knows that the legitimate holder of the warehouse receipt is not the rightful beneficiary shown in the warehouse receipt or if, due to gross negligence, he does not know this.

(3) The delivery of part of the goods is made against a corresponding entry on the warehouse receipt. The entry shall be signed by the warehouse keeper.

(4) The warehouse keeper is liable to the legitimate holder of the warehouse receipt for the damage which results from the fact that he has delivered the goods without having had the warehouse receipt returned to him or without having made an entry of partial delivery.

## § 475f Einwendungen

Dem aus dem Lagerschein Berechtigten kann der Lagerhalter nur solche Einwendungen entgegensetzen, die die Gültigkeit der Erklärungen im Lagerschein betreffen oder sich aus dem Inhalt des Lagerscheins ergeben oder dem Lagerhalter unmittelbar gegenüber dem aus dem Lagerschein Berechtigten zustehen. Eine Vereinbarung, auf die im Lagerschein lediglich verwiesen wird, ist nicht Inhalt des Lagerscheins.

## § 475f Objections

The warehouse keeper can only raise objections against the rightful holder of the warehouse receipt that concern the validity of the declarations made in the warehouse receipt or that result from the content of the warehouse receipt or that the warehouse keeper is directly entitled to vis-à-vis the rightful holder of the warehouse receipt. An agreement to which the warehouse receipt merely makes reference is not content of the warehouse receipt.

## § 475g Traditionswirkung des Lagerscheins

Die Begebung des Lagerscheins an denjenigen, der darin als der zum Empfang des Gutes Berechtigte benannt ist, hat, sofern der Lagerhalter das Gut im Besitz hat, für den Erwerb von Rechten an dem Gut dieselben Wirkungen wie die Übergabe des Gutes. Gleiches gilt für die Übertragung des Lagerscheins an Dritte.

## § 475g Effect of delivery of warehouse receipt

The issuance of the warehouse receipt to someone whom the warehouse receipt authorises to accept delivery of the goods has, if the goods are in possession of the warehouse keeper, the same effect with respect to the acquisition of rights in the goods as the delivery of the goods. The same applies to the transfer of the warehouse receipt to a third party.

**§ 475h**
**Abweichende Vereinbarungen**

Ist der Einlagerer ein Verbraucher, so kann nicht zu dessen Nachteil von den §§ 475a und 475e Absatz 4 abgewichen werden.

**§ 475h**
**Deviating agreements**

Where the person storing the goods is a consumer, §§ 475a and 475e(4) cannot be deviated from to his detriment.

# B. Supply Chains Due Diligence Act

## *Gesetz über die unternehmerischen Sorgfaltspflichten zur Vermeidung von Menschenrechtsverletzungen in Lieferketten* (*Lieferkettensorgfaltspflichtengesetz* – LkSG)

### Erster Abschnitt Allgemeine Bestimmungen (§§ 1–2)

**§ 1**
**Anwendungsbereich**

(1) Dieses Gesetz ist anzuwenden auf Unternehmen ungeachtet ihrer Rechtsform, die

1. ihre Hauptverwaltung, ihre Hauptniederlassung, ihren Verwaltungssitz oder ihren satzungsmäßigen Sitz im Inland haben und
2. in der Regel mindestens 3.000 Arbeitnehmer im Inland beschäftigen; ins Ausland entsandte Arbeitnehmer sind erfasst.

Abweichend von Satz 1 Nummer 1 ist dieses Gesetz auch anzuwenden auf Unternehmen ungeachtet ihrer Rechtsform, die

1. eine Zweigniederlassung gemäß § 13d des Handelsgesetzbuchs im Inland haben und
2. in der Regel mindestens 3.000 Arbeitnehmer im Inland beschäftigen.

Ab dem 1. Januar 2024 betragen die in Satz 1 Nummer 2 und Satz 2 Nummer 2 vorgesehenen Schwellenwerte jeweils 1.000 Arbeitnehmer.

(2) Leiharbeitnehmer sind bei der Berechnung der Arbeitnehmerzahl (Absatz 1 Satz 1 Nummer 2 und Satz 2 Nummer 2) des Entleihunternehmens zu berücksichtigen, wenn die Einsatzdauer sechs Monate übersteigt.

### Part 1 General provisions (§§ 1–2)

**§ 1**
**Scope of application**

(1) This Act shall apply to companies, irrespective of their legal form, which

1. have their head office, their principal place of business, their administrative headquarters, or their registered office in Germany and
2. generally employ at least 3,000 employees in Germany; employees posted abroad are included.

Deviating from sentence 1 number 1, this Act shall also apply to companies, irrespective of their legal form, which

1. have a branch office in Germany in accordance with § 13d of the Commercial Code and
2. generally employ at least 3,000 employees in Germany.

From 1 January 2024, the thresholds in sentence 1 number 2 and sentence 2 number 2 shall each be 1,000 employees.

(2) Temporary agency workers shall be counted as a part of the receiving company when calculating the number of employees (subsection 1, sentence 1, number 2 and sentence 2, number 2), if the duration of the assignment exceeds six months.

(3) Innerhalb von verbundenen Unternehmen (§ 15 des Aktiengesetzes) sind die im Inland beschäftigten Arbeitnehmer sämtlicher konzernangehöriger Gesellschaften bei der Berechnung der Arbeitnehmerzahl (Absatz 1 Satz 1 Nummer 2) der Obergesellschaft zu berücksichtigen; ins Ausland entsandte Arbeitnehmer sind erfasst.

(3) Within affiliated enterprises (§ 15 of the Stock Corporation Act), the employees of all affiliated companies employed in Germany shall be taken into account when calculating the number of employees (subsection 1, sentence 1, number 2) of the parent company; employees posted abroad shall be included.

## § 2
## Begriffsbestimmung

(1) Geschützte Rechtspositionen im Sinne dieses Gesetzes sind solche, die sich aus den in den Nummern 1 bis 11 der Anlage aufgelisteten Übereinkommen zum Schutz der Menschenrechte ergeben.

(2) Ein menschenrechtliches Risiko im Sinne dieses Gesetzes ist ein Zustand, bei dem aufgrund tatsächlicher Umstände mit hinreichender Wahrscheinlichkeit ein Verstoß gegen eines der folgenden Verbote droht:

1. das Verbot der Beschäftigung eines Kindes unter dem Alter, mit dem nach dem Recht des Beschäftigungsortes die Schulpflicht endet, wobei das Beschäftigungsalter 15 Jahre nicht unterschreiten darf; dies gilt nicht, wenn das Recht des Beschäftigungsortes hiervon in Übereinstimmung mit Artikel 2 Absatz 4 sowie den Artikeln 4 bis 8 des Übereinkommens Nr. 138 der Internationalen Arbeitsorganisation vom 26. Juni 1973 über das Mindestalter für die Zulassung zur Beschäftigung (BGBl. 1976 II S. 201, 202) abweicht;
2. das Verbot der schlimmsten Formen der Kinderarbeit für Kinder unter 18 Jahren; dies umfasst gemäß Artikel 3 des Übereinkommens Nr. 182 der Internationalen Arbeitsorganisation vom 17. Juni 1999 über das Verbot und unverzügliche Maßnahmen zur Beseitigung der schlimmsten Formen der Kinderarbeit (BGBl. 2001 II S. 1290, 1291):
   a) alle Formen der Sklaverei oder alle sklavereiähnlichen Praktiken, wie den Verkauf von Kindern und den Kinderhandel, Schuldknechtschaft und Leibeigenschaft sowie Zwangs- oder Pflichtarbeit, einschließlich der Zwangs- oder Pflichtrekrutierung von Kindern für den Einsatz in bewaffneten Konflikten,
   b) das Heranziehen, Vermitteln oder Anbieten eines Kindes zur Prostitution, zur Herstellung von Pornographie oder zu pornographischen Darbietungen,

## § 2
## Definition of terms

(1) Protected legal positions in the sense of this Act are those arising from the conventions on the protection of human rights listed in numbers 1 to 11 of the Annex.

(2) A human rights risk in the sense of this Act is a condition in which, due to factual circumstances, there is a sufficient probability of a violation of one of the following prohibitions:

1. the prohibition of the employment of a child under the age at which compulsory schooling ends according to the law of the place of employment, whereby the age of employment may not be under 15 years; this does not apply, if the law of the place of employment deviates from this requirement in accordance with Article 2 subsection 4 and Articles 4 to 8 of Convention No. 138 of the International Labour Organisation from 26 June 1973 concerning the minimum age for admission to employment (Federal Law Gazette 1976 II p. 201, 202);
2. the prohibition of the worst forms of child labour for children under 18 years of age; this includes, in accordance with Article 3 of the Convention No. 182 of the International Labour Organisation from 17 June 1999 concerning the Prohibition and Immediate Action for the Elimination of the Worst Forms of Child Labour (Federal Law Gazette 2001 II p. 1290, 1291):
   a) all forms of slavery or practices similar to slavery, such as the sale and trafficking of children, debt bondage and serfdom, as well as forced or compulsory labour, including the forced or compulsory recruitment of children for use in armed conflict,
   b) enticing, finding, or offering a child for prostitution, for the production of pornography or for pornographic performances,

c) das Heranziehen, Vermitteln oder Anbieten eines Kindes zu unerlaubten Tätigkeiten, insbesondere zur Gewinnung von und zum Handel mit Drogen,
d) Arbeit, die ihrer Natur nach oder aufgrund der Umstände, unter denen sie verrichtet wird, voraussichtlich für die Gesundheit, die Sicherheit oder die Sittlichkeit von Kindern schädlich ist;

3. das Verbot der Beschäftigung von Personen in Zwangsarbeit; dies umfasst jede Arbeitsleistung oder Dienstleistung, die von einer Person unter Androhung von Strafe verlangt wird und für die sie sich nicht freiwillig zur Verfügung gestellt hat, etwa in Folge von Schuldknechtschaft oder Menschenhandel; ausgenommen von der Zwangsarbeit sind Arbeits- oder Dienstleistungen, die mit Artikel 2 Absatz 2 des Übereinkommens Nr. 29 der Internationalen Arbeitsorganisation vom 28. Juni 1930 über Zwangs- oder Pflichtarbeit (BGBl. 1956 II S. 640, 641) oder mit Artikel 8 Buchstabe b und c des Internationen Paktes vom 19. Dezember 1966 über bürgerliche und politische Rechte (BGBl. 1973 II S. 1533, 1534) vereinbar sind;
4. das Verbot aller Formen der Sklaverei, sklavenähnlicher Praktiken, Leibeigenschaft oder anderer Formen von Herrschaftsausübung oder Unterdrückung im Umfeld der Arbeitsstätte, etwa durch extreme wirtschaftliche oder sexuelle Ausbeutung und Erniedrigungen;
5. das Verbot der Missachtung der nach dem Recht des Beschäftigungsortes geltenden Pflichten des Arbeitsschutzes, wenn hierdurch die Gefahr von Unfällen bei der Arbeit oder arbeitsbedingte Gesundheitsgefahren entstehen, insbesondere durch:
   a) offensichtlich ungenügende Sicherheitsstandards bei der Bereitstellung und der Instandhaltung der Arbeitsstätte, des Arbeitsplatzes und der Arbeitsmittel,
   b) das Fehlen geeigneter Schutzmaßnahmen, um Einwirkungen durch chemische, physikalische oder biologische Stoffe zu vermeiden,
   c) das Fehlen von Maßnahmen zur Verhinderung übermäßiger körperlicher und geistiger Ermüdung, insbesondere durch eine ungeeignete Arbeitsorganisation in Bezug auf Arbeitszeiten und Ruhepausen oder
   d) die ungenügende Ausbildung und Unterweisung von Beschäftigten;
6. das Verbot der Missachtung der Koalitionsfreiheit, nach der

c) enticing, finding or offering a child for illegal activities, in particular for the purpose of obtaining or dealing drugs,
d) work which, by its nature or the circumstances in which it is carried out, is likely to be harmful to the health, safety or morals of children;

3. the prohibition of the employment of persons in forced labour; this includes any work or service which is demanded of a person under threat of punishment and for which the person did not voluntarily make himself or herself available, for example as a result of debt bondage or human trafficking; excluded from forced labour are work or services which are in conformity with Article 2 subsection 2 of Convention No. 29 of the International Labour Organisation from 28 June 1930 concerning Forced or Compulsory Labour (Federal Law Gazette 1956 II pp. 640, 641) or with Article 8, letters b and c of the International Covenant from 19 December 1966 on Civil and Political Rights (Federal Law Gazette 1973 II pp. 1533, 1534);
4. the prohibition of all forms of slavery, slavery-like practices, serfdom or other forms of domination or oppression in the work environment, such as extreme economic or sexual exploitation and humiliation;
5. the prohibition of disregarding the occupational protections applicable under the law of the place of employment, if this gives rise to the danger of accidents at work or work-related health hazards, particularly due to:
   a) evidently insufficient safety standards in the provision and maintenance of the workplace, the work environment, and the work equipment,
   b) the absence of appropriate protective measures to avoid exposure to chemical, physical or biological agents,
   c) the absence of measures to prevent excessive physical and mental fatigue, particularly through inappropriate labour organisation in terms of working hours and rest breaks, or
   d) inadequate training and instruction of employees;
6. the prohibition of disregarding the freedom to join trade unions, according to which

a) Arbeitnehmer sich frei zu Gewerkschaften zusammenzuschließen oder diesen beitreten können,
b) die Gründung, der Beitritt und die Mitgliedschaft zu einer Gewerkschaft nicht als Grund für ungerechtfertigte Diskriminierungen oder Vergeltungsmaßnahmen genutzt werden dürfen,
c) Gewerkschaften sich frei und in Übereinstimmung mit dem Recht des Beschäftigungsortes betätigen dürfen; dieses umfasst das Streikrecht und das Recht auf Kollektivverhandlungen;

7. das Verbot der Ungleichbehandlung in Beschäftigung, etwa aufgrund von nationaler und ethnischer Abstammung, sozialer Herkunft, Gesundheitsstatus, Behinderung, sexueller Orientierung, Alter, Geschlecht, politischer Meinung, Religion oder Weltanschauung, sofern diese nicht in den Erfordernissen der Beschäftigung begründet ist; eine Ungleichbehandlung umfasst insbesondere die Zahlung ungleichen Entgelts für gleichwertige Arbeit;
8. das Verbot des Vorenthaltens eines angemessenen Lohns; der angemessene Lohn ist mindestens der nach dem anwendbaren Recht festgelegte Mindestlohn und bemisst sich ansonsten nach dem Recht des Beschäftigungsortes;
9. das Verbot der Herbeiführung einer schädlichen Bodenveränderung, Gewässerverunreinigung, Luftverunreinigung, schädlichen Lärmemission oder eines übermäßigen Wasserverbrauchs, die
   a) die natürlichen Grundlagen zum Erhalt und der Produktion von Nahrung erheblich beeinträchtigt,
   b) einer Person den Zugang zu einwandfreiem Trinkwasser verwehrt,
   c) einer Person den Zugang zu Sanitäranlagen erschwert oder zerstört oder
   d) die Gesundheit einer Person schädigt;
10. das Verbot der widerrechtlichen Zwangsräumung und das Verbot des widerrechtlichen Entzugs von Land, von Wäldern und Gewässern bei dem Erwerb, der Bebauung oder anderweitigen Nutzung von Land, Wäldern und Gewässern, deren Nutzung die Lebensgrundlage einer Person sichert;
11. das Verbot der Beauftragung oder Nutzung privater oder öffentlicher Sicherheitskräfte zum Schutz des unternehmerischen Projekts, wenn aufgrund mangelnder Unterweisung oder Kontrolle seitens des Unternehmens bei dem Einsatz der Sicherheitskräfte

a) workers may freely form or join trade unions,
b) the establishment, joining and membership of a trade union shall not be used as a reason for unjustified discrimination or retaliation,
c) trade unions may operate freely and in accordance with the law of the place of employment, which includes the right to strike and the right to collective bargaining;

7. the prohibition of unequal treatment in employment, for example on the grounds of national and ethnic origin, social origin, health status, disability, sexual orientation, age, gender, political opinion, religion or worldview, unless this is justified by the requirements of the employment; unequal treatment includes in particular the payment of unequal remuneration for work of equal value;
8. the prohibition of not paying a fair wage; the fair wage shall be at least the minimum wage determined by the applicable law and shall otherwise be determined by the law of the place of employment;
9. the prohibition of causing harmful soil degradation, water pollution, air pollution, harmful noise emission or excessive water consumption, which
   a) significantly impairs the natural basis for the preservation and production of food,
   b) denies a person access to safe drinking water,
   c) impedes or destroys a person's access to sanitary facilities, or
   d) harms the health of a person;
10. the prohibition of unlawful eviction and the prohibition of unlawful deprivation of land, forests and waters in the acquisition, development, or other uses of land, forests and waters, the use of which secures the livelihood of a person;
11. the prohibition of the engagement or use of private or public security personnel for the protection of the enterprise's project if, due to a lack of instruction or control on the part of the enterprise for the security personnel

a) das Verbot von Folter und grausamer, unmenschlicher oder erniedrigender Behandlung missachtet wird,
b) Leib oder Leben verletzt werden oder
c) die Vereinigungs- und Koalitionsfreiheit beeinträchtigt werden;

12. das Verbot eines über die Nummern 1 bis 11 hinausgehenden Tuns oder pflichtwidrigen Unterlassens, das unmittelbar geeignet ist, in besonders schwerwiegender Weise eine geschützte Rechtsposition zu beeinträchtigen und dessen Rechtswidrigkeit bei verständiger Würdigung aller in Betracht kommenden Umstände offensichtlich ist.

(3) Ein umweltbezogenes Risiko im Sinne dieses Gesetzes ist ein Zustand, bei dem auf Grund tatsächlicher Umstände mit hinreichender Wahrscheinlichkeit ein Verstoß gegen eines der folgenden Verbote droht:

1. das Verbot der Herstellung von mit Quecksilber versetzten Produkten gemäß Artikel 4 Absatz 1 und Anlage A Teil I des Übereinkommens von Minamata vom 10. Oktober 2013 über Quecksilber (BGBl. 2017 II S. 610, 611) (Minamata-Übereinkommen);
2. das Verbot der Verwendung von Quecksilber und Quecksilberverbindungen bei Herstellungsprozessen im Sinne des Artikels 5 Absatz 2 und Anlage B Teil I des Minamata-Übereinkommens ab dem für die jeweiligen Produkte und Prozesse im Übereinkommen festgelegten Ausstiegsdatum;
3. das Verbot der Behandlung von Quecksilberabfällen entgegen den Bestimmungen des Artikels 11 Absatz 3 des Minamata-Übereinkommens;
4. das Verbot der Produktion und Verwendung von Chemikalien nach Artikel 3 Absatz 1 Buchstabe a und Anlage A des Stockholmer Übereinkommens vom 23. Mai 2001 über persistente organische Schadstoffe (BGBl. 2002 II S. 803, 804) (POPs-Übereinkommen), zuletzt geändert durch den Beschluss vom 6. Mai 2005 (BGBl. 2009 II S. 1060, 1061), in der Fassung der Verordnung (EU) 2019/1021 des Europäischen Parlaments und des Rates vom 20. Juni 2019 über persistente organische Schadstoffe (ABl. L 169 vom 26.5.2019, S. 45), die zuletzt durch die Delegierte Verordnung (EU) 2021/277 der Kommission vom 16. Dezember 2020 (ABl. L 62 vom 23.2.2021, S. 1) geändert worden ist;

a) the prohibition of torture and cruel, inhumane or degrading treatment is violated,
b) body or life is injured, or
c) the freedom of association and freedom to join trade unions are impaired;

12. the prohibition of an act or an omission contrary to duty that goes beyond numbers 1 to 11, which is directly suitable to impair a protected legal position in a particularly serious manner and the unlawfulness of which is obvious according to a reasonable assessment of all circumstances under consideration.

(3) For the purposes of this Act, an environmental risk is a condition in which, on the basis of factual circumstances, there is a reasonable likelihood of a breach of one of the following prohibitions:

1. the prohibition of the production of mercury-added products pursuant to Article 4 subsection 1 and Annex A Part I of the Minamata Convention on Mercury from 10 October 2013 (Federal Law Gazette 2017 II p. 610, 611) (Minamata Convention);
2. the prohibition of the use of mercury and mercury compounds in manufacturing processes as defined in Article 5 subsection 2 and Annex B, Part I of the Minamata Convention from the phase-out date specified for the respective products and processes in the Convention;
3. the prohibition of the treatment of mercury waste contrary to the provisions of Article 11 subsection 3 of the Minamata Convention;
4. the prohibition of the production and use of chemicals pursuant to Article 3 subsection 1(a) and Annex A of the Stockholm Convention from 23 May 2001 on Persistent Organic Pollutants (Federal Law Gazette 2002 II p. 803, 804) (POPs Convention), last amended by the Decision from 6 May 2005 (Federal Law Gazette 2009 II p. 1060, 1061), in the version of the Regulation (EU) 2019/1021 of the European Parliament and the European Council from 20 June 2019 on persistent organic pollutants (OJ L 169, 26.5.2019, p. 45), which was last amended by the Delegated Regulation from the Commission (EU) 2021/277 of 16 December 2020 (OJ L 62, 23.2.2021, p. 1);

5. das Verbot der nicht umweltgerechten Handhabung, Sammlung, Lagerung und Entsorgung von Abfällen nach den Regelungen, die in der anwendbaren Rechtsordnung nach den Maßgaben des Artikels 6 Absatz 1 Buchstabe d Ziffer i und ii des POPs-Übereinkommens gelten;
6. das Verbot der Ausfuhr gefährlicher Abfälle im Sinne des Artikel 1 Absatz 1 und anderer Abfälle im Sinne des Artikel 1 Absatz 2 des Basler Übereinkommens über die Kontrolle der grenzüberschreitenden Verbringung gefährlicher Abfälle und ihrer Entsorgung vom 22. März 1989 (BGBl. 1994 II S. 2703, 2704) (Basler Übereinkommen), zuletzt geändert durch die Dritte Verordnung zur Änderung von Anlagen zum Basler Übereinkommen vom 22. März 1989 vom 6. Mai 2014 (BGBl. II S. 306, 307), und im Sinne der Verordnung (EG) Nr. 1013/2006 des Europäischen Parlaments und des Rates vom 14. Juni 2006 über die Verbringung von Abfällen (ABl. L 190 vom 12.7.2006, S. 1) (Verordnung (EG) Nr. 1013/2006), die zuletzt durch die Delegierte Verordnung (EU) 2020/2174 der Kommission vom 19. Oktober 2020 (ABl. L 433 vom 22.12.2020, S. 11) geändert worden ist
   a) in eine Vertragspartei, die die Einfuhr solcher gefährlichen und anderer Abfälle verboten hat (Artikel 4 Absatz 1 Buchstabe b des Basler Übereinkommens),
   b) in einen Einfuhrstaat im Sinne des Artikel 2 Nummer 11 des Basler Übereinkommens, der nicht seine schriftliche Einwilligung zu der bestimmten Einfuhr gegeben hat, wenn dieser Einfuhrstaat die Einfuhr dieser gefährlichen Abfälle nicht verboten hat (Artikel 4 Absatz 1 Buchstabe c des Basler Übereinkommens),
   c) in eine Nichtvertragspartei des Basler Übereinkommens (Artikel 4 Absatz 5 des Basler Übereinkommens),
   d) in einen Einfuhrstaat, wenn solche gefährlichen Abfälle oder andere Abfälle in diesem Staat oder anderswo nicht umweltgerecht behandelt werden (Artikel 4 Absatz 8 Satz 1 des Basler Übereinkommens);
7. das Verbot der Ausfuhr gefährlicher Abfälle von in Anlage VII des Basler Übereinkommens aufgeführten Staaten in Staaten, die nicht in Anlage VII aufgeführt sind (Artikel 4 A des Basler Übereinkommens, Artikel 36 der Verordnung (EG) Nr. 1013/2006) sowie

5. the prohibition of environmentally unsound handling, collection, storage and disposal of waste in accordance with the regulations in force in the applicable jurisdiction under the terms of Article 6 subsection 1(d) numbers i and ii of the Stockholm Convention on persistent organic pollutants;
6. the prohibition of exports of hazardous waste within the meaning of Article 1(1) and other waste within the meaning of Article 1 subsection 2 of the Basel Convention on the Control of Cross-Border Movements of Hazardous Wastes and their Disposal from 22 March 1989 (Federal Law Gazette 1994 II pp. 2703, 2704) (Basel Convention), as last amended by the Third Regulation amending the Annexes to the Basel Convention from 22 March 1989 from 6 May 2014 (Federal Law Gazette II pp. 306, 307), and within the meaning of Regulation (EC) No. 1013/2006 of the European Parliament and of the European Council from 14 June 2006 on shipments of waste (OJ L 190, 12.7.2006, p. 1) (Regulation (EC) No. 1013/2006), as last amended by the Delegated Regulation of the Commission (EU) 2020/2174 from 19 October 2020 (OJ L 433, 22.12.2020, p. 11)
   a) to a party of the convention that has prohibited the import of such hazardous and other wastes (Article 4 subsection 1(b) of the Basel Convention),
   b) to an importing state as defined in Article 2 number 11 of the Basel Convention which has not given its written consent to the particular import, if that importing state has not prohibited the import of that hazardous waste (Article 4 subsection 1(c) of the Basel Convention),
   c) to a state which is not a party to the Basel Convention (Article 4 subsection 5 of the Basel Convention),
   d) to an importing state if such hazardous waste or other waste is not managed in an environmentally sound manner in that country or elsewhere (Article 4 subsection 8 sentence 1 of the Basel Convention);
7. the prohibition of exports of hazardous waste from countries listed in Annex VII of the Basel Convention to countries not listed in Annex VII (Article 4 A of the Basel Convention, Article 36 of Regulation (EC) No. 1013/2006); and

8. das Verbot der Einfuhr gefährlicher Abfälle und anderer Abfälle aus einer Nichtvertragspartei des Basler Übereinkommens (Artikel 4 Absatz 5 des Basler Übereinkommens).

(4) Eine Verletzung einer menschenrechtsbezogenen Pflicht im Sinne dieses Gesetzes ist der Verstoß gegen ein in Absatz 2 Nummer 1 bis 12 genanntes Verbot. [2]Eine Verletzung einer umweltbezogenen Pflicht im Sinne dieses Gesetzes ist der Verstoß gegen ein in Absatz 3 Nummer 1 bis 8 genanntes Verbot.

(5) Die Lieferkette im Sinne dieses Gesetzes bezieht sich auf alle Produkte und Dienstleistungen eines Unternehmens. Sie umfasst alle Schritte im In- und Ausland, die zur Herstellung der Produkte und zur Erbringung der Dienstleistungen erforderlich sind, angefangen von der Gewinnung der Rohstoffe bis zu der Lieferung an den Endkunden und erfasst

1. das Handeln eines Unternehmens im eigenen Geschäftsbereich,
2. das Handeln eines unmittelbaren Zulieferers und
3. das Handeln eines mittelbaren Zulieferers.

(6) Der eigene Geschäftsbereich im Sinne dieses Gesetzes erfasst jede Tätigkeit des Unternehmens zur Erreichung des Unternehmensziels. Erfasst ist damit jede Tätigkeit zur Herstellung und Verwertung von Produkten und zur Erbringung von Dienstleistungen, unabhängig davon, ob sie an einem Standort im In- oder Ausland vorgenommen wird. In verbundenen Unternehmen zählt zum eigenen Geschäftsbereich der Obergesellschaft eine konzernangehörige Gesellschaft, wenn die Obergesellschaft auf die konzernangehörige Gesellschaft einen bestimmenden Einfluss ausübt.

(7) Unmittelbarer Zulieferer im Sinne dieses Gesetzes ist ein Partner eines Vertrages über die Lieferung von Waren oder die Erbringung von Dienstleistungen, dessen Zulieferungen für die Herstellung des Produktes des Unternehmens oder zur Erbringung und Inanspruchnahme der betreffenden Dienstleistung notwendig sind.

(8) Mittelbarer Zulieferer im Sinne dieses Gesetzes ist jedes Unternehmen, das kein unmittelbarer Zulieferer ist und dessen Zulieferungen für die Herstellung des Produktes des Unternehmens oder zur Erbringung und Inanspruchnahme der betreffenden Dienstleistung notwendig sind.

8. the prohibition of the import of hazardous wastes and other wastes from a non-party state to the Basel Convention (Article 4 subsection 5 of the Basel Convention).

(4) A violation of a human rights duty within the meaning of this Act is a violation of a prohibition specified in subsection 2 numbers 1 to 12. A violation of an environmental duty within the meaning of this Act is a violation of a prohibition referred to in subsection 3 numbers 1 to 8.

(5) The supply chain in the sense of this Act refers to all products and services of a company. It includes all proceedings in Germany and abroad that are necessary for the production of the products and performance of services, beginning with the extraction of raw materials up to the delivery to the end customer and includes

1. the actions of a company in its own business sector,
2. the actions of a direct supplier,
3. the actions of an indirect supplier.

(6) For the purposes of this Act, an enterprise's own line of business shall include any activity of the enterprise to achieve the objective of the enterprise. This includes every activity for the production and the use of products as well as the performance of services, irrespective of whether it is carried out at a location in Germany or abroad. In affiliated companies, the parent company's own business includes a company belonging to the group if the parent company exercises a decisive influence on the company belonging to the group.

(7) For the purposes of this Act, a direct supplier is a party to a contract for the supply of goods or the performance of services whose supplies are necessary for the manufacture of the enterprise's product or for the performance and use of the relevant service.

(8) For the purposes of this Act, an indirect supplier is any company which is not a direct supplier and whose supplies are necessary for the manufacture of the company's product or for the performance and use of the relevant service.

## Zweiter Abschnitt
## Sorgfaltspflichten (§§ 3–10)

### § 3
### Sorgfaltspflichten

(1) Unternehmen sind dazu verpflichtet, in ihren Lieferketten die in diesem Abschnitt festgelegten menschenrechtlichen und umweltbezogenen Sorgfaltspflichten in angemessener Weise zu beachten mit dem Ziel, menschenrechtlichen oder umweltbezogenen Risiken vorzubeugen oder sie zu minimieren oder die Verletzung menschenrechtsbezogener oder umweltbezogener Pflichten zu beenden. Die Sorgfaltspflichten enthalten:

1. die Einrichtung eines Risikomanagements (§ 4 Absatz 1),
2. die Festlegung einer betriebsinternen Zuständigkeit (§ 4 Absatz 3),
3. die Durchführung regelmäßiger Risikoanalysen (§ 5),
4. die Abgabe einer Grundsatzerklärung (§ 6 Absatz 2),
5. die Verankerung von Präventionsmaßnahmen im eigenen Geschäftsbereich (§ 6 Absatz 1 und 3) und gegenüber unmittelbaren Zulieferern (§ 6 Absatz 4),
6. das Ergreifen von Abhilfemaßnahmen (§ 7 Absatz 1 bis 3),
7. die Einrichtung eines Beschwerdeverfahrens (§ 8),
8. die Umsetzung von Sorgfaltspflichten in Bezug auf Risiken bei mittelbaren Zulieferern (§ 9) und
9. die Dokumentation (§ 10 Absatz 1) und die Berichterstattung (§ 10 Absatz 2).

(2) Die angemessene Weise eines Handelns, das den Sorgfaltspflichten genügt, bestimmt sich nach

1. Art und Umfang der Geschäftstätigkeit des Unternehmens
2. dem Einflussvermögen des Unternehmens auf den unmittelbaren Verursacher eines menschenrechtlichen oder umweltbezogenen Risikos oder der Verletzung einer menschenrechtsbezogenen oder einer umweltbezogenen Pflicht,
3. der typischerweise zu erwartenden Schwere der Verletzung, der Umkehrbarkeit der Verletzung und der Wahrscheinlichkeit der Verletzung einer menschenrechtsbezogenen oder einer umweltbezogenen Pflicht sowie

## Part 2
## Due diligence (§§ 3–10)

### § 3
### Due diligence

(1) Companies have an obligation to exercise due diligence in their supply chains in accordance with the human rights and environmental requirements set out in this section, with the aim of preventing or minimising human rights or environmental risks or ending the violation of human rights or the violation of environmental obligations. The due diligence obligations include:

1. establishing a risk management system (§ 4 subsection 1),
2. determining the responsible party inside the company (§ 4 subsection 3),
3. performing regular risk analyses (§ 5),
4. submitting a policy statement (§ 6 subsection 2),
5. embedding preventive measures in the company's business operations (§ 6 subsection 1 and 3) and with respect to direct suppliers (§ 6 subsection 4),
6. taking remedial actions (§ 7 subsection 1 to 3),
7. establishing a complaints procedure (§ 8),
8. implementing due diligence with regards to risks in indirect suppliers (§ 9) and
9. documenting (§ 10 subsection 1) and reporting (§ 10 subsection 2).

(2) The appropriate manner of action in accordance with due diligence shall be determined by

1. the nature and extent of the company's business,
2. the company's ability to influence the direct perpetrator of a human rights or environmental risk or of the violation of a human right or environmental obligation,
3. the typically expected severity of the violation, the reversibility of the violation, and the likelihood of the violation of a duty related to human rights or to the environment, as well as

4. nach der Art des Verursachungsbeitrages des Unternehmens zu dem menschenrechtlichen oder umweltbezogenen Risiko oder zu der Verletzung einer menschenrechtsbezogenen oder einer umweltbezogenen Pflicht.

(3) Eine Verletzung der Pflichten aus diesem Gesetz begründet keine zivilrechtliche Haftung. Eine unabhängig von diesem Gesetz begründete zivilrechtliche Haftung bleibt unberührt.

4. the nature of the company's contribution to the human rights or environmental risk or to the violation of a human rights or environmental obligation.

(3) A breach of the obligations under this Act does not give rise to civil liability. Civil liability incurred independently of this Act shall remain unaffected.

## § 4
## Risikomanagement

(1) Unternehmen müssen ein angemessenes und wirksames Risikomanagement zur Einhaltung der Sorgfaltspflichten (§ 3 Absatz 1) einrichten. Das Risikomanagement ist in alle maßgebliche Geschäftsabläufe durch angemessene Maßnahmen zu verankern.

(2) Wirksam sind solche Maßnahmen, die es ermöglichen, menschenrechtliche und umweltbezogene Risiken zu erkennen und zu minimieren sowie Verletzungen menschenrechtsbezogener oder umweltbezogener Pflichten zu verhindern, zu beenden oder deren Ausmaß zu minimieren, wenn das Unternehmen diese Risiken oder Verletzungen innerhalb der Lieferkette verursacht oder dazu beigetragen hat.

(3) Das Unternehmen hat dafür zu sorgen, dass festgelegt ist, wer innerhalb des Unternehmens dafür zuständig ist, das Risikomanagement zu überwachen, etwa durch die Benennung eines Menschenrechtsbeauftragten. Die Geschäftsleitung hat sich regelmäßig, mindestens einmal jährlich, über die Arbeit der zuständigen Person oder Personen zu informieren.

(4) Das Unternehmen hat bei der Errichtung und Umsetzung seines Risikomanagementsystems die Interessen seiner Beschäftigten, der Beschäftigten innerhalb seiner Lieferketten und derjenigen, die in sonstiger Weise durch das wirtschaftliche Handeln des Unternehmens oder durch das wirtschaftliche Handeln eines Unternehmens in seinen Lieferketten in einer geschützten Rechtsposition unmittelbar betroffen sein können, angemessen zu berücksichtigen.

## § 4
## Risk management

(1) Enterprises shall establish an appropriate and effective risk management system to ensure compliance with the due diligence obligations (§ 3 subsection 1). Risk management must be embedded in all relevant business processes through appropriate measures.

(2) Effective measures are those that make it possible to identify and minimise human rights and environmental risks and to prevent, end or minimise the extent of violations of human rights or environmental obligations if the enterprise has caused or contributed to these risks or violations within the supply chain.

(3) The company shall ensure that it has determined who within the company is responsible for monitoring risk management, e.g. by appointing a human rights representative. The management shall be informed regularly, at least once a year, about the work of the responsible person or persons.

(4) In establishing and implementing its risk management system, the enterprise shall give due consideration to the interests of its employees, employees within its supply chains and those who may otherwise be directly affected in their protected legal positions by the economic activity of the enterprise or by the economic activity of an enterprise in its supply chains.

## § 5
## Risikoanalyse

(1) Im Rahmen des Risikomanagements hat das Unternehmen eine angemessene Risikoanalyse nach den Abätzen 2 bis 4 durchzuführen, um die menschenrechtlichen und umweltbezogenen Risiken im eigenen Geschäftsbereich sowie bei seinen unmittelbaren Zulieferern zu ermitteln. In Fällen, in denen ein Unternehmen eine missbräuchliche Gestaltung der unmittelbaren Zuliefererbeziehung oder ein Umgehungsgeschäft vorgenommen hat, um die Anforderungen an die Sorgfaltspflichten in Hinblick auf den unmittelbaren Zulieferer zu umgehen, gilt ein mittelbarer Zulieferer als unmittelbarer Zulieferer.

(2) Die ermittelten menschenrechtlichen und umweltbezogenen Risiken sind angemessen zu gewichten und zu priorisieren. Dabei sind insbesondere die in § 3 Absatz 2 genannten Kriterien maßgeblich.

(3) Das Unternehmen muss dafür Sorge tragen, dass die Ergebnisse der Risikoanalyse intern an die maßgeblichen Entscheidungsträger, etwa an den Vorstand oder an die Einkaufsabteilung, kommuniziert werden.

(4) Die Risikoanalyse ist einmal im Jahr sowie anlassbezogen durchzuführen, wenn das Unternehmen mit einer wesentlich veränderten oder wesentlich erweiterten Risikolage in der Lieferkette rechnen muss, etwa durch die Einführung neuer Produkte, Projekte oder eines neuen Geschäftsfeldes. Erkenntnisse aus der Bearbeitung von Hinweisen nach § 8 Absatz 1 sind zu berücksichtigen.

## § 5
## Risk analysis

(1) As a part of risk management, the enterprise shall conduct an appropriate risk analysis in accordance with subsections 2 to 4 in order to identify the human rights and environmental risks in its own business and its direct suppliers. In cases where an enterprise has improperly structured its relationship to its direct supplier or made a circumvention transaction in order to circumvent the due diligence requirements with regard to the direct supplier, an indirect supplier shall be deemed to be a direct supplier.

(2) The identified human rights and environmental risks must be appropriately evaluated and prioritised. In particular, the criteria set out in § 3 subsection 2 shall be relevant.

(3) The enterprise must ensure that the results of the risk analysis are communicated internally to the relevant decision-makers, such as the management board or the purchasing department.

(4) The risk analysis shall be carried out once a year as well as on an ad hoc basis if the enterprise is expecting a significantly changed or substantially expanded risk position in the supply chain, for example due to the introduction of new products, projects or a new business area. Findings from the processing of notices pursuant to § 8(1) shall be taken into account.

## § 6
## Präventionsmaßnahmen

(1) Stellt ein Unternehmen im Rahmen einer Risikoanalyse nach § 5 ein Risiko fest, hat es unverzüglich angemessene Präventionsmaßnahmen nach den Absätzen 2 bis 4 zu ergreifen.

(2) Das Unternehmen muss eine Grundsatzerklärung über seine Menschenrechtsstrategie abgeben. Die Unternehmensleitung hat die Grundsatzerklärung abzugeben. Die Grundsatzerklärung muss mindestens die folgenden Elemente einer Menschenrechtsstrategie des Unternehmens enthalten:

1. die Beschreibung des Verfahrens, mit dem das Unternehmen seinen Pflichten nach § 4 Absatz 1, § 5 Absatz 1, § 6 Absatz 3 bis 5, sowie den §§ 7 bis 10 nachkommt,

## § 6
## Preventive measures

(1) If an enterprise identifies a risk within the framework of a risk analysis pursuant to § 5, it shall immediately take appropriate preventive measures pursuant to subsections 2 to 4.

(2) The enterprise shall issue a policy statement on its human rights strategy. The company's management shall issue the policy statement. The policy statement shall contain at least the following elements of a human rights strategy of the enterprise:

1. a description of the procedure by which the enterprise fulfils its obligations under § 4 subsection 1, § 5 subsection 1, § 6 subsections 3 to 5, and §§ 7 to 10,

2. die für das Unternehmen auf Grundlage der Risikoanalyse festgestellten prioritären menschenrechtlichen und umweltbezogenen Risiken und
3. die auf Grundlage der Risikoanalyse erfolgte Festlegung der menschenrechtsbezogenen und umweltbezogenen Erwartungen, die das Unternehmen an seine Beschäftigten und Zulieferer in der Lieferkette richtet.

(3) Das Unternehmen muss angemessene Präventionsmaßnahmen im eigenen Geschäftsbereich verankern, insbesondere:

1. die Umsetzung der in der Grundsatzerklärung dargelegten Menschenrechtsstrategie in den relevanten Geschäftsabläufen,
2. die Entwicklung und Implementierung geeigneter Beschaffungsstrategien und Einkaufspraktiken, durch die festgestellte Risiken verhindert oder minimiert werden,
3. die Durchführung von Schulungen in den relevanten Geschäftsbereichen,
4. die Durchführung risikobasierter Kontrollmaßnahmen, mit denen die Einhaltung der in der Grundsatzerklärung enthaltenen Menschenrechtsstrategie im eigenen Geschäftsbereich überprüft wird.

(4) Das Unternehmen muss angemessene Präventionsmaßnahmen gegenüber einem unmittelbaren Zulieferer verankern, insbesondere:

1. die Berücksichtigung der menschenrechtsbezogenen und umweltbezogenen Erwartungen bei der Auswahl eines unmittelbaren Zulieferers,
2. die vertragliche Zusicherung eines unmittelbaren Zulieferers, dass dieser die von der Geschäftsleitung des Unternehmens verlangten menschenrechtsbezogenen und umweltbezogenen Erwartungen einhält und entlang der Lieferkette angemessen adressiert,
3. die Durchführung von Schulungen und Weiterbildungen zur Durchsetzung der vertraglichen Zusicherungen des unmittelbaren Zulieferers nach Nummer 2,
4. die Vereinbarung angemessener vertraglicher Kontrollmechanismen sowie deren risikobasierte Durchführung, um die Einhaltung der Menschenrechtsstrategie bei dem unmittelbaren Zulieferer zu überprüfen.

2. the priority human rights and environmental risks identified by the enterprise on the basis of the risks analyses, and
3. the definition, based on the risk analysis, of the human rights and environmental expectations that the company has of its employees and suppliers in the supply chain.

(3) The company must embed appropriate prevention measures in its own business operations, in particular:

1. implementing the human rights strategy set out in the Declaration of Principles in relevant business processes,
2. developing and implementing appropriate procurement policies and practices that prevent or minimise the identified risks,
3. implementing training courses in the relevant business areas,
4. implementing risk-based control measures to verify compliance with the human rights strategy contained in the Declaration of Principles in its own business area.

(4) The enterprise must embed appropriate prevention measures regarding a direct supplier, in particular:

1. the consideration of human rights and environmental expectations when selecting a direct supplier,
2. the contractual assurance from a direct supplier that it will comply with the human rights and environmental expectations required by the enterprise's management and adequately address them along the supply chain,
3. the implementation of training and further education to enforce the contractual assurances of the direct supplier according to number 2,
4. the agreement on appropriate contractual monitoring mechanisms and their risk-based implementation to verify compliance with the human rights strategy by the direct supplier.

(5) Die Wirksamkeit der Präventionsmaßnahmen ist einmal im Jahr sowie anlassbezogen zu überprüfen, wenn das Unternehmen mit einer wesentlich veränderten oder wesentlich erweiterten Risikolage im eigenen Geschäftsbereich oder beim unmittelbaren Zulieferer rechnen muss, etwa durch die Einführung neuer Produkte, Projekte oder eines neuen Geschäftsfeldes. Erkenntnisse aus der Bearbeitung von Hinweisen nach § 8 Absatz 1 sind zu berücksichtigen. Die Maßnahmen sind bei Bedarf unverzüglich zu aktualisieren.

(5) The effectiveness of the preventive measures shall be reviewed once a year and on an ad hoc basis if the enterprise expects a significantly changed or significantly expanded risk situation in its own area of business or at the direct supplier, for example, due to the introduction of new products, projects or a new area of business. Findings from the processing of notices pursuant to § 8 subsection 1 shall be considered. The measures must be updated immediately if necessary.

## § 7
## Abhilfemaßnahmen

(1) Stellt das Unternehmen fest, dass die Verletzung einer menschenrechtsbezogenen oder einer umweltbezogenen Pflicht in seinem eigenen Geschäftsbereich oder bei einem unmittelbaren Zulieferer bereits eingetreten ist oder unmittelbar bevorsteht, hat es unverzüglich angemessene Abhilfemaßnahmen zu ergreifen, um diese Verletzung zu verhindern, zu beenden oder das Ausmaß der Verletzung zu minimieren. § 5 Absatz 1 Satz 2 gilt entsprechend. Im eigenen Geschäftsbereich im Inland muss die Abhilfemaßnahme zu einer Beendigung der Verletzung führen. Im eigenen Geschäftsbereich im Ausland und im eigenen Geschäftsbereich gemäß § 2 Absatz 6 Satz 3 muss die Abhilfemaßnahme in der Regel zur Beendigung der Verletzung führen.

(2) Ist die Verletzung einer menschenrechtsbezogenen oder einer umweltbezogenen Pflicht bei einem unmittelbaren Zulieferer so beschaffen, dass das Unternehmen sie nicht in absehbarer Zeit beenden kann, muss es unverzüglich ein Konzept zur Beendigung oder Minimierung erstellen und umsetzen. Das Konzept muss einen konkreten Zeitplan enthalten. Bei der Erstellung und Umsetzung des Konzepts sind insbesondere folgende Maßnahmen in Betracht zu ziehen:

1. die gemeinsame Erarbeitung und Umsetzung eines Plans zur Beendigung oder Minimierung der Verletzung mit dem Unternehmen, durch das die Verletzung verursacht wird,
2. der Zusammenschluss mit anderen Unternehmen im Rahmen von Brancheninitiativen und Branchenstandards, um die Einflussmöglichkeit auf den Verursacher zu erhöhen,
3. ein temporäres Aussetzen der Geschäftsbeziehung während der Bemühungen zur Risikominimierung.

## § 7
## Remedial measures

(1) If the enterprise discovers that a violation of a human rights or environmental obligation has already occurred or is imminent in its own business or at a direct supplier, it shall immediately take appropriate remedial action to prevent or terminate the violation or to minimise the extent of the violation. § 5 subsection 1 sentence 2 shall apply accordingly. In the company's own business division in Germany, the remedial action must lead to an end of the infringement. In the company's own business division abroad and in its own business area pursuant to § 2 subsection 6 sentence 3, the remedial measure must normally lead to the termination of the infringement.

(2) If the violation of a human rights or environmental obligation at a direct supplier is such that the enterprise cannot end it in the foreseeable future, it must immediately develop and implement a concept to end or minimise it. The plan must contain a concrete timeline. When drawing up and implementing the concept, the following measures in particular must be taken into consideration:

1. the joint development and implementation of a plan to end or minimise the infringement with the company causing the infringement,
2. joining forces with other companies within the framework of industry initiatives and industry standards in order to increase the possibility of influencing the perpetrator,
3. a temporary suspension of the business relationship during the risk minimisation efforts.

(3) Der Abbruch einer Geschäftsbeziehung ist nur geboten, wenn

1. die Verletzung einer geschützten Rechtsposition oder einer umweltbezogenen Pflicht als sehr schwerwiegend bewertet wird,
2. die Umsetzung der im Konzept erarbeiteten Maßnahmen nach Ablauf der im Konzept festgelegten Zeit keine Abhilfe bewirkt,
3. dem Unternehmen keine anderen milderen Mittel zur Verfügung stehen und eine Erhöhung des Einflussvermögens nicht aussichtsreich erscheint.

Die bloße Tatsache, dass ein Staat eines der in der Anlage zu diesem Gesetz aufgelisteten Übereinkommen nicht ratifiziert oder nicht in sein nationales Recht umgesetzt hat, führt nicht zu einer Pflicht zum Abbruch der Geschäftsbeziehung. Von Satz 2 unberührt bleiben Einschränkungen des Außenwirtschaftsverkehrs durch oder aufgrund von Bundesrecht, Recht der Europäischen Union oder Völkerrecht.

(4) Die Wirksamkeit der Abhilfemaßnahmen ist einmal im Jahr sowie anlassbezogen zu überprüfen, wenn das Unternehmen mit einer wesentlich veränderten oder wesentlich erweiterten Risikolage im eigenen Geschäftsbereich oder beim unmittelbaren Zulieferer rechnen muss, etwa durch die Einführung neuer Produkte, Projekte oder eines neuen Geschäftsfeldes. Erkenntnisse aus der Bearbeitung von Hinweisen nach §8 Absatz 1 sind zu berücksichtigen. Die Maßnahmen sind bei Bedarf unverzüglich zu aktualisieren.

(3) The termination of a business relationship is only required if

1. the violation of a protected legal position or an environmental duty is assessed to be very serious,
2. the implementation of the measures developed in the plan does not remedy the situation after the time specified in the plan has elapsed,
3. the company has no other mitigating means at its disposal and an increase in its ability to exert influence does not appear promising.

The mere fact that a state has not ratified one of the conventions listed in the Annex to this Act or has not implemented it in its national law shall not lead to an obligation to terminate the business relationship. Restrictions on foreign trade by or based on federal law, European Union law or international law shall remain unaffected by sentence 2.

(4) The effectiveness of the remedial measures shall be reviewed once a year and on an ad hoc basis if the enterprise expects a significantly changed or significantly expanded risk situation in its own business area or at the direct supplier, for example due to the introduction of new products, projects or a new field of business. Findings from the processing of notices pursuant to §8 subsection 1 shall be taken into account. If necessary, the measures shall be updated without delay.

## §8
## Beschwerdeverfahren

(1) Das Unternehmen hat dafür zu sorgen, dass ein angemessenes unternehmensinternes Beschwerdeverfahren nach den Absätzen 2 bis 4 eingerichtet ist. Das Beschwerdeverfahren ermöglicht Personen, auf menschenrechtliche und umweltbezogene Risiken sowie auf Verletzungen menschenrechtsbezogener oder umweltbezogener Pflichten hinzuweisen, die durch das wirtschaftliche Handeln eines Unternehmens im eigenen Geschäftsbereich oder eines unmittelbaren Zulieferers entstanden sind. Der Eingang des Hinweises ist den Hinweisgebern zu bestätigen. Die von dem Unternehmen mit der Durchführung des Verfahrens betrauten Personen haben den Sachverhalt mit den Hinweisgebern zu erörtern. Sie können ein Verfahren der einvernehmlichen Beilegung anbieten. Die Unternehmen können sich stattdessen an einem entsprechenden externen Beschwerdeverfahren beteiligen, sofern es die nachfolgenden Kriterien erfüllt.

## §8
## Complaints procedure

(1) The enterprise shall ensure that an appropriate internal complaints procedure is in place in accordance with subsections 2 to 4. The complaints procedure enables persons to point out human rights and environmental risks as well as violations of human rights or environmental obligations which have arisen as a result of the economic activities of an enterprise in its own business area or of a direct supplier. The whistle-blowers must be given confirmation of receipt of the information. The persons entrusted by the company with the implementation of the procedure shall discuss the facts with the whistleblowers. They may offer an amicable settlement procedure. Companies may instead participate in an external complaints procedure, provided that it fulfils the following criteria.

(2) Das Unternehmen legt eine Verfahrensordnung in Textform fest, die öffentlich zugänglich ist.

(2) The enterprise shall establish rules of procedure in writing which shall be publicly accessible.

(3) Die von dem Unternehmen mit der Durchführung des Verfahrens betrauten Personen müssen Gewähr für unparteiisches Handeln bieten, insbesondere müssen sie unabhängig und an Weisungen nicht gebunden sein. Sie sind zur Verschwiegenheit verpflichtet.

(3) The persons entrusted by the enterprise with the conduct of the proceedings must offer a guarantee of impartiality, in particular, they must be independent and not bound by instructions. They must be bound to secrecy.

(4) Das Unternehmen muss in geeigneter Weise klare und verständliche Informationen zur Erreichbarkeit und Zuständigkeit und zur Durchführung des Beschwerdeverfahrens öffentlich zugänglich machen. Das Beschwerdeverfahren muss für potenzielle Beteiligte zugänglich sein, die Vertraulichkeit der Identität wahren und wirksamen Schutz vor Benachteiligung oder Bestrafung aufgrund einer Beschwerde gewährleisten.

(4) The enterprise shall make publicly available, in an appropriate manner, clear and comprehensible information on the accessibility, responsibility, and the implementation of the complaints procedure. The complaints procedure shall be accessible to potential stakeholders, maintain confidentiality of identity and provide effective protection against discrimination or punishment because of a complaint.

(5) Die Wirksamkeit des Beschwerdeverfahrens ist mindestens einmal im Jahr sowie anlassbezogen zu überprüfen, wenn das Unternehmen mit einer wesentlich veränderten oder wesentlich erweiterten Risikolage im eigenen Geschäftsbereich oder beim unmittelbaren Zulieferer rechnen muss, etwa durch die Einführung neuer Produkte, Projekte oder eines neuen Geschäftsfeldes. Die Maßnahmen sind bei Bedarf unverzüglich zu wiederholen.

(5) The effectiveness of the complaints procedure shall be reviewed at least once a year and on an ad hoc basis if the company expects a significantly changed or substantially expanded risk situation in its own business area or at the direct supplier, for example, due to the introduction of new products, projects or a new business area. The measures are to be repeated immediately if necessary.

## § 9
## Mittelbare Zulieferer; Verordnungsermächtigung

## § 9
## Indirect supplier; ordinance authorisation

(1) Das Unternehmen muss das Beschwerdeverfahren nach § 8 so einrichten, dass es Personen auch ermöglicht, auf menschenrechtliche oder umweltbezogene Risiken sowie auf Verletzungen menschenrechtsbezogener oder umweltbezogener Pflichten hinzuweisen, die durch das wirtschaftliche Handeln eines mittelbaren Zulieferers entstanden sind.

(1) The enterprise must set up the complaints procedure in accordance with § 8 in such a way that it also enables persons to point out human rights or environmental risks as well as violations of human rights or environmental obligations that have arisen through the economic activities of an indirect supplier.

(2) Das Unternehmen muss nach Maßgabe des Absatzes 3 sein bestehendes Risikomanagement im Sinne von § 4 anpassen.

(2) The enterprise shall adapt its existing risk management plan according to subsection 3 within the meaning of § 4.

(3) Liegen einem Unternehmen tatsächliche Anhaltspunkte vor, die eine Verletzung einer menschenrechtsbezogenen oder einer umweltbezogenen Pflicht bei mittelbaren Zulieferern möglich erscheinen lassen (substantiierte Kenntnis), so hat es anlassbezogen unverzüglich

1. eine Risikoanalyse gemäß § 5 Absatz 1 bis 3 durchzuführen,

(3) If an enterprise has factual indications that make a violation of a human rights or an environmental obligation at indirect suppliers appear possible (substantiated knowledge), it shall immediately and as warranted

1. conduct a risk analysis in accordance with § 5 subsections 1 to 3,

2. angemessene Präventionsmaßnahmen gegenüber dem Verursacher zu verankern, etwa die Durchführung von Kontrollmaßnahmen, die Unterstützung bei der Vorbeugung und Vermeidung eines Risikos oder die Umsetzung von branchenspezifischen oder branchenübergreifenden Initiativen, denen das Unternehmen beigetreten ist,
3. ein Konzept zur Verhinderung, Beendigung oder Minimierung zu erstellen und umzusetzen und
4. gegebenenfalls entsprechend seine Grundsatzerklärung gemäß § 6 Absatz 2 zu aktualisieren.

(4) Das Bundesministerium für Arbeit und Soziales wird ermächtigt, Näheres zu den Pflichten des Absatzes 3 durch Rechtsverordnung im Einvernehmen mit dem Bundesministerium für Wirtschaft und Energie ohne Zustimmung des Bundesrates zu regeln.

## § 10
## Dokumentations- und Berichtspflicht

(1) Die Erfüllung der Sorgfaltspflichten nach § 3 ist unternehmensintern fortlaufend zu dokumentieren. Die Dokumentation ist ab ihrer Erstellung mindestens sieben Jahre lang aufzubewahren.

(2) Das Unternehmen hat jährlich einen Bericht über die Erfüllung seiner Sorgfaltspflichten im vergangenen Geschäftsjahr zu erstellen und spätestens vier Monate nach dem Schluss des Geschäftsjahrs auf der Internetseite des Unternehmens für einen Zeitraum von sieben Jahren kostenfrei öffentlich zugänglich zu machen. In dem Bericht ist nachvollziehbar mindestens darzulegen,

1. ob und falls ja, welche menschenrechtlichen und umweltbezogenen Risiken oder Verletzungen einer menschenrechtsbezogenen oder umweltbezogenen Pflicht das Unternehmen identifiziert hat,
2. was das Unternehmen, unter Bezugnahme auf die in den §§ 4 bis 9 beschriebenen Maßnahmen, zur Erfüllung seiner Sorgfaltspflichten unternommen hat; dazu zählen auch die Elemente der Grundsatzerklärung gemäß § 6 Absatz 2, sowie die Maßnahmen, die das Unternehmen aufgrund von Beschwerden nach § 8 oder nach § 9 Absatz 1 getroffen hat,
3. wie das Unternehmen die Auswirkungen und die Wirksamkeit der Maßnahmen bewertet und
4. welche Schlussfolgerungen es aus der Bewertung für zukünftige Maßnahmen zieht.

2. establish appropriate preventive measures regarding the offender, such as the implementation of control measures, assistance in the prevention and avoidance of a risk or the implementation of sector-specific or cross-sector initiatives to which the company is a party,
3. establish and implement a plan for prevention, cessation or minimisation; and
4. if necessary, update its policy statement in accordance with § 6 subsection 2.

(4) The Federal Ministry of Labour and Social Affairs shall be authorised to regulate the details of the obligations under subsection 3 by ordinance in agreement with the Federal Ministry for Economic Affairs and Energy without the consent of the Bundesrat.

## § 10
## Documentation and reporting obligation

(1) The fulfilment of the due diligence obligations pursuant to § 3 shall be documented on an ongoing basis within the company. The documentation shall be kept for at least seven years from its creation.

(2) The enterprise shall prepare an annual report on the fulfilment of its duties of care in the previous financial year and make it publicly available free of charge on the enterprise's website for a period of seven years no later than four months after the end of the financial year. The report shall at minimum state in a comprehensible manner,

1. whether and if so, which human rights and environmental risks or violations of a human rights or environmental obligation the company has identified,
2. what the enterprise has done to fulfil its due diligence obligations, with reference to the measures described in §§ 4 to 9; this also includes the elements of the policy statement pursuant to § 6 subsection 2, as well as the measures taken by the enterprise as a result of complaints pursuant to § 8 or § 9 subsection 1,
3. how the enterprise evaluates the impact and effectiveness of the measures, and
4. what conclusions it draws from the evaluation for future measures.

(3) Hat das Unternehmen kein menschenrechtliches oder umweltbezogenes Risiko und keine Verletzung einer menschenrechtsbezogenen oder einer umweltbezogenen Pflicht festgestellt und dies in seinem Bericht plausibel dargelegt, sind keine weiteren Ausführungen nach Absatz 2 Satz 2 Nummer 2 bis 4 erforderlich.

(4) Der Wahrung von Betriebs- und Geschäftsgeheimnissen ist dabei gebührend Rechnung zu tragen.

(3) If the enterprise has not identified any human rights or environmental risk and no violation of a human rights or environmental obligation and has plausibly explained this in its report, no further explanations pursuant to § 2 sentence 2 numbers 2 to 4 are required.

(4) Due consideration shall be given to the protection of business and trade secrets.

## Dritter Abschnitt Zivilprozess (§ 11)

### § 11 Besondere Prozessstandschaft

(1) Wer geltend macht, in einer überragend wichtigen geschützten Rechtsposition aus § 2 Absatz 1 verletzt zu sein, kann zur gerichtlichen Geltendmachung seiner Rechte einer inländischen Gewerkschaft oder Nichtregierungsorganisation die Ermächtigung zur Prozessführung erteilen.

(2) Eine Gewerkschaft oder Nichtregierungsorganisation kann nach Absatz 1 nur ermächtigt werden, wenn sie eine auf Dauer angelegte eigene Präsenz unterhält und sich nach ihrer Satzung nicht gewerbsmäßig und nicht nur vorübergehend dafür einsetzt, die Menschenrechte oder entsprechende Rechte im nationalen Recht eines Staates zu realisieren.

## Part 3 Civil procedure (§ 11)

### § 11 Special litigation right

(1) Any person claiming to have his or her outstandingly important protected legal position pursuant to § 2 subsection 1 violated may authorise a trade union or non-governmental organisation in Germany to take legal action to enforce his or her rights.

(2) A trade union or non-governmental organisation may be authorised under subsection 1 only if it maintains a long-term presence and, in accordance with its own statutes, is engaged in a non-commercial and non-temporary basis in the realisation of human rights or equivalent rights in the national law of a State.

## Vierter Abschnitt Behördliche Kontrolle und Durchsetzung (§§ 12–21)

### § 12 Einreichung des Berichts

(1) Der Bericht nach § 10 Absatz 2 Satz 1 ist in deutscher Sprache und elektronisch über einen von der zuständigen Behörde bereitgestellten Zugang einzureichen.

(2) Der Bericht ist spätestens vier Monate nach dem Schluss des Geschäftsjahres, auf das er sich bezieht, einzureichen.

### §§ 13–21

[...]

## Part 4 Regulatory control and enforcement (§§ 12–21)

### § 12 Submission of the report

(1) The report pursuant to § 10 subsection 2 sentence 1 shall be submitted in German and electronically via an access point provided by the responsible authority.

(2) The report shall be submitted no later than four months after the end of the financial year to which it relates.

### §§ 13–21

[...]

## Fünfter Abschnitt Öffentliche Beschaffung (§ 22)

### § 22

[...]

## Part 5 Public procurement (§ 22)

### § 22

[...]

## Sechster Abschnitt Zwangsgeld und Bußgeld (§§ 23–24)

§§ 23–23
[...]

## Part 6 Penalty payment and fine (§§ 23–24)

§§ 23–23
[...]

# C. Product Liability Act

## *Gesetz über die Haftung für fehlerhafte Produkte* (*Produkthaftungsgesetz* – ProdHaftG)

### § 1 Haftung

(1) Wird durch den Fehler eines Produkts jemand getötet, sein Körper oder seine Gesundheit verletzt oder eine Sache beschädigt, so ist der Hersteller des Produkts verpflichtet, dem Geschädigten den daraus entstehenden Schaden zu ersetzen. Im Falle der Sachbeschädigung gilt dies nur, wenn eine andere Sache als das fehlerhafte Produkt beschädigt wird und diese andere Sache ihrer Art nach gewöhnlich für den privaten Ge- oder Verbrauch bestimmt und hierzu von dem Geschädigten hauptsächlich verwendet worden ist.

(2) Die Ersatzpflicht des Herstellers ist ausgeschlossen, wenn

1. er das Produkt nicht in den Verkehr gebracht hat,
2. nach den Umständen davon auszugehen ist, dass das Produkt den Fehler, der den Schaden verursacht hat, noch nicht hatte, als der Hersteller es in den Verkehr brachte,
3. er das Produkt weder für den Verkauf oder eine andere Form des Vertriebs mit wirtschaftlichem Zweck hergestellt noch im Rahmen seiner beruflichen Tätigkeit hergestellt oder vertrieben hat,
4. der Fehler darauf beruht, dass das Produkt in dem Zeitpunkt, in dem der Hersteller es in den Verkehr brachte, dazu zwingenden Rechtsvorschriften entsprochen hat, oder
5. der Fehler nach dem Stand der Wissenschaft und Technik in dem Zeitpunkt, in dem der Hersteller das Produkt in den Verkehr brachte, nicht erkannt werden konnte.

### § 1 Liability

(1) If, as a result of a defect of a product, a human being is killed, injured or affected in his health, or a thing is damaged, the manufacturer is obliged to compensate the person who suffered the damage resulting therefrom. In the case of damage to property this rule applies only if an object other than the defective product is damaged and if this object is normally intended for private use or consumption and has been used by the injured person for this purpose primarily.

(2) The manufacturer's liability for damages is excluded if

1. he has not put the product into circulation;
2. it is to be assumed under the circumstances that the product was not yet defective when it was put into circulation by the manufacturer;
3. he has neither manufactured the product for sale or for any other form of distribution with economic purpose nor has he manufactured the product in the course of his occupational activities;
4. the defect derives from the fact that at the time when the manufacturer put the product into circulation it complied with mandatory legal provisions;
5. the defect could not yet be detected, having regard to the state of the art of science and technique at the time when the manufacturer put the product into circulation.

(3) Die Ersatzpflicht des Herstellers eines Teilprodukts ist ferner ausgeschlossen, wenn der Fehler durch die Konstruktion des Produkts, in welches das Teilprodukt eingearbeitet wurde, oder durch die Anleitungen des Herstellers des Produkts verursacht worden ist. Satz 1 ist auf den Hersteller eines Grundstoffs entsprechend anzuwenden.

(3) In addition, the liability of the manufacturer of a subproduct is excluded, where the defect was caused by the construction of the product into which the subproduct was inserted or by the instructions of the manufacturer of the product. Sentence 1 applies to a manufacturer of a basic substance by analogy.

(4) Für den Fehler, den Schaden und den ursächlichen Zusammenhang zwischen Fehler und Schaden trägt der Geschädigte die Beweislast. Ist streitig, ob die Ersatzpflicht gemäß Absatz 2 oder 3 ausgeschlossen ist, so trägt der Hersteller die Beweislast.

(4) The person who has suffered damage bears the burden of proof for the defect the damage and the causal connection between defect and damage. In case of dispute as to whether the liability is excluded pursuant to subsection 2 or 3, the manufacturer bears the burden of proof.

### § 2 Produkt

Produkt im Sinne dieses Gesetzes ist jede bewegliche Sache, auch wenn sie einen Teil einer anderen beweglichen Sache oder einer unbeweglichen Sache bildet, sowie Elektrizität.

### § 2 Product

Product in the meaning of this Act is every moveable object, even if it forms part of another moveable or immovable object as well as electricity.

### § 3 Fehler

(1) Ein Produkt hat einen Fehler, wenn es nicht die Sicherheit bietet, die unter Berücksichtigung aller Umstände, insbesondere

a) seiner Darbietung,
b) des Gebrauchs, mit dem billigerweise gerechnet werden kann,
c) des Zeitpunkts, in dem es in den Verkehr gebracht wurde,

berechtigterweise erwartet werden kann.

(2) Ein Produkt hat nicht allein deshalb einen Fehler, weil später ein verbessertes Produkt in den Verkehr gebracht wurde.

### § 3 Defect

(1) A product is defective if it does not provide the degree of safety which can be justifiably expected, having regard to all the circumstances, in particular

(a) its presentation;
(b) its use which may be reasonably expected;
(c) the time when it was put into circulation.

(2) A product is not defective for the sole reason that at a later point in time an improved product was put into circulation.

### § 4 Hersteller

(1) Hersteller im Sinne dieses Gesetzes ist, wer das Endprodukt, einen Grundstoff oder ein Teilprodukt hergestellt hat. Als Hersteller gilt auch jeder, der sich durch das Anbringen seines Namens, seiner Marke oder eines anderen unterscheidungskräftigen Kennzeichens als Hersteller ausgibt.

(2) Als Hersteller gilt ferner, wer ein Produkt zum Zweck des Verkaufs, der Vermietung, des Mietkaufs oder einer anderen Form des Vertriebs mit wirtschaftlichem Zweck im Rahmen seiner geschäftlichen Tätigkeit in den Geltungsbereich des Abkommens über den Europäischen Wirtschaftsraum einführt oder verbringt.

### § 4 Manufacturer

(1) Manufacturer in the meaning of this Act is a person who has manufactured the final product, a basic substance or a subproduct. Furthermore, whoever represents himself as a manufacturer by attaching his name, trademark or other distinctive mark is regarded as manufacturer.

(2) Furthermore, a person is also deemed to be a manufacturer who, within the range of his commercial activity, imports or places into the area covered by the contracting states of the European Economic Area Agreement a product with the purpose to sale, rent, lease or to distribute it in any other form.

(3) Kann der Hersteller des Produkts nicht festgestellt werden, so gilt jeder Lieferant als dessen Hersteller, es sei denn, dass er dem Geschädigten innerhalb eines Monats, nachdem ihm dessen diesbezügliche Aufforderung zugegangen ist, den Hersteller oder diejenige Person benennt, die ihm das Produkt geliefert hat. Dies gilt auch für ein eingeführtes Produkt, wenn sich bei diesem die in Absatz 2 genannte Person nicht feststellen lässt, selbst wenn der Name des Herstellers bekannt ist.

(3) If the manufacturer of the product cannot be ascertained, every distributor is treated as its manufacturer, unless he indicates to the injured person within one month of receiving the latter's relevant request who is the manufacturer or the person who supplied him with the product. The same applies to an imported product in respect of which the person referred to in subsection 2 cannot be ascertained, even if the name of the manufacturer is known.

## § 5 Mehrere Ersatzpflichtige

Sind für denselben Schaden mehrere Hersteller nebeneinander zum Schadensersatz verpflichtet, so haften sie als Gesamtschuldner. Im Verhältnis der Ersatzpflichtigen zueinander hängt, soweit nichts anderes bestimmt ist, die Verpflichtung zum Ersatz sowie der Umfang des zu leistenden Ersatzes von den Umständen, insbesondere davon ab, inwieweit der Schaden vorwiegend von dem einen oder dem anderen Teil verursacht worden ist; im Übrigen gelten die §§ 421 bis 425 sowie § 426 Abs. 1 Satz 2 und Abs. 2 des Bürgerlichen Gesetzbuchs.

## § 5 Several tortfeasors

If several manufacturers are co-liable for the damage, they are jointly and severally liable. Between the tortfeasors themselves, in the absence of provisions to the contrary, the liability to pay compensation and its extent depends upon the circumstances, in particular as to whether the damage has been caused predominantly by one or the other of them; furthermore, §§ 421 to 425, § 426(1), sentence 2 and subsection 2 Civil Code apply.

## § 6 Haftungsminderung

(1) Hat bei der Entstehung des Schadens ein Verschulden des Geschädigten mitgewirkt, so gilt § 254 des Bürgerlichen Gesetzbuchs; im Falle der Sachbeschädigung steht das Verschulden desjenigen, der die tatsächliche Gewalt über die Sache ausübt, dem Verschulden des Geschädigten gleich.

(2) Die Haftung des Herstellers wird nicht gemindert, wenn der Schaden durch einen Fehler des Produkts und zugleich durch die Handlung eines Dritten verursacht worden ist. § 5 Satz 2 gilt entsprechend.

## § 6 Reduction of liability

(1) If the injured person is partly to be at fault for having caused the damage, § 254 Civil Code applies; in case of property damage, any fault of the person having physical control over the object is treated as that of the injured party.

(2) If the damage has been caused simultaneously by a defect of the product and by the act of a third party, the liability of the manufacturer is not reduced. § 5 sentence 2 applies.

## § 7 Umfang der Ersatzpflicht bei Tötung

(1) Im Falle der Tötung ist Ersatz der Kosten einer versuchten Heilung sowie des Vermögensnachteils zu leisten, den der Getötete dadurch erlitten hat, dass während der Krankheit seine Erwerbsfähigkeit aufgehoben oder gemindert war oder seine Bedürfnisse vermehrt waren. Der Ersatzpflichtige hat außerdem die Kosten der Beerdigung demjenigen zu ersetzen, der diese Kosten zu tragen hat.

## § 7 Extent of damages in case of death

(1) In case of death, the expenses incurred in an attempt to restore health must be compensated together with the pecuniary loss suffered by the deceased in consequence of the loss or reduction of his earning capacity or of his increased needs. Damages also include the funeral expenses payable to the person that has to bear those costs.

(2) Stand der Getötete zur Zeit der Verletzung zu einem Dritten in einem Verhältnis, aus dem er diesem gegenüber kraft Gesetzes unterhaltspflichtig war oder unterhaltspflichtig werden konnte, und ist dem Dritten infolge der Tötung das Recht auf Unterhalt entzogen, so hat der Ersatzpflichtige dem Dritten insoweit Schadensersatz zu leisten, als der Getötete während der mutmaßlichen Dauer seines Lebens zur Gewährung des Unterhalts verpflichtet gewesen wäre. Die Ersatzpflicht tritt auch ein, wenn der Dritte zur Zeit der Verletzung gezeugt, aber noch nicht geboren war.

(3) Der Ersatzpflichtige hat dem Hinterbliebenen, der zur Zeit der Verletzung zu dem Getöteten in einem besonderen persönlichen Näheverhältnis stand, für das dem Hinterbliebenen zugefügte seelische Leid eine angemessene Entschädigung in Geld zu leisten. Ein besonderes persönliches Näheverhältnis wird vermutet, wenn der Hinterbliebene der Ehegatte, der Lebenspartner, ein Elternteil oder ein Kind des Getöteten war.

(2) If at the time of injury the deceased was standing in a relationship to a third party according to which he had a maintenance obligation or a potential maintenance obligation to such third party, and if the third party lost his right to maintenance in consequence of the death, such third party is entitled to damages in so far as the deceased during the period of his life expectancy would have been liable to maintain him. This liability arises also if the third party was sired at the time of death but not yet born.

(3) The party liable to pay damages must make appropriate financial compensation to the surviving dependent who at the time of the injury was in a particularly close personal relationship with the deceased party for the emotional distress caused to the surviving dependent. A particularly close personal relationship is assumed when the surviving dependent was the spouse, the life partner, a parent or a child of the deceased party.

## § 8
## Umfang der Ersatzpflicht bei Körperverletzung

Im Falle der Verletzung des Körpers oder der Gesundheit ist Ersatz der Kosten der Heilung sowie des Vermögensnachteils zu leisten, den der Verletzte dadurch erleidet, dass infolge der Verletzung zeitweise oder dauernd seine Erwerbsfähigkeit aufgehoben oder gemindert ist oder seine Bedürfnisse vermehrt sind. Wegen des Schadens, der nicht Vermögensschaden ist, kann auch eine billige Entschädigung in Geld gefordert werden.

## § 8
## Extent of damages in case of personal injury

If injury was caused to the body or health, the expenses incurred in restoring health must be compensated together with the pecuniary loss suffered by the injured person resulting from the temporary or permanent loss or reduction of his earning capacity or from his increased needs. Fair compensation in money can also be demanded for non-pecuniary loss.

## § 9
## Schadensersatz durch Geldrente

(1) Der Schadensersatz wegen Aufhebung oder Minderung der Erwerbsfähigkeit und wegen vermehrter Bedürfnisse des Verletzten sowie der nach § 7 Abs. 2 einem Dritten zu gewährende Schadensersatz sind für die Zukunft durch eine Geldrente zu leisten.

(2) § 843 Abs. 2 bis 4 des Bürgerlichen Gesetzbuchs ist entsprechend anzuwenden.

## § 9
## Damages by way of periodical payments

(1) Damages arising due to the total or partial loss of earning capacity and of increased needs of the injured person together with the damages payable to a third party in accordance with § 7(2) are to be compensated for the future by periodical payments.

(2) § 843 subsections 2 to 4 Civil Code applies accordingly.

## § 10
## Haftungshöchstbetrag

(1) Sind Personenschäden durch ein Produkt oder gleiche Produkte mit demselben Fehler verursacht worden, so haftet der Ersatzpflichtige nur bis zu einem Höchstbetrag von 85 Millionen Euro.

## § 10
## Maximum amount of damages

(1) Where damage to persons was caused by a product or by products of the same kind affected by the same defect, the liability to pay damages is limited to a maximum of 85 million euro.

(2) Übersteigen die den mehreren Geschädigten zu leistenden Entschädigungen den in Absatz 1 vorgesehenen Höchstbetrag, so verringern sich die einzelnen Entschädigungen in dem Verhältnis, in dem ihr Gesamtbetrag zu dem Höchstbetrag steht.

(2) If the damages payable to several injured persons exceed the maximum rate set out in subsection 1, the individual damages are reduced in proportion of their total to the maximum rate allowable.

**§ 11**
**Selbstbeteiligung bei Sachbeschädigung**

Im Falle der Sachbeschädigung hat der Geschädigte einen Schaden bis zu einer Höhe von 500 Euro selbst zu tragen.

**§ 11**
**Extent of compensation in case of damage to property**

Where property is damaged, the person who suffered the damage has to bear the loss up to 500.

**§ 12**
**Verjährung**

(1) Der Anspruch nach § 1 verjährt in drei Jahren von dem Zeitpunkt an, in dem der Ersatzberechtigte von dem Schaden, dem Fehler und von der Person des Ersatzpflichtigen Kenntnis erlangt hat oder hätte erlangen müssen.

(2) Schweben zwischen dem Ersatzpflichtigen und dem Ersatzberechtigten Verhandlungen über den zu leistenden Schadensersatz, so ist die Verjährung gehemmt, bis die Fortsetzung der Verhandlungen verweigert wird.

(3) Im Übrigen sind die Vorschriften des Bürgerlichen Gesetzbuchs über die Verjährung anzuwenden.

**§ 12**
**Limitation**

(1) A claim pursuant to § 1 prescribe in three years from the time when the claimant knew or could have known of the damage and of the person liable to pay damages.

(2) Until the continuation of negotiations has been abandoned, limitation is suspended where negotiations are pending between the person liable to pay and the person entitled to receive compensation.

(3) Additionally, the provisions of the Civil Code relating to the statute of limitation apply.

**§ 13**
**Erlöschen von Ansprüchen**

(1) Der Anspruch nach § 1 erlischt zehn Jahre nach dem Zeitpunkt, in dem der Hersteller das Produkt, das den Schaden verursacht hat, in den Verkehr gebracht hat. Dies gilt nicht, wenn über den Anspruch ein Rechtsstreit oder ein Mahnverfahren anhängig ist.

(2) Auf den rechtskräftig festgestellten Anspruch oder auf den Anspruch aus einem anderen Vollstreckungstitel ist Absatz 1 Satz 1 nicht anzuwenden. Gleiches gilt für den Anspruch, der Gegenstand eines außergerichtlichen Vergleichs ist oder der durch rechtsgeschäftliche Erklärung anerkannt wurde.

**§ 13**
**Extinction of claims**

(1) A claim according to § 1 expires ten years from the date when the manufacturer against whom the claim is made has put the product into circulation. This does not apply where an action or a delinquency procedure is pending.

(2) Subsection 1 sentence 1 does not apply to a claim which has become *res judicata* or to a claim covered by another enforcement title. The same applies to a claim which is the subject-matter of an out-of-court settlement or which has been recognised by agreement.

**§ 14**
**Unabdingbarkeit**

Die Ersatzpflicht des Herstellers nach diesem Gesetz darf im Voraus weder ausgeschlossen noch beschränkt werden. Entgegenstehende Vereinbarungen sind nichtig.

**§ 14**
**Mandatory character**

The liability of a manufacturer in accordance with this Act cannot be excluded or restricted in advance. Any agreement to the contrary is void.

**§ 15**
**Arzneimittelhaftung, Haftung nach anderen Rechtsvorschriften**

(1) Wird infolge der Anwendung eines zum Gebrauch bei Menschen bestimmten Arzneimittels, das im Geltungsbereich des Arzneimittelgesetzes an den Verbraucher abgegeben wurde und der Pflicht zur Zulassung unterliegt oder durch Rechtsverordnung von der Zulassung befreit worden ist, jemand getötet, sein Körper oder seine Gesundheit verletzt, so sind die Vorschriften des Produkthaftungsgesetzes nicht anzuwenden.

(2) Eine Haftung aufgrund anderer Vorschriften bleibt unberührt.

**§ 15**
**Pharmaceutical liability, liability according to other legal provisions**

(1) If, due to the application of a pharmaceutical product that is destined for human use and sold in the area of application of the German Pharmaceuticals Act and is subject to approval or that has been released from approval by means of regulations, a person is killed or his body or health is affected otherwise, the provisions of the Product Liability Act do not apply.

(2) Liability in accordance with other provisions remains unaffected.

**§ 16**
**Übergangsvorschrift**

Dieses Gesetz ist nicht auf Produkte anwendbar, die vor seinem Inkrafttreten in den Verkehr gebracht worden sind.

**§ 16**
**Transitional provision**

The Act does not apply to products put into circulation before it has entered into force.

**§ 17**
**Erlass von Rechtsverordnungen**

Der Bundesminister der Justiz wird ermächtigt, durch Rechtsverordnung die Beträge der §§ 10 und 11 zu ändern oder das Außerkrafttreten des § 10 anzuordnen, wenn und soweit dies zur Umsetzung einer Richtlinie des Rates der Europäischen Gemeinschaften auf der Grundlage der Artikel 16 Abs. 2 und 18 Abs. 2 der Richtlinie des Rates vom 25. Juli 1985 zur Angleichung der Rechts- und Verwaltungsvorschriften der Mitgliedstaaten über die Haftung für fehlerhafte Produkte erforderlich ist.

**§ 17**
**Issue of statutory instruments**

The Federal Minister of Justice is authorised by means of statutory instrument to amend the amounts stipulated in §§ 10 and 11 or to order the expiration of § 10 if and to the extent that this is necessary to implement a directive of the Council of the European Community on the basis of Articles 16(2) and 18(2) of the Directive of the Council of the European Community dated 25 July 1985 for the approximation of the laws, regulations and administrative provisions of the member states concerning the liability for defective products.

**§ 18**
**Berlin-Klausel**

[...]

**§ 18**
**Berlin clause**

[...]

**§ 19**
**Inkrafttreten**

Dieses Gesetz tritt am 1. Januar 1990 in Kraft.

**§ 19**
**Entry into force**

This Act enters into force on 1 January 1990.

# PART III
# GERMAN-ENGLISH GLOSSARY

| | |
|---|---|
| **Abrechnungszeitraum** | accounting period |
| **Absichtserklärung** | letter of intent |
| **Abtretungsverbot** | prohibition of assignment |
| **abwerben** | to entice away |
| **Abwicklungsgeschäft** | process agreement |
| **Aktiengesellschaft** | stock corporation |
| **Alleinbelieferungsverpflichtung** | exclusive supply obligation |
| **Alleinbezugsverpflichtung** | exclusive purchase obligation |
| **Alleinvertretung** | exclusive agency |
| **Alleinvertriebsrecht** | exclusive distribution right |
| **Alleinvertriebsvertrag** | exclusive distributorship agreement |
| **Allgemeine Deutsche Spediteurbedingungen** | German forwarding agents standard terms and conditions |
| **Allgemeine Geschäftsbedingungen** | standard terms and conditions |
| **Amtsgericht** | District Court |
| **Änderungskündigung** | notice of termination with an option to continue |
| **Anfechtung** | avoidance |
| **Annahme** | acceptance |
| **Anscheinsvollmacht** | apparent authority |
| **Antrag, Angebot** | offer |
| **Anwartschaft** | prospective entitlement |
| **arglistige Täuschung** | deceit |
| **aufbewahren** | taking custody |
| **auflösende Bedingung** | resolutive condition |
| **aufrechnen** | to set-off |
| **Aufwendung** | disbursement |
| **Aufwendungsersatz** | reimbursement of expenditure |
| **Ausführungsvertrag** | accomplishment agreement |
| **Ausgleichsanspruch** | claim for termination compensation |
| **Auslegung** | interpretation |
| **Ausreißer** | outlier |
| **außerordentliche Kündigung** | extraordinary notice of termination, or termination for cause |
| **Ausweichklausel** | escape clause |
| **Auswirkungsprinzip** | effects doctrine |
| | |
| **Bargeschäft** | privileged cash transactions |

| | |
|---|---|
| **Belieferungspflicht** | delivery obligation, or supply obligation |
| **Berufungsgericht** | appellate court |
| **Beschenkter** | receiver |
| **Beweislastumkehr** | reversal of the burden of proof |
| **Bezirksvertretung** | district agency |
| **Bruttozahlung** | gross payment |
| **Bundesagentur für Arbeit** | Federal Employment Agency |
| **Bundesarbeitsgericht** | Federal Labour Court |
| **Bundesfinanzhof** | Federal Finance Court |
| **Bundesgerichtshof** | Federal Court of Justice |
| **Bundesverfassungsgericht** | Federal Constitutional Court |
| **Bürgschaft** | suretyship |
| | |
| **Dauerschuldverhältnis** | ongoing continuing obligation |
| **Deliktsfähigkeit** | tort responsibility |
| **Drohung** | threat |
| **Duldungsvollmacht** | tolerated authority |
| **Durchführungsgesetz zum Montrealer Übereinkommen** | Act Implementing the Montreal Convention |
| | |
| **Eigenlager** | self-owned warehouse |
| **Eigenschaftsirrtum** | mistake as to the characteristics |
| **Eigentumsvorbehalt** | retention of title |
| **Eigenverwaltung** | self-administration |
| **Einfirmenvertreter** | single-firm agent |
| **Einlagerer** | storing party |
| **Erfolgsort** | place where the damage occurred |
| **Erfüllungswahlrecht** | option of performance |
| **Erklärungsirrtum** | mistake of expression |
| **Erstbemusterung** | initial sampling |
| **Europäischer Gerichtshof** | European Court of Justice |
| | |
| **Fabrikationsfehler** | error concerning the production process |
| **Fachhändler** | authorised dealer |
| **Fachhändlervertrag** | authorised dealer agreement |
| **faktischer Geschäftsführer** | *de facto* managing directors |
| **Feststellung des Anspruchs zur Insolvenztabelle** | registration of the claim |
| **Franchisegeber** | franchisor |
| **Franchisenehmer** | franchisee |
| | |
| **Garantie** | guarantee |
| **Gebiets- und Kundenschutz** | territory or customer protection |
| **gebrochene Beförderung** | fractional transport |

| | |
|---|---|
| **Gefährdungshaftung** | strict liability |
| **gegenseitiger Vertrag** | mutual contract |
| **geltungserhaltende Reduktion** | validity preserving reduction |
| **Gerichtsstandklausel** | jurisdiction clause |
| **Geschädigter** | aggrieved party |
| **Geschäftsbesorgungsvertrag** | business management contract |
| **Geschäftsfähigkeit** | capacity to contract |
| **Gesellschaft mit beschränkter Haftung** | limited liability company |
| **gewöhnlicher Aufenthalt** | habitual residence |
| **Gläubiger** | obligee |
| **Gläubigerbenachteiligung** | disadvantaging the creditors |
| **Grundlagengeschäft** | fundamental transaction |
| **Grundstück** | plot of land |
| **Gruppenfreistellung** | block exemption |
| **Gruppenfreistellungsverordnung** | group exemption regulation |
| **Güterkraftverkehrsgesetz** | Law on road haulage of goods |
| | |
| **Handelsregister** | commercial register |
| **Handelsvertreter** | commercial agent |
| **Handelsvertretervertrag** | commercial agency agreement |
| **Handlungsbevollmächtigung** | commercial power of attorney |
| **Handlungsort** | place where the injuring act was carried out |
| **Hemmung** | suspension |
| | |
| **in Verkehr gebracht** | marketed |
| **Inhaltsirrtum** | mistake of content or meaning |
| **Inhaltskontrolle** | content review |
| **Insolvenzanfechtung** | insolvency annulment |
| **Insolvenzforderungen** | insolvency claims |
| **Insolvenzverschleppung** | insolvency delay |
| **Instanzenzug** | appeals system |
| **Instruktionsfehler** | instruction error |
| **Internationales Privatrecht** | private international law |
| | |
| **Juristische Person** | corporate body/legal person |
| | |
| **Kammergericht** | Higher Regional Court of Berlin |
| **Kardinalpflicht** | core obligation |
| **Kauf auf Probe** | purchase on approval |
| **Kaufmännisches Bestätigungsschreiben** | commercial letter of confirmation |
| **kaufmännisches Zurückbehaltungsrecht** | commercial right of retention |
| **Klagehäufung** | consolidation of claims |
| **Kommissionsvertrag** | commission agency agreement |
| **Konsignationswarenlager** | consignment stock warehouse |

| | |
|---|---|
| **Konstruktionsfehler** | construction error |
| **Kündigung** | termination |
| **Kündigungserklärung** | declaration of termination |
| **Kündigungsfrist** | notice period for termination |
| | |
| **Lager, lagern, einlagern** | warehouse, warehousing |
| **Lagerhalter** | warehouse keeper |
| **Lagerschein** | warehouse warrant |
| **Lagervertrag** | warehousing contract |
| **Landessozialgericht** | Higher Social Court |
| **Landgericht** | Regional Court |
| **Lizenzgeber** | licensor |
| | |
| **Mahnbescheid** | demand for payment |
| **Mangelbeseitigung** | rectification of defects |
| **Mangelfolgeschaden** | consequential damage |
| **Masseverbindlichkeiten** | claims against the insolvency estate |
| **mehrseitiger Vertrag** | multilateral agreement |
| **Mitursächlichkeit** | concurrent causation |
| | |
| **Nachbesserung** | repair |
| **Nachlieferung** | replacement |
| **nachrangige Insolvenzgläubiger** | subordinated creditors of the insolvency proceedings |
| **nachvertragliches Wettbewerbsverbot** | post-contractual prohibition of competition |
| **Neben- und Schutzpflichten** | subsidiary and protective obligations |
| **Nebenintervention** | third-party intervention |
| **Neubeginn** | recommencement |
| **Nutzungen** | emoluments |
| | |
| **Obergrenze** | capping level |
| **Oberlandesgericht** | Higher Regional Court |
| **öffentliche Sicherheit und Ordnung** | public policy |
| **Optionsvertrag** | option contract |
| **ordentliche Kündigung** | termination with notice, or ordinary notice of termination |
| | |
| **Pfandrecht** | lien |
| **positive Fortführungsprognose** | positive continuation prognosis |
| **Preisanpassungsklausel** | price adjustment clause |
| **Preisbindung** | price maintenance |
| **Produktabruf** | release order |
| **Prokura** | general commercial authority |
| **Prokurist** | authorised officer |

| | |
|---|---|
| **Prozessführung vor staatlichen Gerichten** | litigation |
| **Prüfungstermin** | creditors' meeting |
| **Querlieferungsverbot** | restriction of cross supplies |
| **Quote** | percentage of recovery |
| **Rechtsbindungswille** | intention of legal responsibility |
| **Rechtsfähigkeit** | capacity to act |
| **Rechtswahlklausel** | choice of law clauses |
| **Reichsgericht** | Supreme Court of the German Reich |
| **Rohausgleich** | raw compensation |
| **Rückgewährschuldverhältnis** | obligation of restitution |
| **Rückstellungen** | accruals |
| **Rücktritt** | rescission |
| **scheinselbstständig** | pseudo self-employed person |
| **Schenker** | giver |
| **Schiedsgericht** | arbitral tribunal |
| **Schiedsverfahren** | arbitration proceeding |
| **Schriftformklausel** | written form clause |
| **Schuldner** | obligor |
| **Schutzgesetz** | protective law |
| **Schutzschirmverfahren** | protective shield proceedings |
| **schwacher vorläufiger Insolvenzverwalter** | weak preliminary insolvency administrator |
| **schwarze Klausel** | hardcore restriction |
| **Selbsteintrittsrecht** | commission agent's right to self-substitution |
| **Sittenwidrigkeit** | violation of *bonos mores* |
| **Sorgfaltspflicht** | duty of care |
| **Sprunglieferungsverbot** | wholesale dealers' prohibition of direct supply to end customers |
| **Stillhalteabkommen** | standstill agreement |
| **Streckengeschäft** | third-party deal |
| **Streitgenossenschaft** | joinder |
| **Sukzessivlieferungsvertrag** | contract for delivery by instalments |
| **Suspendierung** | suspension |
| **Tausch** | exchange |
| **typengemischter Vertrag** | mixed contract |
| **Überhangprovision** | backlog commission |
| **Übermittlungsirrtum** | mistake of transmission |
| **überschuldet** | overindebted |
| **Verbrauchsgüterkauf** | purchase of consumer goods |
| **verjähren** | to lapse |

| | |
|---|---|
| **Verjährung** | limitation |
| **Verschleierung** | concealment |
| **Versender** | shipper |
| **Versendung, Warenlieferung** | shipment |
| **Versicherungsvertragsgesetz** | Insurance Contracts Act |
| **Vertragsabbruch** | abandonment of negotiations |
| **Vertragshändlervertrag** | distribution agreement, or distributorship agreement |
| **Vertragsstrafe** | rules on contractual penalties |
| **Vertretungsmacht** | power of representation |
| **Verwahrungsvertrag** | contract on safe-keeping |
| **Vollmacht** | proxy, or power of attorney, or power of representation |
| **Vorauszahlung** | prepayment |
| **Vorkauf** | preemption |
| **vorläufiger Insolvenzverwalter** | preliminary insolvency administrator |
| **Vorstand** | management board |
| **Vorvertrag** | pre-contract |
| **Warenausgangsprüfung** | distribution inspection |
| **Wareneingangsprüfung** | incoming inspection |
| **Wegfall der Geschäftsgrundlage** | frustration of purpose |
| **Weiterverarbeitungsgebot** | obligation to process purchased products |
| **Weiterverarbeitungsverbot** | prohibition to process purchased products |
| **Wettbewerbsverbot** | non-compete obligation |
| **wichtiger Grund** | compelling reason, or good reason, or cause |
| **Widerruf** | revocation |
| **Wiederkauf** | repurchase |
| **Willenserklärung** | declaration of intent |
| **Wucher** | usury |
| **Zahlungsstockung** | temporary liquidity squeeze |
| **Zahlungsunfähigkeit** | illiquidity |
| **zusammengesetzter Vertrag** | combined contract |
| **zwingende Regelung** | mandatory provision |
| **zwingendes Recht** | mandatory law |

# Index